Excel

Get the Results You Want

HSC

LEGAL STUDIES

A brand-new format that makes even better use of your study time ✓

Belinda Brassil & Dimity Brassil

PASCAL PRESS

© 2011 Belinda Brassil, Dimity Brassil and Pascal Press
Reprinted 2012, 2013, 2014
Updated 2016, 2019
Reprinted 2022, 2024

ISBN 978 1 74125 353 5

Pascal Press
PO Box 250
Glebe NSW 2037
(02) 9198 1748
www.pascalpress.com.au

Publisher: Vivienne Joannou
Project editor: Mark Dixon
Edited by Scharlaine Cairns
Reviewed and answers checked by Matt Peacock
Cover and page design by DiZign Pty Ltd
Typeset by Grizzly Graphics (Leanne Richters)
Photos by iStock and Dreamstime
Printed by Vivar Printing/Green Giant Press

Students
All care has been taken in the preparation of this study guide but please check
with your teacher or the NSW Education Standards Authority about the exact
requirements of the course you are studying as these can change from year
to year.

The validity and appropriateness of the internet addresses (URLs) in this book
were checked at the time of publication. Due to the dynamic nature of the
internet, the publisher cannot accept responsibility for the continued validity or
content of these web addresses.

HSC Legal Studies

Contents

Conquer the syllabus with *Excel*: the comprehensive study guide!

Before you start your revision, a word about the syllabus ...

▶ If you look at the first page of each chapter, you will see the syllabus content in an easy-to-understand form (see extract (**a**) below)—*this way you can cut through the jargon and understand what's required of you!*

▶ Then, if you look at the margin of every page of the ***Excel*** guide, you will see that every syllabus dot point in the HSC Legal Studies syllabus is covered (see extract (**b**) below)—*this way you can be completely confident that you are covering all the syllabus, as you have it all there at your fingertips, on every page of the **Excel** guide!* (You can also print out the whole syllabus yourself by going to the NESA website—www.educationstandards.nsw.edu.au—and clicking on the HSC syllabus link on the home page.)

▶ When you look at the main headings in each chapter (1.1, 2.1, etc.), you will see they are directly from the syllabus, word for word (see extract (**c**) below)—*this way you can easily match the **Excel** guide notes to the syllabus document!*

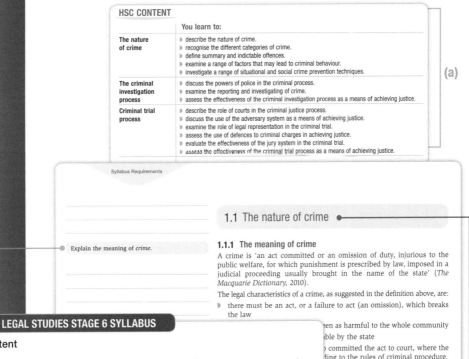

HSC CONTENT

	You learn to:
The nature of crime	▷ describe the nature of crime. ▷ recognise the different categories of crime. ▷ define summary and indictable offences. ▷ examine a range of factors that may lead to criminal behaviour. ▷ investigate a range of situational and social crime prevention techniques.
The criminal investigation process	▷ discuss the powers of police in the criminal process. ▷ examine the reporting and investigating of crime. ▷ assess the effectiveness of the criminal investigation process as a means of achieving justice.
Criminal trial process	▷ describe the role of courts in the criminal justice process. ▷ discuss the use of the adversary system as a means of achieving justice. ▷ examine the role of legal representation in the criminal trial. ▷ assess the use of defences to criminal charges in achieving justice. ▷ evaluate the effectiveness of the jury system in the criminal trial. ▷ assess the effectiveness of the criminal trial process as a means of achieving justice.

(**a**)

Syllabus Requirements

Explain the meaning of *crime*.

1.1 The nature of crime

1.1.1 The meaning of crime

A crime is 'an act committed or an omission of duty, injurious to the public welfare, for which punishment is prescribed by law, imposed in a judicial proceeding usually brought in the name of the state' (*The Macquarie Dictionary*, 2010).

The legal characteristics of a crime, as suggested in the definition above, are:

▶ there must be an act, or a failure to act (an omission), which breaks the law

...een as harmful to the whole community ...able by the state

...o committed the act to court, where the ...ding to the rules of criminal procedure.

..., and the offender is tried by the state. ... and the state.

...ute and common law. Common law still ...w, for example causation (see Section ...ourts play a major role in interpreting ...ion 1.1.4. page 4).

... *Constitution Act* (the Constitution of ...ake laws between state and federal ...government legislates for some criminal ...te law. The major statute in NSW is the ...ists offences and prescribes maximum ...amended as types of criminal offences

(**c**)

LEGAL STUDIES STAGE 6 SYLLABUS

Content

Principal focus: *Through the use of a range of contemporary examples, students investigate criminal law, processes and institutions and the tension between community interests and individual rights and freedoms.*

Students learn to:
• describe the nature of crime
• recognise the different categories of crime

Students learn about:

the nature of crime

• the meaning of crime
• the elements of crime: *actus reus*, *mens rea*
• strict liability offences
• causation

(**b**)

Five steps to HSC success!

STEP 1

Read and understand—then summarise and memorise

- Always begin your revision programme by reading each syllabus requirement in the margin a couple of times—*this way you will be completely focused on what exactly you have to know for the HSC Exam!*
- Then study the section, highlighting any key concepts, and make your own notes in the margin—*by summarising each section in your own words, you will memorise the work effectively so that it's lodged in your short-term memory!*
- Now go straight to Step 4 and answer the *End of chapter questions* as you study each section. Look for the *KCq* and *HSC* icons at the end of sections—*answering questions along the way tests you to see if you have really understood the work!*
- Remember to study in time 'bites': study hard, but also give yourself short breaks—*concentrate hard when you study, but always remember to recharge your batteries now and then!*

STEP 2

Scan and memorise

Scan all the definitions in the *Key definitions and concepts* section and make sure you know all of them by heart. Go through and memorise the definitions that you don't know—*this is an efficient way of learning all the definitions in one go!*

STEP 3

Double-check and review

Read each syllabus question in the *Chapter syllabus checklist* and as you go through them, mentally check that you know all of them. This might seem 'over the top' … but is actually very important, as it will help you check that you know all the material in each chapter and at the same time lodge it in your long-term memory—*if you can answer all these syllabus questions, then you know all the work by heart, and can now aim for top marks in the HSC!*

STEP 4

Answer and check

This is a little like learning to drive a car: it's one thing to know all the theory, but you need to practise actually driving the car! Likewise with your HSC Exam: once you know the theory—the content in each chapter—you must practise by doing; in this case, the questions in each chapter. Let's face it, that's what the HSC is: a whole lot of questions. The first questions are the *Key Concept questions*. You will have lots of these to answer to ensure that you know the content thoroughly (that's why there are so many questions!)—make sure you do all of them and always check your answers! Then you have the HSC-like questions: these are very important, as they are the type of questions you will be answering in your HSC—*if you can answer all these questions, then you are ready for the main event: the HSC Exam!*

STEP 5

Practice runs

The two sample papers are based as much as possible on recent HSC papers, so it is worth your while doing them in an exam-like environment—*this is the real thing now!*

NESA key words

account for	state reasons for; report on
(give an) account of	narrate a series of events or transactions
analyse	identify components and the relationship between them; draw out and relate implications
apply	use, utilise, employ in a particular situation
appreciate	make a judgement about the value of
assess	make a judgement of value, quality, outcomes, results or size
calculate	ascertain/determine from given facts, figures or information
clarify	make clear or plain
classify	arrange or include in classes or categories
compare	show how things are similar or different
construct	make; build; put together items or arguments
contrast	show how things are different or opposite
critically (analyse/evaluate)	add a degree or level of accuracy, depth, knowledge and understanding, logic, questioning, reflection and quality to
deduce	draw conclusions
define	state meaning and identify essential qualities
demonstrate	show by example
describe	provide characteristics and features
discuss	identify issues and provide points for and/or against
distinguish	recognise or note/indicate as being distinct or different from; note differences between
evaluate	make a judgement based on criteria; determine the value of
examine	inquire into
explain	relate cause and effect; make the relationships between things evident; provide why and/or how
explore	look into closely for the purpose of discovery
extract	choose relevant and/or appropriate details
extrapolate	infer from what is known
identify	recognise and name
interpret	draw meaning from
investigate	plan, inquire into and draw conclusions about
justify	support an argument or conclusion
organise	form different parts into a united whole
outline	sketch in general terms; indicate the main features of
predict	suggest what may happen based on available information
propose	put forward (for example, a point of view, idea, argument, suggestion) for consideration or action
recall	present remembered ideas, facts or experiences
recommend	provide reasons in favour
recount	retell a series of events
summarise	express concisely the relevant details
synthesise	put together various elements to make a whole

HSC objectives and outcomes

Outcomes are applicable to all topics. Some may be more relevant to a particular topic than others. Outcomes may be examined.

Objectives	Outcomes
A student develops knowledge and understanding about: 1. the nature and institutions of domestic and international law.	A student: H1: *identifies* and *applies* **legal concepts and terminology.** H2: *describes* and *explains* **key features of and the relationship between Australian and international law.**
2. the operation of Australian and international legal systems and the significance of the rule of law.	H3: *analyses* the **operation of domestic and international legal systems.** H4: *evaluates* the **effectiveness of the legal system in addressing issues.**
3. the interrelationship between law, justice and society and the changing nature of the law.	H5: *explains* the **role of law in encouraging cooperation and resolving conflict, as well as initiating and responding to change.** H6: *assesses* the **nature of the interrelationship between the legal system and society.** H7: *evaluates* the **effectiveness of the law in achieving justice.**
A student develops skills in: 4. investigating, analysing and communicating relevant legal information and issues.	H8: *locates, selects, organises, synthesises* and *analyses* **legal information from a variety of sources including legislation, cases, media, international instruments and documents.** H9: *communicates* **legal information using well-structured and logical arguments.** H10: *analyses* **differing perspectives and interpretations of legal information and issues.**

© NSW Education Standards Authority, *Legal Studies Stage 6 Syllabus*, 2009, p. 8

Chapter 1

Crime

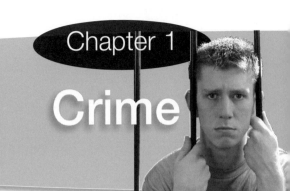

Principal focus

Through the use of a range of contemporary examples, students investigate criminal law, processes and institutions and the tension between community interests and individual rights and freedoms.

Themes and challenges

The following six themes and challenges are also incorporated throughout this chapter, and are summarised in Sections 1.7.1 to 1.7.6 (pages 69–78). They are to be considered throughout your study of this topic.

▶ **1** The role of discretion in the criminal justice system
▶ **2** Issues of compliance and non-compliance in regard to criminal law
▶ **3** The extent to which law reflects moral and ethical standards
▶ **4** The role of law reform in the criminal justice system
▶ **5** The extent to which the law balances the rights of victims, offenders and society
▶ **6** The effectiveness of legal and non-legal measures in achieving justice

HSC CONTENT

	You learn to:
The nature of crime	▶ describe the nature of crime. ▶ recognise the different categories of crime. ▶ define summary and indictable offences. ▶ examine a range of factors that may lead to criminal behaviour. ▶ investigate a range of situational and social crime prevention techniques.
The criminal investigation process	▶ discuss the powers of police in the criminal process. ▶ examine the reporting and investigating of crime. ▶ assess the effectiveness of the criminal investigation process as a means of achieving justice.
Criminal trial process	▶ describe the role of courts in the criminal justice process. ▶ discuss the use of the adversary system as a means of achieving justice. ▶ examine the role of legal representation in the criminal trial. ▶ assess the use of defences to criminal charges in achieving justice. ▶ evaluate the effectiveness of the jury system in the criminal trial. ▶ assess the effectiveness of the criminal trial process as a means of achieving justice.
Sentencing and punishment	▶ discuss factors that affect sentencing decisions, including the purposes of punishment and the role of the victim. ▶ evaluate the effectiveness of different types of penalties, including diversionary programs. ▶ assess the roles of alternative methods of sentencing. ▶ examine the implications of post-sentencing considerations in achieving justice. ▶ evaluate the effectiveness of sentencing and punishment as a means of achieving justice.
Young offenders	▶ discuss the issues surrounding the age of criminal responsibility. ▶ explain why young offenders are treated differently in the criminal justice system. ▶ assess the effectiveness of the criminal justice system when dealing with young offenders.
International crime	▶ define international crime. ▶ describe the various methods used to deal with international crime. ▶ evaluate the effectiveness of the domestic and international legal systems in dealing with international crime.

© NSW Education Standards Authority, *Legal Studies Stage 6 Syllabus*, 2009, pp. 17–19

1.1 The nature of crime

Explain the meaning of *crime*.

1.1.1 The meaning of crime

A crime is 'an act committed or an omission of duty, injurious to the public welfare, for which punishment is prescribed by law, imposed in a judicial proceeding usually brought in the name of the state' (*The Macquarie Dictionary*, 2010).

The legal characteristics of a crime, as suggested in the definition above, are:

▶ there must be an act, or a failure to act (an omission), which breaks the law

▶ the act or omission must be seen as harmful to the whole community

▶ the act or omission is punishable by the state

▶ the state takes the person who committed the act to court, where the offence must be proved according to the rules of criminal procedure.

Criminal law involves the public, and the offender is tried by the state. The case is between the offender and the state.

Criminal law is found in both statute and common law. Common law still covers many areas of criminal law, for example causation (see Section 1.1.4 on pages 3–6), and the courts play a major role in interpreting statutes (see Case Study 1.2, Section 1.1.4. page 4).

The Commonwealth of Australia Constitution Act (the Constitution of Australia) divides powers to make laws between state and federal governments. While the federal government legislates for some criminal offences, most criminal law is state law. The major statute in NSW is the *Crimes Act 1900* (NSW) which lists offences and prescribes maximum penalties. This act is frequently amended as types of criminal offences change. Other statutes include the *Summary Offences Act 1988* (NSW) which mostly deals with public order offences and the *Drug Misuse and Trafficking Act 1985* (NSW) which deals with drug offences (see Section 1.1.5 on pages 5–6). KCq page 87

Explain the elements of crime: *actus reus* and *mens rea*.

1.1.2 The elements of crime

For most types of crime, two elements need to be proved before it can be said that a criminal offence has occurred and that the accused person is criminally liable. To be criminally liable is to be responsible under the law for a criminal offence. The two elements of a crime that must be proved are *actus reus* (the conduct of the offender) and *mens rea* (the mental state of the offender). So a person is generally only guilty if he or she carried out the criminal act with a criminal state of mind.

Actus reus

Actus reus means 'the guilty act'. This means the voluntary commission of an act or the voluntary omission of a duty that breaks the law.

The important features of *actus reus* are:

▶ that the act or omission actually took place

▶ that it was done by the accused person

▶ that it was voluntary. (If a person had a muscular spasm and hit someone during the spasm, he or she would not be acting voluntarily and so *actus reus* would not be proved.)

Mens rea

Mens rea means 'the guilty mind'. Traditionally this means a person is guilty of a crime only if he or she carried out the criminal act (*actus reus*) **and** intended to do so. *Mens rea* includes not only the intention to commit the crime, but can also include recklessness or gross negligence. *Mens rea* is proved if the person committing the criminal act did so with one of the following states of mind:

▶ the intention or specific desire to commit the act or omit the duty

▶ recklessness (which means that the person could foresee the probability of harm, but acted anyway [see Case Study 1.1 below])

▶ negligence (which means that the person failed to exercise the degree of care, skill or foresight that a reasonable person would have exercised in the same circumstances). A very high degree of negligence may be enough to constitute *mens rea* for a criminal act. For example, if a person drove a car in a highly negligent manner and killed someone, he or she could be liable for manslaughter.

CASE STUDY 1.1: *Hyam v the DPP* (1974) 2 All ER 41

Facts

Hyam deliberately set fire to a house in Coventry, England, by pouring half a gallon of petrol through the letterbox and setting it alight. Another woman and her son and two daughters were asleep in the house at the time. While the woman and her son escaped, the two daughters died.

Issue

Was the accused, Hyam, guilty of murder? Hyam argued that she had no intention of harming anyone. She only wanted to scare the occupants of the house. The case went on appeal to the House of Lords.

Decision

The court said that Hyam was guilty of murder because, even though she didn't intend to harm the two daughters, she deliberately exposed them to serious risk of death or grievous bodily harm, with full knowledge of the danger involved. The court said that this was sufficiently reckless to constitute the necessary *mens rea* to be guilty of murder.

 page 87

1.1.3 Strict liability offences

Describe strict liability offences.

In most crimes, both *actus reus* and *mens rea* must be proved for a person to be found guilty of a crime. However, some crimes are strict liability crimes, which means that no *mens rea* needs to be proved. Many traffic offences are strict liability offences. If you speed, it only needs to be proved that you broke the speed limit—your state of mind at the time does not matter. So only *actus reus* needs to be proved. page 87

1.1.4 Causation

Explain the nature of causation.

For a crime to be proved, causation must be shown. This means that the act or omission committed must have caused the specific injury complained of. For example, part of proving the crime of murder is that the actions of the accused person 'caused the death charged' (see Case Study 1.2 on the next page).

Causation can be easily established in most cases. The principles of causation mainly apply to murder and manslaughter charges. In these cases, if the accused had the *mens rea* and the *actus reus* to commit a murder but the victim's death resulted from other means, then the offence of murder is not proved.

Case study 1.2: Murder, the *Crimes Act* and the common law

Murder and the *Crimes Act*

The crime of murder is defined by section 18(1)(a) of the *Crimes Act 1900* (NSW). Part of this section is as follows:

> 'Murder shall be taken to have been committed where the act of the accused, or the thing by him or her omitted to be done, causing the death charged, was done or omitted, with reckless indifference to human life, or with intent to kill or inflict grievous bodily harm upon some person ...'

Interpreting the statute

Though the crime of murder is defined by this statute, the common law has an important part to play in determining what these words mean. For example, there are many cases that deal with the phrase 'causing the death charged'. These cases form the common law of causation. One such case is examined in Case Study 1.3: *Blaue v R* (1975) 1 WLR on the next page.

In murder cases, the law recognises that there are many events which can cause a death. In order for the murder to be proved, the actions of the accused must substantially have caused that death. Circumstances in which the act of the accused (*actus reus*) is said to have caused the death, even though there were other contributing factors include:

- **ordinary natural events**
- **people must take their victims as they find them.**

EXAMPLE **Ordinary natural events**

If you assaulted someone and left him or her lying unconscious in a raging snowstorm and the person died, you would be guilty of murder or manslaughter. That is because a snowstorm is an ordinary natural event and you should have foreseen the death in these circumstances.

EXAMPLE **Taking victims as they find them**

If you hit someone on the head and they died, partly because they had a particularly thin skull, you would still be guilty of murder or manslaughter. This applies to both the physical and mental state of the victim, as shown in the case of *Blaue v R* (1975) 1 WLR (Case Study 1.3, following).

CASE STUDY 1.3: *Blaue v R* (1975) 1 WLR

Facts
The victim was stabbed and, on reaching hospital, she refused a blood transfusion because of her religious beliefs as a Jehovah's Witness. The victim died as a result of refusing treatment.

Issue
Did the accused cause the death of the victim, or was it her own act of refusing a blood transfusion?

Decision
The accused was convicted of manslaughter for the stabbing, because the stabbing was an 'operative and substantial' cause of death. Judge Lawton in the Court of Appeal said, 'Those who use violence on other people must take their victims as they find them. This in our judgement means the whole man, not just the physical man'.

CAN YOU describe the nature of crime?

To describe the nature of crime, you need to be able to:

▷ define the word *crime*, listing all four elements of the definition as shown in Section 1.1.1 (see page 2). You should explain that crimes are behaviours that are seen as harmful to the whole community, not just to the victim of the behaviour, and this is why the conduct is criminalised.

▷ give an example of a crime. Categories of crime that you can use are listed in Section 1.1.5 (see below).

▷ explain that, for most crimes to be proved, the perpetrator needs to have both *actus reus* and *mens rea* (Section 1.1.2, pages 2–3).

▷ explain that some crimes are strict liability offences and what this means (Section 1.1.3, page 3).

▷ explain the meaning of *causation* and give an example (Section 1.1.4, pages 3–5).

KCq page 87

1.1.5 Categories of crime
The criminal law has a far-reaching scope or range. This means it covers a wide variety of behaviour, ranging from breaking the speed limit to murder. Criminal behaviour can be classified by the type of act or omission performed. The different types of criminal offence are as follows.

Describe the categories of crime.

Offences against the person
Crimes against the person are acts or omissions which harm other people. They include murder, assault and sexual assault. (Sexual assault is discussed further in Section 1.3.8 when discussing consent, see page 36).

Offences against the sovereign
These are acts or omissions which aim to disrupt or harm the governing bodies of a country. They are political crimes and are uncommon in Australia. They include spying, treason, illegal demonstrations, and trespass on government land to prevent the government from doing something. Crimes to do with terrorism are crimes against the sovereign

(see Sections 1.2.1 [pages 12–13], 1.6.1–1.6.3 [pages 62–3], 1.7.3 [page 72], and 1.7.5 [page 77]).

Economic offences (property/white collar/computer)

Economic offences involve acts or omissions against people's property or finances and include:

▶ **crimes against property** (These are acts or omissions which damage or remove other people's property. Examples are larceny or theft, break and enter, or damaging property.)

▶ **white-collar crimes** (These are crimes against property carried out by people working in the business world who commit crimes related to money. They include embezzlement and tax evasion.)

▶ **computer crimes**. (These are crimes that are committed using computers and internet technology. They include identity theft and false representations made by persons via the internet in order to gain money.)

Drug offences

These offences include possession of illegal drugs, trafficking, cultivation, manufacture and importation of illegal drugs. *Possession* of an illegal drug means to have enough drugs for personal use only. *Trafficking* means having a trafficable quantity of drugs, which is an amount deemed greater than that which a person could use for himself or herself. T his is a far more serious crime than possession. Drug offences in NSW are covered under the *Drug Misuse and Trafficking Act 1985* (NSW). This act makes possession, trafficking and other drug offences illegal.

Driving offences

Most driving offences are summary or regulatory offences, such as speeding or not wearing a seatbelt. These types of driving offences are strict liability (see Section 1.1.3, page 3). However, driving offences can also be more serious, for example negligent driving and reckless driving.

Public order offences

Public order offences are acts which occur in a public place and are seen as offensive or disruptive to the general population. They are generally minor and include such offences as offensive conduct, obstructing traffic and indecent exposure.

Preliminary crimes (attempts and conspiracy)

To commit a preliminary crime is to try to commit an act or omission, or to plan to do so. It does not matter whether the crime is successfully committed or not. Having the intention to do so is enough. The two main types of preliminary crimes are:

▶ **conspiracy**. This occurs where two or more people agree to do an unlawful act or to do a lawful act by unlawful means.

▶ **attempt**. If a crime is attempted but not successfully committed, then the crime of attempt applies.

EXAMPLE Conspiracy

If two brothers plan to kill another brother but do not actually commit the crime, the two brothers who made the plan could be found guilty of conspiracy.

EXAMPLE Attempt

If the two conspiring brothers did try to shoot their other brother but missed, they could be found guilty of attempted murder.

CAN YOU recognise the different categories of crime?

▶ To show that you can recognise the different categories of crime, you should be able to define and give examples of the seven categories of crime listed on pages 5–6.

KCq page 87

1.1.6 Summary and indictable offences

The two main classifications of a criminal offence are decided upon by the seriousness of the act or omission. These are summary offences and indictable offences.

Summary offences are those heard and decided by a magistrate sitting without a jury. These offences are relatively minor and include driving offences and offensive behaviour. Summary offences are heard by a magistrate in a Local Court.

Indictable offences are serious criminal offences and may be heard by a judge and jury. They include murder, sexual assault and malicious wounding. In practice, many less serious indictable offences are dealt with summarily—that is, without a jury. Sections 1.3.1 (pages 22–5) and 1.3.7 (pages 30–32) explain how summary and indictable offences are dealt with in the legal process.

> Explain the differences between summary and indictable offences.

CAN YOU define *summary* and *indictable* offences?

To define *summary* and *indictable* offences you should mention:

▶ the seriousness of each type of offence

▶ the way each type of offence is heard by a court

▶ an example of each type of offence.

KCq page 87

1.1.7 Parties to a crime

The parties to a crime are the people who have participated in committing a criminal offence. This can be before, during or after the offence. The parties to a crime include:

> Identify the parties to a criminal offence.

▶ **the principal in the first degree**. This is the actual perpetrator of the crime—that is, the person or persons who actually committed the crime.

▶ **the principal in the second degree**. This is a person or persons who were present or who assisted the principal in the first degree in committing the offence.

▶ **the accessory before the fact**. This is a person or persons who helped plan the offence but were not there when it occurred.

▶ **the accessory after the fact**. This is the person or persons who helped the principals after the crime had been committed.

EXAMPLE **Parties to a crime**

John, Bill and Tom planned to rob a service station. On the day, Bill drove John to the service station and waited while John held it up at gunpoint. On leaving the station, Bill and John drove to Sally's house. She helped them dispose of the weapons and car. In this example, John is the principal in the first degree, Bill is the principal in the second degree, Tom is an accessory before the fact, and Sally is an accessory after the fact.

KCq page 87

1.1.8 Factors affecting criminal behaviour

Examine the factors affecting criminal behaviour.

Crime is an aspect of all societies. Crimes change from country to country and from year to year because crime depends on what the public sees as offending public welfare. Sometimes one group in society condemns certain behaviour as being against public welfare while another group sees the behaviour as quite acceptable. Many young people think that marijuana use is quite acceptable, while older people tend to see this behaviour as criminal. Use of marijuana is illegal in NSW.

Most people usually obey most criminal laws all the time. This is because:

▶ a belief, value or custom means a person would follow the legal behaviour anyway. For example, most people do not vandalise public property because they hold the belief or value that public property is for the use of all people, so should be kept undamaged.

▶ many laws simply regulate behaviour which we generally agree should be regulated, for example traffic offences

▶ we are educated to think that certain behaviour should not be allowed, for example urinating in the streets

▶ people fear punishment

▶ people fear public shame or condemnation

▶ people have a general desire for protection which means that people want a legal system to protect them, so will comply with its restrictions.

However, many people do break some criminal laws from time to time. Laws about speeding, for example, are broken by most drivers at some time, usually because of impatience or inattention. Other laws, such as those relating to alcohol consumption or stealing small items, are also broken more often than other criminal laws, because people:

▶ see the law as being unimportant

▶ think that they will not be caught

▶ give in to temptation

▶ see it as thrilling or exciting to break the law.

Some people break criminal laws more often than other people. Crime specialists have sought to explain why some people have a greater tendency to behave in a criminal manner. There are a number of different factors which influence certain individuals to engage in criminal behaviour. These include the factors discussed below.

Social and economic factors

Statistically, people are more likely to commit crimes if they come from a poor or disadvantaged background, though this certainly does not mean that the majority of disadvantaged people are lawbreakers. Differential association theorists argue that, if people are surrounded by or brought up with criminal behaviour around them, they will be more likely to commit crimes themselves because it is seen by them to be socially acceptable to do so.

Genetic factors

Genetic theories state that some people are born criminals—that is, there is something in a person's genetic make-up or personality which means that person has a tendency to commit crime.

Political factors

Sometimes people act in a criminal way because they feel that the law they are breaking is wrong, or the action that they are protesting against is wrong. This is breaking the law for political reasons and is called civil disobedience.

EXAMPLE **Civil disobedience**

Two men painted 'No War' in red paint on the Sydney Opera House in March 2003 as a protest against Australia sending troops to fight in the war against Iraq. Both men were charged with, and found guilty of, malicious damage.

Self-interest

Some members of society may be involved in criminal behaviour for their own personal or economic gain. Economic gain is a major factor contributing to some forms of criminal behaviour. These crimes include drug trafficking, white-collar crime such as tax evasion, and crimes using new technology.

CAN YOU **examine a range of factors that may lead to criminal behaviour?**

To examine the range of factors that may lead to criminal behaviour, you should discuss:

▶ the reasons most people obey the criminal law most of the time

▶ the reasons why many people break some criminal laws sometimes

▶ the factors which may influence the fact that some people are more likely to engage in criminal behaviour than others.

 KCq page 87

1.1.9 Crime prevention: situational and social

There are two main types of crime prevention: situational and social.

Situational crime prevention refers to creating situations where it is difficult for people to break the criminal law.

Describe a range of situational and social crime prevention techniques.

EXAMPLE **Situational crime prevention**

▶ Parents may stop their children from going to a party where a criminal situation could arise. This is private situational crime prevention.

▶ A good security system and locks on a house may discourage potential thieves. This is also private situational crime prevention.

▶ Under the *Children (Protection and Parental Responsibility) Act 1997* (NSW), police have the power to take children home if they are at risk of becoming involved in anti-social behaviour.

▶ An efficient and effective police force and judicial system discourage people from committing crime because they think they will be caught.

▶ Technology such as security cameras and computer encryption technology also prevents and deters people from committing crime.

Social crime prevention occurs through changing the social factors which cause people to be criminals. Some criminals come from low socioeconomic, minority or disadvantaged backgrounds and may have been surrounded by crime from a young age, so that the differential association theory comes into play (see Section 1.1.8, page 8).

To truly prevent crime, the social causes of a cycle of crime should be broken. It is argued that the best crime prevention is through education, employment and a viable social security system.

Education about why laws are established, how they function and why certain acts are illegal is one of the best crime prevention techniques and usually begins in early childhood and continues through life. The morals and ethics of certain groups in society may make crime prevention education difficult. Social and economic disadvantage can also make it difficult for persons to break a cycle of crime through education.

Providing employment or an adequate income through the social security system may also prevent crime because people with sufficient incomes can obtain what they need and want without resorting to crime.

CAN YOU **investigate a range of situational and social crime prevention techniques?**

To investigate a range of situational and social crime prevention techniques, you should discuss:

▶ what is meant by *situational crime prevention*

▶ various examples of situational crime prevention and how effective each is in preventing crime

▶ what is meant by *social crime prevention*

▶ various examples of social crime prevention, such as education and employment, and how effective each is in preventing crime.

 KCq page 87

1.2 The criminal investigation process

The criminal process, also known as the criminal justice system, is the system that operates to bring criminal offenders to justice. There are three main stages in the criminal process, which will be examined in this chapter. They are described below.

▶ **The criminal investigation process**: This is the investigative stage of the criminal process, where crimes are detected and investigated, and evidence is gathered so that an alleged offender may be brought before a court. This is done mainly by the police. The investigative stage of the criminal process is discussed in Sections 1.2.1 to 1.2.7 (pages 11–21).

▶ **The criminal trial process**: This is also known as the adjudication process and is the hearing stage of the criminal process, where the guilt or innocence of a defendant is decided in a court according to the rules of procedure and evidence. The criminal trial process is discussed in Sections 1.3.1 to 1.3.10 (pages 22–43).

▶ **Sentencing and punishment**: This is the punishment stage of the criminal process in which courts decide appropriate punishments for convicted offenders, and sentences are carried out by various sentencing authorities. This is discussed in Sections 1.4.1 to 1.4.9 (see pages 43–56).

The criminal process is not a cohesive system. While all three parts of the system share the basic aim of processing criminal offenders, each part has different specific objectives and functions. Each is also subject to different rules and influences. So conflict arises between the three areas of the criminal justice process and between those areas and the public. Discretion is a major factor in the entire criminal process, and can lead to many of the conflicts in the process. *Discretion* means the choice to do or not do something. Discretion is part of all criminal processes, from reporting crime, and the police deciding what crimes to investigate and which to ignore, to who gets arrested and what charges are decided upon. Police have considerable discretion in enforcing the law and discretion is also demonstrated by the judiciary and other legal personnel in the trial process, in sentencing, and in punishment.

The role of discretion in the criminal justice system is one of the themes and challenges to be incorporated throughout the topic of Crime, and is summarised in Section 1.7.1 (pages 69–71). It is also discussed throughout this chapter. *KCq* page 87

1.2.1 Police powers

The powers which police have in investigating a crime are as follows.

Search and seizure

Police have power to search people, places and motor vehicles, and seize or take evidence. They have the power to search premises in order to investigate a crime, if the occupier of the premises consents, or if the police have a search warrant. Police can search anyone reasonably suspected of possessing stolen property or anything which has been, or is intended to be, used in committing a serious offence. This also applies to motor vehicles. Police may also search a person after arrest (see also Section 1.2.3, pages 15–16).

Access to information

The Computerised Operational Policing System (COPS) operates in NSW, giving police the ability to cross-reference details of all 'persons of interest'. Such persons include people with a criminal history, those with an outstanding warrant, someone who is the subject of an intelligence report or a domestic violence order, anyone who holds a gun licence, a person with a history of mental illness, a victim of a crime or a suspect. Concern has been expressed about the privacy of ordinary citizens being invaded by such a system.

Interrogation

Police have a right to ask questions, but a suspect need not answer them except in special circumstances, which include:

- a driver must produce his or her licence on request
- a person must, if able to do so, give the name and address of a driver who has been involved in a motor accident
- a person must give information to a customs officer about drug smuggling (see Section 1.2.6, page 20).

Police have sometimes been accused of making up false confessions or of using threats of violence in order to force people to make false confessions. Such confessions are called *verbals*.

Most police stations are now equipped to video or audiotape interviews to protect an alleged offender from being verballed. Under changes to the

Describe the powers of the police.

law made in 1995, confessions made to police about a serious crime, but not electronically recorded, generally cannot be used as evidence in court unless the police have a reasonable excuse for not recording the interview. Police must provide to the person being interviewed copies of any video or audiotapes made.

Electronic surveillance

Police may tap phones if they obtain a warrant from a judge first. They do not need a warrant at all in cases of sieges, kidnapping or hostage-taking. Surveillance cameras in public streets have been set up by some local councils, in conjunction with the police, in various locations around Sydney and other NSW centres. They have provided the police with close links to what is happening on the streets and the police have made several arrests on the basis of what the cameras have shown. A significant drop in crime in the areas being watched has been reported. It is also argued that ordinary people feel safer in these areas knowing that there is surveillance, because the cameras seem to deter potential criminals. However, concern has been expressed that such cameras are an invasion of privacy and that they merely shift the crime from the streets under camera surveillance to other localities.

Medical examinations

Police may order an arrested person to undergo a medical examination. This includes giving DNA samples and forensic evidence. Under the *Crimes (Forensic Procedures) Act 2000* (NSW) criminal suspects, volunteers and people convicted of a serious offence can be tested for DNA. This act also provides for the establishment of a DNA database. If a person reasonably suspected of committing a serious crime refuses to consent to giving a sample for the purposes of DNA testing, the police can take a sample of hair by force, or can obtain an order from a magistrate to take a sample by force.

Detention

Police generally may not detain someone unless they are arrested (see Section 1.2.4, pages 16–17). The *Law Enforcement (Powers and Responsibilities) Act 2002* (NSW) allows police to keep a suspect for four hours for investigation. An application must be made to a magistrate or an authorised justice of the peace in order to keep a suspect for up to eight hours. Arrested suspects cannot generally be kept for any longer than eight hours without charges being laid. A drunk and disorderly person may be detained for up to forty-eight hours without arrest. A person can be detained for up to two hours for the purpose of taking samples for DNA testing.

The federal government's *Anti-Terrorism Act (No. 2)* provides for preventative detention. A person suspected of being about to engage in a terrorist activity can be detained in prison for forty-eight hours without charge. Extensions to this time may be granted if police investigations are ongoing.

This law and similar ones enacted by various state governments throughout Australia have been criticised as violating the International Covenant on Civil and Political Rights 1966 (ICCPR), which embodies the principle that people's liberty should only be restricted if there is a criminal charge against them (see Section 2.1.3, pages 106–7). The case of Mohamed Haneef (Case Study 1.4 following) illustrates the danger of this power of detention.

CASE STUDY 1.4: The detention of Mohamed Haneef, July 2007

Facts

On 2 July 2007, Mohamed Haneef, was arrested at Brisbane Airport at the request of British police, following failed terrorist attacks in London and Glasgow on 29 June and 30 June. Haneef was an Indian citizen who had been working in his profession as a doctor on the Gold Coast. He allegedly had connections with the terrorists in Britain.

Haneef was detained by police in Brisbane for twelve days, without charge, until 14 July when he was charged with providing support to a terrorist organisation. Haneef was granted $10 000 bail on 16 July. However, his visa was then cancelled on the grounds that he did not pass the character test, and he was detained in the Villawood migrant detention centre pending the hearing of the charge against him.

On 27 July, following further investigations and media reports, the charges against Dr Haneef were dropped and he was placed in 'residential detention', which allowed him to come and go freely, but not to work. Plans by the government to deport him were abandoned, though he flew to his home in India shortly after.

Issue

Do these powers of detention unreasonably interfere with the individual's rights?

Outcome

The federal government set up an inquiry in 2008 to investigate the circumstances surrounding the arrest and detention of Dr Haneef. The inquiry was conducted by former NSW Supreme Court judge, John Clarke QC. The results of the inquiry, which were released in December 2008, found that Dr Haneef was wrongly charged, and criticised various bodies involved with the case. Dr Clarke also criticised the lack of a cap on the amount of time police could detain a suspect without charging him.

Fingerprints and photographs

Police have the power to take photographs of and fingerprint an arrested person, for identification.

The role of discretion in the exercise of police powers

Police discretion can play a large role in the investigation of criminal offences. Police must decide, because of limited resources, which areas to patrol, which crimes to target and which reports to investigate. They may be more likely to allocate resources in a way that concentrates on Aboriginal people and poor people. For example, in Sydney, they are more likely to patrol Redfern, rather than the more affluent suburb of Vaucluse.

Lack of police resources also affects how thorough the investigation is. In poorer socioeconomic areas it is often easier to find someone to accuse of a crime. Because of this, the crime may not always be as thoroughly investigated as it could be. Police discretion also applies to decisions made by individual officers. An individual police officer uses discretion to decide whether to investigate certain behaviour, whether to charge a suspect or whether to let a young offender go with a caution. The decision of the police officer may be influenced by the alleged offender's race, appearance, family background or address. There is much controversy about whether the police have too much or too little power in the investigation of criminal offences.

CAN YOU discuss the powers of the police in the criminal process?

To discuss the powers of the police in the criminal process, you should describe:

▶ each of the areas where the police can exercise power

▶ concerns about the exercise of police powers (see the table following), including the role of discretion in the exercise of such powers.

Table 1.1 summarises the arguments about whether police have too much power.

Table 1.1 Do police have too much power?

Arguments *against* the idea that police have too much power	Arguments *supporting* the idea that police have too much power
▶ Increasing crime figures mean that police need all their powers in order to combat crime.	▶ Not all crimes have increased, so police do not need wider powers than they already have.
▶ As criminals use more complex technology to commit crimes, police also need wide powers in the use of complex technology in order to detect and investigate crime.	▶ Wide police powers mean that ordinary people lose basic rights. Wide powers of phone tapping, for example, infringe people's privacy, and infringe the presumption of innocence (see Section 1.3.6, page 30).
▶ If police do not have sufficient power to detect and investigate crime, ordinary citizens may be tempted to take the law into their own hands.	▶ Wider police power does not alter the fundamental causes of crime such as drug abuse and social and economic problems.
▶ Police need wide powers to detain people suspected of being about to engage in a terrorist activity, because these people can cause great harm to many innocent people and are well-trained and secretive.	▶ Wider powers of police to detain suspected terrorists without charge infringe on basic human rights (see Case Study 1.4 on page 13).
	▶ More police power does not prevent crime. All it can do is help catch criminals after a crime has been committed.
	▶ More police, not more police power, is the way to improve the detection and investigation of crime.

KCq pages 87–8

Outline the issues involved in reporting crime.

1.2.2 Reporting crime

The reporting of crime is the first step in the criminal investigation process. Most crimes are detected or discovered by private citizens who are either witnesses to or victims of a criminal offence. They report the crime to the police. Many crimes go unreported every year as victims or witnesses exercise their discretion about whether to report a crime or not. Crimes go unreported for many different reasons, including:

▶ reporting a crime may bring the victim's own illegal acts or omissions to the attention of the police

▶ victims may know the alleged offender, who could be a family member, friend or acquaintance. The crimes are not reported due to feelings of fear, loyalty or protection.

▶ solutions can be found between the criminal and the victim. This is usually only true if the victim and alleged offender have previously known each other.

▶ red tape. Often the victim feels that reporting the crime will involve too much red tape and hassle, particularly if they want to forget the incident.

▶ feelings of humiliation/shame. This may occur in the case of sexual assault. Victims feel that they do not want to report the assault because it may bring shame and publicity on themselves.

▶ the belief that reporting does not lead to an arrest/conviction. This may occur in crimes such as domestic violence and sexual assault. Victims feel that, because of police discretion, lack of witnesses and an uninterested legal system, reporting the crime will not lead to further action. The NSW Bureau of Crime Statistics and Research reported in 2006 that 90% of reported sexual assaults did not lead to a conviction (see Section 1.4.4, page 47).

- many sexual assault victims feel that there is sexism in the police force and the judiciary. The evidence of gender bias in the judiciary and the fact that victims of sexual assault are often subjected to gruelling cross-examinations, and can be treated harshly by the legal system, has not helped this perception to change (see Sections 1.3.8 [pages 32–40], 1.4.4 [page 47], and 1.7.5 [pages 75–7]).

Some criminal activities are more likely to be reported than others, depending on who the perpetrator of the crime is. Aboriginal and poor people, for instance, are more likely than others to be reported by a citizen for an alleged criminal offence. For example, shop managers are more likely to report a shoplifter who appears poor than one who appears wealthy. One is regarded as being criminal whereas the other is regarded as being 'disturbed' or 'ill'.

Poor people and Aboriginal people are also more visible than other perpetrators of crime. They are more likely to be noticed or to stand out because of their appearance. They are more visible, so they are more likely to be reported to police, and police on patrol are more likely to notice them.

KCq — page 88

1.2.3 Investigating crime

Police are the main investigators of crime though there are other law enforcers such as:

Outline the procedures involved in investigating crime.

- social security officers, in matters such as social security fraud
- tax officials, in matters of tax evasion
- health and safety inspectors, in matters that relate to breach of safety laws in the workplace and other areas (see Section 5.3.2, pages 342–3)
- local government officials, in matters such as illegal parking in council parking areas.

Gathering evidence

After a crime has been reported or discovered, police investigate the matter further and gather relevant evidence. For example, they might interview possible witnesses, collect a list of stolen property or gather fingerprints and other physical evidence. The powers of police to gather various forms of evidence are discussed in greater detail in Section 1.2.1 (pages 11–14).

Use of technology

Sometimes police use technology to gather and assess evidence. Such technology includes:

- phone taps
- video surveillance
- DNA collection and analysis
- use of data banks, such as COPS.

The powers of police to use technology in the investigation of a crime are examined in Section 1.2.1 (pages 11–14).

Search and seizure

The power of search and seizure means that police and other people, such as customs officers, have the power to search people and their belongings or premises and to take away property that is illegally held or is to be used in evidence. Police have wide powers to search people, places and motor vehicles, and seize or take evidence. The extent of these powers is discussed in Section 1.2.1 (page 11).

Use of warrants

A warrant is a written authorisation issued by a judge or magistrate, which gives the police power to take the action authorised by it. This could be to arrest the person named on the warrant (see Section 1.2.4, below) or to search the premises named on the warrant, or to carry out some other purpose, such as tapping telephone calls.

Generally police need a warrant if they wish to enter and search premises. Police can enter premises without a warrant in some circumstances, such as when:

▶ they wish to arrest a person reasonably suspected of having committed a crime

▶ they have reason to believe, on reasonable grounds, that a domestic violence offence has occurred.

Generally, however, police cannot search premises without either the permission of the occupier, or a warrant.

Police and customs officers can obtain a customs warrant. A customs warrant lasts for a specific period of time and allows the officers to enter and search, at any time, any premises where drugs may be. Police in possession of a customs warrant do not have to show reasonable suspicion and may use force.

CAN YOU **examine the reporting and investigating of crime?**

To examine the reporting and investigating of crime, you should discuss:

▶ who reports crimes and why some crimes are not reported (see Section 1.2.2, pages 14–15)

▶ what is involved in the investigation of crime by police (see Sections 1.2.1 [pages 11–14] and 1.2.3 [pages 15–16])

▶ how police discretion affects the investigation of crime (see Sections 1.2.1 [pages 11–14] and 1.2.3 [pages 15–16]).

The use of police powers is also relevant here, because it forms part of the discussion of how police investigate crime. Police powers are discussed in Section 1.2.3 (see pages 15–16).

KCq page 88

1.2.4 Arrest and charge, summons and warrants

Describe the processes of arrest and charge, summons, and the use of warrants.

There are three ways that the police can bring an alleged offender to court after an investigation. The word *alleged* means that the person is only suspected of having committed the crime—it has not yet been proved that the person committed the offence. The three methods police can use are discussed below.

Information and summons

A summons is an official legal document which commands the person to whom it is addressed to appear at a particular court on a particular day to answer claims made against him or her. The police obtain a summons which is served on (given to) the alleged offender either by the police in person or through the mail.

Information and warrant

An arrest warrant is a written authorisation issued by a judge or magistrate which gives the police power to arrest the person named on it. After a warrant has been issued, the police can arrest the alleged offender wherever and whenever he or she may be found. Other types of warrants are discussed in Section 1.2.3 (page 16).

Arrest without warrant

This is the most usual method of bringing an alleged offender to court. Police may arrest anyone they reasonably suspect of having committed a crime, or being about to commit a crime. They may use whatever force is necessary to carry out the arrest. Armed police must give a clear warning of their intent to use firearms, allow sufficient time for the warning to be heeded and only use firearms when it is 'strictly unavoidable in order to protect life'. Officers, on arrest, must:

- tell the person that he or she is under arrest
- tell the person why he or she is being arrested
- touch the person being arrested.

The use of the term 'reasonably suspect', when referring to the ability of police to arrest, means that police discretion enters into matters of arrest. Police can choose whether to arrest someone for a crime or not. In the case of minor offences, police have the discretion to give a warning or to arrest the offender.

Citizen's arrest

In early English society before police forces developed, it was the right and responsibility of citizens to arrest anyone who committed a felony. This common law right of ordinary people remains in NSW today and is called citizen's arrest. Ordinary people may arrest another person when:

- a crime has been committed or attempted
- there is immediate danger of a crime being committed
- a breach of the peace has been committed or is about to be committed.

An ordinary person cannot arrest someone on a 'reasonable suspicion' of having committed a crime. Only police can do that. Citizen's arrest is a rare occurrence in today's society.

Criminal charges

Police exercise discretion when laying criminal charges against an arrested person. They decide the charges based on the evidence which they have gathered from their investigation, and decide which charge to lay, often in conjunction with the Director of Public Prosecutions (DPP). See Section 1.3.3, page 27.

EXAMPLE Deciding on charges

In the case where A has badly assaulted B who almost died, the police have the discretion to decide what charges A receives. Person A could be charged with assault, with attempted manslaughter, or with attempted murder. Which charge A receives depends on what the investigating police and/or the DPP think is appropriate. Charge negotiation may have an effect on the charge that is laid (see Section 1.3.4, pages 27–8).

KCq page 88

Describe when and why bail may be granted.

1.2.5 Bail or remand

Bail is an agreement to attend court to answer a criminal charge. In NSW the law regarding bail is contained in the *Bail Act* 2013 (NSW). If bail is granted, the defendant is free to go but must attend court on the day specified.

Remand is the term for what happens to the accused when bail is refused. The defendant is remanded in custody (that is, kept in prison, until the day of the court hearing).

Bail can be granted either unconditionally (that is, there are no conditions attached) or conditionally (for example, the defendant must lodge a sum of money or must report to the police station every day). Any money lodged will be returned when the defendant appears in court. Bail can be granted at any stage during the criminal process:

▶ after arrest, the police can grant bail.

▶ at the first court appearance, the magistrate can grant bail

▶ during any adjournments of the court hearing, the judge or magistrate can grant bail.

However, a defendant cannot make an additional application for bail unless new facts are presented to the court, or the defendant did not have legal representation for the first application. Initial studies by the NSW Bureau of Crime Statistics and Research (BOSCAR) reveal a marked increase in the number of juveniles on remand since this amendment was passed ('Recent trends in legal proceedings for breach of bail, juvenile remand and crime', Vignaendra, Moffatt, Weatherburn and Heller, *Crime and Justice Bulletin*, Number 128, May 2009, NSW Bureau of Crime Statistics and Research).

Bail is or is not granted according to the following.

▶ Those accused of minor offences must be granted bail except under very unusual circumstances.

▶ Those accused of more serious offences not involving violence or robbery should be granted bail, unless police have very good reasons for not granting it. This means there is a presumption in favour of bail (that is, it is presumed that the accused will be granted bail).

▶ In the case of people accused of very serious offences involving violence and robbery, there is no presumption in favour of bail. This also applies to those who seriously breach apprehended violence orders (see Section 4.2.4, page 233).

▶ Those accused of drug trafficking, murder or involvement with a terrorist activity are not eligible for bail unless they can satisfy the judge that it should be granted (that is, the presumption is against bail).

Various factors are taken into account when a police officer, magistrate or judge is deciding whether to grant bail. The following must be considered, among other factors:

▶ the likelihood of the accused person coming to court on the appointed day

▶ the interests of the accused person

▶ the protection of the community.

Discretion is involved in the consideration of these factors. Different decision-makers may assess these factors differently.

The importance of bail

Bail is very important because, until the court hearing is over, the defendant is presumed innocent (see Section 1.3.6, page 30). If a person is remanded in custody, that means a person presumed innocent is kept in prison. The person is not guilty of a crime until found guilty by a court, so there must be very good reasons not to grant bail.

The granting of bail becomes even more important when there are delays in the criminal justice system. When a person is charged with a serious offence, the time between when the person is first arrested and the time when the case is heard in court can be well over a year. If bail has not been granted, this means the person can be kept in prison for all this time, even if he or she is eventually found innocent. Some factors which contribute to the delays are:

▶ the fact that we have an adversarial system of trial which is based on confrontation rather than on a quick resolution of the case

▶ courts may sit for only a few hours each day

▶ an increasing number of cases, though this is not true for the Children's Court (see Sections 1.5.3 and 1.5.5 [pages 58–9]).

▶ lack of time management practices by judges, magistrates and lawyers.

Effects of these delays include:

▶ victims can suffer from severe ongoing trauma because the wrongdoer is still free or unpunished

▶ witnesses may forget details, resulting in a case becoming harder to prove

▶ alleged offenders who are on remand and who are eventually found not guilty suffer an enormous infringement on freedom

▶ delays reduce public expectations of the efficiency of the criminal justice system.

 page 88

1.2.6 Detention and interrogation, and the rights of suspects

The rights of people suspected of committing a criminal offence are outlined below and in Section 1.2.1 (see pages 11–14). The extent to which law balances the rights of victims, offenders and society is discussed in Section 1.7.5 (see pages 75–7).

Detention

After a person has been arrested for a crime, he or she is usually detained by the police at the police station and interrogated (questioned). Generally speaking, a person cannot be detained unless he or she is arrested.

As seen in Section 1.2.1 (page 12), police can generally only detain someone for up to eight hours, unless the person is charged with a crime. This does not count travel time, or time spent with a doctor or lawyer.

The allowable detention period varies according to different circumstances, which are outlined in Section 1.2.1 (page 12). Concerns have been expressed about the ability of police to detain suspected terrorists for much longer, as in the case of Mohamed Haneef in 2007 (see Case Study 1.4, Section 1.2.1, page 13). This law has been criticised as violating the International Covenant on Civil and Political Rights 1966 (ICCPR), which embodies the principle that people's liberty should only be restricted if there is a criminal charge against them.

Describe detention and interrogation, and the rights of suspects.

Interrogation and the right to silence

Police may question anyone they like, but all citizens have the right to remain silent—that is, they generally do not have to answer any police questions even if they are under arrest.

Exceptions to this right include:

▶ a driver must produce his or her licence on request

▶ a person must, if able to do so, give the name and address of a driver who has been involved in a motor accident

▶ a person must give information to a customs officer about drug smuggling.

The right to silence extends to the courtroom in the majority of cases. It is not extended to corporations when it comes to documents which might incriminate them. Judges and juries are not supposed to interpret somebody remaining silent as evidence of that person's guilt. Some people argue that the right to silence should be abolished because it only operates to protect the guilty. If someone is innocent, they argue, why would they not speak to show their innocence? However, in practice, the right to silence may be used by people to protect them from having their words twisted by clever barristers, or to protect their friends and families.

Other rights of suspects

Rights regarding privacy

Citizens do not have to allow police to search their persons or their premises except if police have a warrant, or in certain other circumstances outlined in Section 1.2.1 (pages 11–14). A person does not have to supply blood or DNA for forensic tests, unless that person is accused of a serious offence.

Right to communication

Police are supposed to allow a detained person access to facilities to allow that person to contact a friend, relative, solicitor or doctor. This is not a right, but is stipulated in the police code of practice. If an accused person is not given the opportunity for such communication, doubt is cast on the validity of anything he or she may say to police.

Right to a lawyer

An adult has no absolute right to have a lawyer or an independent witness present when being questioned, though the courts have held that a lawyer should be allowed to be present if requested and that the interrogation should be delayed for a reasonable time so that the accused person can attempt to get legal assistance (see Section 1.3.5, page 28).

Young offenders have the right to have an independent adult present when being questioned (see Section 1.5.2, page 58).

Illegal evidence

A confession cannot be used in court unless it is made voluntarily. Confessions made to police but not electronically recorded generally cannot be used as evidence in a court (see Section 1.2.1, pages 11–12). A judge can refuse to admit any evidence which has been illegally obtained. He or she must consider the community's interest, as well as ensuring a fair trial for the accused, when deciding whether to admit or reject evidence. Generally, police have to prove that evidence they have gathered has been obtained legally if it is to be admitted in court.

 KCq page 88

1.2.7 The effectiveness of the criminal investigation process as a means of achieving justice

To assess the effectiveness of the criminal investigation process as a means of achieving justice you should discuss those factors which help ensure justice and those factors which may limit the achievement of justice in the criminal investigation process. Both sets of factors are outlined in Table 1.2.

> Assess the effectiveness of the criminal investigation process as a means of achieving justice.

Table 1.2 Factors affecting the achievement of justice in the criminal investigation process

Factors which *help ensure* the achievement of justice in the criminal investigation process	Factors which may *limit* the achievement of justice in the criminal investigation process
▷ Police need to use technology to combat crime, because many perpetrators are becoming more technologically adept (see Section 1.2.1, pages 11–14).	▷ The exercise of some police powers, such as camera surveillance, DNA collection and COPS, may be an unnecessary violation of privacy (see Section 1.2.1, pages 11–14).
	▷ A significant number of crimes are not reported because people believe nothing effective will be done to the offender. This is particularly true in cases of sexual assault (see Section 1.2.2, pages 14–15).
▷ Police have wide powers of arrest of people who they reasonably suspect of having committed or being about to commit a crime, so the community is protected from criminals (see Section 1.2.4, pages 16–17).	▷ Police have wide discretion in deciding whether to arrest someone or not, particularly when it comes to minor offences. This discretion could be exercised in a discriminatory manner (see Sections 1.2.1 [page 13] and 1.2.4 [pages 16–17]).
▷ Police may only use firearms in limited circumstances (see Section 1.2.4, page 17).	▷ Police may have too much discretion in deciding what charge to lay on an arrested person (see Section 1.2.4, page 17).
▷ People arrested are usually granted bail unless there are good reasons not to do so (see Section 1.2.5, page 18).	▷ The decision to not grant bail is a very serious one, as there is always the chance that an innocent person is kept in detention for a significant period if bail is refused. This can be particularly serious if delays in the criminal process are lengthy (see Section 1.2.5, pages 18–19).
▷ People generally may not be detained by police unless arrested and then only for a limited period (see Section 1.2.6, pages 19–20).	▷ Suspected terrorists can be detained without charge for an indefinite period, which violates a fundamental human right (see Sections 1.2.1 [page 12] and 1.2.6 [page 19])
▷ The right to silence means that people do not have to answer police questions in most circumstances, so they are protected from giving answers which may harm themselves or others (see Section 1.2.6, page 20).	▷ Some argue that the right to silence only operates to protect the guilty (see Section 1.2.6, page 20).
▷ Generally, accused people can communicate with a friend, relative or lawyer (see Section 1.2.6, page 20).	▷ There is no absolute right for an accused person to be able to communicate with a friend or relative (see Section 1.2.6, page 20).
▷ Generally, an accused person is given the opportunity to see a lawyer (see Section 1.2.6, page 20).	▷ There is no absolute right for an accused person to contact a lawyer (see Section 1.2.6, page 20).
▷ Generally, evidence that has been obtained illegally will not be admissible in court (see Section 1.2.6, page 20).	▷ Illegally obtained evidence is admissible in court if it is judged to be in the public interest. This may jeopardise the accused's presumption of innocence (see Section 1.2.6, page 20).

To assess the effectiveness of the criminal investigation process in achieving justice, you should weigh up both sets of factors and decide how effective the system is.

KCq page 88

1.3 Criminal trial process

The criminal trial process is also known as the adjudication process and is the hearing stage of the criminal process, where the guilt or innocence of a defendant is decided in a court according to the rules of procedure and evidence.

1.3.1 Court jurisdiction

Describe court jurisdiction and the role of courts in the criminal justice process.

Jurisdiction means the area over which a court has authority. People in NSW are subject to two court systems because of the constitutional division of power.

As seen in Section 1.1.1 (page 2), *The Commonwealth of Australia Constitution Act* (the Constitution of Australia) divides the powers to make laws between state and federal governments, and most criminal law is state law. So the NSW court system has the jurisdiction to hear most criminal matters, while the Federal Court system hears some criminal matters, such as copyright breaches, and matters arising under the *Competition and Consumer Act 2010* (Cth), such as breaching safety standards (see Section 3.1.5, pages 151–3).

NSW courts: Criminal jurisdiction

The criminal jurisdiction of each court within the NSW court system depends on the type of case and the seriousness of the offence. Figure 1.1 shows the jurisdiction of each court. The arrows indicate the system of appeals, which is discussed later in this section (see page 24).

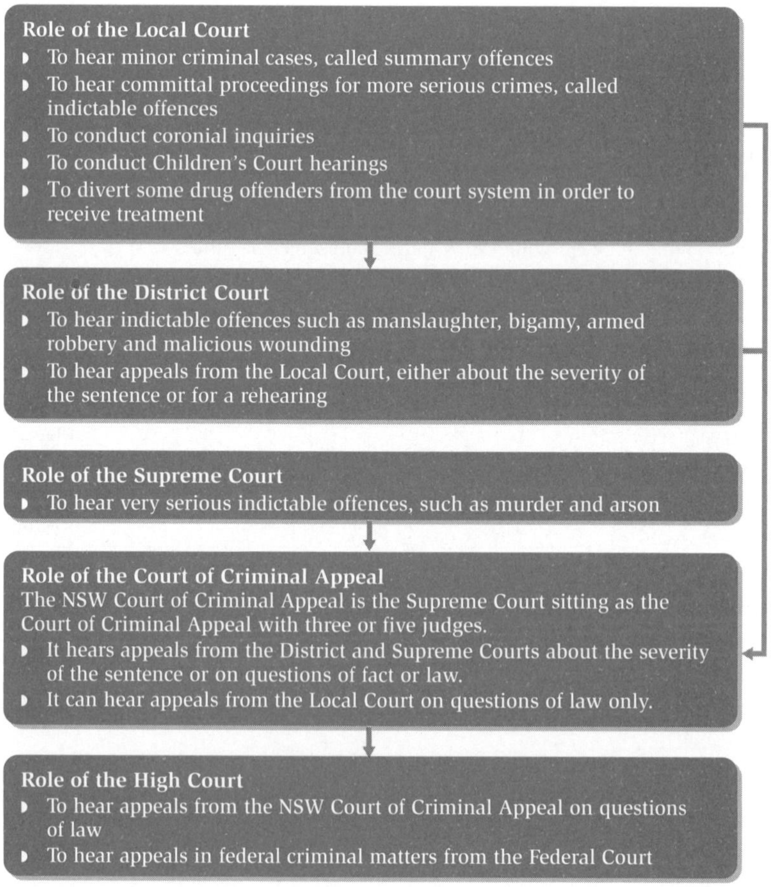

Role of the Local Court
- To hear minor criminal cases, called summary offences
- To hear committal proceedings for more serious crimes, called indictable offences
- To conduct coronial inquiries
- To conduct Children's Court hearings
- To divert some drug offenders from the court system in order to receive treatment

Role of the District Court
- To hear indictable offences such as manslaughter, bigamy, armed robbery and malicious wounding
- To hear appeals from the Local Court, either about the severity of the sentence or for a rehearing

Role of the Supreme Court
- To hear very serious indictable offences, such as murder and arson

Role of the Court of Criminal Appeal
The NSW Court of Criminal Appeal is the Supreme Court sitting as the Court of Criminal Appeal with three or five judges.
- It hears appeals from the District and Supreme Courts about the severity of the sentence or on questions of fact or law.
- It can hear appeals from the Local Court on questions of law only.

Role of the High Court
- To hear appeals from the NSW Court of Criminal Appeal on questions of law
- To hear appeals in federal criminal matters from the Federal Court

Figure 1.1 Jurisdiction of courts in Australia

The Local Court

The Local Court hears summary offences. As seen in Section 1.1.6 (page 7), whether a defendant has a summary hearing or a trial by jury depends on what type of offence he or she has allegedly committed—that is, whether it is a summary or an indictable offence.

In practice, many less serious indictable offences are dealt with summarily—that is, without a jury. Under the *Criminal Procedure Act 1986* (NSW), indictable offences are split into three categories:

- Table One offences, which are those dealt with summarily unless either the prosecution or the accused elects to have the matter dealt with by a judge and jury
- Table Two offences, which are those dealt with summarily unless the prosecution decides to have the offence dealt with by a judge and jury
- strictly indictable offences, which are the most serious offences and must be dealt with by a judge and jury.

As can be seen, discretion plays a part in whether a case is heard summarily or with a jury in the case of Table One and Table Two offences.

Summary hearings

The case is heard in the Local Court and decided by a magistrate alone. The process in a summary hearing is very similar to a trial by jury, except no jury is involved. What happens in a trial by jury is outlined in Section 1.3.7 (pages 31–2).

Committal hearings

Committal hearings are preliminary proceedings for trial by jury. The prosecutor must convince the magistrate there is a *prima facie* case (that is, that there is a sufficiently strong case against the accused to put the matter before a jury). If the magistrate decides there is a *prima facie* case, there is then a trial by jury.

Children's Court hearings

Most charges against people under eighteen years of age are heard in a special Children's Court hearing. The proceedings are much the same as those of a summary hearing with some important exceptions which are outlined in Section 1.5.3 (pages 58–9).

Coronial inquiries

Where there is an unnatural death or an unexplained fire, a coroner will hold an inquest (inquiry) into the circumstances. The proceedings are more inquisitorial than normal court proceedings, and normal rules of evidence and procedure are not followed (see Sections 1.3.2 [page 25] and 1.3.7 [pags 30–32]). If there is evidence of a person committing a serious offence, an indictment will be issued and the person will be tried by a judge and jury in the usual way.

The Drug Court of NSW

This court was established in 1999. It handles non-violent cases committed by adult offenders who are dependent on illegal drugs. This court's aims are not to punish offenders in the prison system but to get the offenders off drugs. By doing this, it aims to reduce drug-related crime and drug addiction.

The Drug Court runs a twelve-month drug court program as an alternative to imprisonment. The program includes judicial and probationary supervision, drug treatment, support services and random drug testing.

If offenders break the conditions of the program, they are sentenced under the normal judicial process.

The District Court

The District Court has jurisdiction over indictable criminal offences, except for murder and other very serious crimes. Criminal matters in the District Court can be heard by a judge and jury. In some cases, such as for Table One and Table Two offences as outlined on page 23, the case can be heard by a judge alone.

In trial by jury, the case is heard by a judge and jury. The court process is the same as that in a summary hearing except that the jury, not the judge, decides the guilt or innocence of the defendant. Trial by jury is used in less than 1% of criminal cases. What happens in a trial by jury is outlined in Section 1.3.7 (pages 31–2).

The District Court also hears appeals regarding decisions by magistrates in most criminal matters. Appeals are discussed below.

The Supreme Court

The Supreme Court hears very serious indictable matters such as murder, complex drug cases and arson. These are heard by a judge and jury. The Supreme Court also sits as the Court of Criminal Appeal.

The Court of Criminal Appeal

The Court of Criminal Appeal has a panel of three or five judges. It hears appeals from:

▶ the Local Court on questions of law

▶ the District Court

▶ single judge decisions in the Supreme Court.

An appeal is when a case is taken to a higher court because either party disagrees with the decision of a lower court. The higher court may then change the decision.

In order for an appeal to succeed, the appellant must show that the lower court judge either wrongly used or misinterpreted the law. No new evidence or fact can be heard.

The *appellant* is the party who disagrees with the decision made and takes the case to a higher court (see also Section 1.4.5, page 48).

Both the federal and state court systems have avenues for lower court decisions to be appealed. The system of appeals helps ensure the effects of wrong decisions made by a judge or magistrate when exercising their discretion are minimised.

The Federal Court of Australia

Though most criminal matters come under state jurisdiction, there are some criminal matters that are heard by the Federal Court of Australia, such as those arising under the *Competition and Consumer Act 2010* (Cth) (see Section 3.1.5, pages 151–3) and breaches of copyright.

The High Court of Australia

In criminal matters, the High Court hears appeals from the Federal Court of Australia and from the NSW Court of Criminal Appeal.

CAN YOU describe the role of the courts in the criminal justice process?

To describe the role of the courts in the criminal justice process, you need to:

▶ explain that a person charged with a criminal offence has his or her guilt or innocence decided in a court hearing

▶ explain that most criminal law is state law so most cases are heard in the NSW court system

▶ explain the types of cases heard in each court in the NSW court system and in the federal system.

▶ explain the system of appeals.

 page 88

1.3.2 The adversarial system

The court process in Australia uses the adversarial system of trial. The inquisitorial system is used in civil law countries, for example France and Italy.

In an inquisitorial system of trial the magistrate or judge collects the evidence from both sides in cooperation with the prosecution after inquiries have been made.

In an adversarial system of trial the two sides of the case try to present and prove their version of the facts and disprove the other side's version. An impartial judge (and sometimes a jury) listens to the evidence and makes a decision as to which side is correct.

Some of the features of an adversarial system of trial which make it different to an inquisitorial system are discussed in Sections 1.3.6 (page 30) and 1.3.7 (pages 30–32). These include:

▶ there are strict rules of evidence, such as those involving hearsay and opinion

▶ there is a presumption of innocence

▶ witnesses are examined orally and can only answer the questions asked

▶ the past record of the accused may only be examined during sentencing.

In an adversarial criminal case:

▶ the case is called a *prosecution*

▶ the party who takes the case to court is called the *prosecution*. The prosecution is usually the state (the government), sometimes called the Crown.

▶ the party against whom the case is brought is called the *defendant*

▶ after the case is decided, the court can sentence the wrongdoer if he or she is found guilty. The court imposes a sanction (punishment). Punishments are discussed in Sections 1.4.1 to 1.4.9 (pages 43–56).

In a criminal case, the prosecution presents evidence to try to prove that the defendant is guilty of the crime with which he or she is charged, while the defence tries to cast doubt on the prosecution's evidence and show that the defendant is not guilty. The way a criminal case is conducted is further outlined in Section 1.3.7 (pages 31–2).

Describe the adversarial system of trial.

CAN YOU **discuss the use of the adversarial system as a means of achieving justice?**

To discuss the use of the adversarial system as a means for achieving justice, you need to weigh up the problems associated with the system against the advantages of the system.

Problems with the adversarial system include:

▶ the adversarial system may be less likely to discover the truth because of the high standard of proof required and the rules of evidence, such as those involving hearsay, opinion and relevance (see Sections 1.3.6 [page 30] and 1.3.7 [page 31])

▶ the adversarial system was developed for juries, which are infrequently used today (see Section 1.3.9, pages 40–42)

▶ oral examination of witnesses, and allowing them to respond only to questions asked, may prevent the full truth being known. Valuable information may never come to light.

▶ the skill of barristers and solicitors may differ; therefore the person with the better lawyer could be advantaged

▶ witnesses, though they may be truthful, can give a bad impression, so they may be disbelieved

▶ some people argue that it is fairer to look at past records of the accused. In the adversarial system, the past record of the accused is generally only admissible during sentencing, not during the trial process itself (see Section 1.4.3, page 46).

Despite these problems, the adversarial system has served common law countries well for centuries. Also, it is argued, the adversarial system does achieve justice in criminal trials because the judge ensures both sides of the case follow the rules of evidence to ensure a just outcome. As well, the system of appeals (see Section 1.3.1. page 24) ensures that, if a mistake is made, there is the opportunity to rectify it.

KCq page 88

1.3.3 Legal personnel

Magistrates and judges

A magistrate decides cases in the Local Court, while a judge decides cases in higher courts, such as the District Court or Supreme Court. In a criminal case, a judge's role differs depending on whether he or she is sitting in a trial by jury or a summary hearing. In both types of cases the magistrate or judge's role is to:

▶ ensure that the trial is conducted legally and in a manner which is fair to the accused

▶ decide questions which arise about the law

▶ impose a punishment if the verdict is that the accused is guilty.

In a summary hearing, the judge or magistrate also decides the guilt or innocence of the accused. In a trial by jury, the judge explains the law to the members of the jury and outlines the questions which must be answered by them for them to reach a verdict.

Police prosecutors

To *prosecute* a case means to present the case in court on behalf of the state. A police prosecutor is a specially-trained officer who usually prosecutes a case in the Local Court. The prosecutor calls on the prosecution witnesses and examines them, and presents other evidence to prove that the alleged offender is guilty of the crime (see also Section 1.3.7, pages 31–2).

> Describe the roles of legal personnel (magistrate, judge, police prosecutor, Director of Public Prosecution, Public Defenders) in the legal system.

Director of Public Prosecutions

The Director of Public Prosecutions (DPP) is the holder of a government office responsible for prosecuting indictable offences heard summarily or in front of a jury. For these offences, a barrister from the office of Director of Public Prosecutions (the DPP) generally prosecutes the case.

Public Defenders

Public Defenders are legal practitioners appointed by the NSW government to represent accused people in the District Court and Supreme Court. So the people represented by Public Defenders are only those accused of serious offences. Public Defenders are only available to people who have been granted legal aid (see Section 1.3.5, pages 28–9). Public Defenders represent accused people in the same way as other defence lawyers (see Sections 1.3.5 [pages 28–9] and 1.3.7 [pages 31–2]). Public Defenders are appointed under the *Public Defenders Act 1995* (NSW).

Other court personnel

The other main participants in the court process are:

▷ the clerk of the court, who is responsible for administrative work in a Local Court.

▷ the registrar, who is responsible for administrative work in a higher court

▷ the tipstaff, who maintains order in the court and administers the oath to witnesses.

KCq page 88

1.3.4 Pleas and charge negotiation

After an alleged offender is charged with a crime, he or she must appear in court for the charge to be heard. When the accused appears in court, he or she will be asked to plead guilty or not guilty to the charge. If the accused pleads guilty, he or she is admitting to the crime. A guilty plea means there is no criminal hearing, the judge or magistrate only needs to consider what penalty to impose (see Sections 1.4.3 [page 46], 1.4.6 [pages 48–52] and 1.4.7 [page 52]). In over 80% of criminal cases, the accused person pleads guilty to the charge.

If the accused person pleads not guilty, then there will be a criminal hearing to determine the guilt of the accused. Types of criminal hearing are described in Section 1.3.1 (pages 22–4).

Sometimes charge negotiation (also known as plea bargaining) occurs. During charge negotiation, the prosecution and defence meet before the trial, and the defence agrees that the accused will plead guilty if the prosecution reduces the charge. Charge negotiation is one of the main ways discretion is used in the court and adjudication processes. The accused and the prosecution decide whether there will be a definite conviction, the nature of the charge and, therefore, the likely severity of the sentence.

EXAMPLE Charge negotiation

An example of charge negotiation would be a person charged with attempted murder agreeing to plead guilty to malicious wounding. This charge carries a much smaller maximum penalty than attempted murder. In return, the prosecution agrees to drop the attempted murder charge. It is hard to determine how many charge negotiations occur in NSW, because it is not an open, officially-recognised practice.

Explain the processes involved in pleas and charge negotiation.

The implications of charge negotiation

Charge negotiation has implications for the notion of justice for the accused, the victim, and for the community as a whole.

The accused

▶ Charge negotiation puts pressure on the accused to plead guilty to something he or she may not be found guilty of in a court hearing, perhaps lessening his or her chance of achieving justice.

▶ The accused may get a lighter sentence than he or she really deserves.

▶ The accused may be prepared to plead guilty to a lesser charge simply because he or she cannot afford the cost of defending the more serious charge.

The victim

▶ Charge negotiation saves the victim from the ordeal of giving evidence and being cross-examined.

▶ The lighter sentence for the accused may mean the victim of the crime feels that the offender was not punished sufficiently.

The community

▶ Charge negotiation saves witnesses in the community from the ordeal of giving evidence and being cross-examined.

▶ Charge negotiation is efficient, quick and inexpensive, because there is no court hearing, except for a sentencing hearing.

▶ The efficiency of charge negotiation saves the community from unnecessary expense.

▶ A lighter sentence may mean that the accused will be more likely to reoffend, resulting in the offender being a greater danger to the community.

▶ Charge negotiation is a secretive process that prevents the court system being seen by the community to operate to achieve justice.

KCq page 89

1.3.5 Legal representation, including legal aid

Describe legal representation, including legal aid.

As seen in Section 1.3.3 (pages 26–7), criminal cases are prosecuted by specially-trained police prosecutors or a barrister from the office of the Director of Public Prosecutions. It is, therefore, important that people charged with a criminal offence receive legal advice and are represented by a lawyer in court. Legal representation is also important in a criminal case because the rules of evidence and procedure can be difficult for a non-lawyer to deal with.

A defence lawyer presents the evidence favourable to the accused and tries to discredit the evidence of the prosecution by cross-examination of witnesses. A solicitor is normally used in a minor case and a barrister is used in a more serious case.

The right to legal representation

Until recently there has been no right to legal representation in Australia. In the High Court case of *McInnes v R* (1979) 14 CLR 575, it was decided that McInnes had a fair trial even though he had to defend himself on a rape charge and could not obtain legal representation. However, in the High Court case of *Dietrich v The Queen* (1992) 177 CLR 292, a limited right to legal representation was established (see Case Study 1.5 following).

CASE STUDY 1.5: *Dietrich v the Queen* (1992) 177 CLR 292

Facts

Dietrich was charged with several drug offences, but was refused legal aid unless he pleaded guilty. During his trial, where he ended up defending himself, Dietrich complained that he did not understand the court process. The trial, nevertheless, continued and Dietrich was found guilty. He appealed to the High Court.

Issue

The High Court was asked to consider whether an accused person has the right to legal representation.

Decision

The High Court found that a judge should refuse to hear a case where a poor person has been accused of a serious crime and has been refused legal aid if an injustice is likely to occur, and that, in such a case, the trial should be delayed indefinitely if necessary until legal representation can be found.

The right to legal representation was only established for serious crimes in this case. There is no general right to legal representation.

Legal aid

Legal aid is the provision of free or cheap legal services to people on limited incomes. The cost of legal representation is very high and many ordinary people cannot afford to hire a solicitor or barrister for an extended period.

The aim of legal aid is to help redress inequalities of access to the legal system by providing legal assistance and, for those on low incomes, legal representation in court hearings. The primary source of legal aid in NSW is Legal Aid NSW. Legal Aid NSW provides a legal practitioner who prepares a case and/or represents the client in court. In serious criminal matters, a Public Defender may be appointed (see Section 1.3.3, page 27).

To receive legal aid, a person must pass:

▶ **a means test** (that is, the person applying for legal aid must show that his or her disposable income is less than a specified amount)

▶ **a merit test** (that is, the person applying for legal aid must have a good chance of winning his or her case). In criminal matters, a merit test is generally only applied in criminal appeals and Supreme Court bail applications. This means that legal aid is available for the vast majority of criminal matters, providing the person applying passes the means test.

▶ **a jurisdiction test** (that is, legal aid will only be granted for certain types of legal matters). Most criminal matters pass the jurisdiction test, though motor traffic offences only attract legal aid if there are exceptional circumstances or the likelihood of a jail sentence.

The provision of legal aid is a very important way to give people access to the legal system. If legal aid is not readily available, the legal system becomes an avenue only available to those with considerable economic power.

However, despite the importance of legal representation, in June 1998, the Senate Legal and Constitutional References Committee found that many people who do not meet the means test still have great difficulty paying for legal assistance. This is largely because of the low level of the means test and the high cost of legal representation.

CAN YOU **examine the role of legal representation in the criminal trial?**

To examine the role of legal representation in criminal trials, you need to:

▶ explain the role of a defence lawyer (see also Section 1.3.7, pages 31–2)

▶ explain why legal representation is important

▶ explain the significance of the Dietrich case (in Case Study 1.5, page 29)

▶ explain how legal aid operates for criminal matters

▶ explain the consequences of not being granted legal aid.

KCq page 89

Describe the burden and standard of proof.

1.3.6 Burden and standard of proof

Rules about the conduct of a trial (that is, about court procedures and presentation of evidence) have developed to ensure that a judge's discretion is exercised so that an accused person receives a fair trial. Some of these rules are fundamental principles of criminal justice. They include the following.

Presumption of innocence

Accused people are innocent until proven guilty. The prosecution must prove their guilt; the accused people do not need to prove their innocence.

Burden of proof

The *burden of proof* means the responsibility for proving something. Because of the presumption of innocence, the burden of proof is on the prosecution—that is, the prosecution must prove that the accused person is guilty of committing the crime alleged. However, the burden of proving a particular defence, such as mental illness, may be on the accused (see Section 1.3.8. page 33).

Standard of proof

The *standard of proof* means the weight or value given to the evidence (that is, how much proof is needed). An accused person must be proved guilty beyond reasonable doubt. If there is a reasonable doubt that the accused person committed the crime, he or she should be acquitted. Some people argue that the introduction of majority verdicts waters down this standard (see Section 1.3.9, pages 40–42).

Other rules regarding the use of evidence and the conduct of the case are discussed in Section 1.3.7, following.

KCq page 89

1.3.7 Use of evidence, including witnesses

Describe the use of evidence, including witnesses.

In a criminal trial, evidence is presented to the court through witnesses. Witnesses are people who know something about the case and who give evidence in court about what they know. The prosecution witnesses include the police officers who investigated the case and arrested the alleged offender. The procedure in a trial by jury is outlined in Figure 1.2. Following Figure 1.2 is more information about the process.

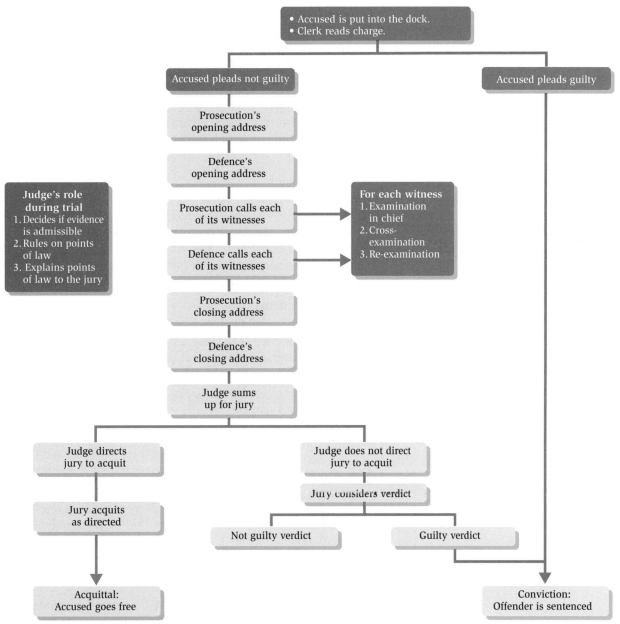

Figure 1.2 The procedure in trial by jury

Examination of witnesses

Witnesses are called by both the prosecution and the defence and are examined orally. This means that they are asked questions by the appropriate lawyer.

Examination-in-chief

This refers to the witness giving his or her evidence. This questioning is undertaken by the prosecution for prosecution witnesses and by the defence lawyer for the defence witnesses. Generally, a witness can only answer the questions he or she is asked. A police officer who has made a statement about the matter soon after the event can read the statement to the jury, rather than memorise it, if the statement has been signed and provided to the defence.

Cross-examination

After a witness has given evidence in the examination-in-chief, he or she can be cross-examined by the lawyer from the other side. Cross-examination gives the opposing side a chance to test the accuracy and objectivity of the evidence.

Re-examination

The prosecution and defence can re-examine their own witness after cross-examination, in order to clarify any issues arising out of cross-examination.

Rules of evidence

There are rules about what questions lawyers can ask and which questions must be answered by a witness. These are the rules of evidence. These rules have been developed in order to try and keep the process fair to both sides. The magistrate or judge presiding over the court hearing determines which questions are permissible.

Some of the rules of evidence involve:

- **hearsay evidence** (witnesses may only tell the court what they saw or heard, not what someone else told them happened)
- **opinion evidence** (a witness cannot give his or her opinion in a court about another person's words or actions unless the witness is an expert in that field)
- **relevance** (only evidence that relates to the matter under scrutiny can be given by a witness)
- **character evidence** (generally, evidence cannot be given about the bad character of the accused).

The right to silence

An accused person does not have to say anything in court at all, though corporations must submit documents even when such documents might incriminate them. Judges and juries are not supposed to interpret somebody remaining silent as evidence of that person's guilt (see Section 1.2.6, page 20).

Confessions

A confession cannot be used in court unless it is made voluntarily. Confessions made to police, but not electronically recorded, generally cannot be used as evidence in a court (see Section 1.2.1, pages 11–12).

Illegally obtained evidence

A judge can refuse to admit any evidence which has been illegally obtained. The judge or magistrate must consider the community's interest, as well as ensuring a fair trial for the accused, when deciding whether to admit or reject evidence. Generally, police must prove that evidence they have gathered has been obtained legally if it is to be admitted in court (see Section 1.2.6, page 20).

KCq page 89

1.3.8 Defences to criminal charges

Outline the defences to criminal charges, including complete defences and partial defences to murder.

A defence to a crime is a legally acceptable reason for committing an act or omitting a duty. If a defence is successfully proved by a defendant and he or she is completely cleared of the offence, it is called a complete defence. A partial defence is only available for murder and, if successfully proved, reduces the defendant's liability from murder to manslaughter.

Complete defences

Complete defences to a crime completely clear a person of the crime. They include mental illness, self-defence, necessity, duress and consent.

Mental illness

It must be proved that, at the time the defendant committed the crime, he or she was of unsound mind (that is, suffering from a mental illness which either prevented him or her from knowing what the criminal action he or she committed was, or from knowing that it was wrong). If this is proved, the defendant is found not guilty, but may well have to be admitted to a mental institution for an indefinite period. *R v Porter* (Case Study 1.6 below) is an example of the successful use of the defence of mental illness.

CASE STUDY 1.6: *R v Porter* (1936) 55 CLR 182

Facts

Porter was separated from his wife and was caring for his eleven-month-old son. He was suffering from depression and sleeplessness. He travelled from Canberra to Sydney to try to reconcile with his wife and threatened to kill himself and his son. She contacted police who found Porter at home crying. The baby was dead and Porter was about to kill himself. Porter was charged with murder.

Issue

Was Porter guilty of murder or not guilty on the grounds of mental illness?

Decision

The jury found that Porter poisoned his son and intended to do so, but that he did not appreciate the wrongness of his action, because he was suffering from mental illness at the time. The jury found that Porter was not guilty on the grounds of mental illness.

CAN YOU assess the use of the defence of mental illness in achieving justice?

The use of this defence achieves justice because:

▶ a person should not be held responsible for doing something he or she did not understand was wrong

▶ the test to prove mental illness as a defence is quite a rigorous one, so that a person who does understand what he or she is doing despite mental illness will not be wholly excused

▶ even when this defence is successfully proved, the community is protected from further harm because the defendant is often placed in a mental institution until he or she is no longer a danger to others.

Self-defence

The defendant admits to committing the criminal offence, knowing that it was wrong, but claims he or she was acting to defend himself or herself or someone else from attack. In these cases the defendant may use only whatever force is reasonably necessary. The case of *Zecevic v DPP* is an important Australian case about self-defence (see Case Study 1.7 following).

Case study 1.7: *Zecevic v DPP* (1987) 162 CLR 645

Facts

The accused had an argument with a neighbour, and returned to his flat where he got a gun and shot his neighbour. Zecevic claimed self-defence, explaining that the neighbour had already stabbed him and threatened to blow his head off. The neighbour was moving towards his car, where the accused believed he kept a gun, when the accused shot and killed the neighbour. The trial judge said that the jury could not consider the defence of self-defence because the force used by the defendant was not reasonable in the circumstances.

Issue

Did the accused act reasonably in defending himself from attack?

Decision

The High Court said that what is reasonable force depends on:

▶ whether the defendant believed it was necessary to use such force

▶ whether that belief was based on reasonable grounds.

The High Court ordered a new trial so that a jury could consider whether the accused's actions were reasonable in the circumstances.

CAN YOU assess the use of the defence of self-defence in achieving justice?

The use of this defence achieves justice because:

▶ the High Court held in the case of *Zecevic v DPP* (1987) that this defence can only be used if the force used in self-defence was necessary and reasonable

▶ people should be able to protect themselves from harm.

Some argue that this defence does not always achieve justice, because people who are only trying to protect themselves or their property can be guilty of a criminal offence if the court finds they used excessive force.

Necessity

The defendant claims that the act or omission committed was necessary to avert serious danger. The action taken must be in proportion to the danger that the defendant was trying to avert. The case of *R v Dudley and Stephens* (1884), outlined in Case Study 1.8 following, is a famous case in the area of necessity.

Case study 1.8: *R v Dudley and Stephens* (1884) 14 QB 273

Facts

In 1884, the ship, the *Mignonette*, was sinking and everyone abandoned ship. Dudley and Stephens were in a lifeboat with two others and were 2000 kilometres from land. By the eighteenth day, they had been without food or water for five days. On the twentieth day, Dudley and Stephens killed one of their companions, who was near death, and all three remaining survivors fed off his corpse. They were found on the twenty-fourth day.

Issues

Was it necessary for Dudley and Stephens to kill their companion in order to live? Is necessity available as a defence to the charge of murder?

Decision

Evidence suggested that the men would have died if they had not killed their companion and that the victim would almost certainly have died anyway. The judges, however, said that the defence of necessity was not available for murder.

CAN YOU **assess the use of the defence of necessity in achieving justice?**

The use of this defence achieves justice because:

▷ the test to prove necessity is rigorous—that is, the act or omission committed must be necessary to avert serious danger and must be in proportion to the danger that the defendant was trying to avert

▷ the defence of necessity is not available for murder.

Duress

The defendant admits to committing the criminal act knowing that it was wrong, but claims that he or she was so frightened by threats of death or serious bodily harm that he or she committed the act anyway. The threat can be either to the defendant or to another person. Duress can be a complete or a partial defence. Duress and necessity are both defences of compulsion. This means, in both defences, that the people claiming the defence argue that they were compelled or forced to act criminally because of other circumstances. A case where duress was successfully pleaded is *R v George Palazoff* (see Case Study 1.9 following).

CASE STUDY 1.9: *R v George Palazoff* (1986) 23 ACrimR 86

Facts

The defendant was convicted of cultivating and possessing Indian hemp (marijuana) for trading purposes, based on the fact that he was the owner of and was found in some glasshouses that contained the plants. Palazoff claimed that he was acting under duress, because another man, Hatsiosifidis, who had leased the glasshouses, had threatened his family if he objected, and he backed up the threat with a pistol shot to Palazoff's feet. The jury at the trial found that Palazoff was guilty. Palazoff appealed against the conviction, claiming that the trial judge did not direct the jury properly regarding the defence of duress.

Issue

Was Palazoff acting under duress sufficient to legally excuse him from the crime?

Decision

The South Australian Court of Criminal Appeal found that the trial judge erred and should have pointed out to the jury that:

▷ threats to the appellant's family were as relevant to the defence of duress as threats to the appellant himself

▷ the threats needed to be sufficient to cause an ordinary person of the appellant's age, sex and circumstances to commit the crime.

The court upheld the appeal, quashed the conviction and ordered a new trial.

CAN YOU assess the use of the defence of duress in achieving justice?

The use of this defence achieves justice because:

▶ the threats needed to prove duress must be sufficient to cause an ordinary person of the defendant's age, sex and circumstances to commit the crime

▶ this defence allows people to act in a reasonable way to protect themselves or their families.

Consent

The defendant claims that he or she acted with the victim's consent. Consent by a victim to his or her own death will not completely excuse the defendant, though it may reduce liability. The defence of consent can be either complete or partial, and is often used in sexual offences when it is a complete defence.

Consent is an important element in sexual assault cases. Often the perpetrator of an alleged sexual assault will claim that the alleged victim actually consented to the sexual act. Sexual assault comes under section 61 of the *Crimes Act 1900* (NSW) and occurs when someone has sexual intercourse with another person without their consent, knowing that they do not consent. To prove a charge of sexual assault, the prosecution must prove that the victim did not consent, and that the accused person was aware that the victim did not consent or was reckless as to whether the victim consented or not.

Consent must be 'freely and voluntarily' given. Consent cannot be obtained by:

▶ force, threats and fear

▶ fraud

▶ mistake as to the identity of the person

▶ mistake as to marriage

▶ mistake as to the purpose (such as thinking it was for some medical purpose).

The case of *R v Mueller* (2005) is a NSW Court of Criminal Appeal case about consent (see Case Study 1.10 following).

CASE STUDY 1.10: *R v Mueller* (2005) NSWCCA 47

Facts

The accused was employed as a caretaker at a home for people with disabilities. The victim was a resident at the home and suffered from Asperger's syndrome. The two were sitting on a couch when the accused allegedly touched, kissed and bit the victim's breasts and proceeded to touch and kiss her genital area outside her clothing, and forced her to touch his penis. The accused admitted to some of these actions but claimed the victim consented.

Issue

Did the victim legally consent to these sexual acts? The prosecution argued that the victim lacked the capacity to consent, and that she did not, in fact, consent.

Decision

The NSW Court of Criminal Appeal held that the victim did not consent. Justice Hunt said that, 'Silence or absence of positive resistance to an unwanted sexual advance is not to be taken as consent, or as communication of consent … submission is not the same as consent'.

CAN YOU assess the use of the defence of consent in achieving justice?

The use of this defence achieves justice because:

▶ it allows people to consent to acts which may, in non-consensual circumstances, be illegal, such as sexual intercourse, or surgery.

▶ the law makes sure consent must be 'freely and voluntarily given', and not obtained by fraud or force.

Some argue that this defence does not always achieve justice because, in the case of sexual assault, criminal justice outcomes are extremely poor. In March 2006, the NSW Bureau of Crime Statistics and Research (BOSCAR) reported that 90% of reported sexual assaults did not lead to a conviction, and only 17% ended up in court. Of these, less than half led to a guilty verdict. The difficulty in gathering sufficient evidence to prove a sexual assault is one reason for this. Most sexual assaults occur without witnesses and the issue of consent often comes down to the perpetrator's word against that of the accused.

Successfully proven defences of mental illness, self-defence, necessity, duress and consent will generally acquit the defendant of the crime (that is, he or she will be found not guilty).

Partial defences to murder

Partial defences to murder include provocation and substantial impairment of responsibility, also called diminished responsibility. Successful defences of provocation and substantial impairment of responsibility are called partial defences because they will generally reduce the liability of the defendant from murder to manslaughter. A successfully proven partial defence to murder does not completely free the defendant from liability.

Provocation

The defendant claims that he or she was aggravated by the victim in such a way that the actions of the murdered person would have caused an ordinary person to lose self-control. The case of The *Queen v Damian Karl Sebo* (see Case Study 1.11 following) is an example of a recent case where the defence of provocation was successfully proved.

CASE STUDY 1.11: *The Queen v Damian Karl Sebo* (2007) Supreme Court of Queensland

Facts

Damian Sebo, a twenty-eight-year-old man, admitted to killing Taryn Hunt, his sixteen-year-old girlfriend, by bashing her to death with a steering wheel lock on 7 September 2005. He claimed that he was provoked by her because she bragged about cheating on him with several other men.

Issue

Were Taryn's actions sufficient to prove provocation? Her alleged sexual taunts must have been sufficient for an ordinary man to have lost control in similar circumstances.

Decision

The jury accepted that Sebo was provoked sufficiently by Taryn to find him guilty of manslaughter rather than murder. Sebo was sentenced to ten years imprisonment. The state appealed against the leniency of the sentence. However, in November 2007, the Queensland Court of Appeal rejected the arguments and Sebo's sentence remained at ten years imprisonment.

In recent years, the courts have considered other factors in proving provocation and/or other defences to a criminal charge, such as self-defence. These factors include:

▶ **battered woman syndrome**, which is being increasingly recognised by courts across Australia for charges of murder. Battered woman syndrome may arise when a woman kills her husband or partner after years of suffering domestic violence (see Section 4.2.4, page 236). In NSW, evidence of battered woman syndrome may help to prove duress, provocation or self-defence. It may also lead to mitigation of the sentence of an offender suffering from the syndrome (see Section 1.4.3, page 46) or a decision by the state not to prosecute.

▶ **the abuse excuse**, which has been recognised in NSW courts in the case of violent crimes such as murder. In two separate cases in 1997, two men were acquitted of murder on the defence that they had suffered, or were protecting those who had suffered, from child abuse.

CAN YOU assess the use of the defence of provocation in achieving justice?

The use of this defence achieves justice because:

▶ it is only provable if the alleged provocation was sufficient for an ordinary person to have lost control in similar circumstances

▶ it does not, in most cases, completely exonerate the offender

▶ it allows women who have suffered years of abuse to reduce their liability if they cause the death of the abuser.

Some argue that this defence does not always achieve justice because allowing battered woman syndrome and the abuse excuse as defences of provocation is allowing people to take the law into their own hands rather than allowing the legal system to deal with the abuser. However, others would argue that it is very difficult to prove such abuse, so the perpetrator may be beyond the reach of the law.

Substantial impairment of responsibility

This partial defence, also known as diminished responsibility, claims that the accused person was not completely in control of his or her mind when he or she committed the murder. This defence is provided by Section 23A of the *Crimes Act 1900* (NSW) and can be proved if:

▶ the accused was suffering from an abnormality of mind caused by either disease or injury

▶ the abnormality impaired the accused person's mental responsibility for the killing.

Intoxication will generally not be taken into account when determining criminal liability for murder or manslaughter, but intoxication by accident or because of a prescribed drug may be considered by the court as a defence to murder. If a person's brain is damaged by long-term use of alcohol or other drugs, this may be sufficient to prove diminished responsibility. In the case of *Chayna v The Queen* (1993) (see Case Study 1.12 following), substantial impairment of responsibility was raised as a defence.

CASE STUDY 1.12: *Chayna v The Queen* (1993) 66 ACrimR 178

Facts

Andre Chayna killed her two daughters and her sister-in-law. She invited her sister-in-law to her house and subjected her to 'frenzied attack', hiding the body in the backyard. Later that night Chayna stabbed her own daughter and left the body in the house for two days. She stabbed her second daughter two days later when she returned from a camp. The defence claimed substantial impairment of responsibility, and conflicting evidence from seven psychiatrists was given as to Chayna's mental state at the time of the killings. The trial judge summed up to the jury on the basis that the evidence of the last psychiatrist did not support the defence of mental illness nor the defence of diminished responsibility but, instead, supported a finding of murder. The jury returned a verdict of murder. The case was appealed in the NSW Court of Criminal Appeal.

Issue

Did Chayna kill her daughters and sister-in-law while suffering from substantial impairment of responsibility?

Decision

The Court of Criminal Appeal substituted a verdict of manslaughter for murder, saying the trial judge had wrongly summed up to the jury on the basis that the evidence of only one of the seven doctors did not support a defence of diminished responsibility.

CAN YOU **assess the use of the defence of substantial impairment of responsibility in achieving justice?**

The use of this defence achieves justice because:

▶ people who are not fully responsible for their actions are not held fully responsible

▶ this defence does not excuse people who deliberately become intoxicated or who use intoxication as an excuse to kill someone

▶ it is only a partial defence, so the defendant is still liable for a criminal act

▶ even when this defence is successfully proved, the community is protected from further harm because the defendant is often placed in a mental institution until he or she is no longer a danger to others.

CAN YOU **assess the use of defences to criminal charges in achieving justice?**

In order to assess the use of defences to criminal charges in achieving justice, you need to discuss:

▶ the use of defences in general. You could argue that it is reasonable to look at all the circumstances of the alleged crime and that, in some cases, the circumstances are such that a complete or partial offence should be considered.

▶ individual defences and cases to decide if justice is served. Arguments for and against the use and application of individual defences are outlined after each defence in the discussion on the preceding pages. The defences in which there is some controversy about whether the use of the defence achieves justice are:

● self-defence

● consent

● provocation, including battered woman syndrome and the abuse excuse.

Describe the role of juries, including verdicts.

1.3.9 The role of juries

In trial by jury, the case is heard by a judge and jury. The court process is the same as that in a summary hearing except that the jury, not the judge, decides the guilt or innocence of the defendant. The process followed in a trial by jury is outlined in Section 1.3.7 (pages 31–2). Trial by jury is used in less than 1% of criminal cases.

The way in which juries are selected and operate is governed by the *Jury Act 1977* (NSW). Some facts about juries follow.

- In criminal cases there are usually twelve people who form a jury. However, under amendments made to the Jury Act in 2006, the court can empanel up to fifteen jurors for lengthy criminal proceedings, though only twelve of them will ultimately determine the verdict.

- Jurors are selected from electoral rolls.

- Jury service is compulsory, unless you are exempt.

- Both the prosecution and defence may reject possible jurors if they feel they will be biased against or in favour of the accused.

- The verdict of the jury can be a majority verdict of 'eleven to one' in NSW criminal trials, under amendments made to the Jury Act in 2006. A majority verdict will only be accepted by the court if the jury has deliberated for at least eight hours and if the court is satisfied, after examination on oath of one or more of the jurors, that it is unlikely that the jurors will reach a unanimous verdict after further deliberation (see Case Study 1.13 following).

CASE STUDY 1.13: Unanimous or majority verdicts?

Background

Periodically, usually after a well-publicised case where there has been a *hung jury* (that is, the jury couldn't reach a unanimous verdict) there are calls for allowing majority verdicts. In May 2006, the *Jury Act 1977* (NSW) was amended to allow for 'eleven to one' majority verdicts when a unanimous verdict could not be reached. The decision to change the law to allow for majority verdicts is a controversial one and sparked much discussion in the media when it was announced in November 2005.

Arguments for majority verdicts

- The need for a unanimous verdict means there must be a retrial if the jurors cannot reach a unanimous decision. Retrials are costly and take up court time.

- Hung juries can occur because of a *rogue juror* (that is, someone who enters the jury room having prejudged the verdict, and refusing to listen to the evidence or the views of the other jurors). This occurred in the trial of former Queensland Premier Sir Joh Bjelke-Petersen, for perjury, in 1991. After deliberating for four days, the jury members reported to the judge that they were unlikely to agree on a verdict, and were discharged. Media reports revealed that the jury had been split 'eleven to one'. The hold-out juror was not only the foreman of the jury panel, but a former president of the Young National Party and a strong supporter of the defendant, who refused to agree with a verdict to convict. 'Eleven to one' majority verdicts would prevent such a situation occurring.

▶ The incidence of hung juries has doubled in NSW since 1985, from 3.5% to 8%.

▶ Majority verdicts are permitted in Victoria, Western Australia, South Australia, Tasmania and the Northern Territory, and in the United Kingdom. There have been no reported cases of injustices occurring because of it.

Arguments for retaining unanimous verdicts

▶ Majority verdicts compromise the criminal standard of proof, 'beyond reasonable doubt', in that there is one juror who has a doubt.

▶ There is a greater risk of convicting the innocent.

▶ Historically, trial by jury is an important right, the protection of which can be traced back to the Magna Carta. In the case of *Cheatle v The Queen* (1993) 177 CLR 541, the High Court found that, on the grounds of 'history, principle and authority' the constitutional right to a trial by jury means the right to a unanimous verdict, unanimity being an essential feature of a jury trial.

▶ The NSW Law Reform Commission inquired into the question of whether to allow majority verdicts, and released its report in 2005 (Report No 111), recommending against the introduction of majority verdicts.

▶ Statistics used by the NSW Law Reform Commission from the NSW Bureau of Crime Statistics and Research (BOCSAR) showed that while 8% of jury trials were hung, the introduction of 'eleven to one' majority verdicts would make little difference because it was usually more than one juror that disagreed with the majority.

▶ The argument that the introduction of majority verdicts would save court time and the expense of a retrial is less powerful given that the BOCSAR research shows that the saving in court time created by 'eleven to one' majority verdicts would be 1.1%.

▶ A lone juror who does not agree with the rest of the jury is not necessarily a 'rogue juror'. He or she may have reasonable doubts that should be discussed.

CAN YOU evaluate the effectiveness of the jury system in the criminal trial?

In order to evaluate the effectiveness of the jury system in the criminal trial, you need to discuss the advantages and disadvantages of the jury system and decide whether the advantages outweigh the disadvantages. You also need to consider the effect of majority verdicts on the effectiveness of the jury system. The advantages and disadvantages of the system are listed below.

Advantages of the jury system in the criminal trial

▶ The jury system is more reliable than a single judge because it draws strength and credibility from numbers. If twelve people find the offender guilty, then the offender must be guilty. This may be undermined by the provision for 'eleven to one' majority verdicts.

▶ Ordinary people are involved in the criminal trial process, so the community is confident that the system is operating fairly.

▶ Current values and community standards are applied.

▶ Trial by jury is a fundamental right which protects the individual from abuses of state power, though the implied right to unanimity in the verdict has been removed in NSW.

Disadvantages of the jury system in the criminal trial

▶ Juries may be inclined to be more emotional than judges, so may not look at the facts objectively.

▶ Juries may not understand court proceedings or technical evidence.

▶ Juries may be easily intimidated, so may be too scared to ask for matters to be explained.

▶ Juries are more likely to acquit the accused.

▶ Juries may be easily swayed by clever barristers.

▶ Trial by jury is more expensive and time-consuming.

▶ Jury duty is an imposition on ordinary people who have their own lives to lead.

▶ Because of exemptions, juries may not be really representative of the community.

▶ Juries may be influenced by the media. Although jurors are instructed to base their verdict only on the evidence they hear in court, in a case in which there has been a lot of media coverage, it may be very difficult for jurors to ignore the media.

▶ The availability of majority verdicts may mean that, in some cases, an accused person may be found guilty even when one person has a reasonable doubt as to his or her guilt.

 page 89

> Assess the effectiveness of the criminal trial process as a means of achieving justice.

1.3.10 The effectiveness of the criminal trial process as a means of achieving justice

To assess the effectiveness of the criminal trial process as a means of achieving justice, you should weigh up those factors which help ensure justice and those factors which may limit the achievement of justice in the criminal trial process, and decide how effective the process is. Table 1.3 outlines both sets of factors.

Table 1.3 The effectiveness of the criminal trial process as a means of achieving justice

Factors which *help ensure* the achievement of justice in the criminal trial process	Factors which may *limit* the achievement of justice in the criminal trial process
▶ The provision of summary offences and Local Courts mean that minor offences can be heard locally, quickly and relatively cheaply (see Section 1.3.1, pages 22–3).	▶ Because so many indictable offences can be heard summarily, accused people may be denied their constitutional right to trial by jury (see Sections 1.3.1 [pages 22–4] and 1.3.9 [page 40]).
▶ The Drug Court of NSW aims to reduce drug-related crime and drug addiction (see Section 1.3.1, pages 23–4).	
▶ The system of appeals helps ensure minimisation of the effects of wrong decisions made by a judge or magistrate when exercising their discretion (see Section 1.3.1, page 24).	
▶ Despite problems with the adversarial system, it has served common law countries well for centuries (see Section 1.3.2, page 25).	▶ There are several problems with the adversarial system of trial as outlined in Section 1.3.2 (see page 25).
▶ The adversarial system achieves justice in criminal trials because the judge ensures both sides of the case follow the rules of evidence to ensure a just outcome (see Sections 1.3.2 [page 25] and 1.3.7 [pages 31–2]).	
▶ Charge negotiation puts pressure on the accused to plead guilty to something he or she may not be found guilty of in a court hearing, perhaps lessening his or her chance of achieving justice (see Section 1.3.4, pages 27–8).	▶ With charge negotiation the accused may get a lighter sentence than he or she really deserves. The lighter sentence of the accused may mean the victim of the crime feels that the offender was not punished sufficiently and that the offender may be more likely to reoffend. (see Section 1.3.4, pages 27–8).
▶ Charge negotiation saves the victim from the ordeal of giving evidence and being cross-examined (see Section 1.3.4, pages 27–8).	
▶ Charge negotiation saves witnesses in the community from the ordeal of giving evidence and being cross-examined (see Section 1.3.4, pages 27–8).	▶ The accused may be prepared to plead guilty to a lesser charge during charge negotiation, simply because he or she cannot afford the cost of defending the more serious charge (see Section 1.3.4, pages 27–8).

Factors which *help ensure* the achievement of justice in the criminal trial process	Factors which may *limit* the achievement of justice in the criminal trial process
▶ Charge negotiation is efficient, quick and inexpensive, because there is no court hearing, except for a sentencing hearing and its efficiency saves the community from unnecessary expense (see Section 1.3.4, pages 27–8).	▶ Charge negotiation is a secretive process that prevents the court system from being seen to operate to achieve justice (see Section 1.3.4, pages 27–8).
▶ The right to legal representation in serious cases has been established in the Dietrich case (1992) (see Section 1.3.5, pages 28–9).	▶ There is no general right to legal representation in Australia (see Section 1.3.5, pages 28–9).
▶ The provision of legal aid helps to redress inequalities of access to the criminal trial process (see Section 1.3.5, pages 28–9).	▶ Many people who do not meet the means test still have great difficulty paying for legal assistance, largely because of the low level of the means test and the high cost of legal representation (see Section 1.3.5, pages 28–9).
▶ The provision of Public Defenders means that those accused of serious offences are adequately represented if they are eligible for legal aid (see Sections 1.3.3 [page 27] and 1.3.5 [pages 28–9]).	
▶ The presumption of innocence, the standard of proof, the burden of proof and other rules of evidence help ensure that a fair trial is achieved (see Section 1.3.6 [page 30] and 1.3.7 [pages 30–32]).	
▶ The use of defences to criminal charges allows the court to look at the whole circumstances of the alleged crime when deciding guilt or innocence (see Section 1.3.8, pages 32–9).	
▶ Arguments for the use and application of individual defences are outlined after each defence in Section 1.3.8 (pages 32–9).	▶ Controversy about whether the defences of self-defence, consent, and provocation achieve justice is discussed in Section 1.3.8 (pages 32–9).
▶ The introduction of majority verdicts in some NSW criminal trials may increase the efficiency of the court process (see Section 1.3.9, pages 40–41).	▶ Majority criminal verdicts may lessen the achievement of justice in criminal trials (see Section 1.3.9, pages 40–41).
▶ The benefits of the jury system in the achievement of justice in the criminal trial process are listed in Section 1.3.9 (pages 40–41).	▶ The limitations of the jury system in the achievement of justice in the criminal trial process are listed in Section 1.3.9 (page 42).
▶ The time taken between arrest and the end of the trial process can be over a year long. This has negative consequences for all involved, and is of particular concern if the alleged offender is kept on remand during this period and then found not guilty (see Section 1.2.5, pages 18–19).	

KCq page 89

1.4 Sentencing and punishment

Once a person pleads guilty or is found guilty of a crime, there is a court hearing to determine the appropriate sentence for the offender. The judge or magistrate decides on the appropriate penalty, according to statutory and judicial guidelines, and after hearing evidence from the prosecutor and the defence as to what sentence is appropriate.

1.4.1 Statutory and judicial guidelines

Judicial discretion is the backbone of the sentencing process. With some exceptions, such as minimum non-parole periods (see the next page), the judiciary has the broad discretion to select the type of sentence to give a convicted offender, and the length of time served (see also Section 1.7.1, pages 69–71). However, judicial discretion is limited by statutory and judicial guidelines, some of which are outlined in this section.

Explain the statutory and judicial guidelines involved in sentencing.

Maximum penalties

The legislation which prescribes the offence usually also prescribes the maximum penalty. Most maximum penalties are found in the *Crimes Act 1900* (NSW). For example, section 59 of the Crimes Act states that anybody who is found guilty of assault occasioning actual bodily harm 'shall be liable to imprisonment for five years'. This is the maximum penalty that can be imposed by the judge. He or she can impose a lesser penalty taking into consideration other factors, as outlined in Section 1.4.3 of this book (page 46).

The Crimes (Sentencing Procedure) Act 1999 (NSW)

This act governs the way judges and magistrates determine sentences, particularly prison sentences, in NSW. This act makes a number of provisions regarding the imposition of a term of imprisonment. Some of these are:

- a court must not impose a full-time prison sentence without considering and rejecting all possible alternatives (see Section 1.4.6, on pages 48–52, for alternatives)

- the court can impose a fixed term of imprisonment or, if the term is over six months, can fix a parole and non-parole period. A non-parole period is the minimum time to be actually spent in prison. A parole period is a time when the offender no longer must be imprisoned, but is freed into the community under supervision (see Section 1.4.8, pages 53–4).

- the parole period is generally a quarter of the total sentence. So an offender who is sentenced to four years in prison would generally serve a three-year non-parole period.

- any sentence of six months or under must be fixed (that is, there is no parole period). So, when the prisoner is released, it is without parole.

Judicial guidelines

Judicial guidelines come in the form of guideline sentences. A guideline sentence is a judgement given about a sentence for a particular crime, which is to be taken into account by courts delivering sentences for similar offences. Guideline sentences are provided for under the *Crimes (Sentencing Procedure) Act 1999* (NSW). The NSW Attorney General can ask the court and the judge to give a guideline sentence for a certain criminal offence. The NSW Court of Criminal Appeal can also give a guideline sentence if it wishes to do so.

EXAMPLE **Guideline sentences**

The first guideline sentence in NSW, which was on the offence of dangerous driving causing grievous bodily harm or death, was handed down in the case of *R v Jurisic* (1998) 45 NSWLR 209 (see Case Study 1.14, Section 1.4.5, page 48) and was later modified in *R v Whyte* (2002) NSWCCA 343.

Mandatory sentencing

Mandatory sentencing refers to the practice of some parliaments of legislating for a particular sentence for a particular crime or series of crimes. All jurisdictions have mandatory sentencing to some degree, such as a mandatory fine for breaking the speed limit by a certain number of kilometres.

However, sometimes mandatory sentencing can have severe repercussions. In the Northern Territory, for example, mandatory sentencing laws for property offences were introduced in 1997. These laws said that a court had to impose prison sentences on all property offenders. For adults, the first property offence meant jail for fourteen days, and the third for 120 days. For youth offenders (aged under seventeen) the third offence meant jail. These laws were repealed in 2000, due to public outcry about the harsh results of such laws, which included the suicide of an Aboriginal teenage boy who had been jailed under these laws for stealing a can of drink.

Mandatory sentencing takes away the exercise of judicial discretion. With mandatory sentencing, the court has no choice but to impose the legislated sentence. It cannot, for example, lessen the sentence because of mitigating factors (see Section 1.4.3, page 46).

In NSW, there have been several forms of mandatory sentencing introduced and repealed over the last twenty years. Since February 2003, amendments to the *Crimes (Sentencing Procedure) Act 1999* (NSW), have prescribed minimum non-parole periods for specific offences, such as ten years for aggravated sexual assault. These amendments also provide for judges and magistrates to take into account aggravating and mitigating circumstances. Nevertheless, it is still a form of mandatory sentencing, in that the court must impose at least the minimum sentence if the features of the listed offence are serious enough. KCq page 89

1.4.2 The purposes of punishment

The purposes of punishment include:

- deterrence (specific and general)
- retribution
- rehabilitation
- incapacitation.

These purposes and the problems with them are discussed in the remainder of this section. Most punishments given by the courts have more than one purpose (see Section 1.4.6, pages 48–52).

Deterrence

Specific deterrence means dissuading the offender from committing a similar crime in the future because of fear of punishment. *General deterrence* means dissuading the general public from committing a similar crime. For example, most people try to keep to the speed limit because the threat of a fine and loss of points is enough to deter them from committing this crime. However, many punishments do not seem to deter offenders from committing another crime. For example, prisons house many recidivists (that is, people who commit crimes again and again).

Retribution

Pure retribution is where the punishment aims to be exactly equivalent to the crime committed—for example, a murderer is put to death. In Australia, this is translated into the idea that, the more serious the crime, the more serious the punishment should be. Pure retribution may be too harsh in a modern society and it is often difficult to find a punishment that exactly matches the crime committed.

Rehabilitation

A punishment that aims to rehabilitate is aimed at changing the behaviour of the offender so that he or she will not wish to commit other crimes because non-criminal behaviour will be seen as preferable. The purpose of diversionary programs (see Section 1.4.6, pages 50–51) is primarily to rehabilitate offenders. However, rehabilitation may not always be successful, and could lead to some offenders being given a different sentence to other offenders who have committed similar crimes. For example, a drug addict who steals may be given a sentence that involves drug rehabilitation, while someone else who steals will not be.

Explain the purposes of punishment.

Incapacitation

Incapacitation means that the punishment aims to isolate the offender, usually in prison, so that he or she is unable to commit another crime. The idea is that the offender should be incapacitated as long as he or she is a danger to society. However, nobody can predict how long an offender is going to be a danger to society and prison imposes a large monetary cost on the public.

KCq page 89

Describe the factors affecting a sentencing decision, including aggravating and mitigating circumstances.

1.4.3 Factors affecting a sentencing decision

The judge or magistrate decides on a suitable punishment for individual offenders within the guidelines set by the *Crimes (Sentencing Procedure) Act 1999* (NSW) and other legislation. Judges and magistrates take into account:

▶ the maximum penalty (see Section 1.4.1, pages 43–4)

▶ other legislative and judicial guidelines (see Section 1.4.1, pages 43–5)

▶ the purposes of punishment (see Section 1.4.2, pages 45–6)

▶ aggravating circumstances (see below)

▶ mitigating factors (see below)

▶ a victim impact statement, if one is given (see Section 1.4.4, page 47).

Weighing up these factors requires the exercise of judicial discretion (that is, the judge/magistrate must make a decision about the sentence, taking into account these factors).

Aggravating factors

Aggravating factors are factors taken into account by the magistrate or judge when determining the sentence. They may result in the maximum penalty being imposed and include the particular circumstances of the offence, the victim, and the offender. These factors are usually put forward by the prosecution at the sentencing hearing to persuade the judge of the severity of the crime. Aggravating factors may include:

▶ whether there was violence or the threat of violence

▶ whether there was a weapon used

▶ whether the crime was planned

▶ the age and disability of the victim

▶ whether there was a relationship of trust with the victim

▶ whether the offender has a prior criminal record.

Mitigating factors

These are matters that persuade the judge that the maximum penalty should not be imposed, and are put forward by the defence. They are factors which lessen the sentence. Some mitigating factors which a judge might consider are:

▶ the offender's past good record

▶ the offender's good character

▶ circumstances surrounding the offence, such as provocation (see Section 1.3.8, pages 37–8)

▶ the effect of a sentence on the offender and his or her family

▶ cooperation with authorities, including providing information leading to other convictions

▶ signs of remorse, including a guilty plea.

KCq page 89

1.4.4 The role of the victim in sentencing

During a sentencing hearing, the prosecutor gives evidence to the magistrate about what sentence to impose, which may include:

▶ the facts of the case, as admitted by the offender or as proved in court

▶ a record of any previous convictions against the accused

▶ a victim impact statement in the case of sexual assault or serious personal injury.

After the prosecution presents their evidence to the court, then the defence is called upon to present any factors in mitigation—that is, any facts which may lessen the sentence (see Section 1.4.3, page 46). This may include evidence of previous good character.

A victim impact statement is a statement read to the court, outlining the full effect of the crime on the victim. A victim impact statement can also be made by the victim, or by a member of the victim's family if the victim has died. Victim impact statements are made available to the defendant and his or her lawyers and the victim can be cross-examined on the statement.

The advantages of victim impact statements are that:

▶ they can provide useful information to the court about the impact of the crime, particularly when the offender has pleaded guilty and the judge has had no opportunity to hear the victim's evidence

▶ they can give the victim a role in the court process, giving the victim and the community greater confidence in the system

▶ they may assist in the rehabilitation of the offender, because he or she gets to hear the impact of his or her actions.

One disadvantage of such statements for the victims is that the delivery of the statement and the possible ensuing cross-examination can prove embarrassing and upsetting, and it may not be in the best interests of the victim to make such a statement.

Victims of crime play a part in youth justice conferencing and circle sentencing (see Sections 1.4.7 [page 52] and 1.5.5 [pages 59–60]). Victims of crime may also be awarded compensation, and have various rights regarding the information they receive about the court case. Victims can also receive assistance from support groups and government authorities, and may be entitled to various protections. These provisions for victims of crime and the extent to which the law balances the rights of victims, offenders and society are discussed in Section 1.7.5 (pages 75–7).

CAN YOU discuss factors that affect sentencing decisions, including the purposes of punishment and the role of the victim?

In order to discuss the factors that affect sentencing decisions, you need to describe each factor affecting the judge's decision and comment on how the consideration of this factor helps achieve the purposes of punishment. The factors you need to consider are:

▶ the maximum penalty (see Section 1.4.1, pages 43–4)

▶ other legislative and judicial guidelines (see Section 1.4.1, pages 43–5)

▶ the purposes of punishment (see Section 1.4.2, pages 45–6)

▶ aggravating circumstances (see Section 1.4.3, page 46)

▶ mitigating factors (see Section 1.4.3, page 46)

▶ a victim impact statement, if one is given (see Section 1.4.4 above).

The effectiveness of various forms of punishment in achieving the purposes of punishment are discussed in Section 1.4.6 (see pages 48–52).

KCq page 89

Explain the role of the victim in sentencing.

1.4.5 Appeals

In criminal cases, appeals can be made either against the conviction or against the sentence. This means that a person found guilty of an offence can appeal against the guilty conviction on certain grounds, or can appeal against the severity of the sentence. The prosecution can appeal against the leniency of the sentence but, generally, cannot appeal against an acquittal. The system of appeals is outlined in Section 1.3.1 (see pages 22–4).

The appeal process for sentencing is important because it allows higher courts to supervise the discretion of magistrates and judges when they are making sentencing decisions, thereby helping to ensure consistency by establishing the maximum and minimum range of sentences for particular offences. The higher courts do this by:

▶ reducing or increasing sentences on appeal

▶ issuing guideline sentences (see Section 1.4.1, page 44).

The case of *R v Jurisic* (1998) 45 NSWLR 209 (see Case Study 1.14 following) is about an appeal by the prosecution against the leniency of the sentence and led to the first guideline sentence in NSW (see also Section 1.4.1, page 44).

CASE STUDY 1.14: *R v Jurisic* (1998) 45 NSWLR 209

Facts

Jurisic pleaded guilty in the Local Court to three charges of dangerous driving occasioning actual bodily harm, after colliding with another car and injuring three people. At the time of the collision, he had a sufficient level of cocaine in his bloodstream to significantly impair his driving. Each of the charges carried a maximum penalty of seven years imprisonment.

At the sentencing hearing in the District Court, it was revealed that Jurisic had several previous driving convictions and his driver's licence had been cancelled three times. Jurisic was sentenced to imprisonment for eighteen months, to be served as home detention, with a minimum term of nine months. He was also disqualified from holding a driver's licence for one year.

Issue

The DPP appealed on the grounds that the sentences were inadequate.

Decision

The Court of Criminal Appeal used the appeal to hand down its first guideline sentence which states that, if the offender in a dangerous driving case has a high moral culpability, he or she should normally be given a full-time prison sentence of at least three years in the case of death and two years in the case of grievous bodily harm. The level of moral culpability will depend on a number of factors including speed, the degree of intoxication or substance abuse, and the number of people put at risk.

Jurisic was sentenced to imprisonment for two years, with a minimum term of one year, and disqualified from driving for two years. **KCq** pages 89–90

1.4.6 Types of penalties

There are many types of penalties available to courts when sentencing. These range from the more traditional types of penalties, such as fines and imprisonment, to diversionary programs such as drug rehabilitation and traffic offenders' programs. Types of penalties available to courts are described in this section.

Traditional penalties

▶ **No conviction recorded:** For trivial matters, the court may find the accused person guilty, but opt to dismiss the charge with no conviction recorded. This means the offender is free to go and has no criminal record.

▶ **Caution:** The offender is cautioned or warned by police, rather than arrested and charged with a criminal offence. Examples of the use of cautions include the 'Cannabis cautioning scheme' (see 'Diversionary programs', page 50) and cautions for young offenders (see Section 1.5.5, page 60).

▶ **Fine:** The offender is ordered to pay a sum of money. Fines are usually expressed in penalty units. In July 2008, one penalty unit equalled $110. People who do not pay a fine can have their driving licence suspended, vehicle registration cancelled, property seized, and wages garnisheed. If these methods fail, a community service order can be imposed and, if this is breached, the offender can be imprisoned or put on periodic detention.

▶ **Bond:** The offender is released but agrees to be on a bond of good behaviour, usually for a period of between one and five years. The court may order that conditions be attached to the bond, such as paying compensation to the victim or accepting the supervision of the Parole Authority (see Section 1.4.8, pages 53–4). If a bond is breached, the offender must go back to court, where another penalty, such as imprisonment, is considered.

▶ **Suspended sentence:** This occurs when an offender is sentenced to a term in prison, but the sentence is not executed. Instead, the offender is released into the community on a bond to be of good behaviour. If the offender breaches the bond, he or she must serve the sentence originally imposed.

▶ **Probation:** A probation order is like a bond but almost always requires the offender to be supervised by the Parole Authority. If breached, the consequences are likely to be more severe than if a bond is breached.

▶ **Criminal infringement notice:** This is a notice issued to people by police, imposing a fine for some minor crimes, such as offensive language and stealing less than $300. It is similar to a fine for a traffic offences. Criminal infringement notices were introduced in November 2007, and have sparked much controversy. Some argue that people issued with them will just ignore them, and 32% were overdue for payment in June 2008 (*The Sydney Morning Herald*, 28 June 2008). The notices may not be effective as a deterrent, though there are consequences of not paying a fine, as outlined above. However, police argue that they are quick, save police and court time and, if the offenders were arrested and charged, they would probably be fined by the court anyway.

▶ **Community service order:** The offender is required to perform some unpaid work or service in the community for up to 500 hours.

▶ **Home detention:** The offender is confined to his or her own home or to a restricted area for a period of up to eighteen months. Home detention was formally introduced as a sentencing option in 1996, and is now governed by the *Crimes (Sentencing Procedure) Act 1999* (NSW) (see Section 1.4.1, page 44). People sentenced to home detention are required to wear an electronic tracking device which is contacted randomly, or are subject to random visits. This sentencing option allows the offender to work and care for his or her family.

- **Periodic detention:** The offender is required to serve his or her prison sentence on consecutive weekends. A six-month period of imprisonment, for example, means twenty-six weekends of detention. A weekend of detention begins at 7:00 pm on Friday night and ends at 4:30 pm on Sunday.

- **Forfeiture of assets:** A person can be ordered to forfeit (give up) his or her property to the government if the court finds that the property was gained with the proceeds of crime, or the property was used to commit crime. Forfeiture of assets is usually only ordered for serious drug offences and some other serious offences, such as organised crime.

- **Imprisonment:** The offender is detained in a prison for at least the length of the non-parole period of the sentence (see Sections 1.4.1 [page 44] and 1.4.8 [pages 53–4]).

Diversionary programs

Traditional ways of dealing with offenders, such as imposing the penalties listed above, are costly and time consuming, and may not be the best way of preventing a person from reoffending. A series of alternatives to the traditional penalties have been developed in the hope that such measures will rehabilitate the offender. These diversionary programs include the following.

- **Magistrates' Early Referral into Treatment Program (MERIT):** This scheme operates in local courts and allows the magistrate to adjourn a case, generally for three months, while the offender undertakes drug rehabilitation. Participation in the scheme is voluntary. Satisfactory completion of the drug rehabilitation program is taken into account when the sentence is being determined.

- **The Drug Court:** This court is discussed in Section 1.3.1 (pages 23–4). It aims to rehabilitate drug offenders so that they are no longer dependent on drugs. There is also the Youth Drug and Alcohol Court which is modelled on the Drug Court and operates in some areas of Sydney (see Section 1.5.5, page 61).

- **Cannabis cautioning scheme:** Police can issue an official caution to an adult charged with possessing a small amount of cannabis. The caution is recorded by police, and, if there is a second caution, the offender must attend a compulsory drug education session. Cautions are also an important part of the law dealing with young offenders (see Section 1.5.5, page 60).

- **Traffic Offenders' Program (TOP):** This program was introduced in 1992 and has been run by various community groups on a voluntary basis since then. A person charged with a driving offence is referred to the program by the magistrate after his or her initial court appearance. The program involves eight lectures over a seven week period, and attendees must complete a compulsory assignment for each lecture. The completion of the program is taken into account when the offender returns to court for sentencing.

- **Sober Driver Program:** This program commenced in 2002 and is aimed at adult repeat drink driving offenders. Courts can order compulsory attendance as part of the sentence for the offence. The program consists of weekly two-hour sessions for nine weeks and teaches offenders about the consequences of drink driving and strategies for avoiding situations which lead to drink driving.

▶ **Circle sentencing and restorative justice:** These represent alternative methods of sentencing the offender and are discussed in Section 1.4.7 (page 52).

As well as the above punishments, the defendant may be ordered to pay compensation to the victim of the crime under the *Victims Rights and Support Act 2013* (NSW) (see Section 1.7.5, page 75).

CAN YOU evaluate the effectiveness of different types of penalties, including diversionary programs?

In order to evaluate the effectiveness of different types of penalties, you need to look at the advantages and disadvantages of each, and decide how well each achieves the purposes of punishment. The advantages and disadvantages of each type of penalty are listed in Table 1.4.

Table 1.4 Effectiveness of penalties

Penalty	Advantages	Disadvantages
No conviction recorded	▶ Inexpensive ▶ Appropriate for minor offences ▶ May be a specific deterrent	▶ Does not rehabilitate ▶ May not seem suitably retributive
Caution	▶ Inexpensive ▶ Appropriate for minor offences ▶ May act as a specific deterrent	▶ Does not rehabilitate ▶ May not seem suitably retributive ▶ May not deter, though there is evidence that youth cautions are successful in cutting reoffending rates (see Case Study 116, Section 155, page 60)
Fine	▶ Inexpensive ▶ Appropriate for minor offences ▶ Flexible	▶ May not deter ▶ May disadvantage poor people who have greater difficulty in paying the fine ▶ Does not rehabilitate
Bond **Suspended sentence** **Probation**	▶ Inexpensive ▶ Can rehabilitate the offender, e.g. a condition of the bond may be to regularly attend a drug rehabilitation centre ▶ Suitable for less serious offences where there is little danger to the community	▶ Offender has opportunity to reoffend ▶ May not deter, though consequences of breaching the conditions imposed may act as a deterrent, particularly with a suspended sentence ▶ May be difficult to supervise conditions imposed on the offender, unless the Parole Authority is involved
Criminal infringement notice	▶ Occurs at the time of the offence ▶ Inexpensive ▶ Saves police and court time	▶ May not be effective as a deterrent ▶ May not be suitably retributive
Community service order	▶ Inexpensive ▶ Assists the general community ▶ Offender may correct damage they have caused, so is suitably retributive, e.g. offenders may have to clean off their own graffiti	▶ May not deter ▶ Offender has opportunity to reoffend ▶ May not rehabilitate offender
Periodic detention	▶ Less costly than imprisonment ▶ Allows offenders to continue with education or employment	▶ May not deter ▶ Offender has opportunity to reoffend
Home detention	▶ Appropriate for those convicted of non-violent crime ▶ Decreases prison population ▶ Can rehabilitate offender ▶ Enables people with family responsibilities to stay at home	▶ Only available in city courts ▶ May not rehabilitate
Forfeiture of assets	▶ May be suitably retributive as the person cannot benefit from the crime	▶ May not rehabilitate
Imprisonment	▶ Incapacitates prisoners so they cannot reoffend ▶ A serious punishment suitable for serious crimes (retributive)	▶ Often does not rehabilitate offenders and may have a negative effect on their behaviour ▶ Imposes hardship on the family of the offender, especially if he or she was the main earner ▶ May not deter ▶ Very costly (it costs over $50 000 to keep a prisoner in jail for one year)

Penalty	Advantages	Disadvantages
Diversionary programs	▸ Can rehabilitate the offender: In March 2000, the first offenders tried under the Drug Court finished the twelve-month program. In the first year of the court, 261 offenders began the program and 168 remained on the program. Independent studies have also shown that offenders who complete the diversionary driving programs are much less likely to reoffend than those who have not. ▸ Relatively inexpensive	▸ Offender has the opportunity to reoffend ▸ May not deter

 page 90

<table>
<tr><td>Describe alternative methods of sentencing, including circle sentencing, restorative justice.</td></tr>
</table>

1.4.7 Alternative methods of sentencing

Alternative methods of sentencing involve diversionary programs, such as those described in Section 1.4.6 (pages 50–51), as well as restorative justice programs. These alternative methods of sentencing are primarily aimed at rehabilitation, so that the offender can avoid further contact with the criminal justice system. They may involve drug or alcohol rehabilitation, or are aimed at a certain group of people, such as Aboriginal or young offenders.

Restorative justice programs aim to both address the causes of criminal behaviour and to allow the offender to rectify the harm he or she has caused. Two forms of restorative justice that operate in NSW are youth justice conferencing (see Section 1.5.5, page 60) and circle sentencing.

Circle sentencing is a restorative justice program for Aboriginal offenders. It was introduced in Nowra in 2002 and has now extended to other areas in the state. Aboriginal offenders are brought before a 'circle' of people involved with the offence, including the victim, the victim's family, community elders, the defence lawyer, the prosecutor and the magistrate. A discussion occurs in which the members of the circle are entitled to speak. The members of the circle discuss the offence, its impact on the victim and the community, ways of rectifying the harm done, and what can be done to help both the victim and the offender in the future. The magistrate ensures the sentence is appropriate to the offence and the circumstances.

CAN YOU assess the roles of alternative methods of sentencing?

In order to assess the role of alternative methods of sentencing, you need to:

▸ **explain where such methods are used**
Circle sentencing and youth justice conferencing are only used for relatively minor offences and only for certain offenders—that is, Aboriginal people in some areas of NSW, and for young offenders.

▸ **explain the benefits of these methods**
The success of circle sentencing, for instance, is evidenced by the fact that the program has expanded across NSW. The program gives support to Aboriginal offenders, helps reduce cultural barriers between Aboriginal people and the courts, involves the community in assisting the offender to rehabilitate and helps redress harm done to the victim.

Youth justice conferencing allows the offender and the victim to meet to work out the best way for the offender to compensate for his or her wrongdoing. It also allows the victim to tell the offender about the impact of the crime (see Section 1.5.5, page 60).

▸ **explain the limitations of such methods**
Despite the fact that youth justice conferencing seems to have reduced the rates of young people reoffending (see Case Study 1.16, Section 1.5.5, page 60), reoffending rates are still high. Youth justice conferencing also does little to address the causes of youth crime. Circle sentencing, on the other hand, involves the offender's community in the process, which may help to address the factors leading to the criminal behaviour.

 page 90

1.4.8 Post-sentencing considerations

After an offender is sentenced to a prison term, various considerations to do with the prison term arise. There are also some other consequences of sentencing which arise for some offenders.

Describe post-sentencing considerations, including security classification, protective custody, parole, preventative detention, continued detention, sexual offenders registration, deportation.

Security classification

On entering a prison, a prisoner is given a security classification by the NSW Classification Committee under the *Crimes (Administration of Sentences) Regulation 2014* (NSW). This classification is based upon the seriousness of the offence committed and the length of the sentence. There are three main security classifications:

▷ **high-risk categories**, which contain male prisoners given an AA, A1 or A2 classification and female prisoners given a 4 or 5 classification. Prisoners in these categories are considered to present a special risk to good order and security and are confined in maximum security prisons with secure physical barriers and towers. About 37% of all prisoners in NSW are in high security prisons.

▷ **medium-risk categories**, which contain male prisoners given a B classification and female prisoners given a 3 classification. These categories of prisoners are confined in medium security prisons which must have secure physical barriers.

▷ **low-risk categories**, which contain male prisoners given a C classification and female prisoners given a 1 or 2 classification. These prisoners are confined in open security prisons which need not have physical barriers and prisoners don't have to be constantly supervised. In NSW, 29% of prisoners are in open institutions.

Implications of security classification

The way a prisoner is classified is important, because it determines in which prison he or she serves the sentence and, consequently, to which rehabilitation programs the prisoner has access. It also determines the privileges to which the prisoner is entitled, and the kinds of offenders the prisoner is likely to serve time with. A high-risk category prisoner generally has fewer privileges and will serve his or her sentence in the company of other serious offenders. These factors have an effect on the offender's prison experience and on his or her chances of integrating back into the community when released from prison.

Protective custody

Prisoners can be subject to violence and harassment from other prisoners for a variety of reasons, such as race, sexual preference, disability, because of the crime they have committed or because they have informed on other criminals. Prisoners who feel they are in danger from their fellow prisoners can ask to be placed in protective custody, which means being separated from the prisoners whom they fear.

Implications of protective custody

While protective custody protects the prisoner from harm, such protection restricts the opportunities for those in custody to work and to access education programs.

Parole

Parole allows prisoners to leave prison before they have completed their full sentence. There are conditions attached to parole and, if a prisoner breaks them, he or she is sent back to prison to complete the original sentence. When and how parole is granted is restricted by the *Crimes (Sentencing Procedure) Act 1999* (NSW) (see Section 1.4.1, page 44). Prisoners who have been sentenced to imprisonment for three years or less are automatically released on parole after they have served the required time in prison. Those with longer sentences can apply for parole after they have served their minimum sentences.

Prisoners on parole are closely supervised by the Parole Authority and are subject to certain restrictions and expectations, such as obtaining and keeping employment and refraining from mixing with certain people or going to certain places.

Implications of parole

One implication of parole is that it encourages prisoners to behave well and undertake rehabilitative activities in the hope of early release. After prisoners are released on parole the close supervision helps to ensure that they reassimilate into society, and so have a greater chance of remaining free from criminal activity. The prospect of returning to prison if parole conditions are breached also encourages parolees to remain free from criminal activity and assimilate into the community.

Preventative detention and continued detention

The term *preventative detention* is used in two ways. First, it is a term used to describe the detention of people detained without charge because they are suspected of terrorist activity, as seen in Section 1.2.1 (page 12). Such people have not been charged with or been found guilty of a criminal offence.

The second use of the term *preventative* (or *preventive*) *detention* applies to the detention of serious offenders who are at risk of reoffending if they are released into the community. In this case, preventative detention refers to the continued detention of serious offenders after their term of imprisonment has expired. Most criminal jurisdictions in Australia have passed legislation allowing such detention. In NSW, the *Crimes (High Risk Offenders) Act 2006* (NSW) provides that serious sexual offenders can continue to be detained after their sentence has expired if they are seen as a threat to the community.

Implications of preventative detention and continued detention

The main reason for preventative and continued detention is to protect the community from possible harm caused by serious offenders reoffending. However, the consequences of this are serious, because people detained under this legislation have already served their sentence. This legislation provides for the detention of people who may do something in the future, not for an offence they have already committed. Some commentators argue that preventive detention violates the International Covenant on Civil and Political Rights (ICCPR) (1966), which provides that: 'No one shall be subject to arbitrary arrest or detention' (see Sections 1.2.1 [page 12] and 2.1.3 [page 107]).

Sexual offenders' registration

All state and territories in Australia have sexual offenders' registers. People who have been convicted of serious sexual offences, particularly those involving children, must register with the police station closest to their residence and provide the police with certain information including any travel plans. The period of registration is for a minimum of eight years for an adult and four years for a juvenile. Serious sexual offenders are also subject to supervision upon release from prison, which may include electronic tagging.

Implications of sexual offenders' registration

The main purpose of registration is to monitor such offenders, so their chances of reoffending are minimised, while they are given support to reassimilate into society. However, if the information becomes public, some residents may object to such a person living in their community. This occurred in 2009, when members of the Ryde community in Sydney objected to a sexual offender living there (see Case Study 1.20, Section 1.7.5, pages 73–4). In some states of the USA, the name, address and photo of such offenders are publicised, and, in three of those states, this has led to the murders of registered individuals.

Deportation

Deportation means the forcible removal of a person from a country and returning that person to his or her country of origin. People who are not Australian citizens and who have been permanent residents for less than ten years can be deported if they are convicted of an offence and sentenced to prison for at least one year.

Implications of deportation

The purpose of deportation is to protect Australian citizens from possible harm from such offenders reoffending. Because such people are not Australian citizens, the government is not obliged to assist them to be reassimilated into the community. Deportation can, however, cause hardship for the offender's family, particularly if the offender is the main income earner.

CAN YOU examine the implications of post-sentencing considerations in achieving justice?

The implications, both positive and negative, of each post-sentencing consideration are examined after the description of each consideration above.

 page 90

1.4.9 The effectiveness of sentencing and punishment as a means of achieving justice

Evaluate the effectiveness of sentencing and punishment as a means of achieving justice.

To evaluate the effectiveness of sentencing and punishment as a means of achieving justice, you should discuss those factors which help ensure justice and those factors which may limit the achievement of justice in the sentencing and punishment process. Both sets of factors are outlined in Table 1.5.

Table 1.5 Factors affecting the achievement of justice in the sentencing and punishment process

Factors which *help ensure* the achievement of justice in sentencing and punishment	Factors which may *limit* the achievement of justice in sentencing and punishment
▸ The provision of statutory and judicial guidelines means that limits are placed on a judge's discretion when sentencing, and this ensures sentencing consistency (see Section 1.4.1, pages 43–5).	▸ Some people feel that judges still have too much discretion when sentencing, and that some sentences are too lenient (see Section 1.4.1, pages 43–5).
▸ There is very limited mandatory sentencing in NSW (see Section 1.4.1, pages 44–5).	▸ Mandatory sentencing does not allow a judge or magistrate to consider the circumstances of the offence and the offender when sentencing (see Section 1.4.1, pages 44–5).
	▸ Many punishments do not seem to deter, as evidenced by reoffending rates (see Sections 1.4.2 [page 45] and 1.4.6 [pages 51–2]).
	▸ Rehabilitation programs for some offenders may result in inconsistency in sentencing (see Section 1.4.2, page 45).
▸ Consideration of many factors in sentencing, including aggravating and mitigating circumstances, help ensure that penalties are appropriate for each individual offence (see Section 1.4.3 page 46).	

Factors which *help ensure* the achievement of justice in sentencing and punishment	Factors which may *limit* the achievement of justice in sentencing and punishment
▶ The provision of victims' impact statements has several advantages for the victim and the community (see Section 1.4.4, page 47).	▶ It may not always be in the best interests of the victim to give a victim impact statement (see Section 1.4.4, page 47).
▶ Sentencing appeals allow higher courts to supervise the exercise of sentencing discretion by magistrates and judges, and this helps to ensure consistency (see Section 1.4.5, page 48).	
▶ The advantages of various types of penalties are outlined in Section 1.4.6 (pages 48–52).	▶ The disadvantages of various types of penalties are outlined in Section 1.4.6 (pages 48–52).
▶ Circle sentencing gives support to Aboriginal offenders, helps reduce cultural barriers between Aboriginal people and the courts, involves the community in assisting the offender to rehabilitate and helps redress harm done to the victim (see Section 1.4.7, page 52).	
▶ Youth justice conferencing allows the offender and the victim to meet to work out the best way for the offender to compensate for his or her wrongdoing. It also allows the victim to tell the offender about the impact of the crime (see Section 1.5.5, page 60).	▶ While youth justice conferencing seems to have reduced the rates of young people reoffending, reoffending rates are still high (see Case Study 1.16, Section 1.5.5, page 60).
	▶ Youth justice conferencing does little to address the causes of youth crime (see Section 1.5.5, page 60).
▶ Protective custody protects the prisoner from harm (see Section 1.4.8, page 53).	▶ Protective custody restricts the opportunities for those in such custody to work and to access education programs (see Section 1.4.8, 52).
▶ Preventative detention and continued detention protect the community from possible harm (see Section 1.4.8, page 54).	▶ Some argue that preventative detention violates the ICCPR (1966) (see Section 1.4.8, page 54).
▶ Sexual offenders' registration monitors such offenders, so their chances of reoffending are minimised, while they are given support to reassimilate into society (see Section 1.4.8, pages 54–5).	▶ If sexual offenders' registration information becomes public, some residents may object to such a person living in their community. In some states of the USA, such information has led to the murders of individuals registered in three of those states (see Section 1.4.8, pages 54–5).
▶ Deportation protects Australian citizens from possible harm caused by non-Australian offenders reoffending (see Section 1.4.8, page 55).	▶ Deportation can cause hardship for the offender's family, particularly if the offender is the main income earner (see Section 1.4.8, page 55).

KCq page 90

1.5 Young offenders

Children are treated differently at every stage of the criminal justice system. The treatment of children accused of crimes is discussed in the following sections.

1.5.1 Age of criminal responsibility

Describe the age of criminal responsibility.

Under the *Children (Criminal Proceedings) Act 1987* (NSW), no-one under the age of ten years can be charged with a criminal offence because it is said that they are not old enough to form the necessary *mens rea*. This is called the principle of *doli incapax*. If a child is between ten and fourteen years, the principle of *doli incapax* can be argued with (that is, the child can be found in court to have the necessary *mens rea* to be held criminally responsible). In this situation, the prosecution must prove that that child knew that what he or she was doing was wrong, and not just naughty. The prosecution was given this task in a trial against a boy who, at ten years old, drowned a six-year-old boy (see Case Study 1.15 following).

CASE STUDY 1.15: The death of Corey Davis, 3 December, 1999

Facts

On 2 March 1998, Corey Davis, a six-year-old boy, was allegedly thrown, struggling, into the Georges River at Macquarie Fields in Sydney. The ten-year-old boy who threw him in the river, allegedly yelled, 'Bad luck,' as Corey, who could not swim, thrashed in the water. The ten-year-old boy later told police, 'Yeah, I pushed him in, so what?' The boy was charged with manslaughter.

Issue

Did the boy know that what he was doing was wrong, not just naughty? In other words, did the boy have the necessary criminal intention to be guilty of manslaughter?

Decision

The prosecution had to prove that the accused boy had the necessary intention. The defence produced witnesses, both psychiatrists and teachers, who gave evidence that the accused boy was mentally at least two years younger than his age. The jury found the accused boy not guilty.

Source: 'Boy cleared of killing', *The Sydney Morning Herald*, 4 December 1999.

CAN YOU **discuss the issues surrounding the age of criminal responsibility?**

The age of criminal responsibility raises media and community interest from time to time, particularly when a child is involved in causing serous harm to others, such as in the death of Corey Davis in 1998 (see Case Study 1.15 above).

Some people argue that the age of criminal responsibility should be lowered, while others argue that the current law regarding the age of criminal responsibility should be retained. These arguments are summarised below.

▶ The principle of *doli incapax* is old-fashioned, and doesn't hold true for modern children. Others argue that *because* the idea is very old, dating back to the seventh century, and has survived so long, we should be wary of changing it.

▶ Modern children have compulsory education from the age of five, and so develop faster both mentally and physically. Others argue that while school may generally contribute to educating children, children who commit offences often do not regularly attend school because of truancy or exclusion. Furthermore, it is the child's social and family environment which influences his or her understanding of right and wrong—not school.

▶ Modern children are more sophisticated, having a greater understanding of the world because of technology. Others argue that technology may actually lessen children's ability to determine what is real—they may expect a seriously injured person to recover quickly, as happens in cartoons or video games. Also, in past centuries, children worked from a young age and were more responsible than they are now.

▶ Children are getting away with crime at the expense of community protection—victims of serious crimes are just as badly hurt, and deserve there to be some sort of punishment for the perpetrator, even if he or she is a child. Others argue that adults are acquitted from criminal serious offences if it is found through a successfully argued defence that they did not have they necessary *mens rea*, so it is inconsistent to treat children more harshly.

 page 90

Describe the rights of children when questioned or arrested.

1.5.2 The rights of children when questioned or arrested

Children have the same rights as adults when questioned or arrested (see Sections 1.2.1 [pages 11–14] and 1.2.6 [pages 19–20]), except that they have extra protections that adults do not have. Most of these are contained in the *Law Enforcement (Powers and Responsibilities) Act 2002* (NSW). These include:

▶ a parent or guardian must be notified if a child is taken into custody by police

▶ children have the right to have an independent adult as a support person present during any police procedure, such as an interview or search. A child cannot waive this right.

▶ the police must tell a child about his or her rights and assist the child to exercise those rights, such as giving them the Legal Aid Hotline number

▶ the powers of search and seizure are the same for adults and children, except that a child under ten may not be strip searched and a support person should be present for the strip search of an older child

▶ children in police custody must not be kept in the same cell as an adult

▶ police must not photograph or take fingerprints of a child under fourteen, unless there is a court order

▶ police may not take a bodily sample, such as blood or hair, from a child without a court order.

Some laws regarding police enforcement may, however, have an unfair impact on children. The powers of police to search and to direct people to move on are more likely to be exercised on young people, according to various reports including the 'Policing Public Safety: Report of the NSW Ombudsman' (1999). There has also been concern that anti-gang laws passed in 2009 may have a greater impact on young people who are more likely to be part of visible groups.

CAN YOU **explain why young offenders are treated differently in the criminal justice system?**

Young offenders are treated differently from adults in the criminal justice system for the following reasons.

▶ Young people are given special protection by the law in many circumstances (see Section 4.1.4, pages 214–19), so it would be inconsistent to treat them as harshly as adults in criminal matters.

▶ Young offenders are more likely to be intimidated by, and less likely to understand, court procedure than are adults.

▶ A young offender does not always understand as well as an adult the consequences of his or her action.

▶ Young offenders have a greater chance of resuming normal life and becoming worthwhile citizens and should be encouraged to do so.

KCq page 90

1.5.3 Children's Court

Unless a child is diverted from court proceedings under the *Young Offenders Act 1997* (NSW) (see Section 1.5.5, pages 59–61), most charges against people under eighteen years of age are heard in a special Children's Court hearing. The operation of the Children's Court is governed by the *Children (Criminal Proceedings) Act 1987* (NSW). The proceedings are much the same as those of a summary hearing except that here, too, there are special protections for children including:

▶ it is a closed court (that is, the public are not allowed at the hearing)

▶ the media may attend the hearing, but may not publish the identity of the offender

▶ the magistrate often specialises in children's cases and will take reasonable measures to ensure that the child understands the proceedings

▶ a conviction is not recorded if the child is under sixteen years of age.

The Children's Court has jurisdiction over most criminal matters involving children, except for traffic offences and serious indictable offences, such as murder. Committal proceedings for serious indictable offences are heard in the Children's Court, but the trial and sentencing hearing are heard in the relevant court, either the District Court or Supreme Court.

The Children's Court also has the power to adjourn court proceedings and to direct parents to attend court under the *Children (Protection and Parental Responsibility) Act 1997* (NSW).

 page 90

1.5.4 Penalties for children

When a child pleads or is found guilty of a criminal offence, the Children's Court must follow principles of sentencing set out in the *Children (Criminal Proceedings) Act 1987* (NSW). Some of these principles are:

▶ it is desirable, if possible, for a child's education to continue uninterrupted

▶ it is desirable, if possible, for a child to live at home

▶ a penalty imposed on a child for an offence should be no greater than that imposed on an adult who commits an offence of the same kind.

Most penalties and sentencing options available to the court are similar to those available for adult offenders (see Section 1.4.6, pages 48–52). These include:

▶ dismissal of the charges, or dismissal with caution

▶ imposing a fine

▶ placing the defendant on a bond

▶ probation

▶ a community service order

▶ a suspended sentence

▶ imprisonment: For juveniles, imprisonment occurs by way of a control order, which is an order sending the child to be detained in a juvenile detention centre.

Other sentencing options available to the court include:

▶ referral to a youth justice conference (see Section 1.5.5, page 60)

▶ adjournment for rehabilitation purposes: This usually occurs when the court is thinking of imposing a serious penalty, but wants to give the child the chance to demonstrate rehabilitation. Usually strict conditions are imposed and the adjournment can be for up to twelve months. At the end of the adjournment the child is likely to receive a less severe penalty, if he or she has complied with the conditions.

KCq pages 90–91

1.5.5 Alternatives to court

For young offenders there are several alternatives to court, the main alternatives being those provided under the *Young Offenders Act 1997* (NSW). Under this act, the police must consider giving the young offender a warning, or a caution, or instructing them to attend a conference. Court proceedings can only be commenced if these options are clearly inappropriate. These options, discussed below, are available for summary offences and less serious indictable matters.

Warnings

A child can be given an on-the-spot warning by police for a minor offence. The child's name is recorded, but the offence does not form part of a child's criminal history.

Cautions

Police can also issue a more formal warning in the form of a caution. A caution can only be given if the child admits to the offence and an independent adult is present. A record of the caution is kept and may be seen by the Children's Court if a further offence is committed. A child may be cautioned up to three times.

Youth justice conferences

The *Young Offenders Act 1997* (NSW) introduced youth justice conferencing. Present at the conference are: the young offender; a parent, guardian, or any other close associate of the offender; the victim; a supporter for the victim; and a mediator. The aim of such conferences is to come up with an agreement which may include an apology for the victim, reparation made to the victim, drug or alcohol rehabilitation for the young offender, or anything else considered appropriate. If the child does not fulfil the agreement then court proceedings may be commenced.

The effect of the use of cautions and youth justice conferences is discussed in Case Study 1.16, following.

CASE STUDY 1.16: Effectiveness of police cautions and youth justice conferencing

A report entitled 'Reoffending among young people cautioned by police or who participated in a youth justice conference' (by S. Vignaendra and Jacqueline Fitzgerald, *Crime and Justice Bulletin*, Number 103, October 2006, NSW Bureau of Crime Statistics and Research) reveals that the introduction of police cautions and youth justice conferences for young people have led to a significant drop in the number of young offenders appearing before the Children's Court. The number has nearly halved, dropping from 16 113 in 1996–97, to 8428 in 2005. This drop has many benefits, including better use of resources.

In 2004–05, approximately 1200 young people completed a youth justice conference. Of those offenders who completed a youth justice conference in 1999, 58% reoffended within five years.

In 2004–05, approximately 9000 young people were cautioned by police and a further 19 000 received a warning. Of those offenders who received a caution in 1999, 42% reoffended within five years.

These reoffending rates are lower than those before the introduction of the *Young Offenders Act*. Of young people appearing in court for the first time in 1995, 63% had reoffended within five years.

These statistics demonstrate that juvenile crime is still significant and that, while diversionary procedures may keep young offenders out of court, reoffending rates are still high. One major criticism concerning the prevention of juvenile crime is that lawmakers have still not addressed the social and economic factors which lead children to break the law and to reoffend.

The Youth Drug and Alcohol Court

The Youth Drug and Alcohol Court was established under the *Children's (Criminal Proceedings) Act 1987* (NSW) and is similar to the Drug Court (see Section 1.3.1, pages 23–4), except that it is for young offenders. It gives young offenders an opportunity to participate in an intensive program of rehabilitation before being sentenced. A program lasts six months and involves detoxification, rehabilitation, and close supervision by the court. Successful completion of the court's program means a lighter sentence.

Intensive program units and mentor programs

These two options are often imposed as a condition of probation or early release from a detention centre. Intensive program units provide specialist psychological counselling to persistent or serious young offenders, or to those with particular psychological problems. Mentor programs are designed for Aboriginal and Torres Strait Islander children or children from non-English speaking backgrounds. Mentor programs provide these offenders with a trained older person to assist them to rehabilitate and avoid further offences.

KCq page 91

1.5.6 The effectiveness of the criminal justice system when dealing with young offenders

Assess the effectiveness of the criminal justice system when dealing with young offenders.

To assess the effectiveness of the criminal justice system when dealing with young offenders, you should discuss those factors which help ensure the effectiveness of the system and those factors which may limit the effectiveness of the criminal justice system when dealing with young offenders. Then come to a conclusion about the overall effectiveness of the system. Both sets of factors are outlined in Table 1.6.

Table 1.6 Factors affecting the criminal justice system when dealing with young offenders

Factors which *help ensure* the effectiveness of the criminal justice system when dealing with young offenders	Factors which may *limit* the effectiveness of the criminal justice system when dealing with young offenders
▶ The law regarding the age of criminal responsibility is effective, because children do not have the experience or mental capacity to truly form the necessary *mens rea* to commit a crime (see Section 1.5.1, page 56).	▶ Some argue that the age of criminal responsibility is too high and that consequently children are excused from crimes for which they should be found guilty (see Section 1.5.1, page 56).
▶ Children are given greater protection by the law at every stage of the criminal justice process because they are more vulnerable and have a greater chance of rehabilitating and becoming responsible citizens (see Section 1.5.2, page 58).	
▶ Children are given greater protection than adults when questioned or arrested by the police because they are more vulnerable (see Section 1.5.2, page 58).	▶ Some laws regarding police enforcement may have an unfair impact on children (see Section 1.5.2, page 58).
▶ Children's Court proceedings are designed to protect children who are charged with a criminal offence, while also holding them accountable for any crime they have committed (see Section 1.5.3, pages 58–9).	
▶ The sentencing principles which apply to sentencing young offenders help ensure they are not treated as harshly as adults (see Section 1.5.4, page 59).	
▶ The provision of separate detention centres for children protects them from the negative impacts of hardened adult criminals (see Section 1.5.4, page 59).	
▶ Sentencing alternatives available to the Children's Court and programs which divert young offenders from court, such as warnings, cautions and youth justice conferences, may assist in rehabilitating young offenders (see Sections 1.5.4 [page 59] and 1.5.5 [pages 59–61]).	▶ Some see sentencing alternatives available to the Children's Court and programs which divert young offenders from court, such as warnings, cautions and youth justice conferences, as soft options which only encourage young offenders to reoffend (see Sections 1.5.4 [page 59] and 1.5.5 [pages 59–61]).

Factors which *help ensure* the effectiveness of the criminal justice system when dealing with young offenders	Factors which may *limit* the effectiveness of the criminal justice system when dealing with young offenders
▶ Youth justice conferencing allows the offender and the victim to meet to work out the best way for the offender to compensate for his or her wrongdoing. It also allows the victim to tell the offender about the impact of the crime (see Section 1.5.5, page 60).	▶ While youth justice conferencing seems to have reduced the rates of young people reoffending, rates of reoffending are still high (see Case Study 1.16, Section 1.5.5, page 60).
▶ Programs such as intensive program units and mentor programs help prevent young offenders from reoffending and this helps protect society (see Section 1.5.5, page 60).	▶ Youth justice conferencing does little to address the causes of youth crime (see Section 1.5.5, page 60).

 page 91

1.6 International crime

1.6.1 Categories of international crime

Describe categories of international crime, including crimes against the international community and transnational crimes.

CAN YOU define international crime?

International crime is crime committed which has international implications in either international law or in the enforcement of domestic criminal law.

There are three main types of international crime:
▶ crimes against the international community
▶ transnational crimes
▶ crimes committed outside the jurisdiction.

To thoroughly define international crime, you should give the definition for and explain the three main types of international crime, with examples.

Crimes against the international community

Crimes against the international community are crimes committed by individuals and states which are seen as wrong by the international community. These crimes may be aimed at the whole international community or at specific groups or members within the community. Crimes against the international community include war crimes, crimes against peace and humanity, genocide, terrorism, apartheid and slavery.

Laws against these crimes are usually contained in declarations and conventions of the United Nations and are linked directly to human rights and responsibilities (see Section 2.2.2, pages 108–9).

One example of a crime against the international community is terrorism. Terrorism is violence by an individual or group against a perceived international enemy, aimed at provoking fear. Terrorist acts are often undertaken by an individual or group who come from outside the nation where the terrorist act takes place. A very famous act of terrorism is the '9/11' attacks on the World Trade Centre in New York in 2001. These acts, the reaction of the international community to them, and terrorism in general, are discussed in Section 6.3.2 (see pages 408–9).

Genocide is another example of a crime against the international community. Genocide means acting with the 'intent to destroy, in whole or in part, a national, ethnic, racial or religious group' (Article II, United Nations Convention on the Prevention and Punishment of the Crime of Genocide 1948). Genocide is usually committed by one ethnic, religious or cultural group upon another, and became an international concern after Nazi Germany's actions concerning Jews, Poles and Slavs in World War II. Over five million Jews were killed in World War II because of their ethnicity and religious beliefs. Genocide still occurs today.

EXAMPLE Genocide

A modern-day example of genocide is the forced expulsion and murder of thousands of ethnic Albanians from Kosovo, led by the Serbian government in 1999 (see Case Study 6.4, Section 6.2.9, page 404). According to United Nations' figures, the bodies of up to 11 000 ethnic Albanians have been found. Crimes such as genocide receive international attention and action. War Crimes tribunals, as well as the International Criminal Court (see Sections 2.2.2 [page 110], 2.2.3 [page 113], 6.2.4 [pages 398–400] and 6.4.5 [pages 423–4]) represent action by the international community to deal with these types of crimes.

Transnational crimes

These crimes occur within a state's legal system but contain an international element. This usually means that the organisations or people involved in the crime could be responsible for that crime in several countries. These crimes are, therefore, handled under both the criminal system of a nation-state and through international criminal provisions.

The main transnational crimes are hostage-taking, terrorism, the drug trade, and pornography (see Case Study 1.19, Section 1.6.2, page 68). The international drug trade has become one of the chief problem areas for international crime enforcement. Because of the growth of the international drug trade since the 1960s, the international community has needed to create conventions concerning illegal drugs.

The United Nations Convention on Narcotic Drugs (1961) states that narcotics, such as heroin, are illegal. The Convention requires states to have laws making possession, cultivation and trafficking of narcotics illegal. It also says that states should cooperate with each other to stop global drug trafficking. The Convention states that offenders are to be prosecuted for drug offences in the state where the offence was committed. This may involve extradition (see Section 1.6.2, pages 66–7). The 1972 protocol, which amends this Convention, states that drug rehabilitation can be an alternative to other punishment. The 1971 Convention on Psychotropic Substances means that psychotropic drugs, such as amphetamines, are subject to the same legal regimes as narcotics.

Crimes committed outside the jurisdiction

These are crimes which take place outside a particular nation's criminal laws, for example piracy and aircraft hijacking. These crimes take place in international waters or airspace, and do not come under the clear-cut jurisdiction of any nation. Crimes committed outside national jurisdiction are covered by treaties, including extradition treaties (see Section 1.6.2, page 66). Piracy and hijacking are also governed by United Nations' declarations. The main declarations involve:

▶ **piracy:** the Convention on the High Seas (1958) and the Convention on the Law of the Seas (1982)
▶ **aircraft hijacking:** the Tokyo Hijacking Convention (1963), the Hague Hijacking Convention (1970), and the Montreal Hijacking Convention (1971).

Piracy and aircraft hijacking are still major international crimes, but are not as prevalent as they were. Hijacking was a common crime in the 1970s and 1980s, due to political terrorism, but has become rare. The hijacking, in late 1999, of an Indian Airlines plane by Pakistani terrorists caused an international crisis. Other crimes which occur in the sea and the air include hostage-taking, murder, theft and terrorism. There are conventions that decide under which national jurisdiction these crimes should be dealt with. KCq page 91

1.6.2 Dealing with international crime

CAN YOU describe the various measures used to deal with international crime?

To do this, you need to describe both international and domestic measures of dealing with international crime.

International measures for dealing with international crime include:

▶ international instruments

▶ international customary law

▶ international criminal tribunals, such as the International Criminal Court (ICC)

▶ sanctions

▶ extradition treaties

▶ international cooperation between countries, particularly between police forces.

Domestic measures for dealing with international crime include:

▶ domestic criminal laws that deal with transnational crimes, such as laws prohibiting the importation of illegal drugs and anti-terrorism laws (see Case Study 1.4 [page 13], Sections 1.2.1 [page 13] and Section 1.1.5 [page 6]).

▶ cooperation between domestic authorities in different nation states, in order to deal with transnational crimes and crimes outside the jurisdiction. An example is the 'Wonderland Club' case described in Case Study 1.19 (page 68). This is also an international measure.

▶ other international measures that require domestic legal action, such as the imposition of sanctions and implementation of extradition procedures (see Case Study 1.18, on page 67).

The above measures, both international and domestic, are described in the following text.

International instruments

These are one of the main measures for dealing with international crime. An international instrument is a formal legal document which has legal force under international law, such as a treaty or convention. There are many international instruments which have been developed with respect to international crime, such as the treaties and conventions mentioned in Section 1.6.1 (pages 62–3). An important international instrument recently ratified is the Rome Statute (1998), which established the International Criminal Court (ICC) (page 65).

Customary international law

This consists of principles and procedures that have grown up through general usage, to the point where they are accepted as being fair and right by the international community. Genocide is an example of international crime which is outlawed by customary international law.

International tribunals

There are several international tribunals which have been developed to hear cases involving international crime.

The International Court of Justice (ICJ) is the judicial organ of the United Nations. The ICJ has fifteen justices who each serve a nine-year term and who are elected by the United Nations General Assembly and the Security Council. The ICJ can only hear cases between nations. It does not hear cases between individuals. So it is only concerned with public (not private) international law. It hears public criminal cases, such as crimes against the international community. The case of *Nicaragua v United States of America* (1986) ICJ 14 (see Case Study 6.2, Section 6.2.4, page 398) is an example of an ICJ case. The effectiveness of the ICJ depends on the cooperation it receives, and this is restricted by the consensual nature of international law.

Several specialist criminal tribunals have been established for specific investigations concerning war crimes and crimes against humanity. The first War Crimes Charter was established after World War II. The war crimes trials of World War II resulted in convictions of specific Nazi offenders. Other war crimes tribunals have dealt with crimes against humanity in the former Yugoslavia and in Rwanda. These are the International Criminal Tribunal for the former Yugoslavia and the International Criminal Tribunal for Rwanda (see Section 6.2.4, page 399). Because of the infrequency of war crime tribunals and the lack of real convictions or even trials, war crimes trials are usually left up to individual states.

Since the first war crimes tribunals in the late 1940s and early 1950s, trials and convictions for serious crimes against the international community have been rare. Despite this, serious crimes, such as genocide, have been committed in Bosnia, Kosovo, Iraq and Rwanda in recent times. Trials are rare because the ICJ, and declarations and conventions regarding war crimes, are not effective international enforcers of these laws. Because of this limited effectiveness, the International Criminal Court was established in 2002.

The International Criminal Court (ICC) began operation in 2002 and has the role of bringing justice to victims of war crimes and other international crimes. The ICC is a permanent court, separate to the United Nations, set up by a multilateral treaty, the Rome Statute 1998. The ICC began operating out of The Hague in July 2002. The ICC is the first permanent court allowing individuals to be tried for crimes against humanity. It is known as a court of 'last resort', meaning it will only hear cases if they are not being investigated or prosecuted by a national judicial system, unless the national systems are not genuine (see also Section 6.2.4, pages 398–9).

As of 2019, there were 123 parties to the Rome Statute, meaning 123 nation-states had agreed to its provisions and to the jurisdiction of the ICC. In July 2008, Human Rights Watch issued a report into the operation of the ICC in it first five years (see Case Study 1.17 following).

CASE STUDY 1.17: The first five years of the ICC

Human Rights Watch reported on the first five years of the operation of the ICC in July 2008 ('ICC: Good Progress Amid Missteps in First Five Years', Human Rights Watch, 11 July 2008). The report stated that the court had made 'notable progress'. Some of its accomplishments and some problems it has encountered are presented below.

ICC accomplishments

▷ The ICC has opened investigations in the Democratic Republic of Congo, northern Uganda, the Darfur region of Sudan, and the Central African Republic.

▷ The ICC has issued twelve warrants against suspects in four countries, four of whom are currently in custody.

▷ The ICC has established viable witness protection programs.

▷ The ICC has made efforts to provide meaningful support to defendants.

ICC problems

▷ The ICC has had to suspend indefinitely the trial of Thomas Lubanga, a Congolese warlord accused of recruiting and using children as soldiers, because of flaws in the prosecution case.

▷ There has been criticism of the court's interaction with the communities worst affected by these types of crimes, such as in the Democratic Republic of Congo and in northern Uganda.

▷ The court has lacked some diplomatic support including enforcement of its arrest warrants.

Sanctions

Sanctions are actions taken by the international community towards a state which is seen to be attempting to, or has broken, recognised international law. There are five main types of sanctions:

▶ **moral sanctions** (these are the mildest sanctions and occur when other states express their disapproval towards an offending state)

▶ **political sanctions** (these can include the breaking of diplomatic relations)

▶ **economic sanctions** (these involve the offending state being punished economically—this punishment can include the refusal to trade with a specific country, disallowing exports and imports, and using boycotts and blockades). The effectiveness of economic sanctions is discussed in Case Study 6.9, Section 6.4.1, page 417.

▶ **financial sanctions** (this involves a state being refused financial assistance or loans from other states)

▶ **physical sanctions** (this is the use of force, which can sometimes result in war—in 1999, the Serbian state of Kosovo had physical sanctions placed on it by NATO [see Case Study 6.4, Section 6.2.9, page 404]).

Sanctions may coerce states into abiding by international criminal law. However, there are limits to their effectiveness. For example, imposing sanctions on one state can harm other states. This can make it difficult to convince these other states to agree to sanctions. Sanctions also often harm the citizens of the offending state and not its leaders. This is particularly true in the case of economic and physical sanctions.

Extradition

This occurs when a person is handed over by one state to another state because that person is accused of a crime in the latter state. Extradition is based on agreement between states. It is determined by specific extradition treaties between countries.

Extradition is based upon the principle that offenders should not be able to escape justice merely by escaping to another country or state. Extradition is a major international method of dealing with fugitive domestic criminals (that is, people who commit a crime under one country's domestic law and then flee the country in order to escape the consequences). Extradition also occurs between Australian states. For example, someone who commits a crime in Victoria and travels to NSW can be arrested by NSW police and extradited to Victoria in order to face trial.

Extradition instruments include:

▶ **bilateral treaties** (for example, Australia and the USA have an extradition treaty called the Treaty on Extradition between Australia and the United States [1974])

▶ **multilateral treaties** (for example, the European Union has the 1957 European Conventions on Extradition)

▶ **United Nations conventions** (some United Nations conventions have a section on extradition, such as the Convention on the Prevention and Punishment of the Crime of Genocide [1948]).

Extradition law is also contained in customary international law.

Not all offences are covered by extradition treaties. The offences which are extraditable must be considered an offence by all members of the treaty. Political, religious and military offences are usually not included in extradition treaties.

International regimes developed to deal with fugitive domestic criminals include cooperation between the police forces of various countries and extradition court hearings. The case of the extradition of Jayant Patel (see Case Study 1.18 following) shows these regimes in action.

CASE STUDY 1.18: The extradition of Jayant Patel (2008)

Background

Dr Jayant Patel was charged in Queensland with three counts of manslaughter, three counts of causing grievous bodily harm while a surgeon and eight counts of fraud. These charges relate to a number of botched operations performed by Dr Patel at Bundaberg Base Hospital in Queensland betwee 2003 and 2005, and to his alleged efforts to conceal a history of professional misconduct in New York and Oregon. Dr Patel is an Indian-born citizen of the United States.

The extradition

The Queensland Department of Public Prosecutions commenced proceedings in 2008 to extradite Dr Patel from the United States to face these charges. Patel was arrested in Oregon on Tuesday 11 March 2008, under the 1974 Treaty on Extradition between Australia and the United States. He faced a court hearing, in which it needed to be decided whether there was 'double-criminality' (that is, that the charges laid against Dr Patel are not only crimes in Australia, but are recognised under the extradition treaty). Only those charges which have been outlined in the arrest warrant issued under the treaty could be brought against Patel in Australia. Dr Patel could also have argued that he would not receive a fair trial in Australia because of the publicity surrounding the case.

Outcome

The US District Court judge who ordered Patel's extradition, ordered that his file be kept secret. However, the extradition was ordered and Patel was extradited to Australia in July 2008 to face criminal charges.

Extradition is an effective enforcement procedure if states consent to signing extradition treaties and obeying them. The main aim of extradition is cooperation between states and for states to be able to enforce their domestic law.

There is no general international agreement on extradition. This is because each nation-state has different moral, ethical and cultural viewpoints. For example, what is an offence in India may not necessarily be an offence in Australia. The nature of domestic law and the role of extradition in international law mean that extradition's effectiveness relies solely on state cooperation and consensus.

Cooperation between nations

Another important method for dealing with international crime is cooperation between enforcement authorities in various countries. Such cooperation has led to the apprehension and conviction of various offenders whose crimes have an international element, such as crimes involving trade in illegal drugs and child pornography. The offenders are tried in the country of their arrest, if that is where the crime occurred, or are extradited to the country in which the crime took place. For example, it is illegal to import illicit drugs, so someone who arrives in Australia with such drugs has committed an offence in Australia. The Wonderland Club child pornography case (see Case Study 1.19, page 68) is an example of international cooperation between police leading to the arrest and conviction of offenders operating transnationally.

CASE STUDY 1.19: The Wonderland Club child pornography club (1998)

Background

The Wonderland Club was a secure internet chat room that shared pornographic images of children. A person wishing to become a member needed to supply a large number of new images in order to join the club. By this means, the club gained possession of hundreds of thousands of images of child pornograpy. It had members in several nations, including Great Britain, Germany, the United States and Australia.

Police cooperation

The police in Great Britain discovered the existence of the club and joined the United States in tracking down the members through their internet providers. In an operation called Operation Cathedral, the police forces of all countries where members of the club resided became involved in tracking down the members, placing them under surveillance and sharing information with the other police forces.

Outcome

On 1 September 1998 the police teams simultaneously raided the homes of club members in different parts of the world. Several dozen arrests were made, including two in Australia. Offenders were charged and tried under each country's domestic laws.

Limitations

The limitations of each measure for dealing with international law have been described in the discussion of these measures on the preceding pages and are summarised in Section 1.6.3 following. KCq page 91

Evaluate the effectiveness of the domestic and international legal systems in dealing with international crime.

1.6.3 The effectiveness of the domestic and international legal systems in dealing with international crime

To assess the effectiveness of the domestic and international legal systems in dealing with international crime, you should discuss those factors which help ensure the effectiveness of both systems and those factors which may limit the effectiveness of the domestic and international legal systems in dealing with international crime. Then come to a conclusion about the overall effectiveness of the both systems. Both sets of factors are outlined below.

The nature of international law

Due to the consensual nature of international law, enforcement of these laws can be very difficult.

The usefulness of laws about specific international crimes

Many international treaties encourage nations to cooperate with each other in order to stop transnational crimes, such as the international traffic in illegal drugs. Some of the illegal traffic has been intercepted because of such cooperation.

However:

- crimes such as terrorism are hard to prevent, because the perpetrators are usually members of secret, well-organised groups
- measures to combat terrorism may also result in the infringement of an individual's basic human rights, such as in the case of Mohamed Haneef (see Case Study 1.4, page 13)
- the crime of genocide is often only discovered after it has occurred, as in the case of ethnic Albanians in Kosovo in 1999 (see Sections 1.6.1 [pages 62–3] and 6.2.9 [page 404]).

The effectiveness of international tribunals

The effectiveness of the ICJ depends on the cooperation it receives, and this is restricted by the consensual nature of international law. For example, the USA ignored the ICJ ruling when found guilty of unlawfully invading the airspace of Nicaragua (see Case Study 6.2, Section 6.2.4 [page 398]). Also, war crime tribunals are infrequent and have rarely led to real convictions or even trials. The ineffectiveness of these tribunals has, however, led to the establishment of the ICC.

The ICC

The accomplishments and the limitations of the ICC in its first five years are listed in Case Study 1.17, Section 1.6.2, page 65.

Sanctions

Sanctions may coerce states into abiding by international criminal law.

However:

▶ imposing sanctions on one state can harm other states. This can make it difficult to get these other states to agree to sanctions.

▶ sanctions often harm the citizens of the offending state and not its leaders. This is particularly true in the case of economic and physical sanctions.

Extradition

Extradition is an effective enforcement procedure if states consent to signing extradition treaties and obeying them.

However:

▶ there is no general international agreement on extradition

▶ the nature of domestic law and the role of extradition in international law means that extradition's effectiveness relies solely on state cooperation and consensus.

Cooperation between nations

Cooperation between nations, particularly between police forces, has led to the arrest and conviction of some transnational criminals.

However, this does not occur frequently enough to deter many transnational crimes. The continued, huge, worldwide trade in illicit drugs is evidence of this.

 KCq page 91

1.7 Themes and challenges

1.7.1 Theme 1: The role of discretion in the criminal justice system

Discretion means the choice to do or not do something. Discretion is part of all criminal processes, from reporting crime, and the police deciding what crimes to investigate and which to ignore, to who gets arrested and what charges are decided upon. Police have considerable discretion in enforcing the law, and discretion is also demonstrated by the judiciary and other legal personnel in the trial process, in sentencing, and in punishment. So discretion plays a part in all aspects of the criminal justice process. Areas where discretion occurs are listed on the next page.

> Explain the role of discretion in the criminal justice system.

▶ **In the reporting of crime**: Victims and witnesses, for various reasons, exercise discretion when deciding whether to report a crime or not (see Section 1.2.2, pages 14–15). This exercise of discretion plays a very important part in which crimes are investigated.

▶ **In the criminal investigation process** (see Sections 1.2.1 to 1.2.7, pages 11–21)—police exercise discretion when deciding:

- which areas to patrol
- which crimes to target
- which reports to thoroughly investigate
- what type of evidence to gather
- what charges to lay, if any
- whether to issue a criminal infringement notice or to arrest the offender
- whether to warn, caution or arrest a young offender (see Section 1.5.5, pages 59–60)
- whether or not to grant bail. Judges and magistrates also exercise discretion in the bail decision process.

▶ **In the criminal trial process** (see Sections 1.3.1 to 1.3.10, pages 22–43) discretion is exercised:

- about whether a case is heard summarily or with a jury
- about what evidence is admissible (though the rules of evidence, the adversary system itself, and the system of appeals help minimise harmful effects of discretion in this instance)
- during charge negotiation.

▶ **In sentencing and punishment** (see Sections 1.4.1 to 1.4.9, pages 43–56): discretion is the backbone of the process, and is exercised by judges and magistrates when deciding a sentence. The judiciary has the broad discretion to select the type of sentence to give a convicted offender, and the length of time served. However, judicial discretion is limited by statutory and judicial guidelines, and influenced by aggravating and mitigating circumstances.

Post-sentencing decisions, such as those about the classification of prisoners, are also discretionary (see Section 1.4.8 pages 53–5).

Problems and benefits with the exercise of discretion

Discretionary decisions are fundamental to the criminal justice system. Police, magistrates, judges and others who must make such decisions are guided: by their knowledge of the law; by the likely effect or outcome of their decision; by practical considerations, such as the use of resources, and the amount of time that will be expended; as well as by ideas of public interest and justice.

It is important to remember that, when discretion is exercised, it is because a decision must be made, and there are several options from which to choose. There is usually more than one suitable or correct option. A discretionary decision is not 'wrong' because another course of action was available, or because another person in the same circumstances would have made a different decision.

In fact, in many situations, the exercise of discretion is crucial to the achievement of justice. No two situations are the same, and the exercise of discretion is necessary to take into account the differences between similar, but not identical, situations. In sentencing, for instance, the judge weighs up all the individual factors surrounding the crime, the victim and the offender, and, in doing so, can achieve the fairest result for all concerned.

There are also many laws to guide and limit the use of discretion, such as those concerned with the exercise of police powers, the operation of the trial process and the making of sentencing decisions. The system of appeals and the trial process itself also help ensure that discretionary decision-making processes are subject to scrutiny and review.

However, the exercise of police and judicial discretion may mean that the law is applied differently to different groups. Some cases involving rape have highlighted the lack of sensitivity of some judges to the effect of rape on women and the right of women to say no to sexual intercourse. There is also evidence that young people are more likely to be stopped by police than older people.

The lack of equality displayed by the criminal justice system towards various groups in society is particularly evident in the case of Aboriginal people. In 2006, for example, despite making up less than 2% of Australia's population, Indigenous Australians accounted for 22% of Australia's prison population (NSW Bureau of Crime Statistics and Research). The imprisonment rate has actually increased since the Royal Commission into Aboriginal Deaths in Custody was tabled in 1991, despite measures aimed at reducing the rate. KCq page 91

1.7.2 Theme 2: Issues of compliance and non-compliance in regard to criminal law

Examine issues of compliance and non-compliance.

Why do people comply with (obey) the law or not comply with (disobey) the law? The reasons for this are outlined in Section 1.1.8 (pages 8–9) and include morals, socioeconomic factors, politics, technology and self-interest. Those people who do not comply with the law do so for a variety of reasons as listed in Section 1.1.8 (pages 8–9). Members of society who are not committed to the legal system may be so because they:

- do not feel they have had any input into the system
- do not agree with the morals and ethics on which it is based
- are not achieving in society
- do not feel that the system is just when it deals with them.

These groups can include the socioeconomically disadvantaged, Aboriginal and Torres Strait Islanders, and children. KCq page 91

1.7.3 Theme 3: The extent to which law reflects moral and ethical standards

Examine the extent to which law reflects moral and ethical standards.

The criminal justice system is designed to deal with breaches of society's moral and ethical conduct, which are very strongly linked. This is because whatever Australian society considers to be a crime is also what the society generally accepts as morally and ethically wrong.

Murder is a crime, for example, because society thinks that it is morally wrong, due to societal, cultural and religious reasons. Offences against a child, such as abuse, are also illegal because society sees them as morally and ethically wrong. In fact, often child sex offenders and killers must be placed in protective custody for their own safety (see Section 1.4.8, page 53). This example demonstrates that the individual's and society's moral and ethical viewpoints shape all areas of criminal law.

Sometimes people disobey the law because of their moral, ethical, political and religious viewpoints (see Section 1.1.8, page 8).

Some groups within society establish their own set of beliefs, ethics and rules that may encourage or even reward criminal behaviour. An example of this is organised crime and criminal gangs. Their ethics deviate from the mainstream society that they are operating within.

Moral and ethical differences are also sources of conflict within the criminal justice system. For instance, victims of crime sometimes feel that sentences are too lenient, even though the sentencing judge also has to take into account mitigating factors when determining a sentence (see Sections 1.4.3 [page 46], 1.4.4 [page 47] and 1.7.5 [pages 75–7]).

Moral and ethical standards are also reflected in the protections the law provides for both suspects and victims (see Sections 1.2.6 [pages 19–20] and 1.7.5 [pages 75–7]). In Western democracies, such as Australia, civil and political rights are highly valued and the law protects these rights to a large extent. The counterterrorism laws, which allow for the detention of suspects without charge for forty-eight hours or more, are a concern to some members of the community who see these laws as infringing basic human rights (see Section 1.2.1, pages 12–13). Others in the community say the infringement is necessary to protect the community from a greater harm.

The types of sentence that can be imposed by the law also reflect the community's standards. Because of this, Australia does not have capital or corporal punishments, and young offenders are treated less harshly than adults (see Section 1.5.2, page 58).

The moral and ethical standards of society are passed on through education of children. Education about why laws are established, how they function and why certain acts are illegal is one of the best crime prevention techniques and usually begins in early childhood and continues through life. However, the morals and ethics of certain groups in society may make crime prevention education difficult. Social and economic disadvantage can also make it difficult for persons to break a cycle of crime through education. KCq page 91

1.7.4 Theme 4: The role of law reform in the criminal justice system

Describe the role of law reform in the criminal justice system.

To *reform* the law means to change the law so that it operates more efficiently and/or more effectively. Law can be reformed by legislation or by adaptation of the common law in courts. Parliament is the primary agency of law reform, though the courts contribute to reform in the law by applying precedent to cases currently under review and making decisions to fit changing circumstances. Courts need to apply legislation, and to follow precedent, and can only make a decision in cases before them, so their contribution to reform is usually slow and piecemeal. However, sometimes the effect of a court decision can be profound, as in the case of *Dietrich v The Queen* (1992) 177 CLR 292 (see Case Study 1.5, Section 1.3.5, page 29).

Pressure to change existing law can come from many sources including:
- the media
- lobby groups
- reports from various government inquiries or organisations, such as the Ombudsman or Law Reform Commissions
- international pressure.

Law Reform Commissions are bodies established by state and federal governments to systematically investigate various areas of the law and make recommendations for change in those areas. The first law reform commission was established in 1966 in NSW. The Commonwealth body, the Australian Law Reform Commission, was set up in 1975. Because most criminal law is state law, the NSW Law Reform Commission is the most relevant commission to the operation of the criminal law for residents of NSW.

While law reform commissions can be valuable agencies for changing the law, they can, however, only recommend changes. Governments are not compelled to implement these recommendations. The NSW Law Reform Commission, for example, inquired into the question of whether to allow majority verdicts, and released its report in 2005 (Report No. 111), recommending against the introduction of majority verdicts. The government, however, ignored the report and introduced 'eleven to one' majority verdicts in 2006 (see Case Study 1.13, Section 1.3.9, pages 40–41). However, the government has largely incorporated recommendations made by other Law Reform Commission inquiries, such as the 1996 report on 'Sentencing' (see below).

Many factors may lead to law reform. Some of these are discussed below.

Perceived failure of existing law and media pressure

Frequently, the failure of existing law, the media coverage that surrounds such failures, and the lobbying of various pressure groups who perceive such failures, leads to law reform. Some examples of law reform that has come about because of perceived failures are:

▷ the NSW Homicide Victims' Support Group lobbied for the introduction of the *Victims Rights Act 1996* (NSW), since replaced by the *Victims Rights and Support Act 2013* (see Section 1.7.5, pages 75–6)

▷ the introduction of majority jury verdicts, made by amendments to the *Jury Act* in June 2006, was largely due to the media coverage that accompanied several prominent cases which involved a hung jury, and was made despite recommendations from the NSW Law Reform Commission not to change this law (see Section 1.3.9, page 40)

▷ the so-called 'Ferguson's Law' was passed by NSW parliament in 2009, largely as a reaction to media pressure and despite concerns about the infringement of the rights of Dennis Ferguson (see Case Study 1.20, following)

▷ the reform of sentencing law in the *Crimes (Sentencing Procedure) Act 1999* (NSW). This act consolidated several pieces of legislation about sentencing that then existed, and followed the 1996 NSW Law Reform Commission report 'Sentencing' *(No. 79)* (see Section 1.4.1, pages 44–5)

▷ in the case of *Dietrich v The Queen* (1992) 177 CLR 292, the High Court established a limited right to legal representation in Australia (see Section 1.3.5, pages 28–9)

▷ battered woman syndrome and the abuse excuse have been increasingly recognised by the courts as proving defences to criminal charges (see Section 1.3.8, page 38).

CASE STUDY 1.20: 'Ferguson's Law'

Background

In 1988, Dennis Ferguson was jailed in Queensland for fourteen years, for kidnapping and sexually molesting three children in a Brisbane motel. After his release, and after being chased out of several Queensland communities, he relocated to the Sydney suburb of Ryde in public housing with a legal tenancy agreement. In September 2009, several nearby residents discovered that he was living in the neighbourhood and staged some public protests to have the government remove him. The protests received wide media attention.

Government response

The NSW government had no power to break Dennis Ferguson's legitimate lease agreement with them. However, the government responded to media pressure and passed the *Housing Amendment (Registerable Persons) Act 2009* (NSW), which allows them to relocate a tenant on recommendation from the NSW Police Commissioner, because of concerns about the safety of the tenant or the community. Mr Ferguson was relocated.

Issue

This case and the government response caused widespread media outcry. Some people felt that the government acted well, because communities need to be protected from convicted paedophiles. Others saw the government action as a violation of the rights of Mr Ferguson, who had served his sentence and should be now free to live a normal life in whatever abode he chooses.

Changing social values and composition of society

As social values change, the law also needs to change to reflect this. Some areas of criminal law where changing social values have contributed to reform are:

▶ decriminalisation of homosexual behaviour in NSW in 1984

▶ recognition of victims' rights (see Sections 1.4.4 [page 47] and 1.7.5 [pages 75–7])

▶ new defences, such as battered woman syndrome (see Section 1.3.8, page 38)

▶ the development of alternative methods of sentencing (see Section 1.4.7, page 52)

▶ the introduction of youth justice conferencing and other laws to divert young people from the criminal justice system (see Section 1.5.5, pages 59–61)

▶ the *Anti-Terrorism Act (No. 2) 2005* (Cth) which, among other things, provides for preventative detention for forty-eight hours without charge (see Section 1.2.1, page 12). This reflects the post '9/11' community value that suspected terrorists are to be treated differently to other alleged offenders, even if they are not charged with anything, because their threat to the fabric of society is so great.

International law

The international human rights treaties and organisations have become reforming tools for Australian domestic law to some degree. This can be seen in their role in attempting to influence the Northern Territory to change its mandatory sentencing laws in 2000 (see Section 1.4.1 page 44). Difficulties with bringing to justice perpetrators of crimes against the international community led to the establishment of the International Criminal Court in 2002 (see Section 1.6.2, page 65).

New technology

The advent of computers, the internet and increased globalisation has meant that new criminal law and enforcement measures are constantly needed in order to handle new technology. This is particularly the case when dealing with the internet which allows criminal activity, such as the distribution of pornographic material, to occur on an international level more easily (see Case Study 1.19, Section 1.6.2, page 68). The technological ability to identify DNA has led to the introduction of laws whereby DNA can be collected from suspects and convicted criminals (see Section 1.2.1, page 12).

KCq page 91

1.7.5 Theme 5: The extent to which the law balances the rights of victims, offenders and society

Rights of offenders

The rights of people charged with a criminal offence are outlined in Sections 1.2.1 (pages 11–14), 1.2.6 (pages 19–20), 1.3.6 (page 30) and 1.3.7 (pages 30–32).

Victims' rights

Victims of crime may suffer severe mental and physical turmoil after the crime has been committed. The suffering of victims has long been ignored by the criminal justice system, though the law has provided more assistance to victims in recent years, such as giving the victim a greater role in sentencing (see Section 1.4.4, page 47). The following legal provisions are also provided to help victims of crime.

Compensation

Under the *Victims Rights and Support Act 2013* (NSW), victims can gain compensation for damage done to them through an act of violence. The victim can apply for compensation to the Victims Compensation Tribunal, which was established by the Victims Rights and Support Act. The tribunal can award compensation out of public money for personal injury or death to primary victims, and compensation to secondary victims, such as distressed witnesses and relatives of a deceased victim. The maximum amount that can be paid to a victim of a crime is $50 000 and the minimum is $7500. Some of the rules regarding the award of compensation under the Victims Rights and Support Act are as follows:

▶ Compensation can be recovered from persons found guilty of a crime.

▶ Compensation for the injury can only be paid once (that is, a person cannot, for instance, be paid by the tribunal and by another source, such as workers' compensation).

▶ Motor vehicle accident victims and convicted inmates may not receive compensation, except in very limited circumstances.

▶ There is a set table for compensation, replacing common law principles.

▶ Shock cannot be compensated. Victims must prove a 'chronic psychological or psychiatric disorder' to gain compensation for mental trauma.

Charter of Victims' Rights

A Charter of Victims' Rights was given legislative force in NSW under the Victims Rights and Support Act. Victims of crime have the right to be informed of:

▶ services and remedies available to them

▶ the withdrawal of charges against alleged offenders

▶ the victim's role in the trial process

▶ the final outcome of proceedings, if requested

▶ special bail conditions designed to protect the victims and their families

▶ the outcome of bail applications in cases involving serious personal violence.

Where they request it, and where it would not prejudice the Crown's case, victims have the right to be informed of:

▶ the progress of investigations

▶ modification of charges

▶ charge negotiation.

Victims have the right to have their residential addresses and telephone numbers withheld, unless it is contrary to the interest of justice. Victims also have the right to have the prosecutor make known to a bail authority their need for protection, and to a court the full effect on them of a crime of sexual assault or serious personal injury.

Victim impact statements

Victims of sexual assault or serious personal injury can make a victim impact statement to a court if they wish (see Section 1.4.4, page 47). However, making such a statement may not be in the best interest of the victim.

Counselling and other services

There are several counselling services available to victims of crime. Some are specialists in one area, such as rape or domestic violence. Others, such as that set up by the Sydney City Mission in 1993, are available to all victims. The *Victims Rights Act 1996* (NSW) set up a Victims of Crime Bureau to provide information to victims, to assist victims of crime in the exercise of their rights, and to coordinate the delivery of support services for crime victims.

Victims' lobby and support groups

Often victims of crime and their families feel that one way to deal with the crime is to meet with others who have shared the same experience. These groups offer support to one another and lobby governments for increased victims' rights, and regarding other law and order issues. One example in NSW is the Homicide Victims' Support Group.

Youth justice conferencing and circle sentencing

Youth justice conferencing and circle sentencing allow the offender and the victim to meet to work out the best way for the offender to compensate for his or her wrongdoing. They also allow the victim to tell the offender about the impact of the crime (see Sections 1.4.7 [page 52] and 1.5.5 [page 60]).

Balance between the rights of the victim and the rights of offenders

The balance between the rights of victims and the rights of the accused have swung more in favour of the victim in recent years, with the introduction of the measures outlined above. However, many victims, particularly victims of sexual assault, still need to undergo aggressive and harrowing examinations in court (see Sections 1.2.2 [pages 14–15], 1.3.8 [page 36] and 1.4.4 [page 47]). For the criminal justice process to be effective, the rights of victims need to be recognised, while the rights of the accused to a fair trial and a just punishment also need to be ensured. Giving too much regard to victims may infringe upon the rights of the accused and of offenders.

Balance between the rights of victims and the rights of society

The community has the right to have the criminal justice process operating efficiently. Problems with funding the Victims' Compensation Scheme, in particular, may interfere with this right. However, most members of the wider community sympathise with and support the rights of victims, and there is generally little conflict between the rights of victims and society.

Balance between the rights of offenders and the rights of society

The counterterrorism laws described in Section 1.2.1 (pages 12–13) are a good example of the law's attempt to balance the rights of individual suspects with the need to protect the community from terrorist attack. It should be remembered that Mohamed Haneef (see Case Study 1.4, Section 1.2.1, page 13) was only a suspect, not an offender. Some members of the community see these laws as infringing basic human rights, while others in the community say the infringement is necessary to protect the community from a greater harm.

Similarly, laws about the granting of bail (see Section 1.2.5, page 18) try to balance the rights of the individual suspect, who has not yet been found guilty of any offence, with the need for the community to be protected from crime.

Another area in which the law tries to balance the rights of suspects to a fair trial with the rights of the community to feel safe and to feel that justice is being done is the application of rules of evidence, such as the right to silence and rules regarding hearsay evidence, relevance and other rules (see Sections 1.3.6 [page 30] and 1.3.7 [page 32]). These rules about the way a trial is conducted, and the right to appeal if the rules are wrongly applied, help ensure that the rights of society and the rights of alleged offenders are kept in balance.

Some crimes make a large emotional impact on the community, and the way the perpetrators are treated by the legal system causes considerable community concern and media comment. The treatment of convicted paedophile Dennis Ferguson, in 2009, by both the community in which he resided and by the government, led to much discussion about whether the proper balance between the rights of offenders and the rights of society were achieved (see Case Study 1.20, Section 1.7.4, pages 73–4).

 page 91

1.7.6 Theme 6: The effectiveness of legal and non-legal measures in achieving justice

Analyse the effectiveness of legal and non-legal measures in achieving justice.

The effectiveness of legal and non-legal measures in achieving justice are discussed throughout this chapter, primarily in Sections 1.2.7 (page 21), 1.3.10 (pages 42–3), 1.4.9 (pages 55–6), 1.5.6 (pages 61–2), and 1.6.3 (pages 68–9). Table 1.7 lists legal and non-legal measures at each stage of the criminal justice process. Each measure is followed by the numbers of Sections of this book within which the effectiveness of each measure is discussed.

Table 1.7 Legal and non-legal measures at each stage of the criminal justice process

Legal measures	Non-legal measures
The criminal investigation process	
▸ Police powers of investigation (Sections 1.2.1 [pages 11–14], 1.2.3 [pages 15–16] and 1.2.7 [page 21]) ▸ Rights of suspects (Sections 1.2.1 [pages 11–14], 1.2.6 [pages 19–20] and 1.2.7 [page 21]) ▸ Bail and remand (Sections 1.2.5 [pages 18–19] and 1.2.7 [page 21])	▸ Reporting of crime (Sections 1.2.2 [pages 14–18] and 1.2.7 [page 21]) ▸ Use of warnings (Sections 1.2.1 [page 13], 1.2.4 [page 17] and 1.2.7 [page 21]) ▸ Use of discretion (Sections 1.2.1–1.2.7 [pages 11–21] and 1.7.1 [pages 69–71])

Legal measures	Non-legal measures
The criminal trial process	
▶ Court jurisdiction (Section 1.3.1, pages 22–5) ▶ The adversarial system (Section 1.3.2, pages 25–6) ▶ Legal representation (Section 1.3.5, pages 28–30) ▶ Rules of evidence (Sections 1.3.6 [page 30] and 1.3.7 [page 32]) ▶ Use of defences (Section 1.3.8, pages 32–40) ▶ Use of juries (Section 1.3.9, pages 40–42)	▶ Diversion from punishment via Drug Court programs (Section 1.3.1, pages 23–4) ▶ Charge negotiation and guilty pleas (Section 1.3.4, pages 27–8) ▶ Legal aid (Section 1.3.5, page 29)
Sentencing and punishment	
▶ Statutory and judicial sentencing guidelines (Section 1.4.1, pages 43–5) ▶ Factors affecting a sentencing decision (Section 1.4.3, page 46) ▶ Provision of victim impact statements (Section 1.4.4, page 47) ▶ Provision of sentencing appeals (Section 1.4.5, page 48) ▶ A range of penalty options (Section 1.4.6, pages 48–52) ▶ Alternative methods of sentencing (Section 1.4.7, page 52) ▶ Post sentencing considerations (Section 1.4.8, pages 53–5)	▶ Diversionary programs (Section 1.4.6, pages 50–51)
Other measures	
▶ Laws regarding the age of criminal responsibility (Section 1.5.1, pages 56–7) ▶ Laws regarding children's dealings with police (Section 1.5.2, page 58) ▶ Children's Court proceedings (Section 1.5.3, pages 58–9) ▶ Sentencing principles for young offenders (Section 1.5.4, page 59) ▶ Diversionary programs for young offenders (Section 1.5.5, pages 59–61) ▶ International instruments and institutions for dealing with international crime (Sections 1.6.2 [pages 64–8] and 1.6.3 [pages 68–9])	▶ Social and situational crime prevention (Section 1.1.9, pages 9–10) ▶ Programs to prevent young offenders from reoffending (Section 1.5.5, pages 59–61) ▶ International cooperation between states when dealing with international crime (Sections 1.6.2 [pages 67–8] and 1.6.3 [page 69])

 page 91

Do you know all the key definitions and concepts for this chapter? Go through each term in the list and check that you know them all. Place a bookmark underneath each definition to cover the one below and slide it down. This way you can focus on each definition by itself.

Abuse excuse: The defence that the perpetrator of a crime had suffered, or was protecting those who had suffered, from child abuse.

Accessory after the fact: A person (or persons) who helped the main perpetrator after a crime was committed.

Accessory before the fact: A person (or persons) who helped plan a criminal offence but was not there when it occurred.

Actus reus: 'The guilty act' (that is, the voluntary commission of an act or voluntary omission of a duty that breaks the law).

Adjournment: A temporary postponement of legal proceedings to recommence at a later date.

Adversarial system of trial: System of trial used in Australia, in which the two sides of the case try to present and prove their version of the facts and disprove the other side's version.

Aggravating factors: Circumstances taken into account by a sentencing judge that may result in a more severe penalty.

Alleged: A person is accused of committing a crime, but has not yet been found guilty.

Appeal: A case is taken to a higher court because either side disagrees with the decision of a lower court.

Appellant: The party who disagrees with a court decision and appeals (that is, takes the case to a higher court).

Attempt: A crime is not successfully committed, despite the offender trying to do so.

Bail: An agreement to attend court to answer a criminal charge. Some surety of attendance is usually required, such as a monetary fee.

Battered woman syndrome: A criminal defence which may arise when a woman kills her husband or partner after years of suffering domestic violence or abuse.

Beyond reasonable doubt: Standard of proof in a criminal case. The judge or jury can only find the accused guilty of a crime if there is no reasonable doubt that the accused person actually did commit the crime.

Bond: A punishment in which the offender is free to go into the community but agrees to be of good behaviour for a certain period.

Burden of proof: The responsibility of proving a case in court. In a criminal case the prosecution has the burden of proof and must prove that the accused is guilty.

Causation: The act or omission committed must have caused the specific injury complained of.

Caution: An offender is warned by police rather than arrested and charged.

Character evidence: Evidence about the character of the accused. Bad character evidence is generally not admissible in court.

Charge negotiation: An agreement between the prosecution and defence, having met before the trial, with the defence agreeing that the accused will plead guilty if the prosecution reduces the charge. Also known as **plea bargaining**.

Circle sentencing: A restorative justice program for Aboriginal offenders in which a 'circle' of people involved with the offence discuss the offence and ways of rectifying the harm done.

Citizen's arrest: The right of citizens to arrest anyone who has committed a crime, only able to be used in certain limited circumstances.

Civil disobedience: Breaking the law deliberately as a protest against the law or against another action by government.

Committal hearing: Preliminary proceedings for trial by jury.

Community service order: A punishment for which the offender is required to perform some unpaid work or service in the community for up to 500 hours.

Complete defence: A criminal defence which, if successfully proved, completely clears a person of a crime.

Compulsion: Criminal defences, such as duress and necessity, in which the people claiming the defence argue that they were compelled or forced to act criminally because of other circumstances.

Computer crimes: Crimes, such as identity theft, that are committed using computers and internet technology.

Consent: A criminal defence in which the defendant claims that he or she acted with the victim's consent.

Conspiracy: Two or more people agreeing to do an unlawful act or to do a lawful act by unlawful means.

Continued detention: The detention of serious offenders after their term of imprisonment has expired. Also called **preventive detention** or **preventative detention**.

Control order: An order made by the Children's Court, sending a child to be detained in a juvenile detention centre.

Convention: A treaty which is agreed to and proclaimed by a large number of nations. Also called a **covenant**.

Coronial inquiry: An inquiry into the circumstances surrounding an unnatural death or an unexplained fire. Also called an **inquest**.

Crime: An act committed or an omission of duty, injurious to the public welfare, for which punishment is prescribed by law, imposed in a judicial proceeding usually brought in the name of the state.

Crimes against property: Acts or omissions which damage or remove other people's property, such as larceny, theft, break and enter, or property damage.

Crimes against the international community: Crimes committed by individuals and states which are seen as wrong by the international community, such as war crimes and terrorism.

Crimes committed outside the jurisdiction: Crimes which take place outside a particular nation's criminal laws, for example piracy and aircraft hijacking.

Criminal infringement notice: A notice issued to people by police, imposing a fine for a minor crime.

Criminal investigation process: The investigative stage of the criminal justice system where crimes are detected and investigated, and evidence is gathered so that an alleged offender may be brought before a court.

Criminal justice system: The system that operates to bring criminal offenders to justice, incorporating the investigation process, the trial process, and sentencing and punishment. Also known as the **criminal process**.

Criminal liability: To be responsible under the law for a criminal offence.

Criminal trial process: The hearing stage of the criminal justice system, in which the guilt or innocence of a defendant is decided in a court according to the rules of procedure and evidence.

Cross-examination: When a witness is asked questions in court by the opposing side, in order to test the accuracy and objectivity of the evidence.

Customary international law: Principles and procedures that have grown up through general usage to the point where they are accepted as being fair and right by the international community.

Customs warrant: A written authorisation issued by a judge or magistrate that gives the police power, at any time, to enter and search any premises where drugs may be.

Defence: A legally acceptable reason for committing a criminal act.

Defendant: The person or group of people against whom a civil or criminal action is brought.

Deportation: The forcible removal of a person from a country in order to return that person to his or her country of origin.

Deterrence: A purpose of punishment which either dissuades the offender from committing a similar crime in the future because of fear of punishment (specific deterrence), or dissuades the general public from committing a similar crime (general deterrence).

Diminished responsibility: A partial criminal defence, claiming the defendant acted while mentally ill or disabled and so is not entirely responsible for his or her actions, or where a normally sane person is so affected by alcohol or other drugs that he or she did not know what he or she was doing. Also known as **substantial impairment of responsibility**.

Discretion: The choice to do or not do something.

Doli incapax: The legal principle that a person under the age of ten years cannot be charged with a criminal offence because it is said that they are not old enough to form the necessary *mens rea*.

Driving offences: Offences that involve breaking the rules of the road, such as speeding or not wearing a seatbelt.

Drug offences: Offences including possession of illegal drugs, trafficking, cultivation, manufacture and importation of illegal drugs.

Duress: A criminal defence in which the defendant admits to committing the criminal act knowing that it was wrong, but claims that he or she was so frightened by threats of death or serious bodily harm that he or she committed the act anyway.

Economic offences: Offences involving acts or omissions against people's property or finances.

Examination-in-chief: A witness giving their own evidence in court, in response to questions.

Extradition: When a person is handed over by one state to another state because that person is accused of a crime in the latter state.

Fine: A sum of money paid by an offender as punishment.

Forfeiture of assets: An order for a person to give up his or her property to the government due to the property being gained with the proceeds of crime, or used to commit a crime.

Genocide: Acting with the intent to destroy, in whole or in part, a national, ethnic, racial or religious group.

Guideline sentence: A judgement given about a sentence for a particular crime which is to be taken into account by courts delivering sentences for similar offences.

Hearsay evidence: Evidence about what someone else told a witness happened, rather than what the witness saw or heard him or herself. Generally not admissible in court.

Home detention: A punishment in which the offender is confined to his or her own home or to a restricted area for a period of up to eighteen months.

Imprisonment: A punishment in which the offender is detained in a prison for at least the length of the non-parole period of the sentence.

Incapacitation: A purpose of punishment, aiming to isolate the offender, usually in prison, so that he or she is unable to commit another crime.

Indictable offences: Serious criminal offences that may be heard by a judge and jury.

Inquest: An inquiry into the circumstances surrounding an unnatural death or an unexplained fire. Also called a **coronial inquiry**.

Inquisitorial system of trial: The system of trial used in civil law countries where the magistrate or judge collects the evidence for both sides in cooperation with the prosecution after inquiries have been made.

Intention: The specific desire to commit a criminal act or omit a duty.

International crime: Crime committed which has international implications in either international law or in the enforcement of domestic criminal law.

International instruments: Formal legal documents, such as treaties, conventions and declarations, which have legal force under international law.

Jurisdiction: The area over which a court has authority, which can be geographical or subject-based.

Jury: A group of ordinary citizens brought to court to decide on the guilt or innocence of an offender.

Legal aid: The provision of inexpensive legal services to people on limited incomes.

Majority verdict: A verdict in which the guilt of an accused person is decided by eleven out of the twelve people on a jury.

Mandatory sentencing: The practice of some parliaments of legislating for a particular sentence to be given for a particular crime or series of crimes.

Maximum penalty: The most severe sentence that can be given for a particular crime.

Mens rea: 'The guilty mind', including the intention to commit the crime, recklessness or gross negligence.

Mental illness: A complete criminal defence which proves that, at the time the defendant committed the crime, he or she was of unsound mind (that is, suffering from a mental illness which either prevented him or her from knowing what the criminal action he or she committed was, or from knowing that it was wrong).

Mitigating factors: Matters that persuade the judge in a sentencing hearing that the maximum penalty should not be imposed.

Necessity: A complete criminal defence in which the defendant claims that the act or omission committed was necessary to avert serious danger.

Negligence: Failing to exercise the degree of care, skill or foresight that a reasonable person would have exercised in the same circumstances.

No conviction recorded: An accused person is found guilty of a criminal offence, but the charge is dismissed and no record is made of conviction.

Non-parole period: The minimum time an offender must actually spend in prison.

Offences against the person: Acts or omissions which harm other people, such as murder, assault and sexual assault.

Offences against the sovereign: Acts or omissions which aim to disrupt or harm the governing bodies of a country, such as spying, treason and illegal demonstrations.

Opinion evidence: A witness cannot give his or her opinion in a court about another person's words or actions, unless the witness is an expert in that field.

Parole period: A time when an offender no longer must be imprisoned, but is freed into the community under supervision.

Partial defence: A criminal defence which, if successfully proved, reduces the defendant's liability, for example from murder to manslaughter.

Parties: People who have participated in committing a criminal offence, either before, during or after the offence.

Penalty unit: An amount of money used to impose fines. In July 2008, one penalty unit equalled $110.

Periodic detention: A punishment for which the offender is required to serve his or her prison sentence on consecutive weekends.

Plea bargaining: An agreement between the prosecution and defence, having met before the trial, with the defence agreeing that the accused will plead guilty if the prosecution reduces the charge. Also known as **charge negotiation**.

Possession: Having enough illegal drugs for personal use.

Preliminary crimes: Attempting to commit a criminal act or omission, or planning to do so.

Presumption of innocence: The presumption in a criminal trial that an accused person is innocent until proved guilty.

Preventative detention: (1) Keeping a person suspected of being about to engage in a criminal activity, for example terrorism, in prison for up to forty-eight hours without charge; (2) The continued detention of serious offenders after their term of imprisonment has expired. Also called **preventive detention** and **continued detention**.

Prima facie case: A sufficiently strong case against the accused to put the matter before a jury.

Principal in the first degree: The actual perpetrator of a crime (that is, the person or persons who actually committed the crime).

Principal in the second degree: A person (or persons) who was present or who assisted the principal in the first degree in committing an offence.

Probation: A punishment in which the offender is released into the community but agrees to be on a bond of good behaviour and is subject to the supervision of the Parole Authority.

Prosecute: To present the case in court on behalf of the state.

Prosecution: The party who brings a criminal case to court—usually the police. Also refers to the name of the case itself.

Protective custody: Separating a prisoner from other prisoners whom he or she fears.

Provocation: A partial criminal defence in which the defendant claims that he or she was aggravated by the victim in such a way that the actions of the murdered person would have caused an ordinary person to lose self-control.

Public Defenders: Legal practitioners appointed by the government to represent accused people who have been granted legal aid in the District Court and Supreme Court.

Public order offences: Acts which occur in a public place and are seen as offensive or disruptive to the general population, such as offensive conduct and indecent exposure.

Recklessness: The committing of a criminal act when the probability of harm could be foreseen, but the offender acted anyway.

Recidivist: A person who commits crimes again and again.

Re-examination: The prosecution or defence questions their own witness again, after he or she has been cross-examined by the other side.

Rehabilitation: A purpose of criminal punishment that aims to change the behaviour of offenders so that they will not wish to commit other crimes.

Relevance: Only evidence that relates to the matter under scrutiny can be given by a witness.

Remand: Bail is refused and the defendant is kept in prison until the day of the court hearing.

Restorative justice programs: Sentencing programs which aim to both address the causes of the criminal behaviour and to allow the offender to rectify the harm he or she has caused.

Retribution: A purpose of punishment which aims to 'pay back' the person who committed the crime.

Rogue juror: A juror who enters the jury room having prejudged the verdict, and refuses to listen to the evidence or the views of the other jurors.

Sanction: (1) Punishment; (2) Action taken by the international community towards a state which is seen to be attempting to break, or has broken, recognised international law.

Search and seizure: The power to search people and their belongings or premises and to take away property that is illegally held or is to be used in evidence.

Security classification: The classification given to a prisoner which determines the type of prison in which he or she is placed.

Self-defence: A complete criminal defence in which the defendant admits to committing the offence knowing that it was wrong, but claims he or she was acting to defend himself or herself or someone else from attack.

Sexual offenders' registration: People who have been convicted of serious sexual offences are required to register with the police station closest to their residence and provide the police with certain information, including any travel plans.

Situational crime prevention: Creating situations in which it is difficult for people to break the criminal law.

Social crime prevention: Changing the social factors which cause people to be criminals.

Standard of proof: The weight or value given to evidence; the amount of proof needed in a court case. In a criminal case, this is 'beyond reasonable doubt'.

State: (1) An independent body with a defined territory that can enter into negotiations with other states and be recognised internationally; (2) A part of a federated nation, such as the state of NSW; (3) another name for government.

Strict liability: No *mens rea* needs to be proved. The *actus reus* is enough for the person to be guilty of the crime.

Substantial impairment of responsibility: A partial criminal defence, claiming the defendant acted while mentally ill or disabled and so is not entirely responsible for his or her actions, or where a normally sane person is so affected by alcohol or other drugs that he or she did not know what he or she was doing. Also known as **diminished responsibility**.

Summary offences: Minor criminal offences heard and decided by a magistrate sitting without a jury.

Summons: An official legal document which commands the person to whom it is addressed to appear at a particular court on a particular day to answer claims made against him or her.

Suspended sentence: A punishment in which an offender is sentenced to a term in prison, but the sentence is not carried out, and the offender is released into the community on a bond to be of good behaviour.

Terrorism: Violence by an individual or group against a perceived international enemy, aimed at provoking fear.

Trafficking: Having a quantity of illegal drugs deemed greater than that which the person could use alone.

Transnational crimes: Crimes which occur within a state's legal system but contain an international element.

Treaty: An international agreement between states, in written form and governed by international law.

Unanimous verdict: When all the members of the jury agree on the guilt or innocence of an accused person.

Verbals: False confessions, either fabricated by the police or obtained using threats of violence to force people to confess.

Victim impact statement: A statement made to the court outlining the full effect of the crime on the victim.

Warning: A sanction given on the spot by police for a minor offence. Some offenders, such as children, may be given a warning. In which case, the child's name is recorded, but this does not form part of the child's criminal history.

Warrant: A written authorisation issued by a judge or magistrate which gives the police power to take the action authorised by it, such as arresting the person named on it, or searching premises.

White-collar crimes: Crimes against property, carried out by people working in the business world who commit crimes related to money, such as embezzlement and tax evasion.

Witness: A person who gives evidence in court about what they know about a particular case.

Youth justice conference: A conference involving a young offender, a parent or guardian, the victim, a supporter for the victim and a mediator. The aim of this conference is to arrive at an agreement which helps rectify the effects of the crime and to prevent reoffending.

Are you able to answer every syllabus question in the chapter? Tick each question as you go through the list if you are able to answer it. If you cannot answer it, turn to the given page to find the answer. Refer to page ix to check the meaning of the NESA key words.

	For a complete understanding of this topic:	Page No.	✓
1	Can I describe the meaning of crime?	2	
2	Can I describe the elements of crime: *actus reus* and *mens rea*?	2–3	
3	Can I describe strict liability offences?	3	
4	Can I describe causation?	3–5	
5	Can I recognise offences against the person?	5	
6	Can I recognise offences against the sovereign?	5–6	
7	Can I recognise economic offences (property/white-collar/computer)?	6	
8	Can I recognise drug offences?	6	
9	Can I recognise driving offences?	6	
10	Can I recognise public order offences?	6	
11	Can I recognise preliminary crimes (attempts and conspiracy)?	6	
12	Can I define summary and indictable offences?	7	
13	Can I identify a party to a crime as the principal in the first degree?	7	
14	Can I identify a party to a crime as the principal in the second degree	7	
15	Can I identify a party to a crime as the accessory before the fact?	7	
16	Can I identify a party to a crime as the accessory after the fact?	7	
17	Can I examine a range of factors that may lead to criminal behaviour?	8–9	
18	Can I investigate a range of situational and social crime prevention techniques?	9–10	
19	Can I describe police powers?	11–14	
20	Can I discuss the powers of police in the criminal process?	14	
21	Can I outline the issues involved in reporting crime?	14–15	
22	Can I explain the procedures involved in gathering evidence when investigating crime?	15	
23	Can I explain the use of technology in investigating crime?	15	
24	Can I explain the procedures of search and seizure in investigating crime?	15–16	
25	Can I explain the use of warrants in investigating crime?	16	

	For a complete understanding of this topic:	Page No.	✓
26	Can I examine the reporting and investigating of crime?	16	
27	Can I describe arrest and charge, summons and warrants?	16–17	
28	Can I describe when and how decisions about bail and remand are made?	18–19	
29	Can I describe detention, interrogation and the rights of suspects?	19–20	
30	Can I assess the effectiveness of the criminal investigation process as a means of achieving justice?	21	
31	Can I describe court jurisdiction?	22–4	
32	Can I describe the role of the courts in the criminal justice process?	25	
33	Can I describe the adversarial system?	25	
34	Can I discuss the use of the adversarial system as a means of achieving justice?	26	
35	Can I describe the role of a magistrate in the legal system?	26	
36	Can I describe the role of a judge in the legal system?	26	
37	Can I describe the role of a police prosecutor in the legal system?	26	
38	Can I describe the role of the Director of Public Prosecutions in the legal system?	27	
39	Can I describe the role of Public Defenders in the legal system?	27	
40	Can I explain the processes involved in pleas and charge negotiation?	27–8	
41	Can I describe legal representation, including legal aid?	28–9	
42	Can I examine the role of legal representation in the criminal trial?	30	
43	Can I describe the burden and standard of proof?	30	
44	Can I describe the use of evidence, including witnesses?	30–32	
45	Can I describe complete defences to criminal charges?	33–7	
46	Can I describe partial defences to murder?	37–9	
47	Can I assess the use of defences to criminal charges in achieving justice?	39–40	
48	Can I describe the role of juries, including verdicts?	40	

For a complete understanding of this topic:	Page No.	✓
49	Can I evaluate the effectiveness of the jury system in the criminal trial?	41–2	
50	Can I assess the effectiveness of the criminal trial process as a means of achieving justice?	42–3	
51	Can I explain statutory and judicial guidelines?	43–5	
52	Can I describe the purposes of the punishment of deterrence (specific and general)?	45	
53	Can I describe the purposes of the punishment of retribution?	45	
54	Can I describe the purposes of the punishment of rehabilitation?	45	
55	Can I describe the purposes of the punishment of incapacitation?	46	
56	Can I describe factors affecting a sentencing decision: aggravating and mitigating circumstances?	46	
57	Can I explain the role of the victim in sentencing?	47	
58	Can I discuss factors that affect sentencing decisions, including the purposes of punishment and the role of the victim?	47	
59	Can I describe appeals?	48	
60	Can I describe the penalty of no conviction recorded?	49	
61	Can I describe the penalty of a caution?	49	
62	Can I describe the penalty of a fine?	49	
63	Can I describe the penalty of a bond?	49	
64	Can I describe the penalty of a suspended sentence?	49	
65	Can I describe the penalty of probation?	49	
66	Can I describe the penalty of a criminal infringement notice?	49	
67	Can I describe the penalty of penalty units?	49	
68	Can I describe the penalty of a community service order?	49	
69	Can I describe the penalty of home detention?	49	
70	Can I describe the penalty of periodic detention?	50	
71	Can I describe the penalty of forfeiture of assets?	50	
72	Can I describe the penalty of imprisonment?	50	
73	Can I describe the penalty of diversionary programs?	50–51	
74	Can I evaluate the effectiveness of different types of penalties, including diversionary programs?	51–2	
75	Can I describe alternative methods of sentencing including circle sentencing and restorative justice?	52	

For a complete understanding of this topic:	Page No.	✓
76	Can I assess the roles of alternative methods of sentencing?	52	
77	Can I describe security classification as a post-sentencing consideration?	53	
78	Can I describe protective custody as a post-sentencing consideration?	53	
79	Can I describe parole as a post-sentencing consideration?	52–4	
80	Can I describe preventative detention as a post-sentencing consideration?	54	
81	Can I describe continued detention as a post-sentencing consideration?	54	
82	Can I describe sexual offenders' registration as a post-sentencing consideration?	54–5	
83	Can I describe deportation as a post-sentencing consideration?	55	
84	Can I examine the implications of post-sentencing considerations in achieving justice?	55	
85	Can I evaluate the effectiveness of sentencing and punishment as a means of achieving justice?	55–6	
86	Can I describe the age of criminal responsibility?	56	
87	Can I discuss the issues surrounding the age of criminal responsibility?	57	
88	Can I describe the rights of children when they are questioned or arrested?	58	
89	Can I explain why young offenders are treated differently in the criminal justice system?	58	
90	Can I describe the Children's Court procedures and operation?	58–9	
91	Can I describe penalties for children?	59	
92	Can I describe alternatives to court?	59–61	
93	Can I assess the effectiveness of the criminal justice system when dealing with young offenders?	61–2	
94	Can I define international crime?	62	
95	Can I describe the categories of international crime, including crimes against the international community?	62	
96	Can I describe the categories of international crime, including transnational crimes?	63	
97	Can I outline domestic and international measures for dealing with international crime?	64–8	
98	Can I describe the various measures used to deal with international crime?	64–8	
99	Can I outline the limitations of the measures for dealing with international crime?	68–9	

For a complete understanding of this topic:	Page No.	✓
100 Can I evaluate the effectiveness of the domestic and international legal systems in dealing with international crime?	68–9	
101 Can I discuss the role of discretion in the criminal justice system?	69–71	
102 Can I discuss issues of compliance and non-compliance in regard to criminal law?	71	
103 Can I explain the extent to which law reflects moral and ethical standards?	71–2	

For a complete understanding of this topic:	Page No.	✓
104 Can I explain the role of law reform in the criminal justice system?	72–4	
105 Can I discuss the extent to which the law balances the rights of victims, offenders and society?	75–7	
106 Can I evaluate the effectiveness of legal and non-legal measures in achieving justice?	77–8	

Useful resources

Acts

Anti-Terrorism Act (No. 2) 2005 (Cth) (See Section 1.2.1, page 12.)

Bail Act 2013 (NSW) (See Section 1.2.5, page 18.)

Children (Criminal Proceedings) Act 1987 (NSW) (See Section 1.5.1, page 56.)

Children (Protection and Parental Responsibility) Act 1997 (NSW) (See Section 1.5.3, page 58.)

Competition and Consumer Act 2010 (Cth) (See section 1.3.1, page 24.)

Crimes Act 1900 (NSW) (See Section 1.1.1, page 2.)

Crimes (Administration of Sentences) Regulation 2008 (NSW) (See Section 1.4.8, page 53.)

Crimes (Forensic Procedures) Act 2000 (NSW) (See Section 1.2.1, page 12.)

Crimes (Sentencing Procedure) Act 1999 (NSW) (See Section 1.4.1, page 44.)

Crimes (High Risk Offenders) Act 2006 (NSW) (See Section 1.4.8, page 54.)

Criminal Procedure Act 1986 (NSW) (See Section 1.3.1, page 23.)

Drug Misuse and Trafficking Act 1985 (NSW) (See Section 1.1.5, page 6.)

Housing Amendment (Registerable Persons) Act 2009 (NSW) (See Case Study 1.20, Section 1.7.4, pages 73–4.)

Jury Act 1977 (NSW) (See Section 1.3.9, page 40.)

Law Enforcement (Powers and Responsibilities) Act 2002 (NSW) (See Sections 1.2.1 [page 12] and 1.5.2 [page 58].)

Public Defenders Act 1995 (NSW) (See Section 1.3.3, page 27.)

Summary Offences Act 1988 (NSW) (See Section 1.1.1, page 2.)

Victims Rights and Support Act 2013 (NSW) (See section 1.7.5, page 75.)

Young Offenders Act 1997 (NSW) (See Section 1.5.5, page 60.)

Treaties/Conventions

Convention on Narcotic Drugs (UN, 1961) (See Section 1.6.1, page 63.)

Convention on Psychotropic Substances (UN, 1971) (See Section 1.6.1, page 63.)

Convention on the High Seas (UN, 1958) (See Section 1.6.1, page 63.)

Convention on the Law of the Seas (UN, 1982) (See Section 1.6.1, page 63.)

Convention on the Prevention and Punishment of the Crime of Genocide (UN, 1948) (See Section 1.6.1, page 62.)

European Conventions on Extradition (1957) (See Section 1.6.2, page 66.)

Hague Hijacking Convention (1970) (See Section 1.6.1, page 63.)

International Covenant on Civil and Political Rights (ICCPR) (1966) (See Section 1.2.1, page 12.)

Montreal Hijacking Convention (1971) (See Section 1.6.1, page 63.)

Rome Statute (1998) (See Section 1.6.2, page 64.)

Tokyo Hijacking Convention (1963) (See Section 1.6.1, page 63.)

Treaty on Extradition between Australia and the United States (1974) (See Section 1.6.2, page 66.)

Case studies

Blaue v R (1975) 1 WLR (Case Study 1.3, Section 1.1.4, page 5.)

Chayna v The Queen (1993) 66 ACrimR 178 (See Case Study 1.12, Section 1.3.8, page 39.)

Cheatle v The Queen (1993) 177 CLR 541 (See Case Study 1.13, Section 1.3.9, pages 40–41.)

Dietrich v The Queen (1992) 177 CLR 292 (See Case Study 1.5, Section 1.3.5, page 29.)

Hyam v the DPP (1974) 2 All ER 41 (See Case Study 1.1, Section 1.1.2, page 3.)

McInnes v R (1979) 14 CLR 575 (See Section 1.3.5, page 25.)

Nicaragua v United States of America (1986) ICJ 14 (See Section 1.6.2 [page 65] and Case Study 6.2, Section 6.2.4, [page 65].)

The Queen v Damian Karl Sebo (2007) Supreme Court of Queensland (See Case Study 1.11, Section 1.3.8. page 37.)

R v Dudley and Stephens (1884) 14 QB 273 (See Case Study 1.8, Section 1.3.8, page 34.)

R v George Palazoff (1986) 23 ACrimR 86 (See Case Study 1.9, Section 1.3.8, page 35.)

R v Jurisic (1998) 45 NSWLR 209 (See Case Study 1.14, Section 1.4.5, page 48; and Section 1.4.1, page 44.)

R v Mueller (2005) NSWCCA 47 (See Case Study 1.10, Section 1.3.8, page 36.)

R v Porter (1936) 55 CLR 182 (See Case Study 1.6, Section 1.3.8, page 33.)

R v Whyte (2002) NSWCCA 343 (See Section 1.4.1, page 44.)

Zecevic v DPP (1987) 162 CLR 645 (See Case Study 1.7, Section 1.3.8, page 34.)

Other documents

'Boy cleared of killing', *The Sydney Morning Herald*, 4 December, 1999 (See Case Study 1.15, Section 1.5.1, page 57.)

'ICC: Good Progress Amid Missteps in First Five Years', Human Rights Watch, 11 July 2008 (See Case Study 1.17, Section 1.6.2, page 65.)

'Policing Public Safety: Report of the NSW Ombudsman' (1999) (See Section 1.5.2, page 58)

'Recent trends in legal proceedings for breach of bail, juvenile remand and crime', Vignaendra, Moffatt, Weatherburn and Heller, *Crime and Justice Bulletin*, Number 128, May 2009, NSW Bureau of Crime Statistics and Research. (See Section 1.2.5, page 18.)

'Reoffending among young people cautioned by police or who participated in a youth justice conference', S. Vignaendra and Jacqueline Fitzgerald, *Crime and Justice Bulletin*, Number 103, October 2006. (NSW Bureau of Crime Statistics and Research) (See Case Study 1.16, Section 1.5.5, page 60.)

'Sentencing' (1996), NSW Law Reform Commission Report No. 79 (See Section 1.7.4, page 73.)

Organisations and websites

Australian Institute of Criminology: www.aic.gov.au

Corrective Services NSW: www.correctiveservices.justice.nsw.gov.au

Commonwealth Director of Public Prosecutions (See Section 1.3.3, page 27): www.cdpp.gov.au

Homicide Victims' Support Group (Aust) Inc. (See Section 1.7.5, page 76): www.hvsgnsw.org.au

Human Rights Watch (See Section 1.6.2, page 65): www.hrw.org

International Court of Justice (See Section 1.6.2, pages 64–5): www.icj-cij.org

International Criminal Court (See Section 1.6.2, page 65): www.icc-cpi.int

Interpol: www.interpol.int

Law Reform Commission of NSW (See Section 1.7.4, pages 72–3): www.lawlink.nsw.gov.au/lrc

Legal Aid NSW (See Section 1.3.5, page 29): www.legalaid.nsw.gov.au

NSW Bureau of Crime Statistics and Research (BOCSAR): www.bocsar.nsw.gov.au

NSW Police Force: www.police.nsw.gov.au

Parole Authority (NSW) (See Section 1.4.8, page 54): www.paroleauthority.nsw.gov.au

Public Defender (See Section 1.3.3, page 27): www.publicdefenders.nsw.gov.au

United Nations International Criminal Tribunal for Rwanda (See Section 1.6.2, page 65): www.unictr.org

United Nations International Criminal Tribunal for the Former Yugoslavia (See Section 1.6.2, page 65): www.un.org/icty

Victims' Compensation Tribunal (See Section 1.7.5, page 75): www.lawlink.nsw.gov.au/vs

Victims of Crime Bureau (See Section 1.7.5, page 76): www.lawlink.nsw.gov.au/vs

Other useful websites

Australian Broadcasting Commission (ABC): www.abc.net.au

Australian federal government: australia.gov.au

Findlaw: www.findlaw.com

Legal Information Access Centre (LIAC): www.legalanswers.sl.nsw.gov.au/about

NSW Government: www.nsw.gov.au

The Sydney Morning Herald: www.smh.com.au

End of chapter questions

KCq Key Concept questions

These questions test whether you have grasped the key ideas in each subsection. They are not difficult questions, but will test your recall of knowledge of the material you have read. If you are unsure what a question is asking you to do, refer to page ix to check the meaning of the NESA key words. If you can answer all these questions, you will know you have a sound knowledge of content.

Refer to pp. 445–53 for Answers

1.1 The nature of crime

1.1.1 The meaning of crime

1. List the four legal characteristics of a crime.

1.1.2 The elements of crime

2. Name the two elements of a crime which must generally be proved for a person to be found guilty of a crime.
3. Name three features of *actus reus* that must be proved for *actus reus* to be proved.
4. Identify and define the three states of mind that can constitute sufficient *mens rea* to prove criminal liability.

1.1.3 Strict liability offences

5. Explain how strict liability offences differ from other crimes.

1.1.4 Causation

6. Define *causation*.
7. Name two circumstances in which the act of the accused is said to have caused a death, even though there were other contributing factors.
8. List the items which should be included in order to describe the nature of crime.

1.1.5 Categories of crime

9. List seven categories of crime.
10. Describe two types of preliminary crime.
11. Explain what you need to do to show that you are able to recognise the different categories of crime.

1.1.6 Summary and indictable offences

12. State two examples of a summary offence and two examples of an indictable offence.

13. Describe the different ways the legal system deals with an offence, depending on whether it is summary or indictable.
14. Explain what you should mention in order to define *summary offences* and *indictable offences*.

1.1.7 Parties to a crime

15. Identify four different parties to a crime in the following scenario:

    James lights a fire and burns down a local school, with the intention of destroying it. Helen goes with him and urges him to put a match to the petrol he has been given by Ruth, who approves of the plan. As a result of the fire, the clothing of James and Helen is singed and they receive a couple of minor burns. They go to Tyson's place and he cleans their clothes and dresses their injuries.

1.1.8 Factors affecting criminal behaviour

16. Explain, with an example, why some people see some behaviour as criminal and others do not.
17. List six reasons why most people obey most criminal laws all the time.
18. List four reasons why some criminal laws are broken more often than others.
19. List the five types of factors which can affect whether people may engage in criminal behaviour.
20. Explain what you need to do in order to examine a range of factors that may lead to criminal behaviour.

1.1.9 Crime prevention: situational and social

21. Describe two ways in which ordinary citizens might engage in situational crime prevention.
22. Explain the idea of social crime prevention.
23. Explain what you need to do in order to investigate a range of situational and social crime prevention techniques.

1.2 The criminal investigation process

24. Identify the three stages of the criminal justice system.
25. Define *discretion*.

1.2.1 Police powers

26. Describe the police power of search and seizure.
27. Explain the circumstances under which a person must answer police questions.
28. Explain the circumstances under which police may tap phones.

29. Identify the legislation which allows police to take DNA samples.

30. Describe the circumstances under which police can force a person to provide material to be tested for DNA.

31. Identify the legislation which allows police to detain people.

32. Identify the circumstances and the length of time for which a person can be detained by police.

33. Explain the circumstances of the Haneef case, and why this case has raised concerns.

34. Explain what you need to do in order to discuss the powers of police in the criminal process.

1.2.2 Reporting crime

35. Identify who reports most crimes and outline the reasons for this.

36. List five reasons why crimes may go unreported.

37. Explain how discretion is exercised in the area of reporting crime.

1.2.3 Investigating crime

38. Identify the main investigators of crime, as well as three other crime investigators.

39. List three activities police may undertake when gathering evidence.

40. List four examples of the use of technology by police when investigating a crime.

41. Define the term *warrant*.

42. Explain one occasion when a warrant must generally be used.

43. Identify three areas you need to discuss in order to examine the reporting and investigating of crime.

1.2.4 Arrest and charge, summons and warrants

44. List the three ways in which a person can be brought before a court on a criminal charge.

45. Describe the three things a police officer must do to make a lawful arrest.

46. Explain, with an example, how discretion may be used by a police officer when charging a person for a criminal offence.

1.2.5 Bail or remand

47. Define the terms *bail* and *remand*.

48. Identify the legislation which governs the granting of bail in NSW.

49. Explain why the granting of bail is so important.

50. Explain, using examples, when bail may be granted and by whom.

51. Explain when there is a presumption in favour of bail and what this means.

52. Identify the three factors that must be taken into account when bail is being considered.

53. Explain how discretion is exercised in the area of granting bail.

1.2.6 Detention and interrogation, and the rights of suspects

54. Explain the circumstances in which the right to silence operates.

55. Explain a suspect's right to privacy.

56. Explain the extent to which an accused person has a right to communication.

57. Explain the extent to which an accused person has the right to a lawyer.

1.2.7 The effectiveness of the criminal investigation process as a means of achieving justice

58. List eight factors which help ensure the achievement of justice in the criminal investigation process.

59. List ten factors which may limit the achievement of justice in the criminal investigation process.

1.3 Criminal trial process

1.3.1 Court jurisdiction

60. Name four types of criminal hearings which take place in the Local Court.

61. Explain how discretion plays a role in whether an indictable offence is heard summarily.

62. Explain the purpose of the Drug Court.

63. Outline the difference between cases that are heard in the District Court and those heard in the Supreme Court.

64. Describe the role of the NSW Court of Criminal Appeal.

65. Explain the grounds on which an appeal can be made to a higher court.

66. Identify two criminal matters which are heard by the Federal Court of Australia.

67. Describe the role of the High Court in criminal matters.

68. Identify the four areas you need to explain in order to describe the role of the courts in the criminal justice process.

1.3.2 The adversarial system

69. Explain how the adversarial system and the inquisitorial system of trial differ.

70. Explain what you need to do in order to discuss the use of the adversarial system as a means of achieving justice.

1.3.3 Legal personnel

71. Explain the difference between a *magistrate* and a *judge*.

72. Explain the role of a magistrate/judge in a summary hearing.

73. Explain how the role of a judge differs in a trial by jury.

74. Describe the role of a prosecutor in a criminal case.

75. Describe the role of a Public Defender.

1.3.4 Pleas and charge negotiation

76. Explain the difference between what happens after a person pleads guilty and what happens when a person pleads not guilty.

77. Describe how charge negotiation occurs, using an example.

78. Describe the implications of charge negotiation for the notion of justice for the accused, the victim, and the community.

1.3.5 Legal representation, including legal aid

79. State two reasons why it is important for someone to be represented in a criminal case.

80. Describe the role of a defence lawyer.

81. Explain why the case of *Dietrich v The Queen* is important, and cite it correctly.

82. Identify the three tests which must be passed for a person to receive legal aid.

83. Explain what you need to do in order to examine the role of legal representation in the criminal trial.

1.3.6 Burden and standard of proof

84. Define *presumption of innocence*.

85. Explain the term *burden of proof* and where that burden rests in a criminal case.

86. Explain the term *standard of proof* and what the standard is in criminal cases.

1.3.7 Use of evidence, including witnesses

87. Briefly outline the procedure in a criminal trial by jury.

88. Explain how the criminal trial procedure differs in a summary hearing.

89. Explain why rules of evidence and procedure have been developed.

90. Explain what is meant by the *right to silence*.

91. Explain the rules regarding the use of confessions as evidence.

92. Explain the rules regarding the use of evidence which has been illegally obtained.

1.3.8 Defences to criminal charges

93. Explain the difference between a *complete defence* and a *partial defence*.

94. List five complete defences, explain what must be proved for each to be successful, and give an example of each one.

95. List two partial defences and explain what must be proved for each to be successful. Give an example of each one.

96. Explain what you need to do in order to assess the use of defences to criminal charges in achieving justice.

1.3.9 The role of juries

97. Explain why trial by jury is used in less than 1% of criminal cases.

98. Identify the legislation which governs the operation and selection of juries.

99. Explain the role the prosecution and defence have in selecting a jury.

100. Describe the circumstances under which a majority verdict can be returned in NSW.

101. Explain what you need to do in order to evaluate the effectiveness of the jury system in criminal trials.

1.3.10 The effectiveness of the criminal trial process as a means of achieving justice

102. Explain what you need to do in order to assess the effectiveness of the criminal trial process as a means of achieving justice.

103. List fifteen areas of the criminal trial process you could discuss to assess its effectiveness as a means of achieving justice.

1.4 Sentencing and punishment

1.4.1 Statutory and judicial guidelines

104. Define *maximum penalty* and give an example.

105. Name two statutes which restrict judicial discretion at a sentencing hearing.

106. Explain when a court may impose a prison sentence.

107. Explain the terms *non-parole period* and *parole period*.

108. Identify the usual length of a parole period in a prison sentence.

109. Explain the term *guideline sentence* and give an example.

1.4.2 The purposes of punishment

110. List and define the purposes of punishment.

1.4.3 Factors affecting a sentencing decision

111. List six factors which influence the court when making a sentencing decision.

112. Explain what *aggravating factors* are, and give three examples of such factors.

113. Explain what *mitigating factors* are, and give six examples of such factors.

1.4.4 The role of the victim in sentencing

114. Explain the role of the prosecution and the defence in a sentencing hearing.

115. Identify three advantages and one disadvantage of a victim impact statement.

116. Explain what you need to do in order to discuss factors that affect sentencing decisions.

1.4.5 Appeals

117. Identify the types of appeals that can be made after an offender is found guilty.

118. State two reasons why the sentencing appeal process is important for achieving justice.

1.4.6 Types of penalties

119. List and define twelve types of penalties available in NSW.

120. Explain what a *penalty unit* is and name two types of penalties for which penalty units are relevant.

121. Explain the purpose of diversionary programs and name five such programs.

122. State two reasons why the penalties of no conviction recorded and cautions are sometimes criticised.

123. Identify three traditional punishments which are likely to help rehabilitate an offender, and explain your choices.

124. Explain three disadvantages of imposing a fine as punishment.

125. Identify two disadvantages that are common to bonds, probation orders and community service orders.

126. Explain what you need to do in order to evaluate the effectiveness of different types of penalties.

1.4.7 Alternative methods of sentencing

127. Name three alternative methods of sentencing.

128. Explain the primary purpose of alternative methods of sentencing.

129. Explain the aim of restorative justice programs.

130. Identify who circle sentencing is designed to deal with.

131. List the people involved in circle sentencing.

132. List the matters which come under discussion during circle sentencing.

133. Explain three benefits and two limitations of restorative justice programs.

134. Explain what you need to do in order to assess the roles of alternative methods of sentencing.

1.4.8 Post-sentencing considerations

135. Explain the terms *security classification, protective custody,* and *parole.*

136. Name the three broad categories of security classification, and identify the type of imprisonment each classification brings with it.

137. Identify one advantage and one disadvantage of protective custody.

138. Explain three benefits of parole.

139. Describe the two ways in which the term *preventative detention* is used.

140. Explain how preventive detention operates in NSW, and cite the relevant legislation.

141. State one positive and one negative implication of continued detention.

142. State one positive implication and one negative implication of sexual offenders' registration.

143. Explain the term *deportation* and the circumstances under which it can arise.

144. State one positive implication and one negative implication of deportation.

145. Explain what you need to do in order to examine the implications of post-sentencing considerations in achieving justice.

1.4.9 The effectiveness of sentencing and punishment as a means of achieving justice

146. Explain what you need to do in order to assess the effectiveness of sentencing and punishment as a means of achieving justice.

147. List eight areas of the sentencing and punishment process you could discuss to assess its effectiveness as a means of achieving justice.

1.5 Young offenders

1.5.1 Age of criminal responsibility

148. Cite the legislation that contains the law about the age of criminal responsibility.

149. Identify the age at which children can be held criminally responsible in NSW.

150. Explain what you need to do in order to discuss the issues surrounding the age of criminal responsibility.

1.5.2 The rights of children when questioned or arrested

151. In what ways are the rights of children who are being questioned or arrested better protected than those of adults?

152. Name the legislation that protects the rights of children when they are questioned or arrested.

153. List four reasons why young offenders are treated differently in the criminal justice system.

1.5.3 Children's Court

154. Describe four ways in which a Children's Court hearing differs from an adult hearing.

155. Name the legislation that governs the operation of the Children's Court.

156. List two criminal matters regarding children which are not heard in the Children's Court.

1.5.4 Penalties for children

157. Name the legislation which contains the principles for the sentencing of children, and list three of these principles.

158. What is a *control order*?

159. Name three sentencing options available to the Children's Court which are not available when sentencing adults.

1.5.5 Alternatives to court

160. Name the legislation that provides alternatives to court for young offenders.

161. Identify and describe the three main alternatives to court available to young offenders.

162. What is one major criticism levelled at youth sentencing diversionary programs?

1.5.6 The effectiveness of the criminal justice system when dealing with young offenders

163. Explain what you need to do in order to assess the effectiveness of the criminal justice system when dealing with young offenders.

1.6 International crime

1.6.1 Categories of international crime

164. Define *international crime*.

165. Identify, define and give an example of the three main types of international crime.

1.6.2 Dealing with international crime

166. List six international and three domestic measures for dealing with international crime.

167. Identify two international instruments which have developed with respect to international crime.

168. Define *customary international law*, and give an example.

169. Explain the main limitation to the effectiveness of the ICJ.

170. Explain why the International Criminal Court (ICC) was established.

171. Identify the types of crime that are dealt with by the ICC.

172. Identify and briefly describe the five types of sanctions that can be used to combat international crime.

173. Define *extradition* and *fugitive domestic criminals*.

174. Explain how extradition is determined.

175. Explain how extradition proceedings can be effective.

1.6.3 The effectiveness of the domestic and international legal systems in dealing with international crime

176. Explain what you need to do to evaluate the effectiveness of the domestic and international legal systems in dealing with international crime.

177. List six measures you should discuss in order to evaluate the effectiveness of the domestic and international legal systems in dealing with international crime.

1.7 Themes and challenges

1.7.1 Theme 1: The role of discretion in the criminal justice system

178. What is *discretion*?

179. List five areas of the criminal justice process in which discretion is exercised.

180. List five areas in which the police exercise discretion.

181. State two areas in which the judiciary exercise discretion.

182. List three areas in the lead-up to a criminal trial in which discretion is exercised.

183. Explain why the exercise of discretion is crucial to achieving justice in the criminal justice system.

184. Using an example, explain one problem with the exercise of discretion in the criminal justice process.

1.7.2 Theme 2: Issues of compliance and non-compliance in regard to criminal law

185. Identify five reasons why people comply with or don't comply with the criminal law.

1.7.3 Theme 3: The extent to which law reflects moral and ethical standards

186. Explain how moral and ethical standards are reflected in the law about murder.

187. Explain how a conflict of moral and ethical standards can arise in the exercise of judicial discretion in sentencing.

188. Explain two ways in which the sentencing process reflects society's moral and ethical standards.

1.7.4 Theme 4: The role of law reform in the criminal justice system

189. List four sources of pressure to reform the law.

190. Explain, with an example, why Law Reform Commissions are not always effective agencies of reform.

191. List four factors which give rise to reform and give an example of a reform to the criminal law arising from each.

1.7.5 Theme 5: The extent to which law balances the rights of victims, offenders and society

192. Identify four general rights of suspects.

193. Identify six ways in which the law protects and recognises victims' rights.

194. Explain why it is important not to give too much regard to victims' rights.

195. Describe how bail laws and counterterrorism laws attempt to balance individual rights with society's rights.

1.7.6 Theme 6: The effectiveness of legal and non-legal measures in achieving justice

196. List ten legal measures and ten non-legal measures for achieving justice.

HSC *Sample HSC questions*

Now for the real thing! The following questions are modelled on the types of questions you will face in the HSC. Think about it: if you get extensive practice at answering these sorts of questions, you will be more confident in answering them when it comes to the HSC Exam. It makes sense, doesn't it?

Another reason is that the answers given at the back of this guide are structured in a way that helps you learn strategies on how to answer HSC-like questions. This will help you aim for full marks! The questions in this section match the numbered syllabus areas in the chapter, so you can test yourself on each section while you read through the study guide or at the end of the chapter if you prefer.

▶ For each objective-response question there will be the correct answer, a section reference where you can find the correct answer in the chapter and, where required, an explanation and reasons why all the other answers are incorrect.

▶ For each extended-response question you will have a detailed answer with an explanation of what the question is asking you to do and also, when needed, an examiner's plan to help you get full marks with a section reference where you can find the answer in the chapter.

When you mark your work, highlight any questions you found difficult and earmark these areas for extra study.

Refer to pp. 453–4 for

IN THE HSC EXAM

- Material from this chapter will be examined in Sections I and II of the exam.
- The objective-response part of Section I for this chapter is worth 15 marks. You have 22 minutes and 30 seconds to complete it by selecting the alternative (A, B, C or D) that best answers the question. There are 15 questions worth 1 mark each, so you should spend 1 minute and 30 seconds on each question— two questions should take you 3 minutes, and so on.
- The extended-response question in Section II Part B is worth 15 marks. You have 30 minutes to answer this question.
- Look for the ⏱ min in each section and time yourself. This tells you approximately how much time you will have to answer these questions in the HSC Exam.

OBJECTIVE-RESPONSE QUESTIONS 22 min 30 sec

1. When considering sentences for criminal offences, how are judges restricted by the NSW *Crimes Act*?
   A It provides for standard parole periods.
   B It provides for mandatory sentencing.
   C It provides for maximum penalties.
   D It ensures that the victim's views are taken into account. (1 mark)

2. Which of the following systems form the basis for proceedings in a criminal trial in Australia?
   A the civil law system
   B the adversarial system
   C the inquisitorial system
   D the system of investigation (1 mark)

3. Which of the following best describes *actus reus*?
   A the intention of a person to commit a criminal offence
   B the absence of intention of a person to commit a criminal offence
   C not considering the consequences of a criminal action
   D acts or omissions involved in a criminal offence (1 mark)

4. Which of the following punishments has incapacitation as its main purpose?
   A a community service order
   B a fine
   C imprisonment
   D a suspended sentence (1 mark)

5. John assists Shaun in hiding the knife with which Shaun has just stabbed someone. Which of the following best describes John?
   A an accessory before the fact
   B a principal in the first degree
   C a principal in the second degree
   D an accessory after the fact (1 mark)

6. Which of the following would normally be brought up by the prosecution at a sentencing hearing?
   A the offender's past good record
   B aggravating factors
   C mitigating factors
   D a defence to a charge (1 mark)

7. Which of the following best describes circle sentencing?

A a diversionary program for minor drug offenders

B an alternative method of sentencing for Aboriginal offenders

C an alternative method of sentencing for young offenders

D a rehabilitative program for drink-driving offenders (1 mark)

8. At what age can children be held criminally responsible in NSW?

A seven years of age

B ten years of age

C twelve years of age

D fourteen years of age (1 mark)

9. In March 2003, two men painted 'No War' on the Sydney Opera House as a protest against the war in Iraq. Of what is this an example?

A civil disobedience

B criminal disobedience

C situational crime prevention

D social crime prevention (1 mark)

10. Sometimes a court makes a decision about a sentence for a particular crime and this is to be taken into account by other courts delivering sentences for similar offences. Which of the following best describes this?

A the doctrine of precedent

B a mandatory sentence

C a guideline sentence

D a maximum penalty (1 mark)

11. Which of the following is an essential element of a crime?

A It must harm another person.

B It must be seen as harmful to the whole community.

C It must be proved on the balance of probabilities.

D It must be legislated against by parliament. (1 mark)

12. Which of the following is the main way that an alleged offender is brought before the court?

A information and summons

B information and warrant

C arrest without warrant

D bail or remand (1 mark)

13. In which of the following courts would a charge of murder first be considered?

A the Local Court

B the District Court

C the Supreme Court

D the NSW Court of Criminal Appeal (1 mark)

14. Which of the following statements is true about the role of the jury in NSW?

A A jury must reach a unanimous verdict.

B A jury can, in certain circumstances, reach an 'eleven to one' majority verdict.

C Hung juries are a frequent occurrence.

D Juries often have 'rogue jurors'. (1 mark)

15. John claims that he was forced to kill Joanne because he thought that she was going to shoot him. This scenario best describes which of the following defences?

A provocation

B duress

C necessity

D self-defence (1 mark)

EXTENDED-RESPONSE QUESTIONS 1 h 30 min

- There will be one extended-response question to the value of 15 marks.
- In your answer you will be assessed on how well you:
  - use your knowledge and relevant legal case study/studies;
  - communicate using relevant legal terminology and concepts;
  - present a logical, well-structured answer to the question.
- The expected length of each response will be around four pages of an examination writing booklet (approximately 600 words).

Question 1 30 min

Duncan is a thirteen-year-old boy who is arrested for stealing a car. Explain four processes that Duncan may undergo in his dealings with the criminal justice system. Explain how and why children are treated differently to adults in the criminal justice system.

(15 marks)

Question 2 30 min

Describe the role of court personnel in a trial by judge and jury, and assess the effectiveness of the jury in achieving justice in the criminal process.

(15 marks)

Question 3 30 min

Describe the role of discretion in two phases of the criminal justice system and assess its importance.

(15 marks)

Chapter 2

Human rights

Principal focus

Through the use of a range of contemporary examples, students investigate the notion of human rights and assess the extent to which legal systems embody such human rights and promote them in practice.

Themes and challenges

The following five themes and challenges are incorporated throughout this chapter, and also summarised in Sections 2.4.1 to 2.4.5 (pages 129–34). They are to be considered throughout your study of this topic.

▶ 1 The changing understanding of the relationship between state sovereignty and human rights

▶ 2 Issues of compliance and non-compliance in regard to human rights

▶ 3 The development of human rights as a reflection of changing values and ethical standards

▶ 4 The role of law reform in protecting human rights

▶ 5 The effectiveness of legal and non-legal measures in protecting human rights

HSC CONTENT

	You learn to:
The nature and and development of human rights	▶ define human rights. ▶ outline how human rights have changed and developed over time. ▶ investigate the evolving recognition and importance of universal human rights. ▶ examine major human rights documents and explain their contribution to the development of human rights.
Promoting and enforcing human rights	▶ assess the role of state sovereignty in promoting and enforcing human rights. ▶ evaluate the effectiveness of international responses in promoting and enforcing human rights. ▶ outline how human rights are incorporated into Australian domestic law. ▶ evaluate the effectiveness of Australian responses in promoting and enforcing human rights. ▶ discuss the arguments for and against a Charter of Rights for Australia.
Investigating a contemporary issue which illustrates the promotion and/or enforcement of human rights	▶ investigate a contemporary human rights issue and evaluate the effectiveness of legal and non-legal responses to the issue.

© NSW Education Standards Authority, *Legal Studies Stage 6 Syllabus*, 2009, pp. 20–21

2.1 The nature and development of human rights

2.1.1 The definition of human rights

A *right* is something to which you are entitled. There are many types of rights including moral rights, customary rights, legal rights, human rights, domestic rights and international rights.

Human rights are fundamental rights. They are things to which every human being is entitled for just being a human being. Generally, it is recognised that human rights are:

▶ **universal** (that is, to be enjoyed by all individuals regardless of their nationality, gender, race or status)

▶ **indivisible** (that is, all human rights are equally important)

▶ **inherent** (that is, the birthright of all humans and are to be enjoyed by all people simply by reason of their humanity)

▶ **inalienable** (that is, people cannot agree to give them up or have them taken away).

The indivisibility and universality of human rights is recognised in the Charter of the United Nations 1945 and in the Universal Declaration of Human Rights 1948. These documents are discussed in Section 2.1.3 (see pages 106–7).

Types of human rights

There are three types of human rights:

▶ civil and political rights

▶ economic, social and cultural rights

▶ collective rights, such as environmental and peace rights and the right to self-determination.

Civil and political rights

Civil and political rights are also called 'first generation' rights, because they were the first to be recognised historically.

▶ Civil rights are entitlements belonging to all humans and are to do with being a free citizen of a nation (for example freedom of thought and freedom of religion).

▶ Political rights are entitlements belonging to all humans and are to do with full participation in government (for example the right to vote).

Civil rights and political rights both protect the individual from the arbitrary exercise of power by the state. These rights are set out in Articles 3 to 21 of the Universal Declaration of Human Rights 1948 and in the International Covenant on Civil and Political Rights (ICCPR) 1966 (see Section 2.1.3, page 107).

These rights are:

▶ the right of life, liberty and security of person

▶ the right to freedom from slavery

▶ the right to freedom from torture or from cruel, inhuman or degrading treatment or punishment

▶ the right to self-determination

▶ the right to recognition everywhere as a person before the law

▶ the right to equality before the law

What are *human rights*?

- the right to an effective judicial remedy
- the right to freedom from arbitrary interference with privacy, family, home or correspondence
- the right to freedom of movement and residence
- the right of freedom to leave and return to one's country
- the right to asylum
- the right to a nationality
- the right to marry and found a family
- the right to own and not be arbitrarily deprived of property
- the right to freedom of thought, conscience and religion
- the right to freedom of opinion and expression
- the right to peaceful assembly and association
- the right to take part in the government of one's country and to equal access to public service in one's country.

Many civil and political rights are considered 'negative' rights because the state, rather than performing certain actions, is required to refrain from certain actions against the individual in order to protect these rights. These 'negative' civil and political rights include the rights to: freedom from slavery; freedom from torture or from cruel, inhuman or degrading treatment or punishment; freedom from arbitrary interference with privacy, family, home or correspondence; freedom of movement and residence; freedom to leave and return to one's country; freedom of thought, conscience and religion; and freedom of opinion and expression.

While these require the state *not* to interfere in order to protect civil and political rights, the state can also be required to take positive action in order to protect other civil and political rights, such as acting to establish appropriate institutions (for example courts), as well as training the police and the judiciary.

Economic, social and cultural rights

Economic, social and cultural rights are known as 'second generation' rights because they came to be recognised after civil and political rights. They are concerned with the material and cultural wellbeing of people.

- Economic rights are the rights concerned with the production, development and management of material for the necessities of life.
- Cultural rights are the rights which assist in preserving and enjoying one's cultural heritage.
- Social rights are rights that give people security as they live and learn together, such as the rights involving schools and other institutions.

These rights are set out in Articles 23 to 27 of the Universal Declaration of Human Rights 1948 and in the International Covenant on Economic, Social and Cultural Rights (ICESCR) 1966 (see Section 2.1.3, page 107).

Economic, social and cultural rights include the right to:

- social security (a social right)
- work, and just and favourable conditions of work
- equal pay for equal work
- join and form trade unions
- rest and leisure
- education
- an adequate standard of living (an economic right)

- enjoyment of the highest sustainable standard of physical and mental health
- participate in the cultural life of the community (a cultural right).

Economic, social and cultural rights usually require government action. For example, an adequate health system requires the government to spend money on health centres and hospitals.

Environmental rights, peace rights and the right to self-determination

Environmental and peace rights, along with the collective right of self-determination, are all examples of 'third generation' rights, which have emerged in recent years. These 'third generation' rights do not necessarily belong to the individual, as do other human rights, but rather to 'peoples' as a whole. In other words, these rights are collective rather than individual in nature (see below).

Collective rights are rights that do not belong to an individual but to a group of people (for example the right to continued survival of a race of people). This particular collective right is protected by the prohibition of genocide. The right to self-determination (as discussed in Section 2.1.2, page 104) is the collective right of peoples to govern themselves. Some rights of individuals are also collective in their nature, such as the right to freedom of association and freedom of religion.

The status of third generation rights in international law is not yet clear, although some have been recognised at least partially in various international treaties and declarations. Environmental rights, peace rights and the right to self-determination are discussed in more detail in Section 2.1.2 (pages 104–6).

CAN YOU define human rights?

To define human rights, you need to explain that:

- human rights are fundamental things to which every human being is entitled for just being a human being
- human rights are universal, indivisible, inherent and inalienable
- human rights are recognised at an international level through the *Charter of the United Nations* 1945 and the *Universal Declaration of Human Rights* 1948
- there are three types of human rights:
  - civil and political rights
  - economic, social and cultural rights
  - collective rights, such as environmental and peace rights, and the right to self-determination.

KCq page 139

2.1.2 Developing recognition of human rights

Outline how human rights concepts and movements have changed and developed over time.

The term *human rights* emerged relatively recently, in the 1940s. However, the concept of human rights has its roots in ancient times, and some essential freedoms and rights of individuals were recognised in ancient civilisations. The Ancient Babylonians recognised the need to help the poor, while early Confucianism focused on virtue and compassion. Ancient Greek and Roman civilisations also recognised the essential dignity of all humans through the notion of natural law.

The development of concepts of human rights have been influenced by:

- the idea of state sovereignty (discussed in Section 2.2.1, page 108)
- 'natural law' doctrine (see below)
- historic constitutional documents and international agreements (see below)
- movements to recognise certain human rights.

The 'natural law' doctrine

The philosophy of natural law is based on the idea that there exist certain 'natural' laws which apply to all humanity and which maintain the basic dignity of human beings. This idea was developed in Ancient Greece by philosophers such as Plato and Socrates, and was adopted by later philosophers, such as Saint Augustine (354–430 CE). Natural law theorists argued that certain fundamental natural laws applied to humans and that these could not be taken away by a king or any other power. The philosophy of natural law underpins the development of European law and the idea of individual rights. The 'natural law' doctrine has contributed to concepts of human rights by promoting the idea that humans have certain fundamental freedoms that cannot be taken away, even by a king or queen.

Historic constitutional documents

Human rights have gradually been recognised through various documents which have become part of the constitutions of individual nations, as well as through international agreements. Some of the documents that have contributed to the development of concepts of human rights are described below.

The Magna Carta 1215 and English common law

English law, upon which Australian law is based, first recognised that the king had limited power over individuals in the Magna Carta 1215. This document included the principles that:

- every citizen has a right to freedom
- anyone accused of a crime must be brought before the courts
- there must be equality of all before the laws
- property cannot be confiscated by the king without compensation.

The English common law also developed principles protecting the rights of individuals, such as:

- everyone is entitled to the due process of the law
- the writ of *habeas corpus* (which means that people cannot be imprisoned without good reason).

The Declaration of Rights 1689 (UK)

The principles of the Magna Carta and the common law eventually found clearer expression in the Declaration of Rights 1689. The primary purpose of this document was to establish the supremacy of parliament over the king. It also established some individual rights, such as freedom of speech, and protection against cruel and unusual punishments.

Declarations of America and France

The increasing emphasis on the individual's right to be free from the arbitrary power of the state can be seen in both the American Declaration of Independence 1776 and the French Declaration of the Rights of Man and the Citizen 1789.

The American Declaration of Independence states: 'We hold these truths to be self-evident, that all men are created equal, that they are endowed by their Creator with certain unalienable Rights, that among these are Life, Liberty and the pursuit of Happiness'. The French Declaration of the Rights of Man and the Citizen 1789 states that: 'All men are born and remain free and equal in rights'.

These two documents are important in the development of human rights law because they represent systematic attempts to enshrine individual human rights and freedoms in the laws of specific nations.

Movements recognising human rights

The movement towards the protection of human rights has been influenced by the struggle for:

- the abolition of slavery
- trade unionism and labour rights
- universal suffrage
- universal education
- self-determination
- environmental rights
- peace rights.

Movements for the abolition of slavery

The right to freedom from slavery is recognised in the ICCPR, in Article 8 (see Section 2.1.3, page 107). However, this right was recognised, both within nations and internationally, long before the advent of modern international human rights protection. Slavery was the first human rights issue to arouse wide international concern.

The existence of slavery

Most ancient civilisations (including those of Egypt, Greece and Rome) had slaves. From the Middle Ages, Europeans went to Africa to obtain slaves. The Africans were taken by force and sold to other European nations and, from the seventeenth century, to North America. The movement to end the slave trade and end slavery began in the late eighteenth century in Europe. The right to freedom from slavery was fought for both domestically and internationally. Those who fought to end slavery were known as *abolitionists*.

Domestic efforts

The abolitionist movement gained strength and publicity throughout the nineteenth century and succeeded in gaining legal protections against slavery in various countries. France was the first country to pass a decree abolishing slavery, which it did in 1794, following the Declaration of the Rights of Man and the Citizen in 1789.

In Britain, the slave trade from Africa stopped in 1807, and the keeping of slaves was abolished in 1838. Most European nations had stopped exporting slaves from Africa by 1838.

In the United States, slaves were part of the economy of the southern states from well before the Declaration of Independence in 1776. Many Americans questioned whether slavery should exist in a nation which had declared that 'all men are created equal'. The fight to end slavery in the United States led to civil war. Slavery was finally abolished by Amendment 13 to the Constitution of the United States of America in 1865.

In Australia, Polynesian islanders were used as slaves on sugar and cotton plantations in Queensland from the 1860s. This forced-labour system was abolished by the Queensland government in 1890 but only effectively came to an end in 1904 when the federal government agreed to offset any losses to sugar planters caused by the end of the system.

International efforts

After it was abolished in Europe and America, the trade in African slaves continued in the Muslim nations of South-West Asia, in Arab nations and in India. This slave trade had its roots in the seventeenth century. The British government attempted to stop this trade through treaties and force throughout the nineteenth century, but it became apparent that only international effort could effectively break the trade.

In 1885, European nations met in Berlin to attempt to end the trade in African slaves. In 1890, they met again in Brussels and signed the General Act of Brussels. This was the first international treaty abolishing slavery. The Slavery Convention 1926 was signed in Geneva and was amended in 1953. The Supplementary Convention on the Abolition of Slavery, the Slave Trade and Institutions and Practices Similar to Slavery 1956 came into effect in April 1957 and is one of three international conventions operating to eliminate slavery today.

Slavery today

These days, the United Nations Working Group on Contemporary Forms of Slavery monitors the compliance of nations with the three international conventions mentioned above. Forms of slavery that still exist include child labour, traffic in children and women for prostitution purposes, debt bondage, and the sale of children. These practices are still widespread in many parts of the world.

EXAMPLE Child labour

The use of children on sugarcane plantations in El Salvador is an example of child labour occurring today.

Other organisations which help combat slavery in the contemporary world include the International Labour Organisation (ILO), the World Health Organisation (WHO) and Anti-Slavery International.

Trade unionism and labour rights

A trade union is an association of wage earners which exists in order to maintain and improve the working conditions of its members. Trade unions developed to fight for what are now recognised as fundamental human rights. These include some of the rights listed in the ICESCR 1966 (see page 107), such as:

- the right to the enjoyment of just and favourable conditions of work (Article 7)
- the right to form and join trade unions (Article 8)
- the right to an adequate standard of living (Article 11).

The need for trade unions

Trade unions first appeared in England in the early nineteenth century. They developed in response to the Industrial Revolution which had overtaken England and other parts of the Western world during the previous century. The Industrial Revolution meant that the processes of production changed radically. Manufacturing took over from small craft-based industry and agriculture. Factories grew up in cities and employed thousands of people who had previously been servants or labourers. This factory work was characterised by:

▶ low wages

▶ long working hours

▶ unhealthy and unsafe working conditions.

Because of the poor working conditions, workers joined together in an effort to improve conditions. It was only through combined action that workers could improve their conditions. An employer could not fire his or her workers if all people who worked in an industry demanded the same improvements and refused to work without them. This resulted in workers forming trade unions, or *combinations* as they were called.

Domestic efforts

When trade unions first formed in England they were outlawed by acts of Parliament called *Combination Acts*. These were repealed in 1824. However, the use of collective action by trade union members continued to be punished under criminal laws until the 1870s. In Australia, the Shipwrights Union emerged in 1829 as the first trade union. Laws to restrict collective action of union members remained in force, however, until after the maritime strikes and shearers strikes of the 1890s.

While England and Australia were two of the first nations in which trade unions were formed to protect the rights of workers, other nations also recognised the need to protect these rights.

International efforts

International concern about the conditions of workers was raised in the mid-nineteenth century by two industrialists, Robert Owen (Wales) and Daniel Legrand (France), who called for an international organisation to protect workers. The International Association for Labour Legislation was founded in Basel in 1901 and the ideas of Owen and Legrand were incorporated into the International Labour Organization (ILO) which was created in 1919 at the World War I Peace Conferences in Paris and Versailles.

The ILO was formed to improve conditions of workers internationally and, when it first met in 1919, it passed several conventions to improve conditions for workers, including conventions relating to hours of work, night work and minimum ages for work. Since then, the ILO has passed numerous conventions which relate to human rights.

Rights of workers today

While many workers in developing countries continue to be exploited and to work in poor conditions, the work of the ILO and the trade union movement has continually improved the human rights of workers around the world. In Australia, trade unions have ensured:

▶ minimum wages, based on maintaining an adequate standard of living

▶ the right to form trade unions

▶ equal pay for equal work

▶ occupational health and safety requirements

▶ a 40-hour working week.

Working conditions and trade unions in Australia are discussed at greater length in Chapter 5.

Universal suffrage

Suffrage means the right to vote in government elections. *Universal suffrage* means the right of all adults to vote in government elections. The right to vote is recognised, in Article 1 of both the ICCPR and the ICESCR, as the right to self-determination. This right encompasses the right of all people to suffrage (see page 104). When all adults have the right to vote, then they are able to elect a government that will protect their rights and freedoms. It is in this way that citizens of a nation can ensure their human rights are protected because, at the next election, they can vote out any government that infringes such rights.

At the beginning of the nineteenth century, only a few men and no women were permitted to vote in elections. Indigenous peoples and racial minorities were disenfranchised (unable to vote) in many countries. During the nineteenth and twentieth centuries, the struggle for the right to vote was fought and won in many countries around the world.

Male suffrage

Up until the late eighteenth century, governments in most nation-states were run by a monarchy and the aristocracy. The idea that ordinary people should have a say in government was regarded by most as ill-advised and dangerous. Ordinary people were considered unfit to govern themselves.

The notion that people have the right to choose their own government, or to form a government, can first be found in the American Declaration of Independence 1776 and the Declaration of the Rights of Man and the Citizen 1789 (France) (see Section 2.1.2, pages 98–9). Both these documents arose out of revolutions in which the existing governments were overthrown.

In France, in 1791, the new regime established nearly total male suffrage. This was a revolutionary idea and was isolated to France at that time. However, in 1795, France's political turmoil resulted in suffrage being restricted to men with a certain amount of property. Universal male suffrage was eventually re-established there in 1848. In the United States, nearly all the states had achieved universal male suffrage by 1825.

In other countries, the granting of universal male suffrage was more slowly established and was not the result of revolution. In 1800, in Britain, as elsewhere, the vote was only given to men who owned a certain amount of land. The push to include all men began in Britain in the 1800s and by 1830 was a popular idea among the middle classes. The *Great Reform Act 1832* (UK) allowed one in five males to vote. While male suffrage was gradually widened over the next eighty years, universal male suffrage was not gained in Britain until 1918, when the franchise was extended to all men over twenty-one years of age.

In Australia, election of members to the NSW Legislative Council began in 1842, with the passing of the *Australian Constitution Act (No. 1) 1842* (UK). This act allowed two-thirds of the New South Wales Legislative Council to be elected by men who owned a certain amount of property, while the other one-third was appointed by the Crown. By 1854, 25% of the adult male population were able to vote. New South Wales granted universal male suffrage in 1858.

Female suffrage

In the second half of the nineteenth century, the call for female suffrage gained momentum in many Western democracies, particularly after male suffrage was granted. In some countries, the fight by women for the right to vote was very long and bitter.

New Zealand was the first country to give women the right to vote, in 1893. Australia was the second nation to grant this right. Women were given the right to vote in South Australia in 1894, and in NSW and the Commonwealth in 1902. American women did not gain this right until 1920 and British women gained suffrage in 1928. Most other nations granted women suffrage between 1920 and 1950. Switzerland did not grant women suffrage until 1971. The right of women to vote is now almost universal and, at the beginning of 2010, there were only two nations that did not allow women suffrage within the existing electoral system—the Vatican City and Saudi Arabia.

Racial minorities

The granting of women's suffrage is often regarded as the achievement of true universal suffrage. However, in many countries, racial minorities were denied the right to vote until well into the twentieth century.

In the USA, while black men were legally given the right to vote in 1870, discriminatory laws and practices in many states prevented many black Americans from exercising their right to vote until the passing of the *Voting Rights Act* in 1965. In South Africa, Indians were not given the vote until 1984 and black South Africans did not achieve suffrage until 1994.

In Australia, Aboriginal people were not given the right to vote in NSW until 1926. Only Aboriginal people who had been in the defence forces, who owned property and who were not wards of the state were entitled to vote in the Northern Territory until 1962. In 1961, only eighty-nine out of approximately 17 000 Aboriginal people were not wards of the state. In 1962, the franchise was extended to all Aboriginal people throughout Australia.

Universal education

Accompanying the struggles for justice in the workplace and for the right to vote was the struggle to gain at least a basic education for all children. The right to an education is enshrined in Articles 13 and 14 of the ICESCR.

Lack of universal education

In the eighteenth century, education was only available to the aristocracy. The education of aristocratic women concentrated on accomplishments such as music, needlework and decorative arts. Some people in the lower classes were given a rudimentary education, but the vast majority of the population in most nation-states were illiterate.

The French Revolution and the Industrial Revolution led to new ideas about, and new practical demands for, education for all people. During the early nineteenth century, individuals and churches began to recognise the need for universal education in many countries around the world. The gradual widening of suffrage during the 1860s and 1870s helped to achieve universal education because it became widely recognised that people needed to be educated to effectively exercise their right to vote.

In Britain, the Church of England provided many schools during the first half of the nineteenth century and, in 1833, the government began to provide financial aid to such schools, although they certainly did not cater for all children. In France and Germany, governments also began to finance schools for all children. In 1870, the British parliament passed the *Education Act* which provided almost free elementary schools for all children. Education for children under twelve became compulsory in 1880.

Australia's experience

It was estimated in 1810 that only 19% of children in NSW were receiving any education. In the 1830s, the NSW government began to give funding to some churches and other private schools. In 1844, the NSW Legislative Council conducted an inquiry into education and found that only 50% of children aged between four and fourteen received any education at all. In 1866, the *Public Schools Act* (NSW) established a system of state elementary schools throughout NSW. Primary education became compulsory throughout the Australian states in the 1870s.

The education of women

While girls were included in the drive for universal education, they were not given equal access to secondary and university education. In Britain, women were permitted to attend classes at Oxford University from 1921, but some other universities did not allow female attendance until many years later. In Australia, women were permitted to attend some universities from 1867 but few women completed even secondary education. By 1969, only 25% of Australian university students were women. Today women account for over 50% of Australian university students, although few still graduate in male-dominated fields, such as engineering.

The situation today

In developed nations, the right to education has long been established and education between the ages of six and fifteen is compulsory. Even so, universal education has not been achieved worldwide. Around the world, 130 million children aged between six and eleven still do not have access to primary education.

Other developing concepts of human rights

Self-determination

Self-determination means the right of peoples to govern themselves and to choose their own form of government. It is a very important collective right, recognised both within and between nations.

The importance of this right is shown by its prominence in the Charter of the United Nations 1945 where it is referred to in Articles 1(2) and 55, and by its inclusion in Article 1 of both the ICCPR and ICESCR. It is regarded as a fundamental principle of international relations. Some important features of the right to self-determination are:

- it involves the right of colonised peoples to establish their independence. Many African and Asian countries achieved independence in the 1960s by invoking the right to self-determination.

- it involves the right of people within a nation to freely choose their own form of government and to elect their own government

- it is linked to the principle of sovereign equality of all United Nations member states, irrespective of their size or power. This means that all member nations have an equal footing in the United Nations and all have one vote in the General Assembly.

The most controversial aspect of the right to self-determination is the right claimed by indigenous peoples to control their own traditional lands and economy. This right is referred to in the Declaration on the Rights of Indigenous Peoples 2006 which was adopted by the United Nations General Assembly in 2007.

Environmental rights

Environmental rights encompass the right to a clean, healthy and sustainable environment. Various treaties and declarations have been signed in attempts to protect these rights.

EXAMPLE **Treaties protecting environmental rights**

The Kyoto Protocol 1998 is designed to protect the environment from greenhouse gas emissions by compelling nation-states to cut their greenhouse gas emissions by agreed amounts within certain timeframes.

If only some countries agree to these treaties, their effectiveness is limited because worldwide environmental problems will continue to occur unless all nations agree to prevent them. This is one of the key issues with the Kyoto Protocol. Some nations, including the USA and, until recently, Australia, have refused to sign this protocol. However, with the election of a new Australian government in November 2007, immediate ratification of the Kyoto Protocol by Australia took place.

The 2015 Paris Agreement is the latest international agreement to combat climate change. It commits to keeping the global temperature rise this century to under two degrees Celsius above pre-industrial levels.

Peace rights

The right to peace is the right of people to have their government maintain peace and eliminate war. The Charter of the United Nations 1945 obliges nations to 'settle their international disputes by peaceful means…' [Article 2(3)], and to refrain from acts of war, except in self-defence or by resolution of the Security Council.

Peace was recognised as an international right by the Declaration on the Right of Peoples to Peace, a non-binding resolution of the UN passed in 1984. One binding treaty that exists with the purpose of promoting peace is the Treaty on the Non-Proliferation of Nuclear Weapons 1968. This treaty prohibits signatories from buying or building new nuclear weapons and commits the signatory nations who already have nuclear weapons to work towards disarmament (see Section 6.1.4, page 390). Peace and war are discussed in greater detail in Chapter 6.

CAN YOU **outline how human rights have changed and developed over time?**

To outline the changes to human rights, you should examine the development of core human rights concepts and documents over time.

▶ Concepts: Explain the 'natural law' doctrine, focusing on the promotion of the idea that humans have fundamental freedoms that cannot be taken away.

▶ Documents: List the following core documents and explain the ideas about human rights that were established by each.

- The Magna Carta 1215
- The Declaration of Rights 1689 (UK)
- The Declaration of Independence 1776
- The Declaration of the Rights of Man and the Citizen 1789.

▶ Movements: Explain the list of rights following and outline the movements that worked to establish and support these fundamental human rights and how they did so.

- abolition of slavery
- trade unionism and labour rights
- universal suffrage
- universal education
- self-determination
- environmental rights
- peace rights

CAN YOU **investigate the evolving recognition and importance of universal human rights?**

To investigate how human rights have evolved over time, it is important to look at the growth of the movements listed above. These movements for fundamental human rights globally are:

▶ abolition of slavery

▶ trade unionism and labour rights

▶ universal suffrage

▶ universal education

▶ self-determination

▶ environmental rights

▶ peace rights.

Section 2.4.3 (page 131) explores the development of human rights as a reflection of changing values and ethical standards. It explores:

▶ how human rights can arguably be seen as essentially a Western concept and therefore not universally applicable

▶ emerging arguments saying that economic and social rights are more important than civil and political rights (that is, people need to be fed and sheltered before civil rights become important)

▶ the way the growth of collective rights has watered down the importance of individual rights

▶ how interfering with human rights nationally impacts on state sovereignty

▶ whether the values of national security are contrary to the achievement of human rights.

KCq pages 139–40

2.1.3 Formal statements of human rights

Describe formal statements of human rights.

The atrocities of World War I and World War II led to wider recognition of a wider range of human rights. The establishment of the United Nations in 1945, the Charter of the United Nations 1945 (United Nations Charter) and the Universal Declaration of Human Rights 1948 marked the beginning of true international recognition of human rights and of their protection around the world.

The United Nations Charter established the United Nations in 1945, and is a treaty which binds all members of the United Nations. The United Nations Charter has, as one of its fundamental purposes, the promotion of respect for human rights (contained in Articles 1, 55 and 56). In 1971, the International Court of Justice said that these provisions in the charter bind member states to observe and respect human rights.

The International Bill of Rights is made up of the three documents below.

▶ The Universal Declaration of Human Rights 1948: This document lists the human rights to which every person is entitled. Each of its thirty articles sets out a particular human right or set of rights.

▶ The International Covenant on Civil and Political Rights 1966 (ICCPR) was drawn up in order to give legal force to part of the Universal Declaration of Human Rights. The ICCPR protects civil and political rights (see Section 2.1.1, pages 95–6).

▶ The International Covenant on Economic, Social and Cultural Rights 1966 (ICESCR) gives legal force to the second part of the Universal Declaration of Human Rights. It protects economic, social and cultural rights (see Section 2.1.1, pages 96–7).

These three documents, together with their protocols, form what is known as the International Bill of Rights. A total of 165 countries have agreed to be bound by the provisions in the ICCPR and the ICESCR.

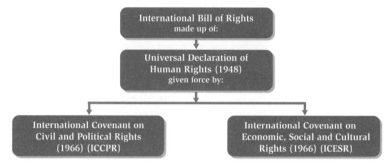

Figure 2.1 Structure of the International Bill of Rights

There are numerous other treaties which deal with specific human rights. These include:

▶ the Convention on the Elimination of All Forms of Racial Discrimination 1965

▶ the Convention on the Elimination of All Forms of Discrimination against Women 1979

▶ the Convention on the Prevention and Punishment of the Crime of Genocide 1948

▶ the Convention against Torture and other Cruel, Inhuman or Degrading Treatment or Punishment 1984

▶ the Convention on the Rights of the Child 1989

▶ the Declaration on the Right of Peoples to Peace 1984

▶ the Declaration on the Rights of Indigenous Peoples 2006.

There are also regional treaties for the protection of human rights, such as:

▶ the European Convention for the Protection of Human Rights and Fundamental Freedoms 1953

▶ the African Charter on Human and People's Rights 1981.

CAN YOU examine major human rights documents and explain their contribution to the development of human rights?

In order to explain the contribution of major human rights documents to the development of human rights, you need to list the three documents that make up the International Bill of Rights and explain their applications, as well as list the other treaties dealing with specific human rights.

 KCq page 140

2.2 Promoting and enforcing human rights

2.2.1 State sovereignty

Define the concept of *state sovereignty* and assess its role in promoting and enforcing human rights.

The idea of *state sovereignty* means that within one country or nation-state there is a group, person or body with supreme lawmaking authority. The notion of sovereignty means that the domestic affairs of a nation are under the control of that nation. It is only the relationships between countries that are or should be subject to international law. State sovereignty means that international law cannot interfere with what happens within a state without that state's consent.

Before the eighteenth century, the usual view of state sovereignty was that it lay with the king or queen and he or she could do whatever he or she pleased within the nation-state. Gradually, the idea of *popular sovereignty* developed, which meant that the people themselves were sovereign. This meant that the people could delegate their power to a parliament and revoke that power if necessary.

EXAMPLE **Popular sovereignty**

In France in 1789, the people drew up the Declaration of the Rights of Man and the Citizen (see Section 2.1.2, pages 98–9), which said that the state could not interfere with the rights of ordinary citizens.

Such rights only applied to citizens of nations who were willing to proclaim and protect these rights on behalf of their citizens. They did not apply to all members of humanity—in particular, they did not apply to slaves, prisoners of war or stateless persons. The idea of national sovereignty was supreme—so, nation-states without such declarations could treat their citizens or subjects as they wished without interference.

CAN YOU **assess the role of state sovereignty in promoting and enforcing human rights?**

To assess the role of state sovereignty in promoting and enforcing human rights, you need to consider that the protection of human rights internationally undermines the idea of national sovereignty because it means interfering with a nation's domestic affairs. However, it is increasingly recognised that nations do have a responsibility to protect human rights within their own borders and that scrutiny of this protection is a legitimate international concern. While resenting interference in their own domestic human rights protection, some nations also do recognise that the international community should interfere to stop human rights violations if such violations endanger world peace and security.

 page 140

2.2.2 The roles of various organisations in international responses

Outline the role of the United Nations, intergovernmental organisations, international courts and tribunals, independent statutory authorities, non-government organisations and the global media in responding to human rights issues.

The United Nations (UN)

The United Nations was established through the United Nations Charter in 1945. Article 1 of the UN Charter outlines the five core purposes of the United Nations—one of which is to promote respect for human rights.

Office of the High Commissioner for Human Rights

The Office of the High Commission for Human Rights (OHCHR) offers its support and expertise to the various human rights monitoring bodies and systems within the UN. The OHCHR oversees the Human Rights Council (see below), the Universal Periodic Review (see below) and the eight human rights treaty bodies who monitor the implementation of major human rights treaties (discussed later in this section, see page 111).

The Human Rights Council

The UN Human Rights Council was established in 2006 as a subsidiary of the UN General Assembly. It consists of forty-seven member states responsible for the promotion and protection of human rights globally. It replaced the United Nations Commission on Human Rights. Its chief purpose is to examine situations in which human rights violations are occurring and make recommendations for action back to the UN General Assembly. The Human Rights Council can also request that the UN Security Council take action to stop human rights violations. These recommendations could include sanctions or direct action.

The Universal Periodic Review

The Human Rights Council runs the Universal Periodic Review. This is a review of the human rights record of all 192 UN member states every four years. It is expected to have reviewed the human rights records of all countries by 2011. This review is based on the will of each member state—it is up to the representatives of each state to declare what actions they have taken to address human rights violations and to meet obligations.

UN Security Council

The UN Security Council is the chief decision-making arm of the UN and consists of fifteen member nations. Five of the members are permanent (United Kingdom, USA, France, Russia and China) and ten other states sit on the council on a two-year rotation The five permanent members each have the power of veto over any Security Council decision.

The UN Charter allows the UN Security to 'take such action by air, sea or land forces as may be necessary to maintain or restore international peace and security'. This ability (known as humanitarian intervention) has been used four times to intervene in human rights abuses, in the former Yugoslavia in 1991, Somalia in 1993, Rwanda in 1994 and East Timor in 1999. The UN Security Council can also intervene to stop defined mass atrocities (genocide, war crimes, crimes against humanity and ethnic cleansing) by force, by using the international Responsibility to Protect (RtoP) principles. (See Section 6.3.1, page 406.)

Intergovernmental organisations

Regional intergovernmental organisations (IGOs) are powerful instruments for protecting against human rights abuses within member states. The membership conditions of many major IGOs include respect for human rights and a good human rights record.

EXAMPLE **IGO membership conditions**

To be a member of the European Union (EU), states must be democracies that: uphold the rule of law; respect and uphold universal human rights; and adhere to the UN Charter on the use of force. Members of the North Atlantic Treaty Organisation (NATO) have the same membership requirements as the EU.

The ability of IGOs to sanction member states on their human rights records varies. Members of the Commonwealth of Nations must abide by the political principle of democracy and respect for human rights. These rights can be enforced by current members, and states can be suspended or expelled from the Commonwealth due to non-compliance. Fiji, Nigeria, Pakistan and Zimbabwe have all been suspended due to infringements, and Zimbabwe voluntarily withdrew completely in 2003. Members of the Association of Southeast Asian Nations (ASEAN) developed an ASEAN Charter in 2008 and agreed on the promotion and protection of human rights. In 2009 ASEAN decided to establish a human rights body (see example below). This is a significant achievement for an organisation such as ASEAN, particularly as some members are authoritarian governments with poor records on human rights, such as Burma and Vietnam. This body does not have any enforcement powers and there are no sanctions for member states, however this action is viewed as a positive step forward.

Courts

International Criminal Court

The International Criminal Court (ICC) is the permanent international court and hears cases relating to the most serious of international crimes and gross human rights abuses, namely genocide, war crimes and crimes against humanity (see Section 6.1.4, page 391). The ICC is the first permanent court allowing individuals to be tried for crimes against humanity and human rights infringements. It is known as a court of 'last resort', meaning it will only hear cases if they are not being investigated or prosecuted by a national judicial system, unless the national systems that are investigating or prosecuting are not genuine. As of March 2010, there were 111 parties to the Rome Statute governing the ICC, meaning 111 nation-states have agreed to the statute's provisions and the jurisdiction of the ICC. The USA is not a party to the Rome Statute.

Tribunals

Ad hoc international tribunals

There have been two UN *ad hoc* tribunals in recent years, set up by the Security Council under the rules of the UN Charter. Individuals could be prosecuted for crimes against humanity in these tribunals. The International Criminal Tribunal for the former Yugoslavia was established in 1993 to hear cases involving breaches of the Geneva Conventions (that is, war crimes) and human rights crimes that were committed during the breakup of the former Yugoslavia in 1991. The second tribunal, the International Criminal Tribunal for Rwanda, was set up in 1994 to hear cases of genocide committed in Rwanda in 1994.

EXAMPLE **Other international tribunals**

Examples of other international tribunals are:

▶ **the European Court of Human Rights**. This has jurisdiction over human rights issues in the EU and its decisions are taken seriously by the Council of the European Union (the governing body of the EU). This court does have some enforcement powers, in that any EU member that does not comply with its ruling could face the sanction of being expelled from the Council.

▶ **ASEAN Intergovernmental Commission on Human Rights**: This commission was established in 2009. Its aim is to promote and protect human rights in its member states. It has no formal enforcement powers and members cannot be punished for human rights infringements.

Independent statutory authorities

There are eight human rights treaty bodies, which are committees of independent experts that monitor compliance with the chief international human rights treaties by signatory states. These committees are created in accordance with the provisions of the treaty they monitor. The committees are:

▶ the Human Rights Committee (OHCHR). The Centre for Civil and Political Rights (CCPR) works to promote the participation of non-government organisations in the work of this committee.

▶ the Committee on Economic, Social and Cultural Rights (CESCR)

▶ the Committee on the Elimination of Racial Discrimination (CERD)

▶ the Committee on the Elimination of Discrimination Against Women (CEDAW)

▶ the Committee Against Torture (CAT), and the added Optional Protocol to the Convention against Torture (OPCAT)—Subcommittee on Prevention of Torture (SPT)

▶ the Committee on the Rights of the Child (CRC)

▶ the Committee on Migrant Workers (CMW)

▶ the Committee on the Rights of Persons with Disabilities (CRPD)

The roles of these treaty bodies include:

▶ considering the reports made by states to the bodies. States are required to report to these bodies about their treaty compliance. As with the Universal Periodic Review (see page 109), such reports are based on the will of each member state—it is up to the state to declare what actions they have taken to meet treaty obligations

▶ considering individual complaints or communications (see Case Study 2.2, Section 2.2.5, page 117)

▶ publishing general comments on the treaties and organising discussions and forums on their purposes and themes.

Non-government organisations

A non-government organisation (NGO) is an organisation that works towards a certain cause and operates separately to any government. As concepts of human rights have evolved, both internationally and within the Australian legal system, and as the interest in human rights protection has grown among ordinary citizens, the establishment of NGOs concerned with human rights has increased. Non-government organisations were instrumental in establishing the UN Charter and the International Bill of Rights, and many of them operate as observers with the UN and other specialised government agencies in the upholding of human rights around the world. Major international NGOs working in the field of human rights include Amnesty International and Human Rights Watch.

The media

The media plays an extremely important role in raising awareness of human rights abuses around the world and rallying public and government action to end such abuses. The growth of dedicated twenty-four hour news channels and the Internet means global news is now broadcast instantly around the world, twenty-four hours a day. The increasing role of the media is both a positive and a negative influence on the reporting of human rights abuses and on subsequent action. The effectiveness and ineffectiveness of the media in promoting and enforcing human rights is discussed in Section 2.2.3 following. KCq page 140

2.2.3 The effectiveness of international responses in promoting and enforcing human rights

While the international legal system has been reasonably effective in promoting and publicising protection of human rights, there have been limits to its success in actually providing protection. The failure of the system in protecting human rights has been dramatically shown in the 'ethnic cleansing' campaigns in Rwanda in 1994 and Bosnia in 1998, as well as in the bloodshed that followed the East Timorese vote for independence in 1999, abuses against Rohingya Muslims in Myanmar in 2018, and the continued and ongoing bloodshed in parts of Western Africa, including the Sudan. Some of the limits to the effectiveness of international law in protecting human rights are:

▶ **not all countries are party to human rights treaties**. So individuals in those countries which are not party to the treaties are not protected by those treaties. However, many would argue that the Universal Declaration of Human Rights has the force of customary law and, therefore, binds all nations whether or not they are party to human rights treaties. A state may also be obliged to protect human rights within its own territory solely by reason of its membership of the United Nations and its acceptance of its obligations under the United Nations Charter.

▶ **lack of adequate enforcement mechanisms**. The enforcement mechanisms of the United Nations and its bodies (which include hearing complaints and conducting investigations) do not apply to all human rights treaties, and some of them are optional rather than compulsory, depending on which treaty is being implemented. Even if a nation has agreed to a treaty, it may not have agreed to the enforcement mechanisms of the treaty. As seen in Section 2.2.6 (page 121). For example, Australia has not agreed to enforcement mechanisms under the Committee on the Elimination of Discrimination Against Women (CEDAW). Many states have been slow to report to the relevant committees, even when they have agreed to do so.

▶ **enforcement by consensus**. Enforcement of any international law is problematic because it relies on consensus, reciprocity and notions of legal responsibility. Nations do not always feel compelled by these reasons to follow international law.

▶ **reliance on state reporting**. The Human Rights Council, with its Universal Periodic Review program, for example, relies on each member state to accurately report its own human rights infringements and the actions it takes towards addressing them. This reliance on state reporting means states who do not wish to comply can simply choose not to report certain situations.

▶ **lack of Security Council action**. The Security Council has only used the powers of humanitarian intervention four times and, each time, to varying degrees—in the former Yugoslavia in 1991, Somalia in 1993, Rwanda in 1994 and East Timor in 1999. In fact, the UN Security Council did not sufficiently intervene to stop mass genocide in Rwanda in 1994 and was widely criticised by the media, NGOs and others for allowing known ethnic cleansing to happen by non-interference. It was this inadequate intervention which directly led to the development of the Responsibility to Protect (RtoP) principles (see Section 6.3.1, page 406, for more details).

Generally, the UN Security Council has proved to be extremely wary of intervening to stop human rights abuses occurring in sovereign states, despite the existence of the humanitarian intervention and RtoP principles.

▶ **war crimes tribunals**. The war crimes tribunals for Rwanda and the former Yugoslavia represent a willingness by the international community to create structures to enforce human rights in times of war. However, the effectiveness of the tribunals is hampered by the fact that they may actually help entrench the conflict rather than end it. Other gross violations of human rights have also been committed in times of war in recent years (for example in Afghanistan), and no similar structures have been instituted to deal with these. It was hoped that the establishment of the International Criminal Court in 2002 would improve the enforcement of human rights in cases where abuse amounts to crimes against humanity, but the court has not made any major impact to date.

▶ **lack of funding**. As discussed in Section 2.2.2 (pages 108–10), the United Nations has established many specialist international organisations which have a role in protecting human rights. For example, the United Nations High Commissioner for Refugees (UNHCR) was established in 1951 and has the role of providing international protection to refugees. Like all United Nations organisations, human rights organisations suffer from a chronic lack of funding which hampers their ability to be fully effective.

▶ **informal recognition of NGOs**. The reporting procedures of nations to UN bodies have been criticised because, it is argued, they do not provide unbiased information. NGOs can and do provide independent information to the UN. However, the role in reporting human rights violations to international organisations has been informal. A more formalised recognition of NGOs in this area is needed for their impact to be fully effective.

▶ **effectiveness of the media**. The media is effective because it can quickly mobilise public action against human rights abuses. Public action can call upon the governments and international organisations to uphold human rights. NGOs are also able to use the media to gain access to the public.

However, the media is all-consuming and twenty-four hour news channels and access to constant news over the internet mean that the general public can quickly get 'compassion fatigue' from being exposed to too many horrors via the media. The news can present a human rights abuse and, once the initial outcry has subsided, the story may then be ignored. The media also has a tendency to be broad but not deep in its coverage—so, while the public knows about the 'what' of the situation, it knows little about the 'why'.

 page 140

2.2.4 The incorporation of human rights into Australian domestic law

Protection of human rights in Australia has generally been of a high standard when compared to that of many other nations, although some court decisions and statutes have placed limitations on human rights, as have some other government practices, particularly in relation to asylum seekers and Aboriginal and Torres Strait Islander peoples. Human rights are protected in Australia through the following legal measures:

▶ the Australian Constitution

▶ common law

▶ statute law

▶ non-interference

List the ways in which human rights are incorporated into Australian law.

▸ courts and tribunals

▸ bills of rights enacted within the ACT and Victoria

▸ a proposed Australian Charter (or Bill) of Rights

In addition, government and non-government organisations, along with the media, assist in the promotion and monitoring of the protection of human rights in Australia.

 page 140

Describe the roles of various legal frameworks and organisations in Australian responses to the protection of human rights.

2.2.5 The roles of various legal frameworks and organisations in Australian responses

When the nation of Australia was first formed in 1901, there was very little recognition of human rights compared to today. This is reflected in the minimal protection of such rights in the Australian Constitution. However, Australia's protection of human rights has evolved as worldwide recognition of such rights has increased. More and more human rights have become protected in Australia through common and statute law, and government bodies, such as the Australian Human Rights Commission, have been established to help promote the recognition and protection of human rights.

The Australian Constitution

Under the division of powers, the federal government has exclusive powers over international affairs—the 'external affairs power' means that only the Australian government can enter into international agreements, including any human rights agreements. Due to this division of power, state and territory governments can act to mirror any international human rights through their own legislation but they do not have the power to ratify human rights agreements themselves or to enact enabling legislation.

The Australian federal government has agreed to uphold the human rights standards set out in a number of international treaties and declarations, including:

▸ the International Covenant on Civil and Political Rights (ICCPR)

▸ the International Covenant on Economic, Social and Cultural Rights (ICESCR)

▸ the Convention on the Rights of the Child (CRC)

▸ the Convention on the Elimination of All Forms of Discrimination against Women (CEDAW)

▸ the Convention on the Elimination of All Forms of Racial Discrimination (CERD)

▸ the Universal Declaration of Human Rights (UDHR)

▸ the Convention Against Torture (CAT)

▸ the Convention on the Rights of Persons with Disabilities (CRPD).

This means that Australia is obliged to give effect to the human rights obligations contained in these documents.

The separation of powers divides the power of government into three separate institutions—the legislature, the executive and the judiciary. Maintaining the independence and separation of each arm of government ensures basic civil and political rights are protected and that no one arm can hold too much power. One criticism of any entrenched Charter of Rights (as discussed later in this section) is that it will override the separation of powers, especially in relation to the independence of the judiciary.

A small number of human rights are guaranteed under the Australian Constitution. These are:

- the right to vote (section 40)
- the right to trial by jury in courts of Commonwealth jurisdiction for serious offences (section 80)
- the right to freedom of religion (section 116)
- the right to just compensation for property acquired by the Commonwealth (section 51[3])
- the right to freedom of speech, which was said to be implied in a limited way by the High Court in 'political advertising' cases during the 1990s, such as *Lange v Australian Broadcasting Corporation* (High Court, 8 August 1997).

Compared to many other nations, Australia's constitutional guarantee of human rights is quite limited. The first ten amendments to the United States' constitution, for example, guarantee all citizens rights including the express right to free speech, the right to bear arms, the right to a speedy trial, the right not to incriminate oneself, and the right to be free from the infliction of cruel and unusual punishment.

Rights conferred by common law

In Australia, the common law gives some rights to people—such as the right of a tenant to quiet enjoyment of the property he or she rents. However, the common law has also restricted the rights of Australians in some cases, as is shown in the protection of the right to legal representation. In *McInnes v The Queen* (1979) 143 CLR 570, it was found that there was no right to legal representation in Australia despite the fact that those with representation have a much greater chance of being acquitted. However, in the case of *Dietrich v The Queen* (1992) 177 CLR 292, it was decided that, in a serious matter, a case could be delayed indefinitely until an accused person acquired legal aid (see Section 1.3.5, pages 28–9).

The Mabo case of 1992 is an important case in the recognition of human rights in Australia (see Case Study 2.1 below). This case established for the first time that Aboriginal and Torres Strait Islander peoples have rights to some lands in Australia.

CASE STUDY 2.1: *Mabo and others v the State of Queensland (No. 2)* (1992) 175 CLR 1

Facts

Eddie Mabo and four other Murray Islanders (the Meriam people) began proceedings in the High Court in 1982 seeking a declaration on behalf of the Meriam people that they had a prior title to the Murray Islands. They did this because they did not want to participate in the Queensland land rights scheme which would make their land subject to the regulation of parliament.

Issue

The High Court had to decide whether Eddie Mabo and the other Murray Islanders had any right to the land, and if this right existed independently of the Queensland government.

Decision

The High Court decided that there was such a thing as 'native title' to land if the Indigenous occupiers of the land could demonstrate an ongoing traditional connection with the land and if the title had not been extinguished by a valid government action.

Statute law and parliaments

Statute law, together with non-interference (see below), remains the main way that human rights are protected in Australia.

EXAMPLE **Statutes protecting human rights in Australia**

Examples of statutes that protect human rights in Australia include:

▶ anti-discrimination laws, such as the *Racial Discrimination Act 1975* (Cth)

▶ discrimination on the basis of disability laws found in the *Disability Discrimination Act 1992* (Cth)

▶ the *Social Security Act 1991* (Cth) which aims to ensure that all people receive the income necessary to supply themselves with an adequate standard of living.

In addition, bodies such as the NSW Anti-Discrimination Board and the federal Australian Human Rights Commission (AHRC) have been established by legislation to examine cases where rights have been violated. Established in 1986 as the Human Rights and Equal Opportunity Commission (HREOC), the now AHRC is an independent statutory authority which administers federal human rights legislation, including anti-discrimination legislation and privacy legislation. The AHRC's role is to investigate and conciliate complaints about abuses of human rights in legislation under its jurisdiction. However, the AHRC does not have the power to make legally binding decisions.

Parliamentary committees and law reform bodies investigate the protection of human rights in Australia and make recommendations for change. The federal parliament's Human Rights Subcommittee is an example of one such body.

Non-interference

Many human rights exist for Australian citizens simply because the law does not interfere with them. Freedom of movement is one such right. People in Australia are free to move from town to town and are free to walk around wherever they like within certain restrictions (for example a person may not trespass on another person's private property and prisoners are confined to jail). There are few other restrictions on where a person may go and when he or she may go there.

Courts and tribunals

Australia is a signatory to many human rights treaties, some of which are listed in Section 2.1.3 (page 107). Generally, these treaties have no force in Australia unless there has been legislation passed in Australia's domestic law enacting the provisions of the treaties. The *Racial Discrimination Act 1975* (Cth), for example, enacts the provisions contained in the Convention on the Elimination of All Forms of Racial Discrimination (1965) (see Section 2.1.3, page 107).

However, many of the human rights treaties that Australia has signed have not been made part of domestic law by the federal government. The ICCPR and the ICESCR, for example, have merely been attached as schedules to the *Australian Human Rights Commission Act 1986* (Cth). This does not make them part of domestic law.

Courts and tribunals, both international and domestic, have had a role in protecting human rights in Australia, even when there is no Commonwealth legislation protecting the right.

Domestic courts and tribunals

As seen earlier, the AHRC does not have the power to make legally binding decisions. Several state tribunals across Australia do, however, have this power in protecting certain human rights. The NSW Civil and Administrative Tribunal (NCAT), for example, can hear complaints about discrimination and make legally binding decisions about the matter (this can include an award of damages of up to $40 000). One such case is the case of *Abdulrahman v Toll Pty Ltd* (2006) (see Case Study 5.9, Section 5.3.1, page 334). Both the ACT and Victorian courts can also hear and make decisions about the abuse of human rights contained in their legislative Charter of Rights (see page 118).

International tribunals

There have been several cases which have shown that international human rights law can have an effect on Australian law, even when there is no domestic legislation enacting the provisions of the treaties. In areas where there is no domestic legal protection for rights in Australia, people whose rights have been adversely affected can lodge a complaint with various international bodies. This occurred with varying degrees of effectiveness in the cases of *Toonen v Australia* and *A v Australia*, in which complaints were made to the United Nations Human Rights Committee (UNHRC) about Australia's protection of human rights. As can be seen in Case Studies 2.2 and 2.3, the finding of the UNHRC led to legislative changes in Toonen's case, but the UNHRC's finding in the case of *A v Australia* had no effect on Australia's protection of human rights. The Australian government ignored this case and several similar cases that have occurred subsequently. These laws remain in force.

CASE STUDY 2.2: *Toonen v Australia*, UNHRC (1994)

Facts

Nicholas Toonen complained to the UNHRC about Tasmania's criminal laws which made homosexuality illegal.

Issue

Toonen claimed that the laws contravened Articles 17 and 26 of the ICCPR because the laws interfered with his right to privacy and non-discrimination.

Decision

The UNHRC agreed with Toonen. The federal parliament responded to the UNHRC's findings by passing the *Human Rights (Sexual Conduct) Act 1994* (Cth) in an attempt to override Tasmania's laws. The validity of the federal law has not been tested because, in 1997, Tasmania repealed its laws making homosexual acts illegal.

CASE STUDY 2.3: *A v Australia*, UNHRC (1997)

Facts

Mr A arrived on a boat from Cambodia in 1989 seeking refugee status in Australia. He was detained for four years while his status as a refugee was being determined.

Issue

Mr A complained that his rights to liberty and security of person were violated by the Australian federal government.

Decision

The UNHRC agreed that Mr A's rights were violated under Article 9 of the ICCPR. However, Australia rejected the finding and argued that the UNHRC was wrong.

Non-government organisations

Many non-government organisations in Australia work to protect human rights domestically. Some of these are:

▶ Amnesty International

▶ The Red Cross

▶ The Australian Human Rights Institute at the University of New South Wales, which provides information about human rights and publishes material about current developments that affect human rights law

▶ The NSW Council for Civil Liberties which monitors and comments on developments that may affect civil rights.

These are just a few of the groups that lobby governments about human rights issues and which publicise human rights concerns in Australia.

Media

The Australian media plays an important role in reporting human rights infringements within Australia and rallying public action. The effectiveness of the media in this area is discussed in Section 2.2.6 (page 122).

The possibility of a Charter of Rights

A Declaration of Rights, or Charter of Rights, is a document which sets out the basic rights to which every human should be entitled. More and more nations have incorporated a Charter of Rights into their domestic law so that, today, Australia is the only Western democracy that does not have a Charter (or Bill) of Rights. Since 2004, both the Australian Capital Territory and Victoria have incorporated a Charter of Rights into their legal systems. A domestic Charter of Rights can be part of a country's laws in two ways:

▶ it can be entrenched

▶ it can be legislative (that is, part of normal legislation).

There have been calls for Australia to do more as the international recognition of human rights has grown. In recent years, many people within Australia have argued that international human rights treaties need to become part of our statute law, because many such treaties do not have domestic legislation to implement them. People also argue that the common law has failed to adequately protect human rights and that legislation is needed to remedy this. The Commonwealth has the power to pass such legislation but it has been unwilling to interfere in what are often regarded as state matters. Further criticisms of Australia's human rights record can be found in Section 2.2.6 (pages 120–22).

Criticisms of Australia's human rights laws have led to the suggestion that Australia should have its own Charter of Rights (or Bill of Rights) to ensure adequate protection of human rights. One of the key recommendations of the 2009 National Human Rights Consultation Committee was to introduce a Federal *Human Rights Act* enshrining human rights in

Australian legislation. The Australian government announced in 2010 that such legislation would not be introduced (see Section 2.2.6, pages 120–22). This is still the case.

An entrenched Charter (or Bill) of Rights

An entrenched Charter (or Bill) of Rights is part of the constitution of a country. Such charters are difficult to change, which means that citizens are protected no matter who is in government. With an entrenched Charter of Rights, no government can pass a law which contradicts a right given by that charter.

The main problem with an entrenched Charter of Rights is that, sometimes, it needs to be amended because of changing social values, but governments can do little about this. The United States has an entrenched Bill of Rights and has great difficulty in controlling the ownership of guns because, under the Bill of Rights, every citizen has the right to bear arms. While this may have been necessary when the bill was first drawn up, it now is less necessary and contributes to murder and violence within the country.

A legislative Charter of Rights

A legislative Charter of Rights is passed by a parliament in the same way as any other law is passed. The proposed Human Rights Act (rejected by the government) would have been a legislative Charter of Rights. A legislative Charter of Rights can, of course, be changed by the legislature too, so citizens do not have the same level of protection as with an entrenched Charter of Rights. However, some argue that this does not matter because the population can simply elect another government if the current one tries to remove too many rights. Britain, New Zealand, Victoria and the ACT all have a legislative Charter of Rights.

CAN YOU discuss the arguments for and against a Charter of Rights in Australia?

The arguments for and against a Charter of Rights in Australia are outlined in Table 2.1.

Table 2.1 A Charter of Rights for Australia

Arguments *for* a Charter of Rights for Australia	Arguments *against* a Charter of Rights for Australia
▶ The common law has not protected human rights adequately, as seen in various court cases such as *McInnes v The Queen* (see page 115). ▶ A Charter of Rights would protect minority groups who are not adequately protected at present, such as Aboriginal people. ▶ The common law is too slow to meet contemporary needs, such as those posed by technological advances, for example electronic surveillance. ▶ A Charter of Rights would protect people from government interference in basic human rights. At present, governments can make laws that infringe on these rights and people can do little to challenge these laws. ▶ A Charter of Rights would adopt a major recommendation of the National Human Rights Consultation Committee, whose report was released in October 2009, after one of the largest public consultations in Australia's history.	▶ Human rights are already adequately protected through international agreements and common and statute law. ▶ A Charter of Rights can only protect people within the limits of the rights it lists. There is a danger that people will have no rights, except for those within the charter. ▶ A Charter of Rights may mean that the judiciary would take on a political role because it would have to decide whether laws infringed the Charter of Rights. ▶ An entrenched Charter of Rights is difficult to change and may become irrelevant or inappropriate over time. ▶ A legislative Charter of Rights is too easy to change and can be amended according to the political policies of the party in power.

CAN YOU **outline how human rights are incorporated into Australian domestic law?**

In order to do this, you need to describe, with examples, the ways in which human rights are incorporated into Australian domestic law—that is, through:

- rights guaranteed under the Australian Constitution (such as the right to vote, freedom of religion, and the right to trial by jury)
- federal statutory law (such as anti-discrimination laws)
- state and territory statutory law (such as separate anti-discrimination legislation)
- the common law (such as the right of a tenant to enjoy his or her rented property and Indigenous native title rights through the Mabo decision)
- courts and tribunals (such as the NSW ADT) and international complaints mechanisms (such as UNHRC)
- the fact that the law does not interfere with the enjoyment of basic human rights (the concept of non-interference)
- publicity and pressure from NGOs
- publicity and pressure from the media
- the development of a state Charter of Rights in Victoria and in the Australian Capital Territory only (but there being no federal or Australian Charter of Rights).

KCq page 140

Evaluate the effectiveness of Australian domestic responses in promoting and enforcing human rights?

2.2.6 The effectiveness of Australian domestic responses in promoting and enforcing human rights

Australia has, by and large, a good record on human rights—and has also had a prominent role in the international arena in the promotion of human rights. Australia has been active in drafting important human rights documents, such as the Universal Declaration of Human Rights and the ICCPR and ICESCR, as well as other more recent documents.

However, there have been several factors which have limited the effectiveness of legal measures in addressing human rights issues. These are discussed below.

- The role of the AHRC has been criticised because it does not have sufficient power or resources to adequately protect human rights. Its decisions and advice are not legally binding. The AHRC has made recommendations to government about human rights issues but has frequently been ignored.
- There has been unwillingness by governments to adopt laws and practices to address some of the challenges facing Australia in the area of human rights. Some areas that need to be addressed will be discussed later in this section. They include:
  - counterterrorism laws
  - the lack of a Charter of Rights
  - reluctance to sign some international treaties
  - treatment of Aboriginal and Torres Strait Islander peoples
  - mandatory detention of asylum seekers, and timeframes for processing claims for refugee status.

Counterterrorist laws

There have been several counterterrorism laws passed by Australia's federal and state governments since the '9/11' terrorist attacks in the USA in 2001.

EXAMPLE **Counterterrorism laws**

In 2005, the Australian federal government passed the *Anti-Terrorism Act (No. 2)* which amended the *Criminal Code Act 1995* to, among other things, provide for:

▶ **'control' orders** which can be imposed by a court and can restrict the movements of people within Australia for up to twelve months. People under a control order can be made to wear a tracking device and can be restricted from contacting specified other people.

▶ **preventative detention**. A person suspected of being about to engage in a terrorist activity can be detained in prison for forty-eight hours without charge. Extensions to this time may be granted if police investigations are ongoing.

Both control orders and preventative detention are imposed on people who have not been charged with any offence and who have not been involved in any trial.

These laws, and similar ones enacted by various governments in Australia, have been criticised as violating the ICCPR which embodies the principle that people's liberty should only be restricted if there is a criminal charge against them. Dr Mohamed Haneef was detained for twelve days under these laws in 2007. He was released without charge. This provoked media and public outcry and led to an inquiry into the laws which found that Dr Haneef was completely innocent (see Case Study 1.4, Section 1.2.1, page 13).

Lack of a Charter of Rights and failure to ratify human rights treaties

Australia is now the only Western democracy in the world without a Charter of Rights. There is continued criticism of the Australian government, both within Australia and in the international community, for its failure to enact a Charter of Rights (see Section 2.2.5, pages 118–19) and its failure to sign some international human rights treaties. Australia finally signed the Optional Protocol to the Convention on the Elimination of All Forms of Discrimination Against Women 1979 (CEDAW), in 2008, and the Convention Against Torture and Other Cruel, Inhuman or Degrading Treatment or Punishment 1984, in 2009. These protocols allow individual complaints to the United Nations bodies which monitor these conventions and unrestricted visiting rights by these bodies to examine Australia's compliance with the treaties. Australia had, until November 2007, also refused to sign the Kyoto Protocol, which protects environmental rights (see Section 2.1.2, page 105).

Treatment of Aboriginal and Torres Strait Islander peoples

Australia's record in ensuring rights for Aboriginal people has come under considerable criticism both within Australia and internationally. Past government policies, such as removal of children and the denial of land rights, have clearly infringed the rights of Aboriginal people, although these have now been replaced by other policies more concerned with ensuring human rights.

However, the average life expectancy of Aboriginal people is still twelve years lower than that of the rest of the population and the infant mortality rate is twice as high. Aboriginal people are more heavily policed, eleven times more likely to be imprisoned and have limited land rights. The *Native Title Act 1993* (Cth) and its amendments have been criticised for limiting the ability of Aboriginal people to protect their property rights.

The *Northern Territory National Emergency Response Act 2007* (Cth), commonly referred to as the NT Intervention, operated in seventy-three Indigenous communities in the Northern Territory. The intervention included the quarantining of welfare payments and income management measures, as well as placing community land under government control. It was put in place as an emergency measure, chiefly to respond to high instances of Indigenous child abuse linked to severe alcohol and drug abuse. The act has also been criticised nationally and internationally for breaching fundamental human rights and federal and state anti-discrimination legislation. The *Racial Discrimination Act 1975* (Cth) was suspended for the purposes of the NT Intervention legislation. This Act has now been repealed. The *Stronger Futures in the Northern Territory Act 2013* (Cth) uses a similar program but runs alongside racial discrimination legislation.

On the international stage, Australia was one of four countries who voted against the Declaration on the Rights of Indigenous Peoples 2006 in the UN General Assembly. The other three were New Zealand, Canada and the US. In 2009, Australia changed its vote to support the declaration.

Australia's Aboriginal people continue to face discrimination and to struggle for self-determination, land rights and economic, social and cultural equality, as do other Indigenous peoples around the world.

Mandatory detention of asylum seekers

The mandatory detention of asylum seekers is an important human rights issue in Australia and is discussed in further detail in Sections 2.3.2 and 2.3.3 (pages 123–9).

Non-government organisations and the media

Non-government organisations have become a very important method of ensuring human rights protection. Some NGOs that operate in Australia are listed in Section 2.2.5 (page 118). The success of these groups in promoting human rights depends on how much pressure they can assert and how much publicity they receive. The media in Australia often gives such groups wide publicity and knowledge about human rights is generally widespread. However, because of state sovereignty, it is up to governments to change laws regarding human rights concerns and, as has been seen above, they may not do so despite widespread publicity and pressure from both within and outside Australia.

CAN YOU **evaluate the effectiveness of Australian domestic responses in promoting and enforcing human rights?**

In order to do this, you need to:

▷ point out that Australia's human rights record is generally good compared to that of other countries

▷ point out that there are some areas in which Australia's human rights protection has been limited

▷ describe Australia's limitations in regard to promoting and enforcing human rights, as outlined in this section.

KCq page 140

2.3 Investigation of a contemporary human rights issue

2.3.1 Contemporary struggles for human rights

The recognition and protection of human rights internationally has grown enormously since the Universal Declaration of Human Rights was drawn up in 1948. However, the record for human rights protection has been limited. The subjects of contemporary struggles for human rights are listed below:

- genocide
- treatment of refugees (the contemporary issue of the treatment of refugees is discussed at length in Sections 2.3.2 and 2.3.3, pages 123–9)
- asylum seekers (this issue is partially discussed in relation to Australia's response to refugees in Sections 2.3.2 and 2.3.3, pages 123–9)
- child soldiers
- abuse of children
- torture
- capital punishment
- arbitrary detention
- religious discrimination
- discrimination against women
- exploitation of workers
- human trafficking and slavery
- limitations on free speech
- suspension of democracy, and political imprisonment.

 page 140

> List current contemporary struggles for human rights.

2.3.2 The contemporary human rights issue of the treatment of refugees

> Describe the contemporary human rights issue of the treatment of refugees.

The nature and extent of the issue

The 1951 UN Convention relating to the Status of Refugees (the 1951 Refugee Convention) defines a refugee as someone who 'owing to a well-founded fear of being persecuted for reasons of race, religion, nationality, membership of a particular social group or political opinion, is outside the country of his nationality, and is unable to or, owing to such fear, is unwilling to avail himself of the protection of that country'.

According to the United Nations High Commissioner for Refugees (UNHCR) 2009 'Global Trends Report', by the end of 2009 there were 43.3 million forcibly displaced people internationally. Of these, 27.1 million were displaced internally, meaning they had been uprooted within their countries due to internal conflict, and 15.2 million fall under the formal definition of a refugee.

Most refugees end up in a nation-state close to the nation-state from which they fled, often in holding or internment camps. This means over 80% of all refugees live in developing countries. Many will never return to their homeland, and for many others it will be decades before they do return.

In 2009, more than one in four refugees worldwide originated from Afghanistan (2.9 million). Most of these refugees fled Afghanistan due to ethnic prosecution, ongoing conflict and religious extremism. They mainly reside in Iran and Pakistan but are spread over seventy-one countries worldwide. Also, in 2009, the top three countries of origin for applications for asylum were Iraq, Afghanistan and Somalia. Of the applications for asylum, 112 400 refugees were admitted to third countries for resettlement by nineteen countries, of which Australia is one.

International legal responses

1951 Refugee Convention

The international legal instrument governing refugees is the 1951 United Nations Convention relating to the Status of Refugees (the 1951 Refugee Convention). Both the Convention and the UNHCR (see below) were established as a direct result of World War II and the resultant world refugee crisis. This key legal document defines a refugee, outlines refugee rights and establishes the refugee obligations of states. The rights of a refugee as outlined in the Convention include the right to freedom of religion and movement, the right to work, the right to education and the right of accessibility to travel documents.

Of the 192 member states of the UN, 144 are parties to the Convention. A key provision of the Convention is that refugees should not be returned to a country where they fear persecution. This provision has entered into customary international law, meaning that even those states who are not party to the Convention must respect this principle.

United Nations High Commissioner for Refugees

The United Nations High Commissioner for Refugees (UNHCR) is the body established to assist refugees internationally. The UNHCR's role is to lead and coordinate international action to protect refugees and resolve refugee issues worldwide. The aim of the UNHCR is to protect the rights and wellbeing of refugees as well as striving to ensure that everyone can exercise their right to seek asylum and find safe refugee in another state, with the options to:

▶ integrate into that state
▶ return home voluntarily (repatriation)
▶ settle in a third state.

The UNHCR also works closely with national governments to ensure the principles of the 1951 Convention are upheld.

In 2010, the UNHCR was operating in over 120 countries worldwide with large scale operations in Afghanistan, Chad, Columbia, the Democratic Republic of Congo, Pakistan, Iraq and the Sudan. Africa and Asia both generate and host the largest number of refugees worldwide.

International non-legal responses

The chief international NGOs in the care and protection of refugees are Amnesty International and Human Rights Watch. Their role is to monitor refugee camps, monitor human rights compliance by states creating or hosting refugees, report on refugee situations to the UN, governments and the media, and campaign for reform. The international media also plays an important role in assisting NGOs in raising awareness and agitating for change.

Australian legal responses

In 2007–08, the Australian government issued 13 014 humanitarian visas under its Refugee and Special Humanitarian Program and set a quota of 13 500 in 2008–09. This placed it 32nd out of the 71 countries who accept refugees and asylum seekers. Refugees and humanitarian entrants arrive directly from overseas and some arrive as onshore asylum seekers. Most of the refugees accepted into Australia apply offshore and are referred from the UNHCR.

A small minority of refugees are accepted from onshore applications including 'unauthorised arrivals', meaning those people who have arrived in Australia and then apply for refugee status. Once a person has applied for asylum he or she is issued a permanent protection visa if he or she has arrived in Australia and meets certain criteria. This visa means the person can live in the community until their application to be accepted as a refugee has been assessed. If their application for refugee asylum is rejected and they have exhausted all appeal channels then they will generally be returned to their home country.

The treatment of 'unauthorised' or 'unlawful' arrivals is slightly different. Since 1992, all people arriving in Australia without proper travel documents have been detained. Under various Commonwealth border security Acts people are detained if they are declared unlawful, and are treated as such if they have:

▶ arrived in Australia without a visa (95% of people seeking asylum in Australia arrive by air and, in 2009, only 1800 people arrived by boat)

▶ overstayed their visa

▶ had their visa cancelled.

People are detained until they are issued a visa or are returned to their home country.

Australian non-legal responses

Global NGOs operate in Australia, including arms of Amnesty International, Human Rights Watch, Oxfam and the Red Cross. The Refugee Council of Australia is the peak body representing the organisations and individuals who support and assist refugees and asylum seekers.

The media plays an important role in shaping Australia's refugee policy and the attitude of Australian citizens towards refugees and asylum seekers. The effectiveness of the Australia media's response is discussed in the following section.

KCq page 141

2.3.3 The effectiveness of legal and non-legal responses to the issue of treatment of refugees

Evaluate the effectiveness of legal and non-legal responses to the issue of treatment of refugees.

No resolution of ongoing conflicts

The numbers of internally displaced people continues to rise worldwide. Fewer refugees have been able to voluntarily return home. The UNHCR reported in 2009 that only 251 000 refugees were able to be voluntarily repatriated to their home countries. This compares badly to the average of one million per year in the last decade. This is largely due to persistent and unresolved inter-state and intra-state conflicts.

The UNHCR reports that ongoing conflicts (such as those in Afghanistan, Somalia, Pakistan and the Democratic Republic of Congo) show no sign of resolution, and that other conflicts that may have been on the path to settlement have stagnated, such as those in Sudan and Iraq.

Until the world acts to find ways to end current conflicts and build global peace and stability the refugee crisis will continue to grow and the effectiveness of the international response through the UNHCR and its bodies will continue to be tested.

Impact of global financial crisis

The world financial crisis which began in 2007 has threatened the jobs and livelihoods of millions. It has led to an increase in economic migrants (see under 'Asylum seekers' below). At the same time as increasing the numbers of people entering abject poverty (a major cause of conflict) it has also affected the responses of the developed wealthy world. Funding to the UNHCR from states has decreased, direct overseas investment in refugee programs has dropped and developed countries have tightened their migration policies.

Developed nations increasingly unwilling to provide refuge

Refugees are reliant on wealthy states, such as Australia, to give them refuge. The 1951 Refugee Convention obliges states to assist refugees, but wealthier states are making this more difficult through domestic legislation. The world's willingness to provide for refugees is decreasing with many European countries, for example, tightening their restrictions on the movement of refugees across their borders. The situation in Europe has been exacerbated through the growth of the European Union and the opening of old borders, allowing access to many countries. The global financial crisis has also impacted upon migration policies.

Surprisingly, figures from the UNHCR have reported some improvement in 2009. As seen in Section 2.3.2 (pages 123–4), the response by developed countries to refugees seeking asylum in 2009 has actually been the best global response in sixteen years.

However, the number of refugees accepted in third countries is still too low to even begin addressing the problem and most countries are still implementing restrictive refugee domestic legislation.

Impact of global terrorism

Since the attacks on 11 September 2001 in the US, and subsequent attacks, many Western citizens and their governments have become less trustful of Muslims. This has led to discrimination, hate crimes and division of communities. Many of the world's asylum seekers come from the Muslim world and they are finding it increasingly hard to find accepting communities. Some domestic governments and sections of the media assist in generating these divisive conditions in communities.

Asylum seekers

'Unauthorised' asylum seekers enter developed countries and then request refugee status in a third country. This is often due to desperation and long internments in refugee camps. This is a significant problem in Europe (where Africans cross from Africa into Europe via border countries such as Spain) and to a lesser extent, Australia where most asylum seekers arrive by air and, far less frequently, by boat from Indonesia. Australia's response to asylum seekers is discussed in further detail on page 128. The major criticisms of these types of asylum seekers include:

▶ they have 'jumped' the refugee queue and thereby disadvantage those currently residing in refugee camps

▶ they are 'economic migrants' and not refugees. An economic migrant is one who is seeking asylum due to economic circumstances, not

- of a well-founded fear of persecution. An asylum seeker will be refused refugee status if he or she is found to be an economic migrant and will be returned to his or her country of origin.
- accepting asylum seekers will encourage further breaches by unscrupulous people smugglers. This is an argument frequently used by the Australian government and the media, although statistics show this is not actually the case.

The numbers of people now seeking asylum has made the developed world and its population less welcoming to all refugees and those seeking asylum generally.

Long-term refugees and internally displaced people

The majority of the world's refugees have been living as refugees for five years or more because they are unable to return home. Many internally displaced people are living within large camps in urban areas of their own countries.

Due to first world developed nations becoming less welcoming and tightening their refugee policy, or to unresolved long-term internal conflict, these people are often unable to satisfactorily find refuge in a suitable third country or return to their homes. In fact, most refugees live in the cities in the developing world (80% of all asylum seekers), usually in substandard refugee camps. Despite the best efforts of NGOs and aid agencies, and of the UNHCR, refugee camps are often overcrowded, unhygienic and lawless. A lack of funding for these humanitarian bodies, as well as domestic political inaction, means refugees continue to live in these conditions for many years.

As a result, a whole generation of people are growing up effectively 'stateless'—they cannot return to their home state, and they cannot make a new life in a second or third state. They are living in abject poverty and with few human rights.

Impacts of climate change and population growth

Climate change and environmental degradation threaten to displace growing numbers of populations in coming years. The effectiveness of the response to refugees currently in developing nations may also be dramatically affected by climate change. Added to this is the fact that world conflicts will increase as the world's population increases and available resources dwindle.

To date, peoples affected by climate change have generally been displaced within their own countries. As the impacts of climate change increase it is anticipated that the numbers of environmental asylum seekers will increase significantly. The need for reform in the definition of a refugee is discussed in Section 2.4.4 (pages 132–3).

The international community has not addressed the threats posed by climate change and increased population. This is an area urgently needing reform.

State sovereignty

The UNHCR 2009 'Global Trends Report' states that 2009 witnessed a growing determination from countries to exercise state sovereignty over international cooperation. This is due to reasons such as the financial crisis, global population growth and the threats of climate change. As states seek to protect their sovereignty at all costs they become less compassionate and make it harder for the UNHCR and NGOs to operate effectively in their countries to aid refugees and internally displaced people.

Effectiveness of non-government organisations

The major NGOs and aid agencies need funds and cooperative governments to aid refugees. The situations described on the previous pages have made it increasingly difficult for NGOS to assist current refugees and lobby to improve refugee and asylum seeker policy.

Role of the media

The media can be both extremely effective and extremely ineffective in assisting refugees and those seeking asylum. The media is essential in taking the plight of refugees to a global audience, reporting the conditions of refugee camps, and discussing treatment of refugees and asylum seekers in host countries. However, the media can also operate to foster fear among populations about accepting refugees and can use its power to encourage discrimination and xenophobia.

Australian response

While Australia's response to accepting offshore refugees under its Refugee and Special Humanitarian Program complies with its responsibilities under the 1951 Refugee Convention, its treatment of onshore asylum seekers has been subject to internal and international criticism.

Australia has been criticised internationally for detaining asylum seekers unfairly and for unreasonably lengthy periods, as in the case of *A v Australia* (UNHRC) (1997), see Section 2.2.5, pages 117–18. In 2004, the Australian Human Rights Commission (then HREOC) released a report into children in immigration detention (entitled *A last resort?)*. This report found that Australia was in breach of several international human rights treaties including the Convention on the Rights of the Child 1989 (CROC).

Since the release of this report, and because of increasing public pressure, all children were removed from detention and some other detainees have been granted visas which allow them to enter into the normal life of the Australian community pending removal from or acceptance into Australia (as discussed in Section 2.3.2, page 125). In addition, in 2005 the Commonwealth Ombudsman was given the power to review the detention of people who have spent two or more years in immigration detention.

Despite these changes, there are still people held for long periods in immigrant detention centres and the policy of mandatory detention continues. In 2004, the High Court found that the indefinite detention of asylum seekers was lawful. Offshore detention centres, such as the one on Christmas Island, continue to operate.

As with the rest of the world, Australia saw a marked increase in the numbers of asylum seekers throughout 2009. In April 2010, the Australian government announced it was freezing all applications for asylum seekers originating from Afghanistan (six month suspension) and Sri Lanka (three month suspension). This suspension was effective immediately. The federal government has been universally condemned for this decision by international and national refugee and human rights bodies. The Australian Human Rights Commission said the changes could see asylum-seekers again being detained indefinitely. It also means that children could again be detained.

Immigration and asylum seeker policy is a tightly-fought government election issue. Some media outlets and commentators help to generate myths surrounding the numbers of unlawful asylum seekers, and the impact of refugees on Australian society generally. Equally, other members of the media work for justice in these areas.

CAN YOU investigate the contemporary human rights issue of the treatment of refugees and evaluate the effectiveness of legal and non-legal responses to this issue?

In order to investigate and evaluate this issue, you need to:

▸ describe the nature and extent of the refugee issue worldwide

▸ describe international legal responses to the treatment of refugees

▸ evaluate the effectiveness of international legal responses to the treatment of refugees

▸ describe international non-legal responses to the treatment of refugees

▸ evaluate the effectiveness of international non-legal responses to the treatment of refugees

▸ describe Australian legal responses to the treatment of refugees

▸ evaluate the effectiveness of Australian legal responses to the treatment of refugees

▸ describe Australian non-legal responses to the treatment of refugees

▸ evaluate the effectiveness of Australian non-legal responses to the treatment of refugees.

 page 141

2.4 Themes and challenges

2.4.1 Theme 1: The changing understanding of the relationship between state sovereignty and human rights

Explain the changing understanding of the relationship between state sovereignty and human rights.

The concept of state sovereignty can help protect the human rights of people in a state where sovereignty rests with the people. However, where a state is governed by one ruler who does not need to heed the wishes of the people, human rights may not be protected. The protection of human rights internationally undermines the idea of national sovereignty because it means interfering with a nation's domestic affairs.

However, it is increasingly recognised that nations do have a responsibility to protect human rights within their own borders and that scrutiny of this protection is a legitimate international concern. Some nations also, while resenting interference in their own domestic human rights protection, recognise that the international community should interfere to stop human rights violations if such violations endanger world peace and security. page 141

2.4.2 Theme 2: Issues of compliance and non-compliance in relation to human rights

Examine issues of compliance and non-compliance in relation to human rights.

States will generally comply with, or obey, human rights law for the following reasons.

▸ As a result of pressure from the international community and the UN to address human rights issues.

▸ Human rights are customary international law and it is international expectation that all countries will abide by them.

▸ Human rights protection is a membership requirement of some very influential IGOs including the European Union and NATO. For example, Turkey is currently being assessed for entry to the European Union and has been required to show compliance with human rights obligations as part of the entry process.

▸ As a result of pressure from international and local media.

- As a result of pressure from international and local NGOs.
- The population of the state may insist that the state's government address human rights violations.
- The existence of the ICC and the war crimes tribunals act as a deterrent, particularly for individuals committing human rights violations because there is now a larger chance they will be caught and prosecuted.

States may choose to not comply with (disobey) human rights treaties for the following reasons.

- Human rights are a Western concept and may, therefore, be seen as not applicable in non-Western nations (see Section 2.4.3, page 131).
- Individual human rights take a secondary priority and are addressed after issues of poverty and inequality in developing nations (see Section 2.4.3, page 131).
- States who have not been instrumental in the development of human rights principles may not feel that these principles apply to them.
- Human rights violations can be viewed as acceptable in a state and/or are popular with the electorate. Examples include the treatment of asylum seekers in Australia, the use of torture on terror suspects in the US, or state-sanctioned capital punishment in many countries.
- Protection of human rights is not deemed as important as other objectives of the state, for example anti-terrorist measures. See Section 2.2.6 (pages 120–21) which discusses how Australia has assessed the importance of preventing terrorism as being of a higher priority than protecting some individual rights. This argument is commonly used when states choose to set aside or override human rights.
- The protection of the rights of groups or individuals may place the rights of other groups or individuals (or self-interest) in danger. For example, it was commonly perceived prior to the Mabo decision that granting Indigenous Australians land rights would infringe on the land rights of non-Indigenous property owners (see Sections 2.2.5 and 2.2.6 [pages 114–22]).
- Sometimes it is argued that it is too expensive to protect human rights. In many countries, particularly developing nations, transnationals and/or governments may decide that protection of human rights will be too expensive to enforce, or will potentially reduce profits. Examples include the protections of trade union rights, or the rights to a living wage.
- It may not be in the state's self-interest to recognise and protect human rights.
- States lack the funds to stop individuals breaking human rights law within their country, for example to stop criminals operating human trafficking rings.
- Due to corruption, states may lack the will to stop individuals from breaking human rights law.
- Enforcement mechanisms are weak so there is no real deterrence.

KCq page 141

2.4.3 Theme 3: The development of human rights as a reflection of changing values and ethical standards

Since the drafting of the Universal Declaration of Human Rights in 1948, there has been an enormous shift in the understanding of human rights worldwide. Human rights have become an important part of international law and human rights abuses are widely publicised and condemned. NGOs have had an important role in promoting knowledge of and compliance with human rights standards. Most countries in the world have also made at least some human rights part of their domestic law.

Some significant challenges facing the global understanding of human rights include the ideas discussed below.

Human rights are a Western concept

While the universality of human rights is seen as fundamental by many, some nations argue that they reflect a Western world-view and do not take into account the quite different cultural perspectives of Asian and other countries. It is argued that the practical observance of human rights needs to be made in the cultural and political context of each country. For example, Australia is sometimes accused of cultural insensitivity when it has criticised Indonesia and Malaysia about human rights. Despite this argument that human rights are basically a Western concept and are not universal, Western, Eastern and developing countries have all contributed to the development of international protection of these rights.

Human rights are indivisible

The indivisibility of human rights has been questioned by some nations who argue that economic and social rights are more important than civil and political rights. This argument is based on the idea that civil and political rights are not of much comfort to people who are starving or in dire economic circumstances. So some nation-states have given priority to developing economic and social wellbeing, even if this means the denial of political and civil rights. This view was expressed by the Chinese government in a statement to the Vienna World Conference on Human Rights in 1993 when it was said: 'When poverty and lack of adequate food and clothing are commonplace and people's basic needs are not guaranteed, priority should be given to economic development. Otherwise, human rights are completely out of the question'.

Collective rights

These are seen by some commentators as an attempt to 'water down' the importance of individual rights. They argue that, while pursuit of such rights is praiseworthy, they should not be seen as overtaking or displacing first and second generation rights.

National security

The 'war on terror' (see Section 6.3.2, pages 408–9) has led to the justification of practices that clearly infringe human rights, such as the detention without trial of suspected terrorists in Guantanamo Bay by the US government, and the new control order and preventative detention laws in Australia (see Section 2.2.6, pages 120–21). Some argue that such measures are necessary to protect national security, while others argue that the fear of terrorist attack should not lead Western democracies to strike down those very freedoms that they most cherish.

KCq page 141

Explain how human rights law is a reflection of changing values and ethical standards.

2.4.4 Theme 4: The role of law reform in protecting human rights

Pressure to reform the existing law can come from many sources including:

▶ the International Law Commission

▶ Law Reform Commissions of nation-states, for example the Australian Law Reform Commission

▶ reports and recommendations from the Australian Human Rights Commission

▶ parliaments of nation-states, for example Australian government commissions and reports

▶ international courts

▶ courts of nation-states

▶ courts of regional federations and intergovernmental organisations

▶ NGOs, including human rights monitoring watchdogs

▶ the media

▶ individuals.

In relation to Australian human rights law, reform can be achieved through legislation or by adaptation of the common law in courts. Parliament is the primary agency of law reform. Australian courts are able to contribute to reform in the law by applying precedent to cases currently under review and making decisions to fit changing circumstances, sometimes with profound results. The recognition of Indigenous land rights in the Mabo decision is an example [*Mabo and Others v the State of Queensland (No. 2)* (1992) 175 CLR 1]. See Section 2.2.5 (page 115).

An example of reform arising from a government commission is the investigation into a Charter of Rights for Australia. The federal government's 2009 National Human Rights Consultation Committee suggested the government introduce a *Federal Human Rights Act* enshrining human rights in Australian legislation. The Australian government announced, in 2010, that they would not be introducing any such legislation. This is an area still requiring reform. See Section 2.2.5 (pages 118–19) for more detail.

Internationally, the International Law Commission can enact reform by reviewing and reporting on legal issues, such as the effectiveness of human rights law. The International Criminal Court (ICC) has played a large role in enacting individual human rights reform since its inception in 2002. It was largely through the work of the ICC and the *ad hoc* war crimes tribunals of Rwanda and the former Yugoslavia that the recognition of rape as a war crime was brought about. Separate international courts and tribunals can also bring about state reform, as in the case of *Toonen v Australia*, United Nations Human Rights Committee (UNHRC) (1994) (see Section 2.2.5, page 117).

For more information, refer to Figure 6.2 on page 422 (which outlines the key law reform bodies in international law and explains how each body works to bring about reform).

EXAMPLE Areas of human rights law requiring reform

▶ **Australia's incorporation of a Charter of Rights**: The Australian government announced they would not be implementing suggestions for an Australian Charter of Rights. See Section 2.2.5 (pages 118–19).

▶ **Australia's response to asylum seekers**: International and national criticism of the current asylum seeker policy, as well as the recent suspension of the processing of claims from those originating in Afghanistan and Sri Lanka, demonstrate that this is an area requiring reform.

▷ **International definition of** *refugee*: Those refugees impacted upon by climate change are referred to as climate change or environmental refugees even though they do not fit the 1951 Refugee Convention definition of *refugee*. People escaping slavery are also not included in the definition. The formal definition of a refugee is an area requiring law reform.

▷ **Global response to the treatment of refugees**: The global conditions that give rise to refugees are changing rapidly and 2009 saw a large increase in the number of internally displaced peoples and refugees around the world. Ongoing conflict, climate change, rapid population growth and the financial crisis are all contributing to increased numbers of refugees and displaced peoples. The current international response to refugees is clearly not working and reform is needed in this area.

KCq page 141

2.4.5 Theme 5: The effectiveness of legal and non-legal measures in protecting human rights

> Investigate the effectiveness of legal and non-legal measures in protecting human rights internationally and in Australia.

The effectiveness of the legal and non-legal measures in protecting international human rights are discussed in detail in Section 2.2.3 (pages 112–13) and through the study of the contemporary human rights issue of refugees in Sections 2.3.2 and 2.3.3 (pages 123–9).

The effectiveness of both the legal and non-legal measures taken by Australia to protect human rights are discussed in detail in Section 2.2.6 (pages 120–22) and through the study of the contemporary human rights issue of refugees in Sections 2.3.2 and 2.3.3 (pages 123–9).

The main points are presented in Tables 2.2 and 2.3.

Table 2.2 Legal and non-legal measures for protecting human rights internationally

Effectiveness of international responses		
International response	Effective	Ineffective
Legal measures		
International Bill of Rights and other treaties	165 countries have agreed to be bound by the International Bill of Rights—meaning the world is united in recognising a need for the protection of human rights.	Not all states are party to human rights treaties.
Enforcement mechanisms		International mechanisms (conventions, treaties, the ICC, tribunals and treaty-based authorities) have inadequate or no enforcement mechanisms. Enforcement is generally through nation-state consensus only.
Universal Periodic Review	The Universal Periodic Review means the human rights records of all states are examined and judged by the international community.	There is a reliance on nation-states reporting their own human rights abuses to UN bodies and the community—therefore they can provide biased, slanted or simply incorrect information.
Use of force	The Human Rights Council has some powers to recommend intervention by the Security Council.	The Security Council is hesitant to use force on the basis of humanitarian intervention.
War crimes tribunals and the ICC	War crimes tribunals for Rwanda and Yugoslavia are an attempt to enforce human rights treaties through the mechanisms of international law. War crimes tribunals and the ICC have both raised the profile of individual perpetrators of abuses War crimes tribunals and the ICC present the threat of capture and punishment to individual perpetrators, which may act as a deterrent.	The effectiveness of the war crimes tribunals is hampered because they may entrench the conflict rather than solve it. War crime tribunals have not been established for other areas where large scale human rights abuses have taken place, such as in the Afghanistan and Iraq conflicts. The US is not a signatory to the ICC and does not accept its jurisdiction.

Effectiveness of international responses		
International response	Effective	Ineffective
Legal measures		
Funding		There is a general lack of funding for all UN bodies.
Intergovernmental organisations (IGOs)	Major regional associations (such as the EU, NATO and Commonwealth) have the upholding of human rights as a membership requirement.	Major regional associations have no enforcement mechanism to ensure member states comply with human rights—the states can be suspended from membership of the organisation, but this may not act as a significant deterrent.
Non-legal measures		
The media	The international media raises awareness of human rights infringements around the world. Awareness of issues can lead to subsequent public and government action.	Too much news means the public can easily get 'compassion fatigue' and ignore abuses. Media coverage can be broad but not deep so that the issues behind the story are not uncovered.
Non-government organisations (NGOs)	NGOs are essential in reporting human rights abuses around the world. NGOs can act as observers for the UN and provide information to it.	The role of information-provider to the UN played by NGOs is too informal.

Table 2.3 Legal and non-legal measures for protecting human rights in Australia

Effectiveness of Australia's responses		
Australia's response	Effective	Ineffective
Legal measures		
Australian Human Rights Commission (AHRC)	Australia has a strong human rights body in the Australian Human Rights Commission, which is independent of government.	The AHRC can only make recommendations, not binding decisions. Federal anti-terrorist legislation allowing for control orders and preventative detention have been criticised for violating the ICCPR.
Legal protections	Many human rights in Australia are protected through non-interference.	Australia has failed to sign some core human rights treaties leading to international criticism.
Treatment of Aboriginal and Torres Strait Islander peoples	The treatment and quality of life for Aboriginal and Torres Strait Islanders continues to improve and previous government legislation which was clearly discriminatory has ceased (for example, the legislation involved in the Stolen Generations).	Aboriginal and Torres Strait Islander peoples still are discriminated against, have lower life expectancy, and have limited land rights. There is still a long way to go. The ongoing NT Intervention breaches anti-discrimination legislation and human rights treaties.
Australian Constitution and a Charter of Rights.	The Australian Constitution already contains some core human rights protection and a separate charter is not needed. In addition, entrenched charters can be inflexible and lead to an infringement of the 'separation of powers' doctrine.	The Australian government refused to look at enacting a Charter of Rights as recently as 2010.
Non-legal measures		
The media	The Australian media raises awareness of human rights infringements in Australia. Awareness of issues can lead to subsequent public and government action.	Despite pressure from the media and NGOs the government can choose to still implement policies which infringe human rights. Some media support current initiatives which may infringe human rights—for example initiatives related to asylum seekers, and the NT Intervention. This provides support to the government and the public to continue infringements.
Non-government organisations (NGOs)	NGOs are essential in reporting human rights abuses —for example the treatment of asylum seekers.	

KCq page 141

Do you know all the key definitions and concepts for this chapter? Go through each term in the list and check that you know them all. Place a bookmark underneath each definition to cover the one below and slide it down. This way you can focus on each definition by itself.

Abolitionist: A person who fights to end slavery.

Asylum seeker: A person who seeks refugee status, (that is, refuge and protection in another country).

Bonded labour: People who are forced to work for an indefinite period in order to pay off a debt.

Charter of Rights: A document which sets out the basic rights to which every human should be entitled.

Civil rights: Entitlements belonging to all humans to do with being a free citizen of a nation, such as freedom of thought and religion.

Collective rights: Entitlements that do not belong to an individual but to a group of people, such as the continued survival of a race of people.

Control order: An order which restricts the movements and communications of people within Australia

Cultural rights: Entitlements to assist in preserving and enjoying one's cultural heritage.

Democracy: A system of government in which lawmaking authority is given to representatives elected by the whole adult population.

Deportation: Forcibly removing a person from the country.

Disenfranchised: Not having the right to vote.

Division of power: The distribution of power between the federal and state governments.

Domestic right: An entitlement that a person has within his or her own country.

Economic migrants: People who are seeking asylum in another country for economic reasons, not because they fear persecution.

Economic rights: Entitlements concerned with the production, development and management of material for the necessities of life.

Entrenched Charter of Rights: A document that is part of the constitution of a country, which sets out the basic rights to which every human should be entitled.

Environmental rights: The entitlement to a clean, healthy and sustainable environment.

Human rights: Fundamental rights to which all people are entitled simply because they are human.

Inalienability: A characteristic of human rights which means they cannot be given up or taken away.

Indivisibility: A characteristic of human rights which means that all human rights are equally important.

Inherent: A characteristic of human rights which means they are the birthright of all humans.

Intergovernmental organisation: An organisation comprised of several sovereign states working for a common cause.

International right: An entitlement recognised internationally as being a fundamental right of all people.

Legal responsibility: The idea that nations want to be seen by other nations as law-abiding.

Legislative Charter of Rights: A document that is passed as an act of parliament, which sets out the basic rights to which every human should be entitled.

Natural law: A philosophy based on the idea that there exist certain 'natural' laws which apply to all humanity and which maintain people's basic dignity.

Non-government organisation (NGO): An organisation that works towards a certain cause and operates separately from any government.

Peace rights: The entitlement of people to have their government maintain peace and eliminate war.

Political prisoner: A person who is imprisoned because he or she disagrees with the government.

Political rights: Entitlements belonging to all humans, that are to do with full participation in government, such as the right to vote.

Preventative detention: The imprisonment, without charge, of someone who is suspected of being about to engage in a terrorist activity.

Protocol: A treaty that changes another treaty, for example by adding additional procedures or provisions.

Reciprocity: The idea that nations obey international law because they want other nations to do the same.

Refugees: People who are outside their country of origin and who can prove that they have a well-founded fear of persecution because of religion, nationality, membership of a particular social group, or political opinion if they return to their country of origin.

Right: Something to which a person is entitled.

Self-determination: The right of peoples to govern themselves and to choose their own form of government.

Separation of powers: The distribution of power between the legislature, the executive and the judiciary.

Social rights: Entitlements that give people security as they live and learn together, such as rights involved in schools and other institutions.

Sovereignty: The existence within one country or nation-state of a group, person or body with supreme lawmaking authority.

Suffrage: The right to vote in elections.

<table>
<tr><td>Trade union: An association of wage earners which exists in order to maintain and improve the working conditions of its members.</td><td>Universal suffrage: The situation in which all adults have the right to vote in elections.</td></tr>
<tr><td>Treaty: A formal agreement between two or more independent nation-states.</td><td>Universality: A characteristic of human rights which means they are to be enjoyed by all individuals regardless of their gender, race or status.</td></tr>
</table>

Chapter syllabus checklist

Are you able to answer every syllabus question in the chapter? Tick each question as you go through the list if you are able to answer it. If you cannot answer it, turn to the given page to find the answer. Refer to page ix to check the meaning of the NESA key words.

	For a complete understanding of this topic:	Page No.	✓
1	Can I define *human rights*?	95–7	
2	Can I outline how human rights have changed and developed over time in regard to the abolition of slavery?	99–100	
3	Can I outline how human rights have changed and developed over time in regard to trade unionism and labour rights?	100–1	
4	Can I outline how human rights have changed and developed over time in regard to universal suffrage?	102–3	
5	Can I outline how human rights have changed and developed over time in regard to universal education?	103–4	
6	Can I outline how human rights have changed and developed over time in regard to self-determination?	104	
7	Can I outline how human rights have changed and developed over time in regard to environmental rights?	105	
8	Can I outline how human rights have changed and developed over time in regard to peace rights?	105	
9	Can I investigate the evolving recognition and importance of universal human rights?	106	
10	Can I describe the Universal Declaration of Human Rights as a formal statement of human rights?	106–7	
11	Can I describe the International Covenant on Civil and Political Rights as a formal statement of human rights?	107	
12	Can I describe the International Covenant on Economic, Social and Cultural Rights as a formal statement of human rights?	107	
13	Can I examine major human rights documents and explain their contribution to the development of human rights?	107	
14	Can I define the concept of state sovereignty?	108	
15	Can I assess the role of state sovereignty in promoting and enforcing human rights?	108	

	For a complete understanding of this topic:	Page No.	✓
16	Can I describe the role of the United Nations in international responses to human rights issues?	108–9	
17	Can I describe the role of intergovernmental organisations in international responses to human rights issues?	109–10	
18	Can I describe the role of courts, tribunals and independent statutory authorities in international responses to human rights issues?	110–11	
19	Can I describe the role of non-government organisations in international responses to human rights issues?	111	
20	Can I describe the role of the media in international responses to human rights issues?	111	
21	Can I evaluate the effectiveness of international responses in promoting and enforcing human rights?	112–13	
22	Can I outline how human rights are incorporated into Australian domestic law?	113–14	
23	Can I describe the role of the Australian Constitution, including division of powers and separation of powers, in Australia's domestic responses to human rights issues?	114–15	
24	Can I describe the role of common law in Australia's domestic responses to human rights issues?	115	
25	Can I describe the role of statute law in Australia's domestic responses to human rights issues?	116	
26	Can I describe the role of courts and tribunals in Australia's domestic responses to human rights issues?	116–17	
27	Can I describe the role of non-government organisations in Australia's domestic responses to human rights issues?	118	
28	Can I describe the role of the media in Australia's domestic responses to human rights issues?	118	

Useful resources

Acts

Australia

Anti-Terrorism Act (No. 2) 2005 (Cth) (See Section 2.2.6, page 121.)

Australian Constitution Act (No. 1) 1842 (UK) (See Section 2.1.2, page 102.)

Australian Human Rights Commission Act 1986 (Cth) (See section 2.2.5, page 116.)

Disability Discrimination Act 1992 (See Section 2.2.5, page 116.)

Human Rights (Sexual Conduct) Act 1994 (Cth) (See Section 2.2.5, page 117.)

Native Title Act 1993 (Cth) (See Section 2.2.6, page 122.)

Northern Territory National Emergency Response Act 2007 (Cth) (See Section 2.2.6, page 122.)

Public Schools Act 1866 (NSW) (See Section 2.1.2, page 104.)

Racial Discrimination Act 1975 (Cth) (See Section 2.2.5, page 116.)

Social Security Act 1991 (Cth) (See Section 2.2.5, page 116.)

Stronger Futures in the Northern Territory Act 2013 (Cth) (See section 2.2.6, page 122.)

Other jurisdictions

Education Act 1870 (UK) (See Section 2.1.2, page 103.)

Great Reform Act 1832 (UK) (See Section 2.1.2, page 102.)

Voting Rights Act 1965 (US) (See Section 2.1.2, page 103.)

Treaties/Conventions

African Charter on Human and Peoples' Rights 1981 (See Section 2.1.3, page 107.)

Charter of the United Nations 1945 (See Sections 2.1.1 [page 95] and 2.1.3 [page 106].)

Convention Against Torture and Other Cruel, Inhuman or Degrading Treatment or Punishment (UN, 1984) (See Section 2.1.3, page 107.)

Convention on the Elimination of All Forms of Discrimination Against Women (UN, 1979) (CEDAW) (See Section 2.1.3, page 107.)

Convention on the Elimination of All Forms of Racial Discrimination (UN, 1965) (See Section 2.1.3, page 107.)

Convention on the Prevention and Punishment of the Crime of Genocide (UN, 1948) (See Section 2.1.3, page 107.)

Convention on the Rights of the Child (UN, 1989) (See Section 2.1.3, page 107.)

Convention relating to the Status of Refugees (UN, 1951) (See Section 2.3.2, page 124.)

Declaration on the Right of Peoples to Peace 1984 (See Section 2.1.3, page 107.)

Declaration on the Rights of Indigenous Peoples 2006 (See Sections 2.1.2 [page 104] and 2.1.3 [page 107].)

European Convention for the Protection of Human Rights and Fundamental Freedoms 1953 (See Section 2.1.3, page 107.)

General Act of Brussels 1890 (See Section 2.1.2, page 100.)

International Covenant on Civil and Political Rights 1966 (ICCPR) (See Sections 2.1.1 [page 95] and 2.1.3 [page 107].)

International Covenant on Economic, Social and Cultural Rights 1966 (ICESCR) (See Sections 2.1.1 [page 96] and 2.1.3 [page 107].)

Kyoto Protocol 1998 (See Section 2.1.2, page 105.)

Paris Agreement on Climate Change 2015 (See Section 2.1.2, page 10.)

Slavery Convention 1926 (See Section 2.1.2, page 100.)

Supplementary Convention on the Abolition of Slavery, the Slave Trade and Institutions and Practices Similar to Slavery 1956 (See Section 2.1.2, page 100.)

Treaty on the Non-Proliferation of Nuclear Weapons 1968 (See Section 2.1.2, page 105.)

Universal Declaration of Human Rights 1948 (See Sections 2.1.1 [page 95] and 2.1.3 [page 106].)

Case studies

A v Australia, UNHRC, (1997) (See Case Study 2.3, Section 2.2.5, pages 117–18.)

Abdulrahman v Toll Pty Ltd NSW ADT (2006) (See Section 5.3.1, page 334.)

Dietrich v The Queen (1992) 177 CLR 292 (See Section 2.2.5, page 115.)

Lange v Australian Broadcasting Corporation, High Court, 8 August 1997 (See Section 2.2.5, page 115.)

Mabo and Others v State of Queensland (No. 2) (1992) 175 CLR 1 (See Case Study 2.1, Section 2.2.5, page 115.)

McInnes v The Queen (1979) 143 CLR 570 (See Section 2.2.5, page 115.)

Minister for Immigration and Citizenship v Haneef (2007) FCAFC 203 (See Case Study 1.4, Section 1.2.1, page 13.)

Toonen v Australia, UNHRC, (1994) (See Case Study 2.2, Section 2.2.5, page 117.)

Other documents

Constitution of the United States of America, and amendments (US) (See Section 2.1.2, page 99.)

Declaration of Independence 1776 (US) (See Section 2.1.2, page 99.)

Declaration of Rights 1689 (UK) (See Section 2.1.2, page 98.)

Declaration of the Rights of Man and the Citizen 1789 (France) (See Section 2.1.2, page 99.)

Magna Carta 1215 (UK) (See Section 2.1.2, page 98.)

Organisations and websites

Australia

NSW Civil and Administrative Tribunal (NSW) (See Section 2.2.5, page 117): www.ncat.nsw.gov.au

Anti-Discrimination Board (NSW) (See Section 2.2.5, page 116): www.lawlink.nsw.gov.au/adb

Australian Human Rights Centre (See Section 2.2.5, page 118): www.austlii.edu.au/ahric

Australian Human Rights Commission (Cth) (AHRC) (See Section 2.2.5, page 116): www.hreoc.gov.au

Australians for Native Title and Reconciliation: www.antar.org.au

Australian Red Cross: www.redcross.org.au

Australian Treaties Library: www.austlii.edu.au/dfat

NSW Council for Civil Liberties (See Section 2.2.5, page 118): www.nswccl.org.au

Refugee Council of Australia (See Section 2.3.2, page 125): www.refugeecouncil.org.au

International

American Civil Liberties Union: www.aclu.org

Amnesty International (See Sections 2.2.2 [page 111] and 2.2.5 [page 118]): www.amnesty.org

Anti-Slavery International (See Section 2.1.2, page 100): www.antislavery.org

Association of Southeast Asian Nations (See Section 2.2.2, page 110): www.asean.org

Commonwealth of Nations (See Section 2.2.2, page 110): www.thecommonwealth.org

Derechos (This is an international human rights organisation whose website contains information on human rights situations around the world): www.derechos.org

European Court of Human Rights (See Section 2.2.2, page 110): www.echr.coe.int

European Union (See Section 2.2.2, page 109): www.europa.eu

Human Rights Internet: www.hri.ca

Human Rights Watch (See Section 2.2.2, page 111): www.hrw.org

International Criminal Court (See Section 2.2.2, page 110): www.icc-cpi.int

International Criminal Tribunal for the former Yugoslavia (See Section 2.2.2, page 110): www.icty.org

International Federation of Red Cross and Red Crescent Societies (See Section 2.2.5, page 118): www.ifrc.org

International Labour Organisation (ILO) (See Section 2.1.2, page 100): www.ilo.org

North Atlantic Treaty Organisation (NATO) (See Section 2.2.2, page 109): www.nato.int

Oxfam International (See Section 2.3.2, page 125): www.oxfam.org

United Nations: www.un.org

United Nations Human Rights, Office of the High Commissioner for Human Rights: www.ohchr.org [Information can be found on this website about the following committees: Committee on Economic, Social and Cultural Rights (CESCR); Committee on the Elimination of Discrimination Against Women (CEDAW); Committee on the Elimination of Racial Discrimination (CERD); Committee Against Torture (CAT) and Optional Protocol to the Convention against Torture (OPCAT); Committee on the Rights of the Child (CRC); Committee on Migrant Workers (CMW); Committee on the Rights of Persons with Disabilities (CRPD)] (See Section 2.2.2, page 109).

United Nations Security Council (See Section 2.2.2, page 109): www.un.org/securitycouncil

Working group for an ASEAN Human Rights Mechanism (See Section 2.2.2, page 110): www.aseanhrmech.org

World Council of Churches: www.oikoumene.org

World Health Organisation (See Section 2.1.2, page 100): www.who.int

End of chapter questions

KCq Key Concept questions

These questions test whether you have grasped the key ideas in each subsection. They are not difficult questions, but will test your recall of knowledge of the material you have read. If you are unsure what a question is asking you to do, refer to page ix to check the meaning of the NESA key words. If you can answer all these questions, you will know you have a sound knowledge of content.

Refer to pp. 454–7 for Answers

2.1 The nature and development of human rights

2.1.1 The definition of human rights

1. Define *human rights*.

2. List and explain four fundamental properties of human rights.

3. Define *civil rights* and *political rights*, giving an example of each.

4. Define *economic rights*, *social rights* and *cultural rights*, giving an example of each.

5. List three examples of 'third generation' rights.

6. Explain what you need to do in order to define *human rights*.

2.1.2 Developing recognition of human rights

7. List three factors which have contributed to the developments of concepts of human rights.

8. Identify four movements that have contributed to the development of concepts of human rights.

9. When did the movement to end slavery begin?

10. Which European country was the first to abolish slavery?

11. Describe slavery in Australia. When did it end?

12. When was the first international agreement regarding the abolition of slavery signed?

13. Describe the incidence of slavery today.

14. Explain how the Industrial Revolution prompted the development of trade unions.

15. What is the ILO, and when and why was it formed?

16. List three benefits the trade union movement has secured for Australian workers.

17. Define *universal suffrage*.

18. When was each of the following gained in Australia?

    a universal male suffrage

    b female suffrage

    c complete universal suffrage

19. Discuss how Australia's record on universal suffrage compares to that of other nations.

20. Why is education for all seen as a right?

21. When was universal education established in Australia?

22. How widespread is the right to universal education today?

23. Define and give two examples of *collective rights*.

24. Define and give two examples of *self-determination*.

25. Why is it difficult to protect environmental rights?

26. What is the *right to peace*?

27. Explain what you need to do in order to outline how human rights have changed and developed over time.

28. Explain what you need to do in order to investigate the evolving recognition and importance of universal human rights.

2.1.3 Formal statements of human rights

29. Why is the United Nations Charter important in the development of the protection of human rights?

30. What do ICCPR and ICESCR stand for?

31. What three documents make up the *International Bill of Rights*?

32. List four other treaties which protect human rights.

33. Explain what you need to do in order to examine major human rights documents and explain their contribution to the development of human rights.

2.2 Promoting and enforcing human rights

2.2.1 State sovereignty

34. What is *state sovereignty*?

35. List three points you can make to assess the role of state sovereignty in promoting and enforcing human rights.

2.2.2 The roles of various organisations in international responses

36. What is the purpose of the United Nations Human Rights Council?

37. Explain what the *Universal Periodic Review* is.

38. Name four IGOs which promote the protection of human rights.

39. Explain the role of the ICC in protecting human rights.

40. List four international tribunals which have had, or now have, a role in protecting human rights.

41. Name four treaty-based committees who monitor compliance with various human rights treaties.

42. List three roles of human rights treaty based authorities.

43. Explain what an NGO is and give an example of one that operates in the field of human rights.

44. List two roles the media plays in protecting human rights.

2.2.3 The effectiveness of international responses in promoting and enforcing human rights

45. List nine factors which limit the effectiveness of international responses in promoting and enforcing human rights.

2.2.4 The incorporation of human rights into Australian domestic law

46. List the ways that human rights are protected in Australia.

2.2.5 The roles of various legal frameworks and organisations in Australian responses

47. To what extent does the division of powers prevent the protection of human rights in Australia?

48. Describe how well the Australian Constitution protects human rights.

49. State one example of how the common law has protected human rights in Australia.

50. State one example of how the common law has restricted human rights in Australia.

51. State an example of one statute that protects human rights in Australia.

52. Describe the role of the Australian Human Rights Commission.

53. Explain how international treaties become part of Australia's domestic law.

54. State one example of how domestic courts and tribunals have protected human rights in Australia.

55. Explain the significance of the Toonen case and the case of *A v Australia*.

56. Briefly describe the role played by NGOs in protecting human rights in Australia.

57. Briefly describe the role played by the media in protecting human rights in Australia.

58. What is a *Charter of Rights*?

59. State one argument for and one argument against the proposition that Australia should have a Charter of Rights.

60. Explain what you need to do in order to outline how human rights are incorporated into Australian domestic law.

2.2.6 The effectiveness of Australian domestic responses in promoting and enforcing human rights

61. Describe Australia's overall record on human rights compared to other nations.

62. Explain what you need to do in order to evaluate the effectiveness of Australian domestic responses in promoting and enforcing human rights.

2.3 Investigation of a contemporary human rights issue

2.3.1 Contemporary struggles for human rights

63. List three contemporary struggles for human rights.

2.3.2 The contemporary human rights issue of the treatment of refugees

64. Define *refugee*.

65. In 2009, how many people fell under the formal definition of a *refugee*?

66. Name the international convention governing refugees, and name three of its provisions.

67. Describe the aim of the UNHCR.

68. List three options that are available for refugees.

69. List two NGOs whose work is in the area of refugees, and list four of their functions.

70. How many refugees were granted asylum in Australia in 2007–08? How does this compare with other countries?

71. When can people be detained under Australia's *Border Security Legislation Amendment Act 2002*?

2.3.3 The effectiveness of legal and non-legal responses to the issue of treatment of refugees

72. State two reasons why citizens in the developed Western-world may be becoming less compassionate towards those seeking asylum.

73. Explain how the media is both effective and ineffective in its response to the treatment of refugees.

74. Explain why Australia has been criticised for its treatment of onshore asylum seekers, and explain Australia's response to these criticisms.

75. Explain what you need to do in order to investigate the contemporary human rights issue of the treatment of refugees and evaluate the effectiveness of legal and non-legal responses to this issue.

2.4 Themes and challenges

2.4.1 Theme 1: The changing understanding of the relationship between state sovereignty and human rights

76. Explain how the concept of state sovereignty can assist in the protection of human rights.

77. Explain how the concept of state sovereignty can hinder the protection of human rights.

2.4.2 Theme 2: Issues of compliance and non-compliance in relation to human rights

78. List three reasons why states choose to comply with international human rights law.

79. List three reasons why states may choose not to comply with international human rights law.

2.4.3 Theme 3: The development of human rights as a reflection of changing values and ethical standards

80. Describe the growth in understanding of human rights.

81. Explain what is meant by the statement that 'human rights are a Western concept'.

2.4.4 Theme 4: The role of law reform in protecting human rights

82. List three agencies that bring about legal reform in the area of human rights protection.

83. Identify one area of human rights law that is in need of reform.

2.4.5 Theme 5: The effectiveness of legal and non-legal measures in protecting human rights

84. Outline two factors which limit the effectiveness of human rights protection in Australia.

85. Outline two factors which have limited the effectiveness of international human rights protection.

HSC Sample HSC questions

Now for the real thing! The following questions are modelled on the types of questions you will face in the HSC. Think about it: if you get extensive practice at answering these sorts of questions, you will be more confident in answering them when it comes to the HSC Exam. It makes sense, doesn't it?

Another reason is that the answers given at the back of this guide are structured in a way that helps you learn strategies on how to answer HSC-like questions. This will help you aim for full marks! The questions in this section match the numbered syllabus areas in the chapter, so you can test yourself on each section while you read through the study guide or at the end of the chapter if you prefer.

▶ For each objective-response question there will be the correct answer, a section reference where you can find the correct answer in the chapter and, where required, an explanation and reasons why all the other answers are incorrect.

▶ For each short-answer question you will have a detailed answer with an explanation of what the question is asking you to do and also, when needed, an examiner's plan to help you get full marks with a section reference to where you can find the answer in the chapter.

When you mark your work, highlight any questions you found difficult and earmark these areas for extra study.

Refer to pp. 458–60 for Answers

OBJECTIVE-RESPONSE QUESTIONS 15 min

1. Which of the following is an example of an economic right?

   A universal suffrage

   B the right to own and not be arbitrarily deprived of property .

   C an adequate standard of living

   D education   (1 mark)

2. By which of the following methods are human rights primarily protected in Australia?

   A the Australian Bill of Rights

   B the United Nations Declaration of Human Rights

   C the Australian Constitution

   D statute law   (1 mark)

3. Which of the following could best be classified as protecting collective rights?

   A the International Covenant on Civil and Political Rights

   B the Convention on the Elimination of All Forms of Discrimination against Women

   C the Kyoto Protocol

   D the Convention on the Rights of the Child
                                            (1 mark)

4. Which of the following is one way in which NGOs can assist in the protection of human rights?

   A expelling non-compliant member states

   B making official reports to the UN

   C raising public awareness of human rights abuses

   D applying sanctions to states that abuse human rights   (1 mark)

5. Which of the following documents does **not** form part of the International Bill of Rights?

   A the Charter of the United Nations

   B the International Covenant on Civil and Political Rights

   C the International Covenant on Economic, Social and Cultural Rights

   D the Universal Declaration of Human Rights
                                            (1 mark)

6. What is the primary organisation that monitors compliance with human rights treaties?

   A the Human Rights Council

   B the UN Security Council

   C the Office of the High Commissioner for Human Rights

   D the Universal Periodic Review   (1 mark)

7. Which of the following best describes the role of the ICC in protecting human rights?

   A It acts as an international human rights complaint mechanism.

   B It can hear cases about gross violations of human rights.

   C It can impose sanctions on nations that breach human rights treaties.

   D It can compel the Security Council to undertake humanitarian intervention.   (1 mark)

8. The argument that economic development is more important than individual political freedom goes against which of the following characteristics of human rights?

   A Human rights are inalienable.

   B Human rights are inherent.

   C Human rights are indivisible.

   D Human rights are universal.   (1 mark)

9. Which of the following exists in Australia to aid in the protection of human rights?

   A a legislative Charter of Rights

   B an entrenched Bill of Rights

   C a national human rights court

   D the separation of powers   (1 mark)

10. Which of the following is a valid criticism of the Australian Human Rights Commission?

    A It has too much power.

    B It does not listen to complaints from individuals.

    C It has no power to make binding orders.

    D It is not independent from the government of the day.   (1 mark)

SHORT-ANSWER QUESTIONS 1 h

In your answer you will be assessed on how well you:
- use your knowledge and relevant legal case study/studies
- communicate using relevant legal terminology and concepts
- present a logical, well-structured answer to the question.

Question 1 10 min

a Explain the idea of national sovereignty.   (2 marks)

b Explain how the idea of national sovereignty can limit the protection of human rights internationally.   (3 marks)

(TOTAL 5 marks)

Question 2 12 min

Describe three ways in which human rights are incorporated into domestic Australian law.   (6 marks)

Question 3 10 min

a Define the terms *intergovernmental organisation* and *non-government organisation*.   (2 marks)

b Using an example, explain how one intergovernmental organisation contributes to the protection of human rights.   (3 marks)

(TOTAL 5 marks)

Question 4 12 min

Describe two movements that have contributed to the developing recognition of human rights.   (6 marks)

Question 5 8 min

Describe how two collective human rights are protected internationally.   (4 marks)

Question 6 8 min

'Australia is the only Western democracy which does not have a Charter of Rights.'

Argue for **or** against the proposition that Australia should have a Charter of Rights.   (4 marks)

Chapter 3

Consumers

Principal focus

Through the use of contemporary examples, students investigate the legal rights of consumers and the effectiveness of the law in achieving justice for consumers.

Themes and challenges

The following five themes and challenges are incorporated throughout this chapter, and are summarised in Sections 3.4.1 to 3.4.5 (pages 187–95). They are to be considered throughout your study of this topic.

▶ **1** The role of the law in encouraging cooperation and resolving conflict in regard to consumers
▶ **2** Issues of compliance and non-compliance
▶ **3** Laws relating to consumers as a reflection of changing values and ethical standards
▶ **4** The role of law reform in recognising the rights of consumers
▶ **5** The effectiveness of legal and non-legal responses in achieving justice for consumers

HSC CONTENT

	You learn to:
The nature of consumer law	▶ outline the developing need for consumer protection. ▶ outline the objectives of consumer law. ▶ examine the nature, function and regulation of contracts. ▶ evaluate the effectiveness of the regulation of marketing, advertising and product certification in achieving consumer protection. ▶ examine the role of occupational licensing in achieving consumer protection.
Consumer redress and remedies	▶ recognise the importance of awareness and self-help. ▶ examine the range of different remedies available to consumers. ▶ evaluate the effectiveness of non-legal and legal measures in achieving justice for consumers.
Contemporary issues concerning consumers	▶ identify and investigate contemporary issues involving the protection of consumers and evaluate the effectiveness of legal and non-legal responses to these issues.

© NSW Education Standards Authority, *Legal Studies Stage 6 Syllabus*, 2009, pp. 22–3

3.1 The nature of consumer law

3.1.1 The developing need for consumer protection

Changes to consumerism

Today, there are many laws that protect consumers from various business practices. These laws have developed over the last century because the economic structure of society has changed radically over the last 200 years, and there has been a developing need for consumer protection.

Rural subsistence society

Before the Industrial Revolution, in the eighteenth and nineteenth centuries, most people provided their own goods and services. They lived in villages and towns, grew their own grains, fruit and vegetables and raised their own livestock which were used for both food and clothing. They knew the makers and sellers of the few items they needed to buy, and there were not very many products to choose from.

The Industrial Revolution

With the Industrial Revolution, people moved from their small local market situations to large cities. They worked in factories and no longer supplied their own essential needs. Instead, they manufactured products and received wages, which were then used to buy goods or services people had previously supplied themselves (such as vegetables, meat and clothing). People needed to rely on goods produced by individuals or companies they didn't know and which were often produced in factories miles away from the place of purchase. Also, a wide range of new products became available.

Caveat emptor and laissez faire

In the altered circumstances described above, it became easier for consumers to be misled or to be sold an inferior or defective product. The concept of *caveat emptor* ('Let the buyer beware') operated. This meant that, if a consumer was mistreated by someone who sold them something, there was very little he or she could do about it. There was no government interference in the deals made between buyers and sellers. The philosophy that governments should not interfere in private negotiations between people is termed *laissez faire*.

It became evident that the notions of *caveat emptor* and *laissez faire* did not provide sufficient protection to consumers in the marketplace so, gradually, laws were developed that prevented unfair business practices and protected consumers. The state has become increasingly involved in protecting consumers by passing laws of this type.

Early consumer protection laws

Both common law and statute law gradually recognised the necessity for protecting consumers from unfair business practices. For example, the case of *Donoghue v Stevenson* (1932) AC 562, is a famous case in the development of the common law which recognised that manufacturers have a duty to consumers to provide goods of a certain quality (see Case Study 3.4, Section 3.1.7, page 155).

An early example of statute law intervening in consumer affairs is the *Factories and Shops Act 1912* (Cth) which was passed to deal with, among other things, deceptive and misleading advertising. Another early example of consumer protection law is the *Sale of Goods Act 1923* (NSW).

This act, which still operates today, was a landmark piece of legislation because it put into statute law the concept that goods should be of merchantable quality (see Section 3.1.5, page 151).

Advertising grew because of the advancement of technology and because of the new methods available to sell products (such as cinema, radio and telephone). These changes led to increased use of credit, and consumers were exposed to new hazards involving harsh credit arrangements. Legislation was also passed to deal with these changes, including the *Hire Purchase Agreement Act 1941* (NSW). The issue of credit is discussed in Section 3.3.1 (pages 170–76).

The urban mass-consumption/production society

As the twentieth century progressed, the mass production of goods became more efficient and goods that were once considered luxury items (such as cars) became cheaper and more available to ordinary people. As technology increased, many new products were also developed and ordinary people had a greater range of products from which to choose. With this increase in consumption, protection of consumers became a matter of concern to many ordinary citizens.

The modern consumer movement

In the 1960s, a grassroots self-help consumer movement developed as many Western consumers became dissatisfied with inferior and unsafe products. In the USA and Britain, in particular, the call for consumer protection from ordinary people was strong. Ralph Nader's book, *Unsafe at Any Speed: The designed-in dangers of the American automobile* (Grossman, New York, 1965), and the effects of the drug thalidomide, sparked similar calls from Australians. This worldwide consumer attitude led to the establishment of consumer groups, such as the Australian Consumer Association, in 1959 (see Section 3.2.6, page 167), and the International Organisation of Consumer Unions (IOCU).

The IOCU was established in 1960 by the USA, Australia, the UK, Belgium and the Netherlands. It is now called Consumers International. The modern consumer movement led to international recognition of consumer rights as well as to more extensive laws to protect consumer rights in Australia.

International consumer rights

The movement for consumer rights led to the establishment of a list of basic consumer rights, in 1962, by the US President John Kennedy, and this list was later added to by the IOCU. The eight rights the list outlines are:

- the right to safety
- the right to be informed
- the right to choose
- the right to be heard
- the right to satisfaction of basic needs
- the right to redress
- the right to consumer education
- the right to a healthy environment.

The United Nations adopted these rights in the United Nations Guidelines for Consumer Protection in 1985, and they were updated in 1999.

The challenges of globalisation and technology

Globalisation refers to the growing economic and social interdependence and interconnectedness of countries worldwide, part of which is the process whereby goods and services available in one country are the same as those offered worldwide.

Globalisation brings new challenges to consumer protection because many goods and services are now produced, marketed and distributed for a global market. The gap between the knowledge and power of consumers and that of suppliers is even greater in a global market.

Other challenges for consumers today are raised by recent advances in technology (such as the advances involving the internet and genetically modified food). The law is just beginning to deal with these new challenges.

CAN YOU outline the developing need for consumer protection?

To outline the developing need for consumer protection, you need to be able to:

- describe the rural subsistence economy
- describe the effects of the Industrial Revolution
- describe the concepts of *caveat emptor* and *laissez faire*
- list early consumer laws
- describe the modern consumer movement
- describe the impact of globalisation on consumers.

 page 189

3.1.2 The definition of *consumer*

Define the term *consumer*.

There are many different laws relating to consumers and they differ in the way they define *a consumer*. Generally, the law defines a consumer as a person who acquires goods and services in a transaction for his or her own personal or household use. He or she may acquire these goods and services through full cash payment or through credit arrangements.

Some consumer laws include as *consumers* small businesses which acquire products for their business, while other laws exclude them. For example, under the *Competition and Consumer Act 2010* (Cth) consumers are defined as those people who acquire goods and services under $40 000, or goods and services of a kind normally used for personal or domestic purposes.

 page 189

3.1.3 Objectives of consumer laws

Outline the objectives of consumer laws.

As has been seen in Section 3.1.1 (pages 145–7), as the modern consumer marketplace has developed, the gap between the knowledge and power of consumers and that of manufacturers and retailers has widened, with consumers becoming more reliant on what is told to them by manufacturers and sellers.

All consumer transactions are based on contracts (see Section 3.1.4, pages 148–51). The basis of contract law is that all parties to a contract are in equal bargaining positions. However, this is not the case in most consumer transactions. The law recognises this anomaly and tries to remedy the imbalance. Both the common law and legislation are aimed to ensure that there is justice in consumer contracts and that consumers are not treated unfairly. The law does this by:

- regulating exclusion clauses (Section 3.1.4, page 150)
- implying standards into contracts (see Sections 3.1.4 [page 150] and 3.1.5 [pages 151–2])

▶ protecting consumers against unfair contracts, through legislation such as the *Contracts Review Act 1980* (NSW) (see Section 3.1.6, pages 153–4)

▶ making allowances for problems of language and literacy (see Section 3.1.6, page 154).

▶ providing remedies for breaches of contract (see Section 3.1.6, page 154)

▶ regulating advertising and marketing, including product certification (see Section 3.1.8, pages 156–7)

▶ licensing occupations (see Section 3.1.9, pages 159–62)

▶ providing avenues for consumer redress and remedies (see Sections 3.2.1 to 3.2.9 [pages 162–70])

▶ providing legal responses to contemporary issues concerning consumers, including product certification and marketing innovations (see Sections 3.3.1 to 3.3.2 [pages 170–77]).

So the objectives of consumer law can be summarised as:

▶ to equalise the bargaining power between consumers and manufacturers and sellers

▶ to protect the rights of consumers (see Section 3.1.1, pages 145–7)

▶ to assist in resolving disputes between consumers and suppliers (see Sections 3.2.2 to 3.2.8 [pages 163–9])

▶ to provide redress when problems between consumers and suppliers arise (see Section 3.2.8, pages 167–9)

CAN YOU outline the objectives of consumer law?

To outline the objectives of consumer law, you need to be able to:

▶ list the four objectives referred to above

▶ list the rights of consumers, as shown in Section 3.1.1 (page 146)

▶ explain why consumer protection laws have become increasingly necessary.

KCq page 189

Describe contracts (types, elements, terms, exclusion clauses).

3.1.4 Contracts

A *contract* is a legally binding agreement. The law of contract is the basis of law about consumer rights, because every consumer transaction involves a contract. The law of contract is founded in common law but there are also many statutes in this area.

State and federal governments act concurrently in the area of consumer protection. The Australian Constitution limits the ability of federal government to make laws in this area. The *Trade Practices Act 1974* (Cth) is the major piece of federal legislation regarding consumer contracts and can apply only to practices by corporations. Therefore, this legislation can only protect consumers who have dealings with corporations. The Trade Practices Act has now been replaced by the *Competition and Consumer Act 2010* (Cth) with the purpose of establishing a national consumer law using the best practice of state and territory governments. The effect of this on consumer contracts within NSW, if any, remains to be seen (see Section 3.4.4, pages 180–2).

In NSW, the *Fair Trading Act 1987* (NSW) duplicates most of the consumer protection measures contained in the Competition and Consumer Act and so consumers are also protected when dealing with suppliers of goods and services that are not corporations. These statutes are only two of the many that exist to protect consumers in a wide range of transactions. The common law also plays an important role in the area of consumer contracts. The common law applies unless an act of parliament states otherwise.

Types of consumer contracts

The law of contract is the basis of law about consumer rights. Every consumer transaction involves a contract. There are two main types of consumer contract:

▶ a contract for goods and services. This is the main type of consumer contract and involves one party (the supplier) supplying goods (the product) or service to the other party (the consumer) in exchange for money. This type of contract is discussed in this section, and in Sections 3.1.5, 3.1.6 and 3.1.7 (see pages 151–5).

▶ a contract for credit.

Elements of a contract

For an agreement to be a contract—that is, for an agreement to be legally enforceable (binding)—there must be three basic elements: offer and acceptance, consideration and the intention to enter into legal relations.

Offer and acceptance

For there to be a contract, one party must offer something and the other party must accept that offer—otherwise there is no agreement, which is the essence of a contract. When you buy a product from a shop, handing over the money constitutes an offer by you (the consumer). Taking the money constitutes acceptance of the offer by the shop (the supplier). If you wish to pay a lower price for the product, perhaps because it is faulty, you make a different offer to the shop proprietor who can accept or reject your offer.

Consideration

This is the term for the exchange of value between the parties. In a normal consumer transaction, one party pays a sum of money and the other provides goods or services. So something of value has been exchanged. A gift to someone is not an example of a contract, because value has gone only one way. The giver of the gift does not receive something of value in return.

Intention to enter legal relations

Though it is seldom stated in consumer transactions, it is clearly the intention of both parties (the buyer and the seller) to enter into legal relations. The seller would expect to be able to use the law to force the buyer to pay for goods or services, and the buyer would also expect the law to uphold his or her rights. An agreement between friends, or between a husband and wife, often does not have any such intention behind it and is, therefore, not a contract.

Written and oral contracts

When most people think of contracts, they think of signing documents. However, a contract can also be an oral agreement. An oral contract is only enforceable once it has been carried out, whereas a written contract can be enforced before it is carried out. For example, if someone says that he or she will sell you his or her car for $1000, you cannot force that person to do so. But if there is a signed document containing that promise, it can be enforced in a court.

Terms of contracts

A *term of a contract* is a promise contained within a contract that makes up an agreement. Terms can be categorised as follows.

▶ An *express term* is one that is actually spoken or written into a contract. An example of an express term is as follows: One party says, 'I will sell you a chair for $30.' The other party accepts. An express term of the contract is that the price is $30.

▶ An *implied term* is a promise that a statute or common law puts into a contract, even though such a term was not discussed by either party to the contract. For example, when one party says, 'I will sell you a chair for $30' and the other party accepts and pays the money, it will be implied by the law that the chair will be fit to sit on. Neither party has discussed whether or not this is the case, but the court will imply that this is a term of the contract. The terms implied into consumer goods and services contracts are described in Section 3.1.5 (pages 151–2).

▶ A *condition* is a term fundamental to the contract. Without the condition, the contract does not exist. In the case of the $30 chair, for example, it is a condition of the contract that one party pays $30. If he or she only pays $15, there is no contract.

▶ A *warranty* is a term that is part of the contract but is not fundamental. If a warranty is breached (or broken), the contract still exists.

The distinction between conditions and warranties is important because different remedies are available if breaches occur. If a condition is breached, the contract is rescinded (that is, it can be put aside and avoided). If a warranty is breached, the contract is not rescinded but damages may be payable to the party suffering loss (see Section 3.2.8. page 167).

Regulating exclusion clauses

Many traders have tried to make the terms implied by the law inapplicable to their contract through exemption or exclusion clauses. Through such clauses, traders try to restrict their liability if something goes wrong. However, they cannot always do this because of provisions that are in place. For example, terms implied by the *Fair Trading Act 1987* (NSW) and the *Competition and Consumer Act 2010* (Cth), such as those described in Section 3.1.5 (pages 151–2), cannot be excluded.

In common law, an exclusion clause is part of a contract for which there is a signed document. However, an exclusion clause which is not part of a signed document will only operate if the trader took reasonable steps to draw the clause to the attention of the consumer before the contract was made. A famous case that illustrates this is *Thornton v Shoe Lane Parking Ltd* (1971) 2 QB 163, outlined in Case Study 3.1 below.

The common law will also often interpret an exclusion clause narrowly; saying it only applies to very particular circumstances, not to all the circumstances intended by the trader.

CASE STUDY 3.1: *Thornton v Shoe Lane Parking Ltd* (1971) 2 QB 163

Facts

Thornton drove into the parking station, taking a ticket from an automatic machine as he did so. On the ticket was a clause exempting the parking station from all liability for any damage done to the car, its contents and to people. When Mr Thornton returned to the car park to collect his car, he suffered an injury. The injury was caused, at least in part, by the negligence of the parking station.

Issue

Was the parking station liable for an injury sustained by Mr Thornton while he was in the parking station, or did the exclusion clause operate to exempt it from liability?

Decision

The court said that the clause did not operate because the driver had no opportunity to reject the contract and, therefore, the clause. Once the ticket was taken by Mr Thornton, the contract was made; he had agreed to enter the parking station. The company did not take reasonable steps to draw the exemption clause to the attention of the consumer before the contract was made.

 page 189

3.1.5 Standards implied by statutes

Explain standards implied by statutes.

Implied standards

The common law, the *Competition and Consumer Act 2010* (Cth), the *Sale of Goods Act 1923* (NSW) and the *Fair Trading Act 1987* (NSW) all imply terms into consumer contracts that relate to the standard of goods or services sold. This means that both common law and statute law put promises or terms into contracts that the parties may never have discussed, but that the law says are there anyway (see Section 3.1.4, page 150).

The Competition and Consumer Act only applies to goods and services supplied by corporations. The Sale of Goods Act only applies to goods, not to services, and applies to goods bought via a written contract for personal or domestic use. The terms implied by the Fair Trading Act do not apply to consumer contracts made before 28 June 2003. The common law applies to other circumstances not covered by the acts.

There are five basic standards implied into consumer contracts which cannot be excluded from a contract. These were first implied by the common law but are now also implied by the statutes listed above. These basic standards are:

- **the person supplying the goods has the right to do so**. It is a condition of a contract that the supplier of the goods owns the goods or has been given the right to sell them by the owner. For example, if you sell your uncle's car without his permission, you have breached a condition of the contract.

- **the goods fit the description**. This is a condition of a consumer supply contract. If a consumer buys goods on the basis of a description given by a supplier, then the goods must answer that description or comply with promotional material. For example, if you order a black lamp and receive a red one, a condition of the contract has been breached.

- **the goods are of merchantable quality**. This means that the goods are of a standard fit for the purpose or purposes for which they are usually sold, taking into consideration the price and description of the goods. For example, if you buy a chair that breaks as soon as you sit on it, that chair is not of merchantable quality and a condition of the contract has been breached. Exceptions to this are:
  - if the goods have been examined by the buyer and there are defects that the buyer should have seen

  - if the buyer bought the goods knowing they were defective. For example, if a consumer bought a dress that was stained for a cheaper price because of this defect, that consumer cannot later claim a refund because the dress is stained.

Case Study 3.7, in Section 3.2.5 (page 166), is an example of a case about merchantable quality.

- **the goods are fit for their purpose**. It is a condition of a contract that goods sold must be fit for the purpose for which they are sold, when the seller has been made aware of the purpose for which the goods are required by the buyer. Because this overlaps with the implied term that goods are of merchantable quality, it mostly applies if the goods are sold for an unusual purpose.

- **the goods must conform to a sample**. If a consumer buys goods, such as carpet, by reference to a sample, then it is a condition of the contract that the whole conforms to the sample. If the carpet sample is brown and the carpet arrives with a blue streak in the middle, this condition would have been breached.

The above five standards apply to contracts for goods (products). There are also some standards that apply to the supply of a service. Services, such as the repair of an item, must all be carried out in a reasonable and competent manner. This is a warranty rather than a condition, because the contract for the supply of the repaired goods that needed servicing is not completely overturned if this term is not met. Services also must be carried out with parts fit for the purpose.

The *Competition and Consumer Act 2010* (Cth) requires manufacturers and importers to ensure that spare parts and repair facilities are reasonably available. What is reasonable is determined by the nature of the product and its 'expected useful life'. Generally, a manufacturer or importer is not obliged to ensure spare parts and repair facilities are available after ten years from the sale of the product.

Voluntary and mandatory standards

As well as the implied terms of contract outlined above, published standards operate. These standards are published documents that set out criteria necessary to ensure that a material or method will consistently do the job it is intended to do. There are two types of standards, voluntary and mandatory, as described below.

Voluntary standards

Primarily, voluntary standards are developed by Standards Australia, a body whose function is to write standards. Manufacturers and suppliers are not obliged to follow voluntary standards, but many do so because they can then assure consumers that their products are of good quality and meet established standards. If they meet such standards, manufacturers and suppliers can certify their products as meeting these standards. Product certification is the process that confirms that a product or service meets the relevant or necessary standards (see Sections 3.1.8 [page 157] and 3.3.1 [pages 170–3]).

Mandatory standards

Mandatory standards are standards which are made compulsory by legislation such as the *Competition and Consumer Act 2010* (Cth) and the *Fair Trading Act 1987* (NSW). Some mandatory standards were developed first as voluntary standards and then became mandatory. These include the standards for sunglasses and for children's toys.

Food standards are mandatory and are developed by Food Standards Australia New Zealand (FSANZ). State and territory health departments enforce these standards. For example, the NSW Food Authority, ensures compliance with the standards under the *Food Act 2003* (NSW) (see Sections 3.1.8 [pages 156–9], 3.2.2 [page 163] and 3.3.1 [page 170]).

The Australian Competition and Consumer Commission (ACCC) (see Section 3.2.3, page 164) enforces other mandatory standards by:

- undertaking random market surveys
- responding to complaints
- acting promptly against offending suppliers
- issuing mandatory product recalls.

Suppliers of goods that are banned or do not comply with a mandatory product standard may be subject to fines of up to $1.1 million for corporations and $220 000 for individuals, under the Competition and Consumer Act. The same fines also apply for failure to comply with a mandatory recall order. Case Study 3.2 below is an example of court action against a supplier of baby products which breached mandatory standards.

Product recall

Product recall refers to a product being removed from availability for sale and an announcement being made for the return of any of the products which have already been sold. Under both the Fair Trading Act and the Competition and Consumer Act, products which are unsafe can be recalled. Recalls are usually voluntary and it is up to the consumer to respond to the recall and return the defective item. Products can also be recalled if they do not meet mandatory standards.

CASE STUDY 3.2: *Australian Competition and Consumer Commission v Skippy Australia Pty Ltd (2006) FCA 1343*

Facts

The Commonwealth Director of Public Prosecutions (DPP), following information provided by the ACCC, laid several charges against Skippy Australia Pty Ltd on 20 April 2006. The DPP alleged that two types of baby walkers and one type of cot supplied by Skippy Australia Pty Ltd failed to meet mandatory safety standards.

Decision

The Federal Court found that both types of baby walker failed to comply with safety features prescribed in the Australian standard for baby walkers, which had been mandatory since November 2002, and that the cot failed to comply with safety standards for cots which had applied since 1998. The court fined the company a total of $860 000.

KCq page 189

3.1.6 Unjust contracts

> Describe unjust contracts (common law and statutory protection).

The *Contracts Review Act 1980* (NSW), the *Competition and Consumer Act 2010* (Cth) and the common law operate so that contracts that are unjust are not enforceable. The Contracts Review Act offers the widest protection in this area, though it only applies to consumer contracts. The Contracts Review Act defines the term 'unjust' as including 'unconscionable, harsh or oppressive'.

Under this act, in deciding whether or not a contract is unjust, the court will look at all the circumstances surrounding entry into the contract. Some factors the court can consider are:

- the age, education and literacy of the parties
- the mental capacity and state of intoxication of the parties

▶ the way in which the contract is expressed

▶ whether any undue pressure was applied to either party to sign the contract

▶ the opportunity for negotiation and for obtaining independent legal advice.

If a contract is found to be unjust, the court can vary, cancel or refuse to enforce part or all of that contract. A well-known case in this area is that of *Blomley v Ryan* (1956) 99 CLR 362 (see Case Study 3.3 below).

CASE STUDY 3.3: *Blomley v Ryan* **(1956) 99 CLR 362**

Facts

Ryan, while in a state of intoxication, contracted to sell his farming property to Blomley. Blomley knew that Ryan was intoxicated and uneducated, and contracted to buy the property for far below its market value.

Issue

Was this contract unjust?

Decision

The court said that this was an unjust contract and so could not be enforced. This case was decided under common law rules.

Problems of language and literacy

The *Competition and Consumer Act 2010* (Cth), the *Contracts Review Act 1980* (NSW) and the common law will not enforce contracts if one party, because of language problems, did not understand the contract.

Remedies for breach of contract

Remedies available to consumers for breach of contract are discussed in Section 3.2.8 (pages 167–9) and include repair, refund, replacement, payment of damages, rescission and modification of contract, special orders, injunctions and specific performance. The types of remedy that will apply in a particular situation will depend on what legislation applies and the nature of the breach.

CAN YOU **examine the nature, function and regulation of contracts?**

To examine the nature, function and regulation of contracts, you need to be able to:

▶ define *contract*

▶ list the two main types of consumer contracts

▶ explain that the function of consumer contracts is to regulate the behaviour between consumers and sellers, and between consumers and credit providers

▶ explain the nature of a contract, by describing its elements

▶ explain how terms, both express and implied, form contracts, and how the common law and statutes imply terms about the quality of goods and services into contracts

▶ list the laws which regulate contracts

▶ describe the circumstances under which a contract will be found to be unjust

▶ list remedies for breach of contract.

KCq pages 189–90

3.1.7 The role of negligence in consumer protection

The people who enter into a contract are called the *parties to a contract*. For example, in a consumer contract for goods, the consumer enters into a contract with the seller of the goods—the consumer and the seller are the parties to the contract. The manufacturer of the goods does not have a contract with the consumer. The manufacturer is not a party to the contract.

Under the doctrine of privity of contract, only the parties to a contract can have the contract enforced. Other people (third parties), who may suffer loss because of breach of the contract (such as negligence on the part of one of the parties) cannot have it enforced. However, the doctrine of privity of contract has been modified by the law, through the common law of torts and through statutory amendments, including product liability laws.

The law of torts provides a way for third parties to a consumer contract to receive damages for loss. So, if a consumer suffers damage because of the negligence of a manufacturer, the law of torts provides a remedy, even though there is no contract between the consumer and the manufacturer. *Donoghue v Stevenson* (1932) AC 562 is a famous case in this area. See Case Study 3.4 below.

> Explain the role of negligence in consumer contracts.

CASE STUDY 3.4: *Donoghue v Stevenson* (1932) AC 562 (House of Lords)

Facts

Mrs Donoghue visited a café with a friend who bought her a bottle of ginger beer, which she drank. The bottle of ginger beer contained a decomposed snail. Mrs Donoghue suffered severe bouts of nausea and gastroenteritis.

Issue

Was the manufacturer of the ginger beer liable for the damages suffered by Mrs Donoghue? Mrs Donoghue's friend had a contract with the seller, not the manufacturer, and Mrs Donoghue had no contract with anyone. Under the rule of privity of contract there is no claim against the manufacturer because Mrs Donoghue had no contract with the manufacturer.

Decision

The court decided that under the law of torts, a person who could reasonably have foreseen that negligent action on his or her part could affect another person owes a duty of care to that person. So, the manufacturer owed a duty of care to the possible consumer of the goods manufactured, even if this person was not the purchaser. Therefore, Mrs Donoghue was paid damages by the manufacturer even though she had no contract with him.

The *Competition and Consumer Act 2010* (Cth) also stipulates that manufacturers and importers must make certain guarantees, one of which is a guarantee of the merchantable quality of goods. So consumers can claim against manufacturers and importers covered by this act even though they have no contract with them. Product liability laws were introduced under amendments made to the *Trade Practices Act 1974* in 1992. These laws allow any person who is injured as a result of defective goods to claim compensation from the manufacturer. There is no need for that person to prove negligence, breach of contract or breach of statutory duty.

KCq page 190

Explain the regulation of marketing and advertising: statutory protection, and non-statutory controls on advertising.

3.1.8 Regulation of marketing and advertising

Advertising, while often irritating, offers a valuable service to consumers because it informs them of the range and price of available products, thereby giving them information and freedom of choice. Businesses are free to advertise their goods and services but they are not free to deceive, mislead or harass consumers. So consumers are protected from exploitation. The regulation of marketing and advertising includes regulation through legislation and statutory authorities, as well as self-regulation by industries themselves.

Statutory controls

General standards

As production and consumption moved away from rural subsistence, consumers needed to rely on the honesty and ethics of the producers and hope that the advertising claims they made for their products were true. This expectation was called the 'general standard' and could be enforced under common law.

The *Competition and Consumer Act 2010* (Cth) and the *Fair Trading Act 1987* (NSW) both operate to protect consumers from unfair advertising and marketing practices. Both contain general provisions which state that sellers of goods and services cannot engage in conduct that is misleading, deceptive or unconscionable (unfair). This includes a wide range of practices. Case Study 3.5 below is a recent example of misleading advertising.

CASE STUDY 3.5: *Australian Competition and Consumer Commission v Prouds Jewellers Pty Ltd* (2008) FCA

Facts

Prouds jewellers advertised certain jewellery using price comparisons, such as 'Was $199/Now $99.50'. These advertisements appeared in the February 2006 *Summer of Love* catalogue and the May 2006 *Love You Mum* catalogue. However, the products advertised had not, in fact, been offered for sale at the 'Was' prices during the period immediately prior to the sale period when the 'Now' prices applied.

Issue

Was the 'Was/Now' advertising misleading, given that the products were not available at the 'Was' price during the period immediately prior to the sale period?

Decision

The Federal Court held that the advertising conduct by Prouds was, in fact, misleading and in breach of the *Trade Practices Act 1974* (Cth). This was because hypothetical consumers would reasonably assume that they would save the difference between the 'Was' and 'Now' prices if they bought the products in the sale period, and this was not the case. Prouds consented to implement a trade practices compliance program.

Specific requirements

Both the *Competition and Consumer Act 2010* (Cth) and the *Fair Trading Act 1987* (NSW) contain specific requirements which prohibit businesses from certain practices, such as:

- bait and switch advertising (in which a business advertises an item at a low price in order to lure a customer into a store, but the product is not available when the customer tries to buy it, and he or she is then offered a similar product at a higher price)

- harassing or coercing a consumer into buying a product
- unordered goods. (Both acts state that unordered goods received by consumers do not need to be paid for, and become the property of the consumer after three months. The consumer is also not responsible for any accidental damage to such goods.)

The *Competition and Consumer Act 2010* and the *Fair Trading Act 1987* restrict many other marketing practices, such as pyramid selling and referral selling. Traders who do engage in unfair marketing and advertising practices are liable to criminal prosecution and penalties, and a consumer who suffers a loss because of such practices is entitled to compensation (see Section 3.2.8, pages 167–9).

Other statutes control advertising and marketing practices. For example, the *Motor Dealers Act 1974* (NSW) states that motor dealers must provide certain information to potential buyers of second-hand cars. They must also offer guarantees for limited periods for cars sold that are less than ten years old and have travelled less than 160 000 kilometres.

Direct commerce refers to practices which involve goods being advertised and then being bought by a consumer from his or her own home, such as door-to-door sales and telephone sales. This includes cases when a consumer is asked to buy a product through the mail. Direct commerce has increased dramatically in Australia in the last ten years, particularly through telephone selling and the advertising of products on the internet. These kinds of direct commerce represent marketing innovations and are discussed in Section 3.3.3 (page 173).

Product certification

Product certification is the process that confirms that a product or service meets the relevant or necessary standards. Many businesses certify that their products comply with certain standards, in order to sell more products. For example, manufacturers of foodstuffs may certify that their product meets the standards required to bear the Heart Foundation tick, or that their product meets other health standards. A growing area of product certification is the claim by some businesses that their product is 'green' (that is, that the products are environmentally-friendly). As for all other advertising, businesses may not make claims about their products, or certify that they meet certain standards if these claims are not true. Product certification is discussed in Section 3.3.1 (pages 170–3).

Non-statutory controls on advertising

Much of the advertising industry is subject to non-statutory controls through industry self-regulation, as well as government imposed regulation, such as the *Competition and Consumer Act 2010* (Cth). The Advertising Standards Bureau (ASB) administers a national system of advertising self-regulation. It can investigate, through the Advertising Standards Board and the Advertising Claims Board, complaints about most forms of advertising, including complaints about the use of language, discriminatory portrayals, violence, sex and nudity.

Both the Advertising Standards Board and the Advertising Claims Board make determinations under the Australian Association of National Advertisers (AANA) Advertiser Code of Ethics. There are also various other self-regulatory codes regarding advertising such as the AANA Code for Advertising and Marketing Communications to Children. These codes are to be adhered to by advertisers. The self-regulation system is based on the idea that advertisers benefit from ensuring that advertisements meet community standards, because consumers are more likely to be influenced by the advertisements if they trust the integrity of the advertising industry.

Consumers who have a complaint about an advertisement can complain to Ad Standards, which can order the withdrawal of the advertisement. If it is an advertisement that is broadcast on radio or television, the consumer can complain to the broadcaster, who must respond within thirty days. If the consumer is still dissatisfied, he or she can complain to Ad Standards or the Australian Communications and Media Authority (ACMA) (see Section 3.2.3, page 164). If the ACMA finds the complaint is justified, this can lead to penalties such as the withdrawal of the advertisement or, in some cases (such as the case discussed in Case Study 3.11 involving Radio 2UE Sydney, see page 175), financial penalties (see Section 3.3.2, pages 173–77).

The effectiveness of non-statutory controls on advertising, such as the AANA Advertiser Code of Ethics, is sometimes called into question. Some argue that self-regulation is not sufficient to regulate the industry. However, these non-statutory controls work in conjunction with statutory controls, such as the *Competition and Consumer Act 2010* (Cth). The effectiveness of statutory and non-statutory controls is illustrated in Case Study 3.6 below.

Case study 3.6: '"Myth-busting" Coke adverts get busted', *The Age*, 3 April 2009

Facts

In October 2008, Coca-Cola ran a series of advertisements in the print media stating that various myths about the detrimental health effects of Coca-Cola had been 'busted'. Part of these advertisements said:

> ▶ Myth: Makes you fat.
>   Busted. No one single product makes you fat...
> ▶ Myth: Packed with caffeine.
>   Busted...
> ▶ Myth: Rots your teeth.
>   Busted... there's no reason why you can't enjoy Coca-Cola.

Complaints made to the Advertising Standards Bureau late in 2008 were dismissed. Complaints were then lodged with the ACCC.

Issue

Were the advertisements misleading and, therefore, illegal under the *Trade Practices Act* 1974?

Decision

The ACCC (see Section 3.2.3, page 164) found that the advertisements were 'totally unacceptable', saying that the advertisements created an impression 'which is likely to mislead, that Coca-Cola cannot contribute to weight gain, obesity and tooth decay. They also had the potential to mislead parents about the potential consequences of consuming Coca-Cola.' Coca-Cola was ordered to publish corrective advertising.

The Australian Consumer Association (see Section 3.2.6, page 167) said that the ACCC's decision underlined that advertisers 'are out of line with community standards' and that this highlighted the failure of the advertising industry to effectively regulate itself.

Source: '"Myth-busting" Coke adverts get busted', *The Age*, 3 April 2009.

CAN YOU evaluate the effectiveness of the regulation of marketing, advertising and product certification in achieving consumer protection?

In order to do this, you need to discuss the factors which enhance, and those which limit, the effectiveness of the regulation of marketing, advertising and product certification in achieving consumer protection. Then you need to decide how effective the regulation is, given the two sets of factors you have discussed. These factors are listed below.

Factors which help ensure the effectiveness of the regulation

(Also refer to Sections 3.3.1 and 3.3.2, pages 170–77.)

▸ Advertising offers a valuable service to consumers because it informs them of the range and price of available products, thereby giving them information and freedom of choice.

▸ Regulation means that businesses may not deceive, mislead or harass consumers.

▸ The legislative framework makes a wide range of advertising practices unacceptable.

▸ There is a range of remedies available to consumers who have suffered because of misleading advertising practices.

▸ The ACCC works with companies who have breached the law, to ensure they know what practices are unacceptable and so prevent future breaches.

▸ There are effective complaints mechanisms for consumers who are offended by an advertisement.

▸ Advertising self-regulation is effective because advertisers benefit from ensuring that advertisements meet community standards, since consumers are more likely to be influenced by the advertisements if they trust the integrity of the advertising industry.

Factors which limit the effectiveness of the regulation

(Also refer to Sections 3.3.1 and 3.3.2, pages 170–77.)

▸ The effectiveness of the regulation of marketing, advertising and product certification relies on consumer awareness.

▸ The ACCC has limited power to deal with false product claims and has called on the federal government to give it more power in this area and to allow for the imposition of heavy fines (see Section 3.3.1, page 173).

▸ Some argue that self-regulation by bodies such as the ASB is ineffective because these industry-funded bodies are not sufficiently aware of prevailing community standards.

KCq page 190

3.1.9 Occupational licensing

Describe occupational licensing.

An *occupational licence* is a permit to practise in a particular profession or occupation. Many occupations (such as tradesmen, builders, architects, lawyers and doctors) are very specialised. The people who practise in such occupations need specialised knowledge, and the consumer usually knows very little about the work being performed. So people in these occupations are given licences, without which they cannot practise. A consumer is then able to know that the person they are dealing with is qualified and competent to do the work required. Licensing protects the consumer from incompetent and faulty work. Occupational licensing occurs through either state regulation or self-regulation.

Self-regulation

Self-regulation occurs when a particular trade or occupation imposes its own licensing restrictions on people who practise in that occupation.

Self-regulation often takes the form of adopting codes of practice which list obligations of members of that particular occupation or industry. For example, most accountants are members of Certified Practising Accountants Australia (CPA Australia). Members of this organisation are required to observe a code of professional conduct. If they do not, they can face disciplinary hearings run by CPA Australia and, if found guilty of breaching the code, can face fines and forfeiture of membership.

The effectiveness of self-regulation is called into question by the finding by the industry-funded Advertising Standards Bureau that some Coca-Cola advertisements were acceptable, when the same advertisements were later found to be totally unacceptable by the ACCC (see Case Study 3.6, Section 3.1.8, page 158).

State regulation

In some industries and occupations, permission to practise is regulated by the state. This means the government, through legislation, gives people in that particular occupation permission to practise. Government regulation is used for many occupations and professions (such as builders, auctioneers, insurance agents, pawnbrokers, and motor car dealers and repairers).

Motor car dealers and repairers

Under the *Motor Dealers and Repairers Act 2013* (NSW), a person must hold a dealer's licence before he or she can undertake business or advertise as a motor car dealer. Licences are granted by the Director-General of the Office of Fair Trading (NSW). If a person operates as a dealer without a licence, he or she can face a penalty in the form of a fine. Dealers who are involved in fraudulent conduct or who fail to comply with the Motor Dealers and Repairers Act can have their licences cancelled.

Licences to repair motor vehicles are granted under the same Act and are overseen by NSW Fair Trading. Disputes between a consumer and repairer are dealt with first by NSW Fair Trading and then, if not resolved, by the NSW Civil and Administrative Tribunal (NCAT). A licence can be removed if the licence holder is dishonest, incompetent or performs substandard work.

Combined state regulation and self-regulation

Some professions or occupations have a combination of self-regulation and state regulation. This is called co-regulation. Regulation of the advertising industry, discussed in Section 3.1.8 (pages 156–9), is an example of co-regulation.

Another example of co-regulation is the regulation of the legal profession which, until recently, was entirely self-regulation. Now a combination of self-regulation and state regulation operates. The Law Society is a self-regulating body which grants certificates of practice to solicitors. The Bar Association, also a self-regulating body, grants permits for barristers to operate. Both bodies may only grant such certificates if the Legal Profession Admission Board, a government body, decides a particular person may be admitted to the legal profession.

In 1994, the Legal Services Commissioner was established through amendments to the *Legal Profession Act 1987* (NSW) because of complaints by consumers about the ineffectiveness of the Law Society and the Bar Association in investigating complaints against legal practitioners. Now all three bodies can investigate consumer complaints against lawyers. If the complaint is very serious, it may be referred to the Administrative

Decisions Tribunal. Lawyers who infringe the *Legal Profession Act 1987* can be reprimanded, ordered to pay compensation to the client concerned or, in very serious cases, be disbarred from practising.

Reviewing licensing decisions

Legislation which provides for occupational licensing also provides for review of decisions by the licensing authority. If a person seeking a licence or certificate is not granted one, or has that licence or certificate removed, he or she can seek a judicial review of the decision (that is, he or she can go to court to have the decision examined). The Consumer and Commercial Division of the NCAT can also examine licensing decisions (see Section 3.2.5, pages 165–6).

Advantages and disadvantages of occupational licensing

The advantages of occupational licensing for consumers include the following.

▶ Some type of licensing of occupations is necessary so consumers can know they are dealing with an honest, skilled and reliable person, and that, if there is a problem, there is a mechanism for addressing it. The recently increased legal control of lawyers has been beneficial to consumers because complaints are better handled than they were previously.

▶ Regulation can force businesses to examine their practices to see if the consumer is being adequately catered for.

▶ Licensing of occupations enhances the reputation of the whole industry and gives consumers increased confidence.

The disadvantages of occupational licensing for consumers include the following.

▶ Occupational licensing may be time consuming and costly for the occupations concerned, and reduce profitability for providers of goods and services. This ultimately harms consumers, because lack of profitability either creates price rises or leads to the failure of businesses which reduces competition between suppliers.

▶ Occupational licensing can create monopolies. If a certain group is the only group with licences, then that group can prevent others from carrying out work and can charge very high fees. For example, when the legal profession was self-regulatory, it prevented anyone else from undertaking conveyancing. Since 1992, others are able to undertake conveyancing. National Competition Policy also prevents monopolies occurring.

▶ Self-regulatory frameworks may not be sufficient to adequately protect consumers (see Case Study 3.6, Section 3.1.8, page 158).

CAN YOU **examine the role of occupational licensing in achieving consumer protection?**

To examine the role of occupational licensing in achieving consumer protection, you need to be able to:

▶ define *occupational licensing*

▶ describe types of occupational licensing, with examples

▶ explain the advantages and disadvantages of occupational licensing for consumers

▶ comment on the importance of occupational licensing for consumers. You should note that occupational licensing is only one method of protecting consumers from shoddy and inadequate workmanship. There are many other remedies as well (see Section 3.2.8, pages 167–9).

 KCq page 190

3.2 Consumer redress and remedies

Consumer redress refers to ways that consumers can achieve a just outcome for a consumer transaction in which they have been wronged. The term *consumer redress* includes both the processes of gaining redress and the remedies available for fixing the problem.

There are numerous ways in which consumers can gain redress if they feel they have been wronged in a consumer transaction. These involve:

▶ self-help

▶ state government organisations

▶ federal government organisations

▶ industry organisations

▶ tribunals and courts

▶ non-government organisations.

There are also numerous bodies and organisations that can assist consumers and can supply information and advice about consumer rights and about particular products.

Remedies available to consumers are also numerous. These are discussed in Section 3.2.8 pages 167–9).

3.2.1 Awareness and self-help

Assess the value of awareness and self-help.

In many consumer matters, the best method of gaining consumer rights is to go directly to the person or business that has wronged the consumer. This means making a complaint to the supplier or manufacturer. Consumers are often best advised to try to remedy a situation themselves.

If a consumer complains about defective goods to the retailer or manufacturer, the business is often only too happy to give a refund or to repair or replace the faulty item. Most businesses rely on good customer relations and wish to keep customers happy (see Section 3.4.2, page 178). The consumer has the right to a refund if goods are defective, and many businesses will give a refund even if the goods are not defective but are merely the wrong size or colour.

Unsatisfactory services can often be dealt with very effectively in a similar manner. If a consumer receives a service with which he or she is unhappy, the situation can usually be remedied satisfactorily by complaining to the provider of that service.

Awareness is vital to consumers. If consumers are aware of their rights and are careful in choosing products when they buy them, many consumer problems can be avoided. It is far better to make a wise decision in the first place than to try to remedy a situation when a defect has been discovered after the product has been purchased. Various government and non-government organisations can assist consumers in making wise choices (see Sections 3.2.2 [below], 3.2.3 [page 164] and 3.2.6 [page 167]).

CAN YOU **recognise the importance of awareness and self-help?**

If consumers are aware of their rights and are careful in choosing products when they buy them, many consumer problems can be avoided. Also, self-help is often the quickest, cheapest way of solving a consumer problem. If a consumer complains about defective goods or services, the business is often only too happy to rectify the problem. Most businesses rely on good customer relations and wish to keep customers happy, to enhance their own profitability.

 page 190

3.2.2 State government organisations

Mediation and conciliation

Describe state government organisations that can assist consumers.

If consumers cannot gain suitable remedies independently, the next most sensible method of obtaining redress is to approach a body which can mediate between the consumer and the retailer or manufacturer. Mediation is the process whereby a third person, called a mediator or conciliator, listens to the two parties to the dispute and makes suggestions in an effort to bring the two parties to agreement. Mediation is also called conciliation. There are several NSW state government organisations that can assist with consumer complaints, some of which use mediation or conciliation to resolve disputes.

The NSW Office of Fair Trading can supply free written information about consumer rights, and will answer particular enquiries over the phone, by e-mail or in person. This organisation has primary responsibility for investigating complaints about unfair or dishonest commercial practices and for taking action against those at fault. It can also investigate a complaint on behalf of a consumer if the consumer has not received suitable redress via his or her own approach to the business concerned. This organisation can negotiate/mediate with the business, but cannot order the business to do anything.

Other NSW state government bodies which can provide redress for consumers include:

- the Legal Services Commissioner, who addresses complaints about lawyers (see Section 3.1.9, page 161)
- compensation funds for consumers who have had dealings with motor dealers or travel agents, set up under licensing legislation (see Section 3.1.9, page 160)
- the Health Care Complaints Commission, which addresses complaints about health professionals, and can refer a matter which may be assisted by conciliation to the Health Conciliation Registry
- the NSW Food Authority which ensures compliance with the *Food Act 2003* (NSW) This authority ensures that the food industry adheres to safe food production and handling, licenses businesses that produce food, and supervises labelling compliance. The NSW Food Authority can act

on complaints received by consumers in many ways, including issuing warnings, making inspections, suspending licences, or taking court action as it did in the case of misrepresentative labelling by Fuze drinks in 2009 (see Case Study 3.8, Section 3.3.1, page 171). KCq page 190

3.2.3 Federal government organisations

Describe federal government organisations that can assist consumers.

▶ **The Australian Competition and Consumer Commission (ACCC)** provides information and guidance to consumers and businesses about their rights and obligations under the law. The ACCC also has investigative and enforcement powers under the *Competition and Consumer Act 2010* (Cth) (see Case Study 3.2, Section 3.1.5 [page 153], Case Study 3.5, Section 3.1.8 [page 156] and Case Study 3.9, Section 3.3.1 [page 172]).

▶ **The Australian Securities and Investments Commission (ASIC)** is responsible for enforcing laws regarding financial services. ASIC can provide information and advice to consumers about how to resolve difficulties they have with a financial service, such as a sharebroker, an insurance provider or a superannuation provider.

▶ **The Australian Communications and Media Authority (ACMA) is** responsible for the regulation of broadcasting, the internet and telecommunications. The ACMA works closely with industry self-regulatory regimes, and ensures industry compliance with licence conditions, codes and standards (see Section 3.1.8 [page 158] and Case Study 3.10, Section 3.3.2 [page 174]).

▶ **The Commonwealth Consumer Affairs Advisory Council (CCAC)** is a federal government organisation which is a part of the Federal Department of Treasury. It provides policy advice to government on consumer protection.

▶ **The Legislative and Governance Forum on Consumer Affairs (CAF)** consists of ministers from the Commonwealth, state, territory and New Zealand governments. It considers consumer policy issues of national significance and tries to develop a consistent approach to these issues. It also provides information on consumer rights (see Section 3.4.4, page 180). KCq page 190

Describe industry organisations that can assist consumers.

3.2.4 Industry organisations

Consumers can also gain assistance and advice from the relevant trade, professional or industry bodies. Many industry organisations have been established and some are willing to put pressure on a member who is not dealing with a consumer complaint adequately. Examples of industry bodies are CPA Australia, which supervises accountants (see Section 3.1.9, page 160); Ad Standards, which regulates the advertising industry (see Section 3.1.8, page 158); and the Law Society of NSW (see Section 3.1.9, page 161). Other bodies have been set up to investigate complaints and resolve disputes in particular industries, such as the Telecommunications Industry Ombudsman and other Ombudsman's offices for other industries.

Some industries have set up their own dispute settling mechanisms for consumers. These mechanisms include mediation and, if that is not successful, arbitration.

Arbitration occurs when a third party listens to the parties to a dispute and makes a decision based on the merits of the case. There are several industry-based and industry-funded dispute resolution schemes, which use conciliation and arbitration to settle disputes between consumers and businesses in the industry. Complaints are heard at no cost to the consumers. Some of these organisations are discussed in detail below.

Australian Financial Complaints Authority (AFCA)

The Australian Financial Complaints Authority (AFCA) commenced operation on 1 November 2018. It replaced the Financial Ombudsman Service (FOS), which was established in 2008. The FOS consolidated services previously supplied by various other organisations, such as the Banking and Financial Services Ombudsman, the Financial Industry Complaints Service, and the Insurance Ombudsman Service. This organisation hears complaints about a wide range of financial services including banking, credit, insurance and investment.

If a consumer is unhappy with a financial, insurance or investment product or service, he or she should complain to the financial service provider in the first instance. If this is unsuccessful, AFCA will offer mediation and, finally, if this fails to reach a solution, makes an award on the matter. This award is binding on the trader if the consumer agrees to it. If the consumer is unhappy with the decision, he or she can pursue the matter in the courts.

The Telecommunications Industry Ombudsman (TIO)

The Telecommunications Industry Ombudsman (TIO) deals with disputes regarding telecommunications services. The process involves referral to the trader, and mediation. The Ombudsman can make an award of up to $10 000 and recommendations up to $50 000. **KCq** page 190

Describe the role of tribunals and courts.

3.2.5 The role of tribunals and courts

If self-help and approaching government, non-government and industry organisations prove ineffective, then the consumer can have the matter determined by a tribunal or court.

Consumer and Commercial Division of the NSW Civil and Administrative Tribunal (NCAT)

The Consumer and Commercial Division of the NSW Civil and Administrative Tribunal (NCAT) can make various orders to redress consumer dissatisfaction.

For claims concerning motor vehicles repairs and consumer matters, the tribunal can hear disputes up to a monetary limit of $30 000, except for cases involving new cars in which the tribunal can make orders for any sum.

The NCAT provides a quick and inexpensive alternative to the court system in consumer matters. Before a hearing takes place, the tribunal must try to bring the disputing parties to agreement through conciliation. If agreement does not occur, then the tribunal will conduct a hearing into the matter.

This division of NCAT must act expeditiously (without undue delay) and, while it does not have to follow the rules of evidence, it does have to follow rules of procedural fairness. Legal representation is *not* generally permitted.

The tribunal has the power to make a wide range of orders which can be enforced by the courts if necessary (see Section 3.2.8, pages 167–9). Appeals can be made to the NSW Supreme Court on a question of law. Case Study 3.7 below is an example of a hearing by the Consumer, Trader and Tenancy Tribunal (CTTT)—in place prior to the NCAT— which was appealed in the Supreme Court.

CASE STUDY 3.7: 'Scratching the surface'

Facts

A consumer applied to the Consumer, Trader and Tenancy Tribunal to have her new car replaced after efforts to remedy defective paintwork on the car failed. Dark marks, which were rough to touch, had appeared all over the vehicle. Both the car owner and the car dealer had tried various ways of removing the marks, but without success.

The tribunal determined that the new car had failed the test of 'merchantable quality' required under section 19 of the *Sale of Goods Act 1923*, and ordered that a new car be provided to the applicant by the company.

Issue

The car company appealed to the Supreme Court, saying that the appropriate remedy was that it be permitted to carry out further repair work, and that the tribunal had made an error in law when it ordered that the owner be given a new car.

Decision

The judge rejected this argument and said the *Consumer Claims Act 1998* allows the tribunal to require a business to replace goods related to a claim. She further said that the standard for merchantable quality is what one might reasonably expect with regard to circumstances, such as the price paid. If the defendant had wanted a car with retouched paintwork, she might have purchased a second-hand car for a lower price.

Source: 'The Consumer, Trader and Tenancy Tribunal Annual Report, 2006–2007', p. 31

The role of the courts

The NSW and Federal Court systems can hear a wide range of civil matters including those to do with consumer transactions arising out of the law about contracts and torts.

The NSW Local Courts can hear matters involving amounts of up to $100 000. The District Court can hear matters involving amounts of between $100 000 and $750 000. The Supreme Court can hear matters involving amounts of over $750 000. Courts are often slow, and legal representation can be expensive—so courts should be regarded as a last resort for consumers. Appeals can also be made to the courts from tribunals. Appeals from the NCAT, for instance, can be made to the Supreme Court on matters of law (see Case Study 3.7 above).

Class actions

A class action is one in which several people who have been harmed by the activities of someone else take the case to court jointly. Such action is also called representative action.

One of the problems with consumer protection laws has been that only individuals could take court action. As most consumer complaints are about relatively small amounts, many people were unwilling to take court action because of the expense involved. However, since amendments made to the *Competition and Consumer Act 2010* in 1992, class actions have become available. Such action can be taken by injured consumers against manufacturers and distributors of dangerous products.

A High Court decision in February 1995 increased the possibility of class action in NSW. This case, *Carnie v Esanda Finance Co. Ltd* (1995) 182 CLR 398, gave a wide interpretation to NSW Supreme Court rules regarding class actions. In 2005, the NSW Civil Procedure Rules were amended to provide a wide scope for class actions similar to those which operate in the federal sphere. The Federal Court already provided wide-ranging rules regarding class action. KCq page 190

3.2.6 The role of non-government organisations

Non-government organisations are very important to consumers because they can provide valuable advice and assistance, particularly in assisting consumers to choose wisely when they buy. Two widely used non-government organisations are:

▶ **Choice** (formerly the Australian Consumers Association [ACA]). This is a large private consumers' organisation which publishes *Choice* magazine. This monthly publication provides members with an analysis of numerous products and their disadvantages and advantages.

▶ **the NRMA**. This organisation advises member consumers about their rights against vehicle sellers and manufacturers. It also assesses cars for sale, on consumer request, and can inform a consumer of any defects a car may have. Unlike Choice (the ACA), which is a not-for-profit organisation, the NRMA is also a business that sells insurance. KCq page 190

Describe the role of non-government organisations.

3.2.7 The role of the media

Newspapers, radio and television often provide information about faulty products and unfair practices conducted by some businesses. The media may also, on occasion, conduct a publicity campaign on behalf of consumers who are dissatisfied with a product or service.

The media also plays an enormous role in consumer affairs by advertising new products. Lifestyle television shows and the like are useful tools for consumers because they can alert them to new products and processes coming onto the market. KCq page 190

Describe the role of the media in consumer protection.

3.2.8 Consumer remedies

A remedy is something that fixes a wrong action. There are numerous remedies available to consumers who have been wronged in a consumer transaction. Some can be gained by consumers themselves. Some can be ordered by statutory bodies, such as tribunals, or by the courts.

Refunds, repairs and replacements

Consumers can usually gain remedies for defective goods or services simply by going to the supplier of the goods or services. A 'no refund' sign in a shop does not apply to defective goods (that is, a consumer has a right to a refund if goods are defective, even if such a sign is displayed). Courts and tribunals also can order refunds, repairs and replacements.

Describe and assess the range of consumer remedies.

Damages

The word *damages* refers to money paid by one party involved in a transaction to the other party, in order to compensate for loss suffered by that party.

Various types of damages can be ordered by a court. These include:

▶ **restitution damages**. The plaintiff is given value for benefits he or she has provided to the defendant so far.

- **reliance damages**. The plaintiff is compensated so that he or she will be in the same position as before the contract was entered into.

- **expectation damages**. The plaintiff is compensated so that he or she is in the position he or she would have been in if the contract had been fulfilled.

- **injured feelings**. These are additional damages awarded to compensate for mental trauma suffered because of a breach of contract.

Rescission and modification of contract

If a contract is unfair or a condition of it has been breached, the contract can be rescinded (that is, the contract is at an end). The buyer does not have to complete his or her part of the bargain and can sue for damages in a court. Rescission of contract can be ordered by a court, and tribunals can make orders with similar effects.

A contract can also be modified or varied by a court to achieve a just outcome (see Section 3.1.6, pages 153–4).

Special orders

Under the *Fair Trading Act 1987* (NSW), the *Competition and Consumer Act 2010* (Cth) and other pieces of legislation, courts and tribunals can make a wide variety of special orders such as:

- an order to vary or void a contract
- an order to perform specific work
- an order to pay money owed
- an order to refund or replace defective goods
- and order to publish corrective advertising. Both the Australian Competition and Consumer Commission (ACCC) and the NSW Office of Fair Trading can order persons to display advertisements which correct a deceptive impression made by an earlier advertisement (see Case Study 3.6, Section 3.1.8 [page 158]). Courts can make similar orders.

Injunctions and specific performance

An *injunction* is an order for someone to do or to refrain from doing something.

Courts and tribunals can order injunctions. Their effect is often to make sure someone completes work he or she promised to carry out, or to stop someone from doing something that would damage the other party.

Specific performance is an order that requires the parties to a contract to do those things which their contract requires, in order to settle and define the parties' rights.

EXAMPLE Specific performance

In a contract for the sale of land, the seller must sign a document that can be registered at the Land Titles Office, transferring ownership to the buyer. If the seller does not sign such a document, an order of specific performance can be made requiring him or her to do so.

Criminal prosecutions

Both the Australian Competition and Consumer Commission (ACCC) and the NSW Office of Fair Trading can initiate criminal prosecutions against persons who contravene various consumer protection statutes. In the case of the *Competition and Consumer Act 2010* (Cth), fines of up to $500 000 for persons and $10 million (or other conditions) for corporations can be imposed for failure to comply with the Australian Consumer Law provisions of the act. Failure to comply with other provisions, such as mandatory product standards can attract much bigger fines (see Case Study 3.2, Section 3.1.5, page 153).

Remedies for society

Criminal prosecutions represent a remedy for society rather than for individual consumers because all of society benefits from the punishment of offenders, and such punishments deter offending traders from committing other offences and prevent them from profiting from their offence. Other traders are also deterred from committing similar offences. Special orders which compel businesses to publish corrective advertising, and product recall orders (see Sections 3.1.5 [page 153], 3.1.8 [pages 157–8] and 3.2.9 [pages 169–70]) also protect the whole of society from unscrupulous traders and defective products.

CAN YOU **examine the range of different remedies available to consumers?**

To do this, you need to describe the remedies outlined in Section 3.2.8 and explain how each assists consumers and society to achieve justice.

 KCq page 190

3.2.9 The effectiveness of non-legal and legal measures in achieving justice for consumers

Table 3.1 summarises the types of consumer redress available, and the advantages and disadvantages of each. Consumer remedies, also listed in the table, are discussed in Section 3.2.8 (pages 167–9).

Table 3.1 Consumer redress: Processes, remedies, advantages and disadvantages

Processes, Remedies	Advantages	Disadvantages
1. **Awareness and self-help** (NON-LEGAL MEASURE) *Remedies:* ▸ refund ▸ repair ▸ replacement	▸ Very inexpensive. ▸ Quick. ▸ Awareness means consumers can make wise decisions in the first place. ▸ Consumers can often get the result they desire.	▸ May not result in a solution.
2. **State and federal government organisations and mediation** (NON-LEGAL MEASURE) *Remedies:* ▸ refund ▸ repair ▸ replacement	▸ Very inexpensive. ▸ Quick. ▸ The solution often suits both parties. ▸ Often a desirable result is reached.	▸ Mediation cannot order suppliers to do something, so a result may not occur.
3. **Industry organisations and arbitration** (NON-LEGAL MEASURE) *Remedies:* ▸ compensation ▸ refund ▸ specific performance	▸ Usually free. ▸ Quick. ▸ Mediation usually also available. ▸ An order is given if no solution is reached.	▸ May operate to protect the industry rather than the consumer. ▸ Limited amounts can be awarded.

Processes, Remedies	Advantages	Disadvantages
4. **The Consumer, Trader and Tenancy Tribunal** (LEGAL MEASURE) *Remedies:* ▶ refund ▶ repair ▶ replacement ▶ contract set aside ▶ wide range of orders	▶ Inexpensive. ▶ Quick. ▶ Often a desirable result for the consumer is reached.	▶ Limited jurisdiction. ▶ Not as quick and cheap as self-help or mediation.
5. **Courts** (LEGAL MEASURE) *Remedies:* ▶ wide range of orders ▶ damages ▶ injunctions and orders for specific performance ▶ criminal prosecution ▶ corrective advertising	▶ A result can be reached. ▶ A wide range of remedies, including damages, is available. ▶ Availability of class actions makes it less expensive for individuals.	▶ Very slow. ▶ Very expensive—often far more expensive than the matter under dispute is worth.
6. **Non-government organisations and the media** (NON-LEGAL MEASURE)	▶ Can increase consumer awareness and so help consumers make better decisions. ▶ Can prevent consumer problems from occurring. ▶ Can place pressure on businesses and governments to act to protect consumers.	▶ These organisations are not able to provide remedies themselves.

CAN YOU **evaluate the effectiveness of non-legal and legal measures in achieving justice for consumers?**

In order to do this, you need to discuss the advantages and disadvantages of each of the measures shown in Table 3.1 and decide whether the advantages outweigh the disadvantages. Then decide how effective each type of measure is. It is also important to state which are the legal measures and which are the non-legal measures.

KCq page 191

3.3 Contemporary issues concerning consumers

3.3.1 Product certification

Describe the issues relating to product certification, and evaluate the effectiveness in protecting the consumer of legal and non-legal responses in relation to product certification.

As seen in Section 3.1.8 (page 157), product certification is the process that confirms that a product or service meets relevant or necessary standards. Product certification is becoming more common, as more businesses claim that their products meet certain safety, health or environmental standards, or that their products are, for example, made in Australia. Businesses certify their products in this way because more and more consumers are conscious of these factors and will buy a healthy or environmentally-friendly product rather than an alternative product that does not have such certification.

However, businesses are not permitted to make claims about their products, or certify that they meet certain standards, if these claims are false or misleading. The common law, the *Competition and Consumer Act 2010* (Cth) and the *Fair Trading Act 1987* (NSW) contain provisions which state that sellers of goods and services cannot engage in conduct that is misleading, deceptive or unconscionable (see Section 3.1.8, pages 156–7). This includes making product certification claims that are false. If descriptions or promotional material are false or misleading, then the buyer has recourse to many remedies, including refund. A supplier or manufacturer may also be ordered to publish corrective advertising.

Various government authorities are responsible for ensuring that the claims made in product certification are true. For example, every state has a Food Authority, to ensure foodstuffs comply with the law. The NSW Food Authority (see Section 3.2.2, page 163) ensures compliance with the *Food Act 2003* (NSW). This includes the requirement that product certification claims made by manufacturers of foodstuffs are, in fact, met. The case of Fuze drinks in Case Study 3.8 below is an example of a manufacturer certifying its products in a misleading way.

CASE STUDY 3.8: Fuze Sparkling Apple Juice Products: Prosecution by the NSW Food Authority, August 2008

Facts

The company, P and N Beverages Australia Pty Ltd, produced a range of carbonated soft drinks with a high fruit juice content, aimed at school children. The main ingredient in the products was reconstituted apple juice. The manufacturers called the product Fuze, to emphasise the fusion of fruit juice and bubbles. The NSW Food Authority prosecuted the company in the Local Court, saying that the company had claimed, falsely, that the drinks were 99% apple juice, contained a certain level of vitamin C, and had no preservatives. The company pleaded guilty to eleven charges under the *Food Act 2003* (NSW) and was fined a total of $76 000. The company appealed to the District Court about the severity of the sentence.

Issue

Was the sentence imposed by the Local Court too severe, given that the company did not intend to mislead the public?

Decision

The judge accepted that there was no intention to mislead, and the false representations were made through carelessness rather than recklessness. However, he also accepted the prosecution argument that the breaches of the *Food Act* 2003 were serious, and that 'many persons purchasing these drinks would be misled into believing that they were a purchasing a very healthy drink with a lot of vitamin C in it'. He imposed penalties totalling $60 000. (Judgment was delivered in the District Court of NSW, Criminal Jurisdiction, 5 June 2009.)

Another area in which product certification has caused concern in recent years is in the area of 'green' certification. An independent 'green' certification can be obtained from Good Environmental Choice Australia (GECA) which uses the highest international standard for eco-labelling, ISO14024 (see Sections 3.1.5 [pages 151–2] and 3.4.4 [page 180]). Products which meet the standard can display the GECA logo. However, many consumers do not know about this logo. One company, Orange Power, that makes cleaning products and has earned the right to display the GECA logo, found that its sales only increased when it obtained paid endorsement from Planet Ark. The issue of 'green' product certification is discussed in Case Study 3.9 following.

Case study 3.9: 'Regulator demands muscle on "green" ads'

An article, appearing in the business section of *The Sydney Morning Herald,* highlights the growing incidence of businesses which make environmentally-friendly claims for their products and the importance of such certification for businesses and consumers. Some of the points made in this article are:

▶ the Australian Competition and Consumer Commission (ACCC) has experienced a sharp rise in the number of complaints about 'green' advertising claims, from almost none in 2007 to about 500 in 2008 and 2009

▶ during 2008 and 2009, the ACCC had discussions with Woolworths, SAAB, Origin Energy and other companies about the environmental claims they have made. Mr Graeme Samuel, chairman of the ACCC said, 'The bigger companies are being very careful. They know the ACCC has made it very clear we won't tolerate excessive claims because we are concerned about consumers being duped'.

▶ in January 2010, the ACCC began action against Global Green Plan (a power supplier), and Prime Carbon (a carbon broker) about misleading 'green' claims

▶ companies making false environmental claims can suffer reputational damage, but there are no financial implications for them

▶ the ACCC has called on the government to pass legislation to give it more power to tackle exaggerated environmental claims, including the ability to issue fines of up to $1.1 million for misleading claims.

Source: 'Regulator demands muscle on "green" ads', *The Sydney Morning Herald,* 26 January 2010.

Effectiveness of legal and non-legal responses to issues involving product certification

Legal and non-legal responses

Two legal responses to issues involving product certification are:

▶ action can be taken by the NSW Food Authority against companies who make claims about foodstuffs which are not met

▶ action can be taken by the ACCC against companies who misrepresent their products.

Non-legal responses include:

▶ the process of certification is usually undertaken by non-government organisations

▶ the effectiveness of product certification relies on the awareness of the consumer

▶ reputational damage can be suffered by businesses who fail to certify their products or who fail to do so properly.

Evaluating effectiveness

Below are listed two sets of factors—those which help ensure, and those which limit, the effectiveness in protecting the consumer of legal and non-legal responses to issues involving product certification.

Factors which help ensure the effectiveness of legal and non-legal responses

▶ Product certification assists consumers to know that the product they are purchasing meets the standards claimed for it.

▶ Businesses which certify that their products meet certain standards or requirements can increase sales because consumers are more willing to buy a certified product than an uncertified one.

▶ It is illegal for companies to make product certification claims that are false, and consumers have recourse to many remedies if false claims are made.

▶ Businesses that make false claims may not only face consumer claims and, in some cases, penalties but can also suffer from reputational damage.

Factors which limit the effectiveness of legal and non-legal responses

▶ The effectiveness of product certification relies on consumers being aware of what the certification stands for. Well-known certification marks, such as the Heart Foundation tick, make such certification effective for both businesses and consumers but, in other cases, such as that of the 'environmentally-friendly' GECA logo, many consumers are not aware of the significance of the logo.

▶ There has been a sharp rise in the number of complaints about exaggerated 'green' claims by companies, indicating that some businesses are unscrupulous in this area.

▶ The ACCC has limited power to deal with false product claims and has called on the federal government to give it more power in this area and to allow for the imposition of heavy fines.

CAN YOU **identify and investigate the contemporary issue of product certification and the protection of consumers, and evaluate the effectiveness of legal and non-legal responses to this issue?**

In order to do this you need to:

▶ explain what *product certification* is, and give examples

▶ explain the importance of reliable product certification for both consumers and businesses

▶ explain the issue of false claims and the increasing number of complaints about them in the area of eco-labelling

▶ describe the legal and non-legal responses

▶ discuss the factors which help ensure, and those which limit, the effectiveness in protecting the consumer of legal and non-legal responses to issues involving product certification

▶ come to a conclusion about the effectiveness of product certification in protecting the consumer.

 page 191

3.3.2 Marketing innovations

Several marketing innovations have increased significantly in recent years. Two of these are product placement and telemarketing.

Describe the issues relating to marketing innovations, and evaluate the effectiveness of legal and non-legal responses to the protection of consumers in relation to such innovations.

Direct commerce

Direct commerce refers to practices where goods are advertised and bought by a consumer from his or her own home (for example door-to-door sales and telephone sales). Direct commerce also includes the situation in which a consumer is asked to buy a product through the mail or via the internet.

Direct commerce has increased enormously in Australia over the last ten years, particularly via phone calls. Direct commerce over the phone is called telemarketing. Its advantages to the consumer include convenience, as well as a wider range of goods and services. Direct marketing is subject to the same advertising and consumer laws as all other forms of selling goods and services.

Telemarketing: Do Not Call Register

People who do not wish to receive telemarketing calls can contact the Do Not Call Register and can list their private or domestic fixed line and mobile numbers. Under the *Do Not Call Register Act 2006* (Cth), it is an offence for a telemarketer to call a number listed on the register. Any business that calls a number on the register can face penalties under the act if it cannot justify the call. Penalties can be imposed upon businesses who fail to comply with the register, as can be seen in Case Study 3.10 (see page 180).

Cooling-off periods

The *Fair Trading Act 1987* (NSW) specifically regulates direct commerce contracts in which the total price to be paid is over $100, or is not disclosed. The Fair Trading Act imposes a five working-day cooling-off period for all such direct commerce contracts. A *cooling-off period* is the time during which a party to a contract can decide not to go ahead with the purchase without penalty. During this time the consumer can cancel the contract, but must do so in writing. The supplier then has twenty-eight days to collect the goods.

CASE STUDY 3.10: 24 × 7 Direct penalised for ringing numbers on the Do Not Call Register

Facts

The Australian Communications and Media Authority (ACMA) (see Sections 3.1.8 [page 158] and 3.2.3 [page 164]), investigated complaints made about the Melbourne company 24×7 Direct Pty Ltd and found that it had made a number of telemarketing calls to numbers on the Do Not Call Register and, therefore, had failing to comply with the *Do Not Call Register Act 2006* (Cth).

Issue

What penalties under the act were appropriate to ensure the future compliance of the company?

Decision

The ACMA accepted a comprehensive enforceable undertaking from the company which aims to ensure its future compliance with the act, and 24×7 Direct Pty Ltd was also fined $8800. The Chairman of the ACMA Mr Chris Chapman said that the penalties showed that the ACMA 'can and will act' if they receive complaints.

Source: '24 × 7 Direct first call centre penalised for ringing numbers on the Do Not Call Register', ACMA Media Release 177/2009, 15 December 2009.

Product placement

Product placement refers to the placement of a sponsored product or brand into the content of entertainment. A famous example of product placement is Reese's Pieces, the favourite food of E.T. in the movie *E.T.*

The Extra-terrestrial. This product enjoyed an estimated 60% surge in sales following the release of the film.

In many European countries, product placement is illegal, because it is seen as covert and deceptive and cannot be filtered out from the entertainment content. In Australia, however, product placement is subject to only a few controls.

Product placement advertising for cigarettes and tobacco products is prohibited in nearly all forms of media. Generally speaking, however, product placement advertising is permitted if it is disclosed (for example if a company has a commercial arrangement with a television or radio station, the media outlet must tell the audience that the product is being advertised). The reasons for this are that consumers need to know that the product is being promoted because the person or program promoting it is being paid to do so, not because of a belief that it is a great product. This issue arose in the 'cash for comment' case against radio station 2UE Sydney, as outlined in Case Study 3.11 following.

CASE STUDY 3.11: Radio 2UE Sydney and the disclosure standard

Facts

Radio 2UE Sydney admitted that, in the final two months of the *John Laws Morning Show* in 2007, John Laws breached the Broadcasting Services (Commercial Radio Current Affairs Disclosure) Standard 2000 (Cth) on thirteen occasions. Complying with the standard is a condition of the broadcasting licence, granted under the *Broadcasting Services Act 1992* (Cth).

The disclosure standard requires broadcasting licensees to broadcast an announcement disclosing the existence of commercial sponsorship arrangements between presenters and sponsors, when the name, products or services of the sponsor are mentioned. In October and November of 2007, Laws breached the disclosure standard in relation to Qantas, Toyota, Hamilton Island and other companies, most of whom paid him over $100000 a year. He had previously done the same thing and 2UE had undertaken to ensure no more breaches occurred. When the 2007 breaches occurred, despite the undertaking made by 2UE to the Australian Communications and Media Authority (see Sections 3.1.8 [page 158] and 3.2.3 [page 164]), the ACMA brought proceedings in the Federal Court against Radio 2UE.

Issue

Because Radio 2UE admitted its failure to comply with the undertaking it had made, the Federal Court had to determine what penalty was suitable.

Decision

Justice Steven Rares found that the breaches were of a serious nature, and imposed penalties totalling $360000. The ACMA welcomed the decision, saying, 'The court has confirmed that, in matters involving serious contraventions, a substantial civil penalty is an appropriate sanction'.

Source: 'Federal court orders Radio 2UE Sydney to pay civil penalty of $360000 for breaches of disclosure rules', ACMA Media Release 89/2009, 17 July 2009.

Effectiveness of legal and non-legal responses to issues involving marketing innovations

Legal and non-legal responses

Five legal responses to issues involving marketing innovations are:

▶ direct commerce, including telemarketing, is subject to the same advertising and consumer laws as all other forms of selling goods and services

▶ a 'cooling-off' period, applies to many direct commerce transactions under the *Fair Trading Act 1987* (NSW)

▶ under the *Do Not Call Register Act 2006* (Cth), it is an offence for a telemarketer to call a number listed on the Do Not Call Register

▶ product placement of cigarettes and tobacco products is prohibited in nearly all forms of media.

▶ product placement advertising for products other than cigarettes and tobacco is permitted if it is disclosed.

Non-legal responses include, the laws and standards that need to be complied with by businesses, for both direct commerce and product placement,. Both government and industry organisations assist businesses to comply with these regulations.

Evaluating effectiveness

Below are listed two sets of factors—those which help ensure, and those which limit, the effectiveness in protecting the consumer of legal and non-legal responses to issues involving marketing innovations.

Factors which help ensure the effectiveness of legal and non-legal responses

▶ Direct commerce and product placement are regulated by several laws.

▶ The ACMA is willing to take legal action against businesses that fail to comply with laws regulating direct commerce and product placement.

Factors which limit the effectiveness of legal and non-legal responses

▶ The effectiveness of laws which protect consumers against unfair or unwanted practices by direct marketeers relies on consumers being aware of the protection the law offers and upon their willingness to make complaints.

▶ Enforcement of product placement disclosure laws relies on compliance by broadcasters and, because it is a covert and insidious form of advertising, consumers may not even be aware that it is occurring.

CAN YOU identify and investigate the contemporary issue of marketing innovations and the protection of consumers, and evaluate the effectiveness of legal and non-legal responses to this issue?

In order to do this, you need to:

▶ explain the two marketing innovations of direct commerce and product placement, and give examples

▶ explain that most responses to the issue of marketing innovations are legal responses

▶ describe the legal and non-legal responses to the issue of marketing innovations

▶ discuss the factors which help ensure, and those which limit, the effectiveness in protecting the consumer of legal and non-legal responses to issues involving marketing innovations

▶ come to a conclusion about the effectiveness of the regulation of marketing innovations in protecting the consumer.

 KCq page 191

3.4 Themes and challenges

3.4.1 Theme 1: The role of the law in encouraging cooperation and resolving conflict in regard to consumers

Assess the role of the law in encouraging cooperation and resolving conflict in regard to consumers.

The role of the law in encouraging cooperation and preventing conflict in the area of consumer protection is extensive. The regulatory framework, which includes the regulation of contracts, implying standards, and occupational licensing, helps to lessen the number of conflicts that arise. Government, industry and non-government bodies monitor compliance with the regulatory framework, thereby reducing the number of non-compliant businesses and, therefore, the number of consumer complaints and disputes.

In the area of consumer protection, the law plays a large role in encouraging cooperation as a means of resolving conflict. As can be seen in Sections 3.2.1 to 3.2.8 (pages 162–9), the legal system encourages consumers to resolve disputes with businesses themselves and provides mediation before any more formal legal action takes place.

The court system is a last resort for consumers. Both federal and state government organisations, such as the ACCC and the NSW Office of Fair Trading, provide advice and assistance to consumers. The NSW Office of Fair Trading, for example, will provide mediation if consumers are unable to resolve a difficulty with a business themselves (see Section 3.2.2, page 163). So cooperation between consumers and businesses is encouraged before the legal system will become involved in resolving a dispute.

Industry organisations, such as the Telecommunications Industry Ombudsman, and the NSW Consumer, Trader and Tenancy Tribunal (CTTT), also provide inexpensive and speedy resolution for consumer complaints if these cannot be resolved by the consumer unaided or through mediation (see Sections 3.2.4 [page 165] and 3.2.5 [pages 165–6]).

Encouraging cooperation extends into every area of consumer protection. For example, in the regulation of marketing and advertising, matters to do with credit, and occupational licensing, consumers and businesses are encouraged to resolve any disputes themselves. Many industries and occupations are self-regulated or subject to co-regulation. Co-regulation encourages cooperation between businesses and government, as well as between consumers and businesses. For example, Ad Standards is an industry-funded body which helps resolve complaints about most forms of advertising, and comes under the umbrella of the government advertising regulator, the ACMA (see Section 3.2.3 page 164).

While cooperation is widely encouraged, the legal system will step in to resolve conflict if the consumer is still not satisfied with the outcome of his or her complaint. This can be seen in the Coca-Cola 'myth-busting' advertisement case (see Case Study 3.6, Section 3.1.8. page 158). In this case, the ACCC ordered Coca-Cola to publish corrective advertising after the Advertising Standards Bureau had dismissed complaints about the advertisement.

The legal system also encourages businesses to cooperate in abiding by regulatory standards, before taking more punitive measures. This can be seen in both the Prouds Jewellers case (Case Study 3.5, Section 3.1.8, page 156) and the 2UE Radio Sydney case (Case Study 3.11, Section 3.3.2. page 175). Prouds consented to implementing a trade practices compliance program, and Radio 2UE was only fined after it failed to comply with an undertaking made with the ACMA.

While cooperation is extensively encouraged within the area of consumer law, the legal system will step in to punish businesses that seriously breach the law. Three examples are the fines imposed on 24 × 7 Direct Pty Ltd (Case Study 3.10, Section 3.3.2, page 174), Fuze Sparkling Apple Juice Products (Case Study 3. 8, Section 3.2.2, pages 156–7) and Skippy Australia Pty Ltd (Case Study 3.2, Section 3.1.5, page 153).

KCq page 191

3.4.2 Theme 2: Issues of compliance and non-compliance

There is generally widespread commitment to consumer law. This is reflected in the fact that there is very little litigation (court action) in the area of consumer law, compared to other areas of civil law. This comparative lack of litigation can be explained by the following factors:

▶ commitment to customer service

▶ effective advice, assistance and mediation services

▶ effective enforcement mechanisms.

Customer service

Suppliers and manufacturers are generally only too happy to repair, replace or give a refund when a product is defective. Many will give a refund even if they are not legally obliged to do so (see Section 3.2.1, page 162), because most businesses rely on good customer service to maintain a profitable business.

Statistics gathered by the Society of Consumer Affairs Professionals in Business Australia Inc. (SOCAP) ('Study of Consumer Behaviour in Australia' 1995) show that:

▶ 73% of people will complain to a business if they are dissatisfied

▶ 66% of those who complain are not satisfied with the way their complaint was handled

▶ 90% of those dissatisfied will not purchase from the business again and will tell another nine people (on average) of their bad experience.

These statistics show that it is in the interests of business to provide good customer service and to handle complaints effectively. Developments to encourage and promote good customer service in Australia include:

▶ the formation of the SOCAP (Society of Consumer Affairs Professionals in Business) for people working in the fields of consumer affairs and customer relations. The members of SOCAP come from business, government and academic circles. This society has lifted the profile of customer service among businesses.

▶ the publication by Standards Australia of several standards to assist businesses in establishing good customer service. One of these is 'Customer satisfaction—Guidelines for complaints handling in oranisations' (AS ISO 10002–2006). This is designed to assist businesses to develop effective systems for handling consumer complaints.

▶ government departments and agencies have established customer service charters at federal, state and local levels to enable such organisations to effectively assist their customers.

Most businesses want to maintain a good reputation in the community, because it means they will do more business. Most businesses will, therefore, comply with consumer laws to avoid reputational damage. This can be seen in the case of product certification (see Case Study 3.9, Section 3.3.1, page 172).

Effective advice, assistance and mediation services

Another reason that suppliers and manufacturers comply with the law is that advice, assistance and mediation for consumers are readily available. If consumers do have a problem with a product or business, these services allow them to rectify the situation quickly and inexpensively. The Consumer, Trader and Tenancy Tribunal also provides a cheap, quick and effective process of redress for consumer complaints (see Sections 3.2.2 to 3.2.8 [pages 163–9]).

Effective enforcement mechanisms

Laws regarding product liability, class actions, mandatory standards and marketing make the consequences of breaking consumer laws costly for suppliers. So it is in the interests of suppliers for them to comply with such laws (see Case Study 3.2, Section 3.1.5 [page 153]; Case Study 3.8, Section 3.2.2 [pages 176–7] and Case Study 3.11, Section 3.3.2 [page 175]).

All these legal provisions are very useful in protecting consumers. The willingness of consumers to seek remedies themselves, along with the many quick, inexpensive forms of consumer redress available to consumers if a manufacturer/supplier breaches the law, means that these laws are extremely useful in protecting the rights of consumers (see Section 3.2.8, pages 168–9).

Though there is widespread commitment to the laws regarding consumer rights, consumers need to be informed and aware to assert their rights and to prevent being subjected to unfair business practices. There are always some suppliers who are willing to take advantage of the unwary consumer.

KCq page 191

3.4.3 Theme 3: Laws relating to consumers as a reflection of changing values and ethical standards

To a large extent, the legal protection of consumers in Australia reflects the dominant morals and ethics of a modern consumer society. The legal system reflects the societal belief that ordinary people have a right to be treated fairly in the marketplace.

However, some have argued that consumer protection laws, introduced since the birth of the modern consumer era in the 1960s, have gone too far and that now traders have too few rights and too little freedom to organise their own affairs. This argument reflects the ethical idea that freedom for people to do what they want is highly important. It is in accordance with this viewpoint that greater self-regulation of occupations is sometimes suggested (see Section 3.1.9, pages 159–60).

To counter this argument there is the ethical view that those with least power need to be protected from those with the greatest power. It is a

> Assess the extent to which the law relating to consumers reflects changing values and ethical standards.

commonly held moral stance that people should be treated equally as far as possible. There is little doubt that, in the modern marketplace, characterised by globalisation and e-commerce, the power of individual consumers is considerably weaker than that of suppliers and manufacturers who are usually large corporations, and have more information and more money at their disposal (see Sections 3.1.1 [pages 146–7], and 3.4.4 [page 180]).

Consumer protection laws, such as the *Competition and Consumer Act 2010* (Cth), have become more far-reaching to take into account this increasing power imbalance. For example, product liability laws introduced in 1992 have given better protection to consumers (see Section 3.1.7, page 155). This reflects the ethical view that people should be responsible for damage or injury they cause to other people.

Other recent changes to the law which attempt to give individual consumers more power in the modern marketplace include:

▶ increased availability of class actions (see Section 3.2.5, pages 166–7)

▶ proliferation of cheap, quick avenues of redress, including the NSW Civil and Administrative Tribunal (NCAT) and industry-based dispute resolution mechanisms (see Sections 3.2.2 to 3.2.6 [pages 163–7]).

Mandatory standards and the laws which enforce them also help protect consumers (see Section 3.1.5, pages 152–3). These standards attempt to place consumers in a position of equality with suppliers by protecting them from unsafe and inferior products and by imposing penalties on the suppliers of such products.

Information is very important if consumers are to be in a position to assert their legal rights. Laws regarding advertising and marketing, as well as bodies which increase the awareness of consumers, help to keep consumers accurately informed (see Sections 3.1.8 [pages 156–9] and 3.2.7 [page 167]).

(KCq) page 191

Examine the role of law reform in recognising the rights of consumers.

3.4.4 Theme 4: The role of law reform in recognising the rights of consumers

Reforming the law

To *reform* the law means to change the law so that it operates more efficiently and/or more effectively. Law can be reformed by legislation or by adaptation of the common law in courts.

Parliaments are the principal lawmakers in our society and are, therefore, the principal agencies of reform to the law. The area of consumer law is governed by many statutes which are amended to keep abreast of changes in society.

While parliament is the primary agency of law reform, the courts contribute to law reform by applying precedent to cases currently under review and making decisions to fit changing circumstances. Courts must apply legislation, must follow precedent, and can only make a decision in cases before them, so their contribution to reform is usually slow and piecemeal. However, sometimes the effect of a court decision can be profound as in the case of *Donoghue v Stevenson* (1932) AC 562 (see Case Study 3.4, Section 3.1.7, page 155), which was the forerunner of modern product liability laws and also the beginning of modern consumer protection laws.

Pressure to change existing law can come from many sources including:

▶ the media

▶ lobby groups

▶ international pressure

▶ reports from various Australian government inquiries or organisations, such as the Ombudsman or Law Reform Commissions.

One area of reform to consumer law suggested by the NSW Law Reform Commission has been reform to the law regarding guarantors ('Guaranteeing someone else's debt', Report No. 107, 2006). Changes to the rules for class actions in the Federal Court in 1992 were a direct result of the Australian Law Reform Commission's report: 'Grouped Proceedings in the Federal Court' (No. 46, 1988).

While Law Reform Commissions can be valuable agencies for changing the law they can, however, only recommend changes. Governments are not compelled to implement these recommendations. For example, the federal government has acted on less than half the recommendations made to it by the Australian Law Reform Commission. This indicates that such organisations may have limited effect, but they serve to raise public awareness about problems within the legal system.

Factors leading to law reform

There are many factors which give rise to the need for law reform. In the area of consumer protection, for example, changes in values and technology have led to several recent reforms in the law.

Changing social values

Changing social values have led to recent law reforms including:

▶ co-regulation of occupations reflecting the view that neither self-regulation nor government regulation are the most effective forms of regulation (see Section 3.1.9, pages 160–61)

▶ greater emphasis on customer service reflecting the emerging idea that businesses are more profitable if they offer good customer service (see Section 3.4.3 pages 188–9)

▶ 'green' certification—the emerging value that products and their manufacturers should try and be as environmentally-friendly as possible has led to a proliferation of companies claiming 'green' credentials for their products.

Failure of existing law

Most law reform comes about because of the failure of existing law, which may not be adequate to meet the needs of a changing society. In the area of consumer law, failure of existing law has led to:

▶ product liability laws (see Section 3.1.7, page 155)

▶ mandatory standards (see Section 3.1.5, pages 152–3).

Product certification is an increasing area of concern, as can be seen in Section 3.3.1 (pages 170–3). Some businesses make exaggerated or false claims about their products.

The Australian Consumer Law was introduced because governments saw a need to establish a national consumer law that ensures consumers are protected no matter the state or territory of Australia in which the supplier is located. The Australian Consumer Law legislation establishes a national consumer law using the best practice of state and territory governments. It introduces provisions regulating unfair contracts at the Commonwealth level, and introduces new penalty, enforcement and consumer redress options. The Australian Consumer Law was implemented through the *Competition and Consumer Act 2010* (Cth) and became effective Australia-wide in 2011. This reform has so far been effective in protecting Australian consumers through one set of laws nationwide.

Technology and marketing innovations

Marketing innovations, such as telemarketing and product placement, have also required new laws to be passed to protect consumers. One such law is the *Do Not Call Register Act 2006* (Cth) (see Section 3.3.2, page 173).

International law

Globalisation of the marketplace has meant that there is a greater need for international cooperation to protect consumers. Section 3.1.1 discusses the challenge of globalisation (see pages 146–7). International cooperation in the area of consumer protection has been occurring for many years and continues to develop as new challenges emerge. Some areas in which international cooperation is occurring are discussed below.

Standardisation

Many products conform to internationally recognised standards. The International Organisation for Standardisation (ISO) and the International Electrotechnical Commission (IEC) are two bodies that ensure many products conform to certain standards, no matter where in the world they are manufactured. For example, ISO standards define the format and size of credit cards and phone cards, so that they can be used worldwide. This kind of cooperation has given consumers around the world access to a wider range of goods and services at cheaper prices. Standards Australia is a member of both the ISO and IEC.

Global trade

The World Trade Organization (WTO) is the international body that deals with the global rules regarding trade between nations. Its main function is to ensure that trade between nations flows as smoothly and freely as possible. Although the work of the WTO is criticised for many reasons, agreements such as the 1997 General Agreement on Tariffs and Trade (GATT) help consumers by providing cheaper goods. For example, when the US limited Japanese car imports in the early 1980s, car prices rose by 41% between 1981 and 1984 (WTO, 1999). Agreements, such as GATT, also allow greater consumer choice, because more products are available from other nations. Australia is a participant in the WTO negotiations and agreements.

Other international organisations

Australia is also a participant in other international organisations such as the Organisation for Economic Cooperation and Development (OECD) and the Asia-Pacific Economic Cooperation (APEC). Other Australian organisations also cooperate internationally in order to protect consumers. For example, ASIC (see Section 3.2.3, page 164) has worked with overseas bodies to recover monies that Australia would have lost in offshore financial scams. In 1999, ASIC recovered $4.7 million in cooperation with financial regulators from other countries. Various free trade agreements negotiated between Australia and other countries also help protect Australian consumers.

Consumer rights groups

International cooperation also exists among consumers and consumer groups. For example, Consumers International provides information to consumers all over the world about how to assert their rights in different countries (see Section 3.1.1, page 146).

KCq page 191

3.4.5 Theme 5: The effectiveness of legal and non-legal responses in achieving justice for consumers

The effectiveness of legal and non-legal measures in achieving justice for consumers is discussed throughout this chapter.

Table 3.2 lists legal and non-legal responses for achieving justice for consumers. Each response is followed by the numbers of the Sections within which the effectiveness of each measure is discussed.

> Analyse the effectiveness of law of legal and non-legal measures in achieving justice for consumers.

Table 3.2 Legal and non-legal responses for achieving justice for consumers

Legal responses	Non-legal responses
Contracts ▷ The law of contract (Section 3.1.4, pages 148–9) ▷ Regulating exclusion clauses (Section 3.1.4, page 150) ▷ Protection against unjust contracts (Section 3.1.6, pages 153–4)	
Implying standards into contracts ▷ Standards implied by statute and the common law (Section 3.1.5, pages 151–2) ▷ Voluntary and mandatory standards (Section 3.1.5, pages 152–3) ▷ Product recall (Section 3.1.5, page 153) ▷ Action for breach of mandatory standards (Section 3.1.5, page 153)	
Negligence ▷ The law of torts (Section 3.1.7, page 155) ▷ Product liability laws (Section 3.1.7, page 155)	
Marketing and advertising ▷ General statutory standards (Section 3.1.8, page 156) ▷ Specific statutory requirements (Section 3.1.8, pages 156–7)	**Marketing and advertising** ▷ Non-statutory controls on advertising (Section 3.1.8, pages 157–8)
Occupational licensing ▷ State regulation (Section 3.1.9, page 160) ▷ Co-regulation (Section 3.1.9, pages 160–61)	**Occupational licensing** ▷ Self-regulation (Section 3.1.9, pages 159–60) ▷ Co-regulation (Section 3.1.9, pages 160–61)
Consumer redress and remedies ▷ Tribunals and courts (Sections 3.2.5 [pages 165–7] and 3.2.9 [page 170]) ▷ A range of legal remedies (Section 3.2.8, pages 167–9) • award of damages • rescission and modification of contract • special orders • injunctions and specific performance • criminal prosecution	**Consumer redress and remedies** ▷ Awareness and self-help (Sections 3.2.1 [pages 162–3] and 3.2.9 [page 169]) ▷ State government organisations (Sections 3.2.2 [pages 163–4] and 3.2.9 [page 169]) ▷ Federal government organisations (Sections 3.2.3 [page 164] and 3.2.9 [page 169]) ▷ Industry organisations (Sections 3.2.4 [pages 164–5] and 3.2.9 [page 169]) ▷ Non-government organisations (Sections 3.2.6 [page 167] and 3.2.9 [page 170]) ▷ The media (Section 3.2.7 [page 167] ▷ A range of non-legal remedies (Section 3.2.8, page 167) • refund • repair • replacement
Product certification ▷ action by the NSW Food Authority (Section 3.3.1, page 170) ▷ action by the ACCC (Section 3.3.1, pages 172–3)	**Product certification** ▷ certification processes (Section 3.3.1, page 170) ▷ consumer awareness (Section 3.3.1, page 172) ▷ reputational damage (Section 3.3.1, page 172)
Marketing innovations ▷ Advertising laws (Section 3.3.2, pages 174–7) ▷ 'Cooling-off' periods (Section 3.3.2, page 174) ▷ *Do Not Call Register Act 2006* (Cth) (Section 3.3.2, page 174) ▷ Prohibition of product placement of cigarettes and tobacco products (Section 3.3.2, pages 174–5) ▷ Product placement disclosure laws (Section 3.3.2, pages 174–5)	**Marketing innovations** ▷ non-statutory standards (Section 3.3.2, pages 174–7)

KCq page 191

Key definitions and concepts

Do you know all the key definitions and concepts for this chapter? Go through each term in the list and check that you know them all. Place a bookmark underneath each definition to cover the one below and slide it down. This way you can focus on each definition by itself.

Arbitration: A third party listens to both parties to a dispute and makes a decision based on the merits of the case.

Borrower: A person who acquires goods and services by using credit.

Caveat emptor: 'Let the buyer beware' (that is, if a consumer is mistreated by a seller there is very little he or she can do about it).

Class action: A court action in which several people who have been harmed by the activities of someone else take the case to court jointly. Also called **representative action**.

Conciliation: The process whereby a third person, called a mediator or conciliator, listens to both parties to a dispute and makes suggestions, in an effort to bring the two parties to agreement. Also called **mediation**.

Condition: A term fundamental to a contract.

Consideration: The exchange of value between the parties to a contract.

Consumer: A person who acquires in a transaction goods and services for his or her own personal or household use.

Contract: A legally binding agreement.

Cooling-off period: A time after a contract is made during which a party can decide not to go ahead with the purchase without penalty. This applies to direct commerce transactions.

Co-regulation: Where occupations or professions are regulated by a combination of self-regulation and state regulation.

Credit: The use of an item before it has been paid for in full by the consumer.

Credit provider: Any business that provides finance to purchase goods, services, and land or to lease goods.

Damages: Money paid by one of the parties of a transaction to the other party, in order to compensate for loss suffered by that party.

Default: Failure to make a payment on a loan.

Direct commerce: The practice of goods being advertised and bought by a consumer from his or her own home (as is the case in door-to-door sales and telephone sales).

Exclusion clause: A clause in a contract by which traders try to restrict their liability if something goes wrong. Also called an **exemption clause**.

Expectation damages: A plaintiff is compensated so that he or she is in the position he or she would have been in if the contract had been fulfilled.

Express term: A promise in a contract that is actually spoken or written into the contract.

Globalisation: The growing economic and social interdependence and interconnectedness of countries worldwide, part of which is the process whereby goods and services available in one country are the same as those offered worldwide.

Guarantor: A person who agrees to pay the debt of another person if that person fails to pay the debt.

Implied term: A promise that a statute or common law will put into a contract even though such a term was not discussed by either party to the contract.

Injunction: An order for someone to do, or to refrain from doing, something.

Interest: Extra money paid by a borrower for the convenience of borrowing money; calculated at a percentage of the amount of money borrowed.

Laissez faire: The philosophy that people should be free to make whatever arrangements they wish and that the government should not interfere in these arrangements by passing laws to control them.

Mandatory standards: Standards that must be met by certain products, and which are made compulsory by legislation.

Mediation: The process whereby a third person, called a mediator or conciliator, listens to both parties to a dispute and makes suggestions in an effort to bring the two parties to agreement. Also called **conciliation**.

Merchantable quality: Goods are fit for the purpose or purposes for which they are usually sold, taking into consideration the price and description of the goods.

Mortgage: An agreement whereby property is provided as security for a loan.

Mortgagee: The person who lends money in a mortgage contract; the **credit provider**.

Mortgagor: The person who borrows money in a mortgage contract; the **borrower**.

Occupational licence: A permit to practise in a particular profession or occupation.

Party: A person who enters into a contract.

Privity of contract: A doctrine that states that only people who actually make a contract (the parties) can enforce it.

Product certification: The process that confirms that a product or service meets the relevant or necessary standards.

Product liability laws: Laws which state that anybody injured by a defective product is able to claim compensation from the manufacturer.

Product placement: The placement of a sponsored such or brand into the content of entertainment.

Product recall: A product is removed from being available for sale and a request is made for the return of any such items which have already been sold.

Redress: Ways consumers can achieve a just outcome in a consumer transaction in which they have been wronged. The term consumer redress includes both processes of gaining redress and the remedies available for fixing the problem.

Reliance damages: A plaintiff is compensated so that he or she is returned to the same position as before the contract was entered into.

Remedy: Something that fixes a wrong action.

Repossession: The credit provider takes possession of goods under a mortgage contract if the borrower fails to make repayments that are due.

Representative action: Court action in which several people who have been harmed by the activities of someone else take the case to court jointly. Also called **class action**.

Rescission of contract A court order saying that the contract is at an end.

Restitution damages: A plaintiff is given value for benefits he or she has provided to the defendant so far.

Security: Any asset over which a credit provider has a claim if the borrower fails to pay his or her debt.

Specific performance: An order that requires the parties to a contract to do those things which their contract requires in order to settle and define the parties' rights.

Telemarketing: The practice of selling goods or services to people by telephoning them at home and offering a product for sale.

Term: A promise contained within a contract that makes up the agreement.

Third party: A person who benefits or suffers loss because of a contract between two other people.

Torts: Wrongful acts (such as negligence) committed by somebody against someone else.

Warranty: A term that is part of the contract but is not fundamental. If a warranty is breached (broken) the contract still exists.

Chapter syllabus checklist

Are you able to answer every syllabus question in the chapter? Tick each question as you go through the list if you are able to answer it. If you cannot answer it, turn to the given page to find the answer. Refer to page ix to check the meaning of the NESA key words.

	For a complete understanding of this topic:	Page No.	✓
1	Can I outline the developing need for consumer protection?	145–7	
2	Can I define *consumer*?	147	
3	Can I outline the objectives of consumer laws?	147–8	
4	Can I describe types of contracts?	149	
5	Can I describe elements of contracts	149	
6	Can I describe terms of contracts?	150	
7	Can I describe exclusion clauses of contracts?	150	
8	Can I explain standards implied by statutes?	151–2	
9	Can I describe unjust contracts—common law and statutory protection?	153–4	
10	Can I examine the nature, function and regulation of contracts?	154	
11	Can I explain the role of negligence in consumer protection?	155	
12	Can I describe statutory protection in the regulation of marketing and advertising?	156–7	
13	Can I describe non-statutory controls on advertising in the regulation of marketing and advertising?	157–9	
14	Can I evaluate the effectiveness of the regulation of marketing, advertising and product certification in achieving consumer protection?	159	
15	Can I describe *occupational licensing*?	159	
16	Can I examine the role of occupational licensing in achieving consumer protection?	162	
17	Can I describe the role of awareness and self-help in regard to consumer redress and remedies?	162–3	
18	Can I describe the role of state government organisations in regard to consumer redress and remedies?	163–4	
19	Can I describe the role of federal government organisations in regard to consumer redress and remedies?	164	
20	Can I describe the role of industry organisations in regard to consumer redress and remedies?	164–5	

	For a complete understanding of this topic:	Page No.	✓
21	Can I describe the role of tribunals and courts in regard to consumer redress and remedies?	165–7	
22	Can I describe the role of non-government organisations in regard to consumer redress and remedies?	167	
23	Can I describe the role of the media in regard to consumer redress and remedies?	167	
24	Can I describe consumer remedies for individuals?	167–9	
25	Can I describe consumer remedies for society as a whole?	169	
26	Can I examine the range of different remedies available to consumers?	169	
27	Can I evaluate the effectiveness of non-legal and legal measures in achieving justice for consumers?	170	
28	Can I identify and describe the contemporary issue of product certification?	170–3	
29	Can I investigate the contemporary issue involving the protection of consumers in regard to product certification, and can I evaluate the effectiveness of legal and non-legal responses to this issue?	173	
30	Can I identify and describe the contemporary issue of marketing innovations?	173–7	
31	Can I investigate the contemporary issue involving the protection of consumers in regard to marketing innovations, and can I evaluate the effectiveness of legal and non-legal responses to this issue?	176–7	
32	Can I assess the role of the law in encouraging cooperation and resolving conflict in regard to consumers?	177–8	
33	Can I examine issues of compliance and non-compliance?	178–9	
34	Can I explain laws relating to consumers as a reflection of changing values and ethical standards?	179–80	
35	Can I explain the role of law reform in recognising the rights of consumers?	180–2	
36	Can I evaluate the effectiveness of legal and non-legal responses in achieving justice for consumers?	183	

Useful resources

Acts

Broadcasting Services Act 1992 (Cth) (See Section 3.3.2, page 175.)

Competition and Consumer Act 2010 (Cth) (See Sections 3.1.4 [page 148] and 3.1.5 [page 151].)

Consumer Claims Act 1998 (NSW) (See Section 3.2.5, page 165.)

Consumer, Trader and Tenancy Tribunal Act 2001 (NSW) (See Section 3.2.5, pages 165–6.)

Contracts Review Act 1980 (NSW) (See Section 3.1.6, page 153.)

Do Not Call Register Act 2006 (Cth) (See Section 3.3.2, page 174.)

Factories and Shops Act 1912 (Cth) (See Section 3.1.1, page 145.)

Fair Trading Act 1987 (NSW) (See Sections 3.1.4 [page 148] and 3.1.5 [page 151].)

Food Act 2003 (NSW) (See Sections 3.1.8 [pages 156–9], 3.2.2 [page 163] and 3.3.2 [page 176].)

Hire Purchase Agreement Act 1941 (NSW) (See Section 3.1.1, page 146.)

Legal Profession Act 1987 (NSW) (See Section 3.1.9, page 161.)

Motor Dealers and Repairers Act 2013 (NSW) (See Section 3.1.9, page 160.)

Sale of Goods Act 1923 (NSW) (See Sections 3.1.1 [pages 145–6] and 3.1.5 [page 151].)

Trade Practices Act 1974 (Cth) (See Sections 3.1.4 [page 148].)

Treaties/International documents

General Agreements on Tariffs and Trade (GATT) 1997 (See Section 3.4.4, page 193.)

United Nations Guidelines for Consumer Protection 1985 (UN) (See Section 3.1.1, page 146.)

Cases

Australian Competition and Consumer Commission v Prouds Jewellers Pty Ltd (2008) FCA 75 (See Case Study 3.5, Section 3.1.8, page 156.)

Australian Competition and Consumer Commission v Skippy Australia Pty Ltd (2006) FCA 1343 (See Case Study 3.2, Section 3.1.5, page 153.)

Blomley v Ryan (1956) 99 CLR 362 (See Case Study 3.3, Section 3.1.6, page 154.)

Carnie v Esanda Finance Co. Ltd (1995) 182 CLR 938 (See Section 3.2.5, page 167.)

Donoghue v Stevenson (1932) AC 562 (See Case Study 3.4, Section 3.1.7, page 155.)

Thornton v Shoe Lane Parking Ltd (1971) 2 QB 163 (See Case Study 3.1, Section 3.1.4, pages 150–51.)

Other documents

'24×7 Direct first call centre penalised for ringing numbers on the Do Not Call Register', ACMA Media release 177/2009, 15 December 2009 (See Case Study 3.10, Section 3.3.2, page 174.)

'Australian Association of National Advertisers (AANA) Advertiser Code of Ethics' (See Section 3.1.8, page 157.)

'Australian Association of National Advertisers (AANA) Code for Advertising and Marketing Communications to Children' (See Section 3.1.8, page 157.)

'Broadcasting Services' (Commercial Radio Current Affairs Disclosure) Standard 2000 (Cth) (See Case Study 3.11, Section 3.3.2, page 175.)

'Customer satisfaction—Guidelines for complaints handling in organisations' (AS ISO 10002–2006), Standards Australia, 2006 (See Section 3.4.2, pages 178–9.)

'Federal court orders Radio 2UE Sydney to pay civil penalty of $360000 for breaches of disclosure rules', ACMA Media Release 89/2009, 17 July 2009 (See Case Study 3.11, Section 3.3.2, page 175.)

'Grouped Proceedings in the Federal Court', Australian Law Reform Commission Report No. 46, 1988 (See Section 3.4.4, pages 180–1.)

'Guaranteeing someone else's debt', NSW Law Reform Commission Report No. 107, 2006 (See Section 3.4.4, page 181.)

'"Myth-busting" Coke adverts get busted', The Age, 3 April 2009 (See Case Study 3.6, Section 3.1.8, page 158.)

'Regulator demands muscle on "green" ads', *The Sydney Morning Herald*, 26 January 2010 (See Case Study 3.9, Section 3.3.1, page 172.)

'Review of Australia's consumer policy framework', Productivity Commission, 2008 (See Section 3.4.4, page 181.)

'Scratching the surface...', A case study from The Consumer, Trader and Tenancy Tribunal Annual Report 2006–2007, p. 31. (See Case Study 3.7, Section 3.2.5, page 166.)

'Study of Consumer Complaint Behaviour in Australia', SOCAP, 1995 (See Section 3.4.2, pages 188–9.)

Unsafe at Any Speed: The designed-in dangers of the American automobile, Ralph Nader, Grossman, New York, 1965 (See Section 3.1.1, page 146.)

Organisations and websites

NSW Civil and Administrative Tribunal (NCAT) (See Section 3.1.9, page 161): www.ncat.nsw.gov.au

Advertising Claims Board (See Section 3.1.8, page 157): www.adstandards.com.au/aboutus/theadvertisingclaimsboard

Advertising Standards Board (See Section 3.1.8, pages 157–8): www.adstandards.com.au/aboutus/theadvertisingstandardsboard

Ad Standards (See Section 3.1.8, page 157): www.adstandards.com.au

Asia-Pacific Economic Cooperation (APEC) (See Section 3.4.4, page 193): www.apec.org

Australian Association of National Advertisers (AANA) (See Section 3.1.8, page 157): www.aana.com.au

Australian Communications and Media Authority (ACMA) (See Sections 3.1.8 [page 158] and 3.2.3 [page 164]): www.acma.gov.au

Australian Competition and Consumer Commission (ACCC) (See Section 3.2.3, page 164): www.accc.gov.au

Australian Consumer Law (including the Ministerial Council on Consumer Affairs [MCCA]) (See Section 3.2.3 page 164): www.consumer.gov.au

Australian Financial Complaints Authority (AFCA) (See Section 3.2.4, page 165) https://www.afca.org.au

Australian Government, Department of the Treasury (for the Commonwealth Consumer Affairs Advisory Council [CCAC]) (See Section 3.2.3, page 164): www.treasury.gov.au/Policy-Topics/Consumer

Australian Government Productivity Commission (See Section 3.4.4, page 191): www.pc.gov.au

Australian Law Reform Commission (See Section 3.4.4, page 191): www.alrc.gov.au

Australian Securities and Investments Commission (ASIC) (See Section 3.2.3, page 164): www.asic.gov.au

Certified Practising Accountants Australia (CPA Australia) (See Section 3.2.4, page 164): www.cpaaustralia.com.au

Choice (formerly the Australian Consumers Association [ACA]) (See Section 3.2.6, page 167): www.choice.com.au

Consumers International (formerly the International Organisation of Consumer Unions [IOCU]) (See Section 3.1.1, page 146): www.consumersinternational.org

Council of Australian Governments (COAG) (See Section 3.4.4, page 191): www.coag.gov.au

Do Not Call Register (Cth) (See Section 3.3.3, page 179): www.donotcall.gov.au

Food Standards Australia New Zealand (FSANZ) (See Section 3.1.5, page 152): www.foodstandards.gov.au

Good Environmental Choice—Australia (GECA) (See Section 3.3.2, page 177): www.geca.org.au

Health Care Complaints Commission (NSW) (See Section 3.2.2, page 163): www.hccc.nsw.gov.au

International Electrotechnical Commission (IEC) (See Section 3.4.4, page 193): www.iec.ch

International Organization for Standardization (ISO) (See Section 3.4.4, page 193): www.iso.org

Law Society of NSW (See Section 3.1.9, pages 161–2): www.lawsociety.com.au

Legal Profession Admission Board (See Section 3.1.9, page 161): www.lawlink.nsw.gov.au/lpab

Legal Services Commissioner (See Sections 3.1.9 [page 161] and 3.2.2 [page 163]): www.lawreform.justice.nsw.gov.au

NRMA (See Section 3.2.6, page 167): www.mynrma.com.au/index.jsp

NSW Bar Association (NSW) (See Section 3.1.9, pages 160–61): www.nswbar.asn.au

NSW Civil and Administrative Tribunal (NCAT) (See Section 3.2.5, pages 165–6) www.ncat.nsw.gov.au

NSW Food Authority (See Section 3.2.2, page 163): www.foodauthority.nsw.gov.au

NSW Law Reform Commission (See Section 3.4.4, page 191): www.lawlink.nsw.gov.au/lrc

NSW Fair Trading (See Sections 3.1.9 [page 160] and 3.2.2 [page 163]): www.fairtrading.nsw.gov.au

Office of the Australian Information Commissioner (OAIC) incorporating the Privacy Commissioner (Cth) (See Section 3.3.4, page 185): www.oaic.gov.au

Organisation for Economic Cooperation and Development (OECD) (See Section 3.4.4, page 193): www.oecd.org

Society of Consumer Affairs Professionals Australia (SOCAP) (See Section 3.4.2, pages 188–9): www.socap.org.au

Standards Australia (See Section 3.1.5, page 152): www.standards.org.au

Telecommunications Industry Ombudsman (See Section 3.2.4, page 165): www.tio.com.au

World Trade Organization (WTO) (See Section 3.4.4, page 193): www.wto.org

End of chapter questions

 Key Concept questions

These questions test whether you have grasped the key ideas in each subsection. They are not difficult questions, but will test your recall of knowledge of the material you have read. If you are unsure what a question is asking you to do, refer to page ix to check the meaning of the NESA key words. If you can answer all these questions, you will know you have a sound knowledge of content.

Refer to pp. 446–50 for

3.1 The nature of consumer law

3.1.1 The developing need for consumer protection

1. Describe the effect of the Industrial Revolution on consumption patterns.
2. Explain the terms *caveat emptor* and *laissez faire*.
3. Explain how globalisation brings new challenges to consumer protection.
4. Explain what you need to do in order to outline the developing need for consumer protection.

3.1.2 The definition of consumer

5. State the general definition of *a consumer*.
6. State the definition of *a consumer* under the *Competition and Consumer Act 2010* (Cth).

3.1.3 Objectives of consumer law

7. Explain why the law has needed to intervene to protect consumers.
8. List four objectives of consumer law.
9. Explain what you need to do in order to outline the objectives of consumer law.

3.1.4 Contracts

10. What is a *contract*?
11. Name the main federal and state statutes that operate in the area of consumer protection.
12. Identify the two main types of consumer contract.
13. Identify the three elements of a contract in the following scenario:

    Jane offers to sell her car to her brother, Michael. He finds out the market value of the car and offers to pay $3000, which is just below market value. Jane accepts the money and signs over the ownership of the car to Michael.

14. Explain the difference between the enforceability of a written contract and that of an oral contract.
15. Explain what *a term* of a contract is.
16. Explain the difference between *express terms* and *implied terms*.
17. Explain the difference between a *condition* and a *warranty*.
18. What is an *exclusion clause*?
19. Name the two statutes that regulate exclusion clauses and explain how they do so.
20. Explain the common law rules about exclusion clauses.
21. Cite a common law case about the regulation of exclusion clauses.

3.1.5 Standards implied by statutes

22. Explain what it means when the law implies terms into contracts.
23. List four sources of terms implied into a contract for goods or services.
24. List the five basic terms implied into consumer contracts for goods.
25. List the two terms implied into service contracts.
26. Describe the obligations imposed by the *Competition and Consumer Act 2010* (Cth) on manufacturers and importers regarding spare parts and repair facilities.
27. Explain the standards that are imposed on suppliers of goods, besides the five basic terms implied into all goods contracts.
28. Explain why many manufacturers and suppliers willingly follow voluntary standards.
29. List three examples of goods which may have mandatory standards applied to them.
30. Name the organisation which monitors compliance with mandatory product standards.
31. Explain the meaning of *product recall*.
32. Using an example, explain the possible consequences for a manufacturer or supplier of breaching mandatory standards.

3.1.6 Unjust contracts

33. Name the laws that regulate unjust contracts.
34. List five of the factors a court will consider when determining whether a contract is unjust.
35. Explain why the contract in *Blomley v Ryan* was found to be unjust, and cite this case correctly.

36. List nine possible remedies for breach of contract.

37. Explain what you need to do in order to examine the nature, function and regulation of contracts.

3.1.7 The role of negligence in consumer protection

38. Explain the relevance of the case of *Donoghue v Stevenson* to privity of contract, and cite it correctly.

39. Explain how product liability laws modify the doctrine of privity of contract.

40. Explain the relevance of negligence under product liability laws.

3.1.8 Regulation of marketing and advertising

41. In what way is advertising of benefit to consumers?

42. Name two ways in which advertising and marketing are regulated.

43. Name the main federal and state statutes that regulate advertising and marketing.

44. Explain the general provisions regarding advertising and marketing contained in this legislation.

45. Outline the rights of a consumer who receives unordered goods.

46. List the legal consequences for traders of engaging in unfair marketing practices.

47. Provide an example of a recent case that involved misleading advertising.

48. Name the three bodies responsible for the self-regulation of the advertising industry.

49. Explain what you need to do in order to evaluate the effectiveness of the regulation of marketing, advertising and product certification in achieving consumer protection.

3.1.9 Occupational licensing

50. What is *occupational licensing*?

51. List three ways occupational licensing occurs in Australia.

52. Explain the benefit to consumers of occupational licensing.

53. Explain the idea of *self-regulation*, giving an example.

54. Giving an example, explain why the effectiveness of self-regulation is sometimes called into question.

55. Explain the idea of *state regulation*, giving an example.

56. Explain the idea of *co-regulation*, giving an example.

57. Explain what you need to do in order to examine the role of occupational licensing in achieving consumer protection.

3.2 Consumer redress and remedies

3.2.1 Awareness and self-help

58. What is *consumer redress*?

59. List six ways in which consumers can pursue redress.

60. Describe the first thing a consumer should do if he or she has been wronged by a supplier or manufacturer.

61. Assess the importance of awareness and self-help.

3.2.2 State government organisations

62. Define the terms *mediation* and *conciliation*.

63. Name the government body that has the primary role in conciliation of consumer complaints in NSW.

64. List three other state government organisations which can assist consumers who have a complaint against a provider.

3.2.3 Federal government organisations

65. Name three federal government organisations that can assist consumers, and briefly outline the areas of their responsibility.

3.2.4 Industry organisations

66. Name four industry organisations that can assist consumers.

67. Choose one industry Ombudsman and explain the process that this Ombudsman goes through when dealing with a consumer complaint.

3.2.5 The role of tribunals and courts

68. State when the Consumer, Trader and Tenancy Tribunal was established, the relevant legislation, and the tribunal it replaced.

69. Name three factors which make the Consumer, Trader and Tenancy Tribunal an effective process of redress for consumers.

70. Explain why the court system should be considered a last resort for consumers.

71. Explain how the provision of class actions assists consumers.

3.2.6 The role of non-government organisations

72. Describe the role of two non-government organisations that can advise and assist consumers.

3.2.7 The role of the media

73. Describe three ways in which the media can assist consumers.

3.2.8 Consumer remedies

74. List and briefly describe ten remedies available to consumers.

75. Explain what you need to do in order to examine the range of different remedies available to consumers.

3.2.9 The effectiveness of non-legal and legal measures in achieving justice for consumers

76. List the legal and non-legal measures available to consumers.

77. Explain what you need to do in order to assess the effectiveness of non-legal and legal measures in achieving justice for consumers.

3.3 Contemporary issues concerning consumers

3.3.1 Product certification

78. Explain *product certification*, giving an example.

79. Explain how product certification is of benefit both to businesses and to consumers.

80. List the laws which limit the ability of companies to certify their products, and explain these limits.

81. List legal and non-legal responses to issues regarding product certification.

82. Explain what you need to do in order to identify and investigate the contemporary issue of product certification and consumer protection, and evaluate the effectiveness of legal and non-legal responses to this issue.

3.3.2 Marketing innovations

83. Explain what *telemarketing* is, and state its benefits to the consumer.

84. Name and explain three legal responses to direct commerce.

85. Define *product placement*, and provide an example.

86. Explain when product placement is permitted and when it is not permitted under Australian law.

87. Giving an example, explain the consequences of breaching product placement regulations.

88. List legal and non-legal responses to issues regarding marketing innovations.

89. Explain what you need to do in order to identify and investigate the contemporary issue of marketing innovations and consumer protection, and evaluate the effectiveness of legal and non-legal responses to this issue.

3.4 Themes and challenges

3.4.1 Theme 1: The role of the law in encouraging cooperation and resolving conflict in regard to consumers

90. Explain how the law assists in preventing conflict through encouraging cooperation.

91. List three ways in which the law encourages cooperation between consumers and business.

92. Name three ways in which consumers can have conflicts resolved, if conciliation and negotiation are ineffective.

3.4.2 Theme 2: Issues of compliance and non-compliance

93. List the three factors which contribute to the high standard of commitment to consumer protection law.

94. Explain how inexpensive and effective processes for consumer redress encourage commitment to the law by traders.

95. List four areas of consumer law that make it costly for suppliers to break the law.

3.4.3 Theme 3: Laws relating to consumers as a reflection of changing values and ethical standards

96. Describe the dominant moral value reflected by the legal system in the area of consumer law.

97. List five ways in which the law tries to reflect the value of equality in the marketplace.

3.4.4 Theme 4: The role of law reform in recognising the rights of consumers

98. State an example from both federal and state parliaments of recent reforms to consumer law.

99. List four sources of pressure to reform the law.

100. State an example of a recent reform brought about by cooperation between state and federal governments.

101. State two examples of consumer law reform resulting from changing social values and the composition of society.

102. Name three reforms to consumer law brought about by a failure of existing law.

103. State an example of a reform to the law brought about by challenges presented by new technology.

104. Name two international bodies which ensure that many products conform to certain standards, no matter where in the world they are manufactured.

3.4.5 Theme 5: The effectiveness of legal and non-legal responses in achieving justice for consumers

105. List seven areas of consumer protection in which there are non-legal responses for achieving justice for consumers.

106. List nine legal measures for achieving justice for consumers in the areas of contracts, standards and negligence.

107. List legal and non-legal avenues of redress for consumers.

108. List legal and non-legal remedies for consumers.

Sample HSC questions

Now for the real thing! The following questions are modelled on the types of questions you will face in the HSC. Think about it: if you get extensive practice at answering these sorts of questions, you will be more confident in answering them when it comes to the HSC Exam. It makes sense, doesn't it?

Another reason is that the answers given at the back of this guide are structured in a way that helps you learn strategies on how to answer HSC-like questions. This will help you aim for full marks!

For each extended-response question you will have a detailed answer with an explanation of what the question is asking you to do and also, when needed, an examiner's plan to help you get full marks with a section reference where you can find the answer in the chapter.

When you mark your work, highlight any questions you found difficult and earmark these areas for extra study.

Refer to pp. 451–2 for **Answers**

IN THE HSC EXAM

- Material from this chapter will be examined in Section III of the exam.
- Each extended-response question in Section III is worth 25 marks. You have 45 minutes to answer each one.
- Look for the min in each section and time yourself. This tells you approximately how much time you will have to answer these questions in the HSC Exam.

EXTENDED-RESPONSE QUESTIONS 1h 30 min

- In Section III of the exam, there will be seven extended-response questions, one for each option. Each question will have two alternatives. You will be required to answer two alternatives, each on a different option.
- In your answer you will be assessed on how well you:
  - demonstrate knowledge and understanding relevant to the question
  - communicate using relevant legal terminology and concepts
  - illustrate your answer with relevant examples, such as legislation, cases, media reports and treaties
  - present a logical, well-structured answer to the question.
- The expected length of response is around eight pages of an examination writing booklet (approximately 1000 words).

Question 1 45 min

Outline the developing need for consumer protection and evaluate the effectiveness of the law in dealing with unfair consumer goods and services contracts.

(25 marks)

Question 2 45 min

Outline the objectives of consumer law and assess how well the law meets at least one of these objectives.

(25 marks)

Chapter 4

Family

Principal focus

Through the use of contemporary examples, students investigate the legal nature of family relationships and the effectiveness of the law in achieving justice.

Themes and challenges

The following five themes and challenges are also incorporated throughout this chapter, and are summarised in Sections 4.4.1 to 4.4.5 (pages 264–75). They are to be considered throughout your study of this topic.

▶ 1 The role of the law in encouraging cooperation and resolving conflict in regard to family

▶ 2 Issues of compliance and non-compliance

▶ 3 Changes to family law as a response to changing values in the community

▶ 4 The role of law reform in achieving just outcomes for family members and society

▶ 5 The effectiveness of legal and non-legal responses in achieving just outcomes for family members

HSC CONTENT

	You learn to:
The nature of family law	▶ discuss the difficulty of defining 'family' and the changing concepts of family. ▶ distinguish between state and federal jurisdiction in family law. ▶ outline the legal requirements of a valid marriage. ▶ explain the legal rights and obligations of parents and children, including those derived from international law.
Responses to problems in family relationships	▶ outline the legal processes involved in dealing with problems in family relationships. ▶ evaluate the effectiveness of the law in protecting victims of domestic violence. ▶ examine the role of non-government organisations and the media in relation to family law. ▶ evaluate the effectiveness of the law in achieving justice for parties involved in relationship breakdowns.
Contemporary issues concerning family law	▶ identify and investigate contemporary issues relating to family law and evaluate the effectiveness of legal and non-legal responses to these issues.

© NSW Education Standards Authority, *Legal Studies Stage 6 Syllabus*, 2009, pp. 26–7

4.1 The nature of family law

4.1.1 The concept of family law

There are many different family arrangements within modern Australian society, all of which shape society's concept of what a family is and what functions it should perform. This chapter discusses different types of families and examines how the law manages and governs different family arrangements.

Family law comprises all the laws that deal with the relationships between family members and the rights and responsibilities of people in families. The family is the basic unit of society. Society places legal obligations upon people in different family arrangements to ensure that members of all families have legal protection.

There are two main functions of families, and these are to take care of children, and of spouses, financially, emotionally and physically. Marriage, for instance, means that both spouses and children have access to property and to income. Society, therefore, protects many people by making married couples financially responsible for each other and for their children, and by distributing property according to marital and parental relationships. Alternative family arrangements are also governed by the law, so that people in such relationships and children of such relationships are financially secure (see Section 4.1.3, pages 199–202).

The definition of *family*

It is difficult to define *family* because, in modern Australian society, there are people living in many different kinds of personal relationships which they regard as a family. The notion of what constitutes a *family* has undergone substantial change over the last thirty years as society has changed. The traditional idea of a family as consisting of a married couple with children is far less common than it was thirty years ago and, therefore, the traditional concept of what a family is has also changed. Every few years, the Australian Bureau of Statistics (ABS) conducts a census which, among other things, surveys the structure of Australian families. The ABS defines a *family* as: 'two or more persons ... who are related by blood, marriage (registered or *de facto*), adoption, step or fostering and who are usually resident in the same household'.

This definition indicates the many different types of families that exist in Australia today. A list of these follows. The percentage figures provided show the number of each type of family compared to the number of households in Australia in 2006, according to the Australian Bureau of Statistics.

▷ **Nuclear family:** This term normally refers to a husband, a wife and their children. Couples with children accounted for 46% of all households in 2006. This figure includes all couples with children—both married couples and unmarried couples.

▷ **Couples without children** (38% of all households)

▷ *De facto* **couples**, with or without children (15%). A *de facto* couple is a couple living together as a married couple without being legally married (see Section 4.1.3, pages 200–1).

▷ **Blended families**: This term refers to married or *de facto* couples with children from previous relationships (see Section 4.1.3, page 210).

- **Extended family**: This term refers to a family with other relatives, besides parents and children, living in the same household. Extended families can include grandparents, aunts and uncles. These families are rare in Australia today.

- **Single-parent families**: This refers to families in which there is one parent raising children. This may be due to many reasons, including death of a spouse, divorce, the breakdown of a *de facto* relationship or an absence of any relationship (16%). (See Section 4.1.3. page 199.)

- **Same-sex couples**, with or without children. In 2001, the Australian census found that there were approximately 20 000 Australian couples of the same gender living in the same home. Of these, about 20% of the female couples were living with children, and about 5% of the male couples were living with children. The rights and laws concerning same-sex relationships are discussed in Sections 4.1.3 (page 200) and 4.3.1 (pages 232–4).

- **Aboriginal and Torres Strait Islander customary law marriages** (see Section 4.1.3, page 199).

The children in all these types of families can be:

- the naturally conceived children of both adults in the family
- related to only one of the adult couple they live with
- the product of artificial reproductive technologies (see Section 4.3.3, page 240)
- foster children
- adopted (see Section 4.1.5, pages 207–9)
- stepchildren.

The rights of children and the responsibilities of parents are discussed in Sections 4.1.4 (pages 202–7), 4.2.2 (pages 211–16) and 4.3.4 (pages 245–51).

Family law governs the relationships between people in all these different types of families.

CAN YOU discuss the difficulty of defining *family* and the changing concepts of family?

To discuss the difficulty of defining *family* and the changing concepts of family, you need to be able to:

- describe the traditional concept of family as a married couple with children
- explain how the traditional concept of family has changed and why it is now difficult to define *family*
- give the ABS definition of *family*
- list and define different types of family relationships
- list the ways children can become part of a family.

This is also discussed in Sections 4.1.3 (pages 199–202) and 4.4.3 (pages 254–7).

 KCq page 268

4.1.2 Legal requirements of marriage

Describe the legal requirements of marriage.

Legal definition of *marriage*

The definition of *marriage* is 'the union of two people to the exclusion of all others, voluntarily entered into for life'. This type of definition was given in the common law in the case of *Hyde v Hyde and Woodmansee* (1866) LR 1 P&D 130 (UK) (see Case Study 4.2, page 197). Under section

51 of the Australian Constitution, the Commonwealth government is given power to make laws about marriage and divorce. So marriage is a matter of federal law. The definition given on page 195 is contained in the *Marriage Act 1961* (Cth).

The legal characteristics of marriage flow from this definition, so a valid marriage must be:

▷ **a union of two people**

▷ **voluntarily entered into**. If one of the partners to a marriage is forced or tricked into it, that marriage is not legally binding (see Case Study 4.3 on page 198)

▷ **for life**. This condition of marriage expresses the intention rather than the actuality of marriage in Australia. While people may intend to remain together for life, divorce is available—allowing a marriage to end legally before the death of either party. Divorce or the dissolution of marriage is discussed in Sections 4.2.1 to 4.2.3 (pages 210–18)

▷ **to the exclusion of all others**. This means that there is a union of two people only. In some societies, people may be married to more than one person at any one time. These societies are polygamous (see Case Study 4.2, page 197, and Section 4.1.3, page 200). Australian society is monogamous, meaning that a person may only be married to one person at a time. Adultery (that is, having sexual relations with a person other than the person to whom you are married) was once a ground for divorce, but this is no longer the case.

CASE STUDY 4.1: *Corbett v Corbett* (1970) 2 WLR 1306 (UK)

Facts

Arthur Corbett applied for a divorce when he discovered the person to whom he was married, whom he thought was a woman, was in reality a man who had undergone a sex change. Corbett's partner also applied for a divorce on the grounds that the marriage had not been consummated (that is, the couple had not had sexual relations).

Issue

Could the couple obtain a divorce?

Decision

The court said the couple could not be divorced because they were not legally married in the first place. The marriage was not valid because it was not a union between a man and a woman. The court held that a man who had undergone a sex change operation was still legally a man.

CASE STUDY 4.2: *Hyde v Hyde and Woodmansee* (1866) LR 1 P&D 130 (UK)

Facts

Mr Hyde was an Englishman and a member of the Mormon faith. He married a Mormon woman in Salt Lake City, Utah, USA, where polygamy, as part of the Mormon religion, was accepted. Mr Hyde moved to Hawaii as a missionary, but later decided Mormonism was wrong and preached against it. He was excommunicated from the Mormon faith and his wife married another man. Mr Hyde returned to England where he applied for a divorce on the grounds of his wife's 'adultery'.

Issue

Was Mr Hyde's marriage valid?

Decision

The judge decided that English law could not exercise jurisdiction over a potentially polygamous union, because it was not 'exclusive of all others'. So Mr Hyde's marriage was not valid in English law.

Requirements of a valid marriage

As well as the four factors outlined in the definition of *marriage* above, there are several other requirements that a marriage must meet to be legally valid. These are outlined in the *Marriage Act 1961* (Cth) and are as described below.

Marriageable age

People can legally marry at the age of eighteen years but may seek special permission from a court to marry at the age of sixteen years. The court will only grant this permission in exceptional circumstances, such as pregnancy, financial independence and, usually, only if parental consent is given. Before amendments to the Marriage Act in 1991, girls could marry at a younger age than boys.

Parental consent is not required for a marriage to be valid, though most people are reluctant to marry without the blessing of their parents. If a person is not of marriageable age, the presence of parental consent may help persuade the judge to allow the marriage.

Prohibited degrees of relationship

A person may not marry his or her descendant, ancestor, brother or sister. This applies to both full-blood and half-blood brothers and sisters, and also to adopted people. An adopted person may not marry his or her adoptive descendant, ancestor, brother or sister.

Notice of marriage

The parties who wish to marry must give at least one month notice of their intention to marry to the celebrant.

Valid marriage ceremony

The way in which a person is married must also meet certain legal requirements. For a valid ceremony to take place, there must be:

▶ two witnesses to the ceremony who appear to be above the age of eighteen. As long as the parties to the marriage reasonably believe the witnesses to be above the age of eighteen, the marriage is valid.

▶ an authorised marriage celebrant to perform the ceremony. If one party to the marriage honestly and reasonably believes the celebrant to be authorised, the marriage is valid.

Marriage certificate

A marriage certificate is issued by the celebrant after the ceremony is completed. This is legal proof that the ceremony was conducted according to the law.

Void marriages

A marriage will be declared void or invalid if:

▶ one of the parties is already married

▶ the parties are related to each other in a prohibited degree

▶ one party did not really consent to the marriage—that is, he or she was forced into the marriage (duress), tricked into the marriage (fraud), or otherwise did not voluntarily enter into the marriage (see Case Study 4.3 below)

▶ one of the parties is not of marriageable age.

CASE STUDY 4.3: *In the marriage of S* (1980) 5 Fam LR 831

Facts

'S' had come to Australia with her family from Egypt. When she was fifteen, her family arranged for her to return to Egypt to become betrothed to a man who the family had selected for her. While 'S' was very upset by the arrangements, she did not wish to upset her family and also succumbed to pressures from her sisters who told her that no one else would marry her. 'S' thought she had no alternative and, on her return to Australia, went through with the marriage. She was distressed throughout the ceremony and, four days later, her husband returned to Egypt without consummating the marriage. 'S' applied to the Family Court for an annulment of the marriage.

Issue

Was the marriage of 'S' valid?

Decision

The court said that 'S' did not freely give her consent and so the marriage was not valid.

CAN YOU outline the legal requirements of a valid marriage?

In order to outline the legal requirements of a valid marriage, you need to be able to explain and give examples of the following requirements:

▶ the marriage must be between two people

▶ both parties must consent to the marriage

▶ the parties must stay married for life, unless divorced

▶ the parties to the marriage can only be married to one person at any one time

▶ the parties must be of marriageable age (eighteen years)

▶ the parties must not be related in a prohibited degree (a person may not marry his or her descendant, ancestor, brother or sister)

▶ there must be one month of notice of marriage

▶ there must be two witnesses

▶ the ceremony must be performed by an authorised celebrant.

KCq page 268

4.1.3 Alternative family relationships

As seen in Section 4.1.1 (pages 194–5), there are many alternative family arrangements to marriage in today's society. These include Aboriginal and Torres Strait Islander peoples' customary law marriages, single-parent families, blended families, same-sex relationships, polygamous marriages, *de facto* relationships and other family arrangements.

Describe alternative family relationships.

Aboriginal and Torres Strait Islander peoples' customary law marriages

An Aboriginal and Torres Strait Islander customary law marriage is one entered into according to tribal custom rather than according to Australian law. Aboriginal people who marry according to tribal custom are not married according to the rules set out in the *Marriage Act 1961* (Cth) (see Section 4.1.2, pages 197–8). These marriages are not recognised by Australian law and are usually treated by the law as *de facto* relationships (pages 200–1).

However, special provisions are made for children of such marriages, in that the Family Court, in determining what is in the best interests of the child, must consider any need to maintain a connection with the lifestyle, culture and traditions of Aboriginal and Torres Strait Islander peoples (see Section 4.2.2, pages 212–13). Adoption laws also consider this when ordering adoption for Aboriginal and Torres Strait Islander children (see Section 4.1.5, pages 207–9).

Two advantages of treating traditional Aboriginal marriages as *de facto* relationships are that:

- full legal recognition would mean that Aboriginal traditional marriages would be moulded into inappropriate European notions of marriage and divorce. Parties to Aboriginal traditional marriage can divorce and remarry simply and quickly.
- there would be little acknowledgement of traditional roles of men, women and children if such unions were fully recognised.

However, treating Aboriginal traditional marriages as *de facto* relationships means that Aboriginal traditional marriages are not seen as legitimate marriages, so have less social status.

Single-parent families

As seen in Section 4.1.1 (page 195), according to the ABS, single-parent families accounted for 16% of all Australian households in 2006. There has been a growth in single-parent families in recent years which can be attributed to:

- the increased divorce rate
- the change in social attitudes which have made unwed mothers more socially acceptable
- greater financial independence of women
- increased government assistance for such families.

Under the Child Support Scheme, first introduced in 1988, and the *Family Law Act 1975* (Cth) as amended in 1995 and 2006, children have a right to know and be cared for by both parents, and to have regular contact with both parents. It is the responsibility of both parents to ensure that children are cared for, whether or not the parents live together (see Sections 4.1.4 [pages 203–7], 4.2.2 [pages 211–16] and 4.3.2 [pages 234–9]).

Blended families

As seen in Section 4.1.1 (page 194), a blended family is a married or *de facto* couple with children from previous relationships. If the couple is married then the children of one spouse are the stepchildren of the other spouse. The law treats the spouses in a blended family according to their marital status—that is, either as a married couple or as a *de facto* couple. However, the stepfather or stepmother is not legally responsible for the children of his or her partner. Nor does he or she have the same rights of discipline as the natural or legal parents. As is the case for all children, it is the responsibility of both natural parents of a child to ensure they are cared for and maintained (see Sections 4.1.4 [pages 203–7], 4.2.2 [pages 211–16] and 4.3.2 [pages 234–9]).

Same-sex relationships

Until 1999, homosexual or same-sex couples were not recognised by the law at all. In 1999, amendments were made to the *De Facto Relationships Act 1984* (NSW), renaming it the *Property (Relationships) Act 1984* (NSW) and including same-sex relationships in NSW *de facto* relationship legislation. In 2003, NSW referred its powers to make laws about *de facto* relationships to the Commonwealth. The majority of states, with the exception of Western Australia and South Australia, also referred their powers. The *Family Law Amendment (De Facto Financial Matters and other Measures) Act 2008* (Cth) commenced on 1 March 2009. Under this act, same-sex couples are treated in the same way in financial matters as *de facto* and married couples. This act relates primarily to the way property is distributed when a couple separate. This is discussed in Section 4.2.3 (pages 216–18).

The recognition of same-sex relationships is discussed in Section 4.3.1 (pages 232–4).

Polygamous marriages

Polygamous marriages are those in which a person has more than one spouse at any one time. *Polyandry* is the term for a woman having more than one husband at any one time. *Polygyny* is the term for a man having more than one wife at a time. Polygyny is much more common than polyandry so, when the term *polygamy* is used, it generally refers to polygyny.

In some countries, particularly Muslim countries, polygamous marriages are recognised. In Australia, polygamous marriages are not permitted (see Section 4.1.2, Case Study 4.2, page 197). However, a party to a polygamous marriage legally made in another country can apply to the Family Court for divorce, property settlement, parenting orders or other orders (see Sections 4.2.1 to 4.2.3, pages 210–18).

De facto relationships

A *de facto* relationship occurs when a man and woman live together as a married couple, though they are not legally married. That is, they are living in a bona fide domestic relationship. The number of people, particularly young people, living in *de facto* relationships has increased dramatically over the last forty years. In 1971, 0.6% of couples were living in *de facto* relationships. In 1982, this figure had risen to 5.7%. This figure rose to 10% in 1996, 12% in 2001 and was approximately 15% in 2006.

A *de facto* relationship is two adult persons living together. For the law to operate for *de facto* couples, it has to be determined whether a bona fide domestic relationship exists. Several different laws, both state and federal, are relevant to *de facto* couples, and the definition of what constitutes a *de facto* couple varies depending on the law which is operating. The *Family Law Amendment (De Facto Financial Matters and other Measures) Act 2008* (Cth), for example, will operate for separating *de facto* couples if any of the following apply:

- the relationship has existed for an aggregate, but not necessarily continuous, period of two years
- there is a child of the relationship
- a party to the relationship can establish a substantial contribution to the relationship that would result in serious injustice if he or she were to be denied the opportunity to bring proceedings under the act.

This legislation is discussed in Section 4.2.3 (pages 216–17).

History of the legal status of *de facto* relationships

In the past, the law gave no recognition to *de facto* relationships because they were viewed as immoral and as an attack on the institution of marriage. This often resulted in hardship for people in these liaisons. For example, a woman whose *de facto* spouse was killed at work was not entitled to workers' compensation. If a *de facto* spouse died, his or her property would be distributed among his or her family and the surviving *de facto* spouse and children of the relationship would receive nothing.

The law has gradually come to recognise these relationships for various purposes. In amendments made to the *Wills, Probate and Administration Act 1898* (NSW) in 1984, if a *de facto* spouse now dies without a will, the surviving spouse may inherit depending on the circumstances. Similar provisions are provided under the *Succession Act 2006* (NSW) (see Section 4.1.4, pages 205–6). In the situation in which a deceased person leaves both a married spouse and a *de facto* spouse, for instance, the *de facto* spouse inherits as a spouse, providing the relationship is of at least two years duration.

In 1984, the *De Facto Relationships Act 1984* (NSW) was passed which amended the law regarding the breakdown of *de facto* relationships. In 1999, the *Property (Relationships) Act 1984* (NSW) included same-sex relationships in the *de facto* relationship legislation in NSW. The De Facto Relationships Act was renamed the *Property (Relationships) Act 1984* (NSW) to accommodate this change. As seen for same-sex couples on the previous page, the *Family Law Act* was amended in 2008, to include *de facto* couples in its provisions about distribution of property after separation. *De facto* couples, whether heterosexual or homosexual, are now covered by the same laws as married couples in these matters (see Section 4.2.3, pages 216–18).

CAN YOU distinguish between state and federal jurisdiction in family law?

Under the Australian Constitution, the federal government has the power to make laws related to marriage and divorce. The states, therefore, have residual powers to make laws about any other family related matters. It is for this reason that there are both state and federal laws about family.

However, the states have agreed to hand their powers to the Commonwealth in certain matters regarding the family. In 1988 and 1990, all the states and territories, except Western Australia, agreed to hand their jurisdiction about the children of *de facto* couples to the Commonwealth. Now, children from all families come under the jurisdiction of the

Family Law Act 1975 (Cth) (see Section 4.2.2, pages 211–16). The law about the care of children after a relationship breaks down is the same for all children, no matter what the marital status of their parents.

As well, as seen earlier, the states also agreed to hand their jurisdiction over *de facto* relationships to the federal government, with NSW doing so in 2003. Since the *Family Law Amendment (De Facto Financial Matters and other Measures) Act 2008* (Cth) came into effect, the *Family Law Act 1975* (Cth) governs financial matters on the breakdown of all family relationships, whether the parties are married or not, and whether the relationships are heterosexual or homosexual.

However, the states still retain jurisdiction over many areas of family law, including:

- adoption (see Section 4.1.5, pages 207–9)
- wills, inheritance and succession (see Section 4.1.4, pages 205–6)
- many aspects of domestic violence (see Section 4.2.4, pages 218–25)
- surrogacy and birth technologies (see Section 4.3.3, pages 239–45)
- the care and protection of children who are at risk of harm (see Section 4.3.4, pages 245–51).

KCq pages 268–9

4.1.4 Legal rights and obligations of parents and children

What is a *child*?

> Describe the legal rights and obligations between parents and children, including those derived from international law.

A *child* is a person under the age of eighteen years. Another term for a child is a *minor*.

Children generally do not have legal rights until they are born. For example, section 20 of the *Crimes Act 1900* (NSW) states that a person cannot be guilty of murdering a child until the child exists. The act says that: 'such child shall be held to have been born alive if it has breathed, and has been wholly born into the world whether it has had an independent circulation or not'.

In 2005, the *Crimes Act* was amended by the *Crimes Amendment (Grievous Bodily Harm) Act 2005* (NSW) which changed the definition of grievous bodily harm to include the destruction by a person of the foetus of a pregnant woman. This amendment came about because of a car accident in 2001, which caused the death of the unborn baby of Renee Shields, who was seven months pregnant. The car in which she was travelling was hit by another driver, Michael Harrigan, in a road rage incident. This amendment is known as Byron's Law, named after the unborn child.

International law

Australia has ratified several international treaties that deal with the treatment of children, the most important one being the United Nations Convention on the Rights of the Child (CROC). This was adopted by the General Assembly of the United Nations in 1989 and was ratified by Australia in 1990.

The United Nations Convention on the Rights of the Child contains forty articles, most of which confer a right for children. The four basic principles of the convention are:

- non-discrimination
- the best interests of the child
- the right to life, survival and development
- the right to have views expressed and respected.

The CROC has been incorporated into Australian law in a limited way. The convention has been made an 'international instrument' under the *Australian Human Rights and Equal Opportunity Act 1986* (Cth). This means that breaches of the CROC can be reported to the Australian Human Rights Commission. However, Australian courts cannot enforce its provisions. Under the convention, Australia reports regularly to the United Nations Committee on the Rights of the Child (CRC).

The CRC gave its 'Concluding Observations on Australia's Combined Second and Third Reports' on 30 September 2005. The committee expressed concern about several aspects of Australia's protection of the rights of children. Among these were:

- disadvantages faced by Indigenous children, including over-representation in juvenile detention facilities
- corporal punishment being permitted in the home
- the increase in homelessness among young people
- the detention of children in immigration detention centres.

The Australian government has responded to some of these concerns—most notably in 2005, amending the laws about the detention of children in immigration detention facilities by adopting the principle of the detention of children being a measure of last resort, and moving all families with children from such facilities to community detention arrangements (see Section 2.3.3, page 128).

Legal rights and obligations of parents and children

Both federal and state governments have passed legislation which aims to ensure that parents uphold their duties to their children. These laws establish that children have certain rights and that it is the obligation of parents and society as a whole to maintain these rights. When examining these rights, it is clear that there are corresponding responsibilities and obligations between parents and children. Some of the important areas in which the rights and obligations between parents and children arise are described below.

Name and nationality

Each child born in Australia must be registered with the Registrar of Births, Deaths and Marriages. Parents are obliged to do this under the *Births, Deaths and Marriages Registration Act 1995* (NSW). Failure to do so could result in a fine or imprisonment. This gives the child a legal name, which is that of the father or, sometimes, the mother—or a hyphenated surname containing both surnames. Under the *Australian Citizenship Act 2007* (Cth), a child born in Australia is automatically an Australian citizen if one parent is an Australian citizen or a permanent resident.

Discrimination

All children have the right to be treated equally by the law. Ex-nuptial children (those born of unmarried parents) were given the same rights as all other children under the *Children (Equality of Status) Act 1976* (NSW), which was replaced by the *Status of Children Act 1996* (NSW). The *Succession Act 2006* (NSW) gives all children the same rights to inheritance (see pages 205–6). Under the *Family Law Act 1975* (Cth), ex-nuptial children are in the same position as all other children in matters regarding parental responsibility (see Sections 4.2.2 [pages 211–16] and 4.3.2 [pages 234–9]). It is illegal to discriminate against anyone because of race, gender or age.

Care and control

Under the *Family Law Act 1975* (Cth), as amended by the *Family Law Reform Act 1995* (Cth) and the *Family Law Amendment (Shared Parental Responsibility) Act* 2006 (Cth), children have a right to know and be cared for by both parents, and to have regular contact with both parents and other 'significant' people. These rights apply unless they would be contrary to a child's best interests. So, it is the responsibility of parents to ensure that children are cared for. This is a responsibility of both parents, no matter what their marital status. If parents fail to care for their children adequately, the children can be removed from the parents by the state (see Section 4.3.4, pages 245–51). Legislation and bodies which provide for the care of children include:

▶ the *Family Law Act 1975* (Cth) (see Section 4.2.2, pages 211–14)

▶ the Family Court (see Sections 4.2.2 [pages 211–15] and 4.2.5 [pages 225–8])

▶ the Child Support Agency (see Section 4.2.2, pages 215–16)

▶ Family and Community Services (formerly DoCS) (see Section 4.3.4, pages 245–8)

▶ the *Children and Young Persons (Care and Protection) Act 1998* (NSW) (see Section 4.3.4, pages 245–6)

▶ the *Child Protection (Working with Children) Act 2012* (NSW), which makes it mandatory to screen all people in child-related employment to determine they have not committed sex-related crimes.

Parents also have a responsibility to control their child and are responsible to a certain degree for their child's behaviour. Parents can be made to pay damages for harm done by their child if they failed to take reasonable steps to supervise that child. Under the *Children (Protection and Parental Responsibility) Act 1997* (NSW), police in certain designated areas of NSW (usually country towns) have the power to take children under the age of fifteen home if they think the children are at risk of becoming involved in anti-social behaviour. If the parents cannot be located, the police must take the children to a refuge.

This legislation also means the courts have the power to bring before a court the parents of a child found guilty of a criminal offence. The parents must undertake before the court that their child will meet his or her sentence requirements. If a parent does not exercise proper care and control of a child and this contributes to the child being guilty of a criminal offence, the parent may also be guilty of an offence under this legislation.

Discipline

Parents, other people given care of a child by the Family Court, and any adults acting *in loco parentis* (in the place of parents) have the right to administer moderate and reasonable corporal punishment to children in their care. What is 'moderate and reasonable' is determined largely by common law. Corporal punishment is banned in all NSW schools—public and private. If a child is physically, sexually or psychologically abused, the person responsible can be charged under the *Children and Young Persons (Care and Protection) Act 1998* (NSW), which came into force during 2000. The person responsible can also be charged under the *Crimes Act 1900* (NSW) (see Section 4.3.4, pages 245–51).

Education

Parents are obliged, under the *Education Act 1990* (NSW), to send their children to a registered school or to make other approved home education arrangements for their children from the age of six until the children reach the school leaving age. From January 2010, amendments to the *Education*

Act became effective, which mean that, in NSW, students are required to complete school to Year 10 and then to continue in either full-time education, training, paid employment, or a combination of these until they are at least seventeen years of age.

Religion

Parents have the right to choose the religion in which their child will be brought up.

Medical treatment

Until a child is fourteen years of age, a parent must seek medical attention for the child when it is in that child's interest, even if they have religious objections to the treatment. In such cases, the *Children and Young Persons (Care and Protection) Act 1998* (NSW) gives doctors the power to carry out necessary medical treatment without parental consent. Family Court permission is needed before certain medical procedures can take place, including sterilisation, termination of life support, organ donation and transplantation, and treatment of children born grossly deformed. Under the *Minors (Property and Contracts) Act 1970* (NSW), people over the age of fourteen can legally give consent to general medical or dental treatment. So a doctor can legally prescribe contraceptives to a girl over fourteen without her parents' knowledge or consent. The case of *Gillick v West Norfolk and Wisbech Area Health Authority* (1985) is relevant here (see Case Study 4.4 following).

CASE STUDY 4.4: *Gillick v West Norfolk and Wisbech Area Health Authority* (1985) 1 All ER 533 (UK)

Facts

Mrs Gillick, a Catholic mother of five girls, was upset and disturbed when she discovered that the Wisbech Area Health Authority was giving contraceptive advice to girls under the age of sixteen, without their parents' knowledge or consent. Mrs Gillick, after writing to the Wisbech Area Health Authority with no result, took the matter to court, seeking a declaration that the Authority's actions were unlawful and interfered with a parent's rights and duties.

Issue

Was the Wisbech Area Health Authority able to give confidential contraceptive advice to children under sixteen, or was parental consent required? (*Note:* It is illegal for a person to consent to sexual intercourse under the age of sixteen.)

Decision

The matter went to the House of Lords, and Mrs Gillick's claim was dismissed. The court decided that children with the maturity to give informed consent should be legally able to do so. The decision was partly based on the idea that parental powers over children 'dwindle' as children grow up and their autonomy increases.

Contracts

The general rule is that people under eighteen are not bound by a contract, lease or other transaction unless it is for their benefit [*Minors (Property and Contracts) Act 1970* (NSW)].

Succession

Succession refers to the transfer of property to the relatives of a deceased person. A will is a document drawn up by a person, stating how his or her property is to be divided upon his or her death. If a person dies without leaving a will, he or she dies intestate.

Parents have a moral duty to provide, in the event of their death, for the maintenance, education and advancement in life of their children, as far as they are able. The legal system enforces this moral duty in the laws about succession. Under these laws, *child* includes an ex-nuptial child, and an adopted child as well. It may also mean a stepchild.

Until recently, laws about succession were contained in the *Wills, Probate and Administration Act 1898* (NSW). In recent years, the states have moved to adopt uniform succession laws across Australia, and the *Succession Act 2006* (NSW) has now replaced the *Wills, Probate and Administration Act 1898* (NSW) as part of this process.

The Succession Act states the law about how a deceased person's property should be divided when there is no will. Any previous will is rendered invalid by a marriage, unless the will clearly states it is made in anticipation of a forthcoming marriage. The rules are, briefly, as follows:

- if one spouse dies intestate, the other will inherit most, if not all, of his or her property
- if there is no surviving spouse, then the children will inherit the estate
- if there is no surviving spouse or children, the parents of the deceased person will inherit the estate
- if there is no surviving spouse, children or parents, the siblings of the deceased person will inherit the estate.

The rules continue in this way, so that the estate is distributed to the next closest surviving relatives.

Even when there is a will, if members of a family are left unprovided for under the will, they can challenge the will under the *Succession Act* 2006 (NSW). Provisions for such family members previously came under the *Family Provision Act 1982* (NSW), which was enacted to remedy the situation in which a person dies and people who are or have been dependent on that person are not adequately provided for. Under this act, and under the new *Succession Act 2006* (NSW), certain people can apply to the court for a share in the deceased person's estate whether or not there was a will and whether or not they were mentioned in it. People who can apply under the Succession Act include:

- the deceased person's spouse at the time of death
- the deceased person's *de facto* spouse at the time of death
- a child of the deceased person
- a former spouse of the deceased person
- another person who has been wholly or partly dependent on the deceased person at some time.

The Succession Act places an emphasis on mediation or conciliation, stating that all matters are to be referred to mediation prior to a court hearing, unless there are special reasons why mediation should not occur.

Autonomy of children

As children grow older they become more autonomous (that is, they are able to make more and more decisions for themselves). Some of the things children are legally able to do before they are legally adult at age eighteen are:

- consent to their own medical treatment at age fourteen (see Case Study 4.4 on page 205)
- work at age fifteen

- leave home at age sixteen (a child does not have a legal right to leave home until aged eighteen, but a child over sixteen would normally not be forced to return home against his or her wishes)
- consent to sexual intercourse at age sixteen [*Crimes Act 1900* (NSW)]
- drive on a provisional license at age seventeen.

CAN YOU explain the legal rights and obligations of parents and children, including those derived from international law?

In order to explain the legal rights and obligations of parents and children, including those derived from international law, you need to be able to discuss two areas.

First, you need to be able to explain:

- the basic provisions of the United Nations Convention of the Rights of the Child (CROC) 1989
- the status of the Convention of the Rights of the Child in Australia
- how well Australia meets its obligations under the convention.

Second, you need to be able to explain the legal rights of children and the responsibilities of parents in the following areas:

- name and nationality
- discrimination
- care and control
- discipline
- education
- religion
- medical treatment
- contracts
- succession
- autonomy of children.

KCq page 269

4.1.5 Adoption

Adoption is the process whereby people become the legal parents of a child born to someone else. Links between changing community values and adoption laws are discussed in Section 4.4.3 (page 254).

Describe the law regarding adoption.

The law about adoption

Adoption is an area for state law and is governed by the *Adoption Act 2000* (NSW). This act represents substantial reforms to the law about adoption (see Section 4.4.4, page 259). Adopted children have exactly the same status and legal rights as a child born into a marriage. They are treated by the law as if they are the natural children of their adoptive parents.

Who can adopt children?

Under the Adoption Act people over twenty-one, either as a couple or single person, can adopt a child. A *couple* was defined as a man and a woman in a married or *de facto* relationship of at least three years duration. Since amendments to the act in September 2010, a same-sex couple may also adopt a child (see also Section 4.3.1, pages 233–4).

Consent

Both the birth mother and biological father must consent to a child's adoption. If the father's name is not on the child's birth certificate, the father must first establish his paternity. Parents of a newborn child cannot consent to the child's adoption until thirty days after the birth. Counselling must generally be given to birth parents before they consent to adoption. A child must also consent to his or her own adoption if he or she is over twelve years of age.

Contact between adopted children and their biological parents

In April 1991, under the *Adoption Information Act 1990* (NSW), it became possible for adopted people over eighteen years of age and their biological parents to identify and contact each other. The provisions of the Adoption Information Act have been incorporated into the *Adoption Act 2000* (NSW). In 1995, an advance notice request system was introduced, in accordance with recommendations made by the NSW Law Reform Commission in 1992. Under this system, an adoptive parent and adopted child or a birth parent can request that they be given advance notice before personal information is released, in order to make suitable arrangements. The advance notice cannot be longer than three months.

If an adopted adult or the biological parents of an adopted adult do not wish to be contacted they can lodge a contact veto with Community Services (formerly DoCS). This makes it illegal for the other party to contact them.

The Adoption Act also allows for adoption plans. This is a plan made by agreement between the adoptive parents and birth parents, and is often called open adoption. These plans deal with issues such as exchange of information, contact, financial and other post-adoption support arrangements, and cultural upbringing. Adoption plans must be approved by the Supreme Court when an adoption order is made. The plan then has the effect of a court order. An adoption plan can also be confirmed, varied or revoked by the court.

Difficulties in adopting children

Because of the increased availability of effective contraception and abortion, and because of the reduced social stigma attached to unmarried mothers and ex-nuptial children, fewer and fewer children are available for adoption. In 1971–72, over 10 000 babies were adopted in Australia, a small percentage of those being from overseas. In 2005–06, 576 children were adopted in Australia, and 421 of those were from overseas. There is a complex screening system for those who wish to adopt children and, if their application is successful, they are placed on a waiting list until the time when a suitable child becomes available for adoption. Because of these difficulties, childless couples have turned to alternatives such as overseas adoption (see below), birth technologies and surrogacy (see Section 4.3.3, pages 239–45).

Overseas adoption

Overseas adoption is complex and tightly controlled. Different countries have different laws on the availability of their children for adoption overseas. The law concerning overseas adoption is governed by the Hague Convention on Protection of Children and Co-operation in respect of Intercountry Adoption 1993. This came into force in Australia in 1998 and the details of the convention are attached to the *Adoption Act 2000* (NSW).

Under the convention, if the adoption of a child from one country to another takes place (if both are signatories to the convention), then that adoption will be formally recognised in any country which has signed the convention. The signing and implementation of this treaty should make the process of overseas adoption easier for Australian couples who are eligible. However, there is still controversy surrounding the whole issue. Table 4.1 presents arguments for and against overseas adoptions.

Table 4.1 The arguments for and against overseas adoption

Arguments *for* overseas adoption	Arguments *against* overseas adoption
▶ Children from poor countries have the opportunity of a level of emotional and material care which they would not receive in their own country. ▶ The level of care a child can receive if adopted by an Australian couple should outweigh any possible cultural difficulties he or she might experience.	▶ Overseas adoption opens the way for exploitation of poor families in other countries. ▶ It is morally wrong for children to be bought and sold, which can occur with overseas adoptions. ▶ Children raised in a different culture may experience great difficulty in attaining a sense of identity and self-esteem because they have been cut off from their cultural heritage.

 page 269

4.2 Responses to problems in family relationships

Many factors can cause problems in family relationships. Some of the more common causes are:

▶ **money** (many couples disagree about how income should be spent and/or worry about how they will meet debts)

▶ **child rearing** (couples argue about how children should be brought up—for example, in what religion they should be raised or what school they should attend)

▶ **behaviour** (parents and children sometimes disagree about what is acceptable behaviour for a child or what tasks they should perform—which can lead to disputes, particularly between adolescents and their parents)

▶ **division of tasks** (as an increasing number of women enter the workforce, the pressure to perform household duties becomes greater—arguments arise as to who should do particular household tasks).

These disputes can lead to:

▶ separation and divorce (see Section 4.2.1, pages 210–11)

▶ children leaving home (see Section 4.3.4, pages 245–51)

▶ violence, usually directed towards women and children (see Sections 4.2.4 [pages 218–25] and 4.3.4 [pages 245–51]).

▶ crises between children. Often children fight among themselves and these arguments can become quite violent. Such arguments also cause tension between parents.

Most legal disputes involving families occur when adults in families separate. The role of the courts and dispute-settling methods are explained in Section 4.2.5 (pages 225–8). The main courts that deal with family disputes are:

▶ the Family Law Court, established in 1975

▶ the Federal Magistrates Court, established in 2000.

Mediation and agreements also play an important role in solving family disputes. Family Relationship Centres, established by the federal government in 2006, are widely used by separating families to assist in resolving disputes, and avoiding court action. State Courts also have a role in some matters concerning families—particularly issues to do with inheritance, domestic violence and the care of children not cared for sufficiently by their parents (see Sections 4.1.4 [pages 203–4], 4.2.4 [pages 211–13] and 4.3.4 [pages 246–9]).

4.2.1 Divorce

Divorce is the legal dissolution of a marriage. After a divorce, the marriage is finished and each party is free to marry another person.

In 1975, the *Family Law Act* (Cth) was passed. This is the statute that currently governs divorce law in Australia. Under this act there is only one ground for divorce and this is to prove that there has been an irretrievable breakdown of marriage. This means that the marriage has broken down to such an extent that there is no possibility of the parties getting back together (reconciling).

To prove that there has been an irretrievable breakdown, a couple must live separately and apart for a period of twelve months before applying for a divorce. Some characteristics of current divorce law are outlined below.

The no-fault concept

The *Family Law Act 1975* (Cth) caused much controversy when it was passed, because of the idea that neither party was to blame for the marriage breakdown. Before this act was passed, the spouse who committed adultery or who left the marriage was seen as the party at fault. When the Family Law Act was first passed, many people felt that one party should be blamed for the breakdown of the marriage and that decisions about property division and the care of children should take into account who was to blame for the failure of the marriage.

The Family Law Act embodies the view that, once a marriage is finished, there is no point in denying the parties the opportunity to divorce or in assigning blame to one party for the break-up. Changes made to the Family Law Act in 1987, and by the *Family Law Reform Act 1995* (Cth) and the *Family Law Amendment (Shared Parental Responsibility) Act 2006* (Cth), have led to the claim that the concept of fault is returning to divorce proceedings. These changes relate to the consideration of family violence when it comes to property division and care of children (see Sections 4.2.2 [pages 212–13], 4.2.3 [pages 217–18] and 4.2.4 [page 225]).

Separately and apart

As seen above, for a couple to prove there has been an irretrievable breakdown of a marriage, they must prove they have been living separately and apart for a period of twelve months. There are three issues involved with proving this. These are described below.

Intention

For a couple to be living 'separately and apart', there must be the intention to end the relationship on the part of at least one of the parties to the marriage. For example, if one spouse travels overseas for a period, though they are living apart from each other, they are not regarded as living 'separately and apart' for the purposes of divorce because there is no intention to end the relationship.

Separation under one roof

A couple may be living separately and apart while still occupying a house together. As long as one has formed the intention to separate, this can be regarded by the law as being sufficient to prove an irretrievable

> Outline the legal processes involved in dealing with divorce.

breakdown of the marriage. In cases such as this, the court will look at evidence, such as separate social lives and separate bedrooms, to prove that the couple is living as two separate individuals rather than as husband and wife.

The 'kiss and make up' clause

Under the Family Law Act, couples who are separated may try living together again for one period of up to three months. If this does not work out, there is no need for the twelve-month separation period to restart. This clause gives couples a chance to reconcile differences and get back together.

Marriages of less than two years

Couples who have been married for less than two years are generally required to receive counselling before a divorce will be granted.

Divorce orders

When the court has decided that an application for divorce is successful, it grants a divorce order. This is an interim order which means that the couple is divorced, but each party may not remarry until the order is made final one month later. This one-month period gives the parties a last-minute chance to change their minds.

KCq page 269

4.2.2 Legal consequences of separation: children

There are two areas of law regarding children that come into play when their parents separate. These are the care of the children and child maintenance.

Outline the legal consequences of separation with regard to children.

The care of children after separation

Laws regarding the care of children after the parents of the children separate are contained in the *Family Law Act 1975* (Cth), which was changed substantially by the *Family Law Reform Act 1995* (Cth) and further by the *Family Law Amendment (Shared Parental Responsibility) Act 2006* (Cth).

Under the Family Law Act parents whether married or not, both have responsibility for the care and welfare of their children. The legislation emphasises the rights of children and the responsibilities of parents (see also Section 4.3.2, page 236). Before the reforms of 1995, parents were granted custody, guardianship and/or access to their children. The 1995 act introduced the terminology of 'residence' and 'contact' orders. These terms no longer apply to decisions about children made by the Family Court. The terms now used under the act are:

▶ 'live with'

▶ 'spend time with'

▶ 'communicate with.

Some important aspects of the law regarding care of children follow.

Parental responsibility

Both parents (whether they are married, divorced, separated or remarried) separately have responsibility for their children. This idea of parental responsibility is the underlying principle of the law regarding children and operates until children reach adulthood. The idea of *parental responsibility* replaces that of *guardianship* which was defined as the long-term responsibility for a child. The *Family Law Act 1975* (Cth) defines parental responsibility as 'all the duties, powers, responsibilities and authority which, by law, parents have in relation to children'. The

2006 amendments mean that, if the court must make an order regarding a child, the presumption will be that it is in the best interests of the child for the parents to have equal shared parental responsibility (see below, and Section 4.3.2, pages 236–9). This presumption does not operate in cases of child abuse or family violence.

Reaching agreement

Most parents who separate reach an agreement about the responsibility for children without interference from the court. These agreements will be accepted by the court when granting a divorce. The agreements can be:

▶ informal

▶ in the form of a parenting plan

▶ consent orders.

A *parenting plan* is an agreement made by parents about the child. It must be signed and dated by both parties and must deal with: parental responsibility; who the child lives with, spends time with, and communicates with; maintenance; and other issues. A parenting plan can be made with the assistance of a legal practitioner, Family Relationship Centre or other family counsellor. Parenting plans have no force legally but will be considered by the court when making a parenting order (see below).

A *consent order* is an enforceable agreement made by separating people about a wide range of matters. A consent order must be registered with the court and will only be granted in the case of children if the best interests of the child are the main consideration. A consent order is as enforceable as any other parenting order made by the court.

Parenting orders

Parenting orders are orders made by the Family Law Courts about the care of and responsibility for children. Parenting orders can deal with:

▶ who the child is to live with (this could be with two or more people who do not live together—for example, a child could live half the week with one parent and half the week with the other parent)

▶ who a child spends time with

▶ who the child communicates with, and how such communications take place

▶ the allocation of parental responsibility, such as equal shared parental responsibility

▶ the way in which parents communicate with each other regarding major long-term decisions

▶ any other aspects of the child's care.

The Family Law Courts will only make parenting orders if the parents cannot agree about the care of their children. In most circumstances, the parents must attempt dispute resolution before they can apply to the court to make a parenting order (see Section 4.2.5, page 225).

Since 1988, any person with an interest in the child may apply for a parenting order. This includes parents, grandparents and the child him or herself.

The best interests of the child

The best interests of the child are of paramount consideration in decisions regarding the care of children. This is the criterion by which the Family Law Courts make all decisions regarding children. In deciding what is in the best interest of the child, the court will consider primary and additional considerations. Primary considerations are:

- the benefit to the child of having a meaningful relationship with both parents
- the need to protect the child from harm.

Additional considerations include:

- the views of the child, but the court will only give these such weight as it considers appropriate. That is, the court may not follow the child's views if they would not serve the child's best interest.
- each parent's willingness and ability to facilitate and encourage a close and continuing relationship between the child and the other parent
- whether the orders made are likely to lead to further dispute. The court tries to make orders that are least likely to do this.
- the effect of changing the existing living conditions of the child
- the attitude to parenting of those who are applying for orders and their capacity to care for the child
- the practical difficulties and expense involved in 'spending time with' and 'communicating with' a parent
- the capacity of each parent and others to provide for the child's needs
- the maturity, gender, lifestyle and background of the child and the parents
- the nature of the relationship of the child with each parent and with other people
- any family violence or family violence order that applies to the child, or his or her family
- any other circumstance the court thinks relevant.

Family violence

The consideration of family violence by the court was introduced under the *Family Law Reform Act 1995* (Cth). Previously, only violence to the child concerned was considered. These provisions recognise that, where there has been violence between spouses, the child can also be adversely affected. It recognises that contact between a child and a violent parent can be detrimental to the child and dangerous to the other parent. The Family Law Courts must ensure that any orders they make are consistent with any family violence orders made by any other court, keeping the best interest of the child as the paramount consideration. The provisions regarding family violence in the *Family Law Act 1975* (Cth) are discussed in Case Study 4.5 (page 214–15) and in Section 4.2.4 (pages 221–3).

Equal shared parental responsibility

As seen above, since 2006, there has been a presumption that it is in the best interests of the child for the parents to have equal shared parental responsibility. This means that the parents must consult each other and agree on 'major long-term issues', such as the child's education, religious and cultural upbringing and the child's name (see Section 4.3.2, page 249). An order for equal shared parental responsibility does not necessarily mean that a child must spend equal time with both parents. The presumption of equal shared parental responsibility does not apply if there has been, or there is a risk of family violence. The presumption can also be rebutted—that is, one parent can argue that equal shared parental responsibility is not in the best interests of the child.

If an order for equal shared parental responsibility is made, the court must then consider making an order for 'equal time' or 'substantial and significant time'. An order for a child spending 'substantial and significant time' with one parent means that the child should spend time with the parent that includes weekends, weekdays and holidays and allows the parent to share daily routines and special occasions with the child. Once again, the best interests of the child is the paramount concern when deciding whether or not to grant equal time or substantial and significant time with both parents The success of these provisions is discussed in Case Study 4.5 below.

Controversy about the care of children under the *Family Law Act*

The 2006 changes to the Family Law Act have prompted much controversy. The two main areas of concern are

▶ the consideration of family violence in the decision-making process

▶ the idea of equal time parenting.

Both of these matters were subject to review during 2009 and are discussed in Case Study 4.5. The treatment of family violence in Family Court decisions about children is also discussed in Section 4.2.4 (pages 222–4).

CASE STUDY 4.5: Review of the 2006 Family Law Reforms, January 2010

On 28 January 2010, the Federal Attorney General, Robert McClelland, released three independent reviews of the reforms relating to shared parental responsibility and equal time parenting introduced by the *Family Law Amendment (Shared Parental Responsibility) Act 2006* (Cth). These reviews are:

▶ 'Evaluation of the 2006 Family Law Reforms' by the Australian Institute of Family Studies. This review is the most comprehensive review ever undertaken of the impact of family law and it involved gathering data from 28 000 people, including 10 000 parents affected by the changes.

▶ 'Family Courts Violence Review: A report' by Professor Richard Chisholm (January 2010). Professor Chisholm is former Justice of the Family Court and was commissioned to undertake the review after a four-year-old girl, Darcey Freeman, died after being thrown off the West Gate Bridge in Melbourne on 29 January 2009, by her father in the presence of her two brothers and many commuters.

▶ 'Improving Responses to Family Violence in the Family Law System' by the Family Law Council.

The best interests of the child and equal time parenting

Together, these reviews found that:

▶ 16% of children spend equal or substantial time with both parents, which is an increase from 9% in 2003

▶ children whose parents are in conflict have more problems than those whose parents cooperate, no matter what the living arrangements

▶ there has been a 22% decline in the number of cases going to court regarding the care of children, and most separating parents are happy with the new network of Family Relationship Centres (see Section 4.2.5, page 226–7)

▶ there was considerable confusion about the shared care provisions of the act both from separating parents and from the ranks of the legal profession. The legislation has led many parents to 'wrongly assume' that the law means that children should spend equal time with both parents, and to confuse the ideas of equal time with shared responsibility.

- Chisholm found that the legislation 'may also have led to the very opposite [of what was] intended, namely the parties thinking about their own entitlements rather than what is best for their children'.

Family violence

The reports found that two provisions of the legislation are potentially putting women and children at risk of family violence, because women are afraid to raise the issue in court.

- The first of these provisions is 'the willingness of each of the children's parents to encourage a close and continuing relationship between the child, and the other parent, after divorce'. The reports found that some women were scared to raise issues of violence for fear that, if they did, the court would view them as the unwilling or 'unfriendly' parent, and grant them less time with the children as a result.

- The second provision about violence that was criticised by the reports involved costs. The act provides for the awarding of costs against a parent who either maliciously raises untrue allegations of violence or makes untrue denials. The reports found that this provision also discouraged women from making reports about family violence.

Child maintenance

Both parents have a duty to maintain their children until they reach the age of eighteen, or even longer if they are still studying. *Maintenance* refers to a payment made by one person to help contribute to the care and welfare of another person.

Until 1989, the Family Court made decisions about maintenance, but two problems emerged:

- the amount of maintenance ordered by the court was often much lower than the real cost of supporting a child, partly because the court took into account social security benefits received by the custodial parent

- over 70% of parents avoided paying child maintenance.

As a result of these two factors, many single parents and children were living in poverty, relying on social security benefits as their only form of income. Also, the community as a whole was left with the financial burden of maintaining these children. The Child Support Scheme was introduced in 1988 to combat these problems.

The Child Support Scheme

From June 1988, child maintenance has been collected by the Child Support Agency. The amount to be paid is deducted from the wages of one parent and paid to the parent with whom the children live, making it much more difficult for people to avoid paying maintenance.

Collection and enforcement of maintenance payments

The Department of Human Services collects maintenance from parents by either:

- arranging for an employer to deduct payments from a parent's pay

- having the parent send money to the agency.

If a liable parent fails to make required payments, the Department of Human Services can:

- garnishee wages, which means the agency can arrange for the payments to be taken out of the liable parent's wages

▶ seize and sell property

▶ sequester an estate

▶ intercept tax refunds.

These enforcement and collection measures have meant that far more liable parents pay child maintenance than was the case before the introduction of the Child Support Scheme.

Private child support agreements

Parents can make private agreements about the amount of child maintenance to be paid and arrangements about its collection, without involving the Department of Human Services. If the carer parent is receiving money from Centrelink, however, the agreement must be approved by Centrelink.

CASE STUDY 4.6: Success of the Child Support Scheme

Background

There is no doubt that, since its introduction in 1988, the Child Support Scheme has significantly increased the number and size of child maintenance payments. The scheme was reviewed in depth in 1994 and 2004 and, subsequently, changed significantly in both 1998 and 2008.

Changes to the formula in 2008

The significant changes that were made to the formula for determining the amount of child maintenance to be paid were reviewed by the Child Support Agency in August 2008 via a survey of 300 payers and 300 payees. This is only a very small proportion of the 1.4 million parents involved in the scheme. The survey found that 63% of those who received support and 76% of those who paid it agreed that the new formula was more balanced.

According to a study conducted by the Department of Families, Housing, Community Services and Indigenous Affairs in August 2008, 50% of recipients of child maintenance have had payments reduced, 37% have had payments increased, and 51% of payers are paying less.

While the new formula seems to meet the approval of the majority of parents, there has been concern expressed that those on very low incomes who rely on government support and who have lost child support income, are not adequately compensated by increases in the family tax benefit. This is particularly true for those who were already receiving the maximum benefit.

Compliance

The Minister for Human Services, Joe Ludwig, reported in October 2008 that figures from the Child Support Agency showed only 50% of paying parents paid child support in full and on time. A large number did not lodge tax returns within a reasonable time and an estimated 30 000 were deliberately avoiding child support through income minimisation schemes. In the previous twelve months, an extra $73 million was collected as a result of stepped up compliance by the agency.

Source: 'Parents back new child support', Adele Horin, *The Sydney Morning Herald*, 11 October 2008, and 'Worthy and unworthy winners', *The Sydney Morning Herald*, 11 October 2008.

 KCq page 269

Outline the legal consequences of separation with regard to property.

4.2.3 Legal consequences of separation: property

When a relationship breaks down, the property that has been shared between the two parties must be divided between them. The *Family Law*

Act 1975 (Cth) determines how the property is to be split. Since the commencement of the *Family Law Amendment (De Facto Financial Matters and other Measures) Act 2008* (Cth), the provisions of the Family Law Act regarding the distribution of property apply not only to divorcing married couples, but also to separating *de facto* couples, both heterosexual and homosexual.

The property of the parties to a marriage or *de facto* relationship is all the property owned by both parties. This can include houses, cars, household goods, bank accounts, shares, gifts and inheritances, compensation, lottery winnings and superannuation. All these can be regarded as joint property, regardless of whose name the property is in.

Court decisions

When deciding how to divide the property between the two parties whose relationship has broken down, the court looks at each case individually and goes through a four-step process which involves:

- deciding what property the parties own and its value
- considering the contributions of each party to the property in the past. This includes the financial and non-financial contributions of each party. Non-financial contributions include maintaining and cleaning the home and grounds, cooking, and looking after children. These are taken into account because if one person takes on these responsibilities the other is free to earn an income.
- considering the present and future needs of each party, including income, earning capacity and the care of children
- considering whether the proposed division is just and equitable in all circumstances.

Superannuation

Deciding how to consider superannuation entitlements in property division is difficult for the court because such money is locked away until a person retires, yet is still a financial asset of the marriage. If one party has a substantial superannuation fund, and the other does not, this is often because one party has had the opportunity to work and accrue superannuation, while the other has made non-financial contributions to the relationship. Sometimes the court has awarded superannuation entitlements to one party and, to compensate, awarded the other party a greater share of other property, such as the family home.

In the case of *Coghlan v Coghlan* (2005) FLC 93-220, the Full Court of the Family Court decided that superannuation should be treated separately to other property. This means the court must deal with two separate pools of property, the non-superannuation and the superannuation property, and apply the four-step process to each pool. The decision in *Coghlan v Coghlan* is currently the basis for making decisions about superannuation. Usually, the superannuation is split into two separate funds, one for each party.

Property division and the no-fault concept

Some argue that the concept of fault has become part of some property orders in that the court may decide that one party has made negative contributions to the property of the marriage. For example, in the case of *Kowaliw v Kowaliw* (1981) FLC 91-092, the financial losses to the property caused by the negligence, alcoholism and gambling of one party did not have to be shared by the other party.

Family violence may also be considered as making a negative contribution to the property. In the case of *Kennon v Kennon* (1997) FLC 92-757, the court considered that the wife's non-financial contributions as a homemaker were increased because they had been made more difficult to perform as a result of the husband's violence towards her.

Agreements

Property settlements are often made by agreement between the parties, which saves the cost of going to court. Before the court will make a property order, parties are obliged to attend a compulsory conciliation conference with the Family Court Registrar who is a lawyer with specialised knowledge of property and maintenance. The Family Court Registrar can help the parties come to an agreement before they go to court. If an agreement is reached at such a conference, the registrar may make a consent order. This is an enforceable agreement, made between separating people, about a wide range of matters, including property allocation.

Binding financial agreements can also be made by the parties who are separating. These became possible under the *Family Law Amendment Act 2000* (Cth), and are agreements that will be enforced by the law dealing with some or all of the financial resources of the parties to a marriage. They can be entered into:

- before a marriage
- during a marriage
- after a marriage has broken down.

For such an agreement to be binding, the agreement must:

- be in writing and be signed by both parties
- have certificates confirming that independent legal advice has been received by both parties.

Agreements can also be terminated or varied by a subsequent agreement. Similar agreements may be made by *de facto* couples. The court may vary such agreements if it would lead to serious injustice.

Spousal maintenance

Spousal maintenance is not often awarded by the court, and then only if one party is unable to support him or herself and if the other party is reasonably able to support him or her. A party is usually in the position of being unable to support him or herself because he or she:

- is caring for children
- cannot obtain work because of illness, age or some other reason.

The Child Support Agency can also collect this type of maintenance.

KCq page 269

4.2.4 Dealing with domestic violence

Explain how the law deals with domestic violence.

About domestic violence

The extent of domestic violence

Domestic violence is actual or threatened violence or harassment within a domestic relationship. Domestic violence does not mean only physical violence. It can also mean verbal and psychological violence, including intimidation, threats and stalking. Shouting abuse or depriving one's spouse of money or freedom can be forms of domestic violence.

In the vast majority of domestic violence cases, women are the victims. It is hard to determine the extent of domestic violence, because it is often unreported. However, 'The Australian Component of the International Violence Against Women Survey', conducted in 2002 and 2003, found that one-third of women surveyed had experienced violence from a current or former partner at some time during their lifetime.

Domestic violence is the most common form of assault in Australia. Domestic violence related assaults accounted for 37% of all assaults reported to NSW police in 2007. The NSW Ombudsmen found that the NSW police responded to approximately 120 000 domestic violence incidents each year ('Domestic Violence: improving police practice', NSW Ombudsman, 2006).

Causes of violence in families

Domestic violence occurs in all age groups, nationalities and socioeconomic backgrounds. Various theories have been put forward to explain why domestic violence occurs, but none explain why it occurs in some families and not in others. Some of these theories are:

▶ the 'cycle-of-violence' theories (which say that violence is more likely to occur when it has been witnessed in childhood—when the child grows up, he or she uses or tolerates violence, and so the cycle is perpetuated). However, this only assists to explain violence in some families. Women's refuge figures show that most women who have sought shelter in refuges from violence have grown up in non-violent families.

▶ structural theories (which say that violence is a response to external pressures, such as poverty, unemployment, alcoholism and cultural displacement)

▶ manifestation-of-male-supremacy theory (which argues that, because men are raised to be aggressive and dominating, they use violence against their spouses when they feel threatened or angry).

Attitudes to domestic violence

The Australian Institute of Criminology published the 'Community Attitudes to Violence Against Women Survey' in 2006, which showed that some attitudes still persist in society that mistakenly minimise the seriousness of domestic violence. For example:

▶ the yelling of abuse, repeated criticism, denial of money and control of a partner's social life were seen as less serious behaviours

▶ domestic violence was seen as excusable if it was because of temporary anger and it led to genuine regret

▶ a belief that women often make up claims of domestic violence in family law disputes to improve their case (see below, and Case Study 4.5, Section 4.2.2, pages 214–15).

The main legal responses to domestic violence

The law responds to domestic violence through:

▶ apprehended violence orders (AVOs), in particular apprehended domestic violence orders (ADVOs)

▶ criminal charges

▶ family court injunctions and other orders.

Apprehended violence orders

An apprehended violence order (AVO) is an order imposed by a Local Court which restricts the behaviour of the defendant for a period of time.

Apprehended violence orders were introduced as part of the *Crimes Act 1900* (NSW) in 1983 and have since been improved and strengthened. The legislation now governing AVOs is the *Crimes (Domestic and Personal Violence) Act 2007* (NSW). These orders are by far the most commonly used legal weapon against domestic violence. The NSW Bureau of Crime Statistics and Research (BOCSAR) shows that, in 2008, over 22 000 Apprehended Domestic Violence Orders were granted.

Obtaining an AVO

An AVO can be obtained by a victim if he or she can prove, on the balance of probabilities, that he or she has reasonable grounds to apprehend (fear), and does in fact fear, personal violence, intimidation or stalking by the defendant.

Apprehended violence orders can be obtained by anyone over sixteen years of age and whole families can be protected by one order. Either the police or the victim, through a chamber magistrate, can start proceedings to obtain an order.

An AVO usually takes effect after there has been a court hearing which proves, on the balance of probabilities, that the person seeking the order has reasonable grounds to fear future violence from the defendant. Apprehended violence orders usually remain in force for twelve months.

Interim AVOs can be obtained over the telephone by police from a magistrate. These can remain in force for up to twenty-eight days and can be issued if the police are satisfied that the person seeking the order is at immediate risk. A provisional AVO remains in force until a court hearing. The order takes effect when it is served on (given to) the defendant, and police can detain a defendant in order to serve the order.

Behaviours restricted by AVOs

Apprehended violence orders are very flexible because the court can order that the defendant restrains himself or herself from a large range of activities, such as:

- assaulting or threatening the victim, or any person who has a domestic relationship with the victim
- possessing firearms
- approaching the victim's home
- stalking or intimidating the victim.

Police have broad powers to search for and seize firearms in a house where there has been a complaint of domestic violence. The police must suspend any firearm licences and seize firearms from a person who is subject to an AVO.

In NSW, it is possible to register a restraining or protection order from another state. So, if a victim of domestic violence has a protection order from another state, that order also applies in NSW.

Breaching an AVO

If the defendant fails to obey an AVO, he or she can be arrested immediately and be found guilty of a criminal offence. Maximum penalties for breach of an AVO are a $5500 fine and/or two years imprisonment.

Under amendments to the *Bail Act 1978* (NSW) there is no presumption in favour of bail where an AVO has been breached by an act of violence and there has been a previous history of violence (see Section 1.2.5, page 18).

ADVOs and APVOs

There are two types of apprehended violence orders available in NSW. These are:

- apprehended domestic violence orders (ADVOs), made to protect people against behaviour from someone with whom they are or have been in a domestic relationship
- apprehended personal violence orders (APVOs), made when the protected person and the defendant are not and have not been in a domestic relationship.

There are several differences between ADVOs and APVOs. These include:

- a police officer has a duty to make an application for an ADVO in cases when the officer suspects that a domestic violence offence has recently been committed, or is about to be committed. There is no such duty for AVPOs
- a chamber magistrate cannot refuse to issue an application for an ADVO, whereas he or she can do so for an AVPO
- a protected person's home address must not be included in an ADVO or an application for an ADVO, except in limited circumstances.

Criminal charges

Under the *Crimes (Domestic and Personal Violence) Act 2007* (NSW), there are a range of offences called domestic violence offences. These are crimes that involve violence between people in a domestic relationship and which are also made illegal under the *Crimes Act 1900* (NSW). Police are required to apply for an ADVO if an offence committed is recorded as a domestic violence offence. Four offences which commonly occur as domestic violence offences are assault, malicious damage, stalking and intimidation.

Assault

The police can charge the perpetrator of a domestic violence attack with assault under the *Crimes Act 1900* (NSW) if an assault has actually taken place. This is like any other assault charge and must be proved beyond reasonable doubt (see Section 1.3.6, page 30). It does not include activities such as harassment.

Stalking and intimidation

These have been made a separate offence under the *Crimes (Domestic and Personal Violence) Act 2007* (NSW). Stalking includes following a person, spying on them and frequenting a place where that person works or lives. Intimidation includes other behaviours, such as nuisance telephone calls or other unwelcome forms of communication, and harassing or threatening someone. These behaviours can be criminal offences when a defendant engages in such acts with the intention or reasonable foresight of putting a victim in fear for his or her personal safety, or for their family's safety. Maximum penalties for these offences are a fine of up to fifty penalty units and five years imprisonment.

Family Court Orders

Under the *Family Law Act 1975* (Cth) and the *Property (Relationships) Act 1984* (NSW), a victim of domestic violence can seek various other orders similar to an AVO. These are described on the following page.

Injunctions

An injunction is a court order which either prevents someone from doing something or orders them to do something. A Family Court injunction can be obtained through the Family Court under the *Family Law Act 1975* (Cth). This injunction operates in much the same way as an AVO but is more difficult to enforce. Breaches of these injunctions carry similar penalties to breaches of an AVO. These injunctions are seldom used because of the ease of obtaining an AVO. Sometimes they are sought when a couple is already before the court because of divorce proceedings or related matters.

Family violence and parenting orders

Under the *Family Law Amendment (Shared Parental Responsibility) Act 2006* (Cth), family violence refers to: 'conduct, whether actual or threatened, by a person towards, or towards the property of, a member of the person's family that causes that or any other member of the person's family reasonably to fear for, or reasonably to be apprehensive about, his or her personal wellbeing or safety'.

When the court is considering a parenting order for a child, it must consider whether there has been family violence or a family violence order made about any member of the family. A family violence order could refer to an AVO or any similar order. The Family Court must ensure that any orders it makes about the future of a child are consistent with existing family violence orders. A Local Court, when granting an AVO, can change a parenting order or parenting plan (see Section 4.2.2, pages 212–15).

As seen in Case Study 4.5, Section 4.2.2 (pages 214–15), recent reports show that some women have been reluctant to reveal family violence to the Family Court because of fear that their applications to care for their children may consequently be viewed unfavourably.

The advantages and disadvantages of the three main legal responses to domestic violence discussed above are listed in Table 4.2.

Table 4.2 The advantages and disadvantages of legal responses to domestic violence

The main legal responses to domestic violence	
Advantages	Disadvantages
Apprehended violence orders (AVOs)	
<ul><li>Very flexible.</li><li>Protect the victim in the future.</li><li>Proceedings can be instituted by police or the victim.</li><li>The victim can be protected immediately because bail conditions and interim orders can be given, and guns can be confiscated. Police can also detain a person in order to serve him or her with a provisional AVO.</li><li>Proof is on the civil standard of 'the balance of probabilities' so it is easier to prove than a criminal offence.</li><li>The perpetrator is guilty of a criminal offence only if he or she breaches the order.</li></ul>	<ul><li>A breach may be hard to prove.</li><li>Police may be reluctant to institute proceedings for an AVO even when required to do so.</li><li>A piece of paper may not be sufficient to stop someone doing something that he or she is determined to do.</li><li>Sometimes the issuing of an AVO may lead to an increase in violence because of resentment felt by the offender.</li></ul>

Criminal charges	
It is acknowledged that the assailant has committed a criminal offence.	This focuses on one incident only and does not look at a history of violence.
The victim can lay charges if the police will not do so.	Standard of proof is 'beyond reasonable doubt', so it is harder to prove than an AVO.
Can lead to police applying for an AVO if the offence is recognised as a 'domestic violence offence'.	Some police and victims are reluctant to pursue criminal charges because they result in a criminal conviction.
Family Court orders	
Injunctions restrict a wide range of behaviours, as does an AVO.	Injunctions are harder to enforce than an AVO.
Deals with violence as part of a larger family problem.	Not as immediately obtainable as an AVO.
Parenting orders recognise the effects of family violence on children.	Women may be reluctant to claim family violence for fear of being viewed unfavourably by the court.

Other responses to domestic violence

Spousal murder

In extreme cases, domestic violence can result in spousal murder. Usually women, and sometimes children, are the victims of such murders. In 2009, the NSW government announced the establishment of a domestic violence homicide review panel to investigate such murders in an effort to prevent these deaths. The Domestic Violence Death Review Team was established by legislation in 2010. This is discussed further in Case Study 4.7 following.

CASE STUDY 4.7: Panel set up to review domestic violence deaths

Background

The NSW Minister for Women stated in a media release on 25 November 2009 that: 'from 2003 to 2008, 215 people died as a result of domestic violence, which equates to 42% of all homicides. Most of those who died were women'.

In November 2008, the NSW Ombudsman, in an interview with the *Sydney Morning Herald*, stated that the government's response to the issue was inadequate and a review would significantly reduce the death toll by identifying the risk factors for domestic violence homicides and identifying where families fall through the cracks. 'You will usually see threats of violence or homicide being made before a death occurs, or find access to weapons, or previous examples of depression, drug or alcohol issues,' he said. Pressure from the media in a series of articles about the matter in November 2008, as well as pressure from lobby groups such as the Domestic Violence Coalition Committee helped convince the government to make this announcement (see Sections 4.2.6 [pages 228–9] and 4.2.7 [pages 229–31])

Calls for a review panel

There have been calls for a domestic homicide review panel in NSW for several years.

- In 2006, the NSW Ombudsman recommended the establishment of a similar team after a review of police practice in response to domestic violence.

▶ In November 2008, the Victorian Attorney General announced the establishment of a similar panel, prompting calls from the media and from lobby groups for NSW to do the same (see Sections 4.2.6 [pages 228–9] and 4.2.7 [pages 229–31]).

▶ The establishment of similar review panels in other jurisdictions, such as in Britain, Canada and some states of the US, has led to a substantial drop in domestic violence related murders. In Santa Clara County, California, for example, there were fifty-one domestic homicides in 1997. With reforms implemented after a homicide review, the number of deaths fell to three in 2007.

The NSW review panel

The NSW review panel, announced in November 2009, will consist of government and non-government members, and will be chaired by the Coroner or a former coronial officer, allowing the panel access to the National Coroner's Information System (NCIS) and, therefore, to information about domestic violence related deaths across Australia. The *Coroners Amendment (Domestic Violence Death Review Team) Act 2010*, establishing the panel, was passed by NSW parliament in June 2010.

Sources: 'Panel set up to review domestic violence deaths', media release, NSW Minister for Women The Hon. Linda Burney MP and Attorney General The Hon. John Hatzistergos MLC, Wednesday, 25 November 2009; and 'Shameful secret of our family murder epidemic', Ruth Pollard, *The Sydney Morning Herald*, 24 November 2008.

Battered woman syndrome

Sometimes a woman who has been a victim of domestic violence over a long period resorts to killing the partner who has subjected her to the violence. Often such women will suffer from 'battered woman syndrome'. This means that the woman suffering feels so helpless that she cannot see any other way out of her situation.

Typically, such women kill their partners when they are asleep or have passed out. Such killings do not usually fall within the rules of either self-defence or provocation (see Section 1.3.8, pages 33–8). However, during recent years the rules regarding both self-defence and provocation have been widened so that they can be available to women who kill while suffering from battered woman's syndrome. Courts have accepted evidence of domestic violence as acting to mitigate sentences and such evidence has led to decisions by the state not to prosecute. This is further discussed in Section 1.3.8 (page 38).

Other responses

There have been several other responses to domestic violence including:

▶ the **women's refuge program**, first established in 1974, which provides a place to stay for women fleeing domestic violence across NSW

▶ the **Staying Home Leaving Violence** program which assists women to stay in their homes by removing the violent offender, providing community support and developing safety plans for women and children which may involve changing locks, installing security doors and a phone alarm system

▶ the **Women's Domestic Violence Court Assistance Scheme** is available at many courthouses and will provide free legal assistance to women when they first go to court to obtain an ADVO, and/or organise the woman a solicitor

▶ the **Start Safely** rental subsidy, which helps domestic violence victims, who have left refuges or their own homes, to move into private accommodation

▶ **victims' compensation** may be available for domestic violence victims (see Section 1.7.5, page 75)

▶ **personal injury claims**. A victim of violence, domestic or otherwise, can also sue the perpetrator in civil proceedings for compensation. This may be an expensive and lengthy option.

CAN YOU evaluate the effectiveness of the law in protecting victims of domestic violence?

In order to do this, you need to discuss the factors which enhance, and those which limit, the effectiveness of the law in protecting victims of domestic violence. Then you need to decide how effective the protection is, given the two sets of factors. These factors are listed below.

Factors which help ensure the effectiveness of the law in protecting victims of domestic violence

▶ The advantages of the legal responses of AVOs, criminal charges and Family Court orders are outlined in Table 4.2 on pages 222–3.

▶ AVOs are a quick, inexpensive, flexible and effective legal measure for dealing with domestic violence and preventing it from recurring, though there are disadvantages, as outlined in Table 4.2 on pages 222–3.

▶ The fact that 22 000 AVOs are issued annually shows that domestic violence victims are willing to take action to prevent it recurring.

▶ The classification of some offences as 'domestic violence offences' means that women can quickly be protected from further violence, because police must apply for an ADVO.

▶ The 2010 establishment of the Domestic Violence Death Review Team may reduce murders stemming from domestic violence.

▶ Various other responses to domestic violence, such as the Staying Home Leaving Violence program, the Women's Domestic Violence Court Assistance Scheme and the Start Safely rental subsidy scheme, can assist domestic violence victims to deal with domestic violence situations and protect themselves and their families from further abuse.

Factors which limit the effectiveness of the law in protecting victims of domestic violence

▶ The extent of domestic violence shows that the legal measures do not prevent the violence from occurring.

▶ The fact that some attitudes which mistakenly minimise the seriousness of domestic violence still persist in the community, means that it is difficult to prevent domestic violence from occurring or from the need to deal with perpetrators when it does occur.

▶ The disadvantages of the legal responses of AVOs, criminal charges and Family Court orders are outlined in Table 4.2 on pages 222–3.

▶ The fact that 22 000 AVOs are issued annually shows that domestic violence is a widespread problem, though it might also indicate that victims are willing to take action to prevent it recurring.

▶ Fear of negative responses from the Family Court when applying for parenting orders may make some women reluctant to raise issues of family violence.

▶ The number of domestic violence related homicides shows that, for these victims, other legal responses to domestic violence have been inadequate.

 KCq page 270

4.2.5 The roles of courts and dispute resolution methods

When problems occur in family relationships, the Federal Courts often only have a role after other dispute-settling methods have failed. This is the case in:

▶ the granting of divorces

▶ making arrangements for the care of children after separation

▶ the division of property after separation.

The role of the courts in these matters is discussed below.

As seen in Section 4.1.3 (page 199), the NSW State Courts have a role in the areas of:

▶ adoption (see Section 4.1.5, pages 207–9)

▶ wills, inheritance and succession (see Section 4.1.4, pages 205–6)

▶ most aspects of domestic violence (see Section 4.2.4, pages 218–25)

▶ surrogacy and birth technologies (see Section 4.3.3, pages 239–45)

▶ care and protection of children (see Section 4.3.4, pages 245–51).

In many family matters, particularly those which come under federal jurisdiction, other dispute-settling methods which encourage parties to come to agreement are very important. These are also discussed in this section.

> Explain the role of courts and dispute resolution methods in responding to problems in family relationships.

The Family Law Courts

The Family Court of Australia was established under the *Family Law Act* in 1975. In 2000, the Federal Magistrates Court was established under the *Federal Magistrates Act 1999* (Cth). This was renamed the Federal Circuit Court in 2013. Couples wanting a divorce have access to both these courts which, together, are known as the Family Law Courts.

The Federal Circuit Court

More than 75% of family law matters are completed in the Federal Circuit Court. This court determines simpler family law matters, and all applications for divorce are filed with the Federal Circuit Court. A divorce will be granted by the court if property matters are suitably agreed upon and if suitable arrangements have been made for any children of the marriage. There will usually be no court hearing if there are no children under the age of eighteen involved (see Section 4.2.1, pages 222–3).

The Family Court of Australia

The Family Court of Australia is a superior court and only hears more complex matters, such as:

- parenting cases which involve multiple parties, allegations of abuse or child welfare agencies
- complex financial matters.

The role of judges

If the parties cannot agree about the dissolution of the marriage, the court will decide for them. When the Family Court of Australia was first opened in 1975, judges did not wear wigs and gowns, and the court was closed to create a non-threatening and private atmosphere in the courtroom. However, this lack of formality helped lead to bombings and bomb threats directed towards judges, their families and courts. People did not see the courts as having the full authority of the law.

Today, judges sometimes wear wigs and gowns and the courts are open, though the names of those involved in a hearing may not be reported in the media. So there is some formality in the courts, the public are aware of what occurs there, and people's privacy is still protected. Since 2006, less adversarial proceedings involving children have been introduced and are called 'child related proceedings'.

Dispute resolution

Both Family Law Courts provide for dispute resolution in the form of counselling, mediation and conciliation to help people sort out their differences and arrive at their own agreements over issues such as the care of children, maintenance and property division. Counsellors must be used if the marriage is less than two years old and if the parties cannot agree about the care of children. Over 90% of dissolutions are resolved at this stage without the necessity for having a decision imposed by the judges.

Counselling and mediation have always been important aspects of the Family Court. Dispute resolution methods for families are provided by Family Relationship Centres (see below) and other community-based dispute resolution organisations. Mediation is the process whereby a third person, known as the *mediator,* listens to the parties to a dispute and helps them to minimise their differences and reach agreement. Counselling is similar to mediation but involves a healing focus. The Family Law Courts normally refer those matters about which parties are in conflict to family dispute resolution providers before making a determination on the matters.

Significant changes were made to the law about dispute resolution in family matters by the *Family Law Amendment (Shared Parental Responsibility) Act 2006* (Cth). Under this act, Family Relationship Centres were established across Australia to provide dispute resolution services for families on a wide range of matters, including disputes about the care of children during the process of dissolving a marriage. If the parents can't agree about the care of their children then, in most circumstances, they must attempt dispute resolution before they can apply to the court to make a decision about the matter.

Advantages of dispute resolution mechanisms

The renewed emphasis on the use of counselling, mediation and other dispute resolution mechanisms reflects the following advantages of these methods over a court hearing:

- it is cheaper
- it is quicker
- often a solution reached this way is best for all parties concerned because they have agreed to it. It is, therefore, less likely that there will be further dispute.

Disadvantages of dispute resolution mechanisms

- Fair and successful mediation depends on equal bargaining power between the parties. Often there is a power imbalance between parties to a marriage because of uneven economic circumstances and, therefore, uneven access to legal help, or because of family violence. However, the *Family Law Amendment (Shared Parental Responsibility) Act 2006* (Cth) dispenses with the requirement for dispute resolution if there has been, or there is a risk of, family violence. Despite this, there is still concern that power imbalances may remain hidden, making the mediation process less likely to result in a fair solution for both parties.

- People may use dispute resolution mechanisms even when it is inappropriate, because it is cheaper.

- Concern has been expressed that dispute resolution mechanisms will be denied to some spouses because of false accusations of family violence.

- Dispute resolution mechanisms mean a lack of court scrutiny and, therefore, the parties' rights are not safeguarded to the same degree as they would be in a court hearing.

CAN YOU outline the legal processes involved in dealing with problems in family relationships?

In order to outline the legal processes involved in dealing with problems in family relationships, you need to, first, name the problems and, second, describe the legal processes involved in dealing with each problem.

The problems and legal processes are listed in Table 4.3. The legal processes involved are further described in each of the sections for which references are given in Table 4.3.

Table 4.3 Legal processes for dealing with problems in family relationships

Problems in family relationships	Legal processes
Divorce (Section 4.2.1, pages 210–11)	- Couples must prove that there has been an irretrievable breakdown of marriage, by living separately and apart for a period of twelve months. - Couples then apply to the Family Courts for a divorce, which will be granted without a hearing if all other issues, such as disputes about children and property, are resolved. If these issues are not resolved, the court will refer the couple to dispute resolution methods before a hearing is able to take place (Section 4.2.5, pages 238–9). - Couples who have been married for less than two years must receive counselling before a divorce is granted.

The care of children after the parents separate This applies to all children no matter what the relationships between their parents (Section 4.2.2, pages 211–16).	▶ Parents must, in most cases, attempt to reach an agreement about the care of children before a court will hear the matter. ▶ Family Relationship Centres were established in 2006 to provide mediation services (Section 4.2.5, page 226). ▶ The 'best interests of the child' are the paramount consideration when the courts make a parenting order. ▶ The presumption is that 'equal shared parental responsibility' is in the best interests of the child. ▶ Family violence is taken into account in the decision-making process, and may mean that mediation need not occur.
Child maintenance This applies to all children no matter what the relationships between their parents (Section 4.2.2, pages 215–16).	▶ Parents are encouraged to reach agreement about child maintenance. Such agreements must be registered with Centrelink if that organisation is involved with paying benefits to either party. ▶ The Department of Human Services determines how much maintenance is to be paid, by applying a formula which was substantially modified in 2008. ▶ The Department of Human Services collects child maintenance payments through a variety of methods.
Distribution of property after separation This applies to married couples and to both heterosexual and homosexual *de facto* couples (Section 4.2.3, pages 216–18).	▶ Parties must attend a compulsory conciliation conference to attempt to reach agreement before the court will hear the matter. ▶ When deciding how property will be distributed, the courts apply a four-step process, which includes looking at the financial and non-financial contributions of each party and their present and future needs. ▶ Superannuation is treated as a separate pool of property.
Domestic violence (Section 4.2.4, pages 218–25)	▶ The three main legal responses are AVOs, criminal charges and Family Court orders. ▶ Battered woman syndrome is sometimes considered as evidence for a defence to a murder charge. ▶ The Domestic Violence Death Review Team was established by legislation in 2010 in an effort to limit deaths caused by domestic violence. ▶ The Women's Domestic Violence Court Assistance Scheme, victims' compensation and personal injury claims are also available to victims of domestic violence.

 KCq page 270

Describe the role of non-government organisations.

4.2.6 The role of non-government organisations

Non-government organisations can and do play a large role in family law. They do this in two ways:

▶ many non-government organisations provide advice and assistance to families experiencing problems, including providing Family Relationship Centres supplying compulsory mediation for separating families

▶ various lobby groups play an important part in pushing for law reform in the area of family law.

These two types of non-government organisations are discussed in this section.

Sources of advice and assistance

There are many non-government organisations that provide advice and assistance to families in a wide range of matters. Some of these include:

▶ charitable organisations, such as the Salvation Army, the St Vincent de Paul Society and Anglicare, which provide physical support to families in terms of emergency accommodation, food and household goods, as well as emotional support (such as counselling)

▶ community-based, not-for-profit organisations (such as Relationships Australia) which provide relationship support services, such as counselling, family dispute resolution and early intervention services. Relationships Australia, and other non-government organisations, are funded by the government to run Family Relationship Centres (see Section 4.2.5, page 227).

▶ women's refuges and other organisations, which assist women who are experiencing domestic violence, by providing emergency accommodation and advice. Other services for women experiencing domestic violence are listed in Section 4.2.4 (pages 224–5).

▶ legal assistance, which can be accessed through private solicitors, through Legal Aid NSW (see Section 1.3.5, page 29), and through non-profit organisations, such as the community based Women's Legal Service NSW.

Lobby groups

A lobby group is a collection of people with specific aims who join together for the purpose of pressuring the government to change the law so as to achieve those aims.

The primary purpose of lobby groups is to pressure governments to reform the law (see Section 4.4.4, page 258), though they also give a voice to people with particular concerns who feel that they cannot be heard by politicians. In order to pressure parliament, lobby groups make representations to government, stage rallies and protests, distribute literature promoting their view, and respond to government inquiries into the operation of the law. Some lobby groups who have large and persuasive memberships and/or capture the attention of the media can be powerful influences on the government. Some of these groups include:

▶ the **Domestic Violence Committee Coalition** (DVCC), which was formed in 2006 with the specific aim of drawing attention to the increasing number of domestic-violence related deaths in NSW, and advocating for change. Its success can be seen in the establishment of the NSW Domestic Violence Death Review Team in 2010 (see Section 4.2.4, pages 224–5).

▶ **Australian Marriage Equality** and the **NSW Gay and Lesbian Rights Lobby**. These are examples of groups that have pressured parliaments to pass laws so that same-sex couples have the same status as heterosexual couples. These gay rights groups have largely been successful, as is evidenced by the changes to the law to recognise gay relationships—though some areas of inequality still exist.

▶ **parents' groups** such as Dads in Distress and the Lone Fathers Association. These groups were very instrumental in having the reforms to family law introduced by the *Family Law Amendment (Shared Parental Responsibility) Act 2006* (Cth) (see Sections 4.2.2 [page 211] and 4.3.2 [page 236]). Former Family Court Chief Justice, Alistair Nicholson, was quoted in *The Age* as saying that the 2006 reforms were 'more or less an attempt to, if you like, pander to the strong pressure that's been put on the Government by various militant fathers' groups'. ('Child custody bill flawed: Nicholson', Jewel Topsfield, *The Age*, 9 December 2005). Groups formed in 2009 and 2010 to protest against or advocate the 2006 reforms include the National Council for Children Post-Separation (NCCPS) and the Shared Parenting Council.

KCq page 284

4.2.7 The role of the media

Describe the role of the media.

The media has a very powerful role in bringing issues to public attention and pressuring parliaments. If the media publishes the views of particular lobby groups, or persistently criticises a government for its policies, reforms to the law frequently will follow. Publicity given to current events can also help persuade the government to review the law. Some examples of the media having had a powerful effect on the actions of governments in the area of family law are described below.

Domestic violence homicide review

The establishment of the NSW Domestic Violence Death Review Team was announced by the government on 25 November 2009 (see Section 4.2.4, pages 236–7). Calls for such a panel were first made by the NSW Ombudsman in 2006. On 24 November 2008, one year before the announcement of the Domestic Death Review Team's establishment, *The Sydney Morning Herald* ran several pages of articles with the pictures and stories of domestic violence homicide victims and such emotive headlines as: 'Shameful secret of our family murder epidemic'; 'Despite all her cries for help, Evelina was left to die'; 'Remembering the victims'; 'Desperate bids for survival'; and 'Call for domestic homicide review'.

This media campaign combined with the renewed calls for the establishment of a Domestic Violence Death Review Panel that arose as a result of yet another domestic violence death—that of Melissa Cook, who was shot fatally by her estranged husband in Sydney on 16 December 2008. This led to the establishment of the Domestic Violence Homicide Advisory Panel by the NSW government, announced on 19 December 2008. The report of the advisory panel in 2009 led, in turn, to the establishment of the NSW Domestic Violence Death Review Team (Section 4.2.4, pages 236–7). The media's frequent and high profile coverage of domestic violence deaths had a major impact on both the establishment of the advisory panel in 2008 and the announcement, in 2009, of the establishment of the permanent NSW Domestic Violence Death Review Team.

The Family Court and domestic violence

Family Courts Violence Review: A report, by Professor Richard Chisholm, was commissioned to review the 2006 reforms to the *Family Law Act* after a four-year-old girl, Darcey Freeman, died after being thrown off the West Gate Bridge in Melbourne on 29 January 2009 by her father in the presence of her two brothers and many commuters. This incident occurred the day after the girl's father was granted less time with his children than he sought. The media coverage of this event assisted in the government decision to commission a review of the legislation, even though two reviews were already underway at the time (see Case Study 4.5, Section 4.2.2, pages 214–15).

Child deaths and the Department of Community Services

There were several highly publicised child deaths in NSW in October and November 2007. Two of these were the death of Shellay Ward, a seven-year old, who died of starvation in her home in NSW in November 2007; and that of Dean Shillingsworth, a two-year-old found dead in a suitcase in a duck pond in Sydney in October 2007. The publicity surrounding these and several other cases, as well as the criticism of the NSW Department of Community Services which accompanied the publicity, led to the establishment of the Special Commission of Inquiry into Child Protection Services in NSW by the NSW Community Services Minister in November 2007. As a result of this inquiry the Department of Community Services, known as DoCS, made several significant changes to policy (see Case Study 4.11, Section 4.3.4, page 246).

CAN YOU examine the role of non-government organisations and the media in relation to family law?

In order to do this, you need to:

▶ state the roles of both non-government organisations and the media in relation to family law.

- The roles of non-government organisations are:
  - to provide advice and assistance to families experiencing problems
  - to lobby for law reform.
- The role of the media is to publicise public events and issues, which can have the effect of pressuring the government to change the law.

▶ give examples of non-government organisations and the media performing these roles.

▶ comment on the impact of these examples in the area of family law.

 KCq page 270

4.2.8 The effectiveness of the law in achieving justice for parties involved in relationship breakdowns

In order to evaluate the effectiveness of the law in achieving justice for parties involved in relationship breakdowns, you need to identify the parties involved and, for each party, discuss the factors which enhance, and those which limit, the effectiveness of the law in achieving justice. Then you need to decide how effective the law is in achieving justice, given the two sets of factors. Table 4.4 lists the parties involved and lists some of the factors which influence the effectiveness of the law in achieving justice for them.

> Evaluate the effectiveness of the law in achieving justice for parties involved in relationship breakdowns.

Table 4.4 The effectiveness of the law in achieving justice for parties involved in relationship breakdowns

Factors which may *enhance* effectiveness	Factors which may *lessen* effectiveness
Parties to a marriage	
▶ Divorce is easy to obtain (Section 4.2.1, pages 210–11). ▶ The 'no fault' concept means no one is to blame, though family violence may be taken into account for decisions about property and children (Sections 4.2.2 [page 211] and 4.2.3 [pages 217–18]). ▶ Agreement about divorce is encouraged, so costs and trauma are reduced (pages 209–10) and Section 4.2.5 [pages 225–9]).	▶ Some argue divorce is too easy to obtain. ▶ Sometimes one party is to blame.
Parties to a *de facto* relationship	
▶ Since 2009, the rules regarding property division for divorcing couples apply to separating *de facto* couples, both heterosexual and homosexual. So the status and the effectiveness of the law for all couples is the same (Sections 4.1.3 [pages 200–1] and 4.2.3 [pages 229–31]).	▶ Some people feel that *de facto* couples should not have the same level of protection from the law, particularly in property disputes. Some argue that if heterosexual *de facto* couples wanted the same level of protection, they would have married.
Parents	
▶ 2006 amendments mean that parents generally have 'equal shared parental responsibility' (Section 4.2.2, pages 2116–18). ▶ Family violence provisions protect victims of domestic violence (Sections 4.2.2 [page 213] and 4.2.4 [pages 218–25]). ▶ 2008 changes to the Child Support formula make it fairer for liable parents (Section 4.2.2, pages 215–16).	▶ 2006 amendments are used by some to lessen child maintenance payments (Section 4.2.2, pages 215–16). ▶ Family violence provisions may be detrimental to women, making them fearful about raising the issue (Sections 4.2.2 [page 213] and 4.2.4 [pages 218–25]). ▶ 2008 changes to the Child Support formula have left some parents worse off (Section 4.2.2, pages 215–16).

Children	
▶ Children are more likely, under the 2006 amendments, to have meaningful relationships with both parents and with other significant people such as grandparents (Section 4.2.2, page 212). ▶ Children's rights rather than parents' rights are emphasised (Sections 4.2.2 [pages 212–13] and 4.3.2 [page 236]).	▶ There have been allegations that family violence is insufficiently catered for and that some children spend 'substantial and significant time' with a violent parent (Section 4.2.2, page 213).
Other people with an interest in the children	
▶ Other people with an interest in the children can apply to the court to see the children (Sections 4.2.2 [page 212] and 4.3.3 [pages 239–40]).	

Note: The effectiveness of the law for victims of domestic violence is discussed in Section 4.2.4, (page 225).

 page 270

4.3 Contemporary issues involving family law

4.3.1 Recognition of same-sex relationships

Describe the contemporary issue relating to family law of the recognition of same-sex relationships, and evaluate the effectiveness of legal and non-legal responses to this issue.

Recognition over time

People in same-sex relationships have only recently been given any legal recognition under the law. In fact, until the 1970s and 1980s, homosexual sexual activity, particularly for males, was a criminal offence. Below is a list outlining some of the timing of the legal steps towards recognition of same-sex relationships in NSW and federally.

1975: South Australia decriminalised homosexual activity; the first Australian state to do so.

1982: The NSW *Anti-Discrimination Act 1977* was amended to prohibit discrimination on the grounds of homosexuality.

1984: Homosexual sexual activity was decriminalised in NSW. The Australian Medical Association removed homosexuality from its list of illnesses and disorders.

1984: The *De Facto Relationships Act 1984* (NSW) was passed which recognised *de facto* relationships and provided for the division of the property of the relationship when the *de facto* couple separated (see Section 4.1.3, pages 200–1).

1990–1995: Several piecemeal instances of legal recognition occurred, such as recognition by some medical insurance companies that a same-sex relationship constitutes a family, and the NSW Industrial Relations Commission's decision in 1995 that up to five days of a worker's sick leave could be used to care for family members and the specific inclusion of same-sex spouses as 'family members'.

1999: The *Property (Relationships) Legislation Amendment Act 1999* (NSW) was passed which amended the *De Facto Relationships Act 1984* (NSW), renaming it the *Property (Relationships) Act 1984* (NSW). This legislation reformed a large number of existing laws to include same-sex couples. Most importantly, same-sex couples were included in the provisions regarding property division that had applied to *de facto* couples since 1984. Other laws affected were those regarding family provision, intestacy, accident compensation and decision-making during illness and after death. NSW was the first state to pass legislation which extended the protection of the law to same-sex couples so comprehensively.

2002: The *Miscellaneous Acts Amendment (Relationships) Act 2002* (NSW) amended twenty laws to include same-sex couples in the definition of *de facto* relationships in such areas as the exception from giving evidence against a spouse in court and employment benefits.

2003: The age for consensual sex was equalised to sixteen in NSW, so that heterosexual and homosexual people can all consent to sexual intercourse at the age of sixteen. Previously, the age for consensual homosexual sex was eighteen.

2003: NSW referred its powers to make laws about *de facto* relationships to the Commonwealth. The majority of states, with the exception of Western Australia and South Australia, also referred their powers.

2008: The passing of the *Miscellaneous Acts Amendment (Same Sex Relationships) Act 2008* (NSW) meant that female same-sex parents, who conceive a child through artificial means, are treated in the same way as opposite-sex parents (see Section 4.3.3, pages 239–40). This act also amended fifty-seven pieces of NSW legislation to ensure that *de facto* couples, including same-sex couples, are treated equally to married couples, including amendments to the *Anti-Discrimination Act 1977* (NSW), so that discrimination against someone because he or she has a same-sex partner is specifically illegal.

2008: The *Family Law Amendment (De Facto Financial Matters and other Measures) Act 2008* (Cth), which commenced on 1 March 2009, treats same-sex couples in the same way as *de facto* and married couples in regard to financial matters. This act relates primarily to the way property is distributed when a couple separates. This is discussed in Section 4.2.3 (pages 216–18).

2008: The *Same-Sex Relationships (Equal Treatment in Commonwealth Laws—General Law Reform) Act 2008* and the *Same-Sex Relationships (Equal Treatment in Commonwealth Laws—Superannuation) Act 2008* were passed by the federal government in December 2008 to remove over 100 discriminatory provisions about same-sex couples in various pieces of Commonwealth legislation. This was in response to the inquiry by the Human Rights and Equal Opportunity Commission (HREOC) which investigated financial and work-related discrimination toward same-sex couples and released its report, 'Same-Sex: Same Entitlements', on 21 June 2007.

2010: The *Relationships Register Act 2010* (NSW) means that same-sex couples can register their relationship with the NSW Registry of Births, Deaths and Marriages. This provides proof of the existence of the relationship for the purposes of the law. It is similar to a civil union in other parts of the world. Similar registration laws apply in the ACT, Victoria and Tasmania.

2010: The *Adoption Amendment (Same Sex Couples) Act 2010* was passed by the NSW parliament in September 2010 and means that same-sex couples are now permitted to adopt children in NSW. This has come about after a lengthy lobbying and parliamentary process. In July 2009, the NSW Legislative Council Standing Committee on Law and Justice released a report: 'Adoption by same sex couples (Inquiry)' (see Sections 4.1.5 [page 207] and 4.2.6 [pages 228–9]). The committee recommended, with a 'four to two' majority, that same-sex couple adoptions should be allowed. However the call to legalise such adoptions was rejected by the government. In June 2010, the *Adoption Amendment (Same Sex Couples) Bill* was introduced in NSW parliament by Clover Moore, an independent parliamentary member, unattached to any major political party. All major political parties in NSW allowed their members a conscience vote on the bill (see Section 4.4.4, pages 260–1), and it was eventually passed, becoming law in September 2010. It is now part of the *Adoption Act 2000* (NSW).

In 2018 an Australia-wide plebiscite overwhelmingly supported marriage equality and the *Marriage Act 1961* was amended so that 'man and woman' was replaced by 'two people'. The last area of true legal inequality for same-sex relationships was removed.

Legal and non-legal responses

Most of the responses to issues involving the recognition of same-sex relationships are legal responses, because the recognition of these relationships refers to their legal recognition which, as can be seen above, has not occurred at all until recently. Legal recognition of same-sex couples has usually followed, rather than led, societal acceptance and recognition.

Non-legal responses include the lobbying activities of various groups, such as the NSW Gay and Lesbian Rights Lobby (see Section 4.2.6, pages 228–9) which have resulted in this legal recognition.

CAN YOU **identify and investigate the contemporary issue relating to family law of the recognition of same-sex relationships, and evaluate the effectiveness of legal and non-legal responses to this issue?**

In order to do this, you need to:

▷ describe the legal recognition of same-sex relationships that has occurred in NSW and Australia since 1975

▷ outline the reasons for recognition and non-recognition, which include:

• successful lobbying

• changes in attitudes and values (see Section 4.4.3, page 255)

• changes in technology which allow women to have children without a male partner (see Section 4.3.3, pages 239–40)

▷ come to a conclusion about the effectiveness of the recognition of same-sex relationships.

(KCq) page 270

Describe the contemporary issue relating to family law of the changing nature of parental responsibility, and evaluate the effectiveness of legal and non-legal responses to this issue.

4.3.2 The changing nature of parental responsibility

The notion of parental responsibility in the past

Parental responsibility is defined in the *Family Law Act 1975* (Cth) as 'all the duties, powers, responsibilities and authority which, by law, parents have in relation to children'. The current emphasis on parental responsibility, discussed also in Section 4.2.2 (pages 211–12), is a relatively recent concept in the law—though parents have always had responsibility for the care of their children. For much of the nineteenth and twentieth centuries, the custody of children was seen as a right, rather than a responsibility of parents.

The early twentiethth century

At the beginning of the twentieth century, women had no custody or guardianship rights over their children. The automatic guardian of any children born to a marriage was the father. If the father died, he could, in his will, appoint another person guardian of his children rather than his wife or the children's mother. In 1916, the *Testator's Family Maintenance and Guardianship of Infants Act 1916* (NSW) was passed, which gave widows automatic custody of their children if their husband died. This act was amended by the *Guardianship of Infants Act 1934* (NSW), which gave women with husbands who were still alive equal rights to the custody of their children. Who was to be granted custody was decided under state law, and the idea of the 'right to a child' rather than 'responsibility for a child' was the underpinning factor in who was granted custody and guardianship.

The Matrimonial Causes Act 1959 (Cth)

With the passing of the *Matrimonial Causes Act 1959* (Cth), the federal government exercised its constitutional powers to make laws about divorce for the first time. The Matrimonial Causes Act provided fourteen grounds for divorce, including adultery, cruelty, insanity, desertion, and separation for five years. When a couple obtained a divorce, one party (usually the mother) was given custody of the children and the other party was ordered to pay maintenance. The party 'at fault' (that is, the one who committed adultery, for example) was generally not awarded custody of the children.

In the minds of many custodial and non-custodial parents, there was a link between the paying of maintenance and having access to the child. If maintenance was not paid, some thought that the liable parent had no right to see the child and, similarly, if the parent did pay maintenance, it was thought that he or she then did have the right to have access to the child. The notion of parental responsibility was less important in the minds of many parents than the rights of access to the child.

The Family Law Act 1975 (Cth)

The *Family Law Act 1975* (Cth) introduced sweeping changes into divorce law in Australia. It:

▶ swept away the idea that one partner to a marriage was at fault for the marriage breakdown

▶ superseded state and territory laws about guardianship, custody, access and maintenance of children of a marriage

▶ introduced the idea of the 'best interests of the child' as the primary consideration for deciding issues about custody of and access to children.

Though the concept of fault was no longer relevant to the custody of children, parents still linked the idea of paying maintenance with access to the child, once again emphasising parental rights, rather than responsibility.

Ex-nuptial children

The position of ex-nuptial children has been different, in the past, to those born within a marriage. As seen in Section 4.1.4 (page 203), ex-nuptial children (those born of unmarried parents) were given the same rights as all other children under the *Children (Equality of Status) Act 1976* (NSW). However, it was not until 1988 that ex-nuptial children came under the jurisdiction of the *Family Law Act 1975* (Cth).

Before this time, many mothers of ex-nuptial children had difficulty collecting maintenance from the father of the child. DNA testing has made the identification of fathers and, therefore, the determination of liability for maintenance easier. Ex-nuptial children are in the same position as all other children in matters regarding parental responsibility and, since 1988, it has become more difficult for fathers to ignore this responsibility.

The United Nations Convention on the Rights of the Child

The United Nations Convention on the Rights of the Child 1989 (see Section 4.1.4, pages 202–3) was adopted by the General Assembly in 1989 and emphasised the rights of the child rather than the rights of parents. Article 9 of the convention states, in part, that signatories: 'shall respect the right of the child who is separated from one or both parents to maintain personal relations and direct contact with both parents on a regular basis, except if it is contrary to the child's best interests'. Australia ratified this convention in 1990.

The *Family Law Reform Act 1995* (Cth)

The *Family Law Act 1975* (Cth) was changed substantially by the *Family Law Reform Act 1995*. These changes were to emphasise the notion of parental responsibility rather than the parental rights to see or have custody of the child. The terms *custody*, *guardianship* and *access* were replaced with *residence, parental responsibility* and *contact*. These changes were to emphasise the fact that parents do not have rights to a child, but that both parents (whether they are married, unmarried, divorced or separated) have parental responsibility for the child, and that children have the right to know both parents.

The *Family Law Reform Act 1995* (Cth) also introduced the consideration of family violence as a factor in determining parental responsibility, residence and contact for a child. These changes were introduced in the hope that conflict between parents in decisions about children would be reduced during divorce proceedings by reducing the winner/loser mentality that has sometimes existed in custody disputes, where the parties saw the children as a 'prize' to be fought for.

Criticisms of the reforms included:

- the idea that the changes were really only changes in terminology, and did not change parents' ideas about parenting
- the place of family violence under the reforms raised concerns, particularly concerning the possibility of women making false allegations about family violence in order to prevent the father from seeing his children.
- The Australian Institute of Family Studies found, in 2005, that 26% of children from broken families saw the non-resident parent, usually the father, less than once a year. Only 6% of children spent close to equal time with both parents.

These concerns show that the idea of parental responsibility did not altogether replace the notion of parental rights in the minds of some parents. These criticisms and strong lobbying from father's groups led to the idea of equal shared parental responsibility which was introduced in the *Family Law Amendment (Shared Responsibility) Act 2006* (Cth) (see also Sections 4.2.2 [pages 213–14] and 4.2.6 [page 229]).

The notion of parental responsibility today

As described in Section 4.2.2 (page 214), the current law regarding the care of children whose parents are separated is described in the Family Law Act as amended by the Family Law Amendment (Shared Responsibility) Act. Children now have a right to be cared for and to have a relationship with both their parents, but parents do not have any rights to see their children. Furthermore, each parent is separately responsible for the child, and it is a presumption under the legislation that it is in the best interests of the child that each parent has 'equal shared parental responsibility', which means that parents must consult each other about long-term decisions affecting the child.

Legal and non-legal responses

The responses to the changing nature of parental responsibility have been legal responses, though they are based on non-legal societal factors, such as changes in values, failure of parents to provide for their children and pressure from lobby groups.

The legal and non-legal responses to the changing nature of parental responsibility, and the relationship between them are outlined in Figure 4.1.

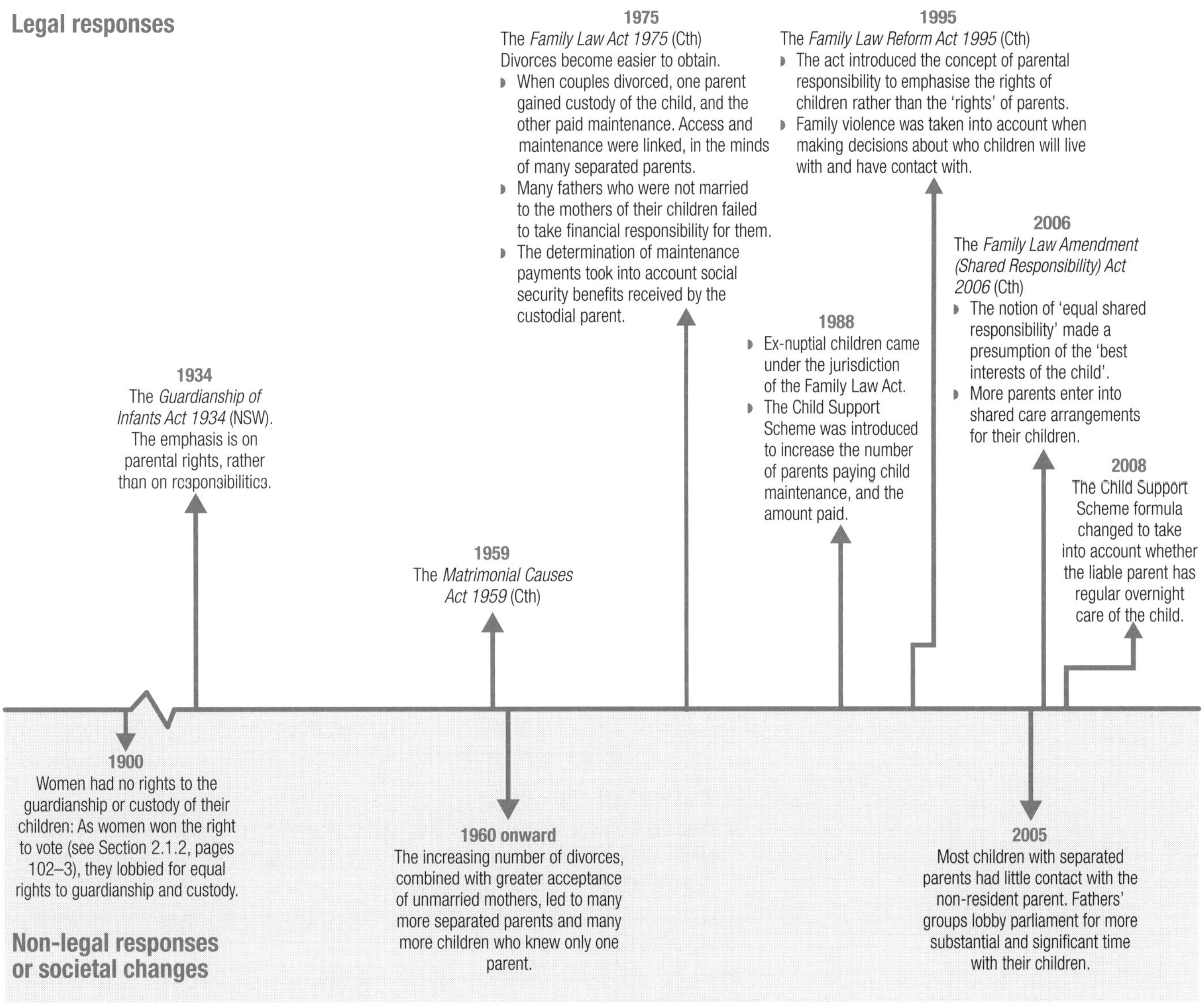

Legal responses

1975
The *Family Law Act 1975* (Cth)
Divorces become easier to obtain.
▸ When couples divorced, one parent gained custody of the child, and the other paid maintenance. Access and maintenance were linked, in the minds of many separated parents.
▸ Many fathers who were not married to the mothers of their children failed to take financial responsibility for them.
▸ The determination of maintenance payments took into account social security benefits received by the custodial parent.

1995
The *Family Law Reform Act 1995* (Cth)
▸ The act introduced the concept of parental responsibility to emphasise the rights of children rather than the 'rights' of parents.
▸ Family violence was taken into account when making decisions about who children will live with and have contact with.

2006
The *Family Law Amendment (Shared Responsibility) Act 2006* (Cth)
▸ The notion of 'equal shared responsibility' made a presumption of the 'best interests of the child'.
▸ More parents enter into shared care arrangements for their children.

1934
The *Guardianship of Infants Act 1934* (NSW).
The emphasis is on parental rights, rather than on responsibilities.

1988
▸ Ex-nuptial children came under the jurisdiction of the Family Law Act.
▸ The Child Support Scheme was introduced to increase the number of parents paying child maintenance, and the amount paid.

2008
The Child Support Scheme formula changed to take into account whether the liable parent has regular overnight care of the child.

1959
The *Matrimonial Causes Act 1959* (Cth)

1900
Women had no rights to the guardianship or custody of their children: As women won the right to vote (see Section 2.1.2, pages 102–3), they lobbied for equal rights to guardianship and custody.

Non-legal responses or societal changes

1960 onward
The increasing number of divorces, combined with greater acceptance of unmarried mothers, led to many more separated parents and many more children who knew only one parent.

2005
Most children with separated parents had little contact with the non-resident parent. Fathers' groups lobby parliament for more substantial and significant time with their children.

Figure 4.1 The legal and non-legal responses to the changing nature of parental responsibility

The success of the current law

As seen in Case Study 4.5, Section 4.2.2 (pages 214–15), the 2006 provisions of the *Family Law Act 1975* (Cth) were subject to several reviews, the results of which were released in 2010.

Below are listed two sets of findings from the reviews: those which show that the idea of equal shared parental responsibility is becoming more prevalent in the care of children whose parents are separated; and those which show that this is not the case.

Factors which indicate the effectiveness of legal and non-legal responses to promoting the idea of parental responsibility

▶ More children are spending substantial or equal time with both parents (16% in 2009, and 9% in 2003), indicating that more parents are embracing the idea that they both have responsibility for their children.

▶ Fewer matters regarding the care of children are going to court, showing that more parents are making agreements about their children—indicating that more parents are accepting that they have joint responsibility for their children.

▶ The changes to the Child Support Scheme formula in 2008 to include the cost of regular overnight care encourages the idea of equal shared parental responsibility and 76% of paying parents approve of the changes (see Case Study 4.6, Section 4.2.2, page 216).

Factors which indicate lack of effectiveness of legal and non-legal responses to promoting the idea of parental responsibility

▶ It is the conflict between parents, not the living arrangements, which have the biggest negative impact on children.

▶ There is considerable confusion about the notion of 'equal shared parental responsibility'.

▶ The 2010 report, 'Family Courts Violence Review: A report', by Professor Richard Chisholm found that some parties are still thinking more about their own entitlements rather than what is best for the children (see Case Study 4.5, Section 4.2.2, pages 214–15).

▶ Provisions about family violence may not be protecting children from having considerable contact with an abusive parent.

▶ Only 50% of paying parents pay child support in full and on time, indicating that many parents do not fully accept responsibility for their children (see Case Study 4.6, Section 4.2.2, page 216).

CAN YOU identify and investigate the contemporary issue relating to family law of the changing nature of parental responsibility, and evaluate the effectiveness of legal and non-legal responses to this issue?

In order to do this, you need to:

▶ describe how the concept of parental responsibility has changed from being focused on the rights of the parents in 1900 to being focused on the responsibilities of parents and the rights of the child in 2010

▶ outline the relationship between the non-legal and legal responses to the changing nature of parental responsibility

▶ discuss the factors which indicate the effectiveness of legal and non-legal responses to promoting the idea of parental responsibility, and factors which indicate a lack of effectiveness

▶ come to a conclusion about the effectiveness of legal and non-legal responses to the changing nature of parental responsibility. In doing this, you should answer the following questions:

  • How well has the law and society embraced the idea of parental responsibility?

- To what extent does the law encourage the idea of parental responsibility and the best interests of the child?

 page 271

4.3.3 Surrogacy and birth technologies

Birth technologies

Birth technologies refer to artificial insemination and in-vitro fertilisation (IVF), which together are referred to as artificial reproductive technology (ART).

This technology allows some infertile couples to produce children with at least some of their own genes. Artificial insemination involves semen being medically implanted into a woman's reproductive system so that she can bear a child. In-vitro fertilisation (IVF), involves the ovum and the sperm being united in a test tube, where they form an embryo which is then implanted into the woman's uterus.

The first child born as a result of IVF technology turned thirty in June 2010 and, by that time, there were over 85 000 children born in Australia as a result of this technology.

Laws in this area are a matter for state governments in Australia though there are some areas in which national laws operate, particularly in the area of research. The National Health and Medical Research Council (NHMRC) gives guidelines and supervises some aspects of this technology, and federal legislation covers some research activities. The *Status of Children Act 1996* (NSW) and the *Assisted Reproductive Technology Act 2007* (NSW), which commenced on 1 January 2010, contain much of the law that operates in NSW about birth technologies.

Who are the child's legal parents?

If the sperm or ova or both have been donated to the couple, the question arises as to who are the resulting child's legal father and mother. In NSW the legal status of parents is as follows:

- under the *Status of Children Act 1996* (NSW), the social father (that is, the man who acts as the father of the child) is the legal father

- the sperm donor is not the legal father of the child, unless he acts as the social father of the child as well [see the case of *Re Patrick* (2002) 28 Fam LR 579, 645, Case Study 4.8 on the following page].

- the woman who bears the child is the legal mother of the child

- until 2008, a child born to a lesbian couple through assisted reproductive technology had only one legal parent, the birth mother. The *Miscellaneous Acts Amendment (Same Sex Relationships) Act 2008* changed the *Status of Children Act 1996* (NSW), so that female same-sex partners who conceive a child through artificial fertilisation are both named on the birth certificate as co-mothers and will have equal status as parents. This replicates laws in other states, such as Western Australia, the ACT and the Northern Territory.

- under the *Family Law Act 1975* (Cth) a non-birth co-mother is not recognised as the child's legal parent even if she is recognised under state law. However, parenting orders may be granted under the act to any person concerned with the care of a child, including a co-mother. The status of homosexual parents, and parental orders granted by the Family Law Court, are discussed in the cases of *Re Patrick*, Case Study 4.8 on the following page, and *Re Mark*, Case Study 4.11 (page 243).

CASE STUDY 4.8: *Re Patrick* (2002) 28 Fam LR 579, 645

Facts

A homosexual man donated his sperm to a lesbian couple who subsequently gave birth to a child. The man, who was the biological father of the child, thought that he would be present at the birth and that he would have twice-weekly contact with the child. The lesbian couple expected that he would be a donor who was not actively involved in the life of the child.

Issue

Did the biological father, who was a sperm donor, have a legal right to have regular contact with his child?

Decision

This case was determined by the Family Court, which declared that a sperm donor is not a parent under the *Family Law Act* 1975 (Cth). However, the man was granted regular contact with the child anyway. The case was decided on the basis of principles applicable to all decisions about children by the Family Court, that is:

▶ decisions are made on a case-by-case basis

▶ the court does not limit orders to biological or legal parents

▶ decisions reflect the court's view of the best interests of the child at the time.

Is it moral?

Some people argue that it is immoral for children to be conceived in this manner. They believe that such technology is 'playing God' and that natural processes, such as conception, should be left to nature. However, there is growing acceptance and widespread support of the use of such technologies in the Australian community.

Developments such as cloning, post-menopausal pregnancy, and choosing the gender of the child have raised much controversy around the world. Many argue that these areas of artificial reproductive technology should not be permitted to continue until issues such as these are resolved by society as a whole.

Gender selection

It is possible for people to choose the gender of their prospective child for non-medical reasons. However, the NHMRC placed a ban on the use of non-medical gender selection across Australia in 2005. This ban is still in place as of 1 July 2016. THe NHMRC is currently reviewing this ban and asked for public consultation in July–September 2015. They are still reviewing their position. The selection of gender for non-medical reasons is also banned in several states in Australia. Gender selection is available overseas and some Australian couples continue to access the technology in the US and other places.

Cloning and embryo experimentation

Another area that raises ethical questions in the community is the issue of cloning and embryo experimentation. The use of stem cells and human embryonic cells for medical purposes is an area in which scientific breakthroughs are continually occurring, and the potential of such cells to develop cures for disease is enormous.

The cloning of human cells is banned in Australia under the *Prohibition of Human Cloning for Reproduction Act 2002* (Cth) and the *Research Involving Human Embryos Act 2002* (Cth).

These laws allow strictly controlled therapeutic cloning and the first licence to allow its use was issued to Sydney IVF in September 2008. This legislation also restricts the use of excess IVF embryos for other purposes, and the creation and use of other embryos in research. Human cloning for reproductive purposes is banned.

Biological knowledge

As the number of children born through ART procedures has increased, the call for information about the donors of sperm and ova has also increased. Children born as a result of IVF sometimes experience 'genetic bewilderment', and there is sometimes a need for them to access information regarding medical conditions which could be linked to their genetic material.

The *Assisted Reproductive Technology Act 2007* (NSW) established a mandatory gamete donor register, commencing on 1 January 2010. Donors of sperm and ova must provide the register with:

▶ their name, date and place of birth

▶ information regarding their ethnicity and physical characteristics

▶ any medical history or genetic test results of the donor or the donor's family that are relevant to the future health of any user of the donation, any child born using the donated material, and any descendants of such a child.

Information from the register will be available to children conceived using donated gametes, once they turn eighteen, as well as to their parents and the donors. Parents can only gain access to non-identifying information, and donors can only gain access to non-identifying information about the gender and date of birth of any child born using their donated gametes.

Rights of access to artificial reproductive technology

Not all people have the same access to the new technologies. Factors which can limit access to ART include family arrangements, cost and age.

Family arrangements

When ART first emerged it was generally only available to infertile married couples. In NSW, ethics committees attached to ART clinics also allowed the treatment of heterosexual couples in *de facto* relationships. Now, all women, no matter what their marital status, are permitted access to IVF treatment in New South Wales under the *Assisted Reproductive Technology Act 2007* (NSW). Medicare funding, however, is only available to couples or single women who are medically infertile. Single women, whether heterosexual or homosexual, may seek IVF because they have no male partner, not only due to medical reasons. These women are 'socially infertile' and so are not eligible for Medicare assistance.

Cost

The cost of new birth technologies is very high and some people feel that our limited health budget would be better spent elsewhere. It is also argued that making such technology available only to those who can afford it means that it becomes a privilege for only the very wealthy and that it would be more difficult for governments to control. In Australia, ART can be claimed on Medicare if the services are 'medically or clinically relevant' to infertility.

Age

Post-menopausal women can give birth using artificial reproductive technology. For example, in June 1994, a sixty-three-year-old Italian woman gave birth to a son and, in 1998, a fifty-three-year-old Adelaide woman gave birth to triplets as a result of ART. In NSW, there is no official age limit for women wishing to use ART but, unofficially, the age limit set by ethics committees has been about fifty.

Surrogacy

Surrogacy, or *surrogate motherhood*, describes when a woman agrees to become pregnant and bear a child on behalf of another couple, who are usually unable to have children of their own. When the child is born, it is given to the couple for adoption. Money is sometimes paid to the surrogate mother (the woman who bears the child) and sometimes the surrogate mother voluntarily performs the task for a close relative. The surrogate mother may use the sperm and/or ova of the childless couple (through such procedures as IVF) or she may use her own ova.

Legal status of surrogacy in NSW

In NSW, commercial surrogacy is banned under the *Surrogacy Act 2010* (NSW), though there is nothing to prevent private surrogacy arrangements taking place for altruistic reasons. In fact, altruistic surrogacy is formally legalised through the Surrogacy Act.

The woman who bears a child is the legal mother of that child. People who make arrangements for a woman to have a baby for them in a surrogacy arrangement are called the *commissioning parents*. A commissioning parent may not use adoption orders to gain legal parental status, because privately arranged adoptions are not permitted. Commissioning parents can apply to the Family Court for parenting orders (see Section 4.2.2, page 212). Case Studies 4.9 (*Re 'Evelyn'*) below and 4.10 (*Re Mark*) on page 243 are about the enforceability of surrogacy arrangements. Both these cases show that, no matter what the parentage, the court will make its decision on what is in 'the best interests of the child'.

The ban on commercial surrogacy in NSW be strengthened by clarifying the reasonable expenses for which the birth mother may be reimbursed in an altruistic surrogacy arrangement; and that courts be given the power to grant a parenting order to commissioning parents in altruistic surrogacy arrangements.

CASE STUDY 4.9: *Re 'Evelyn'* (1998) FamCA 55 (15 May 1998)

Facts

Dr and Mrs S had three children. Their close friends of fifteen years, Mr and Mrs Q, had adopted a little boy of Aboriginal descent, but were unable to have children of their own because of infertility. Mrs S offered to be a surrogate and was inseminated with Mr Q's sperm. In 1996, baby Evelyn was born and lived with the Qs as agreed.

Issue

A year later, the S family applied to the court for the return of baby Evelyn. Were the S family legally entitled to the child? While Mrs S was the child's biological and, therefore, legal mother, Mr Q was the child's biological father.

Decision

The Full Bench of the Family Court found that the surrogate baby of the Q couple should be returned to its birth (surrogate) mother, the woman in the S couple. The High Court upheld this decision. This is the first decision involving a surrogate child to be made by the Family Court. It set a precedent of giving birth rights to the birth mother and deciding against surrogacy contracts. Note that the High Court did not make any ruling on the surrogacy contract, but made its decision on the 'best interests of the child' principle.

Case study 4.10: *Re Mark* (2003) 31 Fam LR 162

Facts

A male homosexual couple conceived a child through a commercial surrogacy arrangement entered into in the US. Mr X, one of the couple, was also the child's genetic father and was named on the birth certificate in the US as the father. The couple applied to the Family Court for parental responsibility of the child.

Issue

Were Mr X and his partner able to be granted parental responsibility for a child born out of such an arrangement?

Decision

The Family Court granted the male homosexual couple shared parental responsibility through a consent order, under the *Family Law Act 1975* (Cth). The judge, Justice Brown, stated that the existence of a commercial surrogacy agreement was irrelevant. The couple were granted parental responsibility on the application of the 'best interests of the child' test. In this case, unlike the *Re 'Evelyn'* case in Case Study 4.9 (page 242), the birth mother did not contest the application for parental responsibility.

Arguments for and against surrogacy

There has been much debate about whether surrogacy should be allowed to take place. Arguments for and against surrogacy are outlined in Table 4.5.

Table 4.5 Arguments for and against surrogacy

Arguments *for* surrogacy	Arguments *against* surrogacy
▶ People have a right to form a family in the way they wish.	▶ A child can be treated as an item for sale.
▶ A woman has the right to use and control her body as she wishes.	▶ The surrogate mother is used as a baby-producing machine.
▶ Surrogacy could be the only option for some childless couples.	▶ Surrogacy can lead to exploitation of poor people.
▶ Private surrogacy arrangements are impossible to prevent, therefore they should be legislated for so that counselling and advice is available.	▶ The surrogate mother and the childless couple will suffer if the surrogate mother changes her mind. Surrogate mothers will inevitably suffer some anguish because they will bond with the child.
▶ Forbidding surrogacy will lead to a black market trade in babies.	▶ The child can be harmed because of confusion about family relationships.
▶ Some surrogacy arrangements are morally commendable (for example, a woman having a baby for her sister).	

Legal and non-legal responses

Most of the responses to issues involving surrogacy and birth technologies are legal responses, because the legal system has made several legislative responses to these issues in recent years as a response to a growing demand for both surrogacy and access to birth technologies. There are still some areas in which the law has not yet responded, and where people have sought non-legal responses if they disagree with the legal response. The legal and non-legal responses to surrogacy and birth technologies are listed below.

Legal responses

▶ Birth mothers and social fathers are the legal parents of children conceived through ART. Lesbian non-birth mothers can be registered as co-mothers (NSW).

▶ The Family Law Court can and does make orders about the care of children in favour of people other than the biological and/or social parents [*Re Patrick* (2002), *Re 'Evelyn'* (1998), and *Re Mark* (2003)]. Like all such decisions, the decisions are based on 'the best interests of the child' (Cth).

- Gender selection is banned (Cth).
- Cloning for reproductive purposes is banned, but restricted and tightly controlled research is allowed (Cth).
- The mandatory donor register (NSW).
- All women have equal access to ART, but do not have equal access to Medicare funding (NSW and Cth).
- Commercial surrogacy is banned (NSW).

Non-legal responses

- Some people travel overseas to access gender selection of children, and sometimes surrogacy arrangements, because these are not available in Australia.
- Most IVF clinics do not provide services to women over fifty.
- Private surrogacy arrangements can be made, but are not legally enforceable.

Evaluating effectiveness

It is difficult to evaluate the effectiveness of legal and non-legal responses to surrogacy and birth technologies, because personal values and ethics affect how each person sees the responses. Generally, the legal system tries to reflect the dominant community values in the area of surrogacy and birth technologies. Below are listed two sets of factors: those which help ensure, and those which limit, the effectiveness of legal and non-legal responses to the contemporary issue relating to family law of surrogacy and birth technologies, bearing in mind that these issues are morally and ethically sensitive.

Factors which may enhance the effectiveness of legal and non-legal responses to issues involving surrogacy and birth technologies

- The ban on gender selection and research involving cloning are because of the legal system's perception that the majority of Australians do not approve of these activities.
- The availability of IVF technology to all women, single or not, is non-discriminatory.

Factors which may limit the effectiveness of legal and non-legal responses to issues involving surrogacy and birth technologies

- The banning of some technological possibilities, such as gender selection, mean that some people travel overseas in order to access them—meaning such technologies only become available for the relatively wealthy.
- The availability of IVF technology to all women, single or not, is non-discriminatory, but may not reflect prevailing community attitudes (see page 240).
- The restriction of Medicare assistance to medically infertile women means that many single or homosexual women can only access IVF if they have sufficient funds for what is an expensive treatment.
- Currently, altruistic surrogacy arrangements are not legally enforceable except for Family Court orders. This may disadvantage some people, though reforms are expected in this area.

CAN YOU **identify and investigate the contemporary issue relating to family law of surrogacy and birth technologies, and evaluate the effectiveness of legal and non-legal responses to this issue?**

In order to do this, you need to:

▶ explain the questions and issues raised by surrogacy and birth technologies

▶ describe the legal and non-legal responses to surrogacy and birth technologies

▶ discuss the factors which may enhance, and those which may limit, the effectiveness of legal and non-legal responses to issues involving surrogacy and birth technologies

▶ come to a conclusion about the effectiveness of legal and non-legal responses to issues involving surrogacy and birth technologies, given that such issues are morally and ethically sensitive.

 page 271

4.3.4 Care and protection of children

Sometimes children are not adequately cared for by their parents or guardians, and are victims of child abuse. Abuse of a child means assault, including sexual assault, ill-treatment of the child and exposing the child to behaviour that psychologically harms him or her. Sometimes children are placed in the care of other people besides their parents. This is called *out of home care*. The number of children who are in out of home care has risen significantly in Australia, as the following figures from The Australian Institute of Health and Welfare's 'Child Protection Australia 2008–2009' show.

> Describe the contemporary issue relating to family law of the care and protection of children, and evaluate the effectiveness of legal and non-legal responses to this issue.

▶ The number of children in out of home care in Australia rose by almost 115%, from 14 470 in June 1998, to 31 166 in June 2008.

▶ 8.4 in every thousand children are in out of home care in New South Wales.

▶ In New South Wales, there were 5603 children in out of home care in 1998. In 2008 this figure more than doubled to 13 566.

▶ Across Australia, of those children removed, 48% were in foster care, 45% were in relative or kinship care, and 5% were in residential care.

▶ The rate of Indigenous children in out of home care was almost nine times the rate of non-Indigenous children.

The *Children and Young Persons (Care and Protection) Act 1998* (NSW) is the main piece of legislation that protects children from harm in NSW. The Department of Human Services, Community Services (formerly called the Department of Community Services or DoCS) is the government department responsible for the protection of children from abuse in NSW.

The number of cases of children reported to DoCS increased dramatically since the *Children and Young Persons (Care and Protection) Act 1998* (NSW) came into operation. Because of some horrific child deaths caused by neglect or abuse, the NSW government commissioned the Special Commission of Inquiry into Child Protection Services in NSW, also known as the Wood Inquiry, the report of which was released in November 2008. The findings of the commission are discussed in Case Study 4.11 on the next page.

CASE STUDY 4.11: The Special Commission of Inquiry into Child Protection Services in NSW, November 2008

Background

Several highly-publicised child deaths in NSW in October and November 2007 led to the establishment of the Special Commission of Inquiry into Child Protection Services in NSW by the NSW Community Services Minister in November 2007. The Commission was headed by former Supreme Court judge, James Wood QC, and presented its report in November 2008. Two of the deaths which led to the Commission's establishment were the death of Shellay Ward, a seven-year old, who died from starvation in her home in NSW in November 2007; and that of Dean Shillingsworth, a two-year-old found dead in a suitcase in a duck pond in Sydney in October 2007.

Findings

One of the main findings of the report was that 'too many reports are being made to DoCS which do not warrant the exercise of its considerable statutory powers'. In 2001–02, just under 160 000 calls were made to the DoCS help line. This had nearly doubled to 300 000 in 2007–08. Consequently, DoCS was being 'swamped' with less serious matters. This prevented it from dealing with serious cases effectively.

Recommendations

There are many recommendations contained in the commission's report, some of the most significant being:

▶ only children at risk of 'significant' harm should be reported to DoCS, thereby reducing the thousands of calls about less serious matters

▶ DoCS should provide feedback to other child welfare agencies, such as the Department of Education and the police, so that these agencies can track a child's progress

▶ some programs, such as early intervention programs, should be run by non-government agencies

▶ DoCS should progressively reduce its role in foster care and allow this to be run by non-government agencies

▶ health services, the police, the Department of Education and Juvenile Justice should each create a special unit to advise their own staff and DoCS when children are at significant risk.

As a response to the Wood Inquiry, the NSW government launched a five year action plan, entitled *Keep Them Safe*, to improve child care and protection in NSW and to implement the recommendations of the Wood Inquiry. The aim of *Keep Them Safe* is to ensure that 'all children in NSW are healthy, happy and safe, and grow up belonging in families and communities where they have opportunities to reach their full potential'.

Legal responses to the care and protection of children

Legislation

The *Children and Young Persons (Care and Protection) Act 1998* (NSW) was amended substantially by the *Children Legislation Amendment (Wood Inquiry Recommendations) Act 2009* (NSW), which implements some of the recommendations made by the Wood Inquiry.

Under the Children and Young Persons (Care and Protection) Act:

▶ it is an offence for someone to abuse a child

▶ schoolteachers and counsellors, among others, must notify Family and Community Services if they have reasonable grounds to suspect that a child is 'at risk of significant harm'. Prior to the implementation of the Wood Inquiry amendments, notification had to be made regarding any children 'at risk of harm'. *Significant harm* means harm which is sufficiently serious to warrant a response by a statutory authority irrespective of the family's consent. The Wood Inquiry amendments make it clear that, in addition to abuse and neglect, parents who withhold children from school may be putting that child at risk of significant harm.

- the protection of the child is the paramount concern

- a police officer or Family and Community Services worker can remove a child from his or her home if it is believed the child is at risk of serious harm. Children can be removed from their homes if they are deemed by a court to be 'in need of care and protection'. Children 'in need of care' do not only include children who have been removed from their home because of neglect or abuse but also children who have run away from home or who have no home or no-one to take care of them. Such children can be placed in the care of relatives, foster parents or an institution.

- parents have a duty to be responsible for their children

- assistance is provided for parents and guardians of children 'at risk of significant harm' and/or 'need of care' so that they can provide a 'safe and nurturing environment'. This is aimed at preventing children needing to be taken into care.

- the different needs of Aboriginal and Torres Strait Islander children must be considered. There is provision under the act for Indigenous community input concerning the placement of Indigenous children into care.

- the act defines *children* as under sixteen, while those who are sixteen and seventeen are defined as 'young persons' and are given greater autonomy (see Section 4.1.4, page 204).

Family and Community Services

Family and Community Services is responsible for services that care for children who are not adequately cared for elsewhere. Family and Community Services also offers assistance to people who fear they will abuse their child. A child or young person can ask for assistance from Family and Community Services, as can a parent, and any other person can also report a child 'at risk of significant harm' to Family and Community Services. As seen above, certain professionals, such as schoolteachers and healthcare workers must report a child whom they suspect is 'at risk of significant harm'.

Once a child is reported to Family and Community Services the matter must be investigated. Family and Community Services can then do several things, including:

- do nothing, if it is perceived there is no risk of significant harm

- make further investigations about the child, which can involve talking to the child's teacher, child care worker and/or relatives. The Wood Inquiry amendments allow for increased sharing of information that relates to the safety and welfare of a child or young person, between a range of agencies, including Family and Community Services, NSW Police, NSW Health and the Department of Education.

- visit the child and family immediately if it seems that the child is in immediate danger. If this is the case, the child can be removed at once.

- notify the police if investigations reveal there may be criminal activity. Then a Joint Investigative Response Team will investigate the allegations. This team comprises specially trained child protection agents from Family and Community Services and the police. They mainly investigate criminal cases, such as sexual abuse or other serious criminal offences. They also provide support for victims and their families.

- arrange for support services to be provided to the family
- make an arrangement with the family for the child to be placed in a temporary care arrangement with Family and Community Services. Such an arrangement can usually only be of three months duration and must include a restoration plan (that is, a plan setting out the circumstances under which the child will be returned to his or her parents).
- develop a care plan with the family to meet the needs of the child. A care plan sets out the steps that will be taken by the family to resolve concerns about the child.
- develop a parental responsibility contract with the primary caregivers of the child. This is a contract entered into by the child's carers, whether or not they are the parents, which contains provisions aimed at improving the carers' parenting skills and making them more responsible for the child's wellbeing. Parental responsibility contracts:
  - must be registered with the Children's Court
  - may not be longer than six months in duration
  - can result in a court hearing about the child if breached (see below)
- remove the child or young person from the family
- make a care application to the Children's Court.

Court proceedings

Children who are found to be 'at risk of significant harm' may be the subject of a court hearing in the Children's Court if a parenting responsibility contract is breached, or if Family and Community Services makes a care application for the child, or in some other circumstances.

The court listens to evidence to see if a child is 'in need of care and protection'. If a child is found to be so, the Children's Court can make a variety of orders, which may involve a child being temporarily or permanently removed from his or her home and placed in the care of someone else, such as a relative or a foster parent.

When determining whether a child should have a care order (that is, the child is 'in need of care and protection'), there are special requirements for court hearings. These include:

- they are to be conducted with as little formality as possible
- they are not to be conducted in an adversarial manner
- the court must be satisfied on the 'balance of probabilities'
- the child in question, any person with parental responsibility, Family and Community Services and the Minister for Family and Community Services have a right to appear before the court
- the child is represented by a legal representative.

Types of orders

The Children's Court can make various types of orders if a child is found to be in need of care and protection. These include:

- an assessment order which authorises a medical or psychiatric assessment of a child or parent
- an order accepting undertakings from the parent about how they will care for the child
- an order for supervision which allows Family and Community Services to regularly meet with the child

- an order for the provision of support services
- an order allocating parental responsibility. This means that parental responsibility for the child is given, in full or in part, to another person.

Other legal responses

There are some other legal avenues available to children who are subject to violence. These include:

- **apprehended violence orders**. An AVO can be taken out by a police officer on behalf of a child. This has the advantage that the offender rather than the child may have to leave the family home (see Section 4.2.4, pages 220–1).
- **victims' compensation**. The Victims Compensation Tribunal can award compensation to a child who has been a victim of sexual or other assault (see Section 1.7.5, page 75).
- the **Family Court** takes family violence into consideration when making decisions about children (see Sections 4.2.2 [page 213] and 4.2.4 [pages 221–3]).
- **legal aid** from the Legal Aid Commission of NSW is available to all children appearing in the Children's Court for any matter. The merit and income tests do not apply to children (see Section 1.3.5, page 29).
- **alternative dispute resolution** is provided for under the *Children and Young Persons (Care and Protection) Act 1998* (NSW).

Non-legal responses to the care and protection of children

There are numerous non-legal responses that are available for children who are in need of care and protection. Since the Wood Inquiry amendments, children may be viewed as at risk of harm which is less than the 'significant harm' stipulated by the amendments. There have been governmental initiatives implemented since the Wood Inquiry to help these children, as well as increased funding for non-government organisations to assist children and families in crisis. Some of these are discussed below.

Child Wellbeing Units

In line with the Wood Inquiry recommendations, Child Wellbeing Units have been established in four government departments and became operational on 24 January 2010. The units have been established in the NSW Department of Health, the NSW Police Force, the Department of Education and Training, and the Department of Human Services. These are the government agencies that made the majority of reports before the 'at risk of harm' mandatory reporting threshold was raised to 'at risk of significant harm'. If someone within these government departments is concerned about a child, but does not think the child is 'at risk of significant harm', he or she is to contact the Child Wellbeing Unit within the department. The Child Wellbeing Units' functions are to:

- assist in assessing the level of risk to the child
- provide advice to the reporter about how the department can assist the child and/or the family
- provide advice about possible referral options and other sources of advice and assistance
- identify whether reports about the child have been made in other departments.

Organisations that do not have a Child Wellbeing Unit should use their own organisational structures and local community contacts to assist and support the child and family.

Non-government organisations

Non-government organisations (NGOs) have always played an important role in the care and protection of children and young people. The Wood Inquiry recommended a greater role for NGOs in the provision of out of home care and early intervention programs and has supplied funding and training to assist NGOs in these roles. In addition, the NSW government has provided the KTS (Keep Them Safe) Support Line, a telephone support service. The following is a short list of the many NGOs that provide services for children and families in need of assistance:

- Relationships Australia
- Anglicare
- Centrecare
- the Youth Off The Streets Outreach Program
- the Association of Children's Welfare Agencies.

Aboriginal children and young people

The Wood Inquiry highlighted the fact that Aboriginal children and young people are vastly over-represented in the child care and protection system in NSW. Several initiatives have been launched to address this, the most important one being an agreement between NSW Community Services and the NSW Aboriginal, Child, Family and Community Care Secretariat (AbSec) signed on 17 March 2010. AbSec is the peak NSW Aboriginal organisation providing policy advice to both government and non-government organisations on child protection issues for Aboriginal families.

The agreement reached between AbSec and Community Services involves:

- the development of an NGO-run Aboriginal specialist advice and support service for child protection, based on the successful Victorian *Lakidjeka* model which emphasises an Aboriginal perspective and the need to work directly with families.
- the establishment of four new Intensive Family Based Services (IFBS) run by NGOs. IFBS is a service that provides an intensive, home-based program for Aboriginal families whose children are either at risk of entering care or whose children have been placed in care and are to be restored to their families.

Evaluating effectiveness

As has been seen earlier, there have been major changes to the provisions for the care and protection of children in NSW since 2008. Most of these changes have been implemented in 2009 and 2010 so, at the time of writing, it is too early to tell how effective these changes are in providing care and protection to children in NSW.

The fact that the NSW government has implemented all the major recommendations of the Wood Inquiry in an effort to improve child care and protection in NSW hopefully means that children will be better protected in NSW in the future.

However, as seen in statistics from the Australian Institute of Health and Welfare, Child Protection Australia, the extent of the need for government and community intervention in the care and protection of children is large. The effectiveness of the new provisions will rely on appropriate government funding, and willingness among all those who come into contact with children to take action and seek appropriate guidance when necessary. The establishment of Family Referral Services, Child Wellbeing Units, and the Families NSW web service and help lines, will hopefully assist people to seek and find appropriate professional assistance when it is required.

CAN YOU **identify and investigate the contemporary issue relating to family law of the care and protection of children, and evaluate the effectiveness of legal and non-legal responses to this issue?**

In order to do this, you need to:

▷ explain the extent of the problem of the care and protection of children in NSW

▷ explain the reasons for the Wood Inquiry, and summarise its findings

▷ describe the legal and non-legal responses to the care and protection of children

▷ discuss the factors which may enhance, and those which may limit, the effectiveness of legal and non-legal responses to the care and protection of children

▷ come to a conclusion about the effectiveness of the legal and non-legal responses to the care and protection of children.

 KCg page 271

4.4 Themes and challenges

4.4.1 Theme 1: The role of the law in encouraging cooperation and resolving conflict in regard to family

Assess the role of the law in encouraging cooperation and resolving conflict in regard to family.

The law has an extensive role in encouraging cooperation as a way of resolving conflict in the area of family law, rather than resolving family conflict through a court ruling. The law is reluctant to step into family matters unless it must, because these matters are seen as private rather than public. Families that cooperate and resolve their own conflicts generally also find a longer-lasting solution than those with a court order telling them what to do. To assist in encouraging cooperation and resolving conflict, the law makes mediation mandatory in some areas of family law before a dispute will be accepted to be considered for a decision by a court.

The role of the law in encouraging cooperation and resolving conflict can be seen in the areas described below.

Dissolution of adult relationships

In the area of the breakdown of adult relationships, the law provides the mechanism for married couples to divorce. Counselling is available for divorcing couples, and couples who have been married for less than two years must have counselling before a divorce is granted. The 'kiss and make up' clause also encourages reconciliation between separating couples (see Section 4.2.1, page 211).

Other non-marital relationships dissolve without any interference from the law, except when there are disputes about the care of children and the distribution of property. As seen in Sections 4.1.3 (pages 199–201), 4.2.3 (pages 216–18) and 4.3.1 (pages 232–4), since 2008, *de facto* couples and same-sex couples are treated in the same way as married couples when it comes to disputes about property. All disputes about children have been settled by the Family Court since 1988.

Family Relationship Centres

These were established by the federal government in 2006 to assist families to resolve disputes and reach agreement over a large range of matters (see Section 4.2.5, page 227). If separating couples cannot agree, they must (except if there is family violence) attempt dispute resolution, and will be referred to a Family Relationship Centre for that purpose. Over 90% of separation matters are resolved by agreement between the parties.

Property disputes

In disputes about property, before imposing a court decision, the law encourages cooperation between the parties by obliging separating couples who cannot come to an agreement to attend a compulsory conciliation conference with a Family Court Registrar. Family Relationship Centres can also assist in this area. Binding financial agreements can also be made by parties (see Section 4.2.3, pages 217–18).

The care of children after separation

As seen in Section 4.2.2 (pages 211–16), the law encourages parents who separate to reach agreement about the care of their children by:

- making it a presumption that it is in the best interests of the child for the parents to have equal shared parental responsibility, which means that parents must consult each other about long-term decisions regarding the child

- specifying that parents must attempt dispute resolution unless there has been family violence

- accepting agreements about the children, which can be informal, in the form of a parenting plan, or in the form of consent orders.

When it comes to the care of children, the role of the law in encouraging agreement is tempered with the need to consider the best interests of the child. For example, a consent order will only be accepted by the court if it is in the best interests of the child. Similarly, the court recognises that mediation is inappropriate if there has been family violence, and that it may not be in best interests of the child to force mediation in these circumstances. If the parents can't agree, the courts will resolve conflict by making orders about parenting.

Parents can also make private arrangements about child support which can be registered.

Succession

As seen in Section 4.1.4 (pages 205–6), under the *Succession Act 2006* (NSW), the law encourages cooperation by providing that all matters regarding disputes about inheriting from a deceased person's estate must be referred to mediation before the court will hear the matter, unless there are special reasons why mediation should not occur.

Adoption

Under the *Adoption Act 2000* (NSW), adoption plans are permitted. These are aimed at reducing potential future conflict between the birth parents, the adoptive parents and the adopted child. The Supreme Court will adjudicate in disputes that arise from such agreements and can vary or revoke the plans if necessary (see Section 4.1.5, pages 207–9).

The care and protection of children

When children are at risk of harm, the law provides mechanisms to protect them. These are discussed in Section 4.3.4 (pages 246–9). These mechanisms include cooperating with parents and other caregivers to help ensure that children are cared for. Restoration plans are one example of cooperation between the legal system and parents to ensure the welfare of children.

Autonomy of children

The legal system allows children greater autonomy as they get older— allowing them greater freedom to make their own decisions, and avoiding conflict with their parents. Some would argue greater autonomy actually creates conflict between parents and children but, by granting children increasing autonomy, the law makes it clear that children have increasing control over their own lives and that the law will support them in exercising these freedoms (see Section 4.1.4, pages 205–6).

 page 271

4.4.2 Theme 2: Issues of compliance and non-compliance

Generally, laws relating to the family are complied with, without coercion from the legal system. For example, the vast majority of marrying couples comply with marriage laws, and there are very few legal disputes in this area. If people do not wish to marry, more and more commonly they choose to live in *de facto* relationships. One area of difficulty with compliance in relation to marriage laws is that some same-sex couples would like to comply with marriage laws, but are excluded from them (see Sections 4.1.2 [page 196], 4.1.3 [page 200] and 4.3.1 [pages 232–4]).

Similarly, as can be seen in Sections 4.2.1 to 4.2.3 (pages 210–18), most people reach agreement when they separate, indicating widespread compliance with the law in this area. Comparatively few couples, either married or *de facto*, need the law to intervene to ensure compliance in the area of dissolution.

There are some areas, however, where compliance with laws about families is less widespread. These areas are discussed below and include:

- laws regarding parental responsibility orders
- payment of child maintenance
- some laws regarding children
- domestic violence.

Orders regarding parental responsibility

Parenting orders are difficult to enforce, particularly those involving the spending of time with a parent with whom the child does not live. Sometimes, access to children (or lack of it) can cause violence in families or even the death of spouses and children at the hand of partners who feel they have not been treated fairly by the law (see Section 4.2.2, pages 212–13.

Maintenance of children

The difficulty of collecting child maintenance and a 70% non-compliance rate led to the establishment of the Child Support Scheme in 1988. Though compliance with payment of child maintenance has vastly improved, there are still difficulties with ensuring compliance in this area. As seen in Case Study 4.6, Section 4.2.2 (page 216), in 2008 only 50% of paying parents paid child support in full and on time.

> Examine issues of compliance and non-compliance in regard to the family.

Children

Most of the laws concerning the rights of children are complied with (see Section 4.1.4, pages 202–7). Areas of the law which cause difficulty are:

▶ the banning of gender selection in IVF treatments in Australia has meant that some people have sought such treatments overseas (see Section 4.3.3, pages 240–1)

▶ the lack of legislation concerning private surrogacy arrangements means that such arrangements cannot be controlled, and compliance with the arrangement cannot be enforced—such as in the case of *Re 'Evelyn'* (see Case Study 4.9, Section 4.3.3, page 242). The NSW government proposed legislation to bring more legal certainty into such arrangements in 2010.

▶ overseas adoption can be difficult to access and can be carried out illegally (see Section 4.1.5, pages 208–9)

▶ the Wood Inquiry revealed the size of the problem regarding care and protection of children, indicating that a significant number of parents are not complying with their legal responsibility to care for their children (see Section 4.3.4, pages 245–6).

Domestic violence

The main issue of compliance concerning domestic violence is the relative ease with which an AVO or Family Court injunction can be broken. The fact that these breaches are such common occurrences also indicates a large lack of compliance with the law in this area (see Section 4.2.4, pages 218–25).

KCq page 271

4.4.3 Theme 3: Changes to family law as a response to changing values in the community

Because the family is the basic unit in society, family law relies heavily upon the morals and ethics of the society it represents. This section describes the ways in which family law reflects the changing values in the community.

The institution of marriage

Marriage rates

The institution of marriage (and its popularity) is a reflection of the moral values of Australian society, both past and present. Marriage has become less popular as the values of the community have changed. In 1986, for example, the figures supplied by the Australian Bureau of Statistics for the crude marriage rate (which is the number of people who get married per 1000 people) was 7.2. By 1996, this rate had declined to 5.8 and was 5.5 in 2006. The drop in the marriage rate has corresponded to a rise in the number of *de facto* couples (see Section 4.1.3, pages 200–1). These changes reflect changes in the morals of society as a whole—in particular, the increased acceptance of sexual relations outside of marriage and the lessening stigma attached to unmarried couples and ex-nuptial children.

Other laws about marriage

In Australia, polygamous marriages are not permitted, people can generally not be married until they are adults, people cannot marry their close relatives, and people cannot be forced into marriage. All these laws about marriage reflect the values of society (see Section 4.1.2, pages 195–8).

> **Assess the extent to which changes to family law are a response to changing values in the community.**

Alternative family relationships

De facto relationships

During the 1960s and 1970s, *de facto* relationships were seen by many as immoral and were described as 'living in sin'. As values have changed, so too has the acceptability of these types of relationships, and the law has responded to this change by giving increasing recognition to *de facto* relationships so that, today, because of the *Family Law Amendment (De Facto Financial Matters and other Measures) Act 2008* (Cth), *de facto* spouses are treated in the same way as married spouses when they separate (see Sections 4.1.3 [pages 200–1], 4.2.3 [pages 216–18] and 4.3.1 [pages 223–4]).

Same-sex relationships

Twenty years ago, same-sex relationships were barely acknowledged. As community values have changed, there has been a growing acceptance of these relationships. This is reflected by the law, with gradual changes to legislation which increasingly equalise the legal recognition of same-sex couples so that, today, they have now achieved marriage equality (see Section 4.3.1, pages 223–4).

Divorce

The concept of 'no-fault' divorce, introduced in the *Family Law Act 1975* (Cth), continues to challenge the values of some in the community. Before 1975, there was usually a party to blame for the breakdown of a marriage, and many agree that this should still be the case (see Section 4.2.1, page 210). As seen in Section 4.3.2 (page 235), the idea of granting custody and ordering maintenance often also involved the idea of fault.

The consideration of fault into property settlements and decisions about children is being reintroduced in some cases concerning domestic violence. Some agree that no-one is to blame for a marriage breakdown and, therefore, no 'punishment' should be given. Others, however, say that, in the case of domestic violence, a victim should be compensated in the dissolution process (see Sections 4.2.1–4.2.3, pages 210–18).

Children

Ex-nuptial children

The issue of ex-nuptial children (see Sections 4.1.4 [page 203] and 4.3.2 [page 235]) is not as morally and ethically problematic as it once was. In the past, children born out of wedlock were seen as the product of an immoral liaison and were not afforded the same legal protections as other children. Similar to the acceptance of *de facto* relationships, the acceptance and recognition of ex-nuptial children has increased as society's moral attitudes towards marriage have changed. Today, all children have the same rights, no matter what the marital status of their parents (see Sections 4.1.4 [pages 202–7], 4.2.2 [pages 211–16] and 4.3.2 [pages 234–9]).

Birth technologies and surrogacy

Birth technologies and surrogacy also raise moral and ethical issues for the community, which are discussed in Section 4.3.3 (pages 239–45). These issues have not been fully resolved, either by society or by the Australian legal system, though there have been some legal responses in both statutes and court decisions. Changes to the law in this area reflect changing community standards. Some of the changes to the law which have occurred in recent years and the changing community values behind these legislative changes are described on the following page.

▶ The *Status of Children Act 1996* (NSW), makes the birth mother the legal mother of the child, and the social father is the legal father.

▶ Various court decisions, such as *Re Patrick* (2002) 28 Fam LR 579, 645 (Case Study 4.8, Section 4.3.3, page 240), confirm that sperm donors have no legal parental status.

▶ The status of lesbian co-mothers has recently been enshrined in NSW law with the passing of the *Miscellaneous Acts Amendment (Same Sex Relationships) Act 2008*. This legislation reflects the change in society's morals regarding homosexual parenting becoming more acceptable (see Section 4.3.1, pages 232–4).

▶ Gender selection for non-medical reasons is banned in Australia.

▶ The *Assisted Reproductive Technology Act 2007* (NSW) established a mandatory gamete donor register, commencing on 1 January 2010, and this reflects the community attitude that children born through such technology should have knowledge about their genetic heritage.

▶ All women have access to birth technology, but those who are 'socially infertile' rather than 'medically infertile' must pay considerably more for the technology because they do not receive Medicare payments for the treatment. This reflects the view held by the majority of community members who do not approve of the use of birth technologies by single and lesbian women (see Case Study 4.9, Section 4.3.3, page 240).

▶ In NSW, commercial surrogacy is banned under the Assisted Reproductive Technology Act, though there is nothing to prevent private surrogacy arrangements taking place for altruistic reasons. Changing attitudes towards altruistic surrogacy have led to calls for legislative change in this area.

▶ In December 2006, the *Prohibition of Human Cloning for Reproduction and the Regulation of Human Embryo Research Amendment Act 2006* (Cth) was passed in a conscience vote in Commonwealth parliament. These amendments allow strictly controlled therapeutic cloning, but restrict the use of excess IVF embryos and the creation and use of other embryos in research. Human cloning for reproductive purposes is banned.

Conscience votes

Conscience votes mean that politicians can vote according to their personal moral beliefs, not according to political party policy. The fact that the 2006 amendments to the legislation about human embryo research and cloning went to a conscience vote shows the highly personal and deeply felt emotions surrounding such issues. The fact that this legislation was passed reflects community values that human embryo cloning should be permitted if it is strictly controlled and can save lives. Changes to adoption laws in NSW in 2010 allowing same-sex adoption were also subject to a conscience vote (see page 257).

Parental responsibility

Changes in values have played an important part in the changing notions of parental responsibility, so that today the law upholds the view that both parents, regardless of their marital status, have equal responsibility for their children (see Section 4.3.2, pages 234–9).

Adoption

Changing community values have led to changes in adoptions and changes in adoption law, and this is discussed in Section 4.1.5 (pages 207–9).

Adoption laws reflect community values in that same-sex couples have, since September 2010, been permitted to adopt. These legislative changes, based on a conscience vote, occurred in 2010 in the NSW parliament, indicating that community attitudes are changing.

Adoption processes also reflect the changing values of the community in that far fewer children are available for adoption than there were twenty to thirty years ago. This reflects an attitudinal shift about unmarried mothers and their children. No longer is an unmarried mother treated as morally inferior and it is now quite acceptable for children to be born out of wedlock. As seen above, and in Sections 4.1.4 (pages 202–7), 4.2.2 (pages 211–16) and 4.3.2 (pages 234–9), there is no legal difference in the treatment of nuptial and ex-nuptial children. Consequently, however, fewer children are available for adoption and people are turning to birth technologies and overseas adoptions instead.

The law now also allows for:

- contact between adopted children and their natural parents
- 'open adoption'
- a thirty-day period after the birth before parents can consent to adoption.

All these legal changes, which have occurred since the 1990s, reflect the changing community attitudes towards unmarried mothers and children, removing the stigma attached to them and recognising the rights of both birth parents and adopted children.

Domestic violence and the care and protection of children

As seen in Section 4.2.4 (pages 218–25), domestic violence and crimes in family relationships are a legal issue facing Australian family law. Domestic violence is the most common form of assault in Australia, and many incidents go unreported. This seems to be because victims are scared, embarrassed or feel that they will not be treated seriously. Attitudes which mistakenly minimise the seriousness of domestic violence still exist, as seen in the Australian Institute of Criminology survey published in 2006. However, the legal system, is increasingly treating the problem of domestic violence seriously, as can be seen by changes to the law in recent years. These changes are discussed in detail in Section 4.2.4 (pages 218–25) and include:

- strengthening of AVOs under the *Crimes (Domestic and Personal Violence) Act 2007* (NSW)
- creating domestic violence offences under the *Crimes* (Domestic and Personal Violence) Act
- taking into account family violence in the consideration of parenting orders by the Family Court. This has been problematic because some people feel that women make false allegations in order to be granted greater care of the children, while others say that women are scared to bring family violence before the court because of a fear that they will be treated as 'unfriendly' by the court.

The area of child care and protection is one that causes great concern in the community. As seen in Case Study 4.11, Section 4.3.4 (page 246), the deaths of two children in 2007 caused community outrage and led to the Wood Inquiry which, in turn, led to substantial changes to the law in this area.

KCq page 272

Examine the role of law reform in achieving just outcomes for family members and society.

4.4.4 Theme 4: The role of law reform in achieving just outcomes for family members and society

To *reform* the law means to change the law so that it operates more efficiently and/or more effectively. Law can be reformed by legislation or by adaptation of the common law in courts.

Parliaments are the principal lawmakers in our society and, therefore, the principal agencies of reform to the law. The area of family law is governed by many statutes which are amended to keep abreast of changes in society. One example of recent law reform is the *Relationships Register Act 2010* (NSW) which allows same-sex couples to register their relationship with the NSW Registry of Births, Deaths and Marriages (see Section 4.3.1, page 233).

While parliament is the primary agency of law reform, the courts contribute to reform in the law by applying precedent to cases currently under review and by making decisions to fit changing circumstances. Courts must apply legislation, must follow precedent and can only make a decision in cases before them, so their contribution to reform is usually slow and piecemeal. However, sometimes the effect of a court decision can be very important, as in the case of *Coghlan v Coghlan* (2005) FLC 93-220 where the Full Court of the Family Court decided that superannuation should be treated separately to other property (see Section 4.2.3, pages 217–18).

Pressure to change existing law can come from many sources including:

- the media (see Section 4.2.7, pages 229–31)
- lobby groups (see Section 4.2.6, page 229)
- reports from various government inquiries or organisations such as the Ombudsman, Law Reform Commissions or government inquiries
- international pressure.

Factors leading to law reform

There are many factors which give rise to the need for law reform. These include:

- **changing social values**. Changes to family law because of changing community values are discussed in Section 4.4.3 (pages 254–6). One example is the increasing recognition of same-sex relationships (see Section 4.3.1, pages 232–4).

- **the changing composition of society**. The shape of Australian families has changed enormously in the last thirty to forty years. There are far more single-parent families, and far more people living in *de facto* relationships and same-sex relationships. The law has been reformed to accommodate these changes. One example of reform to the law because of the changing composition of society is the incorporation into Australian adoption law in 1998 of the Hague Convention on Protection of Children and Co-operation in Respect of Intercountry Adoption 1993 (see Section 4.1.5, pages 208–9). This has come about because of the large decline in Australian children available for adoption, which in turn is a result of greater acceptance of ex-nuptial children and greater use of contraception.

- **failure of existing law**. When existing law fails to achieve just outcomes for family members and/or society, calls are made to change the law. One example is the reforms made to child care and protection in NSW via the *Children Legislation Amendment (Wood Inquiry Recommendations) Act 2009* (NSW), prompted by the failure of the existing system to adequately protect children at risk of harm (see Section 4.3.4, pages 246–7).

▶ **international law**. Sometimes domestic law may need changing to accommodate principles outlined in international law. For example, Australia's ratification of the United Nations Convention on the Rights of the Child in 1990 has led to several reforms, such as the 1995 and 2006 amendments to the *Family Law Act 1975* (Cth) which emphasise the responsibility of parents and enshrine the international right of children to know and be cared for by both parents, and to have regular contact with both parents and other 'significant' people (see Section 4.2.2, pages 211–13).

▶ **new technology**: New technology presents issues which need to be dealt with by both society and the law. This is evident with Artificial Reproductive Technologies (ART) discussed in Section 4.3.3 (pages 239–45). In recent years, there have been several reforms to the law arising from birth technologies, including the cases of *Re 'Evelyn', Re Mark* and *Re Patrick* (see Case Studies 4.8, 4.9 and 4.10, Section 4.3.3, pages 240, 242 and 243, and the *Assisted Reproductive Technology Act 2007* (NSW).

Table 4.6 lists recent reforms to the law which attempt to secure more just outcomes for families, and the factors which have prompted these reforms. Suggested further reforms are also listed.

Table 4.6 Recent law reforms and the factors leading to them

Recent reforms	Factors leading to reform
MARRIAGE (Sections 4.1.3 [pages 200–1] and 4.3.1 [page 233])	
The *Marriage Act 1961* (Cth) was amended to include same-sex marriage.	Changing social values worldwide which increasingly recognise the legitimacy of same-sex relationships.
DE FACTO RELATIONSHIPS (Sections 4.1.2 [pages 200–1], 4.2.2 [pages 211–16] and 4.2.3 [pages 216–18])	
The *Family Law Amendment (De Facto Financial Matters and other Measures) Act 2008* (Cth): *de facto* couples, whether heterosexual or homosexual, are now covered by the same laws as married couples in matters to do with property after separation.	Changing social values which have made *de facto* relationships socially acceptable alternatives to marriage.
RIGHTS OF CHILDREN (Sections 4.1.4 [pages 202–7] and 4.2.2 [pages 211–16])	
The 1995 and 2006 amendments to the *Family Law Act 1975* (Cth) which emphasise the responsibility of parents and enshrine the international right of children to know and be cared for by both parents, and to have regular contact with both parents and other 'significant' people.	Australia's ratification of the United Nations Convention on the Rights of the Child in 1990 led to these reforms. Effective lobbying from fathers' groups was instrumental in the 2006 reforms.
SUCCESSION (Section 4.1.4, pages 205–6)	
The *Succession Act 2006* (NSW)	This reform was to create uniformity in succession laws across Australia, because it is a matter for state law.
ADOPTION (Section 4.1.5, pages 207–9)	
The *Adoption Act 2000* (NSW) reformed the previous law by: ▶ incorporating the birth family into adoption ▶ making open adoption a common practice ▶ making further provisions concerning overseas adoption, in order to make it easier to access, and to comply with adoption treaties ▶ ensuring that the adopted child has access to his or her birth family and culture ▶ ensuring that adoption is a service, first and foremost, to the child concerned.	In 1992, the NSW Law Reform Commission began a review of the *Adoption of Children Act 1965* (NSW). It released its findings in 1997, stating that reform to the legislation was needed. This led to the passing of the *Adoption Act 2000* (NSW). The adoption in 1998 of the Hague Convention on Protection of Children and Co-operation in Respect of Intercountry Adoption 1993 also affected these reforms. * *The suggestion that same-sex couples be allowed to adopt was made by the NSW government inquiry in 2009 and was made law in 2010 (Section 4.3.1, pages 233–4).*

Recent reforms	Factors leading to reform
DIVORCE (Section 4.2.1, pages 210–11)	
The *Family Law Act 1975* (Cth) introduced the 'no-fault' concept which was a fundamental reform to divorce law. Subsequent amendments have reformed the law to increasingly recognise the effect of family violence and to increase the rights of the child. (See also Sections 4.2.2 [pages 211–16], 4.2.3 [pages 216–18], 4.2.5 [pages 225–8] and 4.2.6 [pages 228–9]).	Changing social values have led to all these reforms.
LEGAL CONSEQUENCES OF SEPARATION: RESPONSIBILITY FOR CHILDREN (Sections 4.2.2 [pages 211–16] and 4.3.2 [pages 234–9])	
Reforms to the *Family Law Act* in 1988, 1995 and 2006 have: ▸ made all children subject to these laws ▸ introduced family violence as a factor in determining the best interests of the child ▸ emphasised parental responsibility.	These reforms were brought about by: ▸ perceived failure of existing laws ▸ changing social values ▸ changing composition of society ▸ ratification of the CROC ▸ pressure from lobby groups, such as fathers' groups * *Several reviews into the operation of equal shared parenting laws and the consideration of family violence were released in 2010 and several reforms were suggested, particularly with regard to family violence.*
CHILD MAINTENANCE LAWS (Section 4.2.2, pages 215–16)	
These were radically changed by the introduction of the Child Support Scheme in 1988, which was then substantially reformed in 1998 and 2008.	Changes were brought about by failure of existing laws. Government reviews in 1994 and 2004 led to the 1998 and 2008 reforms.
LEGAL CONSEQUENCES OF SEPARATION: PROPERTY (Section 4.2.3, pages 216–18)	
Reforms to: ▸ who is covered by the laws ▸ the way superannuation is considered ▸ consideration of family violence through legislative changes and court decisions.	These reforms were brought about by: ▸ the perceived failure of existing laws ▸ changing social values ▸ the changing composition of society.
DOMESTIC VIOLENCE (Section 4.2.4, pages 218–25)	
▸ Strengthening of AVOs and other reforms under the *Crimes (Domestic and Personal Violence) Act 2007* (NSW). ▸ Taking into account family violence in the consideration of parenting orders by the Family Court. ▸ The Domestic Violence Death Review Team was established by the *Coroners Amendment (Domestic Violence Death Review Team) Act 2010* (NSW). ▸ Recognition of 'battered woman syndrome' as a criminal defence.	These reforms were brought about by: ▸ the failure of existing laws ▸ changing social values ▸ pressure from lobby groups and the media.
COURTS AND DISPUTE RESOLUTION (Section 4.2.5, pages 225–8)	
The Federal Magistrates Court was established in 2000. Family Relationship Centres were established in 2006 and mediation is mandatory unless family violence is involved.	These reforms were brought about to relieve pressure on the Family Court and to reduce the delays in divorce and child-related proceedings, as well as to make divorce proceedings and related matters cheaper and less likely to lead to further dispute.
RECOGNITION OF SAME-SEX RELATIONSHIPS (Section 4.3.1, pages 232–4)	
There have been many reforms in this area so that same-sex couples are now treated the same as heterosexual couples in nearly every way. This is a very significant change when you consider that homosexual activity was classed as criminal behaviour in NSW until 1984.	These reforms have been brought about by changes in social values and by successful lobby groups. * *The suggestion that same-sex couples be allowed to adopt was made by the NSW government inquiry in 2009 and law was passed in 2010 to enable adoption by same-sex couples.* * *Reform of laws to recognise same-sex marriages has been suggested by some members of the community.*

Recent reforms	Factors leading to reform
THE CHANGING NATURE OF PARENTAL RESPONSIBILITY (Section 4.3.2, pages 234–9)	
The notion of 'equal shared responsibility' introduced under the *Family Law Amendment (Shared Responsibility) Act 2006* (Cth) represents the most recent reform in this area.	These reforms were brought about by: ▷ the perceived failure of existing laws ▷ changing social values ▷ the changing composition of society ▷ successful pressure from lobby groups. * *Inquiries have found that there is some confusion about the latest reforms, and suggestions for change have been made (see Section 4.2.2, pages 214–15).*
SURROGACY AND BIRTH TECHNOLOGIES (Sections 4.3.3 [pages 239–45] and 4.4.3 [pages 255–7])	
There have been many recent reforms in this area, including: ▷ allowing for lesbian co-mothers (2008) ▷ the banning of gender selection for non-medical reasons (2005) ▷ allowing therapeutic human embryo cloning (2006) ▷ the mandatory gamete donor register and laws allowing restricted access to information on that register (2007) ▷ the banning of commercial surrogacy (2007).	These reforms are mainly due to: ▷ new technology ▷ changing social values ▷ the changing composition of society ▷ successful pressure from lobby groups. * *Suggested reforms include legislating for altruistic surrogacy so it can be controlled, and allowing Medicare to contribute for cases of 'socially infertile' women.*
CARE AND PROTECTION OF CHILDREN (Section 4.3.4, pages 245–51)	
Major reforms were made to the law in this area by the Wood Inquiry amendments in 2009.	These reforms were largely brought about by: ▷ the failure of existing law ▷ media pressure ▷ the findings of government inquiries.

KCq page 272

4.4.5 Theme 5: The effectiveness of legal and non-legal responses in achieving just outcomes for family members

The effectiveness of legal and non-legal measures in achieving just outcomes for family members is discussed throughout this chapter, in the following ways:

Analyse the effectiveness of legal and non-legal measures in achieving just outcomes for family members.

▷ **protection of the rights of the child**. The effectiveness of legal and non-legal responses is discussed in Sections 4.1.4 (pages 202–7) and 4.3.4 (pages 245–51).

▷ **adoption**. The effectiveness of these laws is discussed in Section 4.1.5 (pages 207–9).

▷ **domestic violence**. Th effectiveness of legal and non-legal responses is examined in Section 4.2.4 (pages 218–25).

▷ **the roles of courts and alternative dispute resolution mechanisms** in resolving disputes arising from the separation of couples, and their effectiveness, are discussed in Section 4.2.5 (pages 225–8).

▷ **parties involved in relationship breakdown**. The effectiveness of the law in achieving justice for these parties is discussed in Section 4.2.8 (pages 231–2).

▷ **recognition of same-sex relationships**. The effectiveness of legal and non-legal responses to this issue is discussed in Section 4.3.1 (pages 232–4).

▷ **the changing nature of parental responsibility**. The effectiveness of legal and non-legal responses to this issue is discussed in Section 4.3.2 (pages 234–9).

▷ **surrogacy and birth technologies**. The effectiveness of legal and non-legal responses to this issue is discussed in Section 4.3.3 (pages 239–45).

▶ **care and protection of children**. The effectiveness of legal and non-legal responses to this issue is discussed in Section 4.3.4 (pages 245–51).

KCq page 272

Key definitions and concepts

Do you know all the key definitions and concepts for this chapter? Go through each term in the list and check that you know them all. Place a bookmark underneath each definition to cover the one below and slide it down. This way you can focus on each definition by itself.

Aboriginal and Torres Strait Islander peoples' customary law marriage: A marriage entered into according to tribal custom rather than according to Australian law.

Adoption: The process whereby a couple become the legal parents of a child born to someone else.

Adoption plan: A plan made by agreement between the adoptive parents and birth parents, often called **open adoption**.

Apprehended domestic violence order (ADVO): An order made to protect a person against the behaviour of someone with whom they are or have been in a domestic relationship.

Apprehended personal violence order (APVO): An order made to protect a person against the behaviour of someone with whom they have never had a domestic relationship.

Apprehended violence order (AVO): An order imposed by a Local Court which restricts the behaviour of the defendant for a period of time.

Artificial insemination: The practice whereby semen is medically implanted into a woman's reproductive system so that she can bear a child.

Artificial reproductive technology (ART): Technologies that allow women to become pregnant via artificial means, such as artificial insemination and IVF.

Autonomy of children: The ability of children to make more and more decisions for themselves as they grow older.

Binding financial agreements: Agreements that will be enforced by the law and which deal with some or all of the financial resources of the parties to a marriage or *de facto* relationship.

Birth technologies: Technologies that allow women to become pregnant via artificial means, such as artificial insemination and IVF. Also collectively called **artificial reproductive technology (ART)**.

Blended family: A married or *de facto* couple and their children from previous relationships.

Care plan: A plan which sets out the steps that will be taken by a family to resolve the concern that Family and Community Services has about a child.

Child: A person under the age of eighteen years. Also called a **minor**.

Child abuse: Assault of a child, including sexual assault, ill-treatment of a child and exposing a child to behaviour that psychologically harms him or her.

Conciliation: The process whereby a third person, called a mediator or conciliator, listens to both parties to a dispute and makes suggestions, in an effort to bring the two parties to agreement. Conciliation is similar to **mediation** but involves a healing focus and perhaps counselling.

Conscience vote: When politicians vote on legislation according to their personal moral beliefs, not according to political party policy.

Consent order: An enforceable agreement made by separating people about a wide range of matters.

Contact veto: An order lodged with Family and Community Services preventing an adopted adult being contacted by his or her biological parent, or the biological parents of an adopted adult being contacted by that adopted adult.

Counselling: The process whereby a third person listens to the parties to a dispute and helps them to minimise their differences and reach agreement. It involves a healing focus.

De facto relationship: When two people live together as a married couple, though they are not legally married (that is, they are living in a *bona fide* domestic relationship).

Divorce: The legal dissolution of a marriage. The marriage is finished and each party is free to marry another person.

Domestic violence: Actual or threatened violence or harassment within a domestic relationship.

Domestic violence offences: Crimes that involve violence between people in a domestic relationship and which are illegal under the *Crimes Act 1900* (NSW), such as assault, stalking and intimidation.

Equal shared parental responsibility: The presumption that the parents of a child will consult each other and agree on 'major long-term issues', such as the child's education, religious and cultural upbringing and the child's name.

Ex-nuptial child: A child born outside marriage (that is, the parents of the child are not married and were not married when the child was born or conceived).

Extended family: A family with other relatives besides parents and children living in the same household.

Family: 'Two or more persons ... who are related by blood, marriage (registered or *de facto*), adoption, step or fostering, and who are usually resident in the same household' (Australian Bureau of Statistics definition of 'Operational family').

Family violence: 'Conduct, whether actual or threatened by a person towards, or towards the property of, a member of the person's family that causes that or any other member of the person's family reasonably to fear for, or reasonably to be apprehensive about, his or her personal wellbeing or safety' (*Family Law Act 1975*)

Guardianship: The long-term responsibility for a child.

In loco parentis: Literally means 'in the place of parents'. Adults who are acting *in loco parentis* have the same rights and responsibilities regarding the care and control of children as the parents.

Injunction: A court order which prevents someone from doing something or orders them to do something.

Intestacy: A situation in which laws operate to distribute a person's property when that person dies without leaving a will.

Intimidation: Behaviours such as nuisance telephone calls or other unwelcome forms of communication, and harassing or threatening someone.

In-vitro fertilisation (IVF): A practice whereby ovum and sperm are united in a test tube where they form an embryo which is then implanted into a woman's uterus so that she can produce a child.

Irretrievable breakdown of marriage: A marriage has broken down to such an extent that there is no possibility of the parties getting back together (reconciling).

'Kiss and make up' clause: Couples who are separated may try living together again for one period of up to three months. If this does not work out, there is no need to restart the twelve-month separation period required to file for divorce.

Liable parent: A parent who is obliged to pay child maintenance to the other parent.

Lobby group: A collection of people with specific aims who join together for the purpose of pressuring the government to change the law so as to achieve those aims.

Maintenance: A payment made by one person to help contribute to the care and welfare of another person.

Marriage: 'The union of two people to the exclusion of all others, voluntarily entered into for life' [*Marriage Act 1961* (Cth)].

Mediation: The process whereby a third person, called a mediator or conciliator, listens to both parties to a dispute and helps them to minimise their differences and reach agreement. Also called **conciliation**.

Minor: A person under the age of eighteen years. Also called a **child**.

Monogamy: A person may only be married to one person at a time.

Nuclear family: A husband, a wife and their children.

Open adoption: A situation in which there is communication and contact between adoptive parents and birth parents, made by agreement between them via an adoption plan.

Parental responsibility: 'All the duties, powers, responsibilities and authority which, by law, parents have in relation to children' [*Family Law Act 1975* (Cth)].

Parental responsibility contract: A contract entered into by a child's carers, whether or not they are the parents, which contains provisions aimed at improving the carers' parenting skills and making them more responsible for the child's wellbeing.

Parenting order: An order made by the Family Law Courts about the care of and responsibility for children.

Parenting plan: An agreement made by parents about the child, dealing with parental responsibility; who the child lives with, spends time with, and communicates with; maintenance; and other issues. This agreement must be signed and dated by both parents.

Polyandry: A woman having more than one husband at any one time.

Polygamous marriage: A person having more than one spouse at any one time.

Polygyny: A man having more than one wife at any one time.

Property: For the purposes of the *Family Law Act 1975* (Cth) the property of the parties to a marriage or *de facto* relationship is all the property owned by both parties (including houses, cars, household goods, bank accounts, shares, gifts and inheritances, compensation, lottery winnings and superannuation), regardless of whose name the property is in.

Restoration plan: A plan setting out the circumstances under which a child removed into temporary care by Community Services will be returned to his or her parents.

Same-sex couple: Two people of the same gender living together in a *de facto* relationship.

Separation under one roof: A couple may be living separately and apart while still occupying a house together. As long as one of the parties has formed the intention to separate, this can be regarded by the law as being sufficient to prove an irretrievable breakdown of the marriage.

Significant harm: Harm to a child which is sufficiently serious to warrant a response by a statutory authority irrespective of the family's consent.

Single-parent family: A family in which there is one parent raising children.

Social father: A man who acts as the father of a child born as a result of sperm donation.

Stalking: Behaviours such as following a person, spying on them and frequenting a place where that person works or lives.

Substantial and significant time: The description used for the time a child should spend with the parent under a parenting order when such time includes weekends, weekdays and holidays and allows the parent to share daily routines and special occasions with the child.

Succession: The transfer of property to the relatives of a deceased person.

Surrogacy: When a woman agrees to become pregnant and bear a child on behalf of another couple who are usually unable to have children of their own.

Temporary care arrangement: An arrangement made with Community Services for a child to be placed in the care of someone besides his or her family for a period of up to three months.

Unito caro: A common law term which used to be applied to marriages, meaning a husband and wife are 'one flesh', which meant a man could treat his wife as his possession.

Will: A document drawn up by a person to state how his or her property is to be divided upon death.

Chapter syllabus checklist

Are you able to answer every syllabus question in the chapter? Tick each question as you go through the list if you are able to answer it. If you cannot answer it, turn to the given page to find the answer. Refer to page ix to check the meaning of the NESA key words.

	For a complete understanding of this topic:	Page No.	✓
1	Can I describe the concept of family law?	194–5	
2	Can I discuss the difficulty of defining *family*, and the changing concepts of family?	194–5	
3	Can I outline the legal requirements of a valid marriage?	197–8	
4	Can I describe alternative family relationships?	199–201	
5	Can I distinguish between state and federal jurisdiction in family law?	201–2	
6	Can I explain the legal rights and obligations between parents and children, including those derived from international law?	202–7	
7	Can I describe the law relating to adoption?	207–9	
8	Can I describe the law relating to divorce?	210–11	
9	Can I outline the legal consequences of separation with regard to children?	211–16	
10	Can I outline the legal consequences of separation with regard to property?	216–18	
11	Can I explain the role of the law in dealing with domestic violence?	218–25	

	For a complete understanding of this topic:	Page No.	✓
12	Can I evaluate the effectiveness of the law in protecting victims of domestic violence?	225	
13	Can I describe the roles of courts and dispute resolution methods?	225–8	
14	Can I outline the legal processes involved in dealing with problems in family relationships?	227–8	
15	Can I describe the role of non-government organisations?	228–9	
16	Can I describe the role of the media in issues regarding family law?	229–31	
17	Can I examine the role of non-government organisations and the media in relation to family law?	231	
18	Can I evaluate the effectiveness of the law in achieving justice for parties involved in relationship breakdown?	231–2	
19	Can I identify and describe recognition of same-sex relationships?	232–4	
20	Can I investigate the contemporary issue relating to family law of the recognition of same-sex relationships, and evaluate the effectiveness of legal and non-legal responses to this issue?	234	

Useful resources

Acts

Adoption Act 2000 (NSW) (See Section 4.1.5, pages 207–9.)

Adoption Amendment (Same Sex Couples) Act 2010 (See Section 4.3.1, pages 233–4.)

Adoption Information Act 1990 (NSW) (See Section 4.1.5, page 208.)

Anti-Discrimination Act 1977 (NSW) (See Section 4.3.1, pages 232–3.)

Assisted Reproductive Technology Act 2007 (NSW) (See Section 4.3.3, pages 240–2.)

Australian Citizenship Act 1948 (Cth) (See Section 4.1.4, page 203.)

Australian Human Rights Commission Act 1986 (Cth) (See Section 4.1.4, page 203.)

Bail Act 2013 (NSW) (See Section 4.2.4, page 220.)

Births, Deaths and Marriages Registration Act 1995 (NSW) (See Section 4.1.4, page 203.)

Child Protection (Working with Children) Act 2012 (NSW) (See Section 4.1.4, page 204.)

Children and Young Persons (Care and Protection) Act 1998 (NSW) (See Sections 4.1.4 [page 204] and 4.3.4 [page 245].)

Children (Equality of Status) Act 1976 (NSW) (See Section 4.1.4, page 203.)

Children Legislation Amendment (Wood Inquiry Recommendations) Act 2009 (NSW) (See Section 4.3.4, page 246.)

Children (Protection and Parental Responsibility) Act 1997 (NSW) (See Section 4.1.4, page 204.)

Coroners Amendment (Domestic Violence Death Review Team) Act 2010 (NSW) (See Section 4.2.4, page 224.)

Crimes (Domestic and Personal Violence) Act 2007 (NSW) (See Section 4.2.4, pages 220–1.)

Crimes Act 1900 (NSW) (See Sections 4.1.4 [page 202] and 4.2.4 [pages 219–21].)

Crimes Amendment (Grievous Bodily Harm) Act 2005 (NSW) (Byron's Law) (See Section 4.1.4, page 202.)

De Facto Relationships Act 1984 (NSW) (See Section 4.1.3, page 200.)

Education Act 1990 (NSW) (See Section 4.1.4, page 204.)

Family Law Act 1975 (Cth) (See Sections 4.2.1 [page 210] and 4.3.2 [page 236].)

Family Law Amendment Act 2000 (Cth) (See Section 4.2.3, page 217.)

Family Law Amendment (De Facto Financial Matters and other Measures) Act 2008 (Cth) (See Sections 4.1.3 [page 200], 4.2.3 [page 217] and 4.3.1 [page 233].)

Family Law Amendment (Shared Parental Responsibility) Act 2006 (Cth) (See Section 4.2.2, page 211.)

Family Law Reform Act 1995 (Cth) (See Sections 4.2.2 [pages 211–13] and 4.3.2 [page 236].)

Family Provision Act 1982 (NSW) (See Section 4.1.4, page 206.)

Federal Magistrates Act 1999 (Cth) (See Section 4.2.5, page 226.)

Guardianship of Infants Act 1934 (NSW) (See Section 4.3.2, page 235.)

Marriage Act 1961 (Cth) (See Section 4.1.2, page 196.)

Matrimonial Causes Act 1959 (Cth) (See Section 4.3.2, pages 234–5.)

Minors (Property and Contracts) Act 1970 (NSW) (See Section 4.1.4, page 205.)

Miscellaneous Acts Amendment (Relationships) Act 2002 (NSW) (See Section 4.3.1, page 233.)

Miscellaneous Acts Amendment (Same Sex Relationships) Act 2008 (NSW) (See Section 4.3.1, page 233.)

Prohibition of Human Cloning for Reproduction Act 2002 (Cth) (See Section 4.3.3, page 240.)

Prohibition of Human Cloning for Reproduction and the Regulation of Human Embryo Research Amendment Act 2006 (Cth) (See Section 4.3.3, page 240.)

Property (Relationships) Act 1984 (NSW) (See Sections 4.1.3 [pages 200–1] and 4.3.1 [page 233].)

Property (Relationships) Legislation Amendment Act 1999 (See Section 4.3.1 [page 233].)

Relationships Register Act 2010 (NSW) (See Section 4.3.1, page 233.)

Research Involving Human Embryos Act 2002 (Cth) (See Section 4.3.3, page 240.)

Same-Sex Relationships (Equal Treatment in Commonwealth Laws—General Law Reform) Act 2008 (Cth) (See Section 4.3.1, page 233.)

Same-Sex Relationships (Equal Treatment in Commonwealth Laws—Superannuation) Act 2008 (Cth) (See Section 4.3.1, page 233.)

Status of Children Act 1996 (NSW) (See Sections 4.1.4 [page 203] and 4.3.3 [page 239].)

Succession Act 2006 (NSW) (See Section 4.1.4, page 206.)

Surrogacy Act 2010 (NSW) (See Section 4.3.3, page 242.)

Testator's Family Maintenance and Guardianship of Infants Act 1916 (NSW) (See Section 4.3.2, page 235.)

Wills, Probate and Administration Act 1898 (NSW) (See Section 4.1.4, page 206.)

Treaties

Hague Convention on Protection of Children and Co-operation in Respect of Intercountry Adoption 1993 (See Section 4.1.5, pages 208–9.)

United Nations Convention on the Rights of the Child (CROC) 1989 (See Sections 4.1.4 [pages 202–3] and 4.3.2 [pages 235–6].)

Cases

Coghlan v Coghlan (2005) FLC 93-220 (See Section 4.2.3, page 217.)

Corbett v Corbett (1970) 2 WLR 1306 (UK) (See Case Study 4.1, Section 4.1.2, page 196.)

Gillick v West Norfolk and Wisbech Area Health Authority (1985) 1 All ER 533 (UK) (See Case Study 4.4, Section 4.1.4, page 205.)

Hyde v Hyde and Woodmansee (1866) LR 1 P&D 130 (UK) (See Case Study 4.2, Section 4.1.2, page 197.)

In the Marriage of S (1980) 5 Fam LR 831 (See Case Study 4.3, Section 4.1.2, page 198.)

Kennon v Kennon (1997) FLC 92-757 (See Section 4.2.3, page 217.)

Kowaliw v Kowaliw (1981) FLC 91-092 (See Section 4.2.3, page 217.)

Re 'Evelyn' (1998) FamCA 55 (15 May 1998) (See Case Study 4.9, Section 4.3.3, page 242.)

Re Mark (2003) 31 Fam LR 162 (See Case Study 4.10, Section 4.3.3, page 243.)

Re Patrick (2002) 28 Fam LR 579, 645 (See Case Study 4.8, Section 4.3.3, page 240.)

Other documents

'Across the angry divide', Liz Gooch and Jewel Topsfield, *The Age*, 8 December 2005 (See Section 4.2.6, pages 228–9.)

'Adoption by same sex couples', NSW Legislative Council Standing Committee on Law and Justice, July 2009 (See Section 4.3.1, page 233.)

'The Australian Component of the International Violence Against Women Survey' (IVAWS), Australian Institute of Criminology, 2004 (See Section 4.2.4, page 219.)

'Child custody bill flawed: Nicholson', Jewel Topsfield, *The Age*, 9 December 2005 (See Section 4.2.6, page 229.)

'Community attitudes to assisted reproductive technology: A 20-year trend', Kovacs, G.T., Morgan, G., Wood, E.C., Forbes, C. and Howlett, D., *Medical Journal of Australia*, 2003; 179(10) pp. 536–8 (See Case Study 4.9, Section 4.3.3, page 242.)

'Community Attitudes to Violence Against Women Survey: A full technical report', Natalie Taylor and Jenny Mouzos, Australian Institute of Criminology, 2006 (See Section 4.2.4, page 219.)

'Concluding Observations on Australia's Combined Second and Third Reports', United Nations Committee on the Rights of the Child (CRC), 30 September 2005 (See Section 4.1.4, page 203.)

'Domestic Violence: Improving police practice', NSW Ombudsman, 2006 (See Section 4.2.4, page 219.)

'Evaluation of the 2006 Family Law Reforms', Rae Kaspiew, Matthew Gray, Ruth Weston, Lawrie Moloney, Kelly Hand, Lixia Qu and the Family Law Evaluation Team, Australian Institute of Family Studies, December 2009 (See Case Study 4.5, Section 4.2.2, page 214.)

'Family Courts Violence Review: A report', Professor Richard Chisholm, 28 January 2010 (See Case Study 4.5, Section 4.2.2, page 214.)

'Improving Responses to Family Violence in the Family Law System', Family Law Council, 28 January, 2010 (See Case Study 4.5, Section 4.2.2, page 214.)

'Landmark Agreement signed with Peak Aboriginal Organisation', media release, The Hon Linda Burney MP, NSW Minister for the State Plan and Minister for Community Services, 17 March 2010, (See Section 4.3.4, page 250.)

'Legislation on altruistic surrogacy in NSW', report by the Legislative Council Standing Committee on Law and Justice, May 2009 (See Section 4.3.3, page 242.)

'Panel set up to review domestic violence deaths', media release, NSW Minister for Women The Hon. Linda Burney MP, Attorney General and The Hon. John Hatzistergos MLC, 25 November 2009 (See Case Study 4.7, Section 4.2.4, pages 223–4.)

'Parents back new child support', Adele Horin, *The Sydney Morning Herald*, 11 October 2008 (See Case Study 4.6, Section 4.2.2, page 216.)

'Same-Sex: Same Entitlements (National Inquiry into Discrimination against People in Same-Sex Relationships: Financial and Work-Related Entitlements and Benefits)', Human Rights and Equal Opportunity Commission (HREOC), May 2007 (See Section 4.3.1, page 233.)

'Shameful secret of our family murder epidemic', Ruth Pollard, *The Sydney Morning Herald*, 24 November 2008 (See Case Study 4.7, Section 4.2.4, pages 223–4.)

'Report of the Special Commission of Inquiry into Child Protection Services in NSW' (the Wood Inquiry), The Hon James Wood AO QC, November 2008, (See Case Study 4.11, Section 4.3.4, page 246.)

'Rise in support for gay marriage', Ari Sharp, *The Age*, 16 June 2009 (See Section 4.3.1, page 233.)

Women's Experiences of Male Violence: Findings from the Australian Component of the International Violence Against Women Survey (IVAWS), Jenny Mouzos and Toni Makkai, Australian Institute of Criminology, 2004 (See Section 4.2.4, pages 218–25.)

'Worthy and unworthy winners', *The Sydney Morning Herald*, 11 October 2008 (See Case Study 4.6, Section 4.2.2, page 216.)

Organisations and websites

Aboriginal Child, Family and Community Care State Secretariat (NSW) Inc. (AbSec) (See Section 4.3.4, page 250): www.absec.org.au

Anglicare Australia (See Section 4.2.6, page 229): www.anglicare.asn.au

Association of Children's Welfare Agencies (See Section 4.3.4, page 250) www.acwa.asn.au

Australian Bureau of Statistics (See Section 4.1.1, page 194): www.abs.gov.au

Australian Human Rights Commission (formerly the Human Rights and Equal Opportunity Commission) (See Section 4.3.1, page 233): www.humanrights.gov.au

Australian Institute of Criminology (See Section 4.2.4, page 219): www.aic.gov.au

Australian Institute of Family Studies (See Section 4.2.2, page 214): www.aifs.gov.au

Benevolent Society (See Section 4.3.4, page 249): www.bensoc.org.au

Centrelink (See Section 4.2.2, page 216): www.humanservices.gov.au/individuals/centrelink

Child Rights Australia (See Section 4.1.4, pages 202–7): www.childrights.org.au

Children's Court of NSW (See Section 4.3.4, page 248): www.lawlink.nsw.gov.au/childrenscourt

Child Support Agency (See Section 4.1.4, page 204): www.csa.gov.au

Dads in Distress (See Section 4.2.6, page 229): www.dadsindistress.asn.au

Department of Social Services (DSS), formerly FaHCSIA (See Section 4.2.2, page 216): www.dss.gov.au

Department of Family and Community Services (formerly DoCS (See Section 4.3.4, page 245): www.facs.nsw.gov.au

Family Court of Australia (See Section 4.2.5, page 226): www.familycourt.gov.au

Family Law Council (See Section 4.2.2, page 214): www.ag.gov.au/flc

Family Relationship Online (See Section 4.2.5, page 227): www.familyrelationships.gov.au

Federal Circuit Court of Australia (See Section 4.2.5, page 226): www.federalcircuitcourt.gov.au/wps/wcm/connect/fccweb/home

Gay and Lesbian Rights Lobby (See Section 4.2.6, page 229): www.glrl.org.au

Human Services, Families NSW (See Section 4.3.4, page 245): www.families.nsw.gov.au

Joint Investigative Response Teams (See Section 4.3.4, page 247): www.community.nsw.gov.au/for_agencies_that_work_with_us/child_protection_services/joint_investigative_response_teams.html

KTS (Keep Them Safe) Family Referral Services (See Section 4.3.4, page 246): www.keepthemsafe.nsw.gov.au/initiatives/family-referral-services

Legal Aid NSW (See Section 4.2.6, page 229): www.legalaid.nsw.gov.au

Lone Fathers Association of Australia (See Section 4.2.6, page 230): www.lonefathers.com.au

National Council for Children Post-separation (NCCPS) (See Section 4.2.6, page 230): www.nccps.org.au

National Health and Medical Research Council (NHMRC) (See Section 4.3.3, page 239): www.nhmrc.gov.au

NSW Bureau of Crime Statistics and Research (See Section 4.2.4, page 220): www.bocsar.nsw.gov.au

NSW Department of the Premier and Cabinet, Keep Them Safe (See Section 4.3.4, page 246): www.keepthemsafe.nsw.gov.au

NSW Law Reform Commission (See Section 4.1.5, page 208): www.lawlink.nsw.gov.au/lrc

NSW Legislative Council Standing Committee on Law and Justice (See Section 4.3.1, page 233): www.parliament.nsw.gov.au/lawandjustice

NSW Ombudsman (See Section 4.2.4, page 220): www.ombo.nsw.gov.au

NSW Registry of Births, Deaths and Marriages (See Sections 4.1.4 [page 203] and 4.3.1 [page 233]): www.bdm.nsw.gov.au

NSW Women's Refuge Resource Centre (See Section 4.2.4, page 224): www.wrrc.org.au

Office of the High Commissioner for Human Rights, Committee on the Rights of the Child (See Section 4.1.4, page 203): www2.ohchr.org/english/bodies/crc/index.htm

Relationships Australia (See Section 4.2.6, page 229): www.relationships.com.au

Salvation Army (See Section 4.2.6, page 229): www.salvos.org.au

Shared Parenting Council of Australia (See Section 4.2.6, page 229): www.spca.org.au

St Vincent de Paul Society (See Section 4.2.6, page 229): www.vinnies.org.au

Victims Services (See Section 4.3.4, page 249): www.lawlink.nsw.gov.au/vs

Women's Legal Services NSW (See Section 4.2.6, page 229): www.womenslegalnsw.asn.au

Youth off the Streets (See Section 4.3.4, page 250): www.youthoffthestreets.com.au

 End of chapter questions

KCq Key Concept questions

These questions test whether you have grasped the key ideas in each subsection. They are not difficult questions, but will test your recall of knowledge of the material you have read. If you are unsure what a question is asking you to do, refer to page ix to check the meaning of the NESA key words. If you can answer all these questions, you will know you have a sound knowledge of content.

Refer to pp. 452–9 for Answers

4.1 The nature of family law

4.1.1 The concept of family law

1. Outline the purpose of family law.
2. Explain why it is difficult to define *family*.
3. State the Australian Bureau of Statistics' definition of *family*.
4. List eight different types of family arrangements found in Australia.
5. Explain what you need to do in order to discuss the difficulty of defining *family* and the changing concepts of family.

4.1.2 Legal requirements of marriage

6. State the legal definition of *marriage*.
7. Identify the four legal requirements of a valid marriage that flow from its definition.
8. List five other requirements of a valid marriage.
9. List four circumstances in which a marriage will be declared void.
10. Explain what you need to do in order to outline the legal requirements of a valid marriage.

4.1.3 Alternative family relationships

11. Name six alternative family arrangements to a traditional marriage.
12. Describe how Aboriginal and Torres Strait Islander peoples' customary law marriages are usually treated by the legal system.
13. Describe the legal status of polygamous marriages in Australia.
14. Define a *de facto* relationship.
15. List the circumstances under which a *bona fide* domestic relationship is said to exist according to the *Family Law Act* as amended in 2008.
16. Explain why the law has not recognised *de facto* relationships in the past.
17. Explain why there are both state laws and federal laws about families.

18. Name two areas of family law in which the states have handed over their power to the federal government.

19. List five areas of family law in which NSW still exercises jurisdiction.

4.1.4 Legal rights and obligations of parents and children

20. List the four basic principles of the United Nations Convention on the Rights of the Child 1989.

21. Explain the extent to which the CROC has been incorporated into Australian domestic law.

22. Explain what you need to do in order to explain the rights of children and the responsibilities of parents that are derived from international law.

23. List ten areas of the law in which the rights of children are protected in Australia.

4.1.5 Adoption

24. Cite the legislation that allows for adoption of children.

25. List the people who can adopt children.

26. List the people who must consent to an adoption.

27. Describe the requirements which must be met before a newborn child can be adopted.

28. Explain how the advance notice request system and contact vetos protect the interests of adopted people and their biological parents.

29. Explain why it has become increasingly difficult to adopt a child over the last thirty years.

30. Cite the instrument which governs overseas adoptions.

4.2 Responses to problems in family relationships

4.2.1 Divorce

31. Name the statute which currently governs divorce in Australia.

32. Explain what must be proved for a divorce to be granted in Australia.

33. Explain the 'no-fault' concept and why it has been controversial.

34. Explain the three issues involved with proving that a couple are living 'separately and apart'.

4.2.2 Legal consequences of separation: children

35. Name the two areas of law regarding children that become issues when parents separate.

36. Name the legislation which governs the care of children by their parents, and its amending statutes.

37. Describe to whom the legislation governing the care of children by their parents applies.

38. List the terms used to describe orders regarding the care of children under the *Family Law Act* since it was amended in 2006.

39. Describe the main emphasis of the current law regarding the care of children by their parents.

40. List six matters that a parenting order may deal with.

41. Describe the only criterion by which the Family Court can make decisions regarding children.

42. List the two primary considerations and five other considerations that the court may consider in determining the criterion referred to in Question 41.

43. Explain how family violence affects decisions about children made by the Family Court.

44. Outline two criticisms of the family violence provisions in the *Family Law Act 1975* (Cth).

45. Explain the presumption of equal shared parental responsibility, and when it does and does not apply.

46. Explain the term *substantial and significant time* and describe when a court is required to grant such time.

47. Evaluate the effect on the welfare of children of the granting of 'substantial and significant time'.

48. Define *maintenance*.

49. Explain when and why the Child Support Scheme was introduced.

50. List five factors which are considered when determining how much maintenance should be paid by a liable parent.

51. List four actions that can be taken by the Department of Human Services if the liable parent does not meet his or her obligations to pay maintenance.

4.2.3 Legal consequences of separation: property

52. Name the legislation which governs distribution of property after a couple separate, and its 2008 amendment.

53. List the parties to whom the legislation governing distribution of property after a couple separate applies.

54. Define *property* for the purposes of the *Family Law Act 1975*.

55. List four considerations taken into account by the court when determining how property should be divided when a relationship breaks down.

56. Explain why superannuation is treated separately from other property.

57. Explain two kinds of agreement which can be made by couples regarding the division of their property, and the status of these agreements.

4.2.4 Dealing with domestic violence

58. Define *domestic violence*.

59. Give two statistics which show the extent of domestic violence.

60. List three ways in which the law responds to domestic violence.

61. Cite the legislation under which an AVO can be granted, and describe the two different types of AVO available.

62. State the grounds on which an AVO may be granted.

63. State the standard of proof required to obtain an AVO. Explain how this differs from a charge of assault.

64. List four actions which an AVO can prevent.

65. Explain the consequences when an AVO is breached.

66. Define a *domestic violence offence* and explain the consequences when an offence is recorded as a domestic violence offence.

67. Define *stalking* and *intimidation*, and explain when such offences can be regarded as criminal acts.

68. Name two ways in which the Family Law Courts respond to family violence.

69. List six other responses to domestic violence.

70. Explain what you need to do in order to evaluate the effectiveness of the law in protecting victims of domestic violence.

4.2.5 The roles of courts and dispute resolution methods

71. List the family matters heard by State Courts.

72. Name the two courts which deal with divorce in Australia. Name the establishing legislation for each and when both commenced operation.

73. Explain when a matter will be heard by the Family Court of Australia, and how many matters are heard by this court.

74. Identify the approximate number of divorces which do not go to a court hearing.

75. Explain three changes regarding dispute resolution in family matters that have been introduced by the *Family Law Amendment (Shared Parental Responsibility) Act 2006* (Cth).

76. Explain what you need to do in order to outline the legal processes involved in dealing with problems in family relationships, and list the relevant problems.

4.2.6 The role of non-government organisations

77. List four types of advice and assistance available to families experiencing problems. For each one, give an example of a non-government organisation that provides advice and/or assistance.

78. Describe the primary and secondary purposes of a lobby group.

79. List three examples of successful lobby groups, and an example of the success of each.

4.2.7 The role of the media

80. List three actions by the media which can pressure governments to change the law.

81. State two examples of a government responding to media pressure in the area of family law.

82. Explain what you need to do in order to examine the role of non-government organisations and the media in relation to family law.

4.2.8 The effectiveness of the law in achieving justice for parties involved in relationship breakdown

83. Explain what you need to do in order to evaluate the effectiveness of the law in achieving justice for parties involved in relationship breakdown.

84. List the parties who may be involved in relationship breakdown.

4.3 Contemporary issues concerning family law

4.3.1 Recognition of same-sex relationships

85. Outline when and where homosexual activity ceased to be considered illegal in Australia for the first time.

86. Describe the legal recognitions of homosexuality that occurred in NSW in 1982 and 1984.

87. Explain the significance of the *Property (Relationships) Legislation Amendment Act 1999* (NSW) for same-sex couples.

88. List one piece of NSW legislation and three pieces of Commonwealth legislation passed in 2008 which recognised same-sex couples, and explain what recognition each granted.

89. Describe the NSW legislative changes affecting same-sex couples that took place in 2010.

90. Explain why the responses to the issue of same-sex relationships are largely legal responses.

91. Outline one non-legal response to the recognition of same-sex relationships.

92. Explain what you need to do in order to identify and investigate the contemporary issue relating to family law of the recognition of same-sex relationships, and evaluate the effectiveness of legal and non-legal responses to this issue.

4.3.2 The changing nature of parental responsibility

93. Define *parental responsibility*.

94. Describe the rights of parents to the guardianship of their children in 1900.

95. Outline the changes that occurred in child custody and guardianship law from 1900 to 1940.

96. Explain how the ideas of custody, maintenance, access and fault were linked, in the minds of divorced parents, in the 1960s and 1970s.

97. State when, and describe how, the inclusion of ex-nuptial children in the *Family Law Act* changed the nature of parental responsibility.

98. In terms of the idea of parental responsibility explain why the Child Support Scheme was introduced in 1988.

99. Describe how the notion of parental responsibility is enshrined in international law.

100. Describe the terminology changes brought into family law in 1995 and the rationale for these changes.

101. Explain when and why the idea of 'equal shared parental responsibility' was introduced.

102. List three non-legal factors which have contributed to the changing nature of parental responsibility, and give an example of each factor's influence on the law.

103. Explain what you need to do in order to identify and investigate the contemporary issue relating to family law of the changing nature of parental responsibility, and evaluate the effectiveness of legal and non-legal responses to this issue.

4.3.3 Surrogacy and birth technologies

104. Explain the terms *artificial insemination*, *in vitro-fertilisation* and *artificial reproductive technologies*.

105. Describe the legal framework for dealing with birth technologies.

106. Explain when, why and under what legislation the gamete donor register was set up in NSW.

107. Explain how single women and those in a same-sex relationship are disadvantaged in their access to ART compared to women in heterosexual relationships.

108. Explain the term *surrogacy*.

109. Describe the legal status of surrogacy in NSW.

110. State one example of a case about surrogacy, citing it correctly, and stating the legal principle established in the case.

111. List seven legal and three non-legal responses to surrogacy and birth technologies.

112. Explain what you need to do in order to identify and investigate the contemporary issue relating to family law of surrogacy and birth technologies, and evaluate the effectiveness of legal and non-legal responses to this issue.

4.3.4 Care and protection of children

113. Define *child abuse*.

114. State statistics which shows the number of children in out of home care, and how this has risen both in NSW and across Australia.

115. What is Keep Them Safe?

116. Explain the circumstances under which a child may be deemed to be 'in need of care'.

117. Explain what may happen to a child who is 'in need of care'.

118. List the ten options available to Community Services if a child is reported as 'at risk of significant harm'.

119. Explain the following terms: *temporary care arrangement*, *restoration plan*, *care plan*, and *parental responsibility contract*.

120. List five special requirements for a court hearing about whether a child is in need of care and protection.

121. List five types of orders that may be made by a court for a child subject to a court hearing about his or her welfare.

122. List five other legal responses available to protect children.

123. Briefly describe four non-legal responses to the issue of child care and protection in NSW.

124. Explain what you need to do in order to identify and investigate the contemporary issue relating to family law of child care and protection, and evaluate the effectiveness of legal and non-legal responses to this issue.

4.4 Themes and challenges

4.4.1 Theme 1: The role of the law in encouraging cooperation and resolving conflict in regard to family

125. Identify the main way the law resolves conflict in most family matters.

126. Identify the main way the law provides for the breakdown of a marriage.

127. Explain when and why Family Relationship Centres were established.

4.4.2 Theme 2: Issues of compliance and non-compliance

128. Explain one area of difficulty in relation to compliance with marriage laws.

129. Name four areas of family law where compliance is less widespread.

4.4.3 Theme 3: Changes to family law as a response to changing values in the community

130. Describe how the rate of participation in marriage has changed and state one reason for this change.

131. Describe how and why the law has given greater recognition to *de facto* relationships.

132. Explain how divorce laws reflect changing community values.

133. Describe how changes in values have impacted on laws about ex-nuptial children and parental responsibility.

134. Name eight ways in which laws about birth technology and surrogacy reflect changing community values.

4.4.4 Theme 4: The role of law reform in achieving just outcomes for family members and society

135. List one recent law reform that has occurred in each of the following areas: child maintenance, domestic violence, responsibility for children, adoption, *de facto* relationships, and birth technology.

136. List three reforms in the area of family law that have been suggested in recent times but have not yet been achieved.

4.4.5 Theme 5: The effectiveness of legal and non-legal responses in achieving just outcomes for family members

137. List nine areas of family law which you could discuss when evaluating the effectiveness of legal and non-legal responses in achieving just outcomes for family members.

Sample HSC questions

Now for the real thing! The following questions are modelled on the types of questions you will face in the HSC. Think about it: if you get extensive practice at answering these sorts of questions, you will be more confident in answering them when it comes to the HSC Exam. It makes sense, doesn't it?

Another reason is that the answers given at the back of this guide are structured in a way that helps you learn strategies on how to answer HSC-like questions. This will help you aim for full marks!

For each extended-response question you will have a detailed answer with an explanation of what the question is asking you to do and also, when needed, an examiner's plan to help you get full marks with a section reference where you can find the answer in the chapter.

When you mark your work, highlight any questions you found difficult and earmark these areas for extra study.

Refer to pp. 459–60 for

IN THE HSC EXAM

- Material from this chapter will be examined in Section III of the exam.
- Each extended-response question in Section III is worth 25 marks. You have 45 minutes to answer each one.
- Look for the ⏱ min in each section and time yourself. This tells you approximately how much time you will have to answer these questions in the HSC Exam.

EXTENDED-RESPONSE QUESTIONS   1h 30 min

- In Section III of the exam, there will be seven extended-response questions, one for each option. Each question will have two alternatives. You will be required to answer two alternatives, each on a different option.
- In your answer you will be assessed on how well you:
  - demonstrate knowledge and understanding of legal issues relevant to the question
  - communicate using relevant legal terminology and concepts
  - refer to relevant examples such as legislation, cases, media, international instruments and documents
  - present a sustained, logical and cohesive response.
- The expected length of response is around eight pages of an examination writing booklet (approximately 1000 words).

Question 1 45 min

Describe the extent to which alternative family arrangements are recognised by the law, and evaluate how well this recognition reflects community values.

(25 marks)

Question 2 45 min

Evaluate the effectiveness of legal and non-legal responses in protecting victims of domestic violence.

(25 marks)

Chapter 5

Workplace

Principal focus

Through the use of contemporary examples, students investigate legal rights and responsibilities and the effectiveness of the law in achieving justice in the workplace.

Themes and challenges

The following five themes and challenges are incorporated throughout this chapter, and also summarised in Sections 5.4.1 to 5.4.5 (pages 362–72). They are to be considered throughout your study of this topic.

▶ **1** The role of the law in encouraging cooperation and resolving conflict in the workplace

▶ **2** Issues of compliance and non-compliance

▶ **3** Laws relating to the workplace as a reflection of changing values and ethical standards

▶ **4** The role of law reform in recognising rights and enforcing responsibilities in the workplace

▶ **5** The effectiveness of legal and non-legal responses in achieving just outcomes in the workplace

HSC CONTENT

The nature of workplace law	▶ outline the developing need for workplace law. ▶ outline the sources of workplace regulations. ▶ describe the rights and responsibilities of employers and employees in the workplace.
Regulation of the workplace	▶ examine the legal framework for workplace law. ▶ evaluate the effectiveness of dispute resolution processes. ▶ assess the role of the legal system in regulating the workplace. ▶ outline how remuneration is determined. ▶ evaluate the effectiveness of legal and non-legal measures in protecting and recognising workplace rights.
Contemporary issues concerning the workplace	▶ identify and investigate contemporary issues involving workplace law and evaluate the effectiveness of legal and non-legal responses to these issues.

© NSW Education Standards Authority, *Legal Studies Stage 6 Syllabus*, 2009, pp. 33–4

5.1 The nature of workplace law

Describe the changing nature of workplace law over time.

5.1.1 The changing nature of workplace law over time

Workplace law is law about the relationships between employees and employers. An *employer* is a person or organisation who pays wages or a salary to others for performing certain work. *Employees* are the people who perform the work and are paid a wage or a salary to do so. Laws about the workplace have gradually evolved over the centuries. At first there was no legal intervention in the relationships between employers and employees: the relationship was *laissez faire* (see below). Gradually, state intervention has increased in the employment relationship, generally to protect the livelihoods (and lives) of employees.

Some of the stages in the changing nature of workplace law over time are discussed in this section.

Early workplaces

Feudal times

In feudal England, most people who worked either farmed the land or produced goods, such as clothes and household items. Most of these people were villeins, who had few rights and were virtually owned by the people for whom they performed work. They were not *employed* in the modern sense.

The gang system

One of the earliest forms of employment was the gang system. A person contracted to perform a task for another person used a gang of workers to perform the task. This system was used for coalmining and for supplying crews for ships. Payments were made to the whole gang depending on how well they performed their task, and the money was divided among the gang members.

Master–servant relationship

This was another type of early employment relationship. People entered into 'service' for another person. The servants performed tasks for their masters who, in return, provided food, clothing, shelter and perhaps a small allowance. The servants were seen as part of the household and had limited rights.

Conditions of early employment relationships

Besides gang workers, servants and tradesmen, there were very few other forms of employment. Apprentices could learn a trade under the control and supervision of a master tradesman. Anyone who could not support himself or herself was either forced to tend livestock, ejected from the parish where he or she lived, or placed in a workhouse. People in these situations led very harsh lives and often died from starvation or illness.

The Industrial Revolution

In the early eighteenth century, the methods of producing goods were changed radically and, therefore, the relationship between employers and employees was also revolutionised. The Industrial Revolution saw the birth of employer–employee relationships and workplace law as we know it today. Factories were established and people were employed to perform tasks in these factories, for which they were paid a certain amount of money called a *wage*.

Laissez faire

At the start of the Industrial Revolution, the employment relationship was governed by the philosophy of *laissez faire* (the philosophy that employees and employers should be free to make whatever arrangements they wish and that the government should not interfere in these arrangements by passing laws to control them). However, under the philosophy of *laissez faire*, working conditions in the newly established factories were of a very poor standard. Some of the problems of factory work included:

▶ **low minimum wages**. The amount of wages employers paid to workers was often extremely low and did not ensure adequate food and shelter for the worker.

▶ **long working hours**. Workers often had to work for up to sixteen hours a day, seven days a week. This included children, who started working as soon as they were physically able, often as young as seven years old.

▶ **unhealthy and unsafe working conditions**. Factories were often extremely poorly ventilated, noisy and badly lit. Employers did not need to ensure that accidents were avoided or that the factories were clean.

The philosophy of *laissez faire* allowed these conditions to exist because the government did nothing to prevent the conditions from occurring. *Laissez faire* relies on the parties to an agreement having equal bargaining power. But, in the area of employment during the Industrial Revolution, this was not the case because an employer could easily hire another worker from among the many poverty-stricken people moving to the cities, whereas a worker could not always find another job.

State intervention in workplace relations

The poor working conditions in early nineteenth-century England led to the beginning of state intervention in the *laissez faire* nature of workplace relationships. State intervention first took the form of preventing trade unionism but, later, also protected workers from harsh workplace conditions.

Trade unions

A *trade union* is an association of wage earners that exists in order to maintain and improve the working conditions of its members. Aspects of the development of trade unions are discussed in Section 2.1.2 (pages 100–1).

When trade unions first formed in England they were outlawed by the *Combination Act*s. These acts were repealed in 1824, but trade unions continued to be punished under criminal law until the 1870s.

Trade unions also formed in Australia during the nineteenth century. The first union in Australia was the Shipwrights Union. The first strike in Australia was in 1829, held by typographers who worked on *The Australian* newspaper. There were many trade unions in Australia by the 1850s. The influx of working men and women and the growth in prosperity during this period led to stronger trade unions. The role of trade unions in today's workplaces is discussed in Section 5.2.4 (pages 301–8).

The trade union movements in both England and Australia gradually gained important rights for workers, brought about by pressuring the state to intervene in workplace relationships through legislation to protect workers. Some of these laws are discussed on the next page.

Working hours

In England, pressure by trade unions and social reformers led to state intervention to protect workers from long working hours. In 1833, the British parliament passed a law providing that the ordinary working day should begin at 5:00 am and end at 8:00 pm. People between the ages of thirteen and eighteen were only allowed to be employed for twelve hours, and those aged between nine and thirteen for eight hours. Similar laws were passed in Australia.

Safety

In both England and Australia, laws were passed from the 1840s onwards to improve the safety of factories and other workplaces. These laws regulated the use of dangerous equipment and provided protection to workers from other hazards. Today's safety laws are discussed in Section 5.3.2 (pages 323–30).

Settlement of industrial disputes

Another area in which state intervention has occurred is the settlement of industrial disputes. An *industrial dispute* is a dispute about any matter which pertains to the relationship between employers and employees. The Australian government established the Commonwealth Court of Conciliation and Arbitration in 1904. In 1956 this court was replaced by the Conciliation and Arbitration Commission, which was responsible for creating or changing awards only. A new and separate court was also created, the Industrial Relations Court. Dispute settling mechanisms used in today's workplaces are discussed in Section 5.2.3 (pages 297–301).

International intervention

The concept of international protection of workers began in the mid-nineteenth century. The main international organisation protecting workers' rights is the International Labour Organization (ILO) formed in 1919 (see Section 2.1.2, page 101).

The effects of state intervention

The pressure brought on governments by the trade union movement has led to state intervention in the workplace in many areas. While the master–servant relationship of the nineteenth century (in which the employer was the dominant party) is still the basis of the common law of employment in Australia, legislation now regulates nearly all aspects of employment. Much of this state intervention has ensured workers' basic rights, including:

▶ minimum wages (see Section 5.2.5, page 309)

▶ equal pay for equal work (see Section 5.3.1, page 321)

▶ a thirty-eight hour working week (see Section 5.1.4, page 288)

▶ occupational health and safety (see Section 5.3.2, pages 324–8)

▶ the right to form trade unions (see Sections 5.2.4, page 306).

Contemporary Australian workplaces

Australia has seen major changes in the workplace in recent years. There have been major changes in employment patterns, many of which have occurred in response to technological change and globalisation. These technological changes have contributed to changes to the statutory framework that regulates employment. The introduction of enterprise agreements, for example, has made workplaces more flexible and has changed the pay and conditions of many workers (see Section 5.1.3, pages 284–5). Changes in work patterns are examined on the following page.

The impact of technological change on work patterns

Since the Industrial Revolution, technology has advanced rapidly, producing machines which can perform the jobs previously done by people, more quickly and more cheaply than the people could perform them. Automatic teller machines, for instance, are cheaper, quicker and work longer hours than human bank tellers. The advent and development of computers has meant major changes to the workplace. Computers and the internet mean that work patterns can be more flexible; people can work from home, and contact to almost anywhere in the world is simple. This technological change has meant that the number of people needed for factory and manual work has decreased, while jobs for highly-skilled workers have increased, as have jobs in service industries.

In the last twenty years, globalisation of industry and communication has developed because of technological advances. *Globalisation* is the economic and social interdependence and interconnectedness of countries worldwide. Because of globalisation, Australian businesses are under pressure to increase productivity (to produce goods and services at a cheaper rate than previously, so we can compete on a world market). Globalisation has led to restructuring in many industries.

Restructuring means rearranging the duties in the workplace, usually in an attempt to make the workplace more efficient. An example of restructuring is when one branch of a business merges with the activities of another branch. Restructuring of industries has also led to changes in employment patterns.

Changes in employment patterns

In response to technological and statutory changes, the way people are employed has changed significantly in recent years. The number of people working longer hours has grown, while the number of people working part-time has risen significantly since 1979. Australian Bureau of Statistics figures show that the proportion of people working part-time (under thirty-five hours a week) has risen, from 25% in 1979 to 36% in 2006. The number of casual workers and contract workers has also risen significantly.

Casual work

According to Australian Bureau of Statistics figures, the overall proportion of employees defined as casual workers has more than doubled since 1982, rising from 13% of the workforce to 27.9% in 2005. The nature of casual work has also changed. Traditionally, casual work has been short-term, irregular and uncertain. Now it is often regular and continuing and is a central part of staff arrangements.

Contract work

Contract work has also increased, particularly in some industries. The Independent Contractors of Australia estimate that the number of independent contractors has risen, from 16% of total employment in 1978 to 20% in 2004 (see also Section 5.2.4, page 305).

Casual workers and contract workers do not have the same protection as other workers. Neither casual workers nor contract workers have access to holiday pay or sick pay, nor are they (usually) protected by laws about redundancy and unfair dismissals (see Sections 5.3.3 [pages 332–3] and 5.3.4 [page 360]). Contract workers work under a contract for services (see Section 5.1.2, pages 278–9).

outline the developing need for workplace law over time?

In order to do this, you should explain the following.

▶ early forms of employment, such as the gang system and the master/servant relationship

▶ the effect of the Industrial Revolution and the philosophy of *laissez faire* on workplaces and working conditions

▶ the growth of trade unions and state intervention in workplace law because of the hardships caused by the philosophy of *laissez faire*

▶ the impact of technological change in the workplace and changing working patterns in contemporary Australia

KCq page 365

5.1.2 Contracts

A *contract of service* is a legally binding agreement made between an employer and an employee. It is also known as a *contract of employment*. Contracts of service are described below.

Another type of contract that involves someone performing a task for someone else, but does not involve an employer–employee relationship, is a *contract for services* which is also described in this section.

Australian workplace agreements (AWAs) and ITEAs (Individual Transitional Employment Agreements) are individual employment contracts made under the *Workplace Relations Act 1996* (Cth). These have been gradually phased out since March 2008, and are further discussed in Section 5.1.3 (pages 286–7).

Contracts of service

There exists a contract of service, also called a common law contract of employment, between every employer and employee unless they have signed an AWA or ITEA (see Section 5.1.3, pages 286–7). A contract of service exists whether a written contract has been signed or not. The law of contract applies to such agreements (see Section 3.1.4, pages 148–51).

A contract of service contains the rights and duties of individual employees and employers. However, the rights and duties of employers and employees are unlikely to be found in a single document. It is more likely that these rights and duties will be determined by a number of different sources, such as legislation (see Section 5.1.4, pages 287–90), and awards and agreements (see Section 5.1.3, pages 283–7). This is because a common law contract of service cannot remove entitlements granted under legislation or under an applicable award or agreement. Common law contracts operate between the gaps of an award or an agreement to provide for matters not dealt with in the relevant documents. For example, an award may state the salary to be paid to an employee and legislation may stipulate the amount of annual leave to which the employee is entitled, but the common law contract of employment might state the times at which the employee needs to be at work. The rights and duties that arise under a contract of service are described below and in Section 5.1.4 (pages 287–90).

Contracts for services

A *contract for services* differs from the common law contract of employment also called a contract of service. Under a contract for services there is no employer–employee relationship; rather, a person is hired to do a particular task or perform a particular service for a certain

Describe contracts as they occur in the workplace.

sum of money. People who work under this kind of contract are independent contractors, including tradespeople, architects, doctors and solicitors. For example, if a person hires a plumber to fix a drain, that person is not entering into an employer–employee relationship with the plumber. He or she is simply paying the plumber to perform a particular task—that is, to clear the drain.

How is a contract for services determined?

The rules determining whether a person is under a contract of service or a contract for services are contained in the common law. In making its decision, the court will apply two tests:

▶ the multi-factor test

▶ the control test.

The control test: If the person doing the hiring has the right to control the way the task is performed, there is a contract of service rather than a contract for services. (In a contract for services, the hirer has quite limited control over the way a job is done.)

The case of *Zuijs v Wirth Bros Circus* (1955) 93 CLR 56 is a High Court case about the control test. This case is outlined in Case Study 5.1 following.

CASE STUDY 5.1: *Zuijs v Wirth Bros Circus* (1955) 93 CLR 56

Facts

Zuijs claimed workers' compensation after he was injured during his acrobatic performance at the circus. The Workers Compensation Board said that he was not entitled to workers' compensation because he was not employed by Wirth Bros Circus; he was only under a contract for services with them.

Issue

Did Wirth Bros Circus exercise sufficient control over Zuijs for him to be regarded as an employee and, therefore, be entitled to workers compensation?

Decision

The High Court said that Zuijs was an employee because, while Wirth Bros Circus could not really control what occurred in the acrobatic performance because it was a highly skilled task, Wirth Bros Circus did control many other aspects of the working relationship. So Zuijs was deemed an employee and was entitled to workers compensation.

The multi-factor test: When applying the multi-factor test, the court will look at all the circumstances surrounding the contract, including the issue of control. The court examines the totality of the relationship. Other factors, besides the degree of control, which help determine whether there is a contract for services or a contract of service include:

▶ **whether materials are supplied by the hirer** (if they are, then it is most probably a contract of service)

▶ **whether a quote is given for the job** (if there is, then it is most probably a contract for services—in a contract of service, no quote is necessary because wages are paid for the task to be performed)

▶ **whether there is a beginning and completion date for the job** (if there is, then it is most probably a contract for services)

> **the nature and organisation of the business** (if the person claiming to be an employee has the right to hire others to assist him or her, for example, there is probably no contract of service)

> **how income tax is paid** (if it is paid by the employer directly to the Australian Tax Office, then there is probably a contract of service).

The case of *Hollis v Vabu* (High Court, 2001), examined in Case Study 5.2 following, is an example of the application of the multi-factor test.

CASE STUDY 5.2: *Hollis v Vabu* Pty Ltd (2001) HCA 44

Facts

Mr Hollis was injured when a bicycle courier, who was riding illegally on a footpath, collided with him. The rider left the scene without giving his name, but was wearing a jacket with the words 'Crisis Couriers' on it. This was the name of a courier business operated by Vabu Pty Ltd. Circumstances of the contract between the couriers and the company were that:

> Vabu provided radio equipment to the couriers

> the couriers were required to be available at a certain time every day

> Vabu set the rates of payment based on a successful delivery

> the couriers were required to wear a uniform supplied by Vabu

> the couriers had to provide their own bicycle or other vehicle

> the couriers did not receive any annual or sick leave

> the couriers were taxed as independent contractors

> the couriers contributed towards the cost of Vabu's insurance.

Issue

Given all the factors surrounding the arrangements between Vabu and the couriers, were the couriers employees under a contract of service or independent contractors under a contract for services? If they were employees, then Vabu was liable to pay compensation to Mr Hollis under the rule of vicarious liability (see 'Duties of employers implied by the common law', page 296).

Decision

By a majority of five to two, the High Court held that the couriers were employees, not independent contractors.

The importance of a contract of service

It is most important to determine whether a person is working under a contract of services (or employment), or a contract for services. If a person is working under a contract for services, then he or she is not entitled to:

> an award wage

> annual leave

> superannuation

> workers compensation

> sick pay and other leave

These entitlements are often available to people working under a contract of service. Casual workers may not be entitled to everything listed above even though they are employed under a contract of service. For example, casual employees are generally not entitled to annual leave or sick leave (see also Section 5.3.4, page 346).

Sham contracting arrangements and deemed employees

People who work under a contract of service generally have more rights and more secure working conditions than those who are under a contract for services. Over the past few years, there has been a growing trend towards the use of independent contractors hired under contracts for services, because the person hiring the contractor has fewer obligations towards them. This is particularly evident in the meat, road transport and building industries. Because of this trend, both state and federal governments have passed legislation to protect people who are employed as contractors, but whose relationship with the hirer is more like an employer–employee relationship.

Deemed employees

In NSW, some contractors are deemed employees under the *Industrial Relations Act 1996* (NSW). People, such as contract truck and courier drivers, are 'deemed' or treated as employees for the purposes of the legislation. These contractors are entitled to some of the benefits usually kept for those under a contract of employment, such as workers' compensation.

Sham contracting arrangements

Most independent contractors now come under federal law (see Section 5.2.1, page 291). Under the *Fair Work Act 2009* (Cth), sham contracting arrangements are illegal. A sham contracting arrangement occurs when an employer attempts to disguise an employment relationship as an independent contracting arrangement, usually in order to avoid responsibility for employee entitlements. Under the sham contracting provisions of the *Fair Work Act* 2009, an employer cannot:

▶ misrepresent an employment relationship or a proposed employment arrangement as an independent contracting arrangement

▶ dismiss or threaten to dismiss an employee for the purpose of engaging them as an independent contractor (see also Section 5.3.3, particularly Case Study 5.12, page 338)

▶ make a knowingly false statement to persuade or influence an employee to become an independent contractor.

The legislation imposes penalties of up to $33 000 for contraventions of these provisions. The *Fair Work Act 2009* (Cth) and the *Independent Contractors Act 2006* (Cth) also establish a review scheme which has the power to decide whether a contract for services is unfair or harsh.

Express and implied terms

An *express term* is one that is actually spoken or written into a contract. Express terms in a common law contract of service are usually few, and may include hours of work, uniform and pay.

An *implied term* is a promise that is binding on the parties to the contract, put in the contract by the law. It is binding even though the parties to the contract have never discussed it. Both the common law and legislation imply terms into a contract of service (contract of employment). These terms form some of the rights and duties of employers and employees.

Rights and duties of employers and employees

The rights and duties of employees and employers are found in:

▶ express terms of a contract

▶ implied terms of a contract under common law

▶ legislation (see Section 5.1.4, pages 287–90)

▶ agreements (see Section 5.1.3, pages 284–7)

▶ awards (see Section 5.1.3, pages 283–4).

The rights and duties of employers and employees as implied into the contract of employment by the common law are discussed below. These rights and duties complement those enshrined in legislation, awards and agreements. Legislation, agreements and awards are discussed further in Sections 5.1.3 (pages 283–7) and 5.1.4 (pages 287–90). What determines the rights and duties of a particular employee is shown in Figure 5.1 (page 290).

Duties of employers implied by the common law

The duties of employers implied by the common law include:

▶ **the duty to pay reasonable wages**. Usually wages are set by an award or agreement or expressed in the contract. Where this is not the case, the common law states that an employer must pay reasonable wages. What is reasonable is determined by what is customary for that particular occupation.

▶ **the duty to provide work**. Employers have a duty to provide work in two circumstances:

- where the payment of the worker depends on the amount of work done. For example, if a person is paid for every article of clothing he or she makes, the employer must provide sufficient opportunities to make the clothes.

- where the skills of the employee would diminish without constant work. For example, if a surgeon is employed to be a surgeon, the employer has a duty to provide him or her with surgical work so that his or her surgical skills do not diminish.

▶ **the duty to repay an employee** for expenses when the employee has incurred expenses in the course of employment

▶ **the duty to provide a safe system of work**. This duty is now largely imposed by legislation. Occupational health and safety laws are discussed in Section 5.3.2 (pages 324–8).

▶ **the duty to be vicariously liable**. This means that the employer is responsible for the actions and omissions of the employee.

Rights of employers implied by the common law

Employers have the right to expect their employees:

▶ **to work with due skill and care**. Employees are expected to have skills adequate for their job if they have told the employer that they have them. Employees have a duty to use these skills and to use ordinary care when working.

▶ **to obey lawful instructions**

▶ **to act in good faith**. This means that employees must:

- provide the employer with information and money received in the course of employment

- provide the employer with any process of product invented by the employee during the course of employment

- protect trade secrets

- not use the employer's business to benefit personally in a way disapproved of by the employer

▶ **not to commit misconduct**. Employees may not act in a way that is inconsistent with their duties as an employee.

The employer also has the right to dismiss the worker under certain circumstances (see Section 5.3.3, page 330).

Duties of employees implied by the common law

The duties of employees correspond to the rights of employers. This means an employee has the duty:

◗ to use due skill and care

◗ to obey lawful instructions

◗ to act in good faith

◗ not to commit misconduct.

Rights of employees implied by the common law

The rights of employees correspond to the duties of employers. This means an employee has the right to:

◗ be paid reasonable wages

◗ be provided with work in certain circumstances

◗ be repaid by their employer for expenses incurred during their employment

◗ work in a safe environment.

KCq page 365

5.1.3 Awards and agreements

Describe awards and agreements.

As seen in Section 5.1.2, the rights and duties of most employees and employers are determined by more than the contract of service between them. Conditions of employment are usually determined by awards and/or agreements, as discussed below, as well as by legislation (see Section 5.1.4, pages 287–90).

From 1 January 2010, there have been significant changes to the workplace relations system in Australia, with a national system being adopted and applying to the vast majority of employees and employers (see Section 5.2.1, pages 291–2). The only people who remain under NSW industrial relations legislation [the *Industrial Relations Act 1996* (NSW)] are employees of local councils, the NSW public sector and some state owned corporations. Some deemed employees (see Section 5.1.2, page 281), such as contract truck and courier drivers and taxi drivers, also remain covered by NSW legislation. The vast majority of workers now come under the national system. The following discussion of awards and agreements will focus on federal law.

Awards

An *award* is an enforceable document containing minimum terms and conditions of employment in addition to legislated minimum terms (see Section 5.1.4, pages 287–90). An award governs the behaviour between employers and employees in a particular type of employment. Awards will usually state the minimum rates of pay, the holiday leave arrangements and the hours of work, and may contain rules regarding penalty and overtime rates of pay. Awards often only determine minimum conditions, and employers and employees may agree on conditions that are better than the award (see 'Agreements' on the next page). Employers may not breach awards, and penalties can be imposed for breaches. Some industries have no awards at all.

Awards have traditionally been the basis for industrial relations in Australia, but had lost significance in the federal arena with the establishment of enterprise bargaining, AWAs and Work Choices (pages 284–7.)

Federal awards

Federal awards underpin the federal industrial relations statutory framework. The *Fair Work Act 2009* provides for both awards and agreements. On 1 January 2010, modern awards were introduced in the federal arena. The Australian Industrial Relations Commission (AIRC), now replaced by the Fair Work Commission, began the award modernisation process in March 2008 at the request of the government. Modern awards are industry or occupation-based minimum employment standards which apply in addition to the National Employment Standards (see Section 5.1.4, page 302).

There are 122 modern awards that replace the thousands of federal and state awards that previously operated. Modern awards cannot contain conditions less than the National Employment Standards (NES) (see Section 5.1.4, page 302) and must contain:

▶ a flexibility term, which means that individual employers and employees are able to negotiate changes to meet their individual needs relating to issues specified in the flexibility term

▶ dispute settling procedures (see Section 5.2.3, pages 311–15).

Awards often also contain conditions relating to penalty rates, overtime, annual leave loading and many other matters.

NSW awards

Most NSW awards no longer operate because all private sector employees in NSW now come under the national system. Awards for public sector workers and some others still do operate. NSW awards are similar to the federal awards. The relevant legislation is the *Industrial Relations Act 1996* (NSW).

Agreements

There have been several types of workplace agreements available in workplaces around Australia in recent years. These include enterprise agreements, AWAs and ITEAs. But AWAs and ITEAs can no longer be made, and any still in existence will continue to operate until they are terminated or replaced. They are described later in this section.

Enterprise agreements

Enterprise agreements, also called *collective agreements*, are agreements made collectively by all employees in a particular workplace or workplaces with their employer. These agreements override existing awards or agreements. Enterprise agreements can be negotiated at both state and federal levels though, since 1 January 2010, most agreements now come under federal law. The terms contained in such agreements also determine the rights and duties of employees and employers (see Sections 5.1.2 [pages 295–7] and 5.1.4 [pages 301–4]).

At both state and federal levels, enterprise agreements have become more important as more of them come into force and override existing awards.

Some employers prefer enterprise bargaining to industrial awards because they believe it provides a more flexible workplace and, therefore, more competitive business. Enterprise bargaining is also preferred by some workers because they can bargain for the conditions and pay that suit them, rather than have conditions imposed by an industry-wide award.

Federal enterprise agreements

Federal enterprise agreements have been available in a limited way since 1988 and were originally called certified agreements. Provisions allowing for enterprise agreements were expanded in 1993 to allow for non-union agreements (see Section 5.2.4, page 305). Work Choices, introduced in 2006 and now replaced by the *Fair Work Act 2009* (Cth), allowed for both individual agreements (AWAs), since replaced by ITEAs, and collective agreements. All ITEAs, AWAs and collective agreements lodged before 31 December 2009 continue to operate until they are terminated or replaced.

Under the Fair Work Act enterprise agreements can be negotiated between an employer and a group of employees, or between more than one employer and groups of employees. Enterprise agreements can be negotiated to operate above awards and can include a broad range of matters such as:

▶ rates of pay

▶ employment conditions, e.g. hours of work, meal breaks, overtime

▶ consultative mechanisms

▶ dispute resolution procedures

▶ deductions from wages for any purpose authorised by an employee.

There are three types of agreements that can be made under federal law:

▶ **single-enterprise agreements**, involving a single employer, or one or more employers (such as in a joint venture), and employees

▶ **multi-enterprise agreements**, involving two or more employers that are not all in a single enterprise, and their employees

▶ **greenfields agreements**, involving a new enterprise that one or more employers are establishing (or propose to establish) who have not yet employed persons necessary for the normal conduct of the enterprise. Such agreements may be either a single enterprise agreement or a multi-enterprise agreement.

In order to operate, an enterprise agreement must be approved by the Fair Work Commission (see Sections 5.2.1 [page 291] and 5.2.4 [page 301]). Approval will only be given if all the following conditions are met:

▶ the agreement has been made with the genuine agreement of those involved. This involves several steps, including ensuring all parties are informed about the details of the agreement and have adequate time to consider them before voting on the agreement. The bargaining process is explained in more detail in Section 5.2.2 (pages 292–3). Generally, a majority of employees and employers must approve the agreement. A greenfields agreement must be agreed to by each employer and each relevant employee organisation.

▶ the agreement passes the 'better off overall' test (BOOT). To pass this test, each of the employees to be covered by the agreement must be better off overall than under the relevant modern award

▶ the agreement does not include any unlawful terms or designated outworker terms

▶ the group of employees covered by the agreement was fairly chosen

▶ the agreement specifies a date as its nominal expiry date which is not more than four years after the date of approval

▶ the agreement provides a dispute settlement procedure (see Case Study 5.5, Section 5.2.3, page 298)

▶ the agreement includes a flexibility clause and a consultation clause.

Australian workplace agreements (AWAs)

An Australian workplace agreement (AWA) was an individual written agreement between an employee and an employer that set out the terms and conditions of employment. Australian workplace agreements were introduced by the *Workplace Relations Act 1996* (Cth) in 1996 and represented a big innovation in industrial relations in Australia because they were, in effect, individual contracts that had to be registered with the government. Individual contracts have not normally been part of industrial relations in Australia. For the first time, individual contracts (in the form of AWAs) prevailed over existing awards or agreements.

Australian workplace agreements could be negotiated individually or collectively but could only be applied to each individual employee who signed the contract. Unions could be involved in the negotiation of an AWA if the employees requested it. Under the *Workplace Relations Amendment (Transition to Forward with Fairness) Act 2008* (Cth), no new AWAs were allowed to be entered into after April 2008, and employers were able to move employees already under AWAs to Individual Transitional Employment Agreements (ITEAs) which operated for a transitional period until old awards were modernised. Australian workplace agreements and ITEAs are being phased out and replaced by modern awards and enterprise agreements.

There was much community dissatisfaction with the way AWAs operated since the introduction of Work Choices, and various studies confirm that many employees were worse off under AWAs than they were under the previous award or agreement (see Case Study 5.3 following). Australian workplace agreements were also criticised by the International Labour Organization (ILO) who said that their provision put Australia in breach of ILO Conventions 87 and 98, relating to the right to organise and collective bargaining, because they override collective agreements.

Because of community dissatisfaction, the federal government introduced the fairness test, which applied to AWAs and collective agreements lodged after 7 May 2007. This was not sufficient to prevent a change of government in November 2007 and the abolition of AWAs (see Sections 5.4.2 [pages 352–3] and 5.4.3 [pages 354–5], and Case Study 5.3 following.)

CASE STUDY 5.3: The effect of AWAs on the pay and conditions of employees

Background

Australian workplace agreements were introduced in 1996 by the federal government and had to meet the no-disadvantage test. This test was abolished with the introduction of Work Choices in March 2006.

Issue

How well were the pay and conditions of employees protected under Work Choices? On 17 April 2007, *The Sydney Morning Herald* reported that:

- 45% of the agreements stripped away all of the protected award conditions
- 30% allow for no wage rises over the life of the agreement, which is usually five years
- 76% removed shift loadings
- 68% remove penalty rates
- 52% remove overtime loadings
- 27% are possibly in breach of the five minimum standards guaranteed by the legislation.

Outcome

The government introduced a fairness test for AWAs and collective agreements entered into after 7 May 2007. Despite this, criticisms of Work Choices continued and the Howard Liberal/National Party coalition government responsible for the legislation was voted out of office on 24 November 2007. The Rudd Labor government passed the *Workplace Relations Amendment (Transition to Forward with Fairness) Act 2008 (Cth)*, under which no new AWAs were allowed to be entered into as from April 2008, and employers had the option to move employees already under AWAs to Individual Transitional Employment Agreements (ITEAs) which operated for a transitional period until old awards were modernised. All ITEAs had to meet the no-disadvantage test and cease operation at the end of December 2009.

Source: 'Revealed: how AWAs strip work rights', Mark Davis, *The Sydney Morning Herald*, 17 April 2007.

NSW enterprise agreements

Enterprise agreements were introduced in NSW under the *Industrial Relations Act 1991* (NSW). They are now governed by the *Industrial Relations Act 1996* (NSW). Under this act, enterprise agreements will operate when:

▶ both the employer and 65% of the workforce agree to be covered by the agreements, or the employer and relevant union agree to the terms of the enterprise agreement

▶ they meet the 'no net detriment' test (that is, workers must not be disadvantaged by the agreement in relation to their existing terms and conditions of employment)

▶ they comply with anti-discrimination legislation.

The NSW Industrial Relations Commission has had a significant role in supervising enterprise agreements in NSW. It must:

▶ supervise enterprise agreements and ensure they meet the 'no net detriment' test

▶ consider the appropriateness of the negotiation process (that is, ensure that the parties understood the effect of the agreement and that no duress was involved).

When negotiating an agreement without a union, the employer must notify the Industrial Relations Commission's Industrial Registrar who will notify the relevant unions.

From 1 January 2010, all NSW state enterprise agreements for private sector employees and employers moved to the national system and continue to operate within that system until they are terminated or replaced.

KCq page 365

5.1.4 Statutory conditions

Statute law has made a large difference to the traditional common law contract of service. Both federal and state governments have passed many pieces of legislation in the area of employment law, covering many aspects of the relationships between employees and employers. This legislation provides many minimum conditions of employment, the most important of which are the National Employment Standards (NES) the national minimum wage, and general protections. Other rights and obligations of employers and employees are also imposed by statute.

Outline statutory conditions that affect the rights and responsibilities of employers and employees.

National employment standards

As seen in Section 5.1.3, the vast majority of employers and employees now come under federal law. Since 1 January 2010, all employees and employers in the national workplace system established under the *Fair Work Act 2009* (Cth) are covered by the National Employment Standards (NES). There are ten NES entitlements which are set out in the act. These apply to every employee in the national workplace system. The ten entitlements relate to:

1. **maximum weekly hours of work** of thirty-eight hours per week, plus reasonable additional hours

2. **requests for flexible working arrangements** which allow parents or carers of a child under school age or a child under eighteen with a disability, to request a change in working arrangements to assist with the child's care

3. **parental leave and related entitlements** of up to twelve months unpaid maternity, paternity or adoption-related leave for every employee, plus a right to request an additional twelve months (see Section 5.3.4, pages 344–5).

4. **annual leave**—a minimum of four weeks paid leave per year, plus an additional week for certain shiftworkers

5. **personal or carer's leave, and compassionate leave**—every employee has a minimum entitlement of ten days paid personal or carer's leave, two days unpaid carer's leave as required, and two days compassionate leave (unpaid for casuals) as required (see Section 5.3.4, pages 342–3)

6. **community service leave**—there is an entitlement to unpaid leave for voluntary emergency activities and leave for jury service, with an entitlement to be paid for up to ten days for jury service (see Section 5.3.4, page 343)

7. **long service leave**—there is a transitional entitlement for employees who had certain long service leave entitlements before 1 January 2010, pending the development of a uniform national long service leave standard (see Section 5.3.4, pages 343–4)

8. **public holidays**—workers are entitled to a paid day off on a public holiday, except when reasonably requested to work

9. **notice of termination and redundancy pay** of up to four weeks notice of termination (five weeks if the employee is over forty-five and has at least two years of continuous service) and up to sixteen weeks redundancy pay, both based on length of service (see Section 5.3.3, pages 336–7)

10. **provision of a Fair Work Information Statement**—employers must provide this statement to all new employees. It contains information about the NES, modern awards, agreement-making, the right to freedom of association, termination of employment, individual flexibility arrangements, right of entry, transfer of business, and the respective roles of the Fair Work Commission and the Fair Work Ombudsman.

National minimum wage

Under the *Fair Work Act 2009* (Cth), the Minimum Wage Panel of the Fair Work Commission must review the national minimum wage and minimum wages in modern awards. Each year it must set the minimum wage for any employee who does not come under an award or agreement (see Section 5.2.5, page 309).

General protections

Under the *Fair Work Act 2009* (Cth), all people in the national workplace relations system are entitled to general workplace protections. The Fair Work Act provides protections of certain rights, including:

▶ workplace rights, such as compliance with a relevant award, agreement or statute

▶ the right to engage in industrial activities

▶ the right to be free from unlawful discrimination (see Section 5.3.1, page 316)

▶ the right to be free from undue influence or pressure in negotiating individual arrangements.

If an employee is in the situation where one of these general protections is contravened, he or she can complain to the Fair Work Ombudsman (see Section 5.2.4, page 303) who can initiate legal action for penalties of up to $6600 for an individual, or $33000 for a corporation. If the contravention involves the dismissal of an employee then an unlawful termination of employment claim can be made (see Section 5.3.3, page 335).

Other statutory conditions

The industrial relations framework, be it state or federal, includes legislation which establishes and regulates other conditions and instruments of employment, including:

▶ industrial awards (see Section 5.1.3, pages 283–4)

▶ agreements (see Section 5.1.3, pages 284–7)

▶ termination of employment (see Section 5.3.3, pages 330–41)

▶ dispute settling mechanisms (see Section 5.2.3, pages 297–301)

▶ state and federal tribunals (see Section 5.2.4, pages 302–3).

Most of the above matters are contained in the industrial relations acts of the federal and/or state governments. The relevant legislation is:

▶ *Industrial Relations Act 1996* (NSW)

▶ *Fair Work Act 2009* (Cth).

The state and federal industrial relations framework also includes federal and state legislation covering other aspects of the relationship between employees and employers including:

▶ safety in the workplace (see Section 5.3.2, pages 323–30)

▶ workers compensation (see Section 5.3.2, pages 325–7)

▶ discrimination (see Section 5.3.1, pages 316–23)

▶ leave (see Section 5.3.4, pages 341–8).

CAN YOU **outline the sources of workplace regulations?**

In order to do this, you should first, explain that workplace regulations come from:

▶ express and implied terms of the contract of service (see Section 5.1.2, pages 281–3)

▶ industrial awards (see Section 5.1.3, pages 283–4)

▶ workplace agreements, such as enterprise agreements (see Section 5.1.3, pages 284–7)

▶ statute law, with particular reference to the NES and that these are the minimum standards for all employees in the national workplace system.

You should also explain the relationship between these sources of workplace regulations as shown in Figure 5.1 on the next page.

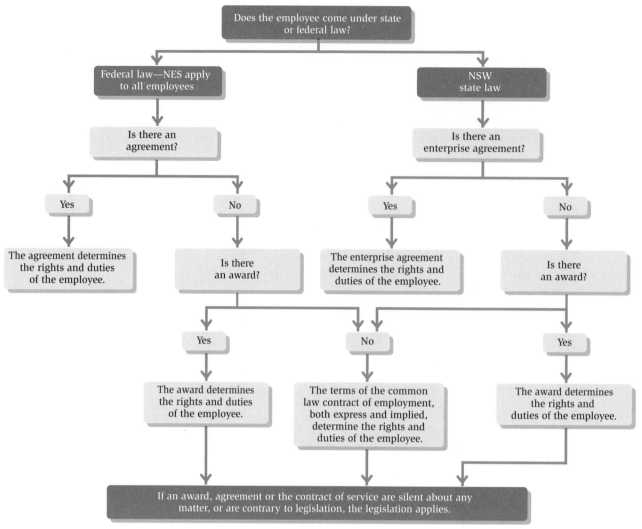

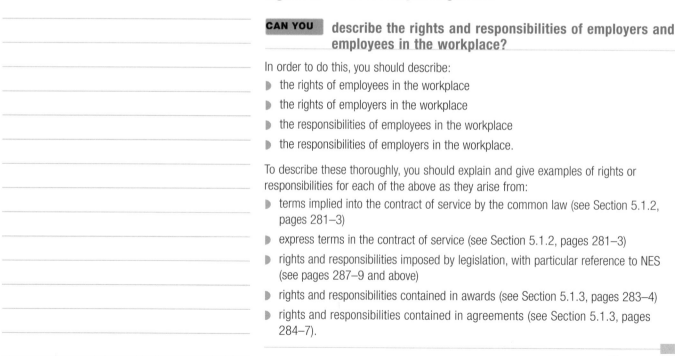

Figure 5.1 Sources of workplace regulations

CAN YOU describe the rights and responsibilities of employers and employees in the workplace?

In order to do this, you should describe:

▶ the rights of employees in the workplace

▶ the rights of employers in the workplace

▶ the responsibilities of employees in the workplace

▶ the responsibilities of employers in the workplace.

To describe these thoroughly, you should explain and give examples of rights or responsibilities for each of the above as they arise from:

▶ terms implied into the contract of service by the common law (see Section 5.1.2, pages 281–3)

▶ express terms in the contract of service (see Section 5.1.2, pages 281–3)

▶ rights and responsibilities imposed by legislation, with particular reference to NES (see pages 287–9 and above)

▶ rights and responsibilities contained in awards (see Section 5.1.3, pages 283–4)

▶ rights and responsibilities contained in agreements (see Section 5.1.3, pages 284–7).

KCq pages 365–6

5.2 Regulation of the workplace

5.2.1 Industrial relations—the state and federal framework

Industrial relations is the term for the relationships between employees and employers. The state and federal framework refers to the legislation and organisations, at both state and federal levels, which regulate these relationships.

The division of power

Since early last century, Australia has had six state industrial relations systems and one federal system. The state systems have regulated the majority of employees and employers in each state, and the federal system has regulated a significant number of employment relationships. This division of power changed fundamentally with the passing of the *Workplace Relations Amendment (Work Choices) Act 2005* (Cth), also known as Work Choices. This legislation has now been replaced by the *Fair Work Act 2009* (Cth).

Until the passing of the Work Choices amendments, the federal government relied on section 51(xxxv) of the Australian Constitution, which gives it power to make laws about 'conciliation and arbitration for the prevention and settlement of industrial disputes extending beyond the limits of any one state'. State governments, therefore, have had the power to make laws about industrial disputes within a state. An industrial dispute is any dispute about any matter which pertains to the relationship between employers and employees.

The Work Choices legislation relied on section 51(xx) of the Australian Constitution, which is called the corporations power. This power allows the federal government to make laws for corporations, whether they go beyond one state or remain within one state. Many small to medium size businesses are corporations but operate within one state and have, until 2006, been subject to state rather than federal industrial relations law. The *Fair Work Act 2009* (Cth) also relies on the corporations power.

According to the Australian Bureau of Statistics, in 1990, 47% of Australian employees were covered by state awards and 31% were covered by federal awards. Gradually the federal government has gained more power over industrial relations so that more and more employees and employers come under federal law. First, Victoria handed over its powers over industrial relations to the federal government in 1996. More significantly, Work Choices and the subsequent Fair Work legislation apply directly to all employers that are corporations and, therefore, to their employees. It is estimated that up to 85% of employees became subject to the federal legislation with the passing of the Work Choices legislation. This represents a fundamental shift in the division of power between state and federal governments in the area of industrial relations.

The *Fair Work Act 2009* (Cth) has an even greater coverage than Work Choices, because all states, with the exception of Western Australia, have handed over their industrial relations powers to the federal government, as from 1 January 2010 when the Fair Work system commenced. Now, the only people who remain under NSW industrial relations legislation [the *Industrial Relations Act 1996* (NSW)] are employees of local councils, the NSW public sector and some state owned corporations. Some deemed employees, (see Section 5.1.2, page 281) such as contract truck and courier drivers and taxi drivers also remain covered by NSW legislation.

Outline the state and federal industrial relations framework.

The federal framework: organisations

There are two main organisations in the federal workplace legislative framework. These are the Fair Work Commission (FWC) and the Office of the Fair Work Ombudsman. These two bodies were created by and operate under the *Fair Work Act 2009* (Cth). Their functions are described in Section 5.2.4 (pages 301–3).

The NSW framework: organisations

There are two main organisations in the NSW workplace legislative framework. These are the NSW Industrial Relations Commission (IRC) and the NSW Industrial Registry. These two bodies operate under the *Industrial Relations Act 1996* (NSW). Their functions are described in Section 5.2.4 (pages 302–4). As seen in the preceding pages of this section, the NSW industrial organisations now only have jurisdiction over employees of local councils, the NSW public sector and some state owned corporations.

CAN YOU **examine the legal framework for workplace law?**

In order to do this, you should:

▶ describe the division of power between state and federal governments in the area of industrial relations, explaining how there has been a fundamental shift of power from state to federal government

▶ list the relevant state and federal legislation

▶ list the relevant state and federal organisations.

KCq page 366

Describe the features of negotiations between employers and employees.

5.2.2 Negotiations between employers and employees

To decide what conditions should apply to a particular employee or a particular workplace, negotiations between employers and employees often take place.

How negotiations take place

Individual and workplace bargaining

Many negotiations between employers and employees about working conditions take place within the workplace informally. Such negotiations can take place between the employer and an individual employee, or between the employer and a group of employees. Individual negotiations between an individual employee and an individual employer often occur in regard to such matters as overtime or time off. Individual negotiations were given greater emphasis when AWAs were introduced, though these can no longer be negotiated (see Section 5.1.3, pages 286–7).

Collective bargaining

This occurs when a group of employees, perhaps represented by a trade union, negotiates directly with an employer. Collective bargaining in individual workplaces has become more common with the introduction of enterprise agreements in the statutory framework at both federal and state level (see Sections 5.1.3 [pages 284–7] and 5.2.1 [page 291]).

Formal bargaining processes

Under the *Fair Work Act 2009* (Cth), when employers and employees wish to make an enterprise agreement, a bargaining process takes place which is legislated for in the act. Generally, the bargaining process occurs in the manner described on the next page.

1. The bargaining process is initiated by the employer, or the employer agrees to bargain with employees. This is called the *notification time*.

2. The employer must notify employees that they have the right to be represented in the bargaining process. The employer must make this notification no longer than fourteen days after the 'notification time' and must notify each employee.

3. Both employers and employees can be represented by a bargaining representative which, in the case of employees, is usually a trade union (see Section 5.2.4, pages 304–8).

4. Those involved in the bargaining process, including bargaining representatives, are required to bargain in good faith. This means that they must:
   ▶ attend and participate in meetings at reasonable times
   ▶ disclose relevant information in a timely manner
   ▶ respond to proposals made by the other side of the bargaining process in a timely manner
   ▶ give genuine consideration to the proposals of other bargaining representatives, and give reasons for the responses to those proposals
   ▶ refrain from capricious or unfair conduct that undermines freedom of association or collective bargaining
   ▶ recognise and bargain with other bargaining representatives for the agreement.

5. A bargaining representative for a proposed enterprise agreement may apply to the Fair Work Commission for assistance in resolving a dispute in relation to the proposed agreement (see Section 5.2.3, pages 297–8).

6. A bargaining representative may apply to the Fair Work Commission for a bargaining order in relation to the agreement if the bargaining representative has concerns that the bargaining process is not being undertaken in good faith, or is not proceeding efficiently (see Section 5.2.3, page 297).

7. Once the bargaining process is complete and there is a draft agreement, the employer must explain the terms of the agreement to the employees and make sure they have a copy at least seven days before voting on the agreement.

8. Voting on the agreement then takes place, and the agreement must be accepted by a majority of employees unless it is a greenfields agreement.

9. The agreement is then sent to the Fair Work Commission for approval.

As seen in Section 5.1.3 (page 287), the NSW Industrial Relations Commission ensures that fair bargaining processes take place when enterprise agreements are being negotiated under state law.

Breakdown in negotiations: industrial action

If negotiations between employers and employees break down, both parties can take industrial action to help give force to their claim. Industrial action by employees includes:

▶ strikes
▶ work-to-rule
▶ demarcation disputes

▶ secondary boycotts.

Other industrial action that is sometimes taken by employees includes picketing and bans. Industrial action by employers includes stand-downs and lock-outs.

Most industrial action by employees is only effective if it is taken collectively. Usually unions are involved in industrial action and organise such action on behalf of their members, though non-unionised workers can also take industrial action.

Some industrial action is unlawful. Industrial action is protected by the law in certain circumstances, which are outlined further in this section. People are breaking the law if they take part in any unprotected industrial action.

People cannot be disadvantaged or discriminated against for taking part in protected industrial action. It is illegal for a worker to be paid while he or she is on strike (see below).

Types of industrial action

Strikes

A strike occurs when employees withdraw their labour from the workplace. This is the most common form of industrial action in Australia. While on strike, workers often attend stop-work meetings to decide on the next stage of their negotiations. The right to strike means the right to withdraw labour from a workplace in an effort to gain improved working conditions. The right to strike is now regarded as a basic human right (see Section 2.1.2, page 101).

Stand-downs

Stand-downs are a form of industrial action used by employers. To *stand a worker down* means to put an employee off work because there is no work for him or her to do because other employees are taking industrial action. For example, if the maintenance crew of an airline was on strike and this prevented the planes from flying, there would be no work for the pilots to do. Employers can stand down employees who are not on strike but who cannot work because of industrial action. This action puts pressure on the union taking industrial action because the industrial action is not just harming the employer, it is also harming other workers.

Lock-outs

A lock-out is another form of industrial action used by employers. In a lock-out an employer closes work premises or refuses to allow employees to work. This tactic is rarely used and is usually aimed at forcing workers to accept certain conditions.

Work-to-rule

This occurs when workers refuse to perform tasks that are outside the strict guidelines of their jobs. In many workplaces, workers perform many tasks that are not actually specified anywhere. Work-to-rule campaigns can cause severe disruptions to work in these workplaces and can, therefore, be an effective form of industrial action.

Demarcation disputes

These are disputes over which workers should perform particular tasks. These disputes usually occur between unions, when a member of one union performs the task reserved for a member of another union. Demarcation disputes cannot be protected under federal law (see 'Protected and unprotected industrial action' on the next page) and will be dealt with as a matter of urgency under NSW law.

Pattern bargaining

Pattern bargaining occurs when a bargaining representative, usually a trade union but sometimes employers, seeks common terms in enterprise agreements across an industry or across different enterprises. Pattern bargaining is illegal under the *Fair Work Act* 2009 (Cth) unless the trade union is genuinely trying to reach agreement.

Secondary boycotts

A secondary boycott occurs when a person or union prevents or substantially hinders a third person, who is not their employer, from engaging in trade or commerce. If a secondary boycott occurs for industrial relations reasons, it is illegal under the *Competition and Consumer Act 2010* (Cth). Most secondary boycott disputes are settled by the Australian Competition and Consumer Commission (ACCC). Secondary boycotts are legal if they are for the purposes of environmental protection or consumer protection.

Protected and unprotected industrial action

Under federal law, most industrial action is only legal if it is protected. As seen above, demarcation disputes, pattern bargaining and secondary boycotts are unlawful in most situations.

Protected industrial action

For industrial action to be protected, it must meet the following criteria:

▶ it is taken after an existing agreement has reached its expiry date
▶ the action is in support of a new enterprise agreement
▶ in the case of employees, the Fair Work Commission has granted an order for a protected action ballot to be held and the employees have voted to take the action
▶ the required notice has been given to the other party
▶ parties involved are genuinely trying to reach agreement.

Generally, protected industrial action is permitted to take place, but may be suspended or terminated by the Fair Work Commission (FWC) in certain circumstances, which include:

▶ when the industrial action is causing significant economic harm to the employer or employers who would be covered by the agreement, and/or the employees who would be covered by the agreement
▶ when it threatens to endanger the life, personal safety, health or welfare of the population, or of part of it, or to cause significant damage to the economy or an important part of it
▶ some cases in which protected industrial action is threatening to cause significant harm to a third party (the FWC acts to allow a cooling off period).

Case Study 5.4 on the next page is a case about the suspension of a period of protected industrial action under the *Fair Work Act 2009* (Cth).

Unprotected industrial action

If an employer or employees take industrial action which is not protected, the Fair Work Commission can make an order to stop the action when it is occurring, or to prevent threatened action from occurring. Where the Fair Work Commission has issued such an order, it is unlawful for that industrial action to occur or continue in contravention of the order. Contravening an order made by the Fair Work Commission can result in penalties of up to $6600 for an individual and $33000 for a corporation. Anybody who has suffered a loss because of the action can also sue for damages caused by the action (see Case Study 5.7, Section 5.2.4, page 303).

Industrial action under NSW law

The *Industrial Relations Act 1996* (NSW) provides that the NSW Industrial Relations Commission (IRC) deals with all industrial disputes by conciliation. If the IRC decides that conciliation will not result in settlement, it can issue a certificate of attempted conciliation. The IRC must consider the effect any industrial action is having on the parties and on the public generally. Once this certificate is issued, arbitration takes place. The IRC can make orders preventing or restraining industrial action after conciliation has broken down. Common law court action may also be commenced (see Case Study 5.7, Section 5.2.4, page 303).

CASE STUDY 5.4: *CFMEU v Woodside Burrup Pty Ltd and Kentz E & C Pty Ltd* [2010] FWAFB 6021

Facts

The Construction, Forestry, Mining and Energy Union (CFMEU) was acting as bargaining representative for twelve employees of Mammoet Australia Pty Ltd, who were contracted to Woodside Pty Ltd as crane and forklift drivers during the construction of Woodside's $9 billion Pluto project on the Burrup Peninsula in north-west Western Australia. Bargaining for a new enterprise agreement was commenced by the employees, represented by the CFMEU, shortly after the nominal expiry date of the Mammoet Australia Pty Ltd Pluto Project Greenfields Agreement 2008.

After bargaining was unsuccessful in producing an agreement, an order was made for a protected action ballot, which was declared, approving protected action. After the commencement of a second twenty-eight-day episode of protected industrial action in late June 2010, Woodside and two contractors affected by the delay in Mammoet's works made an application under the *Fair Work Act 2009* for an order suspending the protected industrial action because of its adverse effect on third parties. The industrial action was suspended for a period of three months. The CFMEU appealed to the full bench of the Fair Work Commission (FWC) against the suspension.

Issue

Was the protected industrial action causing sufficient 'significant harm' to warrant a suspension of the action? The Fair Work Commission must suspend protected industrial action if satisfied 'that the protected industrial action is threatening to cause significant harm to any person other than a bargaining representative...or an employee who will be covered by the agreement' [section 426(3) of the *Fair Work Act 2009*].

Decision

Fair Work Australia decided that the harm caused by the industrial action was not significant enough to warrant a suspension order. the Fair Work Commission found that employees have a right to take protected industrial action in support of a proposed enterprise agreement, and in order to suspend a period of such action, the harm to the third party would need to be significant and more than that of merely suffering a loss, inconvenience or delay.

The FWC observed that effective industrial action will almost always cause harm to an employer which will frequently adversely affect a third party and, as such, 'significant harm' must be beyond the sort of loss, inconvenience or delay commonly caused by industrial action. Unless the harm is out of the ordinary, which is likely to be in very rare cases, the FWA will not be inclined to suspend the action.

KCq page 366

5.2.3 Dispute resolution mechanisms

An *industrial dispute* is any dispute about any matter which pertains to the relationship between employers and employees. Dispute resolution mechanisms in today's workplace include workplace resolution, mediation, conciliation and arbitration. Fines and other penalties can be imposed on parties to a dispute who fail to follow orders made by industrial relations bodies when they are settling a dispute.

Describe and evaluate dispute resolution mechanisms.

Methods of dispute settlement

Workplace resolution

Under the *Fair Work Act* 2009 (NSW) and the *Industrial Relations Act 1996* (NSW) all awards and enterprise agreements must contain dispute settling procedures which must be adhered to before an outside party, such as an Industrial Relations Commission or alternative dispute resolution provider, is consulted. These dispute settling procedures are consensual. This means that both the employer and employee agree to follow the procedures. The aim of workplace dispute settling procedures is to solve the problem quickly and fairly at a workplace level to the mutual satisfaction of both parties.

Workplace dispute settling procedures typically allow for a process similar to the following.

▶ The employees who are party to the dispute meet first with their immediate supervisor. The employees may be represented by a workplace union delegate.

▶ If the matter is not resolved, the employees meet with more senior management who may, perhaps, have a representative of their employer association at the meeting. The employees may invite a union official.

▶ If the matter is still not resolved the employer may refer it to more senior management or a more senior national officer within the employer organisation. The employee may invite a more senior union official to the discussion.

▶ If the matter is still unresolved, either party to the dispute may refer to the relevant industrial relations tribunal for conciliation and/or arbitration (see below and Section 5.2.4, pages 301–2).

In 2010, a case involving Woolworths and the Shop, Distributive and Allied Employees' Association (SDA) made it clear that clauses about dispute settling procedures need not include compulsory arbitration of disputes. See Case Study 5.5 on the next page.

Mediation

Mediation is the process of solving disputes in which a third party, called a *mediator*, listens to the parties in dispute and helps them reach agreement. Mediation may become part of unofficial workplace dispute settling procedures, with either a union representative or an employer organisation representative acting as a mediator. In workplace disputes, mediation is a less formal and unofficial form of conciliation.

If individual or collective bargaining and/or the use of dispute settling procedures do not result in an agreement, employees and employers can seek conciliation and arbitration.

Conciliation and arbitration

Conciliation is the process whereby a third person, called a *conciliator*, listens to the two parties to the dispute and makes suggestions in an effort to bring those parties to agreement. *Arbitration* occurs when a third party listens to the parties to a dispute and makes a decision on the merits of the case. Conciliation and arbitration are the processes of dispute settling used by both FWA and the NSW IRC (see Section 5.2.4, pages 301–2). If there is a dispute, the employer and employees (often represented by a trade union) meet with an Industrial Commissioner to attempt conciliation of the matter. If an agreement is not reached, the Commissioner may arbitrate (that is, make a decision on the disputed matters).

Compulsory conciliation and arbitration

Australia has had a system of compulsory conciliation and arbitration for industrial disputes for most of its history. This has meant that one party to a workplace dispute has been able to require the other party to go before an Industrial Relations Commission to settle the dispute through conciliation or arbitration—though, since the introduction of Work Choices in 2006, this no longer occurs at the federal level.

Since 1996, changes to the law at both state and federal levels have emphasised the negotiation of agreements and made it more difficult to access conciliation and arbitration procedures. As seen above, all awards and agreements in both NSW and federally must contain dispute settling procedures, and conciliation and arbitration procedures will only be used after these dispute settling procedures have failed. In the federal arena, conciliation and arbitration by FWA can occur if the award or agreement allows for it (see Case Study 5.5 following).

Both federal and state courts have a role in settling industrial disputes as well, and this is examined in Section 5.2.4 (pages 302–3).

CASE STUDY 5.5: *Woolworths Ltd trading as Produce and Recycling Distribution Centre* (2010) **FWAFB 1464 (26 February 2010)**

Facts

In January 2010, Commissioner Smith of Fair Work Australia (FWA) rejected an enterprise agreement made between Woolworths (trading as Produce and Recycling Distribution Centre) and the Shop, Distributive and Allied Employees' Association (SDA), because the agreement's dispute settling clause only allowed a dispute to be arbitrated by FWA if both parties agreed. Commissioner Smith said that a dispute settling clause in an enterprise agreement must allow for compulsory arbitration. Woolworths appealed to the full bench of FWA about Commissioner Smith's decision.

Issue

Under the *Fair Work Act 2009* (Cth), must a dispute resolution term in an enterprise agreement allow for disputes to be settled by arbitration, whether the parties want it or not?

Decision

FWA decided that various sections of the *Fair Work Act 2009* (Cth), when taken together, mean that any enterprise agreement negotiated must allow a dispute to be arbitrated either by FWA or by some other independent party if both parties agree. Compulsory arbitration may be included as part of a dispute resolution clause but is not mandatory.

Changes in the number of industrial disputes

In recent years, there has been a significant reduction in the number of industrial disputes in Australia and in the number of working days lost because of such disputes. This trend is discussed in Case Study 5.6 below.

Several factors have contributed to this reduction. First, many changes have occurred to the rules regarding the legitimacy of industrial action over the last twenty years, as can be seen in Section 5.2.2 (pages 293–6). Under current law, industrial action is only permitted if it is 'protected', and some types of industrial action are not permitted at all. There have also been significant changes to the ways industrial disputes are handled, with the system of compulsory conciliation and arbitration becoming largely irrelevant and a growing emphasis on dispute settling procedures becoming a mandatory part of awards and enterprise agreements at both state and federal levels.

These legislative changes have been accompanied by economic factors, such as periods of high unemployment and periods of economic growth, and substantial social changes, including a decline in union numbers and a rise in the number of casual employees and independent contractors (see Sections 5.1.1 [page 277] and 5.2.4 [page 305]).

Case study 5.6: Decline in industrial disputes

Statistics about numbers of industrial disputes

The Australian Bureau of Statistics collects data about industrial disputes in Australia. For the purposes of their data, an *industrial dispute* refers to 'a state of disagreement over an issue or group of issues between an employer and its employees which results in employees ceasing work'.

The number of industrial disputes per year in 1987 was 1519, with working days lost being 1.3 million. In 2007 there were 135 disputes and working days lost equalled 50 000. In the year ending in June 2010, there were 225 industrial disputes with 126 000 working days lost. The large decline in numbers has fluctuated considerably since 1987, but the overall trend is for a significant decline in the number of industrial disputes in Australia.

Reasons for the trends

There are a number of factors identified by the ABS which have contributed to these trends. In the abstract cited above, the ABS says, 'Institutional, legislative and economic changes over the past twenty years have dramatically changed the industrial relations environment in Australia'. Some of the factors influencing this reduction, identified by the ABS, are:

▶ the Prices and Incomes Accords between 1983 and 1996 which encouraged wage restraint and negotiation among employees, employers and governments outside industrial relations processes (see Section 5.2.5, pages 309–10)

▶ the range of legislative initiatives which have affected the legal terms under which industrial action can take place, including how and when such action is lawful. The latest legislative changes to laws about industrial action are contained in the *Fair Work Act 2009* (Cth) (see Section 5.2.2, pages 292–3).

▶ after the economic downturn of the early 1990s, there has been a sustained period of prosperity characterised by strong employment growth and a decline in unemployment. Such conditions usually lead to a decline in industrial disputation.

Other important factors are:

▶ the changes in emphasis from awards to enterprise agreements

▶ the introduction of AWAs (now superseded) which meant many workers went onto individual contracts

▶ the rise in independent contractors (see Sections 5.1.1 [page 277] and 5.2.4 [page 305])

▶ the rise in casual and part-time workers (see Section 5.2.4, page 305)

▶ the provision of mandatory dispute settling procedures in awards and agreements at both state and federal level.

Source: 'Australian Social Trends, 2008: Industrial disputes', Abstract (4102.0) Australian Bureau of Statistics (ABS)

Effectiveness of dispute resolution processes

The effectiveness of industrial dispute resolution processes is difficult to determine, because this depends on what criteria you use to measure effectiveness. One criterion that can be used is the number of industrial disputes in Australia. This is discussed in Case Study 5.6 on page 299. From this case study, it can be said that industrial dispute resolution processes are very effective because there has been a downward trend in the number of disputes in Australia, showing that fewer disputes occur and that more disputes are quickly and informally resolved at workplace level.

However, the reduction in the number of industrial disputes might also indicate that more employees are disempowered in the workplace and do not have the bargaining power to enter into negotiations or disputation in the first place. This view is supported by Case Study 5.3, (Section 5.1.3, pages 286–7) which shows that many people under AWAs lost rights and conditions in the workplace. The increase in casual and contract work described in Section 5.1.1 (page 277) may also mean that these types of employees have less chance of asserting their rights and, therefore, fewer disputes occur.

Table 5.1 examines the advantages and disadvantages of various dispute settling processes in the workplace. The table considers three systems for regulating workplace arrangements:

▶ **a compulsory conciliation and arbitration system** which relies on the determination of awards by an Industrial Relations Commission and the settling of disputes by the legal system. This system relies exclusively on legal methods of regulating workplace arrangements and is the system which has traditionally operated throughout Australia.

▶ **a legislative framework system**, such as that which now operates at both state and federal levels. This system provides for dispute settlement and collective bargaining outside the conciliation and arbitration system by providing for enterprise agreements and dispute settling mechanisms in awards and agreements which may or may not use industrial tribunals.

▶ **pure collective bargaining**. This is a *laissez faire* arrangement in which there is no state intervention in workplace arrangements. Such a system has no external measures to settle disputes or to determine workplace arrangements.

Table 5.1 A comparison of systems for regulating workplace arrangements

Advantages	Disadvantages
Compulsory conciliation and arbitration	
▶ Compulsory conciliation and arbitration means that disputes must be settled. An industrial dispute cannot go on indefinitely. ▶ The making of awards by an external body ensures that parties are treated fairly and that exploitation does not occur.	▶ Parties to a dispute may allow disputes to occur more easily and may not try to settle them themselves. ▶ Disputes could be settled more quickly if the parties did not rely on the external system to settle their differences for them. ▶ The compulsory system fails to take into account the particular circumstances of particular workplaces.
Legislative framework system	
▶ Enterprise agreements allow particular circumstances of particular workplaces to be taken into account. ▶ The possibility of using the conciliation and arbitration system means that disputes will still be settled. ▶ The mandatory dispute settling processes in awards and agreements mean that employers and employees are encouraged to settle disputes themselves.	▶ Enterprise agreements may allow for those in less powerful bargaining positions to be intimidated and exploited. ▶ Many parties to disputes will still rely on the external system of dispute settlement and, therefore, allow disputes to occur and remain unresolved, while waiting for the external system to settle the dispute for them—though the mandatory procedures in awards and agreements should minimise this.
Pure collective bargaining	
▶ Parties are encouraged to reach agreement between themselves. ▶ A fairer outcome may be reached because a decision is not imposed on the parties.	▶ Some disputes may never be settled or may be extremely lengthy and costly to the community and all parties involved. ▶ Parties in a less powerful bargaining position can be intimidated and exploited.

CAN YOU **evaluate the effectiveness of dispute resolution processes?**

In order to evaluate the effectiveness of dispute resolution processes, you should:

▶ describe the processes involved, i.e. workplace resolution, conciliation and arbitration

▶ describe the reduction in the number of industrial disputes in Australia in recent years, and what these figures may mean

▶ compare the advantages and disadvantages of various dispute settling processes

▶ decide whether the current dispute settling processes in Australian workplaces are effective or ineffective, given the alternative dispute settling mechanisms.

 page 366

5.2.4 The roles of courts and other agencies

There are several types of bodies that play an important role in regulating the workplace. These include the following.

▶ Legal institutions, such as:

- tribunals

- courts

- government organisations.

▶ Non-legal institutions and bodies, such as:

- trade unions

- employer associations

- non-government organisations (NGOs)

- the media.

The roles of these bodies in regulating the workplace are discussed in this section.

> Describe the roles of courts and other agencies in regulating the workplace.

Tribunals

A *tribunal* is a specialised body set up to decide disputes in a particular area. For over 100 years there have been federal and state industrial tribunals to decide disputes between employers and employees by compulsory conciliation and arbitration. There are tribunals operating in both the federal and state spheres in the area of industrial relations.

Fair Work Commission

This is the national workplace relations tribunal. It commenced operations on 1 July 2009, replacing the Australian Industrial Relations Commission (AIRC). The Fair Work Commission (FWC) has several functions including:

▶ determining the safety net of minimum wages and employment conditions (see Section 5.2.5, page 309)

▶ ensuring enterprise bargaining occurs according to the law, and approving enterprise agreements (see Sections 5.1.3 [pages 284–7] and 5.2.2 [pages 292–3])

▶ overseeing awards (see Section 5.1.3, pages 283–4)

▶ ensuring any industrial action occurs according to the law (see Section 5.2.2, pages 295–6)

▶ assisting in dispute resolution (see Section 5.2.3, pages 297–8)

▶ making determinations about unfair dismissals (see Section 5.3.3, page 333).

NSW tribunals

The NSW Industrial Relations Commission (IRC) is the most important tribunal for regulation of the workplace for employers and employees who still come under state law. It is the body that has the power to settle industrial disputes that come under NSW law. During arbitration the Industrial Relations Commission can issue orders, such as ordering parties to cease industrial action and return to work, and ordering parties to discontinue a secondary boycott. If a dispute order is ignored or contravened, the IRC can impose a range of penalties, including imposing a penalty of up to $10 000.

The NSW IRC can:

▶ make awards relating to pay and disputes

▶ settle disputes (see above and Section 5.2.3, page 298)

▶ conciliate in the area of enterprise bargaining, and approve agreements (see Sections 5.1.3 [pages 284–7] and 5.2.3 [pages 297–300]).

▶ determine applications regarding unfair dismissal (see Section 5.3.3, pages 333–5).

Another tribunal that operates in the field of workplace relationships is the NSW Civil and Administrative Tribunal (NCAT) (see Section 5.3.1, pages 319–20). Among other matters, NCAT deals with claims about discrimination in the workplace.

Courts

The court system also has a role in regulating the workplace.

Federal Courts

With the advent of the *Fair Work Act 2009* (Cth), a Fair Work Division has been established in both the Federal Circuit Court and the Federal Court. These courts can enforce matters relating to breaches of the National Employment Standards, general protections and breaches of awards and agreements. They can also enforce orders made by the Fair Work Commission, such as those to do with unlawful industrial action (see Section 5.2.2, page 295) and can impose sanctions on parties who breach industrial relations laws.

The Federal Circuit Court deals with small claims in relation to breaches of the National Employment Standards, modern awards, enterprise agreements, workplace determinations, national minimum wage orders, equal remuneration orders or safety net contractual entitlements. The Federal Circuit Court has a small claims jurisdiction, which allows employees' claims in regard to matters under $20 000 to be settled with a quick and simple mechanism. When using the small claims procedure, the Federal Circuit Court is not bound by the rules of evidence or by legal technicalities. Legal representation is permitted, but is usually not necessary.

Common law court action arising from industrial disputes usually occurs in the Federal Court, as can be seen in Case Study 5.7 on page 303. The Federal Court and the High Court played an important role in the waterfront dispute of 1998, because it was court action that brought about the reinstatement of waterfront workers (see Case Study 5.15, Section 5.4.2, page 351). The Federal Court also hears cases regarding unlawful termination of employment (see Section 5.3.3, pages 333–5).

NSW Courts

The NSW Industrial Relations Commission can be constituted as the Industrial Court of New South Wales and has the same status as the Supreme Court. The Industrial Court of New South Wales can make decisions about unfair contracts of employment, breaches of awards and agreements, breaches of dispute orders and other matters. It can impose fines for breaches and can order employers to pay monies owed.

Common law court action

Under common law, employers have been able to sue a union if it has used unlawful methods. These unlawful methods can include unlawful intimidation, conspiracy to cause damage by unlawful means, or interference with contractual relations between parties. However, common law action cannot be pursued by employers when there is protected industrial action. As has been seen in Section 5.2.2 (pages 295–6), if an employer or employees engage in unlawful industrial action, which breaches an order by the Fair Work Commission or the NSW IRC, common law court action can be commenced. The pilots' dispute of 1989 is an example of successful common law court action by an employer against a union (see Case Study 5.7 following).

CASE STUDY 5.7: The pilots' dispute (1989): *Ansett Transport Industries (Operations) Pty Ltd v Australian Federation of Air Pilots* (1991) 1 VR 637

Facts

The Australian Federation of Air Pilots (the union) asked Ansett for a wage rise of 29.47% for the pilots, which well exceeded the 6% granted under National Wage Case guidelines (see Section 5.2.5, pages 309–10). One industrial tactic used by the pilots was to only work from 9:00 am to 5:00 pm.

Issue

The airlines lost a lot of money during the dispute because they were unable to fly their planes outside the hours worked by the pilots. Was the union liable for the losses?

Decision

The case was heard in the Supreme Court of Victoria. The judge stated that the union had been involved in conspiracy and had interfered with the contractual relations between the airlines and their passengers. The Australian Federation of Air Pilots was ordered to pay a large amount of money in damages to Ansett.

Government organisations

The Office of the Fair Work Ombudsman

This is the main federal government organisation that deals with the regulation of the workplace. It commenced operation on 1 July 2009, replacing the Workplace Ombudsman and other government organisations that previously operated in the area of workplace regulation. The Fair Work Ombudsman listens to and investigates complaints or suspected contraventions of workplace laws, awards and agreements, and litigates to enforce workplace laws (see Case Study 5.9, Section 5.3.1, page 320). The Fair Work Ombudsman is the place people should contact if they have a complaint about any matter to do with the national workplace system.

NSW Industrial Relations

NSW Industrial Relations (NSW IR) administers NSW laws regulating shop trading hours, public holidays and long service leave as well as working with the Commonwealth's Fair Work Ombudsman to ensure NSW private sector businesses comply with their responsibilities under the national workplace relations system. It also has the role of prosecuting breaches of awards and agreements and may advise the NSW IRC when required. Breaches of awards and agreements and breaches of industrial relations legislation are heard by the NSW Industrial Relation Commission when it is constituted as the Industrial Court of NSW.

Other government organisations play an important role in regulating the workplace. These include bodies to oversee occupational health and safety, such as Safe Work NSW (see Section 5.3.2, pages 325–7), and the NSW Anti-Discrimination Board (see Section 5.3.1, page 318).

Trade unions

Trade unions have an important role in representing workers, both individually and collectively, in industrial disputes. In order to represent workers in industrial matters, trade unions must be registered under the *Fair Work (Registered Organisations) Act 2009* (Cth). The roles of trade unions are summarised in Table 5.2 below.

Table 5.2 What unions do

Unions represent workers *individually* in:	Unions represent workers *collectively* by:
▶ unfair dismissal claims ▶ occupational health and safety matters ▶ individual disputes with employers ▶ dispute settling procedures	▶ negotiating with employers for better wages and conditions in awards and agreements ▶ organising industrial action to support the claims of members ▶ appearing before the Fair Work Commission, state Industrial Relations Commissions and other bodies for conciliation or arbitration ▶ lobbying governments to change laws and policies to better protect workers. This is generally done by the ACTU and other trade union organisations.

Right of entry requirements

Trade unions had their right to enter workplaces restricted under the *Workplace Relations Act 1996* and further restricted in the 2005 Work Choices amendments. Under the *Fair Work Act 2009* (Cth), right of entry for union officials is firmly established. Unions in the federal arena must obtain a permit to enter a workplace and must usually give employers twenty-four hours notice of their intention to enter, though this can be waived by the Fair Work Commission in certain circumstances. A union official may enter a workplace for the purpose of investigating suspected breaches of the *Fair Work Act 2009* (Cth), suspected breaches of awards and agreements, suspected breaches of Occupational Health and Safety laws and to hold meetings with employees who are eligible to be union members.

The Australian Council of Trade Unions (ACTU)

This is an organisation of trade unions. Most trade unions in Australia are affiliated with the ACTU. The ACTU provides support for unions and negotiates on behalf of unions in national areas, such as in minimum wage reviews (see Section 5.2.5, page 310).

Falling union membership

Trade unions have become less important in modern Australian society. Union membership has decreased and continues to do so. In 1953, 63% of Australian workers were members of trade unions. According to the Australian Bureau of Statistics this figure had fallen to 42% by August 1988, to 28% by August 1998 and to just 20% by August 2009. On the next pages are listed factors which have limited the membership and effectiveness of trade unions, and factors which confirm the power and necessity of trade unions.

Factors which limit the role of trade unions

▷ **Limited relevance**: Unions are seen by some as less relevant than in the past because most workers have satisfactory wages and conditions.

▷ **Changes to wage fixing**: Over the last twenty years, individual unions have had less involvement in wage fixing while the ACTU's involvement has increased because of national wage cases. The Minimum Wage Panel of the Fair Work Commission now fixes minimum wages and, in doing so, must take into account submissions from interested parties including trade union organisations such as the ACTU (see Section 5.2.5, page 310).

▷ **The National Employment Standards (NES)**, introduced in January 2010, now mean that all workers in the national system have certain basic protections (see Section 5.1.4, page 288). So workers may feel that it is not necessary to join a trade union because their entitlements are protected by legislation.

▷ **Enterprise agreements** have become more prominent and can be made without a union (see Section 5.1.3, pages 284–7), though most are made with union involvement. The Australian Centre for Industrial Relations Research and Training found, in 1999, that non-union enterprise agreements are likely to contain lower wage rises and more significant changes to working hours.

▷ **Casual and part-time work**: The increase in casual and part-time work has decreased union participation because such workers are far less likely to belong to unions (see Section 5.1.1, page 277).

▷ **Rise of independent contracting**: The increasing use of contracts for services rather than contracts of employment has meant that unions can no longer represent traditional groups. In both the building and meat industries, for example, contracts for services have been increasingly used (see Section 5.1.1, page 277).

▷ **Voluntary unionism** or the principle of **freedom of association** has led to decreases in union membership. Until the passing of both the *Industrial Relations Act* (NSW) and the *Workplace Relations Act* (Cth) in 1996, it was possible in both state and federal arenas to have closed shop and union preference arrangements. A *closed shop* is a workplace in which the employer agrees to employ only union members. *Union preference* means that union members are given preference over non-union members in matters of hiring, firing and promotion. The purpose of these two measures was to make union membership as attractive as possible. Under both the acts referred to above, and now under the *Fair Work Act 2009* (Cth), people cannot be discriminated against because of their membership or non-membership of a union.

▷ **Restrictions on the right to strike**: As can be seen in Section 5.2.2 (pages 295–6), the right to strike in Australia is limited by the Fair Work Act. Industrial action is only lawful when it is protected. If unions take unprotected industrial action, then they can be liable to penalties and common law court action (see Case Study 5.7, page 317). However, the case of *CFMEU v Woodside Burrup Pty Ltd and Kentz E & C Pty Ltd* (2010) FWAFB 6021 (Case Study 5.4, Section 5.2.2, page 296), shows that the Fair Work Commission is unwilling to suspend protected industrial action except in exceptional circumstances. This means that the right to strike is protected to some degree in

Australian workplaces and, therefore, the place of trade unions is confirmed.

Factors which confirm the power and necessity of trade unions

▶ **Representation of individual workers**: Unions still have an important function in matters regarding workplace safety, dismissal and discrimination.

▶ **Poor outcomes with AWAs and non-union collective agreements**: As seen in Case Study 5.3 (Section 5.1.3, pages 286–7) many workers lost conditions under AWAs, and this may have encouraged people to seek union assistance to regain lost entitlements.

▶ **Raised profile**: The union led 'Your Rights at Work' campaign, which helped oust the Howard coalition government in 2007, lifted the profile of the union movement but, as seen above, only 20% of Australian workers were trade union members in August 2009.

▶ **Discrimination against union members**: The 'freedom of association' principle also means it is illegal to discriminate against someone because of his or her involvement in a trade union. Discrimination against union members was tested in 1998 in the waterfront dispute (see Case Study 5.15, Section 5.4.2, page 351). In this case, the High Court upheld the right of people to belong to a trade union. So, despite attempts by both previous federal governments and some employers to lessen union power, the right of workers to belong to a trade union was reaffirmed in this dispute, and is now enshrined in both state and federal industrial relations legislation.

Employer associations

There are many employer associations which play several roles in the workplace. Like trade unions, in order to represent employers in industrial matters, employer associations must be registered under the *Fair Work (Registered Organisations) Act 2009* (Cth). Some employer organisations are described below.

Industry Associations

An industry association is an organisation that represents the interests of the businesses that operate in a particular industry who are members of that association. One example is the Minerals Council of Australia (MCA), which represents Australia's exploration, mining and minerals processing industry, nationally and internationally. The Mineral Council of Australia's stated objective is to 'advocate public policy and operational practice for a world-class industry that is safe, profitable, innovative, environmentally and socially responsible, and attuned to community needs and expectations'. Another example of an industry organisation is the Australian Meat Industry Council (AMIC) which represents retailers, processors and smallgoods manufacturers. The AMIC confers with members, governments and industry groups to influence policy and provide technical and other advice to the industry. It is registered under *the Fair Work (Registered Organisations) Act 2009* (Cth).

The Australian Chamber of Commerce and Industry (ACCI)

The ACCI is a national organisation that represents businesses and industry associations across Australia. It has a membership of over 350000 businesses. Individual businesses are members of local and regional Chambers of Commerce who, through their state and territory organisations, form a nationwide network. The ACCI also represents industry associations. The ACCI is the largest and most representative business association in Australia.

The Australian Federation of Employers and Industries (AFEI)

The AFEI is another organisation that represents employers. It is a peak employers group and so, like the ACCI, has an important role in formulating the policy of employers in workplace relations issues affecting Australian businesses. It has employment law experts who have played a significant role in test cases in NSW industrial law.

The role of employer associations

Employer associations perform the following functions:

▶ advocating on behalf of their members for policies (both at industry and government levels) that promote the interests of their members

▶ promoting the industry to the community

▶ lobbying governments to make legislative changes which are in the interests of the businesses represented by the association

▶ representing the views of various industries and employer groups to governments and the community. For example, the ACCI and the AFEI both made submissions to the Annual Wage Review 2009–10, conducted by the Minimum Wage Panel of the Fair Work Commission (see Section 5.2.5, pages 309–10)

▶ representing member businesses in international forums, such as the International Labour Organization

▶ conducting relevant research and policy development.

Non-government organisations

The main non-government organisations that have a role in workplace relations are trade unions and employer associations, such as those already described earlier. This is because these bodies represent the interests of those involved in the workplace (that is, employers and employees). These bodies have an important role in representing the interests of their members in industrial negotiations and disputes and in lobbying the government to make law and policy which serves the interests of their members. Other NGOs involved in workplace relations are discussed below.

Self-employed Australia

This not-for-profit organisation was established in 1999 with the purpose of protecting the rights of independent contractors in Australia and providing its members with information about and access to relevant services and government compliance requirements. This organisation, formely known as the ICA, also lobbies government to formulate policy and pass legislation which protects the interests of independent contractors. For example, the ICA was instrumental in developing the *Independent Contractors Act 2006* (Cth) (see Sections 5.1.1 [page 277] and 5.1.2 [page 281]).

Australian Council of Social Service (ACOSS)

This NGO was established in 1956 and represents the views of people involved in community services and welfare. The aims of ACOSS are to develop and promote policy that assists Australians who are vulnerable and are affected by poverty and inequality; and to support NGOs that provide assistance to those in need. In terms of workplace relations, ACOSS has had a significant role in representing the needs of the lowest paid workers in National Wage Cases. For example, it made submissions to the Annual Wage Review 2009–10, conducted by the Minimum Wage Panel of the Fair Work Commission (see Section 5.2.5, pages 310–11).

The media

Newspapers, radio and television have an important role in publicising the views of organisations that have an interest in workplace affairs. Because the media is a powerful influence on the population in general, governments take note of the views expressed in the media and sometimes change policy accordingly. Trade unions, employee associations and NGOs publish media releases in the hope that the media will publicise their views and, therefore, help persuade governments to take action which supports those views.

Both the Cowra Abattoir case of 2006 and the NSW Oakdale Colliery case of 1999 show how powerful the media can be (see Case Study 5.12, Section 5.3.3, page 338 and Case Study 5.13, Section 5.3.3, page 339.) In Cowra, the abattoir withdrew the disputed terminations because of adverse publicity. Similarly, the publicity surrounding the plight of the Oakdale miners eventually led to them receiving their entitlements.

The importance of the role of the media was highlighted in the 2007 federal election campaign. In November 2007, the Howard coalition government was voted out of office as widespread campaigns by trade unions and others highlighted the inequity of some of the provisions of the Work Choices amendments of 2005. The media played an important role in publicising the messages of the 'Your Rights at Work' campaign. The election of the Rudd Labor government in November 2007 was, in part, due to the voting public embracing the ideas behind the 'Your Rights at Work' campaign and rejecting the moral and ethical standards embodied by Work Choices (see Section 5.4.3, pages 354–5).

Another example of the power of the media in the area of workplace law is the publicity surrounding a pregnancy discrimination case brought by the Fair Work Ombudsman in Sydney (see Case Study 5.8, Section 5.3.1, page 319).

CAN YOU assess the role of the legal system in regulating the workplace?

To *assess* something means to make a judgement about it. To assess the role of the legal system in regulating the workplace means to decide how important the role of the legal system is in workplace regulation. In order to assess the role of the legal system in regulating the workplace, you should:

▷ describe the role played by legal and government institutions and agencies in regulating the workplace. These include tribunals, courts and government organisations.

▷ describe the role of non-legal organisations in workplace regulation. These include trade unions, employer associations, other NGOs and the media.

▷ comment on the importance of the legal and non-legal institutions involved in workplace regulation.

Points to consider when making your assessment about the role of the legal system in regulating the workplace are:

▷ one of the most important roles played by non-government institutions is lobbying governments to change the law and representing the views of their members and the wider community to government organisations such as the Fair Work Commission. So non-legal institutions work *within* the legal system.

▷ many workplace negotiations take place informally, and many negotiations take place without the assistance of government agencies, though agreements reached are generally registered with government authorities and must comply with statutes (see Sections 5.2.2, [pages 292–6] and 5.1.4 [pages 287–90]). So non-legal organisations can be very important in determining what happens in particular workplaces and even in larger forums, such as national wage determinations.

 pages 366

5.2.5 Remuneration

Remuneration refers to payment received for services or employment. There are many types of remuneration which are outlined in this section. The ways remuneration is determined are outlined below.

Describe types of remuneration and how remuneration is determined.

How remuneration is determined

There are three main ways that remuneration is determined in Australia:

▷ **national minimum wages**, determined by the Minimum Wage Panel of the Fair Work Commission (FWC). The national minimum wage applies to all workers who do not come under an award or an agreement. The way national minimum wages are established and the way they have been determined in the past are outlined in 'Determination of national wage levels in the past' below.

▷ **awards** which determine what employees are paid in a particular industry (see Section 5.1.3, pages 283–4).

▷ **enterprise agreements** which operate above awards and often grant employees higher remuneration than that allowed for in an award (see Section 5.1.3, pages 284–7).

Determination of national wage levels in the past

For over a century, Australian industrial relations bodies have determined the minimum wage that is payable to Australian workers. The Commonwealth Court of Conciliation and Arbitration was established in 1904 and was renamed the Australian Industrial Relations Commission (AIRC) in 1988. One of its functions was to decide the national minimum wage for Australian workers. Minimum wage fixing was taken over by the Australian Fair Pay Commission (AFPC), which was established by the Work Choices legislation in 2006. Both the AFPC and the AIRC ceased operation during 2009 and were replaced by the Fair Work Commission. The Minimum Wage Panel of the Fair Work Commission (FWC) now makes decisions about national wage levels. Some principles that have been used to determine minimum wage levels, as well as various methods of determining minimum wages are outlined below.

Needs of workers and the Harvester decision

In 1907, Justice Higgins, the President of the Federal Arbitration Court, set the first basic (or minimum) wage in what is known as the 'Harvester decision' [*Ex parte HV McKay (Harvester Case)*, (1907) 2 CAR 1]. He based his decision on the needs of workers (that is, how much a worker and his family needed to support themselves). The basic wage was one that allowed for the 'normal needs of the average employee' living in a 'civilised community'.

'Capacity to pay' principle

This idea was first introduced in the Great Depression of the 1930s. It was decided then, and on later occasions, that the basic wage should not only provide for the needs of workers but should also take into account the capacity of employers to pay the wages.

'Cost of living' principle

During the 1920s, and again on later occasions, the rises in the cost of living were taken into account in the determination of wage levels. This was because, during times of inflation, workers cannot maintain their standard of living unless their wages also rise. During the 1970s, when there were rapid rises in prices, the cost of living principle became very important in wage determination.

'Productivity' principle

Since the 1980s, the efficiency or productivity of workers has become an important factor in determining wage levels. Under this principle, wage rises are given to workers who have been able to show that they have become more efficient in their work.

National Wage Cases and the Prices and Incomes Accords

In 1983, National Wage Cases were introduced. The basic principles used for determining wages were the cost of living and the productivity principle. In a National Wage Case, the AIRC met annually to determine wage rises of all workers employed under federal or state awards. National Wage Case determinations applied to all workers who did not have an enterprise agreement. National Wage Cases were a product of the Prices and Incomes Accords between 1983 and 1996 which encouraged wage restraint and negotiation among employees, employers and governments outside industrial relations processes.

Australian Fair Pay Commission (AFPC)

The AFPC was created under the Work Choices legislation and had the role of setting minimum wages and conditions for all workers, until it was replaced by the Minimum Wage Panel of the Fair Work Commission in 2009. In making its decisions, the AFPC did not need to consider the cost of living but did need to take into account the capacity of the unemployed and low-paid to obtain and remain in employment, as well as productivity and competitiveness. There was no guarantee that minimum wages would be reviewed annually and no obligation for the AFPC to seek advice or opinions.

Determining minimum wages today

The Minimum Wage Panel of the Fair Work Commission (FWC) now makes decisions about national wage levels. This panel is required to conduct a wage review annually. It must review the national minimum wage and modern award minimum wages. After its review, the panel must make a national minimum wage order for employees who do not come under an award or agreement, and may vary modern award minimum wages.

When making its decisions the Minimum Wage Panel must take into account:

- the performance and competitiveness of the national economy, including productivity, business competitiveness and viability, inflation, and employment growth
- increased workforce participation
- relative living standards and the needs of the low paid
- the principle of equal remuneration for work of equal or comparable value
- provision of a comprehensive range of fair minimum wages to junior employees, employees to whom training arrangements apply and employees with a disability.

In reaching its decisions, the Minimum Wage Panel of FWC is required to ensure that all interested parties have a chance to make submissions and comment on the submissions of others. In its first decision, the Annual Wage Review 2009–10 decision, the panel received submissions from the ACTU, ACOSS, and employer associations, among others (see Section 5.2.4, page 301). In the 2009–10 decision, the panel set a new minimum wage (see 'Wages and salaries', page 311) and increased the pay under all modern awards and some enterprise agreements by $26 a week.

Types of remuneration

There are many types of remuneration. Some of these are described below.

Wages and salaries

Wages and salaries are the main types of remuneration for employees. A *wage* is the amount of money a person is paid for a particular type of employment. Wages are usually expressed as an amount paid per hour or per week. For example, the national minimum wage set in the Annual Wage Review 2009–10 decision was $15.00 per hour or $569.90 per week.

Salaries are usually expressed in an amount paid to an employee for a year. Salaries are paid for the job done rather than for the hours worked. For example, a schoolteacher is paid a salary to teach a certain number of classes and to do the activities that go with that, such as assessing students, preparing lessons and writing reports. If a teacher spends time outside of school hours doing these things, he or she does not get any extra pay for the hours worked.

An employee's wage or salary is determined by the national minimum wage or by an award or agreement. The rate of pay depends on such things as the employee's age, experience, level of education, level of responsibility, and the nature of the employment.

Penalty rates

A *penalty rate* is a higher rate of pay for work done outside usual working hours, such as late at night, or on weekends or public holidays. Penalty rates are usually determined by the award or agreement applicable to the employment.

Casual loading

Casual loading is an amount paid to casual employees on top of the normal wage rate. The purpose of a casual loading is to compensate casual employees for not getting certain entitlements that permanent employees receive, such as paid annual leave and personal (sick) leave. Some awards also specify that workers must be paid for at least a certain number of hours for each shift. Casual loading is usually determined by the relevant award or agreement. In its Annual Wage Review 2009–10 decision, the Minimum Wage Panel determined that casual employees who were not under an award or agreement should receive an extra 21% of their wage as casual loading.

Part-time loading

In some awards and agreements, employees who work part-time also receive an extra loading on top of their hourly wage. This is typically lower than a casual loading because part-time employees do receive some annual leave and personal leave.

Overtime

Overtime is usually determined by the relevant award or agreement as time worked in excess of thirty-eight hours or outside of ordinary hours. Overtime work is often paid at a higher rate of pay, which is specified in the relevant award or agreement.

Sometimes, instead of receiving overtime payments, employees may be able to take time off to make up for the extra time they have worked. This is called 'time in lieu'.

Allowances

Employees may be entitled to an extra payment called an allowance if:

- they undertake certain tasks
- they have a particular skill
- they work in unpleasant or hazardous conditions
- they provide their own tools to perform their work
- they use their own car for work
- they wear a uniform that needs to be laundered
- they are supervising other staff, for example as a leading hand.

There are also special allowances for people with a disability, or with particular qualifications. Allowances are provided for in awards and agreements.

Superannuation guarantee

Superannuation is payment made to a person once he or she has retired from work. Many employees contribute to a superannuation scheme while they work so that they will receive enough superannuation when they retire to live comfortably. Employers must also contribute to their employees' superannuation. Under the *Superannuation Guarantee (Administration) Act 1992* (Cth) employers are obliged to pay a minimum level of superannuation for their employees. If employers fail to do this they must pay a tax called the Superannuation Guarantee Charge. Employers must currently pay 9% of an employee's earnings into a superannuation scheme for that employee (see also Section 5.3.3, page 331).

Junior pay rates

People under the age of twenty-one have traditionally been paid lower rates of pay than adults, and junior wage rates are part of many awards and agreements. Such rates are generally based on a proportion of the adult wage, which rises with each year of age. Typically, sixteen year olds are paid 50% of the adult rate, seventeen year olds are paid 60%, eighteen year olds 70%, nineteen year olds 80%, and at twenty years of age the rate payable is 90% of the adult rate. As part of its national minimum wage review of 2010–11 the Minimum Wage Panel is required to set special national minimum wages for juniors and employees who are under training arrangements, such as apprentices.

CAN YOU **outline how remuneration is determined?**

In order to outline how remuneration is determined, you should:

- define *remuneration*
- briefly describe the different types of remuneration
- explain that remuneration is determined by awards, agreements and by national minimum wage decisions
- outline how awards and agreements are determined and, therefore, how remuneration is determined within these industrial instruments (see Section 5.1.3, pages 283–7)
- outline how national minimum wage decisions are made, and explain to whom they apply

 KCq page 367

5.2.6 The effectiveness of legal and non-legal responses in protecting and recognising workplace rights

In order to evaluate the effectiveness of legal and non-legal responses in protecting and recognising workplace rights, we need to:

Evaluate the effectiveness of legal and non-legal responses in protecting and recognising workplace rights.

▷ identify the way workplace rights are protected

▷ explain whether each method is non-legal or legal

▷ discuss those factors which enhance the effectiveness of each method of protection

▷ discuss the factors which limit the effectiveness of each method of protection

▷ decide how effective each legal or non-legal responses is in protecting and recognising workplace rights, given the two sets of factors.

Table 5.3 lists the legal and non-legal responses to protecting and recognising workplace rights and lists some of the factors which influence the effectiveness of each response.

Table 5.3 Legal and non-legal responses to protecting and recognising workplace rights

Factors which may *enhance* the effectiveness of legal and non-legal responses	Factors which may *lessen* the effectiveness of legal and non-legal responses
Common law contract of service (LEGAL RESPONSE) (Section 5.1.2, page 278)	
▷ Some rights are expressed in the contract which can be enforced by the common law. ▷ Parties to the contract have rights implied by the common law which can be enforced by a court. ▷ All employment contracts in the national system must now meet the NES (Section 5.1.4, page 288). ▷ Very few people are only protected by the contract of service. Rights for most workplaces are now determined by awards, agreements and statute (Sections 5.1.3 [pages 283–7] and 5.1.4 [pages 287–90]).	▷ Often parties to a contract do not have equal bargaining power and so the rights of the less powerful person (usually the employee) may be diluted. However, very few people are only protected by the contract of service. Rights for most workplaces are now determined by awards, agreements and statutes.
Contract for services (LEGAL RESPONSE) (Section 5.1.2, pages 278–80)	
▷ Laws about sham contracting arrangements and deemed employees help protect the rights of people hired under contracts for service. ▷ A review scheme has been established under the *Fair Work Act 2009* (Cth) and the *Independent Contractors Act 2006* (Cth) which has the power to decide whether a contract for services is too unfair or harsh.	▷ Independent contractors have far fewer rights than employees. ▷ There has been a marked rise in the number of people hired under contracts for services, which means more people are left unprotected by the rights that flow from a contract of service.
Awards (LEGAL RESPONSE) (Section 5.1.3, pages 283–4)	
▷ Awards must contain at least the NES (Section 5.1.4, page 288), and thus protect rights of workers. ▷ Modern awards contain dispute settling procedures and a flexibility term, allowing people to negotiate workplace arrangements which best suit them. ▷ Many employers and employees negotiate agreements which operate above awards, better protecting rights. ▷ Awards are made or approved by an Industrial Relations body, so meet minimum standards.	▷ May not allow enough flexibility for circumstances in different workplaces, because awards are industry-wide, though flexibility clauses and agreements allow for negotiation.
Agreements (LEGAL RESPONSE) (Section 5.1.3, pages 284–7)	
▷ Agreements are negotiated between employers and employees and thus should suit both parties. ▷ Agreements must be approved by an Industrial Relations body, so are scrutinised by an independent source. ▷ Agreements must meet the 'no net detriment' test (NSW), or the 'better off overall' test (BOOT) (Cth).	

Factors which may *enhance* the effectiveness of legal and non-legal responses	Factors which may *lessen* the effectiveness of legal and non-legal responses
Statutory conditions (LEGAL RESPONSE) (Section 5.1.4, pages 287–90)	
▷ These, particularly the NES and the national minimum wage, ensure that all employees have certain minimum rights protected. ▷ Employers are obliged to give employees a Fair Work Information Statement which outlines their rights and the ways that they can assert those rights if they are impinged. ▷ Penalties can be imposed on employers who fail to uphold the rights of their employers ▷ Employers can dismiss employees who do not perform their responsibilities (Section 5.3.3, page 332).	▷ For employees to assert their rights, they need to know what they are and how to ensure they are upheld. While the provision of Fair Work Information statements can assist them, many workers need assistance to enforce their rights.
Negotiation processes (LEGAL AND NON-LEGAL RESPONSE) (Section 5.2.2, pages 292–6)	
▷ Negotiations between an employer and employee take place at legal and non-legal levels. At an informal workplace level, such negotiations can be quick and to the mutual benefit of both parties. ▷ Formal bargaining processes help ensure that parties are in equal bargaining positions and can thus protect their rights. ▷ Industrial action is allowed in certain circumstances so that employees can add weight to their claims. ▷ Independent tribunals such as the Fair Work Commission can intervene in negotiations if they are harmful or unproductive. ▷ Disputes must be settled eventually as there must be dispute settling procedures in awards and agreements which allow for an independent arbiter (Section 5.2.3, page 298).	▷ Informal negotiations may be to the detriment of one party's rights, if the parties are in uneven bargaining positions. ▷ The right to take industrial action to support claims is restricted. ▷ Enterprise agreements may allow for those in less powerful bargaining positions to be intimidated and exploited.
The role of tribunals (LEGAL RESPONSE) (Section 5.2.4, pages 301–2)	
▷ Federal and NSW state tribunals have wide powers to enforce rights and obligations under legislation, awards and agreements.	
The role of courts (LEGAL RESPONSE) (Section 5.2.4, pages 302–3)	
▷ Federal and State courts have the power to enforce orders made by state and federal tribunals. ▷ The Federal Magistrates Court has a small claims jurisdiction in industrial matters which assists ordinary employees to pursue claims for small amounts quickly and cheaply. ▷ The Fair Work Ombudsman will pursue claims in the Federal Magistrates Court on behalf of complainants in some areas, such a s discrimination which makes it cheap for the individual (see Case Study 5.8, 5.3.1, page 319).	▷ Court action is generally slow and costly, though the small claims jurisdiction and the prosecuting role of the Fair Work Ombudsman alleviate these problems to some degree, at least in the federal arena.
The role of government organisations (LEGAL RESPONSE) (Section 5.2.4, pages 303–4)	
▷ Federal and state government organisations provide advice and assistance to employers and employees about their rights and assist people in asserting their rights. ▷ Federal and state government organisations can prosecute and litigate when industrial laws are broken, thus assisting individuals who are victims of the broken laws (see Case Study 8, 5.3.1, page 319).	
The role of trade unions (NON-LEGAL RESPONSE) (Section 5.2.4, pages 304–6)	
▷ Trade unions have an important role in representing employees individually and collectively in negotiations and disputes with their employer. ▷ Trade unions, particularly umbrella organisations such as the ACTU, have been effective in representing the views of employees to the government and bringing about policy changes as a result. ▷ Right of entry laws mean that trade unions can usually successfully communicate with their members.	▷ Trade union membership numbers have diminished significantly since the 1950s, which means they are less powerful and less well able to protect the rights of workers who are not members. ▷ Some argue that trade unions have too much influence and have convinced governments to change laws to the detriment of businesses and employers.

Factors which may *enhance* the effectiveness of legal and non-legal responses	Factors which may *lessen* the effectiveness of legal and non-legal responses
The role of employer associations (NON-LEGAL RESPONSE) (Section 5.2.4, pages 306–7)	
▶ Employer associations have an important role in representing employers individually and collectively in negotiations and disputes with their employees.	▶ Some argue that employer associations have too much influence and have convinced governments to change laws to the detriment of workers.
▶ Employer associations, particularly umbrella organisations such as the ACCI and the AFEI, have been effective in representing the views of employers to the government and bringing about policy changes as a result.	
▶ Employer associations represent the interests of their members to the community and overseas.	
The role of NGOs (NON-LEGAL RESPONSE) (Section 5.2.4, page 307)	
▶ Other NGOs have been successful in lobbying governments to make laws to support the rights of workers whom they represent.	
▶ Other NGOs have successfully given a voice to the most vulnerable workers such as the lowly paid.	
The role of the media (NON-LEGAL RESPONSE) (Section 5.2.4, page 308)	
▶ The media, by taking up the views of NGOs, such as trade unions and employer associations, have been influential in persuading governments to adopt policies about workplace relations.	▶ Some argue that the media have too much influence on governments, so that they lose touch with the wishes and concerns of ordinary people.
▶ The media has also highlighted particular cases where rights of employees have been breached, thereby bringing attention to these rights.	

Other considerations which may influence the effectiveness of legal and non-legal responses in protecting and recognising workplace rights include:

▶ **casual workers**, whose numbers are increasing, have fewer rights than do permanent employees, though they do receive casual leave loading (see Sections 5.1.1 [page 277], 5.2.5 [page 311] and 5.3.4 [page 346]).

▶ **safety**. While workers have the right to a safe workplace, sometimes safety issues are not addressed by employers, and this can lead to injury or death. New South Wales Occupational Health and Safety laws help protect workers, though figures show an increase of 16% in workplace fatalities between 2003 and 2007, which may indicate that workers are losing ground in this area (see Case Study 5.10, Section 5.3.2, page 325).

▶ **unfair dismissal and redundancy laws**, which also are aimed at protecting workers

▶ the establishment of the **General Employment Entitlements and Redundancy Scheme** (GEERS), which helps protect workers from losing their entitlements if their employer goes bankrupt (see Section 5.3.3, pages 338–9).

▶ **anti-discrimination laws**, which also protect the rights of individual workers (see Section 5.3.1, pages 316–18).

Employers sometimes argue that the laws to protect the rights of workers erode the employers' rights. The move towards more flexible workplaces, however, is designed to give employers greater freedom to organise their workforces in a way that suits them.

KCq page 367

5.3 Contemporary issues concerning the workplace

5.3.1 Discrimination

Discrimination is the treatment of one person differently from another in the same situation due to that person's membership of a particular group in society (such as Aboriginal people, women, migrants or people with physical disabilities). Discrimination occurs in the workplace as it does in other areas of everyday life. Discrimination can be direct or indirect.

Direct discrimination occurs when someone acts directly to treat someone else differently because of their membership of a particular group in society. An example of direct discrimination is when a woman is denied a promotion because she is a woman.

Indirect discrimination occurs when an action is taken which results in one group in society being treated less favourably than another. An example of indirect discrimination is a height requirement being placed on a particular type of employment (that is, requiring a person to be taller than a certain height to do a certain job). Such a requirement could discriminate against groups with a small average height, such as Asian people or women.

Various laws which aim to prevent discrimination in the workplace and in other areas have been passed by state and federal governments.

Legislation about discrimination

Discrimination is illegal under the legislation described below.

NSW legislation

▶ The *Anti-Discrimination Act 1977* (NSW)
▶ The *Industrial Relations Act 1996* (NSW)

Federal legislation

▶ The *Racial Discrimination Act 1975* (Cth)
▶ The *Sex Discrimination Act 1984* (Cth)
▶ The *Australian Human Rights Commission Act 1986* (Cth)
▶ The *Disability Discrimination Act 1992* (Cth)
▶ The *Equal Opportunity for Women in the Workplace Act 1999* (Cth)
▶ The *Age Discrimination Act 2004* (Cth)
▶ *The Fair Work* Act *2009* (Cth)

Adverse action

Under the *Fair Work Act 2009* (Cth) an employer cannot take 'adverse action' against any employee or prospective employee which is discriminatory on any of a number of grounds. 'Adverse action' refers to:

▶ dismissing an employee
▶ damaging an employee's ability to do his or her job
▶ changing an employee's job to his or her disadvantage
▶ treating one employee differently from other employees
▶ refusing to employ a potential employee
▶ not offering a potential employee all the terms and conditions normally associated with a job.

Grounds for which discrimination is illegal

In the workplace, under both state and federal legislation, an employer cannot discriminate against someone because of one of the following attributes:

- **race** (which includes race, colour, nationality, or ethnic or ethno-religious background). An example of discrimination as a result of racism can be seen in the case of *Abdulrahman v Toll Pty Ltd* (2006). See Case Study 5.9 on page 320.

- **gender**. A man or woman cannot be treated in a less favourable way simply because of his or her gender. This kind of discrimination includes sexual harassment, and discrimination because of pregnancy. Case Study 5.8 (page 319) is an example of a case regarding discrimination in the workplace because of pregnancy. Sexual harassment occurs when a person is subject to unwelcome, uninvited conduct or advances. This can happen to both men and women, though women are far more frequently affected. Sexual harassment can range from displaying offensive pictures and publications to sexual assault. If there has been a sexual assault, criminal law can also be applied.

- **physical or mental disability** (which includes intellectual, physical, sensory, psychiatric and learning disabilities). The legislation also covers situations in which a person is discriminated against because it is thought that he or she has a disability or because he or she is associated with a person with a disability. This includes people with HIV/AIDS. In addition, if people with disabilities need special services or facilities to perform their work, employers must make these available, unless it would cause unjustifiable cost or inconvenience.

- **age** (which includes forcing an employee to retire because of age). However, there are also many commonsense exceptions to age discrimination provisions, such as legal age limits for drinking, driving and marrying, and the provision of junior wages.

- **family responsibility**. A person cannot have his or her employment terminated, or cannot be subject to adverse action by an employer, because of family responsibilities. This type of discrimination is usually directed at women because they often have the prime responsibility for other family members, such as children or sick relatives.

- **marital status** (a person cannot be treated differently because he or she is single, married, divorced or living in a *de facto* relationship). It is also unlawful to discriminate against someone because of the marital status of a family member or friend.

- **sexual preference** (it is illegal to discriminate against someone because of his or her sexual preferences or because of the sexual preference of a member of that person's family, their friends or their work colleagues)

- **transgender status**. Under the *Anti-Discrimination Act 1977* (NSW), it is illegal to discriminate against someone because he or she is, or is thought to be, transgender. It is also illegal to discriminate against someone because of the transgender status of a member of that person's family, their friends or their work colleagues.

- **trade union involvement**. Under the *Fair Work Act 2009* (Cth), it is illegal to discriminate against someone because of membership or non-membership of a trade union. In NSW, similar provisions apply under the *Anti-Discrimination Act 1977* (NSW). The right to belong or not belong to a trade union is called *freedom of association* (see Section 5.2.4 [page 306] and Case Study 5.15, Section 5.4.2, [page 351]).

▶ **religious or political opinion**. Adverse action cannot be taken against someone because of his or her religious or political opinions.

▶ **criminal record**. The Australian Human Rights Commission can investigate and conciliate complaints of discrimination due to a criminal record, though such discrimination is not illegal. In NSW, minor criminal convictions go off the record after ten years of crime-free behaviour. This is provided for under the *Criminal Records Act 1991* (NSW).

Taking action against discrimination

If a person feels he or she has been discriminated against, the steps described below should be taken.

Workplace settlement

It is always best to try to settle matters regarding workplace discrimination with the minimum of fuss. If possible, the person discriminated against should first approach the employer or supervisor before taking any further action. The relevant union should then be contacted.

Approaching government bodies

If workplace settlement is not possible or effective, a person who feels he or she has been discriminated against should approach the NSW Anti-Discrimination Board, the Fair Work Ombudsman (Cth) (see Section 5.2.4, page 303) or the Australian Human Rights Commission. These bodies will investigate the complaint and sometimes attempt to conciliate the dispute. Most complaints of discrimination are settled by conciliation. If a complaint is not settled at this level, other action may be taken, including court action and, at a state level, referral to the Equal Opportunity Division of the NSW Administrative Decisions Tribunal (ADT).

Action by the Fair Work Ombudsman (Cth)

The Fair Work Ombudsman only deals with complaints about adverse action because of discrimination under the *Fair Work Act* 2009 (Cth). Complaints about dismissal because of discrimination are dealt with under unfair termination laws (see Section 5.3.3, page 334). The Fair Work Ombudsman will investigate the complaint, but will not generally provide conciliation or mediation. The Ombudsman can recommend litigation, seek enforceable undertakings, issue cautions and provide education and training.

The Fair Work Ombudsman can also bring court proceedings in the Federal Court or the Federal Magistrates Court. The first proceedings of this type, about a discrimination matter, were brought in the Federal Court in July 2010 (see Case Study 5.8, page 319). This represents a significant improvement for people who have been discriminated against in the workplace. Before the commencement of the provisions of the *Fair Work Act* in 2010, people who had complaints about discrimination could bring their own proceeding under state anti-discrimination laws, and only had access to the conciliation in the federal arena in cases of unfair dismissal. The federal Fair Work Ombudsman can investigate and prosecute breaches of discrimination in employment on behalf of employees and the courts can impose penalties on both companies and individuals.

CASE STUDY 5.8: *Wongtas Pty Ltd, Ding Guo Wang and Xiao Yu Zhang; Federal Court of Australia, Sydney (filed 30 June 2010)*

Facts

A thirty-six-year-old woman told her boss at printing company Wongtas Pty Ltd in Riverwood, Sydney, that she was pregnant. The women claimed the company responded by telling her she might not be able to return to her position, and that a second person would be hired and trained to do her job. While she was on sick leave because of complications of the pregnancy, the company hired another full-time office worker and, upon the woman's return, she was told to perform packaging duties instead of office duties—which incurred a lower hourly rate.

According to the employee, her employer had said the pregnancy caused the company 'a lot of inconvenience' for which she must 'bear the consequences', and had told her to leave if she was not satisfied with the new arrangements. When she received a written warning about her performance, she contacted the Fair Work Ombudsman.

Issue

Did the company's treatment of the pregnant woman amount to unlawful discrimination?

Action and outcomes

At the time of writing, the court case had not been finalised, though students will be able to research the result of the case with some research. However, two important outcomes of the court action are:

▸ that the action shows the Fair Work Ombudsman will pursue litigation on behalf of people who have been discriminated against in the workplace

▸ the publicity surrounding the case in the media, and the fact that the Fair Work Ombudsman launched a publicity campaign at the same time as the case was brought, mean that the issue of pregnancy discrimination and the powers of the Fair Work Ombudsman are now widely known.

The Australian Human Rights Commission

The Australian Human Rights Commission can conduct inquiries and make recommendations to the federal government about what action it should take on human rights and discrimination matters. The Australian Human Rights Commission can make determinations to resolve discrimination matters in its jurisdiction. However, the Australian Human Rights Commission does not have the power to make its determinations legally binding. A decision made by the Australian Human Rights Commission can only be enforced if heard in the Federal Court. As seen above, if a person is discriminated against in the workplace in the federal sphere, a complaint to the Fair Work Ombudsman is likely to be far more efficacious than one to the Australian Human Rights Commission.

NSW Civil and Administrative Tribunal (NCAT)

In a discrimination hearing by the NCAT, the complainant has the burden of proof and the civil standard of proof applies. This means that the complainant must prove on the balance of probabilities that the discrimination has occurred. The complaint should be lodged within six months of the alleged discrimination taking place. Orders that can be made by NCAT if discrimination is proved include:

▸ damages of up to $40000

> whatever steps necessary are to be taken to place the complainant in the position he or she would have been in had there been no discrimination

> a court order, such as an injunction, placed on the employer to prevent the discrimination from continuing.

The case of *Abdulrahman v Toll Pty Ltd* (2006) in Case Study 5.9 below is an example of an ADT ruling regarding a complaint of racism.

CASE STUDY 5.9: *Abdulrahman v Toll Pty Ltd trading as Toll Express* (2006) NSWADT 221

Facts

Mr Abdulrahman is a former employee of Toll Express and a Muslim. During his time at Toll Express, he was called 'bombchucker' and 'Osama Bin Laden' by other staff members, including management and a union delegate. Abdulrahman delayed taking his case to the Anti-Discrimination Board because he was afraid of losing his job. However, he eventually did so and the Anti-Discrimination Board referred it to the then NSW Administrative Decisions Tribunal (ADT).

Issue

Was the name-calling discriminatory? The union delegate admitted he had heard the name-calling but argued it was common and inoffensive. He said that he himself had been called a 'wog' and a 'dago' because of his Italian heritage.

Decision

The ADT ruled that the name-calling in the case of Abdulrahman was different to being called 'wog' or 'dago' because it 'suggested that by being a Muslim the [driver] was also a terrorist'. The ADT found that the name-calling was racial discrimination and, because it had occurred over several months and had caused the worker 'a great deal of distress, humiliation and embarrassment', he was awarded damages of $25 000 plus court costs.

NSW Industrial Relations Commission

The NSW Industrial Relations Commission can consider and make orders about any matters covered by the *Anti-Discrimination Act 1977* (NSW) in the area of employment. It has been given this power under the *Industrial Relations Act 1996* (NSW).

Equal employment opportunity

Under the anti-discrimination laws outlined earlier, employers must generally treat their employees equally and not discriminate in an unlawful way. This means that they must give all employees equal employment opportunities. However, some employers are also obliged to practise affirmative action.

Affirmative action is action taken not only to eliminate discrimination but also to relieve the effects of past discrimination and to ensure that future discrimination does not occur. Affirmative action programs have been implemented in Australia to improve the position of women in the workforce. These programs aim to ensure that, over a period of time, workplaces are restructured so that women and men have equality of employment and employment opportunities.

In NSW, the *Anti-Discrimination Act 1977* (NSW) and the *Local Government Act 1993* (NSW) require government departments, statutory bodies and local councils to consider implementation of affirmative action plans to promote equal opportunity for women, racial minorities and people with physical disabilities.

The most far-reaching equal opportunity program is the one introduced by the federal government in October 1986, which is still operating under the *Workplace Gender Equality Act 2012* (Cth). in the *Affirmative Action (Equal Employment Opportunity for Women) Act 1986* (Cth). This act was amended in 1999 to become the *Equal Opportunity for Women in the Workplace Act 1999* (Cth), and was being reviewed in 2009/2010. This legislation requires private sector employers, community organisations, non-government schools, trade unions and group training companies employing over 100 people, as well as higher-education authorities, to implement affirmative action programs for women over a period of time and report their progress annually to the Workplace Gender Equality Agency.

Men are not discriminated against by this legislation because the act states that no woman should be employed simply because she is a woman; she must have comparable skills to any man seeking the position. The bodies that must follow the legislation are required to implement a workplace program designed to remove any discriminatory employment barriers and take action to promote equal opportunity for women.

Equal pay for equal work

Equal pay for equal work means that all people doing the same work receive the same pay irrespective of their gender, race or other differences. In 1959, women and men were granted the same pay for the same job for the first time, when teachers gained equal pay for equal work. In 1972, all workers under federal awards were granted equal pay. In 1974, the male and female minimum wages were made equal.

Despite anti-discrimination legislation, inequalities in the workplace continue to exist, especially in the area of wages. Anglo-Australians earn more on average than Aboriginal people and migrants. According to Australian Bureau of Statistics figures, in October 2010 the average weekly earnings of women were 16.9% below those of men.

Effectiveness of legal and non-legal responses to the issue involving workplace discrimination

Legal and non-legal responses

Legal responses to the issue of discrimination are:

- legislation which prohibits discrimination in the workplace
- state and federal government organisations, tribunal and courts
- litigation in the NSW ADT or the Federal Court, which can be brought by the NSW Anti-Discrimination Board or the Federal Fair Work Ombudsman
- imposition of penalties.

Non-legal responses include:

- workplace settlement of discrimination claims
- provision of information and advice by government bodies
- conciliation by government organisations, such as the NSW Anti-Discrimination Board or the Federal Fair Work Ombudsman.

Evaluating effectiveness

Below are listed two sets of factors—those which help ensure, and those which limit, the effectiveness of legal and non-legal responses to the issue of discrimination in the workplace.

Factors which help ensure the effectiveness of legal and non-legal responses to the issue of discrimination in the workplace

- Many discrimination matters can be resolved in the workplace with little fuss and no expense.

- The Fair Work Ombudsman and the NSW Anti-Discrimination Board offer assistance, including conciliation on occasion, to employees who feel they have been discriminated against.

- The NSW ADT provides a cheap, effective mechanism for employees who come under NSW law to have discrimination complaints heard.

- The capacity and willingness of the Fair Work Ombudsman to litigate in the Federal Court on behalf of employees who have suffered discrimination means that it is now much easier for people who have suffered from discrimination to have their complaint heard by a court.

- Penalties are sufficient under both NSW and federal law to discourage employers from practising discrimination.

- The educative function of the Australian Human Rights Commission, the Fair Work Ombudsman and the NSW Anti-Discrimination Board raises awareness among employers and employees about what constitutes discrimination and that it must be treated seriously.

- Affirmative action laws seem to have improved the position of women in the workforce to some degree.

Factors which limit the effectiveness of legal and non-legal responses to the issue of discrimination in the workplace

- Despite the help available to people who feel they have been discriminated against, discrimination is very hard to prove, because it is difficult to prove that an adverse action taken by an employer is a result of discrimination, rather than as a result of other issues.

- Equal opportunity legislation does not apply to workplaces of less than 100 employees. So, many women do not have the benefit of the legislation.

- The penalties that can be imposed on companies for non-compliance with equal opportunity legislation include: being named in parliament; banning non-complying companies from receiving federal government contracts; and cutting funding to non-complying higher educational authorities. These last two penalties were introduced in 1993 in an effort to ensure greater compliance by companies. Although most companies do comply with the legislation, some still do not.

- Anti-discrimination and affirmative action laws do nothing to redress some fundamental problems faced by women workers, such as lack of adequate childcare facilities.

- The legislation can do nothing to change the attitudes of some men to women in management positions, which continue to prevent women from obtaining promotions.

- Women still receive, on average, remuneration that is 16.9% lower than that of men.

CAN YOU identify and investigate the contemporary issue of workplace discrimination, and evaluate the effectiveness of legal and non-legal responses to this issue?

In order to do this, you need to:

▶ define *discrimination*, both *direct* and *indirect*

▶ list the grounds under which discrimination is illegal in the workplace

▶ list the legislation under which discrimination is illegal in the workplace

▶ describe the action that can be taken by employees to deal with discrimination, including the roles of government organisations, tribunals and courts

▶ list legal and non-legal responses

▶ discuss the factors which help ensure, and those which limit, the effectiveness of legal and non-legal responses to the contemporary issue of workplace discrimination

▶ come to a conclusion about the effectiveness of legal and non-legal responses to the contemporary issue of workplace discrimination.

 page 367

5.3.2 Safety

The meaning of *safety* in the workplace

Safety in the workplace means that employees can perform their work in a safe manner in a workplace that is not injurious to their health. This includes being supplied with a safe system of work, appropriate training and safe equipment. As seen in Section 5.1.1 (pages 274–6), during and after the Industrial Revolution, workers had no guarantees that they would be safe from injury or disease in the workplace. Eventually the common law and legislation provided laws about safety standards in the workplace.

Common law duty of care

Duties of employers

In common law, employers have a duty not to expose employees to unreasonable hazards. This duty arises under the common law of negligence. The employer is negligent in this common law duty if he or she fails to:

▶ employ competent staff and provide proper supervision

▶ provide safe plant and equipment

▶ provide safe means of access to work

▶ ensure a safe system of conducting work.

Duties of employees

Employees have a common law duty to work with due skill and care. This duty imposes safety obligations on employees in that they are obliged to follow safety directions and to work carefully and skilfully, avoiding dangerous practices. Employees do not have to use equipment if it is unsafe and should report unsafe work conditions. Employees are also obliged to take reasonable care for health and safety at work under the *Occupational Health and Safety Act 2000* (NSW).

> Describe the contemporary issue of workplace safety, and evaluate the effectiveness of legal and non-legal responses to this issue.

Statutory duties of employers and employees

Statute laws which impose duties on employers regarding safety in the workplace are described below.

The *Occupational Health and Safety Act 2000* (NSW)

This act applies to all places of work across NSW. Under the *Occupational Health and Safety Act 2000* (NSW), employers must ensure the health, safety and welfare of their employees by:

- providing and maintaining a safe workplace, facilities, plant and work systems
- ensuring the safe use, handling, storage and transport of equipment or substances
- providing proper information, instruction, training and supervision

Each employee's particular circumstances must be taken into account in considering occupational health and safety requirements.

Employees are obliged to take reasonable care for health and safety at work, and must cooperate with initiatives designed to ensure safety at work.

Regulations made under the act also target specific safety issues. The Occupational Health and Safety Regulation 2001 (NSW) is an enormous document which places obligations on employers and employees in a large range of situations. In Chapter 6 of that document, for example, employers are required to identify, assess and control risks arising from the use of hazardous substances in the workplace, as well as train employees in the use of such substances.

The act also provides that, in a workplace of twenty or more employees, an occupational health and safety committee must be established if the majority of employees request it. The committee will be made up of both employees and employers and will have the role of reviewing health and safety matters in the workplace and investigating complaints about such matters.

Union officials may enter workplaces to investigate any suspected breach of occupational health and safety laws. SafeWork NSW inspectors can also visit workplaces and are authorised to investigate a wide range of safety-related activities. They can prohibit further work and impose on-the-spot fines.

Specific statutory regulations

The *Occupational Health and Safety Act 2000* (NSW) incorporates and updates previous legislation specific to certain industries, such as the *Construction Safety Act 1912* (NSW). However, various pieces of legislation specific to particular industries still apply, such as the *Coal Mine Health and Safety Act 2002* (NSW).

Penalties and remedies for breach of workplace safety laws

Penalties can be imposed on employers if they breach statute laws that impose obligations on them in matters of safety. Employers can also be sued for damages if a worker is injured because of an employer's negligence or breach of statutory standards. Penalties of up to $825 000 can be imposed on employers and employees who fail to comply with the *Occupational Health and Safety Act 2000* and its regulations. As well as fines, penalties for breach of statutory duties include seizure of offending articles, and orders to shut down machines and places of work that infringe safety regulations. Despite these laws, Australia continues to suffer from criticism regarding its workplace safety laws. See Case Study 5.10 on the next page.

CASE STUDY 5.10: Australia's workplace safety record

In 1999, it was reported that the number of workplace deaths in Australia was high compared to that of other countries. Australia was ranked eighteenth out of twenty-three established market-based countries, when it came to workplace deaths per head of population. Since that time there has been a National Occupational Health and Safety Strategy and, between 1999 and 2004, Australia's rate of improvement was 11%. In a report by the National Occupational Health and Safety Commission in 2004, Australia was ranked seventh, with Sweden and the United Kingdom having the lowest rates of workplace deaths.

However, on 31 January 2008, it was reported on the ABC's *The World Today* that there was a 16% increase in workplace deaths from 2003 to 2007. Some of the reasons for Australia's continuing problems in this area include:

▶ lack of sufficient funding for adequate government surveillance so that employers and employees have the primary responsibility for workplace safety. For example, lack of funding means a lack of inspectors to ensure safety standards are complied with. The NSW government has recognised this problem to some degree.

▶ increased use of part-time workers, casual workers and independent contractors means that safety problems are less likely to be addressed in the workplace (see Section 5.1.1, page 277)

▶ lack of adequate enforcement procedures when safety standards are breached

▶ lack of prosecutions in this area, though the number of prosecutions in NSW is on the rise because the vigilance of workplace inspectors has increased

▶ insufficient penalties for breach of workplace safety laws. While maximum penalties under the *Occupational Health and Safety Act 2000* (NSW) are high, large penalties are rarely imposed by courts.

▶ 'management by stress' practices which may compromise safe practices (see Section 5.4.2, page 350)

▶ the weakening role of trade unions meaning that occupational health and safety breaches are not as easily detected (see Sections 5.2.4 [pages 304–6] and 5.4.2 [page 353]). Under current NSW law, unions can initiate prosecutions for breach of occupational health and safety laws where the SafeWork Authority has failed to do so, but under the new national system proposed, this would not be possible (see the discussion following).

Sources:

▶ 'Fatal Occupational Injuries: How does Australia compare Internationally?' National Occupational Health and Safety Commission, 2004.

▶ 'Experts criticise workplace safety record', reported by Simon Lauder, *The World Today*, ABC national radio, 31 January 2008.

SafeWork and occupational health and safety

Part of occupational health and safety laws is providing for people who are injured or whose health is adversely affected because of work. This is called workers compensation. In NSW, workers compensation is provided under the SafeWork scheme.

Workers compensation is where employers insure workers against the possibility of suffering injury arising out of or in the course of employment. Workers compensation in NSW is governed by the *Workers Compensation Act 1987* and the *Workplace Injury Management and Workers Compensation Act 1998*, which was further amended in 2001.

These acts provide for workers compensation in NSW, administered by SafeWork NSW. Under the act, all employers who pay annual wages of over $7500 must take out workers compensation for every employee. Fines of up to $55 000 can be imposed on those who do not do so.

Aspects of the current law regarding workers compensation in NSW are discussed below.

Who is paid compensation?

Workers compensation can be paid to all employees and certain others who are 'deemed' employees under the *Workplace Injury Management and Workers Compensation Act 1998* (NSW). Workers compensation can also be paid to the families of workers who die because of a work injury.

When is compensation payable?

Workers compensation is payable for any injury or disease that arises out of the course of employment. The injury need not be caused by the employer's negligence or breach of statutory duty, as it needs to be for the common law to operate. All the person claiming workers compensation needs to prove is that the injury arose during the course of employment. It does not matter, in most cases, if the employee contributed to the cause of the injury.

A worker will not receive compensation if the injury is solely the result of serious or wilful misconduct of the worker, unless death or serious or permanent disablement occurs.

What is 'in the course of employment'?

To be compensated through SafeWork the injury must be sustained 'in the course of employment'. This means that the injury must be sustained while the employee is doing something which is part of, or is incidental to, his or her employment. So compensation can be paid for injuries sustained even when the worker is not actually working. For example, injuries that occur during lunchtime or while the worker is travelling to and from work, can be covered by workers compensation provisions. These are called *journey claims*.

What compensation is payable?

The compensation payments available under SafeWork are smaller than those that can be awarded under common law (see 'SafeWork and common law damages' on page 327). The amounts payable under SafeWork are reviewed twice yearly. Employees who are eligible for workers compensation under SafeWork can be paid:

- for loss of wages for time off work
- a lump sum for a degree of permanent impairment
- for medical, hospital, ambulance, rehabilitation and some travel expenses
- for damage to items of personal property such as clothing or spectacles
- an amount for pain and suffering
- a lump sum to a dependant spouse and/or children on the death of the worker.

Claiming workers compensation

To make a claim for workers compensation, the worker should tell his or her employer of the injury as soon as he or she becomes aware of it. The injured worker will need to see a doctor to obtain a medical certificate, which is then given to his or her employer. The employer must contact the insurer within forty-eight hours if the injury is significant and will result in the worker being unable to work for seven days. The insurer is then obliged to approach the employer, the worker and the treating doctor within three days to initiate an injury management plan (see 'Rehabilitation' below).

Dispute resolution

If there is a dispute about payment of a workers compensation claim any party to the dispute can apply to the Workers Compensation Commission. The Workers Compensation Commission commenced operation on 1 January 2002 and aims to provide independent, fair, quick and cost effective resolution to any dispute arising under both the *Workers Compensation Act 1987* and the *Workplace Injury Management and Workers Compensation Act 1998*.

SafeWork and common law damages

An employee can be entitled to damages under common law only if he or she is injured at work because of an employer's negligence or breach of a statutory duty. However, workers compensation under SafeWork, is payable even if the employer was not to blame for causing the injury.

The right to sue for damages in these matters has been severely restricted by the SafeWork scheme. Common law damages are now only available to workers whose degree of whole person permanent impairment is at least 15%. When deciding how much damages are payable, the judge will consider:

- losses or expenses
- changes to the worker's ability to work and earn in the future
- any permanent physical or mental disability
- potential loss of future enjoyment of life
- the costs of care.

Common law damages are of a potentially higher monetary value than compensation payable under SafeWork. Any dispute must be mediated by the Workers Compensation Commission before court proceedings can commence.

Workplace injuries and diseases

Under workers compensation laws, an *injury* includes:

- anything normally referred to by the word *injury*, such as a cut or a broken bone
- internal damage to the body, such as a hernia or disc lesion
- total or partial loss of limbs or senses, and severe disfigurement or permanent damage to other organs
- death
- a disease contracted during the course of employment, such as asbestosis contracted through working in an asbestos mine
- the aggravation or deterioration of any disease to which the employment is a contributing factor, meaning a worker will be eligible for compensation if he or she suffered from a medical condition which was aggravated because of his or her employment (See Case Study 5.17, Section 5.4.4, page 356).

Rehabilitation

The Workers Compensation Act 1987 (NSW) placed a much greater emphasis on rehabilitation than previous workers compensation law. The *Workplace Injury Management and Workers Compensation Act 1998*

(NSW) places even more emphasis on rehabilitation and aims to achieve an early, safe and lasting return to work for injured workers.

Under this act, all employers are obliged to develop a Return to Work program for their organisation which is compatible with an injury management plan. Insurers are required to develop individual injury management plans for workers with significant injuries. A *significant injury* is one which prevents a worker undertaking some or all of his or her normal duties for more than seven days.

An injury management plan must be made in consultation with the employer, the worker's nominated treating doctor and the injured worker. The employer must provide suitable employment, where practicable, for workers who are able to return to work. The doctor treating the injured worker provides information about the worker's fitness for work and recommends suitable duties for the injured worker. The worker must make all reasonable efforts to return to work and to cooperate with the injury management plan.

Australia's occupational health and safety laws: future directions

*The Work Health and Safety Ac*t *2011* (NSW) commenced in January 2012.

Effectiveness of legal and non-legal responses to the issue involving workplace safety

Legal and non-legal responses

Legal responses to the issue of safety are:

▶ common law duties of employers and employees

▶ workplace safety legislation, most importantly the *Work Health and Safety Act 2011* (NSW)

▶ provision of inspectors

▶ imposition of penalties

▶ workers compensation, specifically the SafeWork NSW scheme

▶ provision of dispute settling procedures through the Workers Compensation Commission

▶ injury management plans.

Non-legal responses include:

▶ workplace occupational health and safety committees

▶ unions' assistance and right of entry into workplaces when there are suspected breaches of safety legislation

▶ injury management plans, which can be seen as a non-legal response because, even though they must be formulated under legislation, the details are determined by the parties involved, not the legal system.

Evaluating effectiveness

Below are listed two sets of factors—those which help ensure, and those which limit the effectiveness of legal and non-legal responses to the issue of safety in the workplace.

Factors which help ensure the effectiveness of legal and non-legal responses to the issue of safety in the workplace

▶ If there are any gaps in the legislation regarding keeping workplaces safe, the common law will still operate to protect every employee.

- Through the use of workplace occupational health and safety committees, employees have a say in how safety issues are managed in the workplace.

- Both union officials and SafeWork NSW inspectors can visit workplaces to investigate suspected breaches of safety laws.

- Harsh penalties can be imposed for breaches of workplace safety laws.

- The SafeWork scheme provides all workers with compensation for injury or illness suffered as a result of their employment, whether they contributed to the injury or not.

- Injury management strategies have proved successful in getting people back to work and in reducing the cost of the workers compensation scheme.

- The Workers Compensation Commission represents a cheap and effective alternative dispute resolution mechanism for employers and employees in the area of workers compensation.

- The introduction of national laws (from January 2012) to protect workplace safety is aimed at streamlining the processes of protecting workers from injury and, hopefully, providing better protection for all workers across Australia.

Factors which limit the effectiveness of legal and non-legal responses to the issue of safety in the workplace

- Australia's workplace safety record has fluctuated in world rankings in recent years.

- Increased use of part-time workers, casual workers and independent contractors means that safety problems are less likely to be addressed in the workplace.

- While maximum penalties for breach of workplace safety laws are high, large penalties are rarely imposed by courts.

- 'Management by stress' practices may compromise safe practices (see Section 5.4.2, page 350).

- Some argue that workers compensation payments, particularly for permanent impairment, are too low.

- NSW has criticised the proposed national workplace safety laws as not being as beneficial to workplace safety as NSW's current laws.

CAN YOU **identify and investigate the contemporary issue of workplace safety, and evaluate the effectiveness of legal and non-legal responses to this issue?**

In order to do this, you need to:

- explain the meaning of *safety* in the workplace

- describe common and statute laws which place obligations on employers and employees to ensure workplaces are safe

- describe Australia's workplace safety record in recent years compared to that of other countries

- explain workers compensation laws

- describe the action that can be taken by employees who are injured during the course of employment, including injury management plans and the settling of disputes by the Workers Compensation Commission

- describe the move towards national workplace safety laws

▶ list legal and non-legal responses to the issue of workplace safety

▶ discuss the factors which help ensure, and those which limit, the effectiveness of legal and non-legal responses to the contemporary issue of safety in the workplace

▶ come to a conclusion about the effectiveness of legal and non-legal responses to the contemporary issue of safety in the workplace.

KCq page 367

> **Describe the contemporary issue concerning the termination of employment, and evaluate the effectiveness of legal and non-legal responses to this issue.**

5.3.3 Termination of employment

Employment can be terminated by either the employer or the employee. The employee can terminate employment through either of the following:

▶ retirement

▶ resignation.

These are discussed in more detail below.

The employer can:

▶ dismiss the employee

▶ make the employee redundant.

Dismissal and redundancy are discussed on pages 332–40, as are the laws which protect employees when they are made redundant, or are dismissed unfairly.

Retirement

Retirement occurs when a person finishes working and does not work again for the rest of his or her life. Retirement usually occurs at sixty to sixty-five years of age but may occur at a younger age. The age of retirement may be written into the contract of employment or the relevant award. As seen in Section 5.3.1 (page 317), it is not permissible to force people to retire because of their age under amendments to the *Anti-Discrimination Act 1977* (NSW) made in 1994, and under the *Age Discrimination Act 2004* (Cth).

The two most important factors which are taken into account when people are deciding when to retire are their desire to work and their income. A person may continue to work past normal retirement age because he or she wants to work, or a person may continue to work simply because they cannot afford to support themselves if they stop work. Income for retirees usually comes from superannuation and/or from the Age Pension.

The ageing population

In recent years, the federal government has become concerned about the increasingly ageing population. According to the Australian Bureau of Statistics, in 2007 there were 2.4 million people aged between sixty-five and eighty-four years. By 2011, the number of people in this age bracket increased by an average of 2.7%, and it is expected to grow by an average of 3.5% per year over the next eleven years, to 4.0 million in 2022. The number of people who have retired is, therefore, a continually increasing proportion of the Australian population. This is of concern to the government because of the need to provide adequate incomes and health care for an increasing number of people. To help deal with the ramifications of an ageing population, the government has made changes to policy regarding access to superannuation and to the Age Pension.

Superannuation

As seen in Section 5.2.5 (page 312), many employees contribute to a superannuation scheme while they work so that they will receive enough superannuation to live comfortably when they retire. Employers must also contribute to their employees' superannuation. Under the *Superannuation Guarantee Charge Act 1992* (Cth) employers are obliged to pay 9% of an employee's earnings into a superannuation scheme for that employee.

Employees can have access to the superannuation when they permanently retire from the workforce, and also reach the minimum age set by law, called the *preservation age*. Until changes to regulations under the *Superannuation Industry (Supervision) Act 1993* (Cth) made in 1999, people could access their superannuation at age fifty-five.

Since the 1999 changes, the age at which someone can access his or her superannuation is determined by their date of birth. These ages are outlined below.

- Those born after June 1964 can access superannuation benefits at age sixty.
- Those born between 1 July 1963 and 30 June 1964 can access benefits at age fifty-nine.
- Those born between 1 July 1962 and 30 June 1963 can access benefits at age fifty-eight.
- Those born between 1 July 1961 and 30 June 1962 can access benefits at age fifty-seven.
- Those born between 1 July 1960 and 30 June 1961 can access benefits at age fifty-six.
- Those born before 1 July 1960 can access superannuation benefits at age fifty-five.

Age pension

Since 1909, people have been able to qualify for the Age Pension at age sixty-five. So, people without any superannuation or any other form of income have been able to retire at age sixty-five and live on the Age Pension.

In May 2009, the federal government announced that, in 2017 the qualifying age for the Age Pension will start to gradually increase from sixty-five to sixty-seven by 2023. The qualifying age for the Age Pension for men and women will be increased by six months every two years, commencing from 1 July 2017 and reaching age sixty-seven on 1 July 2023.

Resignation

Before retirement age, if an employee wishes to leave a job, he or she resigns. The contract of employment or the relevant award or agreement will usually state the conditions under which an employee may do this. In most cases, a person who wishes to resign from his or her job must give notice.

Notice is given when the employee informs the employer of the intention to leave, before he or she actually leaves the job. An employee may be required to give two, three, or more weeks notice (that is, he or she must tell the employer of his or her intention to leave the job two, three or more weeks before he or she actually leaves). Notice must usually be given in writing. If the contract or award does not mention or specify notice, the employee must give reasonable notice. If the employee does not give proper notice, he or she has breached the contract of employment and could be sued for damages. Notice must also be given by employers when dismissing an employee. The necessary periods of notice are discussed under 'Dismissal' below.

Dismissal

Lawful dismissal

Dismissal can occur lawfully in the two ways described below.

▶ **Dismissal with notice:** The employer can dismiss an employee with notice, provided the dismissal is not 'harsh, unjust or unreasonable'. The period of notice required is set out in the National Employment Standards (see 'Dismissal, notice and the National Employment Standards' below), unless it is more favourable to the employee as stated in the relevant award or an agreement.

▶ **Dismissal without notice**, or immediate dismissal, is also called summary dismissal. Under the common law, an employer can summarily dismiss an employee if:

- the employee has been extremely incompetent
- the employee has committed serious misconduct
- the employee has performed a series of cumulative acts and the employer makes it clear each time that such acts are unacceptable.

Most state and federal awards, as well as many contracts, contain similar provisions.

Dismissal, notice and the National Employment Standards

Under the National Employment Standards (NES) set out in the *Fair Work Act 2009* (Cth), an employer is required to give a certain minimum period of notice, or payment in lieu of notice, to any employee whose employment is to be terminated. This notice must normally be given in writing. The period of notice required, depends on the length of time the employee has been employed:

▶ an employee employed for up to one year is entitled to one week of notice

▶ an employee employed for between one and three years is entitled to two weeks of notice

▶ an employee employed for between three and five years is entitled to three weeks of notice

▶ an employee employed for more than five years is entitled to four weeks of notice.

In addition, employees who have been employed by the employer for at least two years and who are over forty-five years of age are entitled to an additional week of notice.

Certain employees are not required to be given notice. These include:

▶ those who are summarily dismissed

▶ casual employees

▶ an employee employed for a specified time or task.

When is it lawful to dismiss an employee?

There are several circumstances in which it is lawful for an employer to dismiss an employee. These include:

▶ if there is a genuine redundancy (see 'Redundancy' on pages 350–53 following)

▶ if the dismissal is not 'harsh, unjust or unreasonable' (see 'Unfair dismissal' below)

▶ if the dismissal is not unlawful (see 'Unlawful termination of employment' on pages 334–5).

Unfair dismissal

Unfair dismissal means the dismissal is judged to be 'harsh, unjust or unreasonable'. When deciding whether a dismissal was unfair, the relevant government authority will generally examine:

▶ whether a genuine reason was given for the dismissal

▶ whether a warning was given

▶ whether the employee was given a chance to explain or defend his or her actions

▶ whether the dismissal came about because of a non-genuine redundancy (see Case Study 5.12 on page 338).

Unfair dismissal can include constructive dismissal, which means a worker resigns because conditions at work leave him or her with no real alternative. An example of constructive dismissal is when an employee resigns because of continued sexual harassment which the employer does nothing to prevent.

If an employee thinks that he or she has been unfairly dismissed, he or she can apply to the Fair Work Commission or to the NSW Industrial Relations Commission to resolve the matter, depending on whether he or she is employed under federal or state law.

Federal or state law?

As seen in Section 5.2.1 (page 291), the vast majority of employees are employed under federal law since the introduction of the national workplace relations system on 1 January 2010. Public sector and local government employees in NSW are still employed under state law. The law about unfair dismissals under NSW jurisdiction is contained in the *Industrial Relations Act 1996* (NSW) and the relevant federal law is contained in the *Fair Work Act 2009* (Cth). Because the laws regarding unfair dismissals are very similar in both jurisdictions and most people are now employed under the national workplace relations system, the following discussion concentrates on the federal law concerning unfair dismissals.

Unfair dismissals and the *Fair Work Act 2009* (Cth)

Only people who are eligible to apply can make an application to the Fair Work Commission about an unfair dismissal. To be eligible to apply a person must either:

▶ have completed a minimum employment period of at least six months (or twelve months if the employer is a small business employer who employs fewer than fifteen employees)

▶ be covered by a relevant award or agreement

▶ be earning less than $113 800 a year.

When a dismissed employee makes an unfair dismissal claim, the Fair Work Commission (FWC) notifies the employer and, usually, conciliation is then arranged. If a resolution cannot be reached, a conference or hearing will be held.

If FWA finds that the dismissal was unfair, the employer can be ordered to either reinstate the employee or pay compensation of up to twenty-six weeks pay, to a maximum amount of $56 900.

The *Fair Work Act 2009* brought in a major reform to unfair dismissal laws in the federal arena. Under the previous legislation, the *Workplace*

Relations Act 1996 (Cth), most employees were not protected by unfair dismissal laws. See Case Study 5.11 below.

CASE STUDY 5.11: Unfair dismissals and Work Choices (2006)

The Work Choices amendments were introduced by the *Workplace Relations Amendment (Work Choices) Act 2005* (Cth) (see Section 5.2.1, page 291) and came into operation in March 2006.

Under Work Choices, employees were not permitted to make a claim for unfair dismissal if any one of the following applied:

▶ the enterprise had less than 100 employees

▶ the employee was employed for a probationary period of less than six months

▶ the employee was a short-term casual employee or a seasonal worker

▶ the employee earned more than $101 300

▶ the business dismissed the employee for 'operational reasons'.

Under Work Choices, very few people could claim that they had been unfairly dismissed. First, most employees did not and do not work in a company with over 100 employees, and so were ineligible to claim unfair dismissal. Second, if an employee was a full-time worker in a company with over 100 employees, the company only needed to claim that the dominant reason for the dismissals was 'operational', which covered technological, organisational or structural change in the company. 'Operational reasons' could cover both genuine and non-genuine redundancies which was the issue at Cowra abattoir in May 2006, as outlined in Case Study 5.12 (page 338).

The Australian Council of Trade Unions (ACTU) estimated that 99% of all private sector employers became exempt from unfair dismissal laws under Work Choices. The *Fair Work Act 2009* (Cth) means that most employees now have access to unfair dismissal laws.

Unlawful termination of employment

Unlawful termination of employment is also called *illegal dismissal*. Unlawful terminations include those in which an employee has been dismissed because of:

▶ unlawful discrimination (see Section 5.3.1, page 318)

▶ temporary absence from work because of illness or injury

▶ absence from work because of maternity or parental leave

▶ temporary absence from work because of the carrying out of a voluntary emergency management activity

▶ raising a health or safety complaint, or other complaint against an employer

▶ union membership or non-membership (see the *Waterfront Dispute*, Case Study 5.15, Section 5.4.2, page 351)

▶ acting as an employee representative.

Federal or state law?

As already noted, since 1 January 2010, the vast majority of employees are employed under federal law and so come under the provisions of the *Fair Work Act 2009* (Cth) in regard to unlawful termination of employment. The law in the NSW jurisdiction about unfair terminations is the same as for unfair dismissals and is contained in the *Industrial Relations Act 1996* (NSW).

Unlawful termination of employment and the *Fair Work Act 2009* (Cth)

If an employee has his or her employment unlawfully terminated, he or she can apply to either the Fair Work Commission or the Fair Work Ombudsman to have the matter dealt with. The restrictions about who is eligible to make an unfair dismissal claim do not apply to unlawful terminations. Any person employed in the national workplace system is entitled to make a claim about unlawful termination of employment.

Terminating someone's employment for any of the reasons outlined above is most likely to be a contravention of the general protections provisions of the *Fair Work Act 2009* (Cth) (see Section 5.1.4, page 289). Such contraventions, including unlawful terminations, can be investigated by the Fair Work Ombudsman. If there has been a contravention of the general protections, the Fair Work Ombudsman can initiate legal action in the Federal Court which can apply penalties of up to $6600 for an individual or $33 000 for a corporation (see Section 5.2.4, page 303).

If an unlawful termination occurs, the Fair Work Ombudsman can also take numerous other courses of action, such as issuing a caution to the employer or entering into an enforceable undertaking with the employer. The Fair Work Ombudsman may seek any underpayment owing to the employee. The employee may also be able to claim up to $20 000 through the small claims procedure (see Section 5.2.4, pages 302–3).

the Fair Work Commission (FWC) will take the following steps if an allegation of unlawful termination is made.

- First, it will have a private conference with the employee and the employer.
- If the FWC finds that all reasonable attempts to fix the matter were or are unlikely to be unsuccessful, it issues a certificate to that effect.
- The employee may use the certificate to apply to a court to resolve the matter.

Possible remedies available for wrongful dismissal

Employees who successfully prove that they have been wrongfully dismissed may be awarded one or more of the following remedies.

- **Compensation and back pay:** Compensation, usually of no more than the equivalent of six months wages, can be awarded to wrongfully dismissed employees. Compensation is calculated on the amount of wages lost since the dismissal (back pay) and the amount of wages the dismissed employee will continue to lose because of the dismissal. The dismissed employee must take reasonable steps to find another job. Usually, compensation awarded in these cases is small because the employee finds another job fairly quickly. Also, no compensation can be awarded for loss of reputation or emotional distress.

- **Reinstatement and re-employment:** Reinstatement is when an unfairly dismissed employee is given his or her job back. Re-employment is when an unfairly dismissed employee is given another suitable job by the employer. Reinstatement and re-employment are often ineffective remedies because of damage caused to the employer–employee relationship. Re-employment can be effective if a large firm is involved, because the worker may be able to be re-employed in a position that involves different people and different surroundings.

Redundancy

Redundancy occurs when an employer either decides he or she no longer wants an employee's job to be done by anyone and terminates the employee's employment (except in cases of ordinary and customary turnover of labour) or becomes insolvent or bankrupt.

Retrenchment is the term used when an employee loses his or her job because of redundancy. Redundancies can occur because of technological change, restructuring, economic recession or insolvency. In times of economic hardship, businesses may find they can no longer employ as many workers as they have done previously or that they must close down altogether. In these situations, jobs become redundant and workers are retrenched.Sometimes workers whose jobs have become redundant may be redeployed to another job in the same organisation. It may be necessary for these workers to undergo retraining in order to fulfil their new duties. *Redeployment* describes the situation when workers are sent to a new place or job.

Redundancy can be very serious for an employee because he or she may need to undergo retraining to find another job, may experience a significant period of unemployment or may have to take up part-time, casual or contract work.

Federal redundancy protections

From 1 January 2010, all employees in the national workplace system are protected by the provisions of the *Fair Work Act 2009* (Cth). The National Employment Standards (NES), which form part of this legislation, provide protections for redundant workers.

Notice

As seen in 'Dismissal' (page 332), employers are required, under the NES, when terminating employment, to give a certain amount of notice to employees, depending on their length of employment. These notice periods also apply to dismissals because of redundancy.

Redundancy pay

In 1984, the Australian Conciliation and Arbitration Commission (now the AIRC) handed down a decision regarding redundancy with the *Termination, Change and Redundancy Test Case* (TCR test case, 1984). This decision was reviewed in the AIRC *Redundancy Case* of 2004. Most federal and state awards have contained provisions which reflect the protections in these cases. The NES now provides protections for redundant workers, which are similar to those provided in the AIRC test case of 2004.

The provisions of the NES regarding redundancy pay are that employees dismissed because of redundancy are entitled to four weeks pay if they have worked more than one year and less than two years with the employer. The amount of redundancy pay increases depending on how long the worker has been employed, so that those who have worked for the employer for between nine and ten years are entitled to sixteen weeks pay. However, employees who have been with the employer for more than ten years are only entitled to twelve weeks redundancy pay. This is to take into account the fact that these workers are often also entitled to ten or more weeks pay because of long service leave owing to them.

When an employee is made redundant, he or she is not only entitled to redundancy pay (also called severance pay), as outlined above, but also is entitled to:

- any outstanding wages or other remuneration still owing
- any payments that are being made in lieu of notice of termination
- pay for any unused annual leave and long service leave.

It should be noted that the provisions in the NES relating to required notice for dismissal apply to all employees across Australia (with the exceptions listed under 'Dismissal' on page 332), while those relating to redundancy pay apply only to employees who are part of the national workplace system (which, as has been seen, is the majority of employees). Those employed under NSW law have similar protections to the protections provided in the NES.

Who is not entitled to redundancy pay?

Redundancy pay is not payable under the NES in some circumstances, which include:

- when the employee has less than twelve months of continuous service
- when the employee was employed for a specified period of time, a specific task or for a specific season
- when the employee is a casual employee
- when the employer employs fewer than fifteen employees.

Genuine and non-genuine redundancies

As discussed above, most redundancies are governed by federal law under the *Fair Work Act 2009* (Cth). This legislation makes a distinction between genuine and non-genuine redundancies.

A genuine redundancy occurs if the employer dismisses an employee because that person's job is no longer needed to be done by anyone because of changes in the operational requirements of the business. For the redundancy to be genuine, the employer must also follow consultation requirements in the relevant award or agreement.

A termination is not a genuine redundancy if the operational requirements of the business have not changed, the employer still needs the employee's job to be done by someone, and if the employer has not followed other requirements set out in the relevant award or agreement. The redundancy also may not be genuine redundancy if it is reasonable for the employee to be redeployed in the employer's business or in a business entity associated with the employer.

The reason why it is important to distinguish between whether a termination is a genuine or non-genuine redundancy is that employers may state that terminations are not redundancies in order to avoid paying severance pays, or for other reasons that disadvantage the employees. This is what occurred in the Cowra Abattoir case outlined in Case Study 5.12 on the next page.

CASE STUDY 5.12: The Cowra Abattoir case (2006)

Facts

On Thursday, 30 March 2006, twenty-nine employees at the Cowra abattoir were given notice of termination. They were to be paid out their entitlements (not including redundancy payments) and were invited to reapply for twenty jobs on new employment contracts, at $180 less a week and with the loss of performance bonuses. After much publicity, the federal government called on the Office of Workplace Services (now defunct) to investigate the legality of the sackings.

Issue

Under Work Choices, introduced in 2006 and since replaced by the *Fair Work Act 2009* (Cth), businesses which employed over 100 people could terminate employment for 'operational reasons'. If the enterprise had less than 100 people, no reason was required to be given for terminations. These provisions meant that employees dismissed for 'operational reasons' were not entitled to redundancy payments or to unfair dismissal claims. Were the terminations at the Cowra abattoir legal under the Work Choices amendments?

Decision

Because of the adverse publicity, Cowra abattoir withdrew its termination notices by Wednesday, 5 April, and did not await a ruling on the legality of the terminations. On Friday, 7 July, the Office of Workplace Services found that the terminations were legal under the Work Choices amendments. Prior to these amendments it was illegal to terminate employment with the intention of dismantling agreed employment conditions.

Under the *Fair Work Act 2009* (Cth) the Cowra abattoir terminations would now not be genuine redundancies.

Fair Entitlements Guarantee (FEG)

One problem that can occur with redundancies is that workers who are made redundant may not receive the money to which they are entitled because the company that has dismissed them is bankrupt. For instance, in the second half of the 1990s, over 3000 workers lost an estimated $30 million in entitlements because their employers were bankrupt and had no money to pay their employees.

As seen above, employee entitlements may include:

▸ unpaid wages
▸ unused annual leave
▸ pay in lieu of notice
▸ redundancy pay
▸ long service leave.

Case Study 5.13 (page 339), about the NSW Oakdale Colliery, is a well-known case in which employees lost their entitlements, and which led eventually to the establishment of the General Employment Entitlements and Redundancy Scheme (GEERS). The GEERs regime has now been replaced by the Fair Entitlements Guarantee (FEG), which applies to all employer insolvency events on or after 5 December 2012. The GEERs still applies in the rare cases before this date.

CASE STUDY 5.13: Loss of employment entitlements at Oakdale Colliery, NSW, May 1999

Facts

In May 1999, the Oakdale Colliery in NSW went into receivership and 125 miners lost their jobs. They were owed collectively approximately $6.3 million in unpaid employee entitlements. There was a general outcry in the media and the community, culminating in protests in Canberra in July and August of 1999 calling on the Federal government to rectify the situation.

Issue

The NSW Attorney-General, the ACTU and the NSW Labor Council called on the federal government to ensure the Oakdale miners were paid and to reform the law to protect the entitlements of all workers if their employer became bankrupt.

Decision

On 18 August 1999, the federal government announced that the Oakdale miners would receive all their entitlements paid from the coal industry long service leave fund. It also announced that it would seek to establish a national scheme in co-operation with the states and employer groups.

Following the Oakdale Colliery closure and several other similar business insolvencies, resulting in large numbers of employees left without entitlements, the Employee Entitlement Support Scheme (EESS) was announced by the federal government in February 2000. This was replaced by the General Employment Entitlements and Redundancy Scheme (GEERS) in September 2001. Under GEERS and now the FEG, outstanding employee entitlements are paid from a fund established by the Commonwealth, state and territory governments. Workers who lose their entitlements because of their employer's bankruptcy can receive from that fund:

▶ up to three months unpaid wages

▶ up to a maximum of five weeks unpaid payment in lieu of notice

▶ all unpaid annual leave

▶ unpaid long service leave

▶ redundancy entitlements in accordance with the NES.

These entitlements are payable for people whose pay is less than the GEERS maximum annual wage ($113 800 for 2010–11). People who earn more than this amount will have their entitlements calculated as if they earned the maximum salary.

As well, the *Corporations Law Amendment (Employee Entitlements) Act 2000* (Cth) was passed to make it illegal for companies to manipulate corporate structures to avoid paying employees their legal entitlements.

Effectiveness of legal and non-legal responses to the issue of termination of employment

Legal and non-legal responses

Legal responses to the issue of termination of employment are:

▶ legislation which prohibits forcing someone to retire because of his or her age

▶ measures to help deal with an ageing population which encourage people to retire at a later age

▶ provisions for employers to dismiss employees at once if they have committed grave misconduct, and with notice in other circumstances

- NES provisions for notice requirements for employees who are being dismissed, which increase with the length of service of the employee
- major reforms introduced by the *Fair Work Act* in 2009 which provide most workers with access to unfair dismissal laws
- the Fair Work Act's protection from unlawful termination of employment for all workers under the national workplace system
- the legislative definition of *redundancy* and the distinction between genuine and non-genuine redundancies
- NES minimums regarding notice requirements and redundancy pay for workers made redundant
- GEERS providing payments to workers whose employers go bankrupt.

Non-legal responses to the issue of termination of employment include:

- provision of conciliation by Fair Work Comission and the Fair Work Ombudsman for unfair dismissal and unlawful termination of employment allegations
- approaches to government bodies, such as the Fair Work Ombudsman, for information and advice.

Evaluating effectiveness

Below are listed two sets of factors—those which help ensure, and those which limit, the effectiveness of legal and non-legal responses to the issue of termination of employment.

Factors which help ensure the effectiveness of legal and non-legal responses to the issue of termination of employment

- Legislation ensures that no one can be forced to retire because of his or her age.
- The federal government has attempted to deal with the economic costs of an ageing population by increasing the age at which people can gain access to superannuation and the Age Pension.
- Major reforms introduced by the Fair Work Act in 2009 mean that most workers have access to unfair dismissal laws whereas, under Work Choices, introduced in 2006, it was estimated that 99% of private sector workers did not have access to such laws.
- The provision that employees of a business which employs fewer than fifteen employees are not eligible to access unfair dismissal or redundancy laws until they have worked for twelve months provides some protection to small businesses.
- Protection from unlawful termination of employment applies to all workers in the national workplace system.
- Penalties can be imposed on employers who unlawfully terminate employment, which dissuades them from acting in an unlawful manner.
- The legislative definition of *redundancy* and the distinction between genuine and non-genuine redundancies protects employees from being unfairly dismissed as the result of an employer attempting to save money by disadvantaging employees, as in the Cowra Abattoir case.
- The NES provides safeguards regarding notice and redundancy pay for employees made redundant.
- GEERS provides payments to workers whose employers go bankrupt.

Factors which limit the effectiveness of legal and non-legal responses to the issue of termination of employment

▶ Increasing the age at which people can gain access to their superannuation funds and to the Age Pension may mean people are forced to work longer than they wish to and longer than those only a couple of years older than them.

▶ The provision that employees of a business which employs fewer than fifteen employees are not eligible to access unfair dismissal or redundancy laws until they have worked for twelve months disadvantages these employees compared to those who work for larger enterprises.

▶ Casual workers and contract workers are generally not protected by unfair dismissal laws or by redundancy laws.

CAN YOU **identify and investigate the contemporary issue of termination of employment, and evaluate the effectiveness of legal and non-legal responses to this issue?**

In order to do this, you need to:

▶ explain the four types of termination of employment and explain that terminations can be initiated by employees or employers

▶ describe the legislative measures which govern resignation

▶ describe the legislation which protects workers from unfair dismissal and unlawful termination of employment

▶ describe the protections given by legislation to workers who are made redundant

▶ list legal and non-legal responses to the issue of termination of employment

▶ discuss the factors which help ensure, and those which limit, the effectiveness of legal and non-legal responses to the contemporary workplace issue of termination of employment

▶ come to a conclusion about the effectiveness of legal and non-legal responses to the contemporary workplace issue of termination of employment.

 pages 367–8

5.3.4 Leave

Leave means permission for an employee to be absent from work for a legitimate reason. This can be because of sickness, family responsibility or because of a leave entitlement, such as the entitlement to annual leave. Leave is usually paid at the same rate as the ordinary pay of the employee, though unpaid leave can also sometimes occur.

There are many different types of leave, which are granted to employees through legislation, awards or agreements. The National Employment Standards (NES) contained in the *Fair Work Act 2009* (Cth) (see Section 5.1.4, page 288) provide minimum standards for various types of leave. All employees governed by the national workplace system are protected by these minimums which became effective on 1 January 2010. Contracts of employment, awards and agreements only apply if they are more advantageous to an employee than the minimums provided by the NES. Leave entitlements guaranteed by the NES are summarised in Table 5.4 on page 346.

> Describe the contemporary issue concerning leave, and evaluate the effectiveness of legal and non-legal responses to this issue.

Types of leave

Most employees are entitled to the following types of leave, as set out in the National Employment Standards.

Annual leave

Annual leave is leave that is given to an employee every year. During a period of annual leave an employee can do whatever he or she chooses.

Under the NES, an employee (other than a casual employee) is entitled to four weeks of paid annual leave for each year of service with the employer. An employee classified as a 'shiftworker' is entitled to five weeks paid annual leave.

Annual leave under the NES does not need to be taken each year, because the entitlement can accumulate. It is up to each employer and employee to agree on when and for how long paid annual leave may be taken. An employer can direct an employee to take annual leave, if such a requirement is reasonable. Such a requirement may be reasonable if, for example, the employee has accrued an excessive amount of paid annual leave, or the business is being shut down for a period (such as between Christmas and New Year).

While on annual leave, the employee receives, as a minimum, the same pay as he or she would earn on the base rate of pay in an ordinary week. Sometimes workers receive an additional amount of pay for their annual leave, usually in the form of annual leave loading. The General Retail Industry Award 2010, for example, provides for an annual leave loading of 17.5% in addition to the base rate of pay. This means employees under this award, while on annual leave, receive their ordinary pay plus an extra amount equal to 17.5% of their ordinary pay.

Under the NES, an employee may agree to cash out unused annual leave at any time. This means an employee can agree to receive money rather than take annual leave.

However, in all cases, the employee must still be entitled to at least four weeks paid annual leave. An employer may not force or try to force an employee to cash out or not cash out their annual leave.

Personal/carer's leave

Personal/carer's leave includes:

- **sick leave**: time off work that can be taken by employees when they can't attend work because they are sick or injured
- **carer's leave**: time off work to provide care or support to a member of an employee's immediate household or family because of illness, injury or unexpected emergency. A member of the employee's immediate family means:
  - a spouse
  - a *de facto* partner
  - a child
  - a parent
  - a grandparent
  - a grandchild
  - a sibling
  - a child, parent, grandparent, grandchild or sibling of the employee's spouse or *de facto* partner.

Under the NES, full-time employees are entitled to ten days paid personal leave per year, which can be accumulated. Many awards and agreements provide greater personal leave allowances than this. Part-time workers receive a *pro rata* entitlement to personal leave based on the number of hours they work. So, if a part-time worker works half the number of full-time hours, he or she is entitled to half the number of personal leave days. A casual employee is also entitled to two days unpaid carer's leave on any one occasion.

The ten day paid leave entitlement can be used for sick leave or carer's leave. In addition to ten days paid personal leave, an employee is entitled to two days of unpaid carer's leave for each occasion when a member of the employee's immediate family or household requires care or support because of a personal illness, injury, or an unexpected emergency. To take personal leave, an employee would normally need to supply evidence of the necessity for the leave, such as a medical certificate.

Under the NES, an employee may not agree to cash out unused personal leave, though he or she can do so if it is permitted under the relevant award or agreement, and if there is a remaining balance of at least fifteen days unused leave. An employer may not force or try to force an employee to cash out or not cash out personal leave.

Compassionate leave

Compassionate leave is time taken off work by an employee to spend with a member of his or her immediate household or family (as listed in 'Personal/carer's leave' on page 342) who has sustained a life-threatening illness or injury, or after the death of a member of an employee's immediate household or family. Compassionate leave is also called bereavement leave when it refers to leave because of a death.

Community service leave

Community service leave is time away from work taken by employees in order to perform a legitimate community service activity. Employees, including casual employees, are entitled to take leave to carry out such activities, which include jury service, including attendance for jury selection, and participating in a 'voluntary emergency management activity'. Voluntary emergency management activities deal with an emergency or natural disaster and involve the employee as a volunteer member of a group which manages such activities. Such groups include the NSW Rural Fire Service and the NSW State Emergency Service.

Community service leave under the NES is unpaid, except for jury service. An employee, other than a casual employee is, however, entitled to 'make-up' pay for the first ten days of his or her absence because of jury service. This means that, for attending jury service, the employee receives the equivalent of his or her normal base rate of pay, partly from the employer and partly from the government.

Long service leave

Long service leave is a period of paid leave for employees who have been working for the same business for a long period of time, usually between seven and fifteen years.

As at January 2011, the NES provides that entitlements to long service leave remain as they were in awards and agreements in force as at 31 December 2009. If an employee would not have had an entitlement under an award or agreement if they had been employed in the same circumstances on 31 December 2009, their entitlement to long service leave generally comes from state or territory long service leave legislation.

In NSW this legislation is the *Long Service Leave Act 1955* (NSW). The federal government intends to replace this with a national long service leave standard yet to be developed.

Long service leave is generally paid at the employee's ordinary rate of pay and cannot be cashed out. If a person leaves employment with long service leave owing, he or she will generally be paid the amount of ordinary pay that covers the amount of long service leave accrued.

Parental leave

Parental leave is leave given to an employee because of the birth or adoption of a child. It can be given to either parent of the child, including same-sex parents. The NES gives unpaid parental leave entitlements to all employees if they have completed twelve months service with their employer. Unpaid parental leave is also available to casual employees if they have been employed by the employer on a regular and systematic basis for at least twelve months and if they would have continued to work for the employer except for the arrival of the child.

Unpaid parental leave is available to either employed parent for up to twelve months each. A parent can request an extension to this from his or her employer for another twelve months but, together, the parents of the child cannot take more than twenty-four months in total.

Paid parental leave

Many awards and agreements provide paid parental leave for a varying number of weeks. However, this varies from industry to industry. In 2008, the federal government commissioned the Productivity Commission to inquire into paid parental leave in Australia and to make recommendations as to whether a government funded paid parental leave scheme needed to be introduced. The inquiry and its results are outlined in Case Study 5.14 below.

CASE STUDY 5.14: Paid Parental Leave: Support for parents with newborn children

Background

In 2008, the federal government asked the Productivity Commission to inquire into the need for, and social and economic impact of, introducing a paid parental leave scheme in Australia. The Productivity Commission is the Australian government's independent research and advisory body on social and economic issues. The Productivity Commission released its report on the issue in February 2009.

Findings

The Productivity Commission found that:

▶ there is 'compelling evidence' that the health and wellbeing of both children and parents benefits from the primary caregiver being absent from work for the first six months of the child's life

▶ while women's participation in the workforce has increased dramatically over the past thirty years, and women now make up 45% of the workforce, during the peak childbearing years, Australian women's workforce participation reduces by a greater amount than for women in other leading industrialised countries

▶ access to employer-funded paid parental leave is highly uneven. In 2007, around 54% of female employees and 50% of male employees had access to some form of paid parental leave, but only one-third of employed women who actually had children received paid parental leave from their employer.

▶ while employers are increasing the availability of paid parental leave to some employees, it is generally not available to part-time, casual and seasonal employees, contractors or the self employed

▶ Australia has been the only OECD country apart from the USA that does not have a comprehensive paid parental leave scheme.

Recommendations

For the reasons outlined above, the Productivity Commission recommended a paid parental leave scheme be introduced and that:

▶ eligible people should have been working for at least ten of the last thirteen months, for at least 330 hours, although not necessarily for one employer

▶ the nominated carer should receive eighteen weeks paid leave at the minimum wage

▶ the leave should be paid for by the employer, who will then be reimbursed by the government.

Action

The *Paid Parental Leave Act* was passed by federal parliament in June 2010, and the paid parental leave scheme, closely following the recommendations of the Productivity Commission, commenced on 1 January 2011.

Source: 'Paid Parental Leave: Support for parents with newborn children', Productivity Commission Report, 28 February 2009.

The paid parental leave scheme

As seen in Case Study 5.14 above, the paid parental leave scheme was introduced on 1 January 2011 under the *Paid Parental Leave Act 2010* (Cth). Details of the scheme are given below.

▶ The scheme provides paid parental leave to primary carers and adoptive parents who have been working and who have a baby or adopt a child on or after 1 January 2011.

▶ To be eligible for the scheme, claimants must pass three tests:

- **the work test**. To meet this test a person must have worked for at least ten of the thirteen months prior to the birth or adoption of the child, and have worked for at least 330 hours in that ten month period (just over one day a week), with no more than an eight week gap between two consecutive working days. This work test can usually be met by casual, part-time, and seasonal workers, as well as by the self-employed and those who change jobs. So paid parental leave is available to many more people than was previously the case (see Case Study 5.14 above).

- **the income test**. To meet this test a person must have a taxable income of less than $150000 in the financial year prior to the date of birth or adoption.

- **residency requirements**. A claimant must be an Australian citizen or permanent resident, or be the holder of one of a number of temporary visas detailed by the Family Assistance Office.

▶ Paid parental leave is for a maximum of eighteen weeks.

▶ The pay for parental leave will be at the rate of the National Minimum Wage. The pay for parental leave will be treated in the same way as other taxable income.

▶ The paid parental leave scheme is funded by the Australian government.

▶ The existing minimum entitlement to twelve months unpaid parental leave for long-term employees, in the National Employment Standards under the *Fair Work Act 2009*, is unchanged.

▶ There is now a small paid non-primary carer parenting payment available.

Leave without pay

As seen already, employees are entitled to some leave without pay in certain circumstances, such as leave for community service activities.

Some awards and agreements also allow for leave without pay to be granted in other circumstances, at the discretion of the employer.

Other leave

Some awards and agreements allow employees to take leave for other purposes such as to attend their own university graduation ceremony, to complete an exam, to undertake study, or to participate in military activities, such as an exercise with the Army Reserve.

Table 5.4 Summary of leave entitlements under the NES

Type of leave	NES entitlement				
	How much annually?	Paid or unpaid?	Can it be accumulated?	Can it be cashed out?	Available for casuals?
Annual leave	4 weeks (5 weeks for shiftworkers)	Paid	Yes	Yes	No
Personal/ carer's leave	10 days	Paid, plus more unpaid	Yes	Under an award or agreement: yes. Under the NES: no.	Only unpaid
Compassionate leave	2 days on each occasion	Paid	No	No	Only unpaid
Community service leave	As necessary	Unpaid, except for jury service to some degree	No	No	Yes, but no payment for jury service unless granted under an award or agreement
Long service leave	Depends on length of service and relevant award, agreement or legislation	Paid	Yes	No	Depends on relevant award, agreement or legislation
Parental leave	12 months, after the birth or adoption of a child	Unpaid (Paid parental leave scheme introduced January 2011)	No	No	Long-term casual employees only

Casual employees and contractors

As seen in Section 5.1.1 (page 277) casual workers and contract workers in Australia form a significant proportion of the workforce, and their numbers continue to rise. These two categories of workers are entitled to few, if any, of the NES leave entitlements. Neither casuals nor contractors are entitled to any paid leave, though, as seen above, casual workers are entitled to two days unpaid carer's leave and two days unpaid compassionate leave per occasion, as well as unpaid community service leave. In addition, casual employees who have been employed for at least twelve months by an employer on a regular and systematic basis, and with an expectation of ongoing employment, are entitled to parental leave (see page 344).

As seen in Section 5.2.5 (page 311), casual employees are entitled to an hourly casual loading for every hour that they work. The casual loading compensates them for entitlements they do not receive, such as paid annual leave and paid personal leave, though many would argue that the loading is insufficient to compensate adequately for the disadvantages of being a casual employee.

The increase in the numbers of casual and contract workers is of concern because it means there are an increasing number of Australians who are not entitled to the same leave as the rest of the workforce. Paid Parental Leave does, however, apply to most casual and contract workers, so they achieve equality with other workers in this regard.

Effectiveness of legal and non-legal responses to the issue of leave

Legal and non-legal responses

Legal responses to the issue of leave are:

- the NES [*Fair Work Act 2009* (Cth)] provides minimum standards for various types of leave, applicable to most Australian employees

- awards and agreements apply if they are more advantageous to an employee than the minimum leave entitlements provided by the NES

- the ability to 'cash out' some leave entitlements under the NES and some awards and agreements

- long service leave is still provided under awards, agreements and state legislation, though there are plans for a national long service leave standard to be developed and to apply under the NES

- the paid parental leave scheme was introduced for parents who give birth to or adopt a child after 1 January 2011, as part of the *Paid Parental Leave Act 2010* (Cth)

Non-legal responses to the issue of leave include that employees and employers are able to negotiate many aspects of leave arrangements to suit both parties, as long as they stay in the parameters set by the law. An example is the decision when to take annual leave.

Evaluating effectiveness

Below are listed two sets of factors—those which help ensure, and those which limit, the effectiveness of legal and non-legal responses to the issue of leave.

Factors which help ensure the effectiveness of legal and non-legal responses to the issue of leave

- The wide application of the NES minimum standards means very few full-time or part-time employees are without adequate leave provisions.

- Employees under an award or agreement with more advantageous leave provisions than the NES benefit from such provisions.

- Employees have the ability to 'cash out' unused annual leave under the NES and unused personal leave under some awards and agreements. The fact that they must have substantial leave entitlements remaining means that they do not lose all leave entitlements.

- Unpaid leave is available to all workers in order to care for family members, to attend to matters relating to a life-threatening situation affecting a family member or to matters relating to a death in the family.

- Employees are able to participate in important activities necessary for the smooth running of society because of community service leave.

- The introduction of paid parental leave means that many people, such as part-time employees, casuals, seasonal employees, contractors and the self-employed, now have access to paid parental leave which they did not have before the introduction of the scheme.

- Casual leave loading operates to compensate casual employees for the fact that they have no paid leave entitlements.

Factors which limit the effectiveness of legal and non-legal responses to the issue of leave

- A national long service leave standard is yet to be developed.

- Casual and contract workers have very few entitlements to leave, particularly paid leave, and the increasing numbers of such workers mean that an increasing number of people in Australia are not entitled to paid leave.

▶ Many would argue that casual leave loading is insufficient to compensate adequately for the disadvantages of being a casual employee, such as no entitlement to paid leave.

CAN YOU **identify and investigate the contemporary issue of leave, and evaluate the effectiveness of legal and non-legal responses to this issue?**

In order to do this, you need to:

▶ describe the leave entitlements under the NES, and to whom they apply

▶ describe leave entitlements and provisions which arise under other legal instruments

▶ describe the provisions of the *Paid Parental Leave Act 2010* (Cth)

▶ describe any non-legal responses to the issue of leave

▶ discuss the factors which help ensure, and those which limit, the effectiveness of legal and non-legal responses to the contemporary workplace issue of leave

▶ come to a conclusion about the effectiveness of legal and non-legal responses to the contemporary workplace issue of leave.

KCq page 368

5.4 Themes and challenges

5.4.1 Theme 1: The role of the law in encouraging cooperation and resolving conflict in the workplace

Assess the role of the law in encouraging cooperation and resolving conflict in the workplace.

The workplace has always been a possible source of conflict, because employers and employees have, to some degree, conflicting interests. Employees wish to maximise their wages and conditions. Employers, on the other hand, wish to maximise profits for their business and, therefore may try to keep wages at a minimum, though many employers recognise that keeping their employees well-paid and with high job satisfaction can increase profits.

As seen in Section 5.1.1 (pages 274–5), as employer–employee relationships emerged in the Industrial Revolution. The law first took a laissez-faire attitude, and did not interfere in the relationships between employers and employees at all. This resulted in very poor conditions for workers because they did not have the bargaining power to negotiate good conditions for themselves.

Governments gradually recognised that they needed to intervene in employer–employee relationships to protect the rights of employees. The law has also acted to encourage employees and employers to negotiate working conditions and wages, and has provided dispute settling mechanisms when negotiations have broken down. Ways in which the law has done this are listed below.

The law encourages cooperation between employers and employees through:

▶ allowing contracts of employment to be negotiated between employers and employees, though these cannot interfere with conditions in statutes, awards or agreements (see Section 5.1.2, pages 278–83)

▶ allowing informal negotiations to take place between employers and employees about numerous matters, such as overtime or leave (see Sections 5.2.2 [pages 292–3] and 5.3.4 [page 341])

- providing for enterprise agreements which allow employers and employees to negotiate for pay and conditions that suit their particular workplace or business rather than be bound by an award (see Section 5.1.3, pages 284–7)
- requiring employers, employees and their representatives to bargain in good faith when enterprise agreements are being negotiated (see Section 5.2.2, page 293)
- allowing for industrial action to take place to give force to negotiations between employers and employees, as long as the action takes place within the limitations prescribed by the law (see Section 5.2.2, pages 293–4)
- clearly delineating the role and the allowable actions of trade unions and employer associations so they can assist in workplace negotiations (see Section 5.2.4, pages 304–7)
- providing for injury management plans, for workers who have sustained a significant injury at work, to be developed through cooperation between the employer, the injured worker and the worker's doctor (see Section 5.3.2, pages 327–8)
- providing for the Fair Work Commission to arrange conciliation when there has been an unfair dismissal claim (see Section 5.3.3, page 333)
- providing that both the Fair Work Commission and the Fair Work Ombudsman will try to bring employers and employees to a resolution about an unfair termination of employment claim before any determinations take place or any orders are made about the matter (see Section 5.3.3, pages 332–6).

Dispute settling provisions for resolving conflicts in the workplace provided for by the legal system include:

- dispute settling mechanisms must be contained in awards and agreements (see Section 5.1.3, pages 284–5)
- the *Fair Work Act 2009* (Cth) prescribes a bargaining process for the negotiation of enterprise agreements, minimising disputes in the process and also providing for dispute settling mechanisms if disputes do occur while negotiations are taking place (see Section 5.2.2, pages 292–3)
- mediation, which can become part of unofficial workplace dispute settling mechanisms with a trade union or employer association acting as the mediator
- mandatory dispute settling procedures in all awards and agreements to encourage the settlement of disputes in the workplace (see Sections 5.1.3 [pages 284–5] and 5.2.3 [page 297])
- conciliation and arbitration are accessible through tribunals [the Fair Work Commission under the Fair Work Act and the NSW Industrial Relations Commission under the *Industrial Relations Act 1996* (NSW)] (see Section 5.2.4, pages 301–2)
- Federal Courts and State Courts can make decisions about disputes relating to a range of industrial matters, and a Fair Work Division has been created in the Federal Court and Federal Magistrates Court (see Section 5.2.4, pages 302–3)
- the Fair Work Ombudsman can investigate complaints and seek resolutions with employees for suspected breaches of workplace law, as well as litigate on behalf of complainants, making the resolution of disputes about suspected breaches of workplace law quicker and cheaper than before the passing of the Fair Work Act (see Sections 5.2.4 [page 303] and 5.3.1 [page 318])

- clear roles and the allowable actions for trade unions and employer associations in the settlement of industrial disputes (see Section 5.2.4, pages 304–7)

- provision of bodies [i.e. the NSW Anti-Discrimination Board, the Fair Work Ombudsman (Cth) and the Australian Human Rights Commission] which can provide conciliation in disputes about discrimination (see Section 5.3.1, pages 318–20)

- provision of quick, inexpensive methods of dispute resolution if conciliation in discrimination matters is not effective through the NSW Civil and Administrative Tribunal (NCAT), and through litigation by the Fair Work Ombudsman in the Federal Court on behalf of complainants (see Section 5.3.1, pages 318–20)

- the NSW Workers Compensation Commission is a tribunal which provides independent, quick and inexpensive resolutions to disputes about workers compensation in NSW (see Section 5.3.2, page 327)

- the Fair Work Commission makes determinations about unfair dismissal and unfair termination of employment claims and can impose penalties and order compensation. The Fair Work Ombudsman can also make orders regarding unfair termination of employment (see Section 5.3.3, pages 333–5).

KCq page 368

5.4.2 Theme 2: Issues of compliance and non-compliance

Commitment to workplace laws is variable. While most employers and employees comply with workplace laws, there are some areas in which compliance does not always occur. This lack of compliance occurs for a variety of reasons, including:

- lack of knowledge of the law
- a desire to save money
- carelessness
- disagreement with the law and/or the values and ethics behind it
- media pressure.

Some of the areas in which issues of compliance and/or non-compliance have and do arise in workplace law are outlined below.

Compliance with safety laws

As seen in Case Study 5.10 (Section 5.3.2, page 325) there was a 16% increase in workplace deaths from 2003 to 2007. Lack of commitment to and non-compliance with safety laws by both employers and employees contributes to this situation. The NSW government has taken steps to improve compliance with occupational health and safety laws by increasing the number of inspectors and prosecutions (see Section 5.3.2, page 328).

The director of the Workplace Research Centre at the University of Sydney, Dr John Buchanan, said in 2008 that the extra deaths were a poor reflection of workplace safety. He said the increase in fatalities can't be explained by a growing workforce alone: 'The cutting back of resources to get jobs done was a management strategy called, in the '90s, "management by stress", but this is a widespread management practice where basically workforces are cut until they're a bit dysfunctional and then managers staff up once they've identified the limits. The other big change in the nature of work has been the weakening role of unions. This has been often policy induced'. ('Experts criticise workplace safety record', reported by Simon Lauder, *The World Today*, ABC national radio, 31 January 2008. See Case Study 5.10, Section 5.3.2, page 325). These

---

Examine issues of compliance and non-compliance in regard to the workplace.

two factors indicate that compliance with workplace safety laws only occurs with union vigilance in some workplaces. The importance of unions in compliance issues is discussed further below.

Since 2008, there has been renewed recognition that Australia's workplace safety laws could be improved. The introduction of national laws, through the *Model Work Health and Safety (WHS) Act 2010* (Cth) released in December 2010 for public comment and due to be implemented from 1 January 2012, is an attempt to improve these laws (see Sections 5.3.2 [page 328] and 5.4.4 [pages 355–8]).

Non-compliance because of conflicting values and ethics

Workplace laws have undergone substantial changes in the last twenty years because of conflicting values and ethics. These conflicting values and ethics are discussed in Section 5.4.3 (pages 354–5). Sometimes, employers or employees disagree with laws about the workplace to such an extent that they refuse to comply with them.

The waterfront dispute

The waterfront dispute of 1998 (see Case Study 5.15 below) is an example of non-compliance by employers with freedom of association principles enshrined in the laws at that time (see also Section 5.2.4, page 306). This situation arose because the employer and its associates wanted to employ non-union instead of union labour, claiming that the union labour on the waterfront was too expensive and too inflexible.

CASE STUDY 5.15: The waterfront dispute (1998): *Patrick Stevedores Operations No. 2 Pty Ltd v The Maritime Union of Australia* (1998) HCA 30

Facts

Late on the night of 7 April 1998, armed, masked security guards, accompanied by guard dogs, forcibly removed 1400 workers from the Patrick Stevedores docks. The workers were thus dismissed from their employment. No notice was given to the workers who were removed and they were given no reasons for their dismissal. By the morning of 8 April 1998, the docks were locked and oncoming shifts were refused entry. Non-union workers supplied by the National Farmers Federation began work on the docks the same day.

Issues

The Maritime Union of Australia (MUA) argued that the employer (Patrick) had breached the *Workplace Relations Act 1996* (Cth), which prohibited an employer dismissing an employee because he or she was a union member.

The MUA also claimed that Patrick, the National Farmers Federation (NFF) and the Minister for Workplace Relations and Small Business, Mr Peter Reith, conspired to breach the Workplace Relations Act. The NFF was included because it had a supply of labour ready to replace the dismissed workers. Mr Reith was included because he presented a bill to parliament on the same day as the dismissals, which provided for a government-run redundancy plan for the MUA workers. So, not only the employer but also the federal government was implicated in non-compliance with its own law.

Decision

The High Court agreed that the workers had been dismissed for a prohibited reason and the dismissed employees were reinstated. The conspiracy claim was never determined because the matter was settled out of court.

This dispute shows non-compliance with dismissal laws being practised by employers and, possibly, by the federal government itself.

Defiance of valid court orders

On some occasions in the past, trade unions and employer organisations have deliberately disobeyed valid orders made by courts and tribunals because they have disagreed with the orders. NSW fire-fighters, for example, went on strike on 1 August 1999 in defiance of an order by the NSW Industrial Relations Commission ordering them back to work. The Fire Brigade Employees Union faced fines of up to $5000 a day for breaching the IRC order.

Defiance of such orders is usually a protest about the directive and also brings publicity to the issues under dispute. Some unionists feel that they have a right to strike and should not be ordered back to work by government authorities.

Media pressure

As seen in Section 5.2.4 (page 318), the media can have an important influence on the outcome of various issues. The Cowra abattoir situation (Case Study 5.12, Section 5.3.3, page 338) shows a company complying with the law, but being persuaded not to because of the harsh impact of the legislation on workers. In this case, the abattoir sacked its workers for 'operational reasons', and attempted to rehire them on less pay. While it was legal for the company to act in this way, it withdrew its dismissal orders because of adverse publicity, which included comments from senior ministers in the government.

Lack of knowledge of and commitment to the law

As was seen in Case Study 5.3 (Section 5.1.3, pages 286–7) up to 27% of AWAs were possibly in breach of the five minimum standards guaranteed by the relevant legislation, the *Workplace Relations Act 1996* (Cth). The failure to comply with the legislation on such a scale could be caused by several factors, such as:

▶ lack of knowledge by both employers and/or employees as to what the five minimum standards were

▶ unequal bargaining power between employees and employers, so that employees were forced to accept conditions less than the legislative requirements or they would not gain employment

▶ lack of scrutiny by trade unions to ensure the standards were complied with

▶ failure by the Workplace Authority to scrutinise the agreements promptly and ensure compliance. By 5 September 2007, the Workplace Authority had only processed 10% of the AWAS that it had received since the fairness test came into existence, on 7 May 2007.

▶ failure of the legislation to ensure compliance by making AWAs come into force as soon as they were lodged instead of making their commencement dependent upon compliance.

A statement of rights for workers

The widespread non-compliance with legislation regarding AWAs is far less likely under the *Fair Work Act 2009* (Cth). This is for several reasons, including:

▶ AWAs are no longer possible

▶ most employees are covered by an award or agreement

▶ all workers in the national workplace system, (which is the vast majority of workers in NSW) are covered by the NES (see Section 5.1.4, page 288) including the provision of a Fair Work Information Statement.

A Fair Work Information Statement must be provided by all employers to all new employees. It contains information about the NES, modern awards, agreement-making, the right to freedom of association, termination of employment, individual flexibility arrangements, right of entry, transfer of business, and the respective roles of the Fair Work Commission and the Fair Work Ombudsman.

The compulsory provision of these information statements means that the lack of knowledge of legislative rights that may have occurred under the *Workplace Relations Act 1996* (Cth), is far less likely under the *Fair Work Act 2009* (Cth). Also, because the Fair Work Information Statement must contain information about the roles of the Fair Work Ombudsman and the Fair Work Commission, both employers and employees know how to ensure that the entitlements under the legislation can be enforced, and this increases the likelihood of compliance.

Weakening power of unions

As has been seen in Section 5.2.4 (page 304), trade unions continue to suffer from falling membership. The rules regarding their behaviour, particularly in relation to industrial action and right of entry have also been made stricter, as have the penalties for non-compliance with these rules. This weakening power has probably contributed to lessening compliance with safety laws and to the significant non-compliance with minimum standards for AWAs outlined on the previous page. Despite this, unions can be a powerful force in ensuring compliance with workplace laws by employers and, in this way, protecting the rights of workers. This can be seen in the waterfront dispute (see Case Study 5.15, page 351), and in the case of JAL Landscape and Construction described in Case Study 5.16 following.

CASE STUDY 5.16: Non-compliance by employers and the effect of trade unions: *JAL Landscape and Construction Pty Ltd, Sydney, 2006*

Facts

JAL Landscape and Construction Pty Ltd hired two teenagers on individual contracts in December 2005. The employees, Brett Conlon and Stephen Pemberton, started to work on a construction site, where they were required to:

▶ work up to fourteen hours a day without payment for overtime

▶ accept total payments of $250 a week

▶ do without overtime, sick leave or public holiday payments.

After not being paid at all, the employees joined the CFMEU, which protested and leafleted passersby.

Outcome

After two weeks of the protesting, the company paid nearly $14 000 in back pay.

Implications

It was only the support of the union that forced the company to comply with the law. This case is an example of the necessity for trade unions to ensure compliance with the law by some employers.

Source: Construction, Forestry, Mining and Energy Union (CFMEU) publicity, authorised by John Sutton, National Secretary.

KCq pages 368–9

5.4.3 Theme 3: Laws relating to the workplace as a reflection of changing values and ethical standards

Throughout the history of Australia, the state has intervened in the common law contract of employment to reflect the values and ethical standards of the Australian population. Much of this state intervention has come about because of the lobbying of trade unions and has ensured workers' basic rights, including:

- minimum wages (see Section 5.2.5, pages 309–11)
- equal pay for equal work (see Section 5.3.1, page 321)
- freedom from discrimination (see Section 5.3.1, page 316)
- a forty-hour week (see Section 5.1.4, page 288)
- the right to occupational health and safety (see Section 5.3.2, pages 323–4)
- the right to form trade unions (see Section 5.2.4, page 306)

So, for much of Australia's history, the principal that workers have rights which need to be protected has been a fundamental part of Australia's workplace legal framework. However, in the area of industrial relations in Australia, there has been a conflict between two ideologies or two sets of values and ethics.

One ideology is represented by the Howard federal government which held power from 1996 to 2007, and is reflected in the *Workplace Relations Act 1996* (Cth). This set of values sees the freedom of individual employers and employees to make their own workplace arrangements as paramount. So, AWAs overrode awards and agreements (see Section 5.1.3, page 286). This ideology seeks to lessen the role of unions and government organisations, such as tribunals, in workplace arrangements (see Section 5.2.4, pages 301–8).

The opposing ideology says that outside intervention in workplace arrangements is vital to protect the rights of workers, especially those who are most vulnerable. This view argues that workers are not in an equal bargaining position with employers unless they are represented by a good union and have access to an independent referee, such as an Industrial Relations Commission. People who hold these values protested against the Workplace Relations Act arguing that it did not uphold a fundamental value in society—that is, that people should be treated equally and protected from exploitation. Public marches and rallies occurred across Australia during 2006 and 2007 in the Your Rights at Work campaign, protesting against Work Choices.

In November 2007, the Howard coalition government was voted out of office, as widespread campaigns by trade unions and others highlighted the inequity of some of the provisions of the Work Choices amendments of 2005. Some of these provisions included:

- the removal of pay and conditions under AWAs (see Case Study 5.3, Section 5.1.3, pages 286–7)
- the removal of unfair dismissal protections for the majority of workers (see Section 5.3.3, page 334)
- the provision of dismissals for 'operational reasons' as highlighted in the Cowra Abattoir case (see Case Study 5.12, Section 5.3.3, page 338).

The election of the Rudd Labor government in November 2007 was, in part, due to the voting public rejecting the moral and ethical standards embodied by Work Choices. The *Workplace Relations Amendment (Transition to Forward with Fairness) Act 2008* (Cth) was introduced and no new AWAs were allowed to be entered into after April 2008. The *Fair Work Act*

2009 (Cth) introduced major reforms to workplace relations across Australia, which better reflect the values and ethics supporting the protection of workers' rights as a fundamental part of Australia's industrial landscape. These reforms are discussed throughout this chapter and briefly listed in Section 5.4.4 following. KCq page 369

5.4.4 Theme 4: The role of law reform in recognising rights and enforcing responsibilities in the workplace

Examine the role of law reform in recognising rights and enforcing responsibilities in the workplace.

To *reform* the law means to change the law so that it operates more efficiently and/or more effectively. Law can be reformed by legislation or by adaptation of the common law in courts.

Parliaments are the principal lawmakers in our society and, therefore, the principal agencies of reform to the law. The area of industrial law is particularly dynamic, and far-reaching changes have been made to the laws in this area because of different values and ethics about what should determine the basis of relationships between employers and employees. *The Fair Work Act 2009* (Cth), for example, is a major reform of industrial relations law. That act replaced the *Workplace Relations Act 1996* (Cth) and the Work Choices amendments of 2005. This legislation, too, introduced major reforms to industrial relations law in Australia (see Sections 5.1.3 [pages 285–7] and 5.2.1 [page 291]).

The *Fair Work Act 2009* (Cth)

The *Fair Work Act 2009* (Cth) introduced major reforms to workplace laws across Australia. Some of the reforms introduced by the Fair Work Act include:

▷ introducing a national workplace system that is applicable to most employees in Australia (see Section 5.2.1, page 291)

▷ making sham contracting arrangements illegal and applying penalties to employers who attempt to make such arrangements (see Section 5.1.2, page 281)

▷ making modern awards central to the conditions of employment in most industries (see Section 5.1.3, pages 283–4) and providing that they must:
  • not contain conditions less than the NES
  • contain a flexibility clause
  • contain dispute settling procedures

▷ establishing the NES and general protections, so that all workers in the national workplace system are protected by minimum conditions (see Section 5.1.4, pages 287–8)

▷ providing for the negotiation of enterprise agreements which must comply with a bargaining process prescribed in the act and must pass the 'better off overall' test (BOOT) (see Sections 5.1.3 [pages 284–7] and 5.2.2 [pages 292–3])

▷ allowing for industrial action to take place, as well as limiting the circumstances under which it can take place, and providing penalties to be imposed on those who take illegal industrial action (see Section 5.2.2, pages 294–6)

▷ making dispute settling procedures mandatory in all awards and agreements to encourage the settlement of disputes in the workplace (see Section 5.1.3 [pages 284–5] and 5.2.3 [pages 298–300])

▷ establishing government bodies (i.e. the Fair Work Commission and the Fair Work Ombudsman) to provide advice, assistance, conciliation and arbitration of disputes (see Section 5.2.4, pages 301–3)

- investing the Fair Work Ombudsman with the power to litigate on behalf of complainants, which makes making the resolution of disputes about suspected breaches of workplace law quicker and cheaper than before the passing of the Fair Work Act (see Sections 5.2.4 [page 303] and 5.3.1 [page 318])
- establishing annual national wage reviews by the Minimum Wage Panel in the Fair Work Commission, which is required to hear submissions from all interested parties (see Section 5.2.5, page 310)
- changing the ways in which discrimination issues can be dealt with in the federal arena, so that employees have greater access to remedies (see Section 5.3.1, pages 318–21)
- making unfair dismissal laws apply to most workers whereas, under the previous legislation, they applied to only about 1% of private sector employers (see Section 5.3.3, page 334)
- making a distinction between genuine and non-genuine redundancies, to prevent employers attempting to disadvantage workers, and providing protections to redundant workers under the NES (see Section 5.3.3, pages 337–8)
- providing minimum standards for various types of leave under the NES (see Section 5.3.4, pages 341–8).

Law Reform Commissions and other agencies review various areas or aspects of the law and make recommendations to parliament about possible legislative changes. For example, as has been seen in Case Study 5.14 (Section 5.3.4, pages 344–5) the Productivity Commission, at the request of the government, inquired into the need for a paid parental leave scheme to be introduced into Australia. As a result of this inquiry, released on 28 February 2009, the federal government introduced such a scheme under the *Paid Parental Leave Act 2010* (Cth) .

While parliament is the primary agency of reform, the courts contribute to reform in the law by applying precedent to cases under review and making decisions to fit changing circumstances. Courts must apply legislation, must follow precedent and can only make a decision in cases before them, so their contribution to reform is usually slow and piecemeal. However, sometimes the effect of a court decision can be profound as in the case of *Scholem v NSW Department of Health*, which led to smoke-free workplaces across Australia (see Case Study 5.17 below).

CASE STUDY 5.17: *Scholem v NSW Department of Health* (NSW District Court, 27 May 1992)

Facts
Liesl Scholem worked in a community health centre run by the NSW Department of Health from 1974 to 1986. Many of her colleagues and her co-workers smoked in the centre. Scholem was an asthmatic and made many requests to her employer to make the workplace smoke-free. The Department's smoke-free workplace policy was not implemented until 1984.

Issue
Scholem claimed that the constant exposure to the smoke exacerbated her asthma and she also eventually developed emphysema.

Decision
The court found that the NSW Department of Health had been negligent under common law and had also breached safety legislation. Scholem was awarded $85 000 in damages.

Implications
This was the first passive smoking case in the world and led to many workplaces around Australia declaring themselves smoke-free so as to avoid similar claims from their workforces.

Factors leading to reform

There are many factors which give rise to the need for law reform. These are discussed below.

Changing social values

The area of workplace law is very dynamic and there have been major changes to industrial relations law in Australia in the last twenty years because of changing social values. This is discussed in Section 5.4.3 (pages 354–5) and includes the law reforms embodied in the *Workplace Relations Act 1996* (Cth) and the Work Choices amendments of 2005, as well as the *Fair Work Act 2009* (Cth).

Changing composition of society

The composition of the workforce has changed significantly in recent years, so that there are now far more casual and part-time workers, as well as contract workers, than there were in 1980 (see Section 5.1.1, page 277). Unfortunately, the law has responded to these changes in a limited way, and many casual and contract workers, in particular, do not enjoy the same protections as the rest of the workforce (see also Sections 5.1.2 [pages 278–80], 5.3.3 [page 333] and 5.3.4 [page 346]). However, the paid parental leave scheme, which commenced in 2011, does apply to casual and contract workers if they can pass the income, work and residency tests necessary for eligibility (see Section 5.3.4, page 345).

Failure of existing law

Most law reform comes about because of a failure of existing law. In the workplace, failure or perceived failure of existing law has led to the following reforms:

- introduction of the NES under the Fair Work Act to protect the rights of workers, because these were being eroded under the Work Choices system (see Sections 5.1.3 [pages 283–7] and 5.1.4 [pages 287–8]).
- changes to the ways in which discrimination issues can be dealt with in the federal arena, so that employees have greater access to remedies (see Section 5.3.1, pages 318–20)
- changes to workers compensation in NSW to make it more efficient and less costly, including the introduction of injury management strategies (see Section 5.3.2, pages 324–8)
- the introduction of national workplace safety laws (from January 2012), aimed at streamlining the processes of protecting workers from injury and, hopefully, providing better protection for all workers across Australia (see Section 5.3.2, pages 324–5)
- the introduction of the GEERS (see Section 5.3.3, page 338)
- the reform of unfair dismissal laws so that they have wider application (see Section 5.3.3, pages 332–5)
- the introduction of the paid parental leave scheme (see Section 5.3.4, pages 344–5).

Whether existing law is failing and still needs reform is often a matter of dispute because of conflicting morals and ethics. For example, those who believe workers' rights were being eroded too much by Work Choices welcomed the change of government in November 2007 and the Fair Work Act (see Section 5.4.3, pages 354–5).

New technology

Technological change is responsible for massive changes in the workplace. These changes have led to the need for reskilling workers, and many employers provide professional development and retraining for workers who require new skills. Laws about redundancy have emerged over the last twenty years to accommodate workplace changes brought about by technological change (see Section 5.3.3, pages 336–7).

KCq page 383

Analyse the effectiveness of legal and non-legal responses in achieving justice in the workplace.

5.4.5 Theme 5: The effectiveness of legal and non-legal responses in achieving justice in the workplace

The effectiveness of legal and non-legal measures in achieving justice in the workplace is discussed throughout this chapter, as described below.

▶ **Dispute resolution mechanisms** in the workplace, and their effectiveness, is discussed in Section 5.2.3 (pages 297–301).

▶ **The role of trade unions:** their effectiveness is discussed in Section 5.2.4 (pages 304–6).

▶ **Protection and recognition of workplace rights:** effectiveness of legal and non-legal responses to the protection and recognition of workplace rights is discussed in Section 5.2.6 (pages 313–15). This discussion includes examining the effectiveness of:

  • contracts of service
  • contracts for services
  • awards
  • agreements
  • statutory conditions
  • negotiation processes
  • the role of tribunals
  • the role of the courts
  • the role of government organisations
  • the role of trade unions and employer associations
  • the role of other NGOS
  • the role of the media.

▶ **Discrimination in the workplace**: the effectiveness of legal and non-legal responses to this issue is discussed in Section 5.3.1 (pages 321–3).

▶ **Safety in the workplace**: the effectiveness of legal and non-legal responses to this issue is discussed in Section 5.3.2 (pages 328–30).

▶ **Termination of employment**: the effectiveness of legal and non-legal responses to this issue is discussed in Section 5.3.3 (pages 339–41). This includes discussion of:

  • resignation
  • unfair dismissal and unfair termination of employment
  • redundancy.

▶ **Leave**: the effectiveness of legal and non-legal responses to this issue is discussed in Section 5.3.4 (pages 347–8). This discussion includes leave entitlements and the paid parental leave scheme.

KCq page 369

Key definitions and concepts

Do you know all the key definitions and concepts for this chapter? Go through each term in the list and check that you know them all. Place a bookmark underneath each definition to cover the one below and slide the bookmark down. This way you can focus on each definition by itself.

Affirmative action: Action taken not only to eliminate discrimination but also to relieve the effects of past discrimination and to ensure that future discrimination does not occur.

Allowance: Extra payment to an employee because of special circumstances attached to the job.

Alternative dispute resolution: Mechanisms for resolving disputes other than the court system. May involve mediation, conciliation or arbitration.

Annual leave: Paid leave that is given to an employee every year at the completion of each year of service.

Annual leave loading: An additional amount of pay included in annual leave pay, calculated as a percentage of the annual leave pay.

Arbitration: When a third party listens to the parties to a dispute and makes a decision on the merits of the case.

Australian Workplace Agreement (AWA): A written agreement between an individual employee and his or her employer, setting out the terms and conditions of employment, governed by the *Workplace Relations Act 1996* (Cth).

Award: An enforceable document containing minimum terms and conditions of employment as well as legislated minimum terms.

Better off overall test (BOOT): The test to which federal enterprise agreements are subject; meaning each of the employees to be covered by the agreement must be better off overall than under the relevant modern award.

Carer's leave: Time off work taken by an employee to provide care or support for a member of his or her immediate household or family because of illness, injury or unexpected emergency.

Cashing out: The process of accepting pay for unused paid leave entitlements, rather than taking the actual leave.

Casual loading: An amount paid on top of the normal wage rate to casual employees to compensate them for not receiving certain entitlements that permanent employees receive.

Closed shop: A workplace in which the employer agrees to employ only union members. This practice is now illegal.

Collective agreements: Agreements, made collectively by all employees in a particular workplace (or workplaces) with their employer, which override existing awards or agreements. Also called **enterprise agreements**.

Collective bargaining: When a group of employees, perhaps represented by a trade union, negotiates directly with an employer.

Community service leave: Time away from work taken by an employee in order to perform a legitimate community service activity.

Compassionate leave: Time off work taken by an employee to spend with a member of his or her immediate household or family who has sustained a life-threatening illness or injury, or after the death of a member of the employee's immediate household or family.

Conciliation: The process whereby a third person, called a conciliator, listens to the two parties to the dispute and makes suggestions in an effort to bring those parties to agreement.

Constructive dismissal: The situation when a worker resigns because conditions at work leave him or her with no real alternative.

Contract for services: A legally binding agreement whereby a person is hired to do a particular task or perform a particular service for a certain sum of money.

Contract of employment: A legally binding agreement made between an employer and an employee. Also known as a **contract of service**.

Contract of service: A legally binding agreement made between an employer and an employee. Also known as a **common law contract of employment**.

Corporations power: Power given to the federal government under section 51(xx) of the Australian Constitution which allows it to make laws for corporations.

Deemed employee: Independent contractors who are treated as employees for certain purposes.

Demarcation disputes: Disputes over which workers should perform particular tasks.

Direct discrimination: When someone acts directly to treat someone else differently because of their membership of a particular group in society.

Discrimination: The treatment of one person differently from another in the same situation because of that person's membership of a particular group in society, such as Aboriginal people, women, migrants or people with physical disabilities.

Dismissal: An employer tells an employee that he or she is no longer required to work for the employer.

Division of power: The division of lawmaking power between the states and the federal government.

Employee: A person who performs work and is paid a wage or a salary to do so.

Employer: A person or organisation who pays others wages or a salary to perform certain work.

Employer association: An organisation that represents the interests of employers.

Enterprise agreements: Agreements made collectively by all employees in a particular workplace (or workplaces) with their employer.

Equal employment opportunity: The treatment of all employees fairly so they are not discriminated against, they all have an equal chance to access workplace opportunities and all have equal protection under the law.

Express term: A promise in a contract that is actually spoken or written into the contract.

Freedom of association: The right to belong or not belong to a trade union.

General protections: Employee rights protected under the *Fair Work Act 2009* (Cth), including compliance with the NES and with conditions under awards and agreement.

Globalisation: The growing economic and social interdependence and interconnectedness of countries worldwide.

Greenfields agreements: Enterprise agreements available under federal law for any new enterprise being established or proposed by one or more employers who have not yet employed persons necessary for the normal conduct of the enterprise.

Implied term: A promise in a contract, binding on the parties to the contract, that is put into the contract by the law.

Independent contractor: A person who is hired to do a particular task or perform a particular service for a certain sum of money.

Indirect discrimination: When an action is taken which results in one group in society being treated less favourably than another.

Individual Transitional Employment Agreements (ITEA): An individual written agreement between an employee and an employer that sets out the terms and conditions of employment, to replace an AWA for a transitional period ending in December 2009.

Industrial action: Action taken by employers and employees to help provide force to their claims if negotiations between them break down.

Industrial dispute: Any dispute about any matter which pertains to the relationship between employers and employees.

Industrial relations: Relationships between employers and employees.

Industry association: An organisation that represents the interests of the businesses operating in a particular industry that are members of the association.

Injury management plan: A plan, made by an injured worker, his employer, the workers compensation insurer and the worker's doctor, to ensure the swift and safe return to work of that injured worker.

Journey claims: Workers compensation claims made for injuries received during journeys to and from work.

Laissez faire: The philosophy that people, including employees and employers, should be free to make whatever arrangements they wish and that the government should not interfere in these arrangements by passing laws to control them.

Leave: Permission for an employee to be absent from work for a legitimate reason.

Lock-out: When an employer closes work premises or refuses to allow employees to work.

Long service leave: A period of paid leave for employees who have been working for the same business for a long period of time, usually between seven and fifteen years.

Mediation: A process of solving disputes in which a third party, called a mediator, listens to the parties in dispute and helps them reach agreement.

Multi-enterprise agreement: An enterprise agreement under federal law involving two or more employers that are not all in a single enterprise and their employees.

No net detriment test: A test applied to NSW enterprise agreements, ensuring that workers are not disadvantaged by the agreement in relation to their existing terms and conditions of employment.

Notice: The informing of one party to a contract of employment (the employer or employee) to the other party of the intention to terminate the employment.

Overtime: Time worked in excess of ordinary hours of work, often paid at a higher rate of pay.

Parental leave: Leave given to an employee because of the birth or adoption of a child.

Part-time loading: An amount paid on top of the normal wage rate to part-time employees to compensate them for not receiving certain entitlements that full-time employees receive.

Pattern bargaining: When a bargaining representative (usually a trade union, but sometimes employers) seeks common terms in enterprise agreements across an industry or across different enterprises.

Penalty rate: A higher rate of pay for work done outside usual working hours, such as late at night or on weekends or public holidays.

Personal/carer's leave: Personal/carer's leave includes leave because an employee is sick (sick leave) or because he or she is caring for a family member who is ill, injured or in an emergency situation (carer's leave).

Preservation age: Age at which an employee can have access to his or her superannuation funds.

Protected industrial action: Industrial action which takes place having met the criteria set out in the *Fair Work Act 2009* (Cth).

Redeployment: To send a person to a new place of work or a new job within the same organisation.

Redundancy: When an employer decides he or she no longer wants an employee's job to be done by anyone and terminates the employee's employment.

Re-employment: The situation in which an unfairly dismissed employee is given another suitable job by the employer who dismissed him or her.

Reinstatement: The situation in which an unfairly dismissed employee is given his or her job back.

Remuneration: Payment received for services or employment.

Resignation: The voluntary termination of the contract of employment by an employee.

Restructuring: The rearrangement of the duties in the workplace, usually in an attempt to make the workplace more efficient.

Retirement: A person finishes working and does not work again for the rest of his or her life.

Retraining: Educating an employee in new skills so that he or she can undertake a different job, either within the same organisation or with a new employer.

Retrenchment: The situation in which an employee loses his or her job because of redundancy.

Salary: The amount of money a person is paid for a particular type of employment, paid for the job done rather than the hours worked, usually expressed as an amount paid per year.

Secondary boycott: When a person or union prevents or substantially hinders a third person, who is not their employer, from engaging in trade or commerce.

Severance payment: Payment made to an employee upon termination of employment because the employee has been made redundant. Also called **redundancy pay**.

Sexual harassment: When a person is subject to unwelcome, uninvited sexual conduct or advances.

Sham contracting arrangement: The situation in which an employer attempts to disguise an employment relationship as an independent contracting arrangement, usually in order to avoid responsibility for employee entitlements.

Sick leave: Time off work that can be taken by employees who can't attend work because they are sick or injured.

Significant injury: An injury received in the course of employment which prevents a worker undertaking some or all of his or her normal duties for more than seven days.

Single-enterprise agreements: An enterprise agreement under federal law involving a single employer, or more employers (such as in a joint venture), and employees.

Stand-down: To put an employee off work when there is no work for him or her to do because other employees are taking industrial action.

Strike: The withdrawal by employees of their labour from the workplace in order to achieve industrial aims.

Summary dismissal: Dismissal without notice, or immediate dismissal.

Superannuation: Payment made to a person, as a funded pension, once he or she has retired from work.

Trade union: An association of wage earners which exists in order to maintain and improve the working conditions of its members.

Tribunal: A specialised body set up to decide disputes in a particular area.

Union preference: The now illegal practice of giving union members preference over non-union members in matters of hiring, firing and promotion.

Vicarious liability: The employer is held liable for the actions and omissions of his or her employees.

Wage: The amount of money a person is paid for a particular type of employment, usually expressed as an amount paid per hour or per week.

Work Choices: The federal statutory framework that governed employment relations, introduced in March 2006 and replaced by the *Fair Work Act 2009*.

Work-to-rule: A form of industrial action in which employees refuse to perform tasks that fall outside the strict guidelines of their job.

Workers compensation: Insurance, provided by employers to workers, against the possibility of suffering injury arising out of or in the course of employment.

Chapter syllabus checklist

Are you able to answer every syllabus question in the chapter? Tick each question as you go through the list if you are able to answer it. If you cannot answer it, turn to the given page to find the answer. Refer to page ix to check the meaning of the NESA key words.

	For a complete understanding of this topic:	Page No.	✓
1	Can I describe the changing nature of workplace law over time?	274–7	
2	Can I outline the developing need for workplace law?	278	
3	Can I describe contracts of service?	278	
4	Can I describe contracts for services?	278–9	
5	Can I describe express and implied terms of contracts?	281–3	
6	Can I describe awards and agreements?	283–7	
7	Can I describe statutory conditions?	287–9	
8	Can I outline the sources of workplace regulation?	289	
9	Can I describe the rights and responsibilities of employers and employees in the workplace?	290	
10	Can I describe industrial relations—the state and federal framework?	291–2	
11	Can I examine the legal framework for workplace law?	292	
12	Can I describe negotiations between employers and employees?	292–6	
13	Can I describe dispute resolution mechanisms?	297–300	
14	Can I evaluate the effectiveness of dispute resolution processes?	301	
15	Can I describe the role of courts and tribunals?	301–3	
16	Can I describe the role of government organisations?	303–4	
17	Can I describe the role of trade unions?	304–6	
18	Can I describe the role of employer associations?	306–7	
19	Can I describe the role of non-government organisations?	307	
20	Can I describe the role of the media?	308	
21	Can I assess the role of the legal system in regulating the workplace?	308	
22	Can I describe types of remuneration?	311–12	

	For a complete understanding of this topic:	Page No.	✓
23	Can I outline how remuneration is determined?	312	
24	Can I evaluate the effectiveness of legal and non-legal measures in protecting and recognising workplace rights?	313–15	
25	Can I identify and describe the contemporary issue of discrimination?	316–21	
26	Can I investigate the contemporary issue of workplace discrimination, and evaluate the effectiveness of legal and non-legal responses to this issue?	321–3	
27	Can I identify and describe the contemporary issue of safety?	323–8	
28	Can I investigate the contemporary issue of workplace safety, and evaluate the effectiveness of legal and non-legal responses to this issue?	328–30	
29	Can I identify and describe the contemporary issue of termination of employment?	330–40	
30	Can I investigate the contemporary issue of termination of employment, and evaluate the effectiveness of legal and non-legal responses to this issue?	340–1	
31	Can I identify and describe the contemporary issue of leave?	341–7	
32	Can I investigate the contemporary issue of leave, and evaluate the effectiveness of legal and non-legal responses to this issue?	347–8	
33	Can I assess the role of the law in encouraging cooperation and resolving conflict in the workplace?	348–50	
34	Can I examine issues of compliance and non-compliance?	350–3	
35	Can I explain laws relating to the workplace as a reflection of changing values and ethical standards?	354–5	
36	Can I explain the role of law reform in recognising rights and enforcing responsibilities in the workplace?	355–8	
37	Can I evaluate the effectiveness of legal and non-legal responses in achieving justice in the workplace?	358	

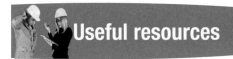

Useful resources

Acts

Age Discrimination Act 2004 (Cth) (See Section 5.3.1, page 316.)

Anti-Discrimination Act 1977 (NSW) (See Section 5.3.1, pages 316–18)

Australian Human Rights Commission Act 1986 (Cth) (See Section 5.3.1, page 316.)

Coal Mine Health and Safety Act 2002 (NSW) (See Section 5.3.2, page 324.)

Combination Acts (1800s) UK (See Section 5.1.1, page 275.)

Competition and Consumer Act 2010 (Cth) (See Section 5.2.2, page 295.)

Construction Safety Act 1912 (NSW) (See Section 5.3.2, page 224.)

Corporations Law Amendment (Employee Entitlements) Act 2000 (Cth) (See Section 5.3.3, page 339.)

Criminal Records Act 1991 (NSW) (See Section 5.3.1, page 318.)

Disability Discrimination Act 1992 (Cth) (See Section 5.3.1, page 316.)

Fair Work Act 2009 (Cth) (See Sections 5.1.4 [page 288] and 5.3.1 [pages 316–18].)

Fair Work (Registered Organisations) Act 2009 (Cth) (See Section 5.2.4, page 304.)

Independent Contractors Act 2006 (Cth) (See Section 5.1.2, page 281.)

Industrial Relations Act 1996 (NSW) (See Sections 5.1.4 [page 289] and 5.3.1 [page 316].)

Local Government Act 1993 (NSW) (See Section 5.3.1, page 321.)

Long Service Leave Act 1955 (NSW) (See Section 5.3.4, page 344.)

Paid Parental Leave Act 2010 (Cth) (See Section 5.3.4, page 345.)

Racial Discrimination Act 1975 (Cth) (See Section 5.3.1, page 316.)

Sex Discrimination Act 1984 (Cth) (See Section 5.3.1, page 316.)

Superannuation Guarantee (Administration) Act 1992 (Cth) (See Section 5.2.5, page 312.)

Superannuation Industry (Supervision) Act 1993 (Cth) (See Section 5.3.3, page 331.)

Trade Practices Act 1974 (Cth) (See Section 5.2.2, page 295.)

Work Health and Safety Act 2011 (NSW) (See Section 5.3.2, page 324.)

Workers Compensation Act 1987 (NSW) (See Section 5.3.2, pages 325–7.)

Workplace Gender Equality Act 2012 (Cth) (See Section 5.3.1, page 321.)

Workplace Injury Management and Workers Compensation Act 1998 (NSW) (See Section 5.3.2, pages 325–7.)

Workplace Relations Act 1996 (Cth) (See Section 5.1.3, page 286.)

Workplace Relations Amendment (Transition to Forward with Fairness) Act 2008 (Cth) (See Section 5.1.3, page 286.)

Workplace Relations Amendment (Work Choices) Act 2005 (Cth) (See Section 5.2.1, page 291.)

Treaties

International Labour Organization Convention No. 87: Freedom of Association and Protection of the Right to Organise, 1948 (See Section 5.1.3, page 286.)

International Labour Organization Convention No. 98: Right to Organise and Collective Bargaining, 1949 (See Section 5.1.3, page 286.)

Cases

Abdulrahman v Toll Pty Ltd trading as Toll Express (2006) NSWADT 221 (See Case Study 5.9, Section 5.3.1, page 320.)

Ansett Transport Industries (Operations) Pty Ltd v Australian Federation of Air Pilots (1991) 1 VR 637 (The pilots' dispute) (See Case Study 5.7, Section 5.2.4, page 303.)

CFMEU v Woodside Burrup Pty Ltd and Kentz E & C Pty Ltd [2010] FWAFB 6021 (See Case Study 5.4, Section 5.2.2, page 296.)

Ex parte HV McKay (Harvester Case) (1907) 2 CAR 1 (See Section 5.2.5, page 309.)

Hollis v Vabu Pty Ltd (2001) HCA 44 (See Case Study 5.2, Section 5.1.2, page 280.)

Patrick Stevedores Operations No. 2 Pty Ltd v The Maritime Union of Australia (1998) HCA 30 (the waterfront dispute) (See Case Study 5.15, Section 5.4.2, page 351.)

Redundancy Test Case, AIRC, 2004 (See Section 5.3.3, page 336.)

Scholem v NSW Department of Health (NSW District Court, 27 May 1992) (See Case Study 5.17, Section 5.4.4, page 356.)

Termination, Change and Redundancy Test Case, ACAC (now AIRC), 1984 (See Section 5.3.3, page 336.)

Wongtas Pty Ltd, Ding Guo Wang and Xiao Yu Zhang; Federal Court of Australia, Sydney, filed: 30 June 2010 (See Case Study 5.8, Section 5.3.1, page 319.)

Woolworths Ltd trading as Produce and Recycling Distribution Centre (2010) FWAFB 1464 (26 February 2010) (See Case Study 5.5, Section 5.2.3, page 298.)

Zuijs v Wirth Bros Circus (1955) 93 CLR 56 (See Case Study 5.1, Section 5.1.2, page 279.)

Other documents

'Australian Social Trends, 2008: Industrial disputes', Abstract (4102.*0)*, Australian Bureau of Statistics (ABS) (See Case Study 5.6, Section 5.2.3, page 299.)

Construction, Forestry, Mining and Energy Union (CFMEU) publicity in regard to non-compliance by employers and the effect of trade unions: JAL Landscape and Construction Pty Ltd, Sydney, 2006, authorised by John Sutton, National Secretary of the CFMEU (See Case Study 5.16, Section 5.4.2, page 353.)

'Experts criticise workplace safety record', reported by Simon Lauder, *The World Today*, ABC national radio, 31 January 2008 (See Case Study 5.10, Section 5.3.2 [page 325], and Section 5.4.2 [page 350].)

'Fatal Occupational Injuries: How does Australia compare Internationally?' National Occupational Health and Safety Commission, 2004. (See Case Study 5.10, Section 5.3.2, page 325.)

'Paid Parental Leave: Support for Parents with Newborn Children', Productivity Commission Report, 28 February 2009 (See Case Study 5.14, Section 5.3.4, pages 344–5.)

'Revealed: how AWAs strip work rights', Mark Davis, *The Sydney Morning Herald*, 17 April 2007. (See Case Study 5.3, Section 5.1.3, pages 286–7.)

Organisations and websites

NSW Civil and Administrative Tribunal (NCAT) (See Section 5.3.1, pages 319–20): www.ncat.nsw.gov.au

Anti-Discrimination Board (NSW) (See Section 5.3.1, page 318): www.lawlink.nsw.gov.au/adb

Australian Bureau of Statistics (ABS) (Cth) (See Section 5.2.3, page 299): www.abs.gov.au

Australian Chamber of Commerce and Industry (ACCI) (See Section 5.2.4, page 306): www.australianchamber.com.au

Australian Council of Trade Unions (ACTU) (See Section 5.2.4, page 304): www.actu.org.au

Australian Federation of Employers and Industries (AFEI) (See Section 5.2.4, page 307): www.afei.org.au

Australian Human Rights Commission (See Section 5.3.1, page 319): www.hreoc.gov.au

Australian Industrial Relations Commission (AIRC) (Cth) (See Section 5.2.4, page 301): www.airc.gov.au

Australian Meat Industry Council (AMIC) (See Section 5.2.4, page 306): www.amic.org.au

Department of Education and Training (Cth) www.education.gov.au

Department of Jobs and Small Business (Cth) www.jobs.gov.au

Fair Entitlements Guarantee (FEG) (Cth) (See Section 5.3.3, page 338): www.jobs.gov.au/fair-entitlements-guarantee-feg

Fair Work Commission (FWC) (See Section 5.2.4, page 301): www.fwc.gov.au

Fair Work Ombudsman (See Section 5.2.4, page 303): www.fairwork.gov.au

Federal Court of Australia (See Section 5.2.4, page 302): www.federalcourt.gov.au

Federal Circuit Court of Australia (See Section 5.2.4, page 302): www.federalcircuitcourt.gov.au/wps/wcm/connect/fccweb/home

Industrial Relations Commission (IRC) (NSW), also Industrial Court of NSW (See Section 5.2.4, page 302): www.lawlink.nsw.gov.au/irc

International Labour Organization (ILO) (See Section 5.1.3, page 286): www.ilo.org

Minerals Council of Australia (MCA) (See Section 5.2.4, page 306): www.minerals.org.au

Industrial Relations NSW, a division of the Department of Services, Technology and Administration (See Section 5.2.4, pages 303–4): www.industrialrelations.nsw.gov.au

Productivity Commission (See Section 5.3.4, pages 344–5): www.pc.gov.au

SafeWork NSW (See Section 5.3.2, page 325): www.safework.nsw.gov.au

Self-employed Australia (See Section 5.2.4, page 307): www.selfemployedaustralia.com.au

Workers Compensation Commission (NSW) (See Section 5.3.2, page 327): www.wcc.nsw.gov.au

Workplace Gender Equality Agency (Cth) (See Section 5.3.1, page 321): www.wgea.gov.au

End of chapter questions

 Key Concept questions

These questions test whether you have grasped the key ideas in each subsection. They are not difficult questions, but will test your recall of knowledge of the material you have read. If you are unsure what a question is asking you to do, refer to page ix to check the meaning of the NESA key words. If you can answer all these questions, you will know you have a sound knowledge of content.

Refer to pp. 460–70 for

5.1 The nature of workplace law

5.1.1 The changing nature of workplace law over time

1. What is workplace law about?
2. Define *employer* and *employee*.
3. Identify three problems that occurred in factories early in the Industrial Revolution.
4. Explain how the philosophy of laissez faire allowed poor working conditions to occur.
5. Describe the form in which state intervention in workplace relations first took place.
6. List four of the legislative protections for working conditions brought about by trade unions.
7. Define *globalisation* and *restructuring* and explain their interrelationship.
8. Describe four significant changes in employment patterns that have occurred in the last thirty years.
9. Explain what you need to do in order to outline the developing need for workplace law over time.

5.1.2 Contracts

10. Define *contact of service* and *contract for services*.
11. Identify the four types of documents that may contribute to the terms of a common law contract of employment.
12. Identify the type of contract used by independent contractors.
13. Name the two tests a court will apply to determine if there is a *contract of service* or a *contract for services* operating.
14. List five factors that would indicate a person was under a *contract for services*.
15. Explain the benefit of being under a *contract of service*.
16. Explain why the law has made some contractors 'deemed' employees.

17. Name the legislation which protects people from sham contracting arrangements, and summarise the protections that it offers.
18. Explain the difference between *express terms* and *implied terms*.
19. Identify the five sources of the rights and duties that may exist in an employment contract for employers and employees.
20. Identify four duties of employers and four rights of employees.
21. Identify four duties of employees and four rights of employers.

5.1.3 Awards and agreements

22. Describe modern awards. To what jurisdiction are they relevant?
23. List three essential ingredients of modern awards.
24. Explain the status of NSW state awards.
25. What is an *enterprise agreement*?
26. Explain the relationship between awards and agreements.
27. Name three types of federal agreements.
28. Name the body that must approve federal agreements.
29. List seven conditions which must be met by federal agreements.
30. Describe the test known as BOOT.
31. Explain how AWAs represented a big innovation in industrial relations in Australia.
32. What is the status of AWAs and ITEAs under current law?
33. Give two reasons why AWAs were criticised.
34. To whom may NSW enterprise agreements apply?
35. Outline the three conditions which must be met by NSW enterprise agreements.
36. Identify the body which supervises the negotiation and legality of NSW enterprise agreements.

5.1.4 Statutory conditions

37. Describe how statute law has, in general, affected the traditional common law contract of service.
38. What does NES stand for?
39. Cite the legislation which provides for the NES.
40. To whom do the NES apply?
41. Briefly list the ten NES entitlements.
42. What are *general protections*?
43. Explain what can occur if general protections are breached.
44. Identify ten areas of workplace regulation provided for by state and federal legislation.

45. Explain what you need to do in order to outline the sources of workplace regulation.

46. Explain what you need to do in order to describe the rights and responsibilities of employers and employees in the workplace.

5.2 Regulation of the workplace

5.2.1 Industrial relations—the state and federal framework

47. Define *industrial relations*.

48. In regard to industrial relations, to what does the 'state and federal framework' refer?

49. Explain, using statistics, how the use of the corporations power in the Work Choices legislation fundamentally changed the traditional division of industrial relations power.

50. Explain why the *Fair Work Act 2009* (Cth) has even greater coverage than the Work Choices legislation.

51. Name the two main organisations under the federal industrial framework, and cite the legislation under which they operate.

52. Name the two main organisations under the NSW state industrial framework, and cite the legislation under which they operate.

53. Explain what you need to do in order to examine the legal framework for workplace law.

5.2.2 Negotiations between employers and employees

54. Identify the ways negotiations between employers and employees may take place.

55. List the steps involved in the formal bargaining process which takes place in the negotiation of federal enterprise agreements.

56. Explain what is meant by the term *bargain in good faith*.

57. List the types of industrial action taken by employees.

58. List the types of industrial action taken by employers.

59. List the criteria which must be met for industrial action to be protected under the *Fair Work Act 2009* (Cth).

60. Citing a relevant example, explain when the Fair Work Commission may suspend protected industrial action.

61. Describe three consequences of taking unprotected industrial action.

5.2.3 Dispute resolution mechanisms

62. Define an *industrial dispute*.

63. List four dispute resolution mechanisms that can be used in the workplace.

64. Explain how industrial relations legislation encourages resolution of disputes in individual workplaces.

65. List the steps involved in a typical workplace dispute settling mechanism.

66. Explain the significance of the case of *Woolworths Ltd trading as Produce and Recycling Distribution Centre* (2010) FWAFB 1464 (26 February 2010).

67. Identify circumstances under which mediation may be used.

68. Describe the process of conciliation, and its possible outcomes.

69. Describe the process of arbitration, and its outcome.

70. What place does compulsory arbitration have in today's industrial landscape?

71. Give one reason why it could be said that industrial dispute resolution mechanisms in Australia are effective.

72. Explain what you need to do in order to evaluate the effectiveness of dispute resolution processes.

5.2.4 The roles of courts and other agencies

73. Name three types of legal institutions and four non-legal agencies that have a role in workplace regulation.

74. Name the federal and state tribunals that operate in the field of industrial relations.

75. Name six functions of the federal industrial relations tribunal.

76. Identify four functions of the NSW industrial tribunal.

77. Name the state and federal courts that have jurisdiction in industrial matters.

78. List two functions of the Fair Work Ombudsman.

79. List three functions of NSW Industrial Relations.

80. List four ways in which a trade union represents workers individually.

81. List four ways in which a trade union represents workers collectively.

82. Describe the ACTU and its primary functions.

83. How do union membership figures today compare with those of the 1950s?

84. List eight factors which might account for the diminishing power of unions.

85. Define *industry association* and give an example.

86. List six roles of employer associations.

87. Name the main two types of NGOs that have a role in workplace relations.

88. With an example, describe how the media can be influential in workplace matters.

89. Explain what you need to do in order to assess the role of the legal system in regulating the workplace.

5.2.5 Remuneration

90. Name the three main ways remuneration is determined in Australia.

91. List and briefly explain four principles that have been used in determining national wage levels.

92. List five considerations the Minimum Wage Panel must take into consideration when making its determinations.

93. Summarise the Annual Wage Review 2009–10 decision.

94. List eight factors which determine the level of an individual's wage or salary.

95. Define *penalty rate*, *casual loading*, *part-time loading*, *overtime* and *allowances*.

96. Briefly describe how the superannuation guarantee scheme works and cite the relevant legislation.

97. Explain what you need to do in order to outline how remuneration is determined.

5.2.6 The effectiveness of legal and non-legal responses in protecting and recognising workplace rights

98. Explain what you need to do in order to evaluate the effectiveness of legal and non-legal responses in protecting and recognising workplace rights.

99. List nine legal responses for protecting and recognising workplace rights.

100. List five non-legal responses for protecting and recognising workplace rights.

5.3 Contemporary issues concerning the workplace

5.3.1 Discrimination

101. Define *discrimination*.

102. Name the legislation, both in NSW and federally, which prohibits discrimination in the workplace.

103. What is meant by *adverse action*?

104. On what grounds is adverse action illegal and under what legislation?

105. Describe the first step that should be taken by someone who feels he or she has been discriminated against in the workplace?

106. Name the organisations with the power to conciliate a discrimination grievance.

107. Name the bodies which have the power to make a determination about a discrimination grievance.

108. Explain the significance of the Wongtas Pty Ltd case (2010).

109. Explain the powers of the Australian Human Rights Commission in matters of workplace discrimination.

110. Describe the penalties under federal and NSW state law that can be applied to employers who discriminate.

111. Describe the most far reaching affirmative action program and name the legislation which governs it.

112. List legal and non-legal responses to the issue of discrimination in the workplace.

113. Explain what you need to do in order to identify and investigate the contemporary issue of workplace discrimination, and evaluate the effectiveness of legal and non-legal responses to this issue.

5.3.2 Safety

114. Define *safety* in regard to the workplace.

115. Explain what, under the common law, employers must refrain from doing in the workplace to ensure the safety of their employees.

116. Name the four common law duties of employers in ensuring the safety of their workers.

117. Explain what is meant by the common law duty to work with due skill and care.

118. Identify the main legislation that imposes workplace safety obligations on employers and employees in NSW.

119. Outline the obligations of employers and employees under the act you identified in Question 118.

120. List the types of penalties that can be imposed for failure to comply with the laws regarding workplace safety.

121. List seven factors that continue to hamper workplace safety in Australia.

122. Explain the aim of workers compensation.

123. List the main pieces of legislation which establish and administer workers compensation in NSW.

124. Outline when workers compensation is payable and to whom it can be paid.

125. Define *significant injury*.

126. Describe the obligations of the employer, employee and insurer if an employee suffers a significant injury in the course of employment.

127. Outline the role of SafeWork NSW and the Workers Compensation Commission.

128. Describe injury management plans and the circumstances under which they are made.

129. Briefly describe the likely future direction of workplace safety laws in Australia.

130. List legal and non-legal responses to the issue of safety in the workplace.

131. Explain what you need to do in order to identify and investigate the contemporary issue of workplace safety, and evaluate the effectiveness of legal and non-legal responses to this issue.

5.3.3 Termination of employment

132. Define *retirement*.

133. Briefly explain the two measures taken by the federal government to encourage people to retire at a later age.

134. Explain why the federal government wishes people to retire at a later age.

135. Define *resignation*.

136. Define *notice*.

137. Define *dismissal*.

138. Identify the circumstances which may lead to summary dismissal.

139. Name three circumstances in which it is lawful to dismiss an employee.

140. List four circumstances which will be examined to determine if a dismissal is unfair.

141. Explain why federal law is relevant to most workers who feel they have been unfairly dismissed.

142. Explain how the *Fair Work Act 2009* represents a major reform to the unfair dismissal laws that operated under Work Choices.

143. List seven reasons for termination of employment that render a dismissal unlawful.

144. Explain to whom laws about unlawful termination of employment apply and how this differs from unfair dismissal laws.

145. List the two bodies that can deal with allegations of unlawful termination of employment.

146. List four possible consequences for an employer who unlawfully dismisses an employee.

147. Describe how much redundancy pay is available to retrenched workers under federal law.

148. List the payments to which a retrenched worker may be entitled.

149. List four categories of employee who are not entitled to redundancy pay.

150. State two factors which must be present for a redundancy to be genuine.

151. Identify the federal legislation that governs redundancies and explain why it makes a distinction between genuine and non-genuine redundancies.

152. Give the full name of GEERS and describe what it can do.

153. List legal and non-legal responses to the issue of termination of employment.

154. Explain what you need to do in order to identify and investigate the contemporary issue of termination of employment, and evaluate the effectiveness of legal and non-legal responses to this issue.

5.3.4 Leave

155. Define *leave*.

156. List three legal instruments which grant leave to employees.

157. Cite the legal instrument which provides minimum leave entitlements to the majority of Australian employees.

158. List the types of leave provided for under the NES.

159. Explain what it means to *cash out* leave.

160. List two types of leave that can be cashed out.

161. Identify the purposes for which personal leave can be taken.

162. Explain the NES entitlement to personal leave for full-time employees, part-time employees and casual employees.

163. Provide three examples of activities that constitute legitimate reasons for taking community service leave.

164. Explain the status of long service leave under the NES.

165. Cite the NSW legislation that governs long service leave, and explain to whom it applies.

166. What is the entitlement to unpaid parental leave under the NES?

167. Identify when paid parental leave was introduced in Australia and under what legislation.

168. Briefly explain three tests which must be passed for a person to be eligible for paid parental leave.

169. Explain the relationship between paid parental leave and the NES entitlement to parental leave.

170. Outline the entitlements of casual workers to paid and unpaid leave.

171. Explain how casual employees are compensated for their lack of leave entitlements.

172. List legal and non-legal responses to the workplace issue of leave.

173. Explain what you need to do in order to identify and investigate the contemporary workplace issue of leave, and evaluate the effectiveness of legal and non-legal responses to this issue.

5.4 Themes and challenges

5.4.1 Theme 1: The role of the law in encouraging cooperation and resolving conflict in the workplace

174. Identify six ways that the law encourages cooperation in the workplace.

175. Identify six dispute settling mechanisms provided by the law for resolving conflict in the workplace.

176. Identify seven bodies which resolve workplace disputes, and briefly explain the function of each.

5.4.2 Theme 2: Issues of compliance and non-compliance

177. List five reasons why there is sometimes a lack of compliance with workplace safety laws.

178. Account for the 16% increase in workplace deaths from 2003 to 2007.

179. Explain the effect of Work Choices on compliance with unfair dismissal laws.

180. List three possible reasons for the failure of a quarter of all AWAs to comply with the law.

181. Explain why the widespread non-compliance that took place with AWAs is unlikely under the *Fair Work Act 2009* (Cth).

182. Describe the effect of unions on compliance with workplace law. Give an example to illustrate your answer.

5.4.3 Theme 3: Laws relating to the workplace as a reflection of changing values and ethical standards

183. Explain the values and ethical standards reflected in most state intervention in workplace law throughout Australia's history.

184. Outline the conflict of ideologies apparent in government approaches to industrial relations laws in Australia since 1996.

5.4.4 Theme 4: The role of law reform in recognising rights and enforcing responsibilities in the workplace

185. List seven important reforms to industrial relations law in Australia introduced by the *Fair Work Act 2009* (Cth).

186. Explain how the Scholem case exemplifies the power of the courts to bring about law reform.

187. List four factors which lead to law reform and give one example of each.

188. List four reforms that have been introduced in the area of workplace law in recent years because of failure, or perceived failure, of existing law.

5.4.5 Theme 5: The effectiveness of legal and non-legal responses in achieving justice in the workplace

189. List seven areas of workplace law which you could discuss when evaluating the effectiveness of legal and non-legal responses in achieving justice in the workplace.

190. List twelve areas you could discuss when assessing the effectiveness of the law in recognising and protecting workplace rights.

Sample HSC questions

Now for the real thing! The following questions are modelled on the types of questions you will face in the HSC. Think about it: if you get extensive practice at answering these sorts of questions, you will be more confident in answering them when it comes to the HSC Exam. It makes sense, doesn't it?

Another reason is that the answers given at the back of this guide are structured in a way that helps you learn strategies on how to answer HSC-like questions. This will help you aim for full marks!

For each extended-response question you will have a detailed answer with an explanation of what the question is asking you to do and also, when needed, an examiner's plan to help you get full marks with a section reference where you can find the answer in the chapter. When you mark your work, highlight any questions you found difficult and earmark these areas for extra study.

Refer to pp. 470–2 for Answers

IN THE HSC EXAM

- Material from this chapter will be examined in Section III of the exam.
- Each extended-response question in Section III is worth 25 marks. You have 45 minutes to answer each one.
- Look for the min in each section and time yourself. This tells you approximately how much time you will have to answer these questions in the HSC Exam.

EXTENDED-RESPONSE QUESTIONS   1h 30 min

- In Section III of the exam, there will be seven extended-response questions, one for each option. Each question will have two alternatives. You will be required to answer two alternatives, each on a different option.
- In your answer you will be assessed on how well you:
  - demonstrate knowledge and understanding of legal issues relevant to the question
  - communicate using relevant legal terminology and concepts
  - refer to relevant examples such as legislation, cases, media, international instruments and documents
  - present a sustained, logical and cohesive response.
- The expected length of response is around eight pages of an examination writing booklet (approximately 1000 words).

Question 1 45 min

Evaluate the effectiveness of the law in achieving justice in the workplace, with particular reference to termination of employment. (25 marks)

Question 2 45 min

Examine the extent to which laws relating to the workplace reflect changing values and ethical standards. (25 marks)

Chapter 6

World order

Principal focus

Through the use of contemporary examples, students investigate the effectiveness of legal and non-legal measures in promoting peace and resolving conflict between nation-states.

Themes and challenges

The following five themes and challenges are incorporated throughout this chapter, and are summarised in Sections 6.4.1 to 6.4.5 (pages 416–27). They are to be considered throughout your study of this topic.

1. The role of the law in encouraging cooperation and resolving conflict in regard to world order
2. Issues of compliance and non-compliance
3. The impact of changing values and ethical standards on world order
4. The role of law reform in promoting and maintaining world order
5. The effectiveness of legal and non-legal responses in promoting and maintaining world order

HSC CONTENT

The nature of world order	• discuss the concept of 'world order'.
	• outline the evolving nature of world order.
	• describe the need for world order.
	• explain the implications of the nature of conflict on achieving world order.
Responses to world order	• examine the role of sovereignty in assisting and impeding the resolution of world order.
	• explain the role of Australia's federal government in responding to world order.
	• evaluate the effectiveness of legal and non-legal measures in resolving conflict and working towards world order.
Contemporary issues concerning world order	• identify and investigate contemporary issues involving world order and evaluate the effectiveness of legal and non-legal responses to these issues.

© NSW Education Standards Authority, *Legal Studies Stage 6 Syllabus*, 2009, pp. 34–5

6.1 The nature of world order

6.1.1 The meaning of *world order*

World order refers to the creation of global relationships and maintenance of world peace. World order governs the relationships between nation-states and other global participants, including transnational corporations, regional federations, intergovernmental organisations and non-government organisations.

KCq page 418

KCq page 418

6.1.2 The need for world order

One of the major changes in world order over the last sixty years is the dramatic growth of international law, including treaties and conventions between nation-states. Without world order, and the bodies and laws that govern relationships between nations and other global participants, there would be international anarchy. This could lead to world conflict and global destruction. If there were no relations between countries, then each nation-state would stand alone, meaning global issues (such as conflicts and global warming) could not be adequately addressed. World order and nation-state interaction are also the backbone of economic interdependence and globalisation. Without world order, each nation-state would be self-reliant and much of the progress of the last five centuries would not have occurred.

CAN YOU describe the need for world order?

This subject is discussed in Section 6.1.2 above. In order to describe the need for world order, you should explain that without world order:

▶ there would be international anarchy

▶ global destruction could eventuate

▶ global issues would not be adequately addressed

▶ economic development and globalisation would not occur.

CAN YOU discuss the concept of world order?

This subject is discussed in Sections 6.1.1 and 6.1.2 above. In order to discuss the concept of world order, you should explain:

▶ that 'world order' refers to the creation and maintenance of relations between the world's nation-states

▶ the consequences of a lack of world order

▶ the concept of world order has been developed over time (see Section 6.1.3 following) and continues to evolve.

KCq page 418

6.1.3 The development of world order over time

European expansionism

Expansionism describes the situation when one nation-state pushes to increase its size or territories and/or increase its influence in the world community. Expansionism has been a feature of world order throughout history and is much of the reason for the current world order.

What is the meaning of *world order*?

Describe the need for world order.

Describe the development of world order over time.

European expansionism began in the seventeenth century and carried through until the twentieth century. The major European powers discovered new territories and claimed them as part of their 'empire' in a process known as imperialism. The territories they claimed became colonies.

The colonies were settled by the European powers. Language, forms of government, religion and institutions of the empire were put in place and the Indigenous inhabitants were often badly treated, resulting in loss of cultural identity and even violence and communal killing. The colonies were often sent to other parts of the globe to fight for their empire, as happened to Australia (a nation of former British colonies) and India (then a British colony) in World War I.

At the start of World War I, in 1914, the European powers of England, Germany, France, Belgium and Holland accounted for less than 1% of the world's surface and 8% of its population, but they ruled over one-third of the world's surface area and one-quarter of its population.

The causes of World War I and World War II were both directly linked to European expansionism, and fighting over the world's colonies. It was after World War II that most of the existing empires handed back their colonies to local rule and the colonies became independent nation-states.

The role of European expansionism is very important to how the world currently operates. Europeans established over 70% of all world borders, including the borders in much of Africa, Asia and South America. The borders they created did not take into account existing tribal groupings, and actually cut across many of them. These borders still exist today, and are part of the reason for ongoing tribal and ethnic conflict throughout the world, particularly in Africa. Another factor is that the Europeans often pulled out of the colonies after they had stripped them of much of their wealth and natural resources. Colonies were often left with poor infrastructure and with political and economic systems imposed upon them by the colonial power.

Impact of imperialism on indigenous peoples and local communities

The United Nations estimates there are 370 million indigenous people from over 5000 groups living in more than seventy countries around the world. All indigenous peoples have suffered at the hands of their governments, most due to the impact of European expansion. Many indigenous groups have had their native lands taken away, had their original culture destroyed and have been attacked by weapons and disease. Indigenous peoples the world over are still suffering: Indian tribal groups live below the poverty line, and the average life expectancy of an Aboriginal Australian is 20 years lower than that of a non-Aboriginal Australian.

Expansionist activity is now on the decrease, and the numbers and conditions of indigenous peoples are on the rise. Indigenous groups are increasingly finding a political voice in their own nation-states and globally. The United Nations has played a role in this. It created the Working Group on Indigenous Populations in 1982 to investigate the rights of the world's indigenous peoples. In 2002, a permanent United Nations body was established, the Permanent Forum on Indigenous Issues.

The rise of the US 'empire'

A *unipolar world* means there is one dominant power. Since the Cold War ended in 1991, the US has risen to superpower status and many world commentators see this as the time of the American 'empire'. This belief has increased since September 11 2001, with US actions, including invading Afghanistan and Iraq, viewed by some as being expansionist. History shows that when there is only one power in a dominant position, another power or powers will rise to challenge it, thereby creating a world where there are two or more dominant powers—a multipolar world. International commentators say that the US dominance cannot last and that emerging powers, such as China, Russia, Japan and the European Union, will come to the fore. It is always a period of uncertainty in international affairs when a major power is challenged, and this could well pose a problem to the current world order.

The rise of the transnational corporation

A transnational corporation is one that engages in foreign investment and owns, or controls, activities in more than one nation-state. Examples include Microsoft, McDonalds, Coca-Cola and Ikea. Transnational corporations have become extremely powerful and are a major global economic force. Corporations can decide to move jobs off-shore in search of cheaper wages or buy local business if there are government restrictions on imports. Actions such as these mean that such corporations wield more economic power than the traditional nation-state. Transnationals are extremely wealthy; the top 200 world corporations hold double the economic power of the bottom 80% of humanity.

Interdependence

All nation-states are becoming increasingly dependent on each other in many ways. They need to work together to improve themselves and the conditions of their people. Nation-states cooperate to fight against common threats, such as war, disease, human trafficking, the drug trade, terrorism, global warming, pollution and famine. Nation-states are realising that, to prosper, indeed to survive, they need to work with each other. Interdependence also means nation-states cooperating for their mutual benefit, chiefly in the area of trade. The increase in global trade and economic cooperation over the last thirty years is part of the phenomenon of globalisation.

Globalisation

The nation-state is not the only player in the newly globalised world. In the era of globalisation there is cooperation and influence from transnational corporations, intergovernmental organisations (such as the United Nations), non-government organisations (such as environmental organisations, political organisations, humanitarian charities and lobby groups) and individuals. Transnational corporations are making global profits. Trade between nation-states is thriving. Intergovernmental and non-government organisations are working on global political issues, for example global warming and debt forgiveness for Africa's debt. Individuals are also going global, due to the advent of international travel and instant international communications systems, such as the internet.

Development of global efforts to prevent war

The international community has been working on a collective solution to prevent war and maintain a peaceful world order for centuries. Table 6.1 on the next page summarises the most important international efforts towards limiting war in society.

Table 6.1 Efforts towards limiting war

Year	Name	Signatories	Purposes
1648	Treaty of Westphalia	▶ The Holy Roman Emperor, the King of France, and allies	▶ Developed the nation-state. ▶ Gave nation-states protection in international law.
1815	Concert of Europe	▶ Britain, Austria, Prussia and Russia	▶ A result of the Napoleonic Wars. ▶ Agreement to maintain stability and prevent further outbreaks of war.
1899 and 1907	The Hague Peace Conferences	▶ Twenty-five European powers	▶ Adopted the Convention for the Pacific Settlement of International Disputes. ▶ States were to use their best efforts to ensure the peaceful settlement of disputes. ▶ Introduced the Permanent Court of Arbitration which made fifteen decisions between 1899 and 1914. ▶ Tried to implement a 'cooling-off' period before nations entered a conflict. ▶ Initiatives fell apart with the outbreak of World War I in 1914.
1919	The League of Nations Covenant	▶ Forty-one nations, including the US, UK, China, France, Greece, Italy and Japan.	▶ Established the League of Nations. ▶ Chief aim was to achieve international peace and security. ▶ Built upon the concepts of mediation and arbitration. ▶ Required all member countries to exhaust all alternatives before resorting to war. ▶ The League of Nations fell apart and could not prevent World War II in 1939.
1928	Pact of Paris (or the Kellogg-Briand Pact)	▶ Sixty-five states signed, including seven that were not members of the League of Nations	▶ The first agreement to renounce war. ▶ Not applicable to non-members. ▶ No mechanism for compliance. ▶ Is still referred to today.
1941	Atlantic Charter	▶ Drawn up by Winston Churchill (UK) and Franklin Roosevelt (US). ▶ Agreed to by World War II allied nation-states.	▶ US and UK pledged to create a world of peace and stability. ▶ Stated that the allied states would seek no territories (colonies or lands) after World War II. ▶ Freedom of the seas. ▶ All nation-states can choose their form of government, have safe boundaries and have access to trade. ▶ Abandonment of use of force and establishment of league of nation-states.
1945	Charter of the United Nations	▶ Fifty-one founding members. ▶ Now 192 members.	▶ Established the United Nations. ▶ Outlawed the use of force except in self defence or through resolutions by the Security Council. ▶ Article 2(3): 'All Members shall settle their international disputes by peaceful means…' ▶ Article 2(4): 'All members shall refrain in their international relations from the threat of use of force…'
1949	Geneva Conventions	▶ 188 signatories (in 1949) ▶ 156 signatories to the two 1977 Additional Protocols	▶ Introduced the international rules of war. ▶ Outlined the humanitarian treatment of wounded military personnel, prisoners of war and civilians caught in conflict.
1968	Nuclear Non-Proliferation Treaty	▶ 189 signatories (all nation-states except India, Pakistan and Israel who have never signed it; and North Korea who formally withdrew in 2003)	▶ Nation-states are prohibited from buying or building new nuclear weapons. ▶ It has commitment from five states that have nuclear weapons to work towards disarmament.

CAN YOU **outline the evolving nature of world order?**

This is discussed in Section 6.1.3 (pages 371–4). In order to outline the evolving nature of world order, you should:

▶ explain that world order is constantly evolving and must continue to do so as new challenges to resolving conflict and maintaining peace arise

▶ outline major world events and international instruments (such as treaties, conventions and declarations) that are essential to explain the evolution of world order to the present day

▶ explain that the evolution of world order is also due to constantly emerging ethics, morality and values held by nation-states and their citizens. See Section 6.4.3 (pages 404–6).

▶ describe the current challenges to maintaining world order, such as terrorism, the threat of nuclear warfare and nuclear non-proliferation measures, wars in Iraq and Afghanistan, civil war in Sudan, the emerging threat of hostilities between North Korea and South Korea, and continuing evidence of war crimes such as genocide and communal killing. See Section 6.3.2 (pages 394–8).

▶ explain that international bodies (such as the United Nations) and instruments (including treaties, conventions and declarations) must continue to evolve (within the constraints of the Westphalian system of state sovereignty and consensual law) in order to create new solutions to world order issues. Current law reform issues are discussed in Section 6.4.4 (pages 406–7).

 KCq page 418

6.1.4 The nature of conflict

There are two main types of international conflict: inter-state and intra-state. Intra-state conflict is between opposing sides in the same nation-state. Inter-state conflict is between two or more different nation-states. This section examines the various forms of inter-state and intra-state conflict.

What forms of conflict disrupt world order?

Guerrilla warfare

This is one of the oldest forms of conflict, because it requires little training, and unsophisticated weapons. Guerrilla fighters normally form small groups, use simple weapons (such as farming tools), and operate using the element of surprise. They are familiar with the land, do not have uniforms and are difficult to find. Their tactics are to harass the enemy, attack small targets and then retreat. They repeat this tactic until the enemy is worn down. Guerrilla fighting is the oldest form of warfare, and was used in Roman times and throughout the Middle Ages. It is successfully used in both intra-state and inter-state conflicts. It was also used, with great success, by the Vietcong against the US Army in the Vietnam War (1954–75).

Conventional warfare

World War I and World War II were both conventional inter-state conflicts. A conventional war is one in which there are professional armies and large, well organised military forces from nation-states fighting against the armies of other nation-states. There are large numbers of troops who fight in units and use extensive amounts of equipment. Conventional warfare originated in the seventeenth century and, until World War I, involved mainly humans fighting against humans using hand-held weapons. As the technology for bombs, land mines and aeroplanes developed, so did the way conventional war was waged.

Conventional warfare is very expensive, due to the weaponry used and the expense of maintaining professional soldiers. Since the 1960s, all conventional wars that resulted in a clear victory have been won in less than six weeks (such as the Gulf War in 1990–91). This is due to the fact that conventional wars now need so much equipment, and are so expensive, that governments cannot hold large reserves. If there has not been a clear victory after that crucial six week period, then the conflict drags on (such as the situations in Iraq and Afghanistan).

Border conflict

As we know, a nation-state is defined by its geographical borders, often created under the European imperial system. Inter-state conflict arises when a nation-state does not recognise the borders of its neighbours and both parties lay 'claim' to an area of land. There are continuing border disputes between Israel and Palestine over the West Bank, and between India and Pakistan over Kashmir.

Nuclear warfare

The huge death tolls of the first and second world wars led to the search for stronger weapons—so strong that they would achieve a quick, clear victory. This led to the creation of nuclear power and the atomic bomb. Atomic bombs have only been used twice in history, when they were dropped on the Japanese cities of Hiroshima and Nagasaki in August 1945. This resulted in an immediate end to World War II and the defeat of the Japanese.

While the bomb that can bring quick victories has been found, it is far too powerful for nation-states to actually use. During the Cold War it was estimated that the US and the USSR possessed over 50 000 nuclear weapons. If either side had used only a few hundred of these then the planet would have been devastated.

Cold War

The Cold War was an ongoing inter-state conflict which began after World War II, when the threat of nuclear warfare breaking out was very real. The Cold War ran from 1947 to 1991 and the name refers to the uneasy peace maintained between the two world superpowers—communist USSR and capitalist US. They were rivals on all levels—politics, economics, even sport—and they each called upon their allies to wage war. This was an uneasy time in the world, because each superpower was racing to create more nuclear weapons than the other.

International instruments

Testing of nuclear weapons by the USSR and US ended in 1963, when they signed the Limited Test Ban Treaty. The chief international treaty in this area is the Treaty on the Non-Proliferation of Nuclear Weapons (NNPT) (1968), which prohibits nation-states that do not already have nuclear weapons from buying or building them.

The impact of nuclear warfare on the current world order is outlined in Section 6.3.2 (page 396).

Chemical and biological warfare

Chemical weapons are weapons which use chemicals (such as nerve gas) to cause harm. Biological warfare refers to the release of agents, like bacteria or viruses, into a population. Chemical warfare was used during World War I and the Vietnam War, in conjunction with more traditional weapons, such as guns, fighter aircraft and bombs. Those soldiers exposed to nerve gas in World War I and Agent Orange in Vietnam suffered effects long after the battles were over. Chemical and biological warfare have not been used often, and usually in inter-state conflicts, but the technology is available for this type of warfare to cause large scale human destruction.

Civil warfare

Civil war is the most basic definition of intra-state conflict—a war between two or more sides within one nation-state. There have been many civil wars throughout history, with the American Civil War (1861–65) and the war in Lebanon in the 1980s being two prominent examples. Civil wars are becoming more prominent as conventional wars decline.

Democide

Democide is another example of intra-state conflict. This refers to the situation when the nation-state wages war on its own people, and includes genocide, mass killing, death squads and state sponsored terror. The most infamous case of democide was the genocide of the Jewish peoples by Nazi Germany in World War II. This began in Germany and then carried over to all nation-states occupied by Germany, and resulted in the deaths of over 6 million Jews.

Communal killing

Communal killing is the term used to describe violence and killing within communities in the nation-state. It is another form of intra-state conflict, and is mainly due to political, economic, social, religious or ethnic differences. Communal killing has been on the increase since the end of the Cold War in the 1990s because, during that time, the two world superpowers (the US and the USSR) could exert some control over the groups within their power. At the end of the Cold War, the former communist state of Yugoslavia was broken into three states: Bosnia, Serbia and Croatia. Mass killing occurred there in the early 1990s. The end of European colonialism has also meant the rival groups in these countries are no longer being 'controlled' by a colonial force.

The African nation-states of Somalia (1993) and Rwanda (1994) experienced communal killing, and it seems certain that communal killing and genocide has been occurring in the Darfur region of Sudan since 2003.

Terrorism

Terrorism is the deliberate use of violence by an individual or group against the enemy in order to provoke fear. The 'enemy' in terrorism can be difficult to define—it can be nation-states, rulers or their governments; an ethnic or religious group; or international concepts, such as communism or democracy. The 'type' of conflict is also difficult to define—it can be either inter-state (for example, the 11 September attacks by the Taliban on the US in 2001) or intra-state (for example, IRA terrorism in Northern Ireland throughout the twentieth century). Terrorists often deliberately attack civilians and civilian infrastructure as their main way to instil terror in the community, such as in the Bali bombings of 2002 and 2005, which targeted a major tourist destination in order to attack Western governments.

State-sponsored terror is what occurs when terrorist activity is supported by a nation-state. Terrorist groups can also operate without the support of any nation-states and across boundaries. What is common to all is that they operate outside international law.

The impact of terrorism in the current world order is outlined in Section 6.3.2 (pages 394–5).

CAN YOU **explain the implications of the nature of conflict on achieving world order?**

In order to do this, you need to:

▶ explain the different types of conflict, as described in Section 6.1.4 (pages 375–7)

▶ discuss the following points about the attempts of nations to control these different types of conflict

- • more 'traditional' types of conflicts, such as conventional warfare, civil war and border conflict, are governed by a large body of international law developed over a long period of time. This includes humanitarian law which governs the conduct of war (see Section 6.3.4, pages 400–1).

- nuclear warfare is also closely governed and controlled by the United Nations and international organisations and there are several conventions and treaties aimed at this (see Sections 6.1.4 [page 390] and 6.3.2 [page 410]).

- genocide, democide and communal killing can also be classified as a traditional form of warfare and are clearly governed by international law. This body of law has not successfully prevented genocide.

- chemical and biological warfare is constantly evolving as new methods of conducting such warfare are discovered. While there is a large body of international law in this area it must be constantly reviewed.

- terrorism is proving to be the most challenging type of conflict in the current world order. The very definition of terrorism makes it a challenge because traditional methods of governing the disputes between separate nation-states do not apply. The treatment of terrorists once they are captured is also a challenge to conventional international law because it can be argued that humanitarian law does not apply (see Section 6.3.2, pages 394–5).

 KCq page 418

6.1.5 Access to resources as a source of conflict

Explain how access to resources between nation-states can be a major source of conflict.

The economic inequality between states is one of the major issues facing the current world order, particularly as traditional state boundaries are broken down by globalisation in areas of trade and investment. Access to and sharing of resources globally is a source of ongoing conflict in developing nations, particularly in former African colonies and in South America. Many factors have led to the fact that poorer states are not accessing resources and creating wealth to the same extent as wealthy, developed nations. These factors include:

▶ the behaviour of unethical transnationals and corrupt corporations

▶ corrupt regimes and undemocratic and repressive governments

▶ the legacy of imperialism and repression of Indigenous populations

▶ inequitable free trade laws and the sanctioning of unjust trade practices.

The fact that poorer states are not accessing resources and creating wealth to the same extent as wealthy, developed nations results in widespread and disproportionate intra-state and inter-state conflict, as well as flow-on global effects, such as illegal immigration, people trafficking, organised crime and human rights infractions.

Addressing inequality

One of the criticisms of globalisation is the view that it is actually making wealthier nations richer, and poorer nations poorer. Inequitable free trade laws, in which wealthier states ensure that some industries and production are protected while developing nations are asked to free up all trade barriers, are a factor in the unequal allocation of resources.

Many non-government organisations and grassroots movements are focused on addressing the economic inequality of poor states (mostly in Africa and South America) compared to wealthy nations (the 'Western' states). In 2005, three billion people attended simultaneous 'Live Aid' concerts throughout the world in an attempt to convince the G8 leaders to cancel African foreign debt—debt which is debilitating to the affected nations and their peoples. The G8 stands for the Group of Eight, which is an organisation of the nation-states who are among the largest economies in the world. The G8 consists of: The United States, the United Kingdom, France, Russia, Canada, Germany, Italy and Japan. This 'Live Aid' movement led to the leaders promising some reduction of

African debt. By 2010, the World Bank and International Monetary Fund (IMF) had approved debt reduction packages for thirty-five countries (twenty-nine of them in Africa) to provide US$51 billion in debt-service relief over time—a long, ongoing process.

The European Union is an example of how a regional organisation can lift the political and economic status of smaller states within it. For example, states such as Ireland and Spain were struggling on the economic world stage prior to their inclusion in the EU—but both nations went through a major economic revival prior to the global financial crisis of 2008–09. The collapse of the Greek economy in 2010, and the subsequent bail-out by the remainder of the EU-currency countries (led by Germany), is an example of larger states assisting smaller states in the event of a crisis. Conversely, it also demonstrates how the economic weakness of Greece has weakened the entire EU financially and led to uncertainty about the future of the organisation.

Foreign aid

Over forty years ago, wealthy United Nations member states agreed to give 0.7% of their gross national product to foreign aid, but many do not reach this target. It is not mandated or enforced and is a suggested target only. There is pressure on rich nations and federations (such as the EU) to provide more aid and funds for development. Well-targeted aid and re-examining trade inequalities may well assist in a more equitable division of resources between states and, in turn, lead to less conflict within the poorer states.

Behaviour of transnationals

The unethical practices of some transnationals are also a factor in the uneven distribution of resources across the world. Some of these companies move their manufacturing operations to countries where the population can be easily exploited and the country itself gains no benefits from the huge profits made by the company. See Case Study 6.1 below.

CASE STUDY 6.1: Coca-Cola and the use of child labour in El Salvador, 2004

'Coca-Cola is indirectly benefiting from the use of child labour in sugarcane fields in El Salvador, according to a new report by Human Rights Watch (HRW), which is calling on the company to take more responsibility to ensure that such abuses are halted'.

Background

By the 1990s sugar, which was produced mainly by state-owned plantations, had become El Salvador's second largest export crop after coffee. In 1995, the industry was privatised. Human Rights Watch (HRW) found, in 2004, that between 5000 and 30 000 Salvadoran children (some as young as eight years old) were working in the sugarcane fields, where injuries such as burns and severe cuts and gashes are common.

Issue

Coca-Cola does not own or buy directly from any of these plantations but its local bottler buys sugar from the central Salvadoran refinery which is supplied by some of these plantations. Coca-Cola has said that neither it, nor its local bottler, has any contracts with these plantations and so is not responsible for the use of child labour.

Action

The HRW has argued that Coca-Cola has known that child labour is used and that it benefits from the cheaper price of sugar which results. Coca-Cola responded to the report by saying they would work with the ILO (International Labour Organisation) to help families involved in Salvadoran sugarcane cultivation.

Source: 'Sweet and Sour' by Jim Lobe, Corpwatch, 2 June 2004 (www.corpwatch.org).

Corruption

The existence of corrupt governments and transnationals means that resources are being unevenly shared across society, which generally results in poverty and hardship for individuals in the community. Corruption is an issue mostly in developing states, particularly in the former colonies of Africa, and is a source of ongoing intra-state and inter-state conflict.

Wealthy countries experience corruption as well, often through the actions of large corporations. For example, the corrupt activities that led to the collapse of Enron in 2002 in the US meant many thousands of Enron employees lost their retirement savings. Unlike developing nations, the corruption of transnationals in wealthy nations does not lead to large scale internal conflict. This is because developed nations have the necessary infrastructure, resources and social systems to ensure that the corrupt actions of a few do not impact upon the nation-state as a whole.

The international community and international law have taken huge steps in improving equality of resource allocation between nation-states in terms of human rights, resources and economic wealth since World War II. However, there is still a lot of work to be done. **KCq** page 418

6.2 Responses to world order

World order is maintained using the following legal and non-legal measures, all operating under the constraints of nation-state sovereignty:

▶ the United Nations
▶ international instruments (declarations and treaties)
▶ international courts and tribunals
▶ intergovernmental organisations (IGOs)
▶ non-government organisations (NGOs)
▶ the Australian federal government
▶ the media
▶ political negotiation and persuasion
▶ force.

6.2.1 The role of the nation-state and state sovereignty

State sovereignty is the underlying concept of the Westphalian nation-state system and is enshrined in the UN Charter. State sovereignty means that each nation-state has the absolute right to control its own affairs within its borders and is not obligated to listen to any outside authority. This is the basis of current world order.

Governments send delegates to represent them at conferences and meetings of international organisations, to debate and to sign international treaties and agreements. It is the governments of the nation-states that decide to sign a treaty and then to implement it into their domestic law, so it becomes applicable in their states. All nation-states are equal under international law, meaning that each nation-state has one vote in the UN and, no matter their size, they have equal rights to sovereignty, their territory and the freedom to run their own country.

The key to a sovereign state is that the national government has the right of control over its own affairs. Sovereign states have the right to refuse to sign treaties and other international instruments. They have the right

Examine the role of state sovereignty in the creation and resolution of world order issues.

to refuse to join international organisations, even the UN (although all 192 states are currently members, except for one non-member observer which is the Holy See).

It has, however, been recognised that there are times when it is legitimate for the international community to intervene in the domestic affairs of a nation, for example when mass atrocities are being carried out on sections of the population. The principles of the 'Responsibility to Protect' and humanitarian intervention provisions allow for international intervention in a sovereign state in such circumstances (see Section 6.3.1, page 392).

CAN YOU **examine the role of sovereignty in assisting and impeding the resolution of world order issues?**

In order to do this, you should explain the following:

State sovereignty and the absolute independence of the nation-state is a major obstacle to accepting world order agreements and maintaining world order, because the activities of nation-states impact on others. For example, where pollution or disease crosses over into neighbouring states, or where a state allows a human rights abuse or internal conflict to occur, other states often want to intervene. The right of a state to create nuclear weapons, although against international law, has the potential to threaten all nation-states.

However, most nation-states follow most international law most of the time. This is for two main reasons:

▶ the idea of reciprocity, which means nations comply with international agreements because they want other nations to do the same

▶ the idea of legal responsibility, which means that nations want to be seen as law-abiding by other nations.

In addition, the right of the international community to intervene in the domestic affairs of a nation is recognised in some circumstances (see Section 6.3.2, pages 394–8).

So, while state sovereignty has the potential to impede the resolution of world order issues, the ideas of reciprocity and legal responsibility assist in resolving world order issues because both ideas encourage sovereign states to resolve issues in their dealings with other nations.

World government

One world government would replace the current system of nation-states. It would have the power to enact laws and, unlike the UN, the power to enforce them. It would have a legislature, a police force and leaders. Supporters of a world government say that, with the increase of interdependence and the rise of issues needing a 'global' solution, the current world order of nation-states will become ineffective.

The idea of a world government is usually criticised. There is a real risk of an undemocratic leader or dictator gaining power and exerting global domination. Individual histories and tensions, cultural and language differences may all be lost. At this stage, the dangers associated with creating one world government outweigh the advantages. **KCq** page 418

6.2.2 The role of the United Nations

The United Nations is the most important body in maintaining world order and was established after World War II. It is the world 'association' of nation-states. It enforces treaties by imposing sanctions, has a judicial

Describe the role and functions of the United Nations in maintaining world order.

arm in the International Court of Justice (ICJ) as discussed in Section 6.2.4 (page 384), creates declarations and customary law, registers treaties, makes decisions on world order issues, and fosters economic and social cooperation between nation-states.

Principles

The UN came into existence in October 1945. After World War II, the allies created the Charter of the United Nations (United Nations Charter). This was agreed to in 1945 by fifty countries. It became effective when the Perm-5 nations of the US, UK, France, China and the USSR (now Russia), and a majority of nations, ratified it on 24 October 1945. The UN had fifty-one foundation members—by 2010 there were 192 member states.

Article 1 of the United Nations Charter outlines the purposes of the UN, which are to:

▶ maintain international peace and security
▶ develop friendly relations between nation-states and strengthen universal peace
▶ achieve international cooperation in solving international problems of a social, economic, cultural or humanitarian nature
▶ promote respect for human rights.

The UN is to achieve these purposes by following the core principles as outlined in the charter, including:

▶ all member states have full, and equal, sovereignty
▶ all members will settle disputes through peaceful means
▶ all members will refrain from force, or the threat of force, against the territorial boundaries or political independence of any state
▶ members will not intervene in the domestic matters of any state (subject to enforcement measures outlined in Chapter VII of the Charter, as discussed in Section 6.3.1, pages 392–3).

The United Nations Charter can only be amended by a two-thirds vote of the member states in the General Assembly and all Perm-5 members of the Security Council.

Structure

The UN has six organs as shown in Figure 6.1: The General Assembly, the Security Council, the International Court of Justice (ICJ), the Economic and Social Council (ECOSOC), the Secretariat, and the Trusteeship Council.

KCq page 418

6.2.3 The role of international instruments

An international instrument is a source of international law, such as a treaty or declaration. A treaty is a written legal agreement between nation-states, and treaties between nation-states are one of the main ways of maintaining world order. Treaties are also called statutes, protocols, covenants or conventions. They are binding on the nation-states that ratify them, and treaty disputes can be settled by the UN and the International Court of Justice (ICJ). To *ratify* a treaty means that a nation-state agrees to ensure that its domestic laws will be implemented to incorporate the requirements of the treaty or international agreement.

Treaties can be made between two nations (bilateral) or between many nations (multilateral). Article 102 of the United Nations Charter requires all treaties to be registered by the UN and there have been over 158 000 treaties and agreements registered since 1946 (some of which are no longer active). There are currently over 500 registered major multilateral treaties.

Describe the role of international instruments and international customary law in maintaining world order.

Figure 6.1 The organs of the United Nations

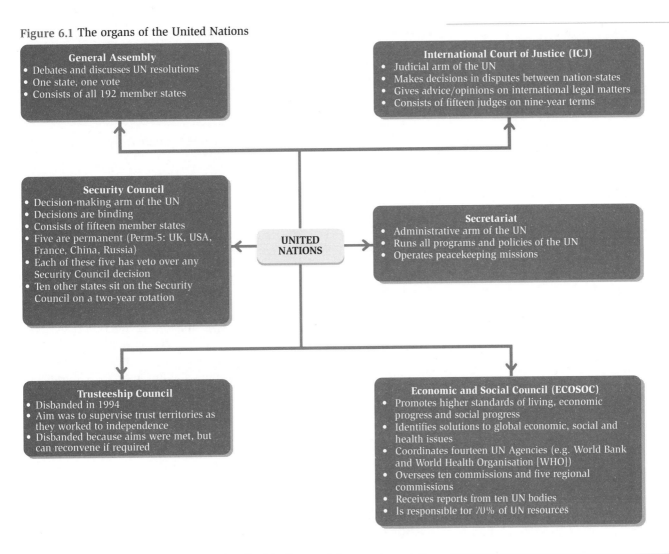

Unlike a treaty, a declaration is not legally binding and does not carry the force of law. A declaration is a formal statement, usually made by the UN General Assembly, outlining a set of values considered to be universally applicable. Nation-states can take the values in a declaration and incorporate them into domestic law. Declarations are also useful because ascertaining whether a nation-state is taking action to support the values in a particular declaration can be the starting point for negotiating a treaty.

International customary law

International customary law is a source of international law drawn from the common practices of governments which, over a period of time, become accepted as legally binding.

Most international customary law has now been incorporated into treaties and declarations, such as the 1984 Convention Against Torture and Other Cruel, Inhuman or Degrading Treatment or Punishment. Human rights and international humanitarian law are part of international customary law.

The chief difference between customary law and treaty law is that customary law is binding on all states, whether they have signed a corresponding treaty or not. This means all nation-states are subject to it. **KCq** pages 418–19

6.2.4 The role of courts and tribunals

There are four types of international courts and tribunals which have a role in maintaining world order:

- the International Court of Justice (ICJ)
- the International Criminal Court (ICC)
- *ad hoc* international tribunals
- intergovernmental organisation and treaty tribunals.

International Court of Justice (ICJ)

The International Court of Justice (ICJ), which has operated since 1946, is the UN's judicial organ and is the closest court to a 'world court' currently in existence. Individuals, NGOs and corporations cannot bring disputes to the ICJ—it can only hear disputes between governments of nation-states. The ICJ can hear two types of cases, as discussed below.

Disputes between nation-states

The ICJ hears disputes between states when each of the states involved agrees to have its case submit to a ruling. Treaties often list the ICJ as having jurisdiction over disputes and, in theory, ICJ decisions are final and binding. However, this is often not the case due to state sovereignty and the consensual nature of international law. Losing states can be unwilling to abide by the decision of the ICJ, and the Security Council is reluctant to enforce the ICJ's decisions. Case Study 6.2, *Nicaragua v United States of America* (1986) ICJ 14 below, is an example of this occurring.

Advisory opinions

The ICJ can also offer a reasoned opinion on any matter of international law brought before it by the UN General Assembly. Advisory opinions are non-binding.

CASE STUDY 6.2: *Nicaragua v United States of America* (1986) ICJ 14

Background

The US was gathering intelligence using high aerial flights over Nicaragua (in Central America). It was also supporting armed rebels by flying in supplies, and was creating 'sonic booms' when aircraft broke the sound barrier.

Issue

Nicaragua claimed the US violated their sovereignty by carrying out armed attacks in their airspace, committing aerial trespass.

Decision

The ICJ found that the US had violated the Nicaraguan airspace, which was contrary to international customary law. The US was to 'cease and refrain' from the 'unlawful use of force' and pay Nicaragua reparations.

Action

The US ignored the ruling.

International Criminal Court

The International Criminal Court (ICC) is a permanent international court and can hear cases relating to the most serious of international crimes, namely genocide, war crimes and crimes against humanity (see Sections 1.6.1 [page 62] and 6.1.4 [pages 375–7]). The ICC is separate from the United Nations and was set up by the Rome Statute, a multilateral treaty.

The Rome Statute was signed by 121 nation-states, including Australia, in 1998. To become effective, the Rome Statute needed to be ratified by sixty states and the ICC began operating out of The Hague in July 2002. The ICC is the first permanent court allowing individuals to be tried for crimes against humanity. It is known as a court of 'last resort', meaning it will only hear cases if they are not being investigated or prosecuted by a national judicial system, unless the national systems are not genuine.

Although separate to the UN, the ICC operates closely with it. Cases can be referred to it in three ways:

▶ by a signatory nation-state

▶ by the UN Security Council

▶ by the ICC prosecutor.

There are limitations: Any one member of the Perm-5 can use its veto powers to stop a case being referred to the ICC; and any case referred to the iCC by the ICC Prosecutor must be approved by a three judge panel to stop politically motivated prosecutions.

As of March 2010, there were 111 parties to the Rome Statute, meaning 111 nation-states have agreed to its provisions and to the jurisdiction of the ICC. The US is not a party to the Rome Statute. The success of the ICC is discussed in Section 6.4.5 (pages 409–10) and Case Study 1.17 (Section 1.6.2, page 65).

Ad hoc international tribunals

An *ad hoc* international tribunal is created for a specific purpose and then disbanded. In recent years, there have been two UN *ad hoc* tribunals, set up by the Security Council under the rules of the United Nations Charter:

▶ the International Criminal Tribunal for the former Yugoslavia was established in 1993 to hear breaches of the Geneva Conventions (war crimes) and international customary law that were committed during the break-up of the former Yugoslavia in 1991

▶ the International Tribunal for Rwanda was set up in 1994 to hear cases of genocide committed there in 1994.

Individuals could be prosecuted for crimes against humanity in these tribunals.

Other international tribunals

International tribunals can also be established through intergovernmental organisations and treaties. Examples include:

▶ **the Court of Justice of the European Communities** (the Court of Justice), which is the formal tribunal for the EU

▶ **the European Court of Human Rights**. This has jurisdiction over human rights issues in the EU and its decisions are taken seriously by the Council of the European Union (the governing body of the EU). This court has some enforcement powers in that any EU member that does not apply with its ruling could face the sanction of being expelled from the council.

▶ **the Appellate Body of the World Trade Organisation (WTO)**, which was established in 1995, and can hear cases relating to trade disputes

▶ **the International Tribunal for the Law of the Sea**, which was established in 1994, and can examine any issue in relation to the law of the seas. It was established through the UN Convention on the Law of the Sea 1982 and parties to this treaty must use this tribunal or the ICJ to resolve disputes.

> ▶ **the International Court of Arbitration**, which was established by the 1958 New York Convention, and arbitrates on international commercial disputes between member nations.

> ▶ **the International Centre for the Settlement of Investment Disputes**, which was established by the Convention on the Settlement of Investment Disputes between States and Nationals of Other States in 1966, and can arbitrate on disputes between member nations and any investors who are nationals of other member countries. **KCq** page 419

6.2.5 The role of intergovernmental organisations

Explain the role of intergovernmental organisations in maintaining world order.

Regional intergovernmental organisations (IGOs) are powerful instruments in maintaining world order. Article 52 of the United Nations Charter encourages member states to form regional alliances and groupings. It allows regional organisations to handle matters pertaining to international peace as long as the aims of the organisation are consistent with the principles of the UN. The charter also requires member states of IGOs who are also members of the UN to settle disputes at the regional level before referring them to the UN Security Council.

There are many regional intergovernmental organisations. The European Union is the most successful and powerful IGO. Through it European countries have been joined together to share in increased wealth and security. The EU has, so far, been successful in stopping another major war in Europe, and is now bringing European influence around the world. It has twenty-seven member states, with a total population of nearly 500 million. Member states must be democracies that uphold the rule of law, respect human rights and adhere to the UN Charter in regards to the use of force.

The North Atlantic Treaty Organisation (NATO) is also a strong and powerful intergovernmental organisation which is focused on security and defence. Its member nations supply forces that can be deployed for peacekeeping missions and into conflicts. It has the same membership requirements as the EU. Case Study 6.4 in Section 6.2.9 (page 390) is one example of a successful NATO mission in the maintenance of world order. Other intergovernmental organisations are the African Union (AU), the Commonwealth, ASEAN (the Association of Southeast Asian Nations) and the Arab League. **KCq** page 419

6.2.6 The role of non-government organisations

Explain the role of non-government organisations in maintaining world order.

A non-government organisation, or NGO, is an organisation that works towards a certain cause and operates separate to any government. NGOs play a very important role in world order, were instrumental in establishing the UN Charter, and work closely with the UN and other specialised government agencies.

NGOs are very powerful political lobby groups and/or providers of humanitarian aid, promoting their causes through international and government bodies and, increasingly, the media. Over 25 000 NGOs campaign across the globe on humanitarian issues (for example Amnesty International, The International Red Cross and Red Crescent Movement, Oxfam International and Greenpeace).

The International Red Cross and Red Crescent Movement

The International Red Cross and Red Crescent Movement, one of the first NGOs, was established by Swiss banker Henry Dunant in 1859. He campaigned for an international organisation to look after the wounded in battle. The Red Cross was instrumental in establishing the Geneva

Conventions, international humanitarian law and preparing the UN Charter. It is responsible for preparing all international humanitarian law and reminds belligerents of their obligations in this area. **KCq** page 419

6.2.7 The role of Australia's federal government

Section 51, subsection 29, of the Australian Constitution refers to the external affairs power. This means that the federal government has exclusive powers over international affairs—only the Australian government can enter into international agreements. For an international agreement to be ratified, it must pass through the Australian federal parliamentary process. So it is reasonably rare for a treaty signed by Australia not to be passes through parliament and be enacted into local law, because the government of the time usually controls the parliament. However, in 2004, the bilateral Free Trade Agreement between Australian and the US was ratified by parliament only after the senate insisted on significant variations to the original agreement. In addition, several human rights treaties which Australia has signed, such as the ICCPR and the ICESCR, have not been enacted into legislation (see Section 2.2.5, page 114).

State governments cannot enter into international agreements. They, like NGOs, can lobby the federal government to sign treaties on Australia's behalf, but the federal government is under no obligation to listen to them. For example, Australia's former refusal (until late 2007) to ratify the Kyoto Protocol 1997, an international agreement linked to the United Nations Framework Convention on Climate Change, was against the wishes of the state governments. The federal government does, however, often consult the states before signing international agreements, and states can enact legislation to mirror international agreements. For example, both Victoria and the ACT have enacted Charters of Rights to put into effect principles of the ICCPR (see Section 2.2.6, page 120).

As well as entering into international agreements for Australia and passing legislation to put such agreements into effect, Australia's federal government has several other roles in maintaining world order. These include:

▶ contributing to foreign aid (see Section 6.1.5, page 379)

▶ sending peacekeeping and other forces to areas of conflict in the world, such as East Timor, Iraq and Afghanistan (see Sections 6.3.2 [pages 394–5] and 6.3.3 [page 399])

▶ extradition of criminals (see Case Study 6.11, Section 6.4.5, page 410)

▶ membership of the UN and relevant IGOs, such as ASEAN (see Sections 6.2.2 [pages 381–2] and 6.2.5 [page 386])

▶ taking part in diplomatic persuasion to encourage other nations to comply with international law (see Case Study 6.3, Section 6.2.9, page 389).

CAN YOU explain the role of Australia's federal government in responding to world order?

In order to do this, you need to describe the seven roles the federal government plays in contributing to the maintenance of world order and give examples of each one.

These seven roles are:
▶ entering into international agreements for Australia
▶ passing legislation to put international agreements into effect
▶ contributing to foreign aid
▶ sending peacekeeping and other forces to areas of conflict
▶ extradition of criminals

Outline the role of Australia's federal government in determining Australia's response to the search for world order.

▶ maintaining membership of the UN and relevant IGOs, such as ASEAN

▶ taking part in diplomatic persuasion.

You should also explain that state and territory governments hold no power in this area but are able to lobby the federal government to sign international agreements on Australia's behalf. States are also able to enact their own legislation that mirrors international agreements.

KCq page 419

6.2.8 The role of the media

Describe the role of the media in the maintenance of world order.

The media has an enormous influence on the maintenance of world order. The information revolution has meant the media, and its power, is expanding rapidly. Conflicts and world issues can now be broadcast instantly across the world, twenty-four hours a day. This media attention can mobilise public action. For example, public action can call on governments and international organisations to settle conflicts, give aid, or uphold human rights.

The increasing role of the media also has a negative influence on achieving world order. The modern media often shows the drama of world order issues with little or no exploration of the reasons behind the issues. News items also grow old very quickly and, once the initial drama or horror is shown, the story is then ignored, even if the situation continues. Media coverage of tragedy can also lead to 'compassion fatigue' in the developed world. The effectiveness and ineffectiveness of the media is discussed further in Section 6.4.5 (page 412).

KCq page 419

6.2.9 Political negotiation, persuasion and the use of force

Outline the role of political negotiation, persuasion and the use of force in maintaining world order.

Besides the role of NGOs and the media, there are three non-legal remedies available for maintaining world order:

▶ political negotiation

▶ persuasion

▶ force. (Note: the use of force is sometimes legal. See page 389.).

Usually, these remedies are used in the following order. First, political negotiations are used if there is a threatened disruption to world order, then persuasion and, finally, force.

Political negotiation

Political negotiation is the simplest, most frequently used tool to settle differences between nations. Nation-states all have diplomats whose job it is to negotiate with representatives of other nations around the globe on issues impacting on their countries. Diplomats and government representatives work together to attempt to resolve conflict peacefully and through negotiation. There is no third party involved, such as the UN, so nations are free to settle issues among themselves. Unfortunately, political negotiation is not always effective because mutual goodwill and willingness to find a solution must be present on both sides.

Persuasion

Persuasion is important in encouraging not only nation-states but also transnationals and other international organisations to comply with international law. Persuasion is normally the next step when political negotiations break down. Persuasion can take many forms, including:

▶ NGOs use persuasion by 'naming and shaming' offending states in reports

- the UN 'names and shames' offending nations in their reports and deliberations on human rights issues

- the threat of international sanctions, including economic and trade sanctions (see Case Study 6.9, Section 6.4.1, page 403)

- expressions of global disapproval, often portrayed through media coverage (see Case Study 6.3 below)

- positive persuasion (states must improve their behaviour if they wish to join world or regional intergovernmental organisations). For example, Turkey wants to join the EU but, to join, it has been asked to improve its political system, economy and compliance with human rights.

CASE STUDY 6.3: Australian Cricket Team withdraws from Zimbabwe tour, 2007

'Prime Minister John Howard earlier today announced the federal government would not allow the scheduled cricket tour of Zimbabwe to go ahead in September. "We don't do this lightly, but we are convinced that for the tour to go ahead there would be an enormous propaganda boost to the [President Robert] Mugabe regime"'.

Background

The people of Zimbabwe are suffering as a result of poverty, political oppression and human rights abuses under the corrupt Mugabe dictatorship.

Issue

There are two opposing thoughts: First, would the Australian cricket team, as representatives of Australia, have been seen as supporting the Mugabe regime by touring there? Second, should the Australian cricket team avoid getting involved in politics, and just play cricket in countries where they are asked to?

Decision

The Australian government decided not to allow the Australian cricket team to take part in the tour. This led to media coverage in Commonwealth countries highlighting the corrupt regime, angered the Mugabe government and led to further international isolation for Zimbabwe. This isolation continues today.

Source: *Sydney Morning Herald*, Sports blog, Alex Brown, 13 May 2007

Force

Historically, the use of force has been the common way to maintain world order, and there is a place for legal force (or military action) in maintaining order internationally. Both the League of Nations and, then, the UN established when the use of force would be legal under international law. The UN Charter, Article 2(4) states:

> 'All members shall refrain in their international relations from the threat of use of force against the territorial integrity or political independence of any state, or in any other manner inconsistent with the Purposes of the United Nations'.

Article 51 of the charter and international customary law allow for force to be used in self-defence. The concept of collective self-defence means that, if a nation-state is threatened, their allies can legally come to their assistance. Pre-emptive self-defence describes the situation in which a nation-state can legally use force if it can prove that it is about to be subject to invasion or force. This is difficult to prove and this justification can only be used within a short timeframe.

Article 42 of the charter allows the UN Security Council to 'take such action by air, sea or land forces as may be necessary to maintain or restore international peace and security'. These powers have been drawn upon since 1990 for humanitarian reasons and to maintain international security. See Sections 6.3.2 [page 395], 6.3.3 [page 399] and 6.3.4 [pages 400–1] for more detail.

Intergovernmental organisations can also use force. This is known as multilateral force. The general rule is that multilateral intervention is authorised by international law if the threat to peace is significant. On the other hand, unilateral action (one nation-state using force) has been illegal since 1945. Case Study 6.4 below presents an example of the legal use of multilateral force.

CASE STUDY 6.4: NATO's use of multilateral force in Kosovo, 1999

Background

In 1998, the Serbian government, led by Slobodan Milosevic, began an ethnic cleansing campaign (genocide) against the Muslim population in Kosovo. There was an international outcry for intervention, particularly in the US and the United Kingdom.

Issue

The Security Council could not pass a resolution authorising the use of force to stop the genocide because Russia and China threatened to use their Perm-5 veto powers.

Action

A force led by the North Atlantic Treaty Organisation (NATO) intervened in March 1999 and successfully ended the genocide. It was only after NATO entered Kosovo that the Security Council called for an international presence in the area and retrospectively authorised the NATO mission.

Status

Was the NATO use of force legal before the Security Council sanctioned it? International law specialists would argue it was, because it was carried out by a multilateral force from an intergovernmental organisation whose principles for membership and aims for international peace are consistent with the UN.

 KCq page 419

6.2.10 The effectiveness of legal and non-legal measures in resolving conflict and working towards world order

The following can be described as the sources of legal measures for resolving conflict and working towards world order:

▶ the United Nations

▶ international instruments (declarations and treaties)

▶ international courts and tribunals

▶ intergovernmental organisations (IGOs)

▶ the Australian federal government.

The following can be described as non-legal measures for resolving conflict and working towards world order:

▶ non-government organisations (NGOs)

▶ the media

▶ political negotiation and persuasion

▶ force.

It is important to note that the use of force is sometimes legal.

The legal and non-legal measures that seek to resolve conflict and work towards achieving world order have limited effectiveness, mostly due to the non-compliance of nation-states. Table 6.2 lists factors which indicate that legal and non-legal measures have been effective in seeking to resolve conflict and work towards world order, and factors which limit the effectiveness of these measures.

Table 6.2 **The effectiveness of measures seeking to resolve conflict and work towards world order**

Factors which *indicate* effectiveness	Factors which *limit* effectiveness
▶ The United Nations system has managed to avoid another major world conflict for over sixty years. ▶ Nuclear weapons have the potential to destroy the entire world, so all nation-states have a vested interest in avoiding conflict and maintaining world order. ▶ *Ad hoc* war tribunals and the ICC have been somewhat effective in bringing individuals and groups who have perpetrated war crimes to justice. There seems to now be a fear by perpetrators that they will be indicted. ▶ IGOs, particularly the EU and NATO, are proving effective in maintaining order, security and prosperity for their member nations. The (non-force) enforcement powers of the EU and its tribunals are more effective than those of the UN. ▶ The media is effective in seeking world order in that local issues are now global and the media's reporting increases public awareness and action. ▶ NGOs are having an increasing impact on creating and maintaining world order through humanitarian programs and lobbying of governments.	▶ A nation-state can refuse to be a member of the UN and to ignore international customary law and treaty law if they choose to do so. ▶ The UN system of treaties and the ICJ have not been effective in stopping issues such as terrorism, and conflicts in Africa and Iraq. ▶ The effectiveness of the ICC has not really been tested. The fact that all nation-states, including the US, do not recognise the jurisdiction of the ICC, means its effectiveness is already limited. ▶ There is criticism that the UN is not allowing the use of force for humanitarian reasons when required. ▶ There are also negative effects of the vast amount of media coverage, as described in Sections 6.2.8 (page 388) and 6.4.5 (page 412).

Section 6.4.5 (pages 421–7) examines the effectiveness of legal and non-legal responses to resolving conflict and maintaining world order.

CAN YOU **evaluate the effectiveness of legal and non-legal measures in resolving conflict and working towards world order?**

In order to do this, you need to:

▶ list legal and non-legal measures for resolving conflict and working towards world order

▶ explain factors which enhance the effectiveness of each measure in resolving conflict and working towards world order, using examples where appropriate

▶ explain factors which limit the effectiveness of each measure in resolving conflict and working towards world order, using examples where appropriate

▶ come to a conclusion about the overall effectiveness of each measure.

To do these things you need to consider the material in Section 6.2.10 (pages 390–1) and the material in Section 6.4.5 (pages 407–13).

KCq page 419

6.3 Contemporary issues concerning world order

6.3.1 The principle of 'Responsibility to Protect'

The 'Responsibility to Protect'

The 'Responsibility to Protect' (RtoP) is an international set of principles which operates to prevent four crimes—genocide, war crimes, crimes against humanity, and ethnic cleansing. These are referred to as 'mass atrocities'. The RtoP is a framework only and is not enshrined in any international conventions or instruments, unlike humanitarian intervention.

The RtoP was established in 2002 as a direct result of the international community's failure to intervene during the genocide in Rwanda, which was clearly a case of ethnic cleansing carried out with the knowledge of the wider international community. The question resulting was: 'When does the international community intervene to protect populations?'

In 2000 the Canadian Government established the International Commission on Intervention and State Sovereignty (ICSS) which released its 'Responsibility to Protect' report in late 2001. The RtoP states that:

▶ a state has the first responsibility to protect its population from genocide, war crimes, crimes against humanity and ethnic cleansing (mass atrocities)

▶ if the state cannot protect its population from these mass atrocities alone, then the international community has a responsibility to assist the state by building its capacity to manage the situation. This could include diplomatic engagements, mediation of conflicts between internal parties, strengthening security, establishing early warning capacities, and many other actions.

▶ If the state is manifestly failing to protect its population from mass atrocities and peaceful measures are not working, then the international community has the responsibility to intervene at first diplomatically, then with more force and, as a last resort, with military force. The power to use military force sits only with a consensus of the UN Security Council.

RtoP is often equated as being the same as humanitarian intervention (explained below). However, the use of force under the RtoP can only be for the four defined mass atrocities and can only be invoked by consensus of the Security Council. Like humanitarian intervention, the RtoP is still chiefly limited by the rights of state sovereignty.

Humanitarian intervention

As has been seen in Section 6.2.1 (pages 380–1), state sovereignty makes it difficult for others to interfere in the internal affairs of a nation-state. Article 2(4) of the United Nations Charter prohibits the use of force in international relations, and Article 2(7) states the UN will not interfere in the domestic affairs of a nation. There are three clear situations in which intervention is permissible:

▶ when the UN Security Council decides that the actions of a nation pose a threat to international peace and security

▶ when a nation intervenes to protect its own citizens caught in a conflict

▶ when a nation must allow inspections for outlawed weapons.

The situations just described are all provided for in Chapter VII of the UN Charter.

Nation-states can only accept humanitarian aid if their government allows it. Because it is often government regimes that lead to famine, poverty and conflict, or government regimes that do not want to be part of international law, the benefits of humanitarian aid and intervention are often denied to the people governed by these regimes. This is a major issue facing the current world order and there has been a slow erosion of the principle that aid can only be delivered with the permission of the nation-state.

Chapter VII of the United Nations Charter deals with 'Action with respect to threats to the peace, breaches of the peace, and acts of aggression'. In recent years, the Chapter VII powers of the UN Charter have been used to intervene in a nation's affairs on humanitarian grounds (See 'Peacekeeping' in Section 6.3.3, page 399).

Chapter VII of the charter establishes the UN peace-enforcement powers and Article 42 states that the UN Security Council can 'take such action by air, sea or land forces as may be necessary to maintain or restore international peace and security'. These powers were first used in 1990 to allow intervention after Iraq's invasion of Kuwait. They have since been used to intervene to stop human rights abuses in the former Yugoslavia in 1991, Somalia in 1993, Rwanda in 1994 and East Timor in 1999.

Effectiveness of legal and non-legal responses to the issue of 'Responsibility to Protect'

Factors which help ensure the effectiveness of legal and non-legal responses

- The existence of the RtoP principle shows that many nations are concerned about stopping mass atrocities around the world.
- There has been a slow erosion of the principle that aid can only be delivered with the permission of a nation-state.
- Peace-enforcement powers have been used to intervene to stop human rights abuses in Kuwait in 1990, the former Yugoslavia in 1991, Somalia in 1993, Rwanda in 1994 and East Timor in 1999.

Factors which limit the effectiveness of legal and non-legal responses

- The RtoP is a framework only and is not enshrined in any international conventions or instruments.
- Like humanitarian intervention, the RtoP is still chiefly limited by the rights of state sovereignty.
- Nation-states can only accept humanitarian aid if their government allows it, though this principle is slowly being eroded.

CAN YOU identify and investigate the contemporary issue involving world order of the principle of 'Responsibility to Protect', and evaluate the effectiveness of legal and non-legal responses to this issue?

In order to do this, you need to
- describe the 'Responsibility to Protect' principle and explain that it has no legal basis
- explain the legal response of humanitarian intervention under the UN Charter

▶ discuss the factors which may enhance, and those which may limit, the effectiveness of legal and non-legal responses to the issue of the principle of 'Responsibility to Protect'

▶ come to a conclusion about the effectiveness of the legal and non-legal responses to the contemporary world order issue of the principle of 'Responsibility to Protect'.

KCq page 419

6.3.2 Regional and global situations that threaten peace and security

This section presents an overview of the following contemporary regional and global situations that threaten peace and security in the current world order:

▶ the war on terror: ongoing conflict in Afghanistan and Iraq

▶ illegal use of force

▶ the threat of nuclear warfare

▶ the conflict between Israel and Palestine

▶ the behaviour of North Korea

▶ the incidence of mass atrocities

The effectiveness of the legal and non-legal responses to these current situations is discussed both within this section and in Section 6.4.5 (pages 407–13).

The war on terror: ongoing conflict in Afghanistan and Iraq

Terrorism is really a political term. A government can decide if an action is terrorism and if a group that opposes that government is defined as a 'terrorist' group. According to Keith Suter, '… one government's "terrorist" is another's "freedom fighter"' (*Contemporary Review*, October 2005).

For example, Nelson Mandela was deemed a terrorist by the South African government in the 1960s and was jailed there until the 1980s. The government regime changed, and Mandela became South Africa's first Black president.

CASE STUDY 6.5: What is the 'war on terror'?

Background

The terrorist attacks on the US in September 2001 led to the then US President, George Bush, formally declaring a war on terror. There have been two chief military actions in the war on terror: the campaign in Afghanistan against the Taliban, launched in October 2001; and the conflict in Iraq, which started on 20 March 2003.

Issue

The campaign in Afghanistan, which formally ended in December 2001, resulted in the Taliban rulers being overthrown. However, the terrorist network Al-Qaeda is still operating and Afghanistan is struggling in the aftermath. Bin Laden was killed by US forces in Pakistan in May 2011.

The US declared the war against Iraq officially over on 1 May 2003. However, conflict is ongoing and casualties on all sides are continuing to rise.

Status

The reported number of casualties varies significantly but Associated Press estimates 110 000 violent deaths (both civilians and military) up to April 2009 in Iraq alone.

Opinion

'It is more the war of error than a war on terror. Who, four years ago, would have put money on Washington bungling its invasion of Iraq so badly? What might the odds have been then on Osama bin Laden surviving to celebrate his 50th birthday?'

Source: 'Bin Laden birthday bash mocks war on terror. Spy chief warns of Pakistan threat.', Paul McGeough, *The Age*, 19 March 2007.

Conflict in Iraq

The conflict in Iraq outlined in Case Study 6.5 above is ongoing. Despite initial victories, the US-led occupation of Iraq continues to the present day. The war in Iraq has become increasingly unpopular in the US, in the United Kingdom, in Australia, across the rest of the world and in Iraq and the Middle East. The continued presence of the US-led force in Iraq has been held to blame for terrorist attacks in Iraq, across the Middle East and in European countries.

Conflict in Afghanistan

The invasion of Afghanistan to find Al-Qaeda and topple the Taliban was legal under international law and was meant to be fast and decisive. However US coalition troops remain in Afghanistan and Al-Qaeda remains at large. The coalition has started making steps to withdraw from Afghanistan once security and peace has been established. Meanwhile, casualities on all sides continue to grow as insurgencies and counter-insurgencies continue. Although the presence of troops in Afghanistan is viewed more favourably than the occupation of Iraq, it is clear that foreign troops need to leave as soon as possible. This ongoing situation is still a threat to world order and a cause of growing unrest across the Middle East.

This conflict and the conflict in Iraq are discussed in Case Study 6.5 (page 394) and Case Study 6.6 (page 396).

Illegal use of force

The legal uses of force have been outlined in Section 6.2.9 (pages 389–90). To return to this subject, all force is illegal except:

▶ in the case of self defence (Article 51 of the UN Charter)
▶ if the Security Council invokes Chapter VII of the UN Charter and intervenes in order to maintain international peace and security.

All other use of force is illegal under international law. Although the UN has made many advances in maintaining world order since 1945, the illegal use of force by nation-states remains a major concern in the international community.

A major concern is the continued existence of nuclear weapons, as discussed on page 396. Major world powers, rogue states and possibly terrorist organisations all have nuclear weapons and weapons of mass destruction. The current world order exists with the threat that any of these groups could use these weapons through an illegal use of force, leading to mass destruction.

Table 6.3 in Case Study 6.6 (page 396) compares the use of force in the US-led invasions of Iraq and Afghanistan and the legal status of the use of force in both situations.

CASE STUDY 6.6: The use of force by the United States in the twenty-first century

Table 6.3 US-led invasions of Afghanistan and Iraq

	US-led use of force in Afghanistan (2001)	US-led use of force in Iraq (2003)
Reason for conflict	▷ Al-Qaeda took responsibility for the attacks on the US, on 11 September 2001. ▷ The Taliban were the ruling authority in Afghanistan and were supporters of Al-Qaeda. ▷ The US requested the Taliban to hand over Al-Qaeda members. The Taliban refused.	▷ The Iraqi government had to allow UN weapons inspectors to check they were destroying their weapons of mass destruction after the end of the Gulf War in 1991 (UN Security Council Resolution 687). ▷ Iraq continuously refused to comply with Resolution 687. ▷ The US-led coalition wanted to force the Iraqi government (led by the dictator Saddam Hussein) to comply with Resolution 687, to remove Hussein as leader and implement regime change.
Legal basis for conflict	▷ The exemption of self-defence under Article 51 of the UN Charter. The US argued they were attacked by Al Qaeda, and the Taliban were harbouring them.	▷ The US and the Security Council cosponsored Resolution 1441 that gave the Iraqi government a final opportunity to comply with Resolution 687. It stated that Iraq would face 'serious consequences' for non-compliance. ▷ The US then used Resolution 1441 as the means to enter Iraq, stating that it was a 'measure of last resort' under Article 42 of the UN Charter. Article 42 says that, when all other measures are deemed inadequate, the Security Council 'may take such action by air, sea, or land forces as may be necessary to maintain or restore international peace and security'.
UN backing	▷ Yes, the Security Council sanctioned the use of force under Article 51.	▷ This is still widely debated. The Security Council did authorise Resolution 1441 but did not explicitly authorise the use of force.
Legal status	▷ Legal	▷ Disputed

The threat of nuclear warfare

Despite the existence of the Treaty on the Non-Proliferation of Nuclear Weapons (NNPT) (1968), as discussed in Section 6.1.4 (page 376) and other treaties in this area, governments are still obtaining and testing nuclear weapons. India and Pakistan (who have not signed or ratified the NNPT) both acquired nuclear weapons in the late 1990s and tested them in 1998. Since the 1950s, India and Pakistan have had a dispute over who owns the territory of Kashmir. Because of the existence of nuclear weapons in both India and Pakistan, the dispute in Kashmir has the potential to escalate into nuclear war if not resolved.

Iran also has a nuclear program in place and is not complying with UN requirements to show the peaceful nature of its nuclear program. It is currently subject to UN Security Council sanctions. The sanctions placed upon Iran in an already unstable Middle East, along with the potential that Iran is developing nuclear weapons, both indicate threats to the current world order.

North Korea also has a nuclear program in place which is discussed in further detail on page 397.

Since September 2001, there has been a fear of terrorists and other forms of guerrilla groups obtaining and using nuclear weapons. Unfortunately, the threat of nuclear weapons being used again is a reality of world order in the twenty-first century.

Conflict between Israel and Palestine

There has been ongoing border conflict between Israel and Palestine since the formation of the nation-state of Israel in 1947. Both Israel and Palestine lay claim to the Gaza Strip and the West Bank, and Israel is the current occupying force. Israel has enforced a blockade of the Gaza Strip since 2007, and the last major conflict in the area was in 2008/2009.

In 2010, Israel launched a military assault on a flotilla, in international waters, which was supplying aid and supplies to the blockaded Gaza Strip. At least nine pro-Palestinian activists were killed, and injuries were sustained on both sides. The UN Security Council was pressured by other states, NGOs, the media and activists to announce that the attack was an illegal use of force. It did condemn the attacks but has not declared them illegal to date. NATO was asked to intervene militarily but did not.

This situation in 2010 is only a recent chapter in one of the world's longest-running conflicts. The complexity of the conflict cannot be understated and it has one of the largest impacts of all conflicts upon the international relations of all other nation-states, particularly between the Middle East and the US as an ally of Israel.

The behaviour of North Korea

North Korea presents a real and continued risk of conflict with South Korea and is known to be developing and testing nuclear weaponry. It has undertaken missile testing throughout the twenty-first century, and it withdrew from the NPTT in 2003, refusing any arms inspections or international oversight of its regime.

North Korea is the most isolated nation-state in the world and operates as a communist dictatorship. It protects the border it shares with democratic South Korea fiercely.

In March 2010, it torpedo-bombed and sunk a South Korean warship, which was viewed as an act of aggression by the international community. South Korea responded forcefully, stating that it would:

▶ take North Korea to the UN Security Council

▶ ban North Korean ships from its waters

▶ suspend all remaining limited trade between the two nations.

The situation in North Korea remains unresolved. Because North Korea remains so isolated its actual nuclear weaponry is unknown and the situation is potentially the most explosive in the current world order.

Incidences of mass atrocities

The war crimes tribunals for Rwanda and the former Yugoslavia represent a willingness by the international community to create structures to enforce human rights and the rules of international humanitarian law in times of war (see Section 6.3.4, pages 400–1). However, the effectiveness of the tribunals is hampered by the fact that they may actually help entrench the conflict rather than end it. Problems with capturing perpetrators and then bringing them to justice are ongoing.

Other gross violations of human rights and international humanitarian law have been committed in times of war in recent years (for example, throughout the Afghanistan and Iraq conflicts) and no structures similar to the war crime tribunals of Rwanda and the former Yugoslavia have been instituted to deal with these.

There are also incidences of genocide and communal killing in internal conflicts and civil wars (including suspected incidences of mass atrocities in Darfur in the Sudan) which do not clearly come under the governance of international humanitarian law, but which are clearly international crimes against humanity and may possibly fall under the 'Responsibility to Protect' (RtoP) principle.

It is hoped that the establishment of the International Criminal Court in 2002 and the presence of the RtoP will continue to improve the enforcement of human rights where abuse amounts to mass atrocities, but there has been no major impact to date.

Effectiveness of legal and non-legal responses to the issue of regional and global situations that threaten peace and security

While each of the regional and global situations discussed in this section has its own set of factors which enhance or limit the legal and non-legal responses to it, some general comments can be made which apply to all the situations discussed.

On the positive side, none of the situations has yet erupted into war on a grand scale involving destruction and death across many nations, indicating that the measures taken by the UN, the Security Council and the network of treaties and regional organisations have prevented large scale conflict, such as occurred in World War I and World War II, from occurring again.

However, the situations as described are continuing to occur, which indicates that the responses to them are ineffective, either because of a lack of will on the part of international bodies to intervene, or because the nations involved are exercising state sovereignty and refusing to comply with international measures designed to resolve the situations.

Sections 6.2.10 (pages 390–1) and 6.4.5 (pages 407–13) discuss in more detail the effectiveness of legal and non-legal responses to situations which threaten global peace and security.

CAN YOU identify and investigate the contemporary issue involving world order of regional and global situations that threaten peace and security, and evaluate the effectiveness of legal and non-legal responses to these issues?

In order to do this, you need to:

▶ identify and describe the regional and global situations that threaten peace and security which have been discussed in this section

▶ explain the legal and non-legal responses to these situations

▶ discuss the factors which may enhance, and those which may limit, the effectiveness of legal and non-legal responses for each of the situations described in this section

▶ come to a conclusion about the effectiveness of the legal and non-legal responses to the contemporary world order issue of regional and global situations that threaten peace and security.

KCq page 419

6.3.3 The success of global cooperation in achieving world order

> Evaluate the success of global cooperation in achieving world order.

The United Nations, and the League of Nations before it, were both formed to stop world war and global conflict. The League of Nations was unsuccessful in its purpose, evidenced by the fact that it could not stop the break out of World War II in 1939. However, the United Nations has so far been successful in this overall aim bcause a third world war has not broken out. Despite this, as seen throughout this chapter, there are ongoing conflicts in many parts of the world.

The nature of modern conflicts, such as terrorism, internal conflict and border disputes, directly challenges how the United Nations and intergovernmental organisations can work to resolve conflict. Humanitarian law and the Geneva Conventions (outlined in Section 6.3.4, pages 400–1) appear outdated when applied to modern conflict, and it is too easy for nation-states to ignore these conventions without consequences. UN-led enforcement and peacekeeping missions, under a consensual system of law, are a final method in which global cooperation is used to achieve world order. Peacekeeping forces are used when other methods of achieving cooperation fail.

United Nations peace enforcement

Chapter VII, Article 47, of the UN Charter established a Military Staff Committee. This committee was to include the Chiefs of Staff of the Permanent 5 (Perm-5) members of the Security Council: Russia, France, the UK, the US and China (the victors in World War II). The Military Staff Committee was to coordinate a UN 'force' that would enforce the decisions of the UN. The reason this article was inserted into the UN Charter was because the League of Nations had no power to enforce its decisions, which was one of the reasons why it could not stop war breaking out in World War II. This initiative was then, and remains now, the most concrete suggestion for a global 'force' to maintain peace.

Due to the Cold War in 1947 the peace-enforcement plan outlined in Chapter VII of the UN Charter has never been implemented. There is still no UN-led force and, while the Chapter VII powers have been drawn upon in more recent years to intervene in situations such as Rwanda and Kosovo, they have never been fully used.

Peacekeeping

The UN peacekeeping program is in place because peace-enforcement has not been implemented. Case Study 6.7 below outlines the first peacekeeping mission ever implemented.

CASE STUDY 6.7: The 'Suez Canal' crisis and the development of UN peacekeeping, 1956

Background

In 1956, Britain, France and Israel invaded Egypt (the 'Suez Canal' crisis) which led to a disagreement between four of the five Perm-5 members. The threat of nuclear war was real.

Decision

The then Secretary of the UN, Dag Hammarskjold, implemented a plan from the Canadian foreign minister to send in a 'peacekeeping' force to oversee a ceasefire in the region. Peacekeeping operations have been in place ever since.

The main features of peacekeeping missions are as follows:

- peacekeepers are sent into areas of conflict to assist in enforcing peace so that diplomatic measures can be used to negotiate an end to the conflict
- agreement of the Perm-5 members of the Security Council is not required
- missions operate out of the UN Secretary General's department
- the UN has requested troops from nations for each mission. Nation-states do not need to send troops, and they have the right to withdraw their troops at any time.
- the UN raises funds for missions from contributions from nation-states, who are often slow to pay.

There have been sixty-four peacekeeping missions since 1948 and they have grown in number and size since the end of the Cold War. There were thirteen missions in the first forty years of the UN, and fifty missions in the last twenty years. In the middle of 2010, there were sixteen peacekeeping missions in operation which involved over 124 000 personnel (both uniformed personnel and civilians) from over 160 nations.

CAN YOU **identify and investigate the contemporary issue of the success of global cooperation in achieving world order, and evaluate the effectiveness of legal and non-legal responses to this issue?**

In order to do this, you need to:

▶ identify and describe the cooperative global measures of peace enforcement and peacekeeping, which are discussed in this section

▶ discuss the factors which may enhance the success of peace enforcement and peacekeeping as methods of global cooperation in achieving world order. These include:

● the fact that no global conflict has broken out since World War II

● the fact that peace enforcement powers have never been used, indicating that global cooperation is being achieved without resort to this measure

● peacekeeping missions have assisted in resolving conflict around the world in an increasing number of cases

● the large number of peacekeeping missions in operation may indicate that global cooperation is ensuring that conflict is being managed and escalation of conflict is being prevented

▶ discuss the factors which may limit the success of peace enforcement and peacekeeping as methods of global cooperation in achieving world order. These include:

● the fact that many more peacekeeping missions have been raised in the last twenty years than in the previous forty years, which may indicate that the number of areas experiencing difficult to resolve conflicts is rising

● the number of peacekeeping missions currently in operation, which indicates that there are many areas of conflict throughout the world

● the number of peacekeeping missions may also indicate that other less intrusive methods of resolving conflict are not effective

▶ come to a conclusion about the effectiveness of the peace enforcement and peacekeeping measures in the success of global cooperation in achieving world order.

KCq page 419

6.3.4 Rules regarding the conduct of hostilities

Outline the main international humanitarian legal regulations regarding the conduct of hostilities.

The rules regarding the conduct of hostilities are collectively known as international humanitarian law. International humanitarian law applies to military personnel and civilians who are caught up in a conflict. It is different to human rights law, which applies to all people at all times. In theory, the combination of international humanitarian law and human rights law means universal protection for individuals in instances in which dignity and safety is threatened.

International humanitarian law has developed over many centuries. Modern humanitarian law was promoted by the Red Cross and Red Crescent movement (an NGO discussed in Section 6.2.6, pages 386–7) which started in 1863 to provide care for wounded soldiers in a conflict. The development of international law in this area culminated in the Geneva Conventions of 1949 and the 1977 Additional Protocols. The Geneva Conventions outline standards to protect civilians in war, wounded combatants, military medical staff and prisoners of war. They cover conventional warfare and international armed conflict.

The 1949 Geneva Conventions provide:

- rules for humane care of sick and wounded combatants on land
- rules for the humane care of sick and wounded combatants at sea
- rules for the humane treatment of prisoners of war
- rules for the protection of civilian persons in time of war.

The 1977 Additional Protocols update the terminology of the 1949 Geneva Conventions and outline the basic rules of war. Protocol I governs the type of warfare that can be waged. It prohibits weapons deemed to cause 'superfluous injury or unnecessary suffering' and warfare that will cause long-term damage to the environment (Article 35). Protocol II requires the application of humane treatment measures to those caught in internal armed conflicts. Case Study 6.8 below is a recent example of the US government side-stepping the rules regarding the conduct of hostilities under the Geneva Conventions.

CASE STUDY 6.8: Guantanamo Bay and the rights of the individual, 2003–07

'All these men had been captured as part of the...war on terror, but they hadn't been held as prisoners of war. Fighting in a war isn't a crime under international law. These men had been placed by the Americans into an entirely new category—enemy combatants—people suspected of being involved with terrorism to be held and interrogated until the United States no longer judged them to pose a threat'.

Background

At the start of the war on terror, the US captured suspected Taliban and Al-Qaeda fighters in Afghanistan and surrounding states. The US then transferred the prisoners to Guantanamo Bay, a jail in Cuba, outside US domestic jurisdiction.

Issue

Prisoners of war (POWs) are subject to international humanitarian law and the Geneva Conventions. These Guantanamo Bay prisoners were denied POW status by the US who, instead, declared them 'unlawful', or 'enemy' combatants, and denied them the right to a trial by either US domestic courts or a military tribunal, as required under the Geneva Conventions.

Action

There has been a lot of international pressure surrounding this issue since 2002. From 2002–09, the US government slowly implemented trials and acquittals or convictions for some of these prisoners. However, many inmates are still classified as unlawful combatants, are still awaiting trial, and are not subject to international humanitarian law. The new US President Barack Obama has set in motion plans to shut down the jail and process inmates as quickly as possible.

Source: 'Inside Guantanamo' broadcast on the *Panorama* program, BBC One, 5 October 2003.

CAN YOU identify and investigate the contemporary issue of the rules regarding the conduct of hostilities, and evaluate the effectiveness of legal and non-legal responses to this issue?

In order to do this, you need to:

- identify and describe the rules regarding the conduct of hostilities discussed in this section
- explain that the US, which promotes itself as an upholder of human rights, side-stepped the rules regarding the conduct of hostilities in its treatment of so-called 'unlawful combatants' in Guantanamo Bay
- explain that pressure from the international community and NGOs encouraged the US to change its treatment of prisoners in Guantanamo Bay
- come to a conclusion about the effectiveness of the rules regarding the conduct of hostilities, given the Guantanamo Bay example in Case Study 6.8 above.

KCq page 420

6.4 Themes and challenges

Explain the role of the law in encouraging cooperation and resolving conflict in regard to world order.

6.4.1 Theme 1: The role of the law in encouraging cooperation and resolving conflict in regard to world order

State sovereignty is the most important concept in international law. It is state sovereignty that limits the ability to resolve conflicts between nation-states and limits the ability of outsiders to interfere in internal conflicts which may be contravening human rights or international humanitarian law. In addition, states often draw upon their sovereign right not to enter into treaties, to disregard the jurisdiction of the ICJ, and not to apply international law and treaties when it does not suit them. The body of international law must operate within this constraint of state sovereignty.

The role of the United Nations in governing the relations of nation-states is also being eroded by the increasing power of transnationals, and intergovernmental and international organisations. The wealth of transnationals means that they can make an impact on a state's decisions regarding environmental, industrial relations, resource and economic issues, as well as conflict. The power of international organisations, such as the World Bank, can have an important influence on states' decisions, particularly smaller and less powerful nation-states.

The concept of world government was discussed in Section 6.2.1 (page 381). For a world government to really work, nation-states would need to give up their sovereignty to another body entirely. This would throw out the entire Westphalian nation-state system, and it also has many dangers.

The challenge for the UN and the international community is to increase compliance with the body of international law and make international law more enforceable within the current system of nation-states and state sovereignty.

Interdependence of nation-states

All states are becoming increasingly interdependent with each other and this has both negative and positive aspects for cooperation between nation-states. No nation-state can fully pull away from interacting with other states, due to economic globalisation and technology. Because of this, all states must now become increasingly interdependent and must cooperate for economic wealth and to address global issues. There are many positives for the state in interdependence and globalisation. However, there are downsides, particularly for less powerful and developing nations, as discussed in Section 6.1.5 (pages 378–80).

International conventions and treaties reflect the expectations of the nation-states that ratify them which, in turn, have led to the creation of international standards. Most nation-states strive for economically successful democracies, where the rule of law, peace and human rights are strongly guarded. International law has been reasonably successful in ensuring that these expectations are met through international standards, such as: international humanitarian law; human rights law; the UN Charter and its rules governing the use of force; and the principles of *jus cogens*. In theory, all nation-states are subject to these laws. When a nation-state does break an international standard, it cannot say it was unaware of it.

Domestic legislation is also influenced by international standards and, domestically, states are increasingly drawing upon international treaties and guidance when passing their own laws, particularly in areas of discrimination and environmental regulation. Sometimes nation-states need to balance their own expectations with international standards, and state sovereignty allows them to meet international standards only to the degree to which they wish. This in turn impacts significantly on how they operate to resolve conflict at an international level.

Enforceability

Most states who sign treaties do so for mutual benefit, so are unlikely to break the treaty. This is integral to the cooperative nature of international law. If the states do break treaties, then that treaty may provide for some form of dispute-settling mechanism, such as a tribunal—an example being the International Tribunal for the Law of the Sea. Just as with the ICJ, however, a state can choose to ignore the ruling. Because of sovereignty, the state can also choose to withdraw from any treaty or convention to which it may be a party.

Sanctions can be used to enforce international law against a nation-state. Economic and political sanctions can put pressure on a state to start complying with the law, as can be seen in Case Study 6.9 below.

Force can be used against nation-states only when there is a serious breach of the law and the Perm-5 of the Security Council can, and has, sanctioned the use of force. See Section 6.2.9 (pages 389–90).

CASE STUDY 6.9: Apartheid in South Africa, and the use of sanctions (1980s)

Background

In 1948, the apartheid regime began in South Africa when the National Party took power. The system of apartheid was that the white minority had all the power and the majority of the population, mostly composed of Black Africans, but also of Indians and 'coloureds', had no political power, and were segregated from the whites. They were restricted in where they could live and travel, and in what jobs they could hold.

International action

As a protest against apartheid, and in an endeavour to make the government change its policy, the United Nations adopted an arms embargo against South Africa in the 1960s, which was followed by an oil embargo imposed by OPEC countries in 1973. In the midst of mounting pressure, the EU imposed some trade and financial sanctions in 1985, followed by similar sanctions by the Commonwealth and the United States; all of which became more stringent in 1986 and thereafter.

Effect of the sanctions

In 1990, Nelson Mandela was released from prison and became the first Black president of South Africa, democratically elected in 1994. While some argue that many other factors led to the end of apartheid, others say that the multilateral economic sanctions imposed in the 1980s were the final straw that made the economic conditions intolerable and forced political change. Upon his release from prison, Mandela stated to a rally in Cape Town: 'To lift sanctions now would be to run the risk of aborting the process towards the complete eradication of apartheid'.

Source: 'South Africa's new era; Mandela, freed, urges step-up in pressure to end white rule', Christopher S. Wren, *The New York Times*, 12 February 1990.

 page 420

Explain the issues of compliance and non-compliance in relation to maintaining world order.

6.4.2 Theme 2: Issues of compliance and non-compliance

Treaties and conventions are based on agreements between nation-states, so there is normally a large commitment to comply from the signatories to treaties. International customary law has developed from the customs and behaviours of state interaction. The UN, international tribunals and intergovernmental organisations are all based on states consenting to rules, protocols and judgements. International law is consensual—it is based solely on sovereign nation-states making agreements and cooperating. In an increasingly interdependent world order, it is usually in the best interest of nation-states to create and comply with international law.

This is the main difference between international and domestic law. Domestic laws have separate enforcement procedures. The police enforce law, and there are clear judicial process and punishments when individuals do not comply. When a state does not comply with international treaties or judgements, then that state can choose to withdraw from the treaty, ignore the decision or even to withdraw from international relations altogether. Political negotiation and persuasion from other states can influence that state to comply with law (See Section 6.2.9, pages 388–9). In more serious situations, the Security Council can impose various sanctions, even force, to ensure compliance. However, this is rare and it must be considered a serious breach of the law for such action to be taken. In reality, nation-states do not comply with certain international laws when they do not agree with them, and often do so with very little consequence.

KCq page 420

Assess the impact of changing values and ethical standards on world order.

6.4.3 Theme 3: The impact of changing values and ethical standards on world order

How law reflects values and ethics

International law is based on the values and ethical standards of the nation-states that create it. It is based on previous values and ethics (such as those in place at the end of World War II relating to the need to prevent another world conflict), emerging values (such as the development of international copyright law) and, more recently, protocols handling pornography and racial vilification on the internet. Human rights law has evolved due to changing standards and philosophies within states. Recent laws regarding terrorism and the control of terrorist behaviour have arisen due to the current war on terror and the resulting moral and ethical dilemmas.

Nation-states enter into treaties and conventions with other states for mutual benefit. As a result of this, treaties and conventions must reflect the values and ethical standards of those states to a large extent. In democracies, the theory is that standards will reflect the views of a majority of the community.

Rule of law

The 'rule of law' is a fundamental underlying principle of the international legal system and the principles of a nation-state. The establishment of the rule of law is a reflection of the moral and ethical standards of a post-World War II world order. Current world conflicts, such as in Darfur in Sudan and in other African states, are taking place in states where there is no rule of law. Human rights abuses are easier to commit in states where the rule of law is not in place.

Jus cogens

International principles of *jus cogens* are accepted philosophies developed due to changes in what the global community will, and will not, accept. When a principle becomes *jus cogens*, it means that all treaties that conflict with it are no longer valid. For example, there were many treaties establishing rules for the slave trade in the eighteenth and nineteenth century. The philosophy that slavery is wrong is now *jus cogens*, so all previous treaties in this area are void (see Section 2.1.2, pages 99–101).

Changing social values and the composition of society

Interdependence and globalisation have changed the composition of the global world. Traditional state boundaries are crossed daily—through trade; through travel by ordinary citizens; through the addressing of social issues, such as poverty and human rights inequalities; through sharing knowledge via new technology; and through the media. As individuals in a society discover more about other cultures and societies as a result of new technology and access to travel, international law needs to change with them.

Prior to World War I, the members of society had little knowledge or education about global issues, and issues such as conflicts, poverty and the social values of each community had little impact outside that community. Media, new technology and an increasingly educated global population mean that politicians must now increasingly answer to world opinion, rather than just national opinion. This has been one of the main areas of change in world order issues since the first half of the twentieth century.

Social values have been integral in the formation of international law. Universal human rights have developed as communities across the world recognised core rights in life. As societal values continue to change, the law will continue to be adapted. The emerging awareness of global warming is leading to a change in values towards the environment, and while the Kyoto Protocol 1997 is the main piece of international law in this area, there is still much more reform needed. The much-anticipated UN Climate Summit, held in Copenhagen at the end of 2009, formally recognised the need for fast international action on climate change but was unable to agree on a new protocol to replace the *Kyoto Protocol*.

In 1945, the UN had fifty-one members. It now has 192. Most of the new member nation-states are former colonies. Changing societal values directly led to the dismantling of the colonies into independent nations. There are many issues left over from expansionism, particularly in Africa. Expansionism not only impacted on the boundaries and formation of states, but on the Indigenous people in those colonies. Recognising the rights of the world's Indigenous peoples, and any rights they may have to self-determination, is now recognised as an important global issue that requires more action.

Society is changing through the emerging power of transnational corporations and their ability to wield economic strength over traditional nation-state borders. The collapse, or corruption, of a world transnational has the ability to damage individuals across the globe. Areas such as trade, corporate governance and industrial relations (in both domestic and international law) are issues needing to be addressed to reflect this change.

Evolving concepts of justice

The evolving values and ethical standards of society have led to the development of new concepts of justice. As discussed above, slavery is now *jus cogens*—this has been a change in the concept of justice, because slavery was accepted, and even commonplace, during the nineteenth century.

Social values and ethical viewpoints are continuously subject to change, and will continue to be so. The recognition that women should be treated equally to men has only really developed in the last sixty years. The instruments of international law need to ensure that current social values and ethical standards are being protected in nation-states and that, as new values and ethics evolve, international law can rise to the challenge of protecting them.

KCq page 420

Outline the role of law reform in the promotion and maintenance of world order.

6.4.4 Theme 4: The role of law reform in promoting and maintaining world order

The need for reform

The United Nations, individual nation-states and the agencies of international law have achieved much since 1945 in creating and maintaining world order. There has been no world war, nuclear weapons have not been used on other states and peoples, and basic human rights have been recognised in the majority of nation-states. These have all been major global achievements and should not be underestimated.

However, there are still many serious issues for individuals, societies, and nations across the globe, which give rise to the need for reform. Three main areas are:

▷ the changing social values and composition of society (see Section 6.4.3, page 405)

▷ new concepts of justice (see Section 6.4.3, pages 405–6)

▷ the effectiveness of existing legal and non-legal responses to current world order issues (see Sections 6.2.10 [pages 390–1] and 6.4.5 [pages 407–13]).

There are other conditions that will continue to give rise to the need for reform to the current world order. These include:

▷ **poverty**. Over 30 000 children die each day due to extreme poverty, and many people say that globalisation is making poverty worse. Despite efforts from grassroots movements, NGOs, governments and foreign aid, it is clear that significant global reform is needed in this area.

▷ **environment**. It is becoming clear that global warming is becoming a major world order issue, and that the international community and all nation-states need to work together to combat this threat. The failure of the Copenhagen Summit in 2009 highlights how reform is needed in this area.

▷ **disease**. Disease spreads across borders, and the threat of increasing global epidemics is real as levels of migration and travel increase. The global swine flu epidemic which surfaced in 2009 demonstrated that global responses are needed to contain and combat outbreaks of disease.

▷ the **erosion of state sovereignty** due to interdependence, transnationals and intergovernmental organisations is a reality in the current world order, and is a challenge to this core principle of the current world order.

The agencies of reform

The agencies able to bring about reform in the current world order are:

▷ the International Law Commission

▷ Law Reform Commissions of nation-states

▷ parliaments of nation-states

▷ international courts

- courts of nation-states
- courts of regional federations and intergovernmental organisations
- non-government organisations
- the media
- individuals.

Figure 6.2 on page 408 illustrates the relationships between the above bodies and how each can bring about reform. (KCq) page 420

6.4.5 Theme 5: The effectiveness of legal and non-legal responses in promoting and maintaining world order

The effectiveness of legal and non-legal responses to world order is summarised in Section 6.2.10 (pages 390–1). Students should reread this section before examining the following material.

Outline the effectiveness of legal and non-legal responses in the promotion and maintenance of world order.

Effectiveness of legal responses

The effectiveness of any legal response to world order issues and to the promotion and maintenance of the world order is limited by state sovereignty and the consensual nature of international law. This is discussed in Sections 6.4.1 (pages 402–3) and 6.4.2 (page 404).

United Nations

The UN has worked very hard at recognising and protecting the values of societies around the world and emerging concepts of justice, and at preventing conflict. The UN has achieved much in its sixty years. However, there is still a lot of work to ensure that all individuals and societies are protected from human rights abuses and suffering caused by conflict and resource inequity, among other things. The UN itself is in need of reform after sixty years because the organisation can be bureaucratic and unwieldy. In 2005, the UN released its first report about the major reforms it saw as worthy of consideration, but world leaders could not agree on implementing the changes.

The structure of the UN means some states are more equal than others, mostly due to the Security Council, which gives veto powers to the Perm-5 members. Reform of the Security Council has been discussed in recent times, and there are now ten additional states which serve on the Security Council on a revolving basis. It has been suggested that more permanent members be added to the Security Council, such as Japan and India, but the veto powers of the original Perm-5 should remain. The power of nations in the UN has a direct impact on how conflicts, such as those in Iraq, Afghanistan, the Gaza Strip and in some African states, are managed.

Reforms, concerning the way nation-states fund foreign aid and the UN itself, are also required. The total amount of money spent by the UN and its agencies every year is approximately US$30 billion. In comparison, the NSW government projected revenues for 2010–11 were AUS$57 billion. Many nations are in arrears on their required dues to the UN and have cut voluntary giving. Peacekeeping missions are also under-funded, and are reliant on states agreeing to fund them, and to supply personnel, for each separate peacekeeping mission.

International Court of Justice (ICJ)

The ICJ can hear disputes between states only when each state agrees to have the case heard, and then agrees to abide by the ICJ's decision. This is the key to the limitations of the effectiveness of the ICJ—the ICJ can pass judgements but enforcement of such decisions is reliant on the state itself.

Figure 6.2 The agencies of reform

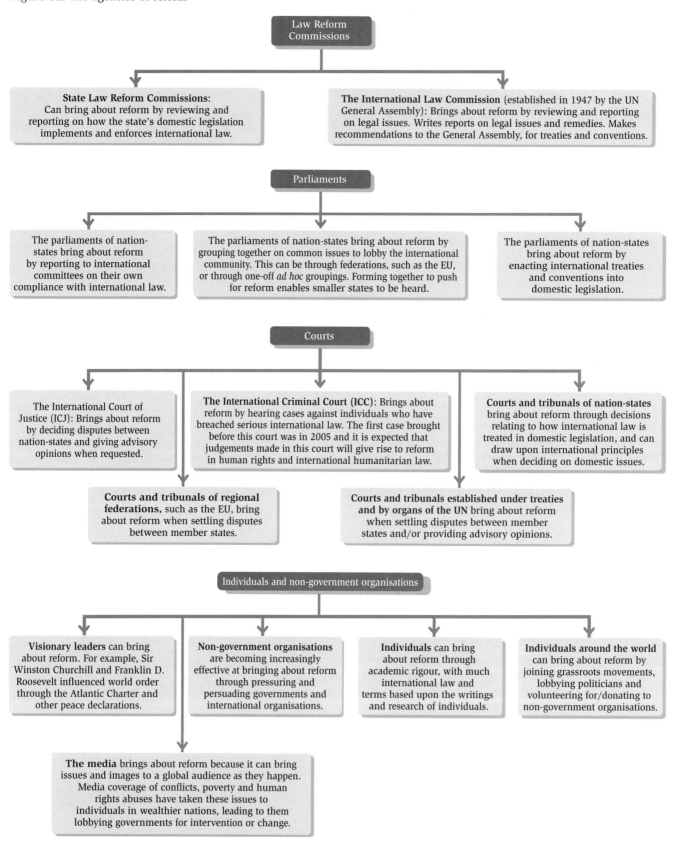

In addition, only states have access to the ICJ—not individuals. Other UN committees and organisations can prepare reports highlighting the abuse of individuals' rights within states, but state sovereignty means that states can choose whether to pay attention to them or not. The cases of *A. v Australia* (UNHRC) (1997) and *Toonen v Australia* (UNHRC) (1994), both heard by the United Nations Human Rights Committee (UNHRC), show the limitations for individuals of these types of cases. In Toonen's case the UNHRC's finding led to a change in the law to protect the rights of individuals who were homosexuals whereas, in the case of *A. v Australia*, the Australian government rejected the findings of the UNHRC regarding unlawful detention violating the rights of a refugee. Both these cases are detailed in Section 2.2.5 (pages 117–18).

International Criminal Court (ICC)

The *Rome Statute* 1998 and the subsequent establishment of the ICC in 2002 have been effective in that there is now a permanent tribunal where individuals and states can access justice, particularly for incidences of mass atrocities. Its effectiveness has yet to be fully tested, and the fact that major powers, such as the US, do not recognise its jurisdiction, severely limits its power.

Unlike the ICJ which does not cater to individuals, the ICC is the first permanent body for cases relating to serious contraventions of international law by individuals, communities or states against individuals and societies. Cases can be referred to it by the UN Security Council and the ICC Prosecutor, which means that cases concerning individual protection can be heard. Victims of crime can present their views and opinions in the ICC for the first time in international law. They may even be eligible for reparation for their suffering, meaning the ICC can force one individual to make payment to another for suffering caused. The effectiveness of the ICC is also discussed in Case Study 1.17, Section 1.6.2, page 65.

While individuals can access international law through the ICC, state sovereignty means that states can choose to ignore the decisions of the ICC and even withdraw from the statute. Therefore, the best mechanism for enforcement of the law for individuals is still through their own state's domestic tribunals and enforcement measures. States with the rule of law are more likely to enforce contraventions of international law. The Lockerbie case, outlined in Case Study 6.10 below, is an example of individuals being punished by a domestic court for offences against world order.

CASE STUDY 6.10: The Lockerbie case [*Her Majesty's Advocate v Abdelbaset Ali Mohmed al Megrahi and Al Amin Khalifa Fhimah* (2001)]

Background
In 1988, Libyan secret service agents bombed a Pan Am passenger airliner over the Scottish town of Lockerbie, with a loss of 270 lives.

Issue
The bombing was sanctioned by the Libyan government. Libya faced international condemnation and severe sanctions. The difficulty was finding a way to prosecute under international law the individual agents responsible.

Decision
The police investigation was conducted by Scottish police and the FBI. Two Libyan secret service agents were prosecuted by three Scottish High Court Judges in the Netherlands. One of the agents was convicted of planting the bomb and was sentenced to twenty-seven years, while the other was acquitted due to lack of evidence.

Perpetrators of human rights abuses are able to be brought to justice through the ICC and *ad hoc* tribunals, but getting them before the court is difficult. There must be a political will for these perpetrators to be found and tried and, normally, a strong commitment is needed from several states—normally powerful ones. In the cases of weaker states and societies, or for human rights abuses and war crimes that do not receive global attention, the perpetrators may never be brought to justice. Case Study 6.11 is an example of Australia extraditing a person accused of mass atrocities in another nation. Extradition is also discussed in Case Study 1.18, Section 1.6.2, page 67.

CASE STUDY 6.11: Extradition to face war crimes (High Court, Australia, 2010)

Background

An Australian citizen, Dragan Vasiljkovic, was indicted for war crimes by the International Criminal Tribunal for the former Yugoslavia.

Issue

Vasiljkovic fought his extradition from Australia to Croatia to face the tribunal, and the full Federal Court ruled he should not be extradited to Croatia on the basis that he might be punished for his political beliefs.

Decision

In early 2010, the High Court deliberated for fifteen minutes and rejected the Federal Court's argument. The extradition order to Croatia was reinstated.

Sanctions

Interestingly, it is often societies and the individuals within them that are victims of international enforcement measures. Political and economic sanctions used to enforce law on nation-states often harm the community the most and not the tyrannical regime. For an example of the successful use of sanctions see Section 6.4.1 (page 403).

Humanitarian intervention and the 'Responsibility to Protect' (RtoP)

While human rights are recognised in many parts of the world, there is still work needed in this area. Genocide, such as in Rwanda in 1994, can still occur. The fact that the global community did not intervene until after the worst of the genocide occurred, demonstrates how ineffective the United Nations and the Security Council can be when seeking to intervene in the affairs of a sovereign state when serious human rights violations are occurring. The formation of the 'Responsibility to Protect' (RtoP) principles has been limited in actual effectiveness. The ongoing situation in Darfur in the Sudan could well be a situation in which RtoP or humanitarian intervention is needed.

Basically, sovereign states that commit mass atrocities and that do not want to protect human rights cannot be forced to do so. The Security Council has used Chapter VII of the UN Charter to use force to intervene for humanitarian purposes in limited cases; however this intervention has normally occurred only when mass genocide or extremely serious human rights abuses have been committed (See Section 6.3.1, pages 392–3).

Development of nuclear weapons

The threat of nuclear war is ever present and the international legal system is still not able to effectively eliminate, through the use of treaties, the production or use of nuclear weapons. Rogue states can simply choose not to sign treaties and this, combined with the fact that some countries (such as Iran and North Korea) are sanctioned for developing weapons, while others (such as Israel) are allowed to do so with little international condemnation, demonstrates the inequities and limited effectiveness of the current measures. While this assessment is damning, it must be remembered that there has been no nuclear warfare since World War II, which is a significant achievement.

Response to terrorism and the war on terror

The 2001 attacks on 11 September in the US, and the resulting war on terror, mean that terrorism has now become a global issue, needing a global response. While the international community responded, through new treaties looking to curb terrorist financing, and weapons restrictions, there have been more terrorist attacks since 2001—and these are ongoing. The UN was powerless to stop the US invading Iraq in 2003, which was a serious blow to the UN's reputation and clearly demonstrated how, without true enforcement, the UN has little power against the rights of state sovereignty (see Section 6.3.2. pages 394–5). In summary, the current international response has not been effective in eliminating or even reducing terrorism or in stopping the resultant war on terror.

States have also enacted legislation to 'find' terrorists, which may infringe on the rights of individuals, and the former prisoner abuses in the US prisons of Abu Ghraib and Guantanamo Bay under the Bush US presidency clearly violated the Geneva Conventions and international humanitarian law.

Access to appeals and review

There is limited access to appeal or review of decisions in international tribunals. This is chiefly because sovereignty means states can reject the jurisdiction of the courts, or decide not to implement a decision. Societies are legally powerless to have a decision reviewed if the state does not wish it reviewed.

Some communities within a nation-state have more rights to review than others, particularly if their states are members of intergovernmental organisations. For example, the European Court of Justice can hear reviews and appeals on matters concerning EU member nations.

Emergence of new technology

International law is always trying to keep up with constantly emerging new technology by developing new regulations—with limited effectiveness. The internet has led to the development of a whole new range of international protocols and global conventions in the area of control, access and ownership. For example, who owns the gateways to the internet? The US owns the domain name servers that direct traffic and, in 2005, this led to an argument between the US and the rest of the world over this control. Governing content on the internet is also problematic, particularly in relation to violent and pornographic material and gambling sites. Another issue is freedom of access to the internet for citizens—in 2010, the transnational search engine company Google entered into discussions with China over its censorship of content delivered through the Google search engine.

Cutting edge technology is also continuously changing the nature of conflict. New weaponry, including nuclear and biological weapons, means that it is now far easier to carry out mass destruction than it has ever been. International law has developing treaties and protocols to govern the use of such technology but, so far, this has not led to disarmament or to new, less destructive, types of weapons being developed.

Effectiveness of non-legal responses

Power of nation-states

Small, new and poor nation-states (such as East Timor) cannot afford to lobby effectively on the world stage. They are less likely to be represented on UN and international committees. Wealthier and stronger nations can influence the international actions and votes of these smaller states in regard to their support on global issues, through promises of aid or economic assistance (or by threatening to withdraw it).

Membership and employees of powerful international organisations are often dominated by powerful and wealthy states, such as the World Bank, which has a large number of US employees and directors. This means that economic powers have a large representation in regard to resource sharing, monetary decisions and trade decisions. A major issue in the current world order between states is the perception that poor nation-states are treated unfairly by rich nation-states in terms of trade, making it difficult for developing states to move forward.

The media

Prior to television, people could not picture the horror of war and poverty unless they were there. The horror of conflict can now be seen on television as we eat dinner, and this can mobilise public action. For example, public action can call on governments and international organisations to settle conflicts, give aid or uphold human rights. Humanitarian disasters, such as the 2004 Boxing Day Tsunami in the Indian Ocean and the 2010 earthquake in Haiti, are shown across the world, driving global assistance and aid. NGOs can use the media to present their cause on the global stage.

When Israel attacked the pro-Palestinian flotilla in 2010, the first news of it was through Twitter updates, video streams and other multi-media messages coming from the persons (including journalists) aboard the flotilla. This meant that the media was integral in spreading the story and its coverage was mostly anti-Israel. This resulted in a 'public relations' disaster for Israel and clearly demonstrates the power of the media in governing international relations.

The role of the media is not all positive. The modern media tends to treat news as entertainment and, in the case of conflict, to show the drama and the violent images, with little or no exploration of the reasons behind the issues. So, while the general public knows about 'what' is going on in the world, it knows little about 'why'. News items also grow old very quickly and, once the initial drama or horror is shown, the story is then ignored—even if the situation continues. Lastly, media coverage of tragedy can lead to 'compassion fatigue' in the developed world—meaning people become immune to suffering due to overexposure.

Media ownership is a significant issue. Print and digital media is increasingly being owned by large transnational companies, such as Fox, and News Ltd, and this trend for the media to be shared across a small pool of companies, is growing. The more concentrated media ownership becomes, the greater the risk of fewer opinions being presented.

CASE STUDY 6.12: Truth is the first casualty of war: media coverage of the Gulf War, 1990–91

Coverage

There was extensive media coverage of the 1990–91 Gulf War. The media gave the impression that the US was using highly accurate 'computer target' bombs on carefully chosen military targets, with little collateral damage or loss of civilian life.

Reality

After the war, the Pentagon stated that only 7% of US explosives used were 'computer bombs' and that 70% of the US bombs that were dropped completely missed their targets. Loss of civilian life was much higher than reported.

Effectiveness of persuasion and political negotiation

The international community can use political negotiation and persuasion to encourage states to comply with human rights and international humanitarian law, but states can still refuse to do so, usually with little consequence.

Non-governmental organisations (NGOs)

Non-government organisations play an extremely important role in the current world order and this is increasingly so as the power of the media and new media grows. This growth of media power gives smaller NGOs access to a wider global audience. The chief limitation to the power of NGOs is that they have no legal authority and they are reliant on fundraising to continue their work. This has the potential to raise conflicts of interest as well as restraints due to lack of finances.

Australia's non-legal response

Australia has always played an important role in global affairs. Historically, Australia was a foundation member of the League of Nations, mostly due to our large contribution in World War I. Many Australian suggestions were implemented in the newly formed United Nations, and we have also supplied many brilliant individuals to work for the UN and on international causes. In fact, Australian Dr H.V. Evatt was the president of the UN General Assembly in 1948–49.

In terms of peacekeeping missions, Australia has also taken its responsibilities seriously since 1947, particularly in the case of peacekeeping in our region. It contributed 1.93% of the total UN peacekeeping budget as of February 2010, placing it twelfth among the world's contributors. Australia's continued effort in the UN peacekeeping mission in East Timor is a current example. Australia has also been involved in peacekeeping missions conducted outside of the UN structure in the Solomon Islands and Fiji and has supplied police forces to Papua New Guinea.

The UN member nations agreed over forty years ago that each nation should give 0.7% of its gross national product (GNP) to foreign aid. Australia, like many developed nations, is giving much less than that. In 2010, the Australian government gave approximately 0.3% of gross domestic product (GDP) to foreign aid, one of the lowest levels of giving from rich developed nations. KCq page 420

Do you know all the key definitions and concepts for this chapter? Go through each term in the list and check that you know them all. Place a bookmark underneath each definition to cover up the one below and slide it down. This way you can focus on each definition by itself.

Anarchy: A state of lawlessness.

Belligerent: Describes a state engaged in, or threatening, warfare.

Bilateral: Involving two nation-states.

Biological warfare: The release of agents such as bacteria or viruses into a population with the intention of causing harm.

Chemical warfare: The use of chemicals (such as nerve gas) to cause harm.

Civil war: War between two or more opposing sides within one nation-state.

Cold War: Running from 1947 to 1991, this was the uneasy peace maintained between the two world superpowers, the communist USSR and the capitalist US.

Collective self-defence: A nation-state can legally come to the assistance of another threatened nation-state.

Colony: A territory that has been successfully invaded or settled by a nation-state through expansionism.

Communal killing: Violence and killing within communities in a nation-state, mainly due to political, economic, social, religious or ethnic differences.

Conventional warfare: The type of warfare in which professional armies and large, well-organised military forces from nation-states fight against the armies of other nation-states.

Declaration: A formal statement, usually made by the UN General Assembly, outlining a set of values considered to be universally applicable

Democide: A nation-state waging war on its own people.

Diplomat: An individual appointed by a nation-state to conduct official negotiations and maintain political, economic, and social relations with another country or countries.

Disarmament: The reduction of weapons, leading to the eventual abolition of a weapon system.

Expansionism: The situation in which one nation-state pushes to increase its size or territories and/or increase its influence in the world community by taking over another country. Also referred to as **imperialism**.

External affairs power: Exclusive powers in world order and international affairs. Section 51(29) of the Australian Constitution gives the federal government these powers.

Force: Violence threatened or committed against individuals, societies or nation-states.

Foreign aid: Aid (including military and economic assistance) given from one nation-state to another.

Genocide: The deliberate and systematic extermination of a national, racial, political, or cultural group.

Global warming: An increase in the average temperature of the Earth's atmosphere, particularly a sustained increase large enough to cause changes in the global climate.

Globalisation: The growing economic and social interdependence and interconnectedness of countries worldwide.

Grassroots movement: A movement driven from members of a community focused on a common issue.

Guerrilla warfare: A type of warfare in which small groups of fighters, familiar with the landscape and using simple weapons, employ tactics to harass the enemy, attack small targets and then retreat.

Imperialism: The situation in which one nation-state pushes to increase its size or territories and/or increase its influence in the world community by taking over another country. Also referred to as **expansionism**.

Intergovernmental organisation (IGO): The grouping together of nation-states that are regionally and/or ideologically close, to achieve common goals and thereby increase each nation's security, status, wealth and position.

International customary law: A source of international law drawn from the common practices of governments which, over a period of time, become accepted as legally binding.

International humanitarian law: The body of law which applies to military personnel, civilians and others who are caught up in a conflict.

International instrument: A source of international law, such as a treaty or declaration.

Inter-state conflict: Conflict between two or more different nation-states.

Intra-state conflict: Conflict between opposing sides within the same nation-state.

Jus cogens: An international philosophical rule which is universally binding. The prohibitions against slavery, genocide and war crimes are all *jus cogens*.

Legal responsibility: The need to be seen as law-abiding by other nations.

Multilateral: More than two nation-states.

Multipolar: Two or more dominant nation-states sharing world power.

Nation-state: The term used in international law for 'country'.

Non-government organisation (NGO): An organisation that works towards a certain cause and operates separate from any government.

Nuclear war: The use of nuclear weapons/atomic bombs against another country.	**Sanction:** Punishment.
Perm-5: The five permanent members of the UN Security Council: Russia, France, the UK, the US and China. These nation-states each have veto powers in the Security Council.	**Sovereignty:** Each nation-state has the absolute right to control its own affairs within its borders and is not obligated to listen to any outside authority.
	State: Country (also referred to as a **nation-state**).
Pre-emptive self-defence: A nation-state can legally use force if it can prove that it is about to be subject to invasion or force.	**State-sponsored terror:** Terrorist activity supported by a nation-state.
Ratify: The agreement by a nation-state to ensure that domestic laws will be implemented to incorporate the requirements of a treaty or international agreement.	**Terrorism:** Violence by an individual or group against its enemy in order to provoke fear; often perpetrated by groups outside a traditional nation-state boundary.
Reciprocity: Nations comply with international agreements because they want other nations to do the same.	**Transnational:** A private corporation that engages in foreign investment and owns, or controls, activities in more than one nation-state.
Regional federation: A cooperative grouping of nation-states that are regionally and/or ideologically close, who work towards common objectives.	**Treaty:** A written legal agreement between nation-states. Also referred to as a statute, protocol, covenant or convention. Treaties can be bilateral or multilateral.
Reparation: Compensation, usually monetary, for wrong or injury done.	**Unipolar:** One dominant world power (nation-state).
Rogue state: A nation-state that does not respect other states in its international actions.	**World government:** One government for all nation-states. A government such as this would be set up with the rule of law and have the power to enact, and enforce, international laws. It would have a legislature, a police force and leaders.
Rule of law: The idea that all peoples and institutions in a nation-state, including the government itself, are governed by, and subject to, the law.	**World order:** The creation of global relationships and the maintenance of world peace.

Chapter syllabus checklist

Are you able to answer every syllabus question in the chapter? Tick each question as you go through the list if you are able to answer it. If you cannot answer it, turn to the given page to find the answer. Refer to page ix to check the meaning of the NESA key words.

	For a complete understanding of this topic:	Page No.	✓
1	Can I define the meaning of *world order*?	371	
2	Can I describe the need for world order?	371	
3	Can I discuss the concept of 'world order'?	371	
4	Can I describe the development of world order over time?	371–5	
5	Can I outline the evolving nature of world order?	375	
6	Can I describe the nature of inter-state conflict?	375–7	
7	Can I describe the nature of intra-state conflict?	375–7	
8	Can I explain the implications of the nature of conflict on achieving world order?	377	
9	Can I describe access to resources as a source of conflict?	378–80	

	For a complete understanding of this topic:	Page No.	✓
10	Can I explain the role of the nation-state and state sovereignty in maintaining world order?	380–1	
11	Can I examine the role of sovereignty in assisting and impeding the resolution of world order issues?	381	
12	Can I describe the role of the United Nations in maintaining world order?	381–2	
13	Can I describe the role of international instruments in maintaining world order?	382–3	
14	Can I describe the role of courts and tribunals in maintaining world order?	384–386	
15	Can I outline the role of intergovernmental organisations (IGOs) in maintaining world order?	386	
16	Can I outline the role of non-government organisations (NGOs) in maintaining world order?	386	

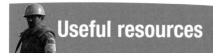

Useful resources

Treaties

Atlantic Charter 1941 (See Section 6.1.3, page 374.)

Charter of the United Nations 1945 (See Sections 6.1.3 [page 374], 6.2.1 [page 380] and 6.2.2 [page 382].)

Comprehensive Nuclear-Test-Ban Treaty (CTBT) 1996 (See Section 6.1.4, page 376.)

Convention against Torture and Other Cruel, Inhuman or Degrading Treatment or Punishment 1984 (See Section 6.2.3, page 383.)

Convention on the Law of the Sea (UN 1982) (See Section 6.2.4, page 385.)

Convention on the Settlement of Investment Disputes between States and Nationals of Other States 1966 (See Section 6.2.4, page 386.)

Covenant of the League of Nations 1919 (See Section 6.1.3, page 374.)

Geneva Conventions 1949 (See Sections 6.1.3 [page 374] and 6.3.4 [pages 400–1].)

Kyoto Protocol 1997 (See Section 6.2.7, page 387.)

Limited Test Ban Treaty 1963 (See Section 6.1.4, page 376.)

New York Convention 1958 (See Section 6.2.4, page 386.)

Pact of Paris (or the Kellogg-Briand Pact) 1928 (See Section 6.1.3, page 374.)

Protocols I and II Additional to the Geneva Conventions 1977 (See Section 6.3.4, pages 400–1.)

Rome Statute 1998 (See Section 6.2.4, pages 374–5.)

Treaty of Westphalia 1648 (See Section 6.1.3, page 374.)

Treaty on the Non-Proliferation of Nuclear Weapons (NNPT) 1968 (See Sections 6.1.3 [page 374] and 6.1.4 [page 376].)

Cases

A. v Australia (UNHRC) (1997) (See Section 6.4.5, page 409.)

Her Majesty's Advocate v Abdelbaset Ali Mohmed al Megrahi and Al Amin Khalifa Fhimah (2001) (The Lockerbie case; see Case Study 6.10, Section 6.4.5, page 409.)

Nicaragua v United States of America (1986) ICJ 14 (See Case Study 6.2, Section 6.2.4, page 374.)

Toonen v Australia (UNHRC) 1994 (See Section 6.4.5, page 409.)

Other documents

'Bin Laden birthday bash mocks war on terror. Spy chief warns of Pakistan threat.', Paul McGeough, *The Age*, 19 March 2007 (See Case Study 6.5, Section 6.3.2, pages 394–5.)

'South Africa's new era; Mandela, freed, urges step-up in pressure to end white rule', Christopher S. Wren, *The New York Times*, 12 February 1990 (See Case Study 6.9, Section 6.3.2, page 403.)

'Sweet and Sour' by Jim Lobe, Corpwatch, 2 June 2004 (www.corpwatch.org). (See Case Study 6.1, Section 6.1.5, page 379.)

Tribunals/courts (and websites)

Appellate Body of the World Trade Organization (See Section 6.2.4, page 385):
www.wto.org › trade topics › dispute settlement

European Union Court of Justice (See Section 6.2.4, page 385):
www.europa.eu/institutions/inst/justice/index_en.htm

European Court of Human Rights (See Section 6.2.4, page 385): www.echr.coe.int

International Centre for Settlement of Investment Disputes (ICSID) (See Section 6.2.4, page 386): www.worldbank.org/icsid

International Criminal Court (ICC) (See Section 6.2.4, pages 374–5): www.icc-cpi.int

International Court of Arbitration (See Section 6.2.4, page 386): www.iccwbo.org/court

International Court of Justice (ICJ) (See Section 6.2.4, page 384): www.icj-cij.org

International Criminal Tribunal for the former Yugoslavia (See Section 6.2.4, page 385): www.icty.org

International Criminal Tribunal for Rwanda (See Section 6.2.4, page 385): www.unictr.org

International Tribunal for the Law of the Sea (See Section 6.2.4, page 385): www.itlos.org

Organisations and websites

African Union (AU) (See Section 6.2.5, page 386): www.au.int

Amnesty International (See Section 6.2.6, page 386): www.amnesty.org.au

Association of Southeast Asian Nations (See Section 6.2.5, page 386): www.aseansec.org

Commonwealth of Nations (See Section 6.2.5, page 386): www.thecommonwealth.org

European Union (EU) (See Section 6.2.5, page 386): www.europa.eu

Greenpeace (See Section 6.2.6, page 386): www.greenpeace.org.au

Human Rights Watch (See Section 6.1.5, page 379): www.hrw.org

International Coalition for the Responsibility to Protect (See Section 6.3.1, page 392): www.responsibilitytoprotect.org

International Commission on Intervention and State Sovereignty (ICISS) (See Section 6.3.1, page 392):
www.responsibilitytoprotect.org/ICISS%20Report.pdf

International Federation of Red Cross and Red Crescent Societies (See Sections 6.2.6 [page 386] and 6.3.4 [page 400]): www.ifrc.org

International Labour Organization (ILO) (See Section 6.1.5, page 379): www.ilo.org

International Law Commission (See Section 6.4.4, page 406): www.un.org/law/ilc

International Monetary Fund (See Section 6.1.5, page 379): www.imf.org

North Atlantic Treaty Organization (NATO) (See Section 6.2.5, page 386): www.nato.int

Oxfam International (See Section 6.2.6, page 386): www.oxfam.org

United Nations (UN) (See Section 6.4.5, page 407): www.un.org

United Nations Permanent Forum on Indigenous Issues (UNPFII) (See Section 6.1.3, page 372): www.un.org/esa/socdev/unpfii

World Bank (See Sections 6.1.5 [page 393] and 6.4.5 [page 412]): www.worldbank.org

End of chapter questions

 KCq *Key Concept questions*

These questions test whether you have grasped the key ideas in each subsection. They are not difficult questions, but will test your recall of knowledge of the material you have read. If you are unsure what a question is asking you to do, refer to page ix to check the meaning of the NESA key words. If you can answer all these questions, you will know you have a sound knowledge of content.

Refer to pp. 472–7 for Answers

6.1 The nature of world order

6.1.1 The meaning of *world order*

1. What is the definition of *world order*?

6.1.2 The need for world order

2. Explain what you need to do in order to describe the need for world order.

3. Explain what you need to do in order to discuss the concept of world order.

6.1.3 The development of world order over time

4. Define *expansionism*.

5. List two impacts of expansionism on the current world order.

6. Identify three negative impacts that conflict and expansionism have had on Indigenous peoples and local communities.

7. Explain the terms *unipolar* and *multipolar*.

8. Define *transnationals* and describe the impact of transnationals on world order.

9. Explain why nation-states are becoming increasingly interdependent.

10. List three non-state participants in the current world order.

11. Identify the chief aim of the League of Nations.

12. Identify the main achievement of the *Pact of Paris* (1928).

13. Explain what you need to do in order to outline the evolving nature of world order.

6.1.4 The nature of conflict

14. Explain the terms *inter-state conflict* and *intra-state conflict*.

15. List five forms of conflict that disrupt world order.

16. Describe the Cold War.

17. Define *terrorism*.

18. List five implications of the nature of conflict for achieving world order.

19. Explain what you need to do in order to explain the implications of the nature of conflict for achieving world order.

6.1.5 Access to resources as a source of conflict

20. Give four reasons why developing states are not creating wealth to the same degree as developed nations.

21. Give an example of an action by a grassroots movement that has effectively assisted in reducing inequality between nation-states.

22. Explain, with an example, how an IGO can help ensure the economic wellbeing of its members.

23. Explain how the UN ensures that foreign aid is available to poor nations.

24. Using an example, explain how transnationals can contribute to resource inequality.

25. Explain why corruption is a more important issue for developing nations than it is for developed nations.

6.2 Responses to world order

26. List nine measures for achieving world order.

6.2.1 The role of the nation-state and state sovereignty

27. Define *state sovereignty*.

28. Outline a world order issue that cuts across traditional nation-state boundaries.

29. Explain the ideas of *reciprocity* and *legal responsibility*.

30. Explain what you need to do in order to examine the role of sovereignty in assisting and impeding the resolution of world order issues.

6.2.2 The role of the United Nations

31. List two of the 'purposes' of the UN as established under the UN Charter.

32. Name four core principles of the UN.

33. List the six original organs of the UN.

34. Explain what the Perm-5 is, list its members and explain its powers.

6.2.3 The role of international instruments

35. Explain the difference between a *treaty* and a *declaration*.

36. What does *ratification of a treaty* mean?
37. Explain the difference between a *treaty* and *international customary law*.

6.2.4 The role of courts and tribunals
38. Identify the types of cases able to be heard by the ICJ.
39. The ICC is a court of last resort. Explain.
40. List two ways a case can be referred to ICC jurisdiction.
41. List two *ad hoc* tribunals and their purpose.
42. List two other international courts.

6.2.5 The role of intergovernmental organisations
43. Outline the circumstances under which the UN Charter allows a regional intergovernmental organisation to address issues concerning world peace.
44. Give an example of a regional federation.

6.2.6 The role of non-government organisations
45. What roles are played by NGOs in achieving world order?
46. What body of the law was the International Federation of Red Cross and Red Crescent Societies instrumental in establishing?

6.2.7 The role of Australia's federal government
47. What is the *external affairs* power?
48. Explain, with an example, the role played by Australia's state governments in promoting world order.
49. List seven ways in which the Australian federal government works to achieve world order.
50. Explain what you need to do in order to explain the role of Australia's federal government in responding to world order.

6.2.8 The role of the media
51. Describe one positive and two negative influences of the media on the maintenance of world order.

6.2.9 Political negotiation, persuasion and the use of force
52. Why is political negotiation not always effective?
53. List three forms of persuasion.
54. Explain when nations may legally use force.
55. Explain the principles of *collective self-defence* and *pre-emptive self-defence*.
56. Citing an example, outline the circumstances in which the use of multilateral force is considered legal under international law.

6.2.10 The effectiveness of legal and non-legal measures in resolving conflict and working towards world order
57. List five legal and four non-legal measures which can resolve conflict and work towards world order.

58. Name one measure that can be seen as both legal and non-legal.
59. Explain what you need to do in order to evaluate the effectiveness of legal and non-legal measures in resolving conflict and working towards world order.

6.3 Contemporary issues concerning world order

6.3.1 The principle of 'Responsibility to Protect'
60. Outline the RtoP principles.
61. What are the three situations in which humanitarian intervention is permissible under international law?
62. Explain the powers contained in Chapter VII of the UN Charter.
63. Explain what you need to do in order to evaluate the effectiveness of legal and non-legal measures for the contemporary world order issue of the principle of 'Responsibility to Protect'

6.3.2 Regional and global situations that threaten peace and security
64. List six regional and global situations that threaten peace and security.
65. Discuss the legal basis of the US-led missions into Afghanistan and Iraq.
66. Identify two current threats to nuclear disarmament.
67. Explain how North Korea presents a threat to world order.
68. Identify three ways the international community has tried to address the incidences of mass atrocities.
69. Explain what you need to do in order to evaluate the effectiveness of legal and non-legal measures for the contemporary world order issue of regional and global situations that threaten peace and security.

6.3.3 The success of global cooperation in achieving world order
70. List three factors which limit the success of the United Nations in preventing conflict.
71. Describe the peace enforcement powers under the United Nations Charter.
72. List five features of peacekeeping missions.
73. Describe the extent to which peacekeeping missions have been used to resolve conflict.
74. Explain what you need to do in order to identify and investigate the contemporary issue of the success of global cooperation in achieving world order, and evaluate the effectiveness of legal and non-legal responses to this issue.

6.3.4 Rules regarding the conduct of hostilities

75. Explain how *international humanitarian law* differs from *human rights*.

76. Who is protected under the Geneva Conventions?

77. Using the treatment of prisoners at Guantanamo Bay as an example, explain what you need to do in order to identify and investigate the contemporary issue of the rules regarding the conduct of hostilities, and evaluate the effectiveness of legal and non-legal responses to this issue.

6.4 Themes and challenges

6.4.1 Theme 1: The role of the law in encouraging cooperation and resolving conflict in regard to world order

78. Explain why nation-states are becoming increasingly interdependent.

79. How is the concept of state sovereignty being eroded?

80. Why are nations unlikely to break treaties they have entered?

81. Using an example, describe a situation in which sanctions have been used successfully.

6.4.2 Theme 2: Issues of compliance and non-compliance

82. Explain why states generally comply with international law.

83. Explain the chief difference between domestic law and international law in relation to compliance and non-compliance.

84. Name three methods used to encourage nation-states to comply with the law.

6.4.3 Theme 3: The impact of changing values and ethical standards on world order

85. Outline two examples of new laws that focus on emerging moral standards.

86. Define *jus cogens* and explain how it reflects moral and ethical standards.

6.4.4 Theme 4: The role of law reform in promoting and maintaining world order

87. Explain how the International Law Commission affects reform.

88. How can parliaments of nation-states bring about reform in the area of world order?

89. List three non-legal agencies of reform.

90. Explain the ways in which disease and poverty give rise to the need for reform to the current world order.

6.4.5 Theme 5: The effectiveness of legal and non-legal responses in promoting and maintaining world order

91. Explain what limits any legal response to world order issues.

92. Describe two areas in which reform to the UN could make it more effective in promoting and maintaining world order.

93. Explain the key to the limited effectiveness of the ICJ.

94. Explain the most effective mechanism for the enforcement of international law for individuals.

95. Explain the significance of the 'Lockerbie case' and the Australian case involving Dragan Vasiljkovic.

96. Explain, using an example, how sanctions can be effective in enforcing international law.

97. Outline why humanitarian intervention and the RtoP measures are generally ineffective in stopping mass atrocities.

98. Why is nuclear disarmament an ongoing world order issue?

99. Outline evidence that suggests that the threats to world order posed by terrorism are not being adequately addressed.

100. Explain why some nation-states have greater access to appeals and reviews than others.

101. Explain how emerging technology is presenting a challenge for the current world order.

102. What factors mean that the nation-states are not equal in the current world order?

103. Assess the effectiveness of Australia's non-legal role in maintaining world order.

104. Explain two factors that indicate that the remedies employed to achieve world order are relatively effective.

105. Explain two factors that indicate that the remedies employed to achieve world order are not effective.

HSC   *Sample HSC questions*

Now for the real thing! The following questions are modelled on the types of questions you will face in the HSC. Think about it: if you get extensive practice at answering these sorts of questions, you will be more confident in answering them when it comes to the HSC Exam. It makes sense, doesn't it?

Another reason is that the answers given at the back of this guide are structured in a way that helps you learn strategies on how to answer HSC-like questions. This will help you aim for full marks!

For each extended-response question you will have a detailed answer with an explanation of what the question is asking you to do and also, when needed, an examiner's plan to help you get full marks with a section reference where you can find the answer in the chapter.

When you mark your work, highlight any questions you found difficult and earmark these areas for extra study.

Refer to pp. 477–8 for **Answers** ▶

IN THE HSC EXAM

- Material from this chapter will be examined in Section III of the exam.
- Each extended-response question in Section III is worth 25 marks. You have 45 minutes to answer each one.
- Look for the ⏱ min in each section and time yourself. This tells you approximately how much time you will have to answer these questions in the HSC Exam.

EXTENDED-RESPONSE QUESTIONS ⏱ 1 h 30 min

- In Section III of the exam, there will be seven extended-response questions, one for each option. Each question will have two alternatives. You will be required to answer two alternatives, each on a different option.
- In your answer you will be assessed on how well you:
  - demonstrate knowledge and understanding of legal issues relevant to the question
  - communicate using relevant legal terminology and concepts
  - illustrate your answer with relevant examples, such as legislation, cases, media reports and treaties
  - present a sustained, logical and cohesive response.
- The expected length of response is around eight examination writing booklet pages (approximately 1000 words).

Question 1 45 min

Describe **two** legal and **one** non-legal response to world order and evaluate the effectiveness of each in resolving conflict and working towards world order.

(25 marks)

Question 2 45 min

Explain how issues of compliance and non-compliance affect the maintenance of world order.

(25 marks)

Sample HSC Examinations

Are you ready to tackle an HSC-like exam paper? Try to complete each paper in as much of an exam-like environment as you can. Give yourself three hours for each exam paper. Do not look at the answers until you complete all the questions. Then mark the exams.

Good exam technique is essential in order for you to maximise your marks.

Allocating your time effectively

Use the suggested times which are set out at the beginning of the paper.

Section I:	Objective-response questions Allow about 30 minutes.
Section II:	Part A: short-answer questions Allow about 30 minutes.
Section II:	Part B: extended-response question Allow about 30 minutes.
Section III:	Extended-response questions Allow about 1 hour and 30 minutes.

▶ Keep track of time. Do not spend too much time on any one section. Move onto a new question where you may gain more marks rather than spending too long on previous questions.

▶ You may answer questions in any order. For example, you can leave the objective-response section till last. Use your reading time to check the general instructions and then find the questions you can best answer first. Come back to the harder questions later.

▶ Stick to the provided time allocations for each section to ensure that you give yourself enough time to complete all questions required adequately.

To answer objective-response questions:

▶ Read the stem of the question carefully. Check what key words are being used (e.g. *calculate*, *identify*).

▶ Look carefully at any related source material provided.

▶ Choose the best response.

▶ If you do not know the answer, make the best choice you can. There are no marks deducted for wrong answers.

To answer short-answer questions:

▶ Read and highlight key words at the beginning of the question. These key words are common to all HSC papers and require you to respond accordingly.

▶ Attempt to fill the entire space provided on the paper for these questions. It has been given to you as a guide to the length your response should be.

▶ Do not restate the question. It is not required and uses up valuable space and time.

▶ You can answer in point form or full-sentence style. In either case, you need to present your response in a logical order.

▶ Do not include irrelevant information in your answer. It will gain no marks and wastes your time.

To answer extended-response questions:

▶ In extended-response questions you must be succinct and make sure you link your ideas together. Do not write anything that comes into your head without linking it to another idea.

▶ Read and highlight key words at the beginning of the questions. These key words are common to all HSC papers and require you to respond accordingly.

▶ It is important that you arrange and organise your argument in a fluent manner. You should structure your response in a traditional essay format with clear introduction, main body and conclusion.

▶ For each new issue or theme you introduce to your argument, ensure that you start a new paragraph.

▶ In discussion questions, make sure you give points for and against.

▶ Continually refer to the question on the exam paper. Make sure that your response is consistent with the question being addressed.

▶ If your answer will not fit in the space provided, you have the right to ask for another booklet.

Check the NESA website resources

Go to the NESA website at www.educationstandards.nsw.edu.au and look through the past exam papers so you can see the types of questions that were asked in previous years. Then look at the sample answers provided for recent papers and also read through the examiners' reports of past papers. These are also very worthwhile as they give insights into the most common student mistakes and misunderstandings. Recognising these common problems will give you an opportunity to learn from other students' mistakes.

See also http://educationstandards.nsw.edu.au/wps/portal/nesa/11-12/hsc/exam-advice-resources/glossary-keywords

Sample HSC Examination 1

General instructions
▶ Reading time — 5 minutes
▶ Working time — 3 hours
▶ Write using blue or black pen.

Total marks — 100

Section I
20 marks
Attempt Questions 1–20.
Allow about 30 minutes for this section.

Section II, Part A
15 marks
Attempt Questions 21–23.
Allow about 30 minutes for this section.

Section II, Part B
15 marks
Attempt Question 24.
Allow about 30 minutes for this section.

Section III
50 marks
Attempt TWO questions from Questions 25–31, each
from a different Option.
Allow about 1 hour and 30 minutes for this section.

Refer to pp. 478–84 for Answers

SECTION I

20 marks
Attempt Questions 1–20.
Allow about 30 minutes for this section.

1. Peter drove his car at 120 km per hour in a
   suburban street. He lost control and crashed into
   another car coming in the opposite direction,
   killing the occupant. Which of the following is the
   ` for this crime?
   A Peter drove recklessly.
   B Peter intended to kill the occupant of the other car.
   C Peter's driving resulted in the death of the
      occupant of the other car.
   D Peter's driving was negligent.   (1 mark)

2. Which of the following best describes the crime of
   murder?
   A a summary offence
   B an economic offence
   C an indictable offence
   D an indictable offence that is heard summarily
                                              (1 mark)

3. Which of the following is an example of
   situational crime prevention?
   A engaging in a public protest about a law with
      which you disagree
   B driving within the speed limit
   C ensuring your house is securely locked and is
      fitted with an alarm system
   D teaching your child not to hit other children
                                              (1 mark)

4. Under which of the following circumstances must
   a person answer questions asked by police?
   A never
   B when arrested
   C when charged with a criminal offence
   D when driving a car and asked to produce a
      driver's licence   (1 mark)

5. Which of the following courts would hear an
   appeal about the severity of a sentence for a
   conviction of assault?
   A the Local Court
   B the District Court
   C the Supreme Court
   D the NSW Court of Criminal Appeal   (1 mark)

6. Which of the following is the correct term for an
   agreement to attend court on a particular day?
   A bail
   B remand
   C charge
   D summons   (1 mark)

7. The prosecution and defence come to an
   agreement that an accused person will plead
   guilty to a charge of assault occasioning actual
   bodily harm rather than face a trial for a charge of
   malicious wounding. Which of the following
   options best describes this scenario?
   A charge negotiation
   B prosecution case
   C defended hearing
   D indictable defence plea   (1 mark)

8. Which of the following is most likely to limit the
   human rights of Australian citizens?
   A counterterrorism laws
   B restrictions on freedom of movement
   C the common law
   D laws about suffrage   (1 mark)

9. Which of the following best protects the rights of Indigenous Australians?

   A the Australian Constitution

   B the *Racial Discrimination Act*

   C the Convention on the Rights of the Child

   D the Northern Territory Intervention   (1 mark)

10. Which of the following best describes how the system of appeals assists in achieving justice?

    A allowing an accused person to opt for a trial by jury

    B minimising the effects of wrong decisions made by judges and magistrates

    C allowing a *prima facie* case to be overturned

    D diverting alleged offenders from the criminal justice process   (1 mark)

11. Which of the following is an example of a civil and political right?

    A the right to equal pay for equal work

    B the right to self-determination

    C the right to an adequate standard of living

    D the right to education   (1 mark)

12. Which of the following best describes the defence of necessity?

    A It is a complete defence.

    B It is a partial defence.

    C The accused person claims that he or she needed to commit the criminal act in order to defend him- or herself.

    D The accused person claims that he or she needed to commit the criminal act because of threats to his or her family.   (1 mark)

13. Which of the following is one difference between citizen's arrest and arrest by police?

    A The police can arrest a person on 'reasonable suspicion' of having committed a crime, but a citizen may not.

    B Police do not need to tell a person why he or she is being arrested, but a citizen does.

    C Police may not use force when making an arrest, but a citizen may.

    D Police must apply for a warrant in order to arrest someone, but a citizen only needs to tell a person that he or she is being arrested.   (1 mark)

14. With which of the following people does the burden of proof lie in a criminal case?

    A the prosecution

    B the defence

    C the judge

    D the accused   (1 mark)

15. Which of the following may persuade a magistrate to mitigate the sentence for a criminal offence?

    A the fact that there was a relationship of trust with the victim

    B the fact that the offender pleaded not guilty

    C the fact that the offender has a prior criminal record

    D the fact that the offender cooperated with the authorities   (1 mark)

16. In order to receive legal aid to defend a serious criminal charge, a person needs to pass which of the following?

    A a merit test

    B a means test

    C a means test and a merit test

    D a means test, a merit test and a jurisdiction test   (1 mark)

17. Which of the following best describes the inalienability of human rights?

    A Human rights are to be enjoyed by all humans regardless of nationality, race or gender.

    B All human rights are equally important.

    C Human rights are the birthright of all humans.

    D Human rights cannot be given up or taken away.   (1 mark)

18. Which of the following is one advantage of a criminal infringement notice?

    A It incapacitates the offender.

    B It is often ignored.

    C It saves the police and the court time.

    D It rehabilitates the offender.   (1 mark)

19. Which of the following best describes the separation of powers?

    A Government power is apportioned between state and federal governments.

    B The powers of police are separate from those of a court.

    C Governmental power is shared between the judiciary, the legislature and the executive.

    D National and international powers of government are separated by treaty arrangements.   (1 mark)

20. Of which of the following is the Treaty on Extradition between Australia and the United States (1974) an example?

    A international customary law

    B a bilateral treaty

    C a political sanction

    D a multilateral treaty   (1 mark)

Section II

Part A — Human rights

QUESTION 21

Identify and briefly describe three major international human rights documents. (3 marks)

QUESTION 22

Explain how one human right is protected in Australia. (2 marks)

QUESTION 23 (10 MARKS)

a Describe the nature and extent of a contemporary issue which illustrates the promotion and/or enforcement of human rights. (4 marks)

b Describe and evaluate the effectiveness of one legal and one non-legal response to the issue of human rights. (6 marks)

Part B — Crime

QUESTION 24

Assess the extent to which the law balances the rights of victims, offenders and society. (15 marks)

Section III — Options

QUESTION 25 — Consumers (25 marks)

a Identify and describe ONE contemporary issue involving the protection of consumers. Describe the legal and non-legal responses to this issue and evaluate the effectiveness of these responses. (25 marks)

OR

b Evaluate the effectiveness of legal and non-legal responses in achieving justice for consumers, with particular reference to the regulation of advertising, marketing and product certification. (25 marks)

QUESTION 26 — Global environmental protection (25 marks)

a Identify and describe ONE contemporary issue involving the protection of the global environment. Describe the legal and non-legal responses to this issue and evaluate the effectiveness of these responses. (25 marks)

OR

b Evaluate the effectiveness of legal and non-legal measures in protecting the global environment, with particular reference to the role of sovereignty in assisting and impeding the achievement of ecologically sustainable development. (25 marks)

Note: there are no sample answers provided for this Option.

QUESTION 27 — Family (25 marks)

a Identify and describe ONE contemporary issue relating to family law. Describe the legal and non-legal responses to this issue and evaluate the effectiveness of these responses. (25 marks)

OR

b Evaluate the effectiveness of legal and non-legal responses in achieving justice for parties involved in relationship breakdowns. (25 marks)

QUESTION 28 — Indigenous peoples (25 marks)

a Identify and describe ONE contemporary issue involving the rights of Indigenous peoples. Describe the legal and non-legal responses to this issue and evaluate the effectiveness of these responses. (25 marks)

OR

b Evaluate the effectiveness of legal and non-legal responses in achieving justice for Indigenous peoples, with particular reference to the role of sovereignty in assisting and impeding the recognition of the rights of Indigenous peoples. (25 marks)

Note: there are no sample answers provided for this Option.

QUESTION 29 — Shelter (25 marks)

a Identify and describe ONE contemporary issue involving the provision of shelter. Describe the legal and non-legal responses to this issue and evaluate the effectiveness of these responses.

(25 marks)

OR

b Evaluate the effectiveness of legal and non-legal responses in protection of tenants, landlords, boarders and lodgers. (25 marks)

Note: there are no sample answers provided for this Option.

QUESTION 30 — Workplace (25 marks)

a Identify and describe ONE contemporary issue involving workplace law. Describe the legal and non-legal responses to this issue and evaluate the effectiveness of these responses. (25 marks)

OR

b Evaluate the effectiveness of legal and non-legal responses in achieving justice for employers and employees, with particular reference to protecting and recognising workplace rights. (25 marks)

QUESTION 31 — World order (25 marks)

a Identify and describe ONE contemporary issue involving world order. Describe the legal and non-legal responses to this issue and evaluate the effectiveness of these responses. (25 marks)

OR

b Evaluate the effectiveness of legal and non-legal responses in working towards world order, with particular reference to the role of sovereignty in assisting and impeding the resolution of world order issues. (25 marks)

Refer to pp. 478–84 for

End of paper

Sample HSC Examination 2

General instructions
▶ Reading time — 5 minutes
▶ Working time — 3 hours
▶ Write using blue or black pen.

Total marks — 100

Section I
20 marks
Attempt Questions 1–20.
Allow about 30 minutes for this section.

Section II, Part A
15 marks
Attempt Questions 21–23.
Allow about 30 minutes for this section.

Section II, Part B
15 marks
Attempt Question 24.
Allow about 30 minutes for this section.

Section III
50 marks
Attempt TWO questions from Questions 25–31, each
from a different Option.
Allow about 1 hour and 30 minutes for this section.

Refer to pp. 484–9 for Answers

SECTION I

20 marks
Attempt Questions 1–20.
Allow about 30 minutes for this section.

1. Which of the following describes a difference between criminal and civil matters?
   A Civil matters are prosecuted, but criminal matters are not.
   B The police are normally involved in criminal matters but not in civil matters.
   C Civil matters are determined by common law, but criminal matters are determined by statute law.
   D Civil matters normally involve the state, but criminal matters do not. (1 mark)

2. Which of the following is an example of a strict liability offence?
   A murder
   B assault
   C speeding
   D theft (1 mark)

3. In which of the following categories of crime would the crime of treason be categorised?
   A offences against the person
   B preliminary crimes
   C public order offences
   D offences against the sovereign (1 mark)

4. Which of the following best describes the provision of legal aid in NSW?
   A It means that everyone who needs legal representation receives it.
   B It ensures the right to legal representation.
   C It does not assist everyone who needs legal representation, because the means test is too low.
   D It is only available for serious criminal matters. (1 mark)

5. Which of the following best describes the role of the Public Defender?
   A to bring a case on behalf of the Crown
   B to defend a person accused of a crime
   C to defend a person accused of a crime, if the person is also eligible for legal aid
   D to defend a person accused of a serious offence, if the person is also eligible for legal aid (1 mark)

6. Which of the following is the required standard of proof in a criminal trial?
   A beyond a shadow of doubt
   B on the balance of probabilities
   C on the standard of natural justice
   D beyond reasonable doubt (1 mark)

7. A person is detained by police for two days because he is suspected of being about to engage in a terrorist activity. Which of the following does the law say about this situation?
   A It is legal because police have the power to do this under counterterrorism legislation.
   B It is legal because police can detain anyone for up to seven days.
   C It is illegal because police can only detain someone if there is a criminal charge against them.
   D It is illegal because police can only keep a suspect for four hours for interrogation purposes. (1 mark)

8. Which of the following best describes the way in which freedom of religion is protected in Australia?
   A through the Australian Constitution
   B through statute law
   C through common law
   D through non-interference (1 mark)

9. Which of the following are defence witnesses generally not permitted to do in a criminal trial?

   A give their opinion about another person's words or actions

   B discuss the good character of the accused

   C explain what they saw with their own eyes

   D be questioned by the prosecution (1 mark)

10. Which of the following types of human rights best describes the right to peace?

    A an economic right

    B a moral right

    C a collective right

    D a social right (1 mark)

11. Which of the following is one feature of an adversarial system of trial?

    A Witnesses may only respond to questions asked.

    B The past record of the accused forms part of the evidence.

    C The judge works with the investigating prosecutor in order to present evidence.

    D Witnesses are obliged to give their opinion about the likely guilt of the accused. (1 mark)

12. Which of the following alternatives best describes the process of one state handing over a fugitive criminal to another state within which the fugitive criminal committed a crime?

    A deportation

    B a physical sanction

    C extradition

    D a transnational agreement (1 mark)

13. Which of the following legal terms refers to the allocation of legislative power between state and federal governments in Australia?

    A state sovereignty

    B the division of powers

    C the separation of powers

    D the unitary system of government (1 mark)

14. Which of the following is the purpose of a coronial inquiry?

    A to discover the circumstances surrounding an unnatural death or an unexplained fire

    B to decide the guilt or innocence of a person involved in an unnatural death or an unexplained fire

    C to decide whether there is a *prima facie* case against the accused

    D to inquire into the likelihood of an accused person breaching bail conditions (1 mark)

15. Which of the following is not a complete defence?

    A provocation

    B consent

    C mental illness

    D self-defence (1 mark)

16. Which of the following rights is protected by the ICCPR?

    A the right to recognition everywhere as a person before the law

    B the right to rest and leisure

    C the right to peace

    D the right to social security (1 mark)

17. On which of the following occasions must a warrant generally be used?

    A to search a motor vehicle

    B to arrest a suspect

    C to take fingerprints

    D to search a premises without the consent of the owner (1 mark)

18. Which of the following responses to crime is available for children but not for adult offenders?

    A a fine

    B a warning

    C dismissal of charges

    D referral for rehabilitation purposes (1 mark)

19. Which of the following is an example of a transnational crime?

    A genocide

    B drug trafficking

    C piracy

    D murder (1 mark)

20. Susannah is continually harassed at her workplace by her male colleagues, who make offensive sexist remarks and gestures to her and about her in her presence. Which of the following courses of action is most likely to result in an order for compensation to be paid to Susannah?

    A lodging a complaint with the Australian Human Rights Commission

    B having the matter heard by the NSW Civil and Administrative Tribunal (NCAT)

    C lodging a complaint with the United Nations Human Rights Committee

    D lodging a complaint with the Committee on the Elimination of Discrimination against Women (1 mark)

Section II

30 marks
Allow about 60 minutes for this section.

Part A — Human rights

15 marks
Attempt Questions 21–23.
Allow about 30 minutes for this section.

QUESTION 21

Choose one domestic or international non-government organisation and describe ONE way it has assisted in the recognition of human rights in recent times.

(4 marks)

QUESTION 22

The following view was expressed by the Chinese government at the Vienna World Conference on Human Rights, 1993:

'When poverty and lack of adequate food and clothing are commonplace and people's basic needs are not guaranteed, priority should be given to economic development. Otherwise, human rights are completely out of the question.'

With reference to the above quotation, explain the nature of human rights. (5 marks)

QUESTION 23

Explain the idea of self-determination, one way in which this right is protected in Australia, and one international protection of this right. (6 marks)

Part B — Crime

15 marks
Attempt Question 24.
Allow about 30 minutes for this section.
In your answers you will be assessed on how well you:
▶ demonstrate knowledge and understanding of legal issues relevant to the question
▶ communicate using relevant legal terminology and concepts
▶ refer to relevant examples such as legislation, cases, media, international instruments and documents
▶ present a sustained, logical and cohesive response.

QUESTION 24

Consider these two cases:

On 23 December 2007, Naomi was found guilty of burglary, after she broke into a house and stole $1000 worth of jewellery. Naomi is a professional thief and often commits such crimes, though she is rarely caught. She has had only one previous conviction. Naomi has the sole care of her two teenage children.

On the same day, Lloyd pleaded guilty to burglary, after he broke into his aunt's house and stole $1000 in cash, which he knew was in the house. Lloyd is twenty-one years old and has a cocaine addiction. He has no previous convictions.

The maximum penalty for these crimes is fourteen years jail.

Describe how the sentencing decisions would have been made in the cases described above. Evaluate the effectiveness of ONE type of criminal penalty that could have been given in either case, and compare that penalty with a sentencing diversionary program that could have been used. (15 marks)

Section III — Options

50 marks
Attempt TWO questions from Questions 25–31, each from a different Option.
Allow 1 hour and 30 minutes for this section.
In your answers you will be assessed on how well you:
▶ demonstrate knowledge and understanding of legal issues relevant to the question
▶ communicate using relevant legal terminology and concepts
▶ refer to relevant examples such as legislation, cases, media, international instruments and documents
▶ present a sustained, logical and cohesive response

QUESTION 25 — Consumers (25 marks)

a   Describe the role of law reform in recognising the rights of consumers, and evaluate the effectiveness of law reform in meeting the challenges of the modern consumer society. (25 marks)

OR

b   Examine the extent to which the law encourages cooperation in regard to preventing and settling consumer complaints. (25 marks)

QUESTION 26 — Global environmental protection (25 marks)

a Describe the role of law reform in protecting the global environment, and evaluate the effectiveness of law reform in meeting the challenges of global environmental protection. (25 marks)

OR

b Examine the impact of state sovereignty on international cooperation in regard to environmental protection. (25 marks)

Note: there are no sample answers provided for this Option.

QUESTION 27 — Family (25 marks)

a Describe the role of law reform in achieving just outcomes for family members and society, and evaluate the effectiveness of law reform in meeting the challenges of modern family relationships. (25 marks)

OR

b Examine the extent to which the law encourages cooperation in regard to resolving family conflict. (25 marks)

QUESTION 28 — Indigenous peoples (25 marks)

a Describe the role of law reform in recognising the rights of Indigenous peoples, and evaluate the effectiveness of law reform in meeting the challenges of recognising these rights in contemporary society. (25 marks)

OR

b Examine the impact of state sovereignty on international cooperation in regard to protecting the rights of Indigenous peoples. (25 marks)

Note: there are no sample answers provided for this Option.

QUESTION 29 — Shelter (25 marks)

a Describe the role of law reform in protecting the rights of those seeking shelter, and evaluate the effectiveness of law reform in meeting the challenges presented by providing shelter in contemporary society. (25 marks)

OR

b Examine the extent to which the law encourages cooperation in regard to providing shelter. (25 marks)

NOTE: There are no sample answers provided for this Option.

QUESTION 30 — Workplace (25 marks)

a Describe the role of law reform in recognising rights and enforcing responsibilities in the workplace, and evaluate the effectiveness of law reform in meeting the challenges of the modern workplace. (25 marks)

OR

b Examine the extent to which the law encourages cooperation in regard to preventing and settling workplace disputes. (25 marks)

QUESTION 31 — World order (25 marks)

a Describe the role of law reform in promoting and maintaining world order, and evaluate the effectiveness of law reform in meeting the challenges of maintaining world order in contemporary society. (25 marks)

OR

b Examine the impact of state sovereignty on international cooperation in regard to maintaining world order. (25 marks)

Refer to pp. 484–9 for Answers

End of paper

Answers

Chapter 1: Crime

KCq Key Concept questions (pages 87–91)

1. i   There must be an act or a failure to act (an omission) which breaks the law.
    ii The act or omission must be seen as harmful to the whole community.
    iii The act or omission is punishable by the state.
    v   The state takes the person who committed the act to court where the offence must be proved according to the rules of criminal procedure.

2. *actus reus* and *mens rea*

3. i   that the act or omission actually took place
    ii that the act or omission was done by the accused person
    iii that the act or omission was voluntary

4. i   intention, which means the specific desire to commit the criminal act or omit the duty
    ii recklessness, which means that the person could foresee the probability of harm, but acted anyway
    iii negligence, which means that the person failed to exercise the degree of care, skill or foresight that a reasonable person would have exercised in the same circumstances

5. In strict liability offences only *actus reus* need be proved, whereas in other crimes both *actus reus* and *mens rea* must be proved.

6. *Causation* means that the act or omission committed must have caused the specific injury complained of.

7. where an ordinary, natural event or the physical or other characteristics of the victim contribute to the death

8. i   the definition of the word *crime*, including all four elements of the definition
    ii an example of a crime, which illustrates the definition
    iii definitions of *actus reus*, *mens rea*, strict liability offences and causation

9. i offences against the person; ii offences against the sovereign; iii economic offences; iv drug offences; v driving offences; vi public order offences; vii preliminary crimes

10. i   conspiracy, which is the case when two or more people agree to do an unlawful act or to do a lawful act by unlawful means
    ii the crime of attempt, which occurs if a crime is attempted but not successfully committed

11. You need to be able to define and give examples of the seven categories of crime.

12. Two summary offences are driving offences and offensive behaviour. Indictable offences include murder, sexual assault and malicious wounding.

13. Summary offences are heard by a magistrate sitting alone in a Local Court. Indictable offences can be heard by a judge and jury.

14. You should mention the seriousness of each type of offence, the way each type of offence is heard by a court, and give examples of each type of offence.

15. James is the principal in the first degree. Helen is the principal in the second degree. Ruth is an accessory before the fact and Tyson is an accessory after the fact.

16. What is deemed to be criminal depends on what the public sees as offending public welfare. Sometimes one group in society condemns certain behaviour as being against public welfare while another group sees the behaviour as quite acceptable. Many young people think that marijuana use is quite acceptable, for example, even though it is a criminal activity.

17. i   because of a belief, value or custom which means a person would follow the legal behaviour anyway
    ii many laws simply regulate behaviour which we generally agree should be regulated
    iii education
    iv fear of punishment
    v   fear of public shame or condemnation
    vi a general desire for protection

18. i   Some people see the law as being unimportant.
    ii People think that they will not be caught.
    iii People give in to temptation.
    iv People see it as thrilling or exciting to break the law.

19. social factors, economic factors, genetic factors, political factors and self-interest

20. You should discuss the reasons most people obey the criminal law most of the time, the reasons why many people break some criminal laws sometimes, and the factors which may influence the fact that some people are more likely to engage in criminal behaviour than others.

21. avoiding situations in which a criminal situation could arise, such as a party; and installing a good security system and locks on a house in order to discourage potential thieves

22. Social crime prevention occurs through changing the social factors which cause people to be criminals.

23. You should discuss what is meant by both situational crime prevention and social crime prevention, and give various examples of both, discussing how effective each is in preventing crime.

24. the criminal investigation process, the criminal trial process, and the processes of sentencing and punishment

25. *Discretion* means the choice to do or not to do something.

26. Police have power to search people, places and motor vehicles, and seize or take evidence, if they are investigating a crime, if the occupier of the premises consents, or if they have a search warrant. Police can search anyone reasonably suspected of possessing stolen property or anything which has been, or is intended to be, used in committing a serious offence. Police may also search a person after arrest.

27. A driver must produce his or her licence on request; a person must, if able to do so, give the name and address of a driver who has been involved in a motor accident; and a person must give information to a customs officer about drug smuggling.

28. Police may tap phones if they obtain a warrant from a judge first. They do not need a warrant at all in cases of sieges, kidnapping or hostage-taking.

29. the *Crimes (Forensic Procedures) Act 2000* (NSW)

30. If a person reasonably suspected of committing a serious crime refuses to consent to giving a sample for the purposes of DNA testing, the police can take a sample of hair by force, or can obtain an order from a magistrate to take a sample by force.

31. the *Law Enforcement (Powers and Responsibilities) Act 2002* (NSW)

32. Police can detain an arrested person for four hours for investigation. Arrested suspects cannot be kept for any longer than eight hours without charges being laid. A 'drunk and disorderly' person may be detained for up to eight hours without arrest. A person can be detained for up to two hours for the purpose of taking samples for DNA testing. A person suspected of being about to engage in a terrorist activity can be detained for forty-eight hours without charge. Extensions to this time may be granted if police investigations are ongoing.

33. In July 2007, Mohamed Haneef was detained without charge for twelve days by Brisbane police because he was suspected of having links to a failed terrorist attack in Britain. On the twelfth day, he was charged with providing support to a terrorist organisation and released on bail, pending deportation under immigration laws. The charges against Haneef were dropped two weeks later. This case has raised concerns because it goes against a fundamental human right and it is a breach of the International Covenant on Civil and Political Rights (ICCPR) 1966 to detain a person without charge.

34. To discuss the powers of the police in the criminal process you should describe each of the areas in which the police can exercise power, and describe concerns about the exercise of police powers, including the role of discretion in the exercise of such powers.

35. Most crimes are detected and, therefore, reported by private citizens who are either witnesses to, or victims of, a criminal offence.

36. Any five of the following: reporting may bring the victim's own illegal acts to the attention of the police; victims may know the alleged offender, and not report due to feelings of fear, loyalty or protection; a solution can be found between the criminal and the victim; red tape; feelings of humiliation/shame; feeling that reporting does not lead to an arrest/conviction; feeling that there is sexism in the police force and the judiciary.

37. Discretion is exercised by people who decide whether or not to report a crime. They may be influenced by the race, sex, age or appearance of the alleged offender.

38. Police are the main investigators of crime. Other crime investigators include social security officers, tax officials, health and safety inspectors, and local government officials.

39. Police might interview possible witnesses, collect a list of stolen property, and gather fingerprints or other physical evidence.

40. phone taps; video surveillance; DNA collection and analysis; use of data banks such as COPS

41. A *warrant* is a written authorisation issued by a judge or magistrate which gives the police power to take the action authorised by it.

42. A warrant must generally be used by police to search premises, unless the occupier of the premises consents to the search.

43. You need to discuss: who reports crimes and why some crimes are not reported; what is involved in the investigation of crime by police, including a discussion of police powers; and how police discretion affects the investigation of crime.

44. information and summons, information and warrant, arrest without warrant

45. Officers, on arrest, must: tell the person that he or she is under arrest; tell the person why he or she is being arrested; and touch the person being arrested.

46. Police decide charges on the evidence they have gathered from their investigation. For example, in the case where A has badly assaulted B who almost died, the police have the discretion to decide whether A is charged with assault, with attempted manslaughter or attempted murder.

47. *Bail* is an agreement to attend court to answer a criminal charge. *Remand* is what occurs when bail is refused. The defendant is remanded in custody (that is, kept in prison) until the day of the court hearing.

48. the *Bail Act 2013* (NSW)

49. Granting bail is very important because, until the court hearing is over, the defendant is presumed innocent. If a person is not granted bail, that means a person who has not been found guilty of a crime is kept in prison.

50. Bail can be granted by the police or by a magistrate or judge. After arrest the police can grant bail. At the first court appearance, the magistrate can grant bail. During any adjournments of the court hearing, the judge or magistrate can grant bail.

51. There is a presumption in favour of bail for those accused of more serious offences not involving violence or robbery. This means they should be granted bail unless police have very good reasons for not granting it.

52. **i** the likelihood of the accused person coming to court on the appointed day; **ii** the interests of the accused person; **iii** the protection of the community

53. Discretion is used in the granting of bail by weighing up the three factors to be considered when granting bail.

54. The right to silence operates when a person is being questioned by the police, even if he or she is under arrest. It also operates in the courtroom, though corporations generally must supply documents even if they are incriminating. Exceptions to the right to silence include: a driver must produce his or her licence on request; a person must, if able to do so, give the name and address of a driver who has been involved in a motor accident; a person must give information to a customs officer about drug smuggling.

55. Citizens are not compelled to allow police to search their persons or their premises except if police have a warrant or in certain other circumstances. A person does not have to supply blood or DNA for forensic tests, unless that person is accused of a serious offence.

56. There is no absolute right for an accused person to communicate with a friend, relative or lawyer but, if an accused person is not given the opportunity for such communication, doubt is cast on the validity of anything he or she may say to police.

57. A lawyer should be allowed to be present if the accused person requests, and the interrogation should be delayed for a reasonable time so that the accused person can attempt to get legal assistance.

58. **i** Police use of technology can help to catch perpetrators who are technologically adept.

ii The police have wide powers of arrest, thereby protecting the community.

iii Police may only use firearms in limited circumstances, and this prevents unnecessary death and injury.

iv People arrested are usually granted bail unless there are good reasons not to do so, and this protects the presumption of innocence, and the community.

v People generally may not be detained by police unless arrested and then only for a limited period, which protects people's right to freedom.

vi People do not have to answer police questions in most circumstances, and so are protected from giving answers which may harm themselves or others.

vii Accused people can generally communicate with a friend, relative or lawyer.

viii Evidence that has been obtained illegally will generally not be admissible in court.

59. **i** The exercise of some police powers, such as camera surveillance, DNA collection and COPS, may be an unnecessary violation of privacy.

ii A significant number of crimes are not reported because people believe nothing effective will be done to the offender.

iii Wide police discretion in deciding whether to arrest someone or not could be exercised in a discriminatory manner.

iv Police may have too much discretion in deciding what charge to lay on an arrested person.

v If bail is not granted, there is always the chance that an innocent person is kept in detention for a significant period.

vi Suspected terrorists can be detained without charge for an indefinite period, which violates a fundamental human right.

vii Some argue that the right to silence only operates to protect the guilty.

viii There is no absolute right for an accused person to be able to communicate with a friend or relative.

ix There is no absolute right for an accused person to contact a lawyer.

x Illegally obtained evidence is admissible in court if it is judged to be in the public interest, which may jeopardise the accused person's presumption of innocence.

60. **i** hearings of minor criminal cases, called summary offences; **ii** committal proceedings for more serious crimes; **iii** coronial inquiries; **iv** Children's Court hearings

61. Many indictable offences can be heard summarily depending on whether the prosecution and/or the accused decide that they want the offence heard in this way.

62. The Drug Court aims to get the offender off drugs rather than punish the offender, thereby aiming to reduce drug-related crime and drug addiction.

63. The District Court hears most indictable offences, such as manslaughter, bigamy, armed robbery and malicious wounding. The Supreme Court only hears the most serious indictable offences, such as murder and arson.

64. The NSW Court of Criminal Appeal can hear appeals from the District Court and Supreme Court about the severity of the sentence or on questions of fact or law. It can also hear appeals from the Local Court on questions of law only.

65. The appellant must show that the judge in the lower court either wrongly used or misinterpreted the law. No new evidence or facts can be heard.

66. matters arising under the *Competition and Consumer Act 2010* (Cth), and breaches of copyright

67. The High Court hears appeals from the NSW Court of Criminal Appeal on questions of law, and appeals in federal criminal matters from the Federal Court.

68. **i** that a person charged with a criminal offence has his or her guilt or innocence decided in a court hearing

ii that most criminal law is state law so most cases are heard in the NSW court system

iii the types of cases heard in each court in the NSW court system and in the federal system

iv the system of appeals

69. In an adversarial system of trial, the two sides of the case try to present and prove their version of the facts and disprove the version of the other side. An impartial judge (and sometimes a jury) listens to the evidence and makes a decision as to which side is correct. In an inquisitorial system of trial the magistrate or judge collects the evidence for both sides, in cooperation with the prosecution, after inquiries have been made. Also, in an adversarial system of trial: there are strict rules of evidence such as hearsay and opinion; there is a presumption of innocence; witnesses are examined orally and can only answer the questions asked; and the past record of the accused may only be examined during sentencing.

70. You need to weigh up the problems associated with the system against the advantages of the system.

71. A *magistrate* decides cases in the Local Court, while a *judge* decides cases in higher courts, such as the District Court or the Supreme Court.

72. The role of a magistrate/judge in a summary hearing is to: ensure that the trial is conducted legally and in a manner which is fair to the accused; to decide questions which arise about the law; to decide the guilt or innocence of the accused; and to impose a punishment if the verdict is guilty.

73. In a trial by jury, the judge explains the law to the jury and outlines the questions which must be answered so that the jury, not the judge, can decide the guilt or innocence of the accused.

74. In a criminal case, the prosecutor calls on each prosecution witness and examines him or her, and presents other evidence to prove that the alleged offender is guilty of the crime.

75. The role of a Public Defender is to represent accused people who have been granted legal aid in the District Court and Supreme Court.

76. When a person pleads guilty, he or she is then sentenced by the court. When a person pleads not guilty, there is a court case to determine his or her guilt.

77. In charge negotiation the prosecution and defence meet before the trial and the defence agrees that the accused will plead guilty if the prosecution reduces the charge. An example is if a person charged with attempted murder agrees to plead guilty to malicious wounding, which carries a much smaller maximum penalty, in return for the prosecution dropping the attempted murder charge.

78. **i** Charge negotiation puts pressure on the accused to plead guilty to something he or she may not be found

guilty of in a court hearing, and the accused may get a lighter sentence than he or she really deserves.

ii Charge negotiation saves the victim from the ordeal of giving evidence and being cross-examined, but the lighter sentence given to the accused may mean the victim of the crime feels that the offender was not punished sufficiently.

iii Charge negotiation saves witnesses in the community from the ordeal of giving evidence and being cross-examined, and its efficiency saves the community from unnecessary pain and expense. However, being given a lighter sentence may mean that the accused will be more likely to reoffend and will, therefore, be a greater danger to the community. Charge negotiation is a secretive process that may prevent the court system from being seen by the community to be operating to achieve justice.

79. i Criminal cases are prosecuted by trained lawyers so it is important that defendants are represented by a lawyer as well.

ii The rules of evidence and procedure can be difficult for a non-lawyer to deal with.

80. A defence lawyer presents the evidence favourable to the accused and tries to discredit the evidence of the prosecution by cross-examination of witnesses.

81. The correct citation is *Dietrich v The Queen* (1992) 177 CLR 292. This case is important because it established a right to legal representation for serious offences.

82. a means test, a merit test and a jurisdiction test

83. You need to: explain the role of a defence lawyer; explain why legal representation is important; explain the significance of the *Dietrich* case; explain how legal aid operates for criminal matters; and explain the consequences of not being granted legal aid.

84. *Presumption of innocence* is the presumption in a criminal trial that an accused person is innocent until proved guilty.

85. *Burden of proof* means the responsibility of proving a case in court. In a criminal case the prosecution has the burden of proof and must prove that the accused is guilty.

86. *Standard of proof* means the weight or value given to evidence; how much proof is needed in a court case. The standard of proof in criminal cases is 'beyond reasonable doubt' (that is, if there is a reasonable doubt in the mind of the judge or jury as to whether the defendant committed the crime, he or she must be acquitted).

87. The procedure is as follows:
• the prosecution gives its opening address
• the defence gives its opening address
• the prosecution calls each of its witnesses, who undergo examination-in-chief, and possibly cross-examination and re-examination
• the defence calls each of its witnesses, who undergo examination-in-chief, and possibly cross-examination and re-examination
• the prosecution gives its closing address
• the defence gives its closing address
• the judge sums up for the jury and may direct the jury to acquit
• the jury delivers its verdict.

88. The procedure outlined above is the same in a summary hearing except that there is no jury, so the judge or magistrate decides the verdict.

89. These rules have developed in order to try and keep the process fair to both sides.

90. The *right to silence* means that an accused person does not have to say anything in court at all, though corporations must submit documents even when such documents might incriminate them.

91. A confession cannot be used in court unless it is made voluntarily. Generally, confessions made to police but not electronically recorded cannot be used as evidence in court.

92. The judge or magistrate must consider the community's interest, as well as ensuring a fair trial for the accused, when deciding whether to admit or reject evidence. Generally, police must prove that evidence they have gathered has been obtained legally if it is to be admitted in court.

93. A *complete defence* is a legally acceptable reason for committing the crime which completely excuses the defendant, so that he or she is found not guilty. A *partial defence* reduces the liability of the accused, so that he or she is found guilty of a lesser offence, such as manslaughter rather than murder.

94. i Mental illness: it must be proved that, at the time the defendant committed the crime, he or she was of unsound mind (that is, suffering from a mental illness which either prevented him or her from knowing what the criminal action he or she committed was, or from knowing that it was wrong). Example: *R v Porter* (1936) 55 CLR 182.

ii Self-defence: the defendant admits to committing the criminal offence knowing that it was wrong but claims he or she was acting to defend him or herself or someone else from attack. Example: *Zecevic v DPP* (1987) 162 CLR 645.

iii Necessity: the defendant claims that the act or omission committed was necessary to avert serious danger. Example: *R v Dudley and Stephens* (1884) 14 QB 273.

iv Duress: the defendant admits to committing the criminal act knowing that it was wrong, but claims that he or she was so frightened by threats of death or serious bodily harm that he or she committed the act anyway. Example: *R v George Palazoff* (1986) 23 ACrimR 86.

v Consent: The defendant claims that he or she acted with the victim's consent. Example: *R v Mueller* (2005) NSWCCA 47.

95. i Provocation: the defendant claims that he or she was aggravated by the victim in such a way that the actions of the murdered person would have caused an ordinary person to lose self-control. Example: *The Queen v Damian Karl Sebo* (2007) Supreme Court of Queensland.

ii Substantial impairment of responsibility, also known as diminished responsibility, claims that the accused person was not completely in control of his or her mind when he or she committed the murder. Example: *Chayna v The Queen* (1993) 66 ACrimR 178.

96. You need to discuss the use of defences in general as well as individual defences and cases to decide if justice is served.

97. i because, in over 80% of criminal cases, the accused pleads guilty

ii Of the remaining 20%, the majority are heard summarily because there are many indictable offences that can be heard summarily.

98. the *Jury Act 1977* (NSW)

99. Both the prosecution and the defence may reject possible jurors if they feel they will be biased against or in favour of the accused.

100. A majority verdict will only be accepted by the court if the jury has deliberated for at least eight hours and if the court is satisfied, after examination on oath of one or more of the jurors, that it is unlikely that the jurors will reach a unanimous verdict after further deliberation.

101. You need to discuss the advantages and disadvantages of the jury system and decide whether the advantages outweigh the disadvantages, and to consider the effect of majority verdicts on the effectiveness of the jury system.

102. You need to weigh up those factors which help ensure justice and those factors which may limit the achievement of justice in the criminal trial process, and decide how effective the process is.

103. **i** provision of summary offences; **ii** provision of local courts; **iii** the Drug Court; **iv** the system of appeals; **v** provision of indictable offences heard summarily; **vi** the adversarial system; **vii** charge negotiation; **viii** the limited right to legal representation; **ix** legal aid and Public Defenders; **x** the presumption of innocence; **xi** rules of evidence; **xii** the use of defences; **xiii** the jury system; **xiv** majority verdicts; **xv** the effect of delays.

104. The *maximum penalty* is the most severe penalty that a court can give for a particular offence, such as five years imprisonment for assault occasioning actual bodily harm.

105. the *Crimes Act 1900* (NSW) and the *Crimes (Sentencing Procedure) Act 1999* (NSW)

106. Only after considering and rejecting all possible alternatives.

107. A *non-parole period* is the minimum time an offender must actually spend in prison. A *parole period* is a time when an offender no longer must be imprisoned, but is freed into the community under supervision.

108. The parole period is generally a quarter of the total sentence.

109. A *guideline sentence* is a judgement given about a sentence for a particular crime, which is to be taken into account by courts delivering sentences for similar offences. An example is the guideline sentence on the offence of dangerous driving causing grievous bodily harm or death, handed down in the case of *R v Jurisic* (1998) 45 NSWLR 209.

110. **i** Rehabilitation: which aims to change the behaviour of offenders so that they will not wish to commit other crimes.
ii Deterrence: which aims to dissuade people from committing crimes.
iii Retribution: which aims to 'pay back' the person who committed the crime.
iv Incapacitation: which aims to isolate the offender, usually in prison, so that he or she is unable to commit another crime.

111. **i** the maximum penalty; **ii** the purposes of punishment; **iii** other legislative and judicial guidelines; **iv** aggravating circumstances; **v** mitigating factors; **vi** a victim impact statement, if one is given.

112. *Aggravating factors* are circumstances taken into account by a sentencing judge that may result in the maximum penalty. Aggravating factors can include the age and disability of the victim, a relationship of trust with the victim, and a prior criminal record.

113. *Mitigating factors* are matters that persuade the judge that the maximum penalty should not be imposed, such as the offender's past good record, the offender's good character, the circumstances surrounding the offence (such as provocation), the effect of a sentence on the offender and his or her family, cooperation with authorities including providing information leading to other convictions, or signs of remorse including a guilty plea.

114. The prosecution puts forward aggravating factors in order to persuade the judge to give a severe penalty, while the defence puts forward mitigating factors in order to persuade the judge to reduce the penalty.

115. Three advantages of a victim impact statement are that:
i the victim can be sure that the court knows the full effects of the crime
ii this gives the victim a role in the court process, giving the victim and the community greater confidence in the system
iii it may assist in the rehabilitation of the offender because he or she gets to hear the impact of his or her actions.

One disadvantage is that the victim can be cross-examined on their statement, which can prove embarrassing and upsetting for the victim.

116. You need to describe each factor affecting the judge's decision and comment on how the consideration of this factor helps achieve the purposes of punishment.

117. The offender can appeal against the conviction or against the severity of the sentence. The prosecution can appeal against the leniency of the sentence.

118. The sentencing appeals process allows higher courts to supervise the discretion of magistrates and judges when they are making sentencing decisions, and helps to ensure consistency by establishing the maximum and minimum range of sentences for particular offences.

119. **i** No conviction recorded: the accused person is found guilty, but the charge is dismissed with no conviction recorded.
ii Caution: the offender is warned by police rather than arrested and charged.
iii Fine: a sum of money is paid by an offender as punishment.
iv Bond: the offender is released but agrees to be on a bond of good behaviour.
v Suspended sentence: the offender is sentenced to a term in prison, but the sentence is not executed, and the offender is released into the community on a bond to be of good behaviour.
vi Probation: the offender is released into the community but agrees to be on a bond of good behaviour and is subject to the supervision of the Parole Service.
vii Criminal infringement notice: police issue these notices, imposing a fine for some minor crimes such as offensive language and stealing less than $300.
viii Community service order: the offender is required to perform some unpaid work or service in the community for up to 500 hours.
ix Home detention: the offender is confined to his or her own home or to a restricted area for a period of up to eighteen months.
x Periodic detention: the offender is required to serve his or her prison sentence on consecutive weekends.
xi Forfeiture of assets: a person is ordered to give up his or her property to the government if the property was gained with the proceeds of crime, or used to commit crime.
xii Imprisonment: the offender is detained in a prison for at least the length of the non-parole period of the sentence.

120. A *penalty unit* is an amount of money used to impose fines. In July 2008, one penalty unit equalled $110. Penalty units are relevant to fines and criminal infringement notices.

121. Diversionary programs are programs which divert offenders away from traditional penalties in the hope that such measures will rehabilitate the offender. Five such programs are the Magistrates Early Referral into Treatment Program (MERIT) scheme, the Drug Court, the cannabis cautioning scheme, the Traffic Offenders Program (TOP), and the Sober Driver Program.

122. They may not rehabilitate or may not seem suitably retributive.

123. A bond, a suspended sentence or probation can all help to rehabilitate an offender because conditions can be imposed on the offender, such as to regularly attend a drug rehabilitation centre.

124. A fine may not deter, it may disadvantage poor people who have greater difficulty in paying the fine, and a fine does not rehabilitate.

125. Bonds, probation orders and community service orders may be insufficiently harsh to deter the offender or the community from committing a similar crime, and the offender has the opportunity to reoffend.

126. You need to look at the advantages and disadvantages of each type of penalty, and decide how well each achieves the purposes of punishment.

127. diversionary programs, youth justice conferencing, and circle sentencing

128. The primary purpose of alternative methods of sentencing is to rehabilitate, so that the offender can avoid further contact with the criminal justice system.

129. The aim of restorative justice programs is to both address the causes of criminal behaviour and to allow the offender to rectify the harm he or she has caused.

130. Aboriginal offenders

131. the offender, the victim, the victim's family, community elders, the defence lawyer, the prosecutor and the magistrate

132. **i** the offence; **ii** the impact of the offence on the victim and the community; **iii** ways of rectifying the harm done; **iv** what can be done to help both the victim and the offender in the future

133. Benefits of circle sentencing include:

    i it gives support to Aboriginal offenders; **ii** it helps reduce cultural barriers between Aboriginal people and the courts; **iii** it involves the community in assisting the offender to rehabilitate; **iv** it helps redress harm done to the victim.

    Benefits of youth justice conferencing are:

    i it allows the offender and the victim to meet to work out the best way for the offender to compensate for his or her wrongdoing; **ii** it allows the victim to tell the offender about the impact of the crime.

    Limitations include that the reoffending rates from youth justice conferencing are still high, and youth justice conferencing does little to address the causes of youth crime.

134. You need to explain where alternative methods of sentencing are used, explain the benefits of these methods and explain the limitations of such methods.

135. A *security classification* is the classification given to a prisoner which determines the type of prison in which he

or she is placed. *Protective custody* means a prisoner is separated from other prisoners whom he or she fears. *Parole* is when an offender no longer must be imprisoned, but is freed into the community under supervision, until his or her sentence is over.

136. **i** high-risk category prisoners, who are confined in maximum security prisons with secure physical barriers and towers

    ii medium-risk category prisoners, who are confined in medium security prisons which must have secure physical barriers

    iii low-risk category prisoners, who are confined in open security prisons which need not have physical barriers and in which prisoners do not need to be constantly supervised

137. One advantage of protective custody is that it protects the prisoner from harm. One disadvantage is that restricts the opportunities for those in custody to work and to access education programs.

138. Parole encourages prisoners to behave well and undertake rehabilitative activities in the hope of early release. The close supervision after release helps to ensure that they reassimilate into society, thereby having a greater chance of remaining free from criminal activity. The prospect of returning to prison if parole conditions are breached also encourages parolees to remain free from criminal activity and assimilate into the community.

139. **i** *Preventative detention* is a term used to describe people detained without charge because they are suspected of terrorist activity.

    ii It also refers to the continued detention of serious offenders after their term of imprisonment has expired.

140. In NSW, the *Crimes (High Risk Offenders) Act 2006* (NSW) provides that serious sexual offenders can continue to be detained after their sentence has expired if they are seen as a threat to the community.

141. One positive implication of continued detention is that it protects the community from possible harm. One negative implication is that some argue that preventative detention violates the ICCPR 1966.

142. One positive implication of sexual offenders' registration is that it monitors such offenders, so their chances of reoffending are minimised, while they are given support to reassimilate into society. One negative implication is that, if sexual offenders' registration information becomes public, some residents may object to such a person living in their community. In some states of the USA, such information has led to the murders of individuals registered in three of those states.

143. *Deportation* means the forcible removal of a person from a country and returning that person to his or her country of origin. People who have been permanent residents for less than ten years can be deported if they are convicted of an offence and sentenced to prison for at least one year.

144. One positive implication of deportation is that it protects Australian citizens from possible harm caused by non-Australian offenders reoffending. One negative implication is that it can cause hardship for the offender's family, particularly if the offender is the main income earner.

145. You need to weigh up the advantages and disadvantages of each post-sentencing consideration.

146. You need to discuss those factors which help ensure justice and those factors which may limit the achievement of justice in the sentencing and punishment process.

147. **i** the discretionary nature of sentencing; **ii** statutory and judicial guidelines which limit discretion; **iii** the purposes of punishment; **iv** factors considered when making a sentencing decision; **v** the provision of victim impact statements; **vi** the advantages and disadvantages of various types of penalties; **vii** the advantages and disadvantages of alternative methods of sentencing; **viii** the implications of post sentencing decisions.

148. the *Children (Criminal Proceedings) Act 1987* (NSW)

149. at the age of ten years old

150. Explain the arguments against the principal of *doli incapax* as it currently stands, and explain the reasons for keeping the principle in its current form.

151. **i** A parent or guardian must be notified if a child is taken into custody by police.
   ii Children have the right to have an independent adult, as a support person, present during any police procedure.
   iii The police must tell a child about his or her rights and assist the child to exercise those rights.
   iv A child under ten may not be strip searched and a support person should be present for the strip search of an older child.
   v Children in police custody must not be kept in the same cell as an adult
   vi Police must not photograph or take fingerprints of a child under fourteen unless there is a court order.
   vii Police may not take a bodily sample, such as blood or hair, from a child without a court order.

152. the *Law Enforcement (Powers and Responsibilities) Act 2002* (NSW)

153. **i** Young people are given special protection by the law in many circumstances, so it would be inconsistent to treat them as harshly as adults in criminal matters.
   ii Young offenders are more likely to be intimidated by, and less likely to understand, court procedure than are adults.
   iii A young offender does not always understand the consequences of his or her actions as well as an adult.
   iv Young offenders have a greater chance of resuming normal life and becoming worthwhile citizens, and should be encouraged to do so.

154. **i** The public are not allowed at the hearing.
   ii The media may attend the hearing but may not publish the identity of the offender.
   iii The magistrate must take reasonable measures to ensure that the child understands the proceedings.
   iv A conviction is not recorded if the child is under sixteen years of age.

155. the *Children (Criminal Proceedings) Act 1987* (NSW)

156. traffic offences and trial proceedings for serious indictable offences, such as murder

157. the *Children (Criminal Proceedings) Act 1987* (NSW); three of the principles of this act are:
   i it is desirable for a child's education to continue uninterrupted
   ii it is desirable for a child to live at home

   iii a penalty imposed on a child for an offence should be no greater than that imposed on an adult who commits an offence of the same kind.

158. A *control order* is an order made by the Children's Court, sending a child to be detained in a juvenile detention centre.

159. **i** referral to a youth justice conference; **ii** adjournment for rehabilitation purposes

160. the *Young Offenders Act 1997* (NSW)

161. **i** Warnings: a child can be given an on-the-spot warning by police for a minor offence.
   ii Cautions: police can also issue a more formal warning in the form of a caution. A caution can only be given if the child admits to the offence and an independent adult is present.
   iii Youth Justice Conferences: these are conferences involving a young offender, a parent or guardian, the victim, a supporter for the victim and a mediator, whose aim is to come up with an agreement which helps rectify the effects of the crime and prevent reoffending.

162. The social and economic factors which lead children to break the law and to reoffend are not addressed by youth sentencing diversionary programs.

163. You should discuss those factors which help ensure the effectiveness of the criminal justice system and those factors which may limit the effectiveness of the system when dealing with young offenders. Then come to a conclusion about the overall effectiveness of the system.

164. *International crime* is crime committed which has international implications in either international law or in the enforcement of domestic criminal law.

165. **i** crimes against the international community, which are crimes committed by individuals and states that are seen as wrong by the international community, such as terrorism and genocide
   ii transnational crimes, which are crimes that occur within a state's legal system but contain an international element, such as the illegal drug trade
   iii crimes committed outside the jurisdiction, which are crimes that take place outside a particular nation's criminal laws, for example piracy and aircraft hijacking

166. International measures for dealing with international crime include:

   i international instruments; **ii** international customary law; **iii** international criminal tribunals, such as the International Criminal Court (ICC); **iv** sanctions; **v** extradition treaties; **vi** international cooperation between countries, particularly between police forces.

   Domestic measures for dealing with international crime include:

   i domestic criminal laws that deal with transnational crimes, such as laws prohibiting the importation of illegal drugs and counterterrorism laws; **ii** cooperation between domestic authorities in different nation-states in order to deal with transnational crimes and crimes outside the jurisdiction; **iii** other international measures that require domestic legal action, such as the imposition of sanctions and implementation of extradition procedures.

167. Two examples are the Rome Statute 1998 and the Tokyo Hijacking Convention 1963. There are many other examples.

168. *Customary international law* consists of principles and procedures that have grown up through general usage, to the point where they are accepted as being fair and right by the international community. An example is the outlawing of genocide.

169. The effectiveness of the ICJ depends on the cooperation it receives, and this is restricted by the consensual nature of international law.

170. The ICC was established in 2002 because of the limited effectiveness of the ICJ and international criminal tribunals in dealing with war crimes.

171. Genocide, war crimes and crimes against humanity.

172. i moral sanctions: when other states express their opinion towards an offending state
ii political sanctions: such as the breaking of diplomatic relations
iii economic sanctions: such as refusing to trade with a specific country, disallowing exports and imports, and using boycotts and blockades
iv financial sanctions: a nation-state is refused financial assistance or loans from other nation-states
v physical sanctions: the use of force, which can sometimes result in war

173. *Extradition* occurs when a person is handed over by one nation-state to another nation-state because that person is accused of a crime in the latter state. A *fugitive domestic criminal* is a person who commits a crime under one country's domestic law and then flees the country in order to escape the consequences.

174. Extradition is determined by specific extradition treaties between countries, and sometimes by sections of UN conventions such as the UN Convention on the Prevention and Punishment of the Crime of Genocide 1948.

175. Extradition proceedings can be effective because they can, as in the case of Jayant Patel, force fugitive domestic criminals to face the legal system in the country where the alleged offence took place.

176. You should discuss those factors which help ensure the effectiveness of both systems and those factors which may limit the effectiveness of the domestic and international legal systems in dealing with international crime. Then come to a conclusion about the overall effectiveness of the both systems.

177. i the nature of international law; ii specific treaties and conventions dealing with various breaches of international criminal law; iii international tribunals; iv sanctions; v extradition; vi cooperation between nations

178. *Discretion* is the choice to do or not do something.

179. i in the reporting of crime; ii in the investigation process; iii in the adjudication process; iv in the sentencing process; v in the determination of post-sentencing considerations

180. Police exercise discretion when deciding (include any five of the following):
i which areas to patrol; ii which crimes to target; iii which reports to thoroughly investigate; iv what type of evidence to gather; v what charges to lay, if any; vi whether to issue a criminal infringement notice or to arrest the offender; vii whether to warn, caution or arrest a young offender; viii whether or not to grant bail.

181. when deciding what evidence to admit and what sentence to give

182. i in the granting or refusal of bail; ii in deciding whether or not to hear a case summarily or with a jury; iii during charge negotiation

183. No two situations are the same, so the exercise of discretion is necessary to take into account the differences between similar, but not identical situations.

184. The exercise of police and judicial discretion may mean that the law is applied differently to different groups. For example, there is evidence that young people are more likely to be stopped by police than are older people.

185. People comply with or do not comply with the criminal law because of morals, socioeconomic factors, politics, technology and self-interest.

186. Murder is a crime because society thinks that it is morally wrong, due to societal, cultural and religious reasons.

187. Victims of crime often feel that sentences are too lenient, while the judge needs to consider mitigating factors as well as the effect of the crime on the victim.

188. i Australia does not have capital or corporal punishment.
ii Young offenders are treated less harshly than adults.

189. i the media; ii lobby groups; iii reports from various government inquiries or organisations, such as the Ombudsman or Law Reform Commissions; iv international pressure

190. Law Reform Commissions are not always effective because the government does not need to implement their recommendations. The NSW Law Reform Commission, for example, in Report No 111 (2005), recommended against the introduction of majority verdicts. The government, however, ignored the report and introduced 'eleven to one' majority verdicts in 2006.

191. i perceived failure of existing law and media pressure, such as the passing of 'Ferguson's Law' in 2009
ii changing social values and the composition of society, such as the decriminalisation of homosexual behaviour in NSW in 1984
iii international law, such as the establishment of the International Criminal Court in 2002
iv new technology, such as the introduction of laws whereby DNA can be collected from suspects and convicted criminals

Note: Other examples could be given.

192. i the right to silence; ii rights regarding privacy; iii the right to legal representation; iv the right to freedom from detention, unless arrested

193. i compensation; ii the Charter of Victims' Rights; iii victim impact statements; iv counselling and other services; v lobby and support groups; vi alternative methods of sentencing, such as youth justice conferencing and circle sentencing

194. Giving too much regard to victims' rights may infringe upon the rights of the accused.

195. Both laws try to balance the rights of the individual suspect, who has not yet been found guilty of any offence, with the need for the community to be protected from harm.

196. **Legal measures:**
• police powers of investigation
• rights of suspects

- bail and remand
- court jurisdiction
- the adversarial system
- legal representation
- rules of evidence
- use of defences
- use of juries
- statutory and judicial sentencing guidelines
- factors affecting a sentencing decision
- provision of victim impact statements
- provision of sentencing appeals
- a range of penalty options
- alternative methods of sentencing
- post sentencing considerations
- law regarding the age of criminal responsibility
- laws regarding children's dealings with police
- Children's Court proceedings
- sentencing principles for young offenders
- diversionary programs for young offenders
- international instruments and institutions for dealing with international crime

Non-legal measures:
- reporting of crime
- use of police warnings
- use of police discretion
- diversion from punishment via Drug Court programs
- charge negotiation and guilty pleas
- legal aid
- diversionary sentencing programs
- social and situational crime prevention
- programs to prevent young offender's from reoffending
- international cooperation between states when dealing with international crime

HSC **Sample HSC questions** (pages 92–3)

1. **C** is the correct answer. The NSW *Crimes Act* contains maximum penalties for the offences described within it. **[1.4.1]**

2. **B** is the correct answer. The system of trial in Australia is the adversarial system. The inquisitorial system (**C**) is the form of trial in a civil law system (**A**). Answer **D** does not exist. **[1.3.2]**

3. **D** is the correct answer. All the other answers refer to the presence or absence of *mens rea*. **[1.1.2]**

4. **C** is the correct answer. Imprisonment is the only one of these penalties that incapacitates. **[1.4.6]**

5. **D** is the correct answer. **[1.1.7]**

6. **B** is the correct answer. Answers **A** and **C** would be brought up by the defence at a sentencing hearing in an effort to have the judge lessen the sentence. Answer **D** would normally be brought up at the trial, not at the sentencing hearing. **[1.4.3 and 1.3.8]**

7. **B** is the correct answer. **[1.4.7]**

8. **B** is the correct answer. The age of criminal responsibility in NSW is ten years of age though, for a child between the ages of ten and fourteen, the prosecution must prove that the child was sufficiently mature to form the necessary *mens rea*. **[1.5.1]**

9. **A** is the correct answer. **[1.1.8 and 1.1.9]**

10. **C** is the correct answer. This process is an example of a guideline sentence. **[1.4.1]**

11. **B** is the correct answer. Answers **A** and **D** need not be an element of a criminal offence. **C** is an element of civil law. **[1.1.1]**

12. **C** is the correct answer. This is the main way that alleged offenders are brought before the court. Answers **A** and **C** are less common methods. Answer **D** is relevant to where an alleged offender is while waiting to go to court, i.e. in prison or free. **[1.2.4]**

13. **A** is the correct answer. A charge of murder is first considered in the Local Court during the committal proceeding. If the *prima facie* case is proved, the case then goes to the Supreme Court. **[1.3.1]**

14. **B** is the correct answer. Because **B** is correct, **A** must be incorrect. Hung juries occur in about 8% of cases, and may occur because of a 'rogue juror'. This is not frequent, so **C** and **D** are incorrect. **[1.3.9]**

15. **D** is the correct answer. **[1.3.8]**

Extended-response questions

Note: **EM** means Examiner Maximiser

Question 1

What you are asked to do

This question asks you to:

- describe four processes that Duncan may undergo. Choose four from different parts of the criminal justice process that illustrate the second part of the question, for example: questioning by the police, trial in the Children's Court, the proving of the age of criminal responsibility, and sentencing.

- explain how and why children are treated differently to adults in the criminal justice system. Explain why first, and then explain how, using Duncan as an example.

EM In order to achieve top marks for your answer to this question, in your answer you should follow the plan below.

Plan

Paragraph 1: Explain why children are treated differently from adults in the criminal justice system. **[1.5.2]**

Paragraph 2: Explain the law regarding a child, such as Duncan, being questioned by police and how this differs to the law for adults in the same situation. **[1.5.2]**

Paragraph 3: Explain how the Children's Court criminal process differs from the adult court process. **[1.5.3]**

Paragraph 4: Explain that, for a thirteen year old, the prosecution needs to prove that he was old enough to form the requisite mens rea. **[1.5.1]**

Paragraph 5: Explain how the sentencing process differs for children and adults. **[1.5.4]**

Conclusion: Sum up that Duncan will be given extra protections at all stages of the criminal justice process because he is a child.

Question 2

What you are asked to do

This question asks you to:

- identify the people involved in a trial by jury and describe what each one does

- come to a conclusion about how effective the jury system is in achieving justice. To do this, you need to explain ways in which the jury system is effective and ways in which its effectiveness is limited. Then decide how effective it is.

EM In order to achieve top marks for your answer to this question, in your answer you should follow the plan below.

Plan

Paragraph 1: Describe the role of the prosecutor, including the Director of Public Prosecutions. **[1.3.3]**

Paragraph 2: Describe the role of the defence lawyer, including the Public Defender. **[1.3.3]**

Paragraph 3: Describe the role of the judge. **[1.3.3]**

Paragraph 4: Describe the role of the jury. **[1.3.9]**

Paragraph 5: Explain ways that the jury system is effective. **[1.3.9]**

Paragraph 6: Explain limitations to the effectiveness of juries. **[1.3.9]**

Conclusion: State how effective the jury is in achieving justice in the light of what you have said previously. **[1.3.9]**

Question 3

What you are asked to do

This question asks you to:

- describe the role of discretion in two phases of the criminal justice process. To do this, you need to choose two stages, such as investigation and sentencing, give examples of the exercise of discretion in each stage, and explain how discretion is curtailed.

- come to a conclusion about how important discretion is in achieving justice. To do this, you need to explain how important discretion is in each phase of the process you discuss, and assess whether there is too much or too little discretion in these two stages of the criminal justice process.

EM In order to achieve top marks for your answer to this question, in your answer you should follow the plan below.

Plan

Paragraph 1: Define *discretion* and explain that it is an integral part of the criminal justice process, from the reporting of crime to post-sentencing considerations. **[1.7.1]**

Paragraph 2: Describe how discretion is used by police in the criminal investigation process. Give examples. **[1.2.1 to 1.2.7]**

Paragraph 3: State the advantages and disadvantages of the use of discretion in the criminal investigation process and explain how important it is. **[1.2.1 and 1.7.1]**

Paragraph 4: Describe how discretion is used by judges and magistrates in the sentencing process. Give examples. **[1.4.1, 1.4.3, 1.7.1 and 1.4.5]**

Paragraph 5: Give the advantages and disadvantages of the use of discretion in the sentencing process and state how important it is. **[1.4.5 and 1.7.1]**

Conclusion: State how important discretion is in these two phases of the criminal justice process. **[1.7.1]**

Chapter 2: Human rights

KCq *Key Concept questions* (pages 139–41)

1. *Human rights* are fundamental rights to which all people are entitled simply because they are human.

2. **i** Human rights are universal (that is, to be enjoyed by all individuals regardless of their nationality, gender, race or status).
   ii Human rights are indivisible (that is, all human rights are equally important).
   iii Human rights are inherent (that is, they are the birthright of all humans and are to be enjoyed by all people simply by reason of their humanity).
   iv Human rights are inalienable (that is, people cannot agree to give them up or have them taken away).

3. *Civil rights* are entitlements belonging to all humans, to do with being a free citizen of a nation (such as freedom of thought and freedom of religion). *Political rights* are entitlements belonging to all humans, to do with full participation in government (such as the right to vote).

4. *Economic rights* are those rights concerned with the production, development and management of material for the necessities of life (such as the right to an adequate standard of living). *Cultural rights* are rights to assist in preserving and enjoying one's cultural heritage (such as the right to participate in the cultural life of the community). *Social rights* are rights that give people security as they live and learn together (such the right to an education and to social security.

5. environmental rights, peace rights and the right to self-determination

6. You need to explain: what human rights are; their characteristics; their international recognition; and that there are three types of international human rights.

7. **i** the idea of state sovereignty
   ii 'natural law' doctrine
   iii historic constitutional documents and international agreements

8. the movements struggling for slavery abolition, trade unionism, universal suffrage and universal education

9. The movement to end slavery began in Europe in the late eighteenth century.

10. France

11. In Australia, Polynesian islanders were used as slaves on sugar and cotton plantations in Queensland from the 1860s. This effectively came to an end in 1904 when the federal government agreed to offset any losses to sugar planters caused by the end of that system.

12. It was signed in 1890 and was called the *General Act of Brussels*.

13. Forms of slavery that still exist include child labour, traffic in children and women for prostitution purposes, debt bondage, and the sale of children. These practices are still widespread in many parts of the world.

14. The Industrial Revolution meant that factories grew up in cities and employed thousands of people. This factory work was characterised by low wages, long working hours, and unhealthy and unsafe working conditions. Because of

these poor working conditions, workers joined together into trade unions in an effort to improve conditions. It was only through combined action that workers could improve their conditions.

15. The ILO is the International Labour Organization, which was created in 1919 to improve conditions for workers internationally.

16. Any three of the following: minimum wages based on maintaining an adequate standard of living; the right to form trade unions; equal pay for equal work; occupational health and safety requirements, and a forty-hour week.

17. *Universal suffrage* is the right of all adults to vote in government elections.

18. **a** In NSW, universal male suffrage was granted in 1858.
   b Female suffrage was granted in 1894 in South Australia, and in 1902 in NSW and the Commonwealth.
   c Complete universal suffrage was granted in 1962.

19. Australia's record compares well. Australia was one of the first nations in the world to grant universal male and female suffrage, though Aboriginal and Torres Strait Islanders did not gain the vote until 1962.

20. It became widely recognised that people needed to be educated to participate equally in society and to exercise their right to vote.

21. Universal primary education became accessible in 1866 when the *Public Schools Act* (NSW) established a system of state elementary schools throughout NSW. Primary education became compulsory throughout the Australian states in the 1870s.

22. In developed nations, the right to education has long been established, and education between the ages of six and fifteen is compulsory. However, around the world, 130 million children aged between six and eleven still do not have access to primary education.

23. *Collective rights* are rights that do not belong to an individual but to a group of people. Two examples are the right to continued survival of a race of people (protected by the prohibition of genocide), and the right to self-determination.

24. *Self-determination* means the right of peoples to govern themselves and to choose their own form of government. Two examples of this right are the right of colonised peoples to establish their independence, and the right claimed by Indigenous peoples to control their own traditional lands and economy.

25. Environmental rights rely on all countries in the world agreeing to protect these rights. For example, if one country decides to emit greenhouse gases, it will affect the rights of people in other countries to a healthy and sustainable environment.

26. The *right to peace* is the right of people to have their government maintain peace and eliminate war.

27. You need to describe the development of core human rights concepts and documents over time, as well as describe movements for the establishment of particular rights.

28. You need to describe the growth of the movements outlined in Section 2.1.2 (pages 97–106), and refer to Section 2.4.3 (page 131) which explores the development of human rights as a reflection of changing values and ethical standards over time.

29. *The Charter of the United Nations* was important because it was the first international treaty to bind all members of the United Nations and it has, as one of its fundamental purposes, the promotion of respect for human rights. The International Court of Justice said that these provisions in the United Nations Charter bind member states to observe and respect human rights.

30. ICCPR stands for the *International Covenant on Civil and Political Rights* 1966. ICESCR stands for the *International Covenant on Economic, Social and Cultural Rights* 1966.

31. The *International Bill of Rights* is made up of: the *Universal Declaration of Human Rights* 1948, the *International Covenant on Civil and Political Rights* 1966 (ICCPR), and the *International Covenant on Economic, Social and Cultural Rights* 1966 (ICESCR).

32. Any four of the following: the Convention on the Elimination of All Forms of Racial Discrimination 1965, the Convention on the Elimination of All Forms of Discrimination against Women 1979, the Convention on the Prevention and Punishment of the Crime of Genocide 1948, the Convention against Torture and Other Cruel, Inhuman or Degrading Treatment or Punishment 1984, the Convention on the Rights of the Child 1989, the Declaration on the Right of Peoples to Peace 1984, and the Declaration on the Rights of Indigenous Peoples 2006.

33. You need to list the three documents that make up the International Bill of Rights and explain their coverage, as well as list the other treaties dealing with specific human rights.

34. *State sovereignty* means that, within one country or nation-state, there is a group, person or body with supreme lawmaking authority, and that the domestic affairs of a nation are under the control of that nation.

35. **i** The protection of human rights internationally undermines the idea of national sovereignty because it means interfering with a nation's domestic affairs.
   ii The scrutiny of a country's protection of human rights within its own borders is a legitimate international concern.
   iii Many countries recognise that the international community should interfere to stop human rights violations if such violations endanger world peace and security.

36. The UN Human Rights Council examines situations in which human rights violations are occurring and makes recommendations for action to the UN General Assembly.

37. The 'Universal Periodic Review' is a review of the human rights record of all 192 member states of the UN every four years.

38. the European Union, NATO, the Commonwealth of Nations and ASEAN

39. The ICC hears cases relating to the most serious of international crimes and gross human rights abuses, namely genocide, war crimes and crimes against humanity.

40. The International Criminal Tribunal for the former Yugoslavia, the International Tribunal for Rwanda, the European Court of Human Rights, and the ASEAN Intergovernmental Commission on Human Rights.

41. Any four of the following: the Human Rights Committee (OHCHR), through the Centre for Civil and Political

Rights (CCPR); the Committee on Economic, Social and Cultural Rights (CESCR); the Committee on the Elimination of Racial Discrimination (CERD); the Committee on the Elimination of Discrimination Against Women (CEDAW); the Committee Against Torture (CAT) and Optional Protocol to the Convention against Torture (OPCAT)—Subcommittee on Prevention of Torture (SPT); the Committee on the Rights of the Child (CRC); the Committee on Migrant Workers (CMW); or the Committee on the Rights of Persons with Disabilities (CRPD).

42. **i** considering the reports made by states to the authorities
 ii considering individual complaints or communications
 iii publishing general comments on the treaties and organising discussions and forums on their purposes and themes

43. An NGO is an organisation that works towards a certain cause and operates separately to any government. Examples in the area of human rights are Amnesty International and Human Rights Watch.

44. The media raises awareness of human rights abuses across the world, and rallies public and government action to end such abuses.

45. **i** Not all countries are party to human rights treaties.
 ii There is a lack of adequate enforcement mechanisms.
 iii Enforcement is by consensus.
 iv There is reliance on states reporting about themselves.
 v There is a lack of Security Council action.
 vi There is limited effectiveness and a limited number of war crimes tribunals.
 vii There is a lack of funding generally.
 viii Informal recognition of NGOs.
 ix Media overload leads to compassion fatigue and disinterest.

46. In Australia, human rights are protected by: common law; statute law; the Australian Constitution; international law; courts and tribunals; non-interference; and Charters of Rights enacted within the ACT and Victoria. Government and non-government organisations also assist in the promotion and monitoring of the protection of human rights in Australia

47. The division of power really does not limit the protection of human rights in Australia because, even though state and territory governments do not have the power to ratify human rights agreements themselves or enact enabling legislation, they can act to mirror any international human rights through their own legislation, as the ACT and Victoria have done with their Charters of Rights.

48. The Australian Constitution does not protect human rights very well because it protects very few rights in Australia. Those few include the right to vote, to trial by jury for serious offences and to freedom of religion.

49. Examples of the common law protecting human rights are the right of a tenant to quiet enjoyment of the property he or she rents, or the Mabo case which granted Indigenous land rights.

50. An example of the common law restricting human rights involves the right to legal representation because that is only a right in serious cases.

51. the *Racial Discrimination Act 1975* (Cth) or the *Social Security Act 1991* (Cth)

52. The role of the Australian Human Rights Commission is to investigate and conciliate complaints about abuses of human rights in legislation under its jurisdiction.

53. An international treaty only becomes part of Australian domestic law if the federal government passes legislation to make the provisions of the treaty part of our law.

54. The NSW Civil and Administrative Tribunal (NCAT) can hear complaints about discrimination and make legally binding decisions about a matter that can include an award of damages of up to $40 000, as it did in the case of *Abdulrahman v Toll Pty Ltd* (2006).

55. Both the Toonen case (1994) and the case of *A v Australia* (1997) are cases heard by the United Nations Human Rights Committee (UNHRC) about Australia's protection of human rights. These cases are significant because they show the influence of international findings on Australian law. In Toonen's case the finding of the UNHRC led to legislative changes, but the UNHRC's finding in the case of *A v Australia* had no effect on Australia's protection of human rights.

56. NGOs lobby governments about human rights issues and publicise human rights concerns in Australia.

57. The Australian media plays an important role in reporting human rights infringements within Australia and mobilising public action.

58. A *Charter of Rights* is a document which sets out the basic rights to which every human should be entitled.

59. One argument put forward by people who call for a Charter of Rights for Australia is that human rights are not adequately protected by existing common and statute law, which are the main ways of currently protecting human rights in Australia. Those against a Charter of Rights for Australia argue that to list rights in a document is to limit them to only those listed. Several other arguments for and against can be found in Section 2.2.5 (pages 118–19).

60. You need to describe, with examples, the ways in which human rights are incorporated into Australian domestic law—that is, through the Australian Constitution, federal statutory law, state and territory statutory law, the common law, courts and tribunals, the fact that the law does not interfere with the enjoyment of basic human rights, publicity and pressure from NGOs and the media, and the development of a state Charter of Rights in Victoria and the Australian Capital Territory.

61. Generally, Australia has a good record on human rights and has been a world leader in the drafting and promoting of some human rights treaties.

62. You need to point out that:
 i Australia's human rights record is generally good compared to other countries
 ii there are some areas in which Australia's human rights protection has been limited (and you need to describe these limitations).

63. Choose three of the following: genocide; treatment of refugees; asylum seekers; child soldiers; abuse of children; torture; capital punishment; arbitrary detention; religious discrimination; discrimination against women; exploitation of workers; human trafficking and slavery; limitations on free speech; or suspension of democracy and political imprisonment.

64. A *refugee* is someone who 'owing to a well-founded fear of being persecuted for reasons of race, religion, nationality, membership of a particular social group or political opinion, is outside the country of his nationality, and is unable to, or owing to such fear, is unwilling to avail himself of the protection of that country.'

65. According to the UNHCR, in 2009, 15.2 million fell under the definition of *refugee*.

66. The UN Convention relating to the Status of Refugees 1951. It defines a refugee, outlines refugee rights and establishes the refugee obligations of states.

67. The aim of the UNHCR is to protect the rights and wellbeing of refugees as well as to strive to ensure that everyone can exercise his or her right to seek asylum and find safe refuge in another state.

68. According to the UN *Convention relating to the Status of Refugees* 1951, refugees have the option to integrate into the nation-state where they are seeking asylum, return home voluntarily (repatriation), or settle in a third state.

69. Amnesty International and Human Rights Watch are two NGOs working in the area of refugees. Four of their functions are to: monitor refugee camps; monitor human rights compliance by states creating or hosting refugees; report to the UN, government and the media on refugee situations; and campaign for reform.

70. About 13 000 refugees were granted asylum in Australia in 2007–08. This ranks Australia thirty-second out of the seventy-one countries who accept refugees.

71. People can be detained under Australia's border security legislation, if they are declared unlawful, and are treated as such if they have arrived in Australia without a visa, overstayed their visa, or had their visa cancelled.

72. Any two of the following: impact of terrorism; the global financial crisis; pressure due to the increasing world population; the threat of climate change; compassion fatigue; impact of the media.

73. The media is effective in that it reports the plight of refugees to a global audience, reports the conditions of refugee camps, and discusses treatment of refugees and asylum seekers in host countries. However, the media can also operate to foster fear among populations about accepting refugees and can use its power to encourage discrimination and xenophobia.

74. Australia has been criticised internationally for detaining onshore asylum seekers unfairly and for unreasonably lengthy periods. In response to these criticisms all children were removed from detention; and some other detainees have been granted visas which allow them to enter into the normal life of the Australian community pending removal from or acceptance into Australia. In addition the Commonwealth Ombudsman has been given the power to review the detention of people who have spent two or more years in immigration detention.

75. You need to: describe the nature and extent of the refugee issue worldwide; describe international legal and non-legal responses to the treatment of refugees and evaluate their effectiveness, and describe Australian legal and non-legal responses to the treatment of refugees and evaluate their effectiveness.

76. If the sovereignty in a nation-state rests with the people, then the people can ensure that their rulers or governments protect their human rights because, if they don't, the people can vote them out of office in the next election.

77. The notion of state sovereignty means that, within a country, the power of the ruling authority is absolute, and international agreements need not have any bearing on what happens within the borders of that country. So, a ruler of a country can violate the human rights of its citizens if he or she wishes to do so.

78. Any three of the following: pressure from the international community; an expectation that rights will be protected; pressure from the media and NGOs; membership requirements of an IGO; the state's population may bring about change; the existence of international enforcement mechanisms.

79. Any three of the following: human rights are a Western concept; human rights are a secondary priority in poor nations; nation-states may feel that human rights are not applicable to them; some violations may be popular domestically; human rights can be sacrificed for other nation-state purposes, such as terrorism prevention; protecting the rights of one group or individual may endanger the rights of another; it is too expensive to protect human rights; states lack the funds and/or the willpower for enforcement against individual perpetrators; states may be corrupt so it is not in their interest to protect human rights; current enforcement mechanisms may not act as a deterrent.

80. Human rights have become an important part of international law, and human rights abuses are widely publicised and condemned. NGOs have had an increasingly important role in promoting knowledge of and compliance with human rights standards. Most countries in the world have also made at least some human rights part of their domestic law.

81. Some nations argue that the idea of human rights reflect a Western worldview and do not take into account the different cultural perspectives of non-Western countries.

82. List three of the following: the International Law Commission; Law Reform Commissions of nation-states; the Australian Human Rights Commission; parliaments of nation-states; international courts; courts of nation-states; courts of regional federations; and intergovernmental organisations, NGOs and individuals.

83. Any of the following: a Charter of Rights in Australia, Australia's response to asylum seekers, definition of a *refugee*, or global treatment of refugees.

84. The AHRC has only advisory powers, and governments have been unwilling to act on some of the challenges currently facing human rights protection in Australia (such as anti-terrorist laws, lack of a Charter of Rights, failure to ratify some human rights treaties, treatment of Aboriginal and Torres Strait Islander peoples and mandatory detention of asylum seekers).

85. Any two of the following: not all countries have been willing to sign human rights treaties; lack of adequate enforcement measures; selectivity when investigating and prosecuting war crimes and other crimes against humanity; continued human rights abuses by some countries.

Sample HSC questions (pages 141–3)

1. **C** is the correct answer. **A** and **B** are civil and political rights. **D** is a social right. **[2.1.1]**

2. **D** is the correct answer. There is no Australian Bill of Rights (**A**). The Australian Constitution (**C**) protects only a few rights. **B** only protects rights in Australia if domestic law also grants the right, which it primarily does through statute law. **[2.2.5]**

3. **C** is the correct answer. **A**, **B** and **D** all protect individual rights. **C** protects environmental rights, which are collective rights. **[2.1.2 and 2.1.3]**

4. **C** is the correct answer. NGOs do not have the power to do any of the actions described in **A**, **B** or **D**. Those alternatives are available to nation-states and IGOs. **[2.2.2]**

5. **A** is the correct answer. **[2.1.3]**

6. **A** is the correct answer. **[2.2.2]**

7. **B** is the correct answer. The International Criminal Court cannot do **C** or **D**. It only hears matters about gross violations of human rights, so does not act as described in alternative **A**. **[2.2.2]**

8. **C** is the correct answer. Human rights are indivisible which means that no one right is more important than the other, so the argument stated in the question goes against that idea. **[2.1.1]**

9. **D** is the correct answer. The separation of powers divides the power of government between the legislature, the executive and the judiciary. Maintaining the independence and separation of each arm of government ensures basic civil and political rights are protected and that no one arm can hold too much power. **A**, **B**, and **C** do not exist in Australia. **[2.2.5]**

10. **C** is the correct answer. The AHRC cannot make binding orders, which means **A** is incorrect. It does listen to individual complaints, so **B** is incorrect. It is an independent statutory authority, so **D** is also incorrect. **[2.2.5]**

Short-answer questions

Note: **EM** means Examiner Maximiser

Question 1a

What you are asked to do

This question asks you to explain what *national sovereignty* means and how it works it.

EM In order to achieve top marks for your answer to this question, in your answer you should:

- define what *national sovereignty* is
- describe how national sovereignty affects lawmaking and the domestic affairs of a country or nation-state.

Answers could include the following:

- The idea of national sovereignty means that, within one country or nation-state there is a group, person or body with supreme lawmaking authority. **[2.2.1]**
- This notion of sovereignty means that the domestic affairs of a nation are under the control of that nation. It is only the relationships between countries that are or should be subject to international law, not domestic matters. **[2.2.1]**
- State sovereignty means that international law cannot interfere with what happens within a nation-state without that nation's consent. **[2.2.1]**

Question 1b

What you are asked to do

This question asks you to explain how the idea of national sovereignty can limit the protection of human rights internationally.

EM In order to achieve top marks for your answer to this question, in your answer you should:

- explain how national sovereignty can negatively affect human rights
- give an example to support your claims.

Answers could include the following:

- National sovereignty means that the domestic affairs of a nation, including the protection of the human rights of the citizens of that nation, are under that nation's control. **[2.4.1]**
- Some nations may resent the outside interference of international bodies which monitor the protection of human rights in nations around the world. This resentment can limit the protection of human rights because the nation may fail to comply with human rights treaties, or may fail to report (or report accurately) to international treaty committees, and there is little the United Nations can do about this. The inability of the UN to act in these situations is evidenced by the case of *A v Australia*, which was a case heard before the UNHRC in 1997 about the detention of asylum seekers. Australia rejected the findings of the UNHRC, which found that Australia had violated the ICCPR. **[2.4.1]**

Question 2

What you are asked to do

This question asks you to:

- state THREE of the ways in which human rights are protected under Australian law.
- explain how each of the ways you listed protects human rights, and give a specific example.

EM In order to achieve top marks for your answer to this question, in your answer you should:

- list any THREE of the following: the Australian Constitution; common law; statute law; non-interference; courts and tribunals; or the Bill of Rights enacted within each of the ACT and Victoria
- explain how each of the three things you listed protects human rights, and give a specific example of each.

Answers could include the following:

- Three ways in which human rights are incorporated into Australian law are through the Australian Constitution, through the common law and through statute law. **[2.2.4]**
- The Australian Constitution protects only a few human rights. For example, section 40 of the Constitution gives all adult Australians the right to vote. This is one of the very few rights contained within our Constitution. **[2.2.5]**
- The common law also protects some rights. For example, the right of tenants to the quiet enjoyment of their property is a common law right. Also, the Mabo case of 1992 recognised the right of Indigenous Australians to hold native title over some lands. This is another example of the common law recognising a human right. **[2.2.5]**
- Most human rights in Australia are protected by statute law. For example, the *Racial Discrimination Act 1975* (Cth) protects people from being discriminated against because of their race. **[2.2.5]**

Question 3a

What you are asked to do

This question asks you to:

- define the term *intergovernmental organisation*
- define the term *non-government organisation*.

EM In order to achieve top marks for your answer to this question, in your answer you should:

- provide a clear explanation of the meaning of *intergovernmental organisation*
- provide a clear explanation of the meaning of *non-government organisation*.

Answers could include the following:

- An intergovernmental organisation (IGO) is an organisation comprised of several sovereign states working for a common cause. **[2.2.2]**
- A non-government organisation (NGO) is an organisation that works towards a certain cause and operates separately to any government. **[2.2.2]**

Question 3b

What you are asked to do

This question asks you to:

- choose an intergovernmental organisation to discuss in regard to its contribution to the protection of human rights
- explain how the intergovernmental organisation you chose contributes to the protection of human rights.

EM In order to achieve top marks for your answer to this question, in your answer you should::

- select an intergovernmental organisation whose contribution to the protection of human rights you are able to discuss
- explain how your chosen intergovernmental organisation contributes to the protection of human rights.

Answers could include the following:

- The European Union (EU) consists of twenty-seven nations located in Europe. To be a member of the EU, states must be democracies that uphold the rule of law, respect and uphold universal human rights and adhere to the UN Charter on the use of force. **[2.2.2]**
- Human rights are protected because the European Court of Human Rights has jurisdiction over human rights issues in the EU and its decisions are taken seriously by the Council of the European Union (the governing body of the EU). The European Court of Human Rights has some enforcement powers in that any EU member that does not comply with its ruling can face the sanction of being expelled from the council. **[2.2.2]**

Question 4

What you are asked to do

This question asks you to:

- choose two of the movements mentioned in the syllabus that have contributed to the developing recognition of human rights
- briefly describe what each of the two movements you chose has achieved and how this has contributed to the recognition of human rights.

EM In order to achieve top marks for your answer to this question, in your answer you should:

- select TWO of the following movements: the movement for abolition of slavery; the movement for trade unionism and labour rights; the movement for universal suffrage; and the movement for universal education
- briefly describe what each movement you chose has achieved and how this contributes to the recognition of human rights.

Answers could include the following:

- Two movements have contributed to the developing recognition of human rights are the movement for the abolition of slavery and the movement for universal suffrage. **[2.1.2]**
- The movement for the abolition of slavery really began in the nineteenth century, though France was the first nation to abolish slavery in 1789. At first, the movement began with many individual nations gradually realising independently that people should not be enslaved if it was accepted that all men were created equal. Most European nations stopped exporting slaves from Africa by 1838. Australia imported slaves to Queensland until 1890. **[2.1.2]**
- Internationally, the General Act of Brussels was signed in 1890 and this was the first international treaty abolishing slavery. **[2.1.2]**
- Three international treaties operate to eliminate slavery today, including the Slavery Convention of 1926. **[2.1.2]**
- Though slavery still exists, it is recognised internationally that to enslave a person interferes with the fundamental human rights of that person. **[2.1.2]**
- Another movement which has contributed to the developing recognition of human rights is the movement towards universal suffrage, or the right to vote for all people. It is a fundamental human right because, if people can vote, they can vote for a government that protects their rights and freedoms. **[2.1.2]**
- The notion that people have the right to choose their government or form a government can first be found in the American Declaration of Independence 1776 and the French Declaration of the Rights of Man and the Citizen 1789. However, even in this case, only men who owned property or had more than a certain income could vote. Gradually it was recognised that all men should be entitled to vote. **[2.1.2]**
- Universal male suffrage was granted in NSW in 1858, though it was not granted in the UK until 1918. Australia and New Zealand were the first countries in the world to grant female suffrage, which they did in the 1890s. Voting rights for many racial minorities around the world were not granted until later. Australia, for example, did not grant suffrage to all Aboriginal people until 1962. **[2.1.2]**

Question 5

What you are asked to do

This question asks you to:

- choose two collective human rights
- briefly explain how each of the two rights you chose is protected internationally.

EM In order to achieve top marks for your answer to this question, in your answer you should:

- select TWO collective human rights from the following: the prohibition of genocide; the right to self-determination; environmental rights; the right to form a trade union; and the right to peace

- briefly explain how each of the collective rights you selected is protected internationally, by listing treaties which protect that right.

Answers could include the following:

- The right to peace is a collective right recognised under the UN Charter 1945, which obliges states to 'settle their international disputes by peaceful means'. **[2.1.2]**
- The UN passed the *Declaration on the Rights of People to Peace* in 1984. This is a non-binding resolution recognising the right to peace as a collective right of all peoples. **[2.1.2]**
- The right to self determination is the collective right of peoples to govern themselves and to choose their own form of government. The importance of this right is shown by its prominence in the UN Charter 1945 where it is referred to in Articles 1(2) and 55, and by its inclusion in Article 1 of both the ICCPR and ICESCR. **[2.1.2]**
- The right to self-determination involves the right of colonised peoples to establish their independence. It also involves the right of people within a nation to freely choose their own form of government and to elect their own government. The most controversial aspect of the right to self-determination is the right claimed by Indigenous peoples to control their own traditional lands and economy. This right is referred to in the *Declaration on the Rights of Indigenous Peoples* 2006 which was adopted by the United Nations General Assembly in 2007. **[2.1.2]**

Question 6

What you are asked to do

This question asks you to:

- choose to argue either for or against the idea that Australia needs a Charter of Rights
- clearly present your argument for or against an Australian Charter of Rights.

EM In order to achieve top marks for your answer to this question, in your answer you should:

- clearly state which side you have chosen to argue, either for or against the idea that Australia needs a Charter of Rights. You should not give arguments on both sides.
- refer to the quote in the question. (If you are arguing *against* the proposition, you can say something like: 'Australia is the only Western democracy which does not have a Charter of Rights' because human rights are already well protected in Australia. If you are arguing *for* the proposition, you can say something like: 'Australia is the only Western democracy that does not have a Charter of Rights', which may indicate that it is time for Australia to consider introducing one, because human rights in Australia may not be as well protected as they could be.
- explain that a nation can have a legislative Charter of Rights or an entrenched Charter of Rights.

Answers arguing for the Charter of Rights could include the following:

- In order to protect human rights, many nations have either an entrenched Charter of Rights or a legislative Charter of Rights. An entrenched Charter of Rights is part of the constitution of the nation and cannot be changed by parliament. The US has such a charter. A legislative Charter of Rights can be changed by parliament through the passing of amending legislation. The UK has a legislative Charter of Rights. Australia has neither. **[2.2.5]**
- Australia is the only Western democracy which does not have a Charter of Rights, which may indicate that it is time

to consider introducing one, because human rights in Australia may not be as well protected as they could be. **[2.2.5]**

- Many argue that human rights in Australia are already well protected. This is certainly true for the majority of Australians, but there are several issues which indicate that not all people's human rights are adequately protected in Australia. For example, the following are actions that have taken place in Australia despite breaching international human rights conventions: the arrest and detention of Mohamed Haneef, under counterterrorism laws in 2007; the Northern Territory Intervention which has been ongoing since 2007; and the prolonged detention of asylum seekers. **[2.2.5]**
- If we had a Charter of Rights, either legislative or entrenched, which enshrined human rights in the Australian law, people affected by breaches of human rights conventions would have recourse in Australian law, which they don't currently have without a Charter of Rights. **[2.2.5]**

Chapter 3: Consumers

KCq *Key Concept questions* (pages 189–91)

1. With the Industrial Revolution, consumers no longer supplied their own food and clothing, but needed to rely on goods produced by individuals or companies unknown to them, and which were often produced in factories miles away from the place of purchase. Also, a wide range of new products became available.

2. *Caveat emptor* means, 'Let the buyer beware', which means that if a consumer is mistreated by a seller there is very little he or she can do about it. *Laissez faire* refers to the philosophy that governments should not interfere in private negotiations between people.

3. Globalisation means many goods and services are now produced, marketed and distributed for a global market, so the gap between the knowledge and power of consumers and of suppliers is even greater than before globalisation.

4. You need to describe the rural subsistence economy, describe the effects of the Industrial Revolution, describe the concepts of *caveat emptor* and *laissez faire*, list early consumer laws, describe the modern consumer movement, and describe the impact of globalisation on consumers.

5. Generally, *a consumer* is a person who acquires goods and services in a transaction for his or her own personal or household use.

6. Under the *Competition and Consumer Act 2010* (Cth), *consumers* are defined as those people who acquire goods and services for under $40 000 or of a kind normally used for personal or domestic purposes.

7. The basis of contract law is that parties to a contract are in equal bargaining positions but, in most consumer transactions, the bargaining power is on the side of the manufacturers and sellers, so the law needs to intervene to redress the balance.

8. The objectives of consumer law are:

   i to equalise the bargaining power between consumers and manufacturers and sellers; **ii** to protect the rights of consumers; **iii** to assist in resolving disputes between consumers and suppliers; **iv** to provide redress when problems between consumers and suppliers arise.

9. You need to list the four objectives of consumer law, list the international rights of consumers, and explain why consumer protection laws have become increasingly necessary.

10. A *contract* is a legally binding agreement.

11. The *Competition and Consumer Act 2010* (Cth) and the *Fair Trading Act 1987* (NSW)

12. contracts for goods and services, and contracts for credit

13. Michael's offer of $3000 for the car and Jane's acceptance of the offer is the first element (offer and acceptance). The exchange of the car for the money is the second element (consideration). The signing over of the car by Jane is the third element (because it shows that there was an intention to enter into legal relations).

14. An oral contract is only enforceable once it has been carried out, whereas a written contract can be enforced before it is carried out.

15. A *term* of a contract is a promise contained within the contract.

16. An *express term* is one that is actually spoken or written into a contract, whereas an *implied term* is a promise that statute or common law will put into a contract even though such a term was not discussed by either party.

17. A *condition* is a term fundamental to a contract, whereas a *warranty* is a term of the contract but it is not a fundamental term.

18. An *exclusion clause* is a clause in a contract by which traders try to restrict their liability if something goes wrong.

19. The *Fair Trading Act 1987* (NSW) and the *Competition and Consumer Act 2010* (Cth) state that terms implied by them cannot be excluded.

20. At common law, an exclusion clause is part of a contract which involves a signed document. An exclusion clause which is not part of a signed document will only operate if the trader took reasonable steps to draw the clause to the attention of the consumer *before* the contract was made.

21. *Thornton v Shoe Lane Parking Ltd* (1971) 2 QB 163

22. The law is able to imply terms into contracts. This means that both common and statute law put promises or terms into contracts that the parties to the contract may never have discussed.

23. The common law, the *Competition and Consumer Act 2010* (Cth), the *Sale of Goods Act 1923* (NSW) and the *Fair Trading Act 1987* (NSW) are all the source of implied terms in contracts.

24. The five basic terms implied into consumer contracts for goods are:

    i the person supplying the goods has the right to do so; **ii** the goods fit the description; **iii** the goods are of merchantable quality; **iv** the goods are fit for the purpose; **v** the goods conform to a sample.

25. Services must be carried out in a reasonable and competent manner, and must be carried out with parts fit for the purpose.

26. The *Competition and Consumer Act 2010* (Cth) requires manufacturers and importers to ensure that spare parts and repair facilities are 'reasonably available', which generally means they are available up to ten years from the sale of the product.

27. As well as the five basic implied terms of contracts, published standards may also apply that set out criteria necessary to ensure that a material or method will consistently do the job it is intended to do.

28. Manufacturers and suppliers willingly follow voluntary standards because they can then assure consumers that their products are of good quality and meet established standards, thereby increasing consumer confidence and the likelihood of purchase.

29. Food, toys and sunglasses are products which may have mandatory standards applied to them.

30. The Australian Competition and Consumer Commission (ACCC)

31. *Product recall* means a product is removed from being available for sale and a request is made for the return of any items which have already been sold.

32. Suppliers of goods that do not comply with a mandatory product standard may be subject to fines of up to $1.1 million for corporations and $220 000 for individuals under the *Competition and Consumer Act 2010* (Cth). In the case of *Australian Competition and Consumer Commission v Skippy Australia Pty* Ltd (2006) FCA 1343, the company was fined $860 000 for supplying non-compliant baby walkers and cots.

33. The *Contracts Review Act 1980* (NSW), the *Competition and Consumer Act 2010* (Cth) and the common law regulate unjust contracts.

34. Factors that a court will consider in deciding if a contract is unjust include:

    i the age, education and literacy of the parties; **ii** the mental capacity and state of intoxication of the parties; **iii** the way in which the contract is expressed; **iv** whether any undue pressure was applied to either party to sign the contract; **v** the opportunity for negotiation and for obtaining independent legal advice.

35. In the case of *Blomley v Ryan* (1956) 99 CLR 362, the court found that the contract was unfair because Blomley knew that Ryan was uneducated and, at the time of entering the contract, that he was also intoxicated.

36. Remedies for breach of contract include:

    i repair; **ii** refund; **iii** replacement; **iv** payment of damages; **vi** rescission of contract; **vii** modification of contract; **viii** special orders; **viii** injunctions; **ix** specific performance.

37. You need to define *contract*, list the two main types of consumer contract; explain that the function of consumer contracts is to regulate the behaviour between consumers and sellers, and between consumers and credit providers; explain the nature of a contract by describing its elements; explain how terms, both express and implied, form contracts, and how the common law and statutes imply terms about the quality of goods and services into contracts; list the laws which regulate contracts; describe the circumstances under which a contract will be found to be unjust; and list remedies for breach of contract.

38. The case of *Donoghue v Stevenson* (1932) AC 562 is relevant because, in this case, the court decided that, under the law of torts, the manufacturer owed a duty of care to the consumer, even though the consumer was not a party to the contract.

39. Product liability laws allow any person who is injured as a result of defective goods to claim compensation from the manufacturer, with whom they don't have a direct contract.

40. Negligence is irrelevant to product liability laws. A person injured as a result of defective goods is still entitled to compensation, whether there was negligence or not.

41. Advertising informs consumers of the range and price of available products, thereby giving them information and freedom of choice.

42. Advertising and marketing are regulated through legislation and statutory authorities, as well as self-regulation by industries themselves.

43. The *Competition and Consumer Act 2010* (Cth) and the *Fair Trading Act 1987* (NSW) regulate advertising and marketing.

44. The general provisions in the *Trade Practices Act 1974* (Cth) and the *Fair Trading Act 1987* (NSW) state that sellers of goods and services cannot engage in conduct that is misleading, deceptive or unconscionable (unfair).

45. The consumer does not have to pay for unordered goods, they become the property of the consumer after three months and the consumer is not responsible for any accidental damage to such goods.

46. Traders who engage in unfair marketing practices are liable to criminal prosecution and penalties, and a consumer who suffers a loss because of such practices is entitled to compensation.

47. The *Australian Competition and Consumer Commission v Prouds Jewellers Pty Ltd* (2008) FCA 75 is a case involving misleading advertising.

48. Ad Standards and the Advertising Claims Board are responsible for the self-regulation of the advertising industry.

49. You need to discuss the factors which enhance, and those which limit, the effectiveness in achieving consumer protection of the regulation of marketing, advertising and product certification. Then you need to decide how effective the regulation is, given the two sets of factors.

50. *Occupational licensing* is the granting of permits to practise in particular professions or occupations.

51. Occupational licensing occurs through self-regulation, state regulation and co-regulation.

52. Occupational licensing means a consumer can know that the person they are dealing with is qualified and competent to do the work required, and it protects the consumer from incompetent and faulty work.

53. *Self-regulation* occurs when a particular trade or occupation imposes its own licensing restrictions on people who practise in that occupation (for example accountants are members of CPA Australia).

54. The finding by the industry-funded Advertising Standards Bureau that some Coca-Cola advertisements were acceptable, when the same advertisements were later found to be totally unacceptable by the ACCC, indicates that self-regulating bodies may not always work in the best interests of the consumer.

55. *State regulation* means that the government, through legislation, gives people in a particular occupation permission to practise. For example, motor car dealers and repairers are given this permission under the *Motor Dealers and Repairers Act 2013* (NSW).

56. *Co-regulation* occurs when occupations or professions are regulated by a combination of self-regulation and state regulation. Two examples are the legal profession and the advertising industry.

57. You need to define *occupational licensing*; describe types of occupational licensing, with examples; explain the advantages and disadvantages of occupational licensing for consumers; and comment on the importance of occupational licensing for consumers. You should note that occupational licensing is only one method of protecting consumers from shoddy and inadequate workmanship. There are many other remedies as well.

58. *Consumer redress* means the ways that consumers can achieve a just outcome to a consumer transaction in which they have been wronged, and it includes both processes and remedies.

59. Consumers can pursue redress through:

    i awareness and self-help; **ii** state government organisations; **iii** federal government organisations; **iv** industry organisations; **v** tribunals and courts; **vi** non-government organisations.

60. Complain directly to the supplier or manufacturer.

61. Both awareness and self-help are very important because consumer awareness helps to prevent consumer problems and self-help is often the quickest, cheapest way of solving the consumer problems that do occur.

62. *Mediation* is the process whereby a third person, called a mediator or conciliator, listens to the two parties to a dispute and makes suggestions in an effort to bring the two parties to agreement. Another word for *mediation* is *conciliation*.

63. The NSW Office of Fair Trading is the primary conciliator in NSW.

64. Other state government organisations which can assist consumers are the Legal Services Commissioner, the Health Care Complaints Commission and the NSW Food Authority.

65. **i** The Australian Competition and Consumer Commission (ACCC) provides information and guidance to consumers and businesses about their rights and obligations under the law.

    ii The Australian Securities and Investments Commission (ASIC) provides information and advice to consumers about how to resolve difficulties they have with a financial service such as sharebrokers, insurance providers and superannuation providers.

    iii The Australian Communications and Media Authority (ACMA) is responsible for the regulation of broadcasting, the internet and telecommunications.

66. Any four of the following; CPA Australia; the Advertising Standards Bureau; the Law Society of NSW; the Australian Financial Complaints Authority (AFCA); and the Telecommunications Industry Ombudsman (TIO).

67. Variety of answers acceptable. For example: After a consumer has unsuccessfully tried to resolve the matter him or herself, the Financial Ombudsman Service refers to the financial institution for settlement, then tries to solve the matter by mediation and, finally, if these methods fail to reach a solution, makes an award on the matter via arbitration. This award is binding on the trader if the consumer agrees to it. If the consumer is unhappy with the decision, he or she can pursue the matter in the court.

68. The Consumer, Trader and Tenancy Tribunal began operation in 2002 under the *Consumer, Trader and Tenancy Tribunal Act 2001* (NSW), and replaced the Fair Trading Tribunal. It is now the NSW Civil and Administrative Tribunal (NCAT).

69. Any three of the following:
   i before a hearing takes place, NCAT must try to bring the disputing parties to agreement through conciliation
   ii NCAT must operate without regard to technicalities or legal forms
   iii NCAT must act expeditiously (without undue delay)
   iv NCAT must follow rules of procedural fairness
   v legal representation is not generally permitted by NCAT which makes it inexpensive
   vi NCAT has the power to make a wide range of orders which can be enforced by the courts if necessary.

70. Courts should be a last resort because they are often slow, and legal representation can be very expensive.

71. Class actions mean that several consumers can take a case to court jointly, splitting the cost between them and thereby reducing the cost to each individual consumer.

72. The Australian Consumers Association and the NRMA both provide information to consumers and can assist them to choose wisely when they buy various products.

73. The media can assist consumers by providing information about faulty products and unfair practices, by conducting publicity campaigns on behalf of consumers who are dissatisfied with a product or service, and by advertising new products.

74. i Refund: the supplier takes back a faulty product and gives the consumer back his or her money.
   ii Repair: the supplier repairs a faulty product.
   iii Replacement: the supplier replaces a faulty product.
   iv Damages: money is paid by one party to the other party of the transaction, in order to compensate for loss suffered by that party.
   v Rescission of contract: the consumer contract is decided to be at an end.
   vi Modification of contract: the consumer contract is varied.
   vii Special orders: courts and tribunals can make a wide variety of special orders, such as to pay money owed, to refund or replace defective goods, or to publish corrective advertising.
   viii Injunction: an order is made for someone to do or to refrain from doing something.
   ix Specific performance: an order is made that requires the parties to a contract to do those things which their contract requires, in order to settle and define the parties' rights.
   x Criminal prosecution: the supplier or manufacturer is prosecuted if he or she has contravened particular consumer laws, and fines or other penalties may be imposed.

75. You need to describe the ten remedies available to consumers and explain how each assists consumers and society to achieve justice.

76. **Non-legal measures are**: awareness and self-help; state and federal government organisations; mediation/conciliation; industry organisations and arbitration; non-government organisations; and the media. **Legal measures are**: the Consumer, Trader and Tenancy Tribunal; and the courts.

77. You need to discuss the advantages and disadvantages of each legal and non-legal measure available to consumers and decide whether the advantages of each outweigh its disadvantages. Then decide how effective each type of measure is.

78. *Product certification* is the process that confirms that a product or service meets relevant or necessary standards, such as safety, health or environmental standards.

79. Product certification benefits business because more and more consumers are conscious of such matters and will buy a healthy or environmentally-friendly product rather than an alternative product that does not have such certification. Consumers can be assured that the product they purchase meets certain standards.

80. Businesses are limited in their ability to certify their products by the common law, the *Competition and Consumer Act 2010* (Cth) and the *Fair Trading Act 1987* (NSW). All of these contain provisions which state that sellers of goods and services cannot engage in conduct that is misleading, deceptive or unconscionable. This includes making product certification claims that are false.

81. Two legal responses to issues involving product certification are: action taken by the NSW Food Authority against companies which make claims about foodstuffs which are not met; and action by the ACCC against companies which make misrepresentations about their products. Non-legal responses include: the process of certification is usually undertaken by non-government organisations; the effectiveness of product certification relies on the awareness of the consumer; and the reputational damage that can be suffered by businesses who fail to certify their products or who fail to do so properly.

82. You need to: explain what *product certification* is and give examples; explain the importance of reliable product certification for both consumers and businesses; explain the issue of false claims and the increasing number of complaints about these in the area of eco-labelling; describe legal and non-legal responses; discuss the factors which help ensure, and those which limit, the effectiveness in protecting the consumer of legal and non-legal responses to issues involving product certification; and come to a conclusion about the effectiveness of product certification in protecting the consumer.

83. *Telemarketing* is the practice of selling goods or services to people by telephoning them at home and offering the product for sale. Its advantages to the consumer include convenience, as well as a wider range of goods and services.

84. i The laws about advertising and consumer transactions under the *Competition and Consumer Act 2010* (Cth) and the *Fair Trading Act 1987* (NSW) apply to direct commerce as they do to all other forms of selling goods and services.
   ii The Fair Trading Act also imposes a five working-day cooling-off period for most direct commerce contracts.
   iii People who do not wish to receive telemarketing calls can contact the Do Not Call Register and list their private or domestic fixed-line and mobile numbers under the *Do Not Call Register Act 2006* (Cth).

85. *Product placement* refers to the placement of a sponsored product or brand into the content of entertainment, such as the biscuits Reese's Pieces in the movie *E.T. The Extra-terrestrial.*

86. Product placement advertising for cigarettes and tobacco products is not permitted under Australian law. Other product placement advertising is permitted if it is disclosed.

87. Heavy penalties can be imposed on a broadcaster who contravenes the disclosure laws. For example, Radio 2UE Sydney was fined a total of $360 000 when one of its presenters, John Laws, failed to make the requisite disclosures several times in October and November of 2007.

88. Five legal responses are: generally applicable advertising and consumer laws under the *Competition and Consumer Act 2010* (Cth) and the *Fair Trading Act 1987* (NSW); a 'cooling-off' period applies to many direct commerce transactions under the *Fair Trading Act 1987* (NSW); the *Do Not Call Register Act 2006* (Cth) makes it an offence for a telemarketer to call a number listed on the register; product placement of cigarettes and tobacco products is prohibited in nearly all forms of media; and product placement advertising for other products is permitted if it is disclosed. A non-legal response is that both government and industry organisations assist businesses to comply with the legal requirements for direct commerce and product placement.

89. You need to: explain the two marketing innovations of direct commerce and product placement and give examples; explain that most responses to the issue are legal responses; describe the legal and non-legal responses to the issue; discuss the factors which help ensure, and those which limit, the effectiveness in protecting the consumer of the responses; and come to a conclusion about the effectiveness of the regulation of marketing innovations in protecting the consumer.

90. First, the government provides a regulatory framework, within which industry must operate. Second, government, industry and non-government bodies monitor compliance with the regulatory framework, thereby reducing the number of non-compliant businesses and, as a result, the number of consumer complaints and disputes.

91. The law encourages cooperation between consumers and business in these ways:
    i consumers must try to resolve disputes themselves before seeking government assistance.
    ii government authorities offer advice and mediation.
    iii other bodies, such as industry organisations, have dispute settling procedures.

92. If conciliation and negotiation are ineffective, consumers can have conflict resolved through industry organisations, such as the Telecommunications Industry Ombudsman, NSW Civil and Administrative Tribunal (NCAT) and the court system.

93. Three factors which contribute to the high standard of commitment to consumer protection law are:
    i commitment to customer service; ii effective advice, assistance and mediation services; iii effective enforcement mechanisms.

94. It is sensible for traders to keep consumers happy because the processes of redress available to consumers are quick, cheap and easily accessible. So businesses will probably be forced to rectify the situation anyway.

95. Four areas of consumer law that make it costly for suppliers to break the law are laws regarding: product liability; class actions; mandatory standards; and marketing.

96. The dominant moral value reflected by the law is that ordinary people have a right to be treated fairly in the marketplace.

97. The law tries to reflect the value of equity in the marketplace by:
    i product liability laws; ii increased availability of class actions; iii proliferation of cheap, quick avenues of redress; iv introduction of the *Consumer Credit Code*; v mandatory product standards.

98. A federal example is the *Do Not Call Register Act* 2006 (Cth), which aims to protect consumers from being harassed by unwanted telemarketing calls.

99. The sources of pressure to reform the law are: the media; lobby groups; reports from various government inquiries or organisations, such as the Ombudsman or Law Reform Commissions; and international pressure.

100. The Australian Consumer Law of 2010 developed because of cooperation between federal, state and territory governments through the MCCA and COAG. This law reform draws on the conclusions of the 2008 Productivity Commission's report: 'Review of Australia's consumer policy framework'.

101. Two examples of consumer law reform resulting from changing social values and the composition of society are: greater use of co-regulation by industry; and greater emphasis on customer service.

102. Two reforms to consumer law brought about by a failure of existing law are:
    i product liability laws; ii mandatory product standards.

103. Non-legal responses for achieving justice for consumers include:
    i marketing and advertising; ii occupational licensing; iii consumer redress and remedies; iv credit; v product certification; vi marketing innovations; vii technology.

104. Legal responses for achieving justice for consumers include:
    i the law of contract; ii regulating exclusion clauses; iii protection against unjust contracts; iv standards implied by statute and the common law; v voluntary and mandatory standards; vi product recall; vii action for breach of mandatory standards; viii the law of torts; ix product liability laws.

105. Legal avenues for redress for consumers are tribunals and courts. Non-legal avenues include: awareness and self-help; state government organisations; federal government organisations; industry organisations; non-government organisations; and the media.

106. Legal remedies for consumers include: an award of damages; rescission and modification of a contract; special orders; injunctions and specific performance; and criminal prosecution for the supplier. Non-legal remedies for consumers are: refund; repair; and replacement.

Extended-response questions

Note: **EM** means Examiner Maximiser

Question 1

What you are asked to do

This question asks you to:

- outline the developing need for consumer protection
- evaluate how effectively the law deals with unfair contracts.

EM In order to achieve top marks for your answer to this question, in your answer you should:

- explain how the current consumer situation has developed from the past
- outline the current issues in regard to consumer protection
- describe how the law deals with unfair contracts
- explain whether the law today effectively protects the consumer.

Your answer could follow the plan below.

Plan

Paragraph 1 (Introduction):

- Since the seventeenth century, society has changed from a rural subsistence society to an urban mass consumption/production society. Consumer law developed from contract law. Contracts are regulated in several ways including provisions made to modify or rescind unfair contracts, thereby protecting the consumer. The law regarding contracts is effective in protecting the consumer.

Paragraph 2:

- Ways in which society has changed from a rural subsistence society to an urban mass consumption/production society.
- The Industrial Revolution, the philosophy of *laissez faire* and *caveat emptor* and why and how governments departed from this philosophy. **[3.1.1]**

Paragraph 3:

- The basis of consumer law is contract law.
- Define *contract*.
- Describe the nature and function of contracts. **[3.1.4]**

Paragraph 4:

- Describe some of the ways contracts are regulated: implied standards; mandatory standards; exclusion clauses; product liability.
- Unfair contracts can be modified or rescinded. **[3.1.4, 3.1.5, 3.1.6 and 3.1.7]**

Paragraph 5:

- The laws that protect people from unfair contracts.
- The circumstances in which a contract will be found to be unjust (giving an example).
- The remedies available for those who are involved in an unjust contract. **[3.1.6]**

Conclusion:

- Summarise the developing need for consumer protection.
- Summarise the way in which the law regulates consumer contracts.

- Comment on the effectiveness of the law in dealing with unfair consumer good and services contracts.

Question 2

What you are asked to do

This question asks you to:

- outline the objectives of consumer law
- assess how well the law deals with at least one of these objectives.

EM In order to achieve top marks for your answer to this question, in your answer you should:

- state and briefly explain the objectives of consumer law
- choose one (or two) of the objectives you listed
- describe **how** the law meets the chosen objective(s)
- explain whether the law effectively meets the objective(s).

Your answer could follow the plan below.

Plan

Paragraph 1 (Introduction):

- Consumer laws are based on the law of contract, which relies on the parties being in equal bargaining positions. In the modern, global consumer marketplace, the bargaining positions are unequal. Law tries to even the balance.
- So objectives are:
  - to equal the balance
  - to protect consumers
  - to assist in dispute resolution
  - to provide redress.
- Discuss objectives to assist in dispute resolution and provide redress.

Paragraph 2. List ways that the law assists in resolving disputes: advice; assistance and mediation through government authorities; tribunals and courts. **[3.2.2, 3.2.3, 3.2.5 and 3.2.9]**

Paragraph 3:

- The best method is self-help.
- Government organisations will not intervene until self-help has been tried.
- State the effectiveness of self-help. **[3.2.1 and 3.2.9]**

Paragraph 4:

- List state and federal organisations which will supply advice, assistance and mediation.
- State the effectiveness of these state and federal organisations. **[3.2.2 and 3.2.3]**

Paragraph 5:

- Describe the NSW Civil and Administrative Tribunal (NCAT), and provide an example of its dealings.
- State the effectiveness of the NSW CCCT. **[3.2.5]**

Paragraph 6:

- Consumers always have the option of going to court.
- Discuss the availability of class actions.
- State the effectiveness of court action. **[3.2.5]**

Conclusion:

- List the objectives of consumer law.
- The law is very successful in assisting in dispute settlement and providing redress.

- Summarise the methods of dispute resolution, stating advantages and disadvantages.
- All these avenues of redress and the wide variety of remedies available mean that the law is very effective in meeting these two objectives in NSW.

Chapter 4: Family

KCq Key Concept questions (pages 268–72)

1. Family law deals with the relationships between family members and the rights and responsibilities of people in families.

2. It is difficult to define *family* because the notion of what constitutes a 'family' has undergone substantial change over the last thirty years as society has changed. In modern Australian society, there are people living in many different kinds of personal relationships which they regard as being 'family'.

3. The ABS defines *family* as: 'Two or more persons ... who are related by blood, marriage (registered or *de facto*), adoption, step or fostering and who are usually resident in the same household'.

4. i nuclear families
   ii couples without children
   iii *de facto* couples
   iv blended families
   v extended families
   vi single parent families
   vii same-sex couples
   viii Aboriginal and Torres Strait Islander customary law marriages

5. You need to: describe the traditional concept of family as a married couple with children; explain how the traditional concept of family has changed and why it is, therefore, difficult to define *family*; give the ABS definition of family; list and define different types of family relationships; and list the ways children can become part of a family.

6. *Marriage* is: 'The union of two people to the exclusion of all others, voluntarily entered into for life'.

7. A marriage must be between two people; both parties must consent to the marriage; the parties stay married for life, unless divorced; the parties to the marriage can only be married to one person at any one time.

8. The parties to a marriage must be of marriageable age; they must not be related in a prohibited degree; there must be one month notice of marriage; there must be two witnesses; and the ceremony must be performed by an authorised celebrant.

9. A marriage will be declared void: if one of the parties is already married; if the parties are related to each other in a prohibited degree; if one party did not really consent to the marriage; or if one of the parties is not of marriageable age.

10. You need to be able to explain and give examples of the following requirements: the marriage must be between two people; both parties must consent to the marriage; the parties stay married for life, unless divorced; each party to the marriage can only be married to one person

at any one time; the parties must be of marriageable age (eighteen years); the parties must not be related in a prohibited degree (a person may not marry his or her descendant, ancestor, brother or sister); there must be one month notice of marriage; there must be two witnesses; and the ceremony must be performed by an authorised celebrant.

11. Aboriginal and Torres Strait Islander peoples' customary law marriages; single parent families; blended families; same-sex relationships; polygamous marriages; and *de facto* relationships

12. Aboriginal and Torres Strait Islander peoples' customary law marriages are treated as *de facto* relationships.

13. Polygamous marriages are not recognised or permitted in Australia.

14. A *de facto* relationship occurs when a man and woman live together as a married couple, though they are not legally married. That is, they are living in a *bona fide* domestic relationship.

15. Under the *Family Law Amendment (De Facto Financial Matters and other Measures) Act 2008* (Cth), the law will operate for *de facto* couples who are separating: if the relationship has existed for an aggregate, but not necessarily continuous, period of two years; if there is a child of the relationship; or if a party to the relationship can establish a substantial contribution to the relationship that would result in serious injustice if he or she is denied the opportunity to bring proceedings under the act.

16. *De facto* relationships were viewed as immoral and as an attack on the institution of marriage.

17. Under the Australian Constitution, the federal government has power to make laws related to marriage and divorce. The states have residual powers to make laws about any other family related matters.

18. States have handed over their powers to the federal government to make laws about the parental care of children, and about the distribution of property after the breakdown of a *de facto* relationship, whether it be heterosexual or homosexual.

19. i adoption
    ii wills, inheritance and succession
    iii most aspects of domestic violence
    iv surrogacy and birth technologies
    v the care and protection of children

20. The four basic principles of the United Nations Convention on the Rights of the Child (CROC) 1989 are: non-discrimination; the best interests of the child; the right to life, survival and development; and the right to have views expressed and respected.

21. The CROC has been made an 'international instrument' under the *Australian Human Rights Commission Act 1986* (Cth), which means that breaches of the CROC can be reported to the Australian Human Rights Commission, but Australian courts cannot enforce its provisions.

22. You need to be able to explain: the basic provisions of the CROC; the status of the CROC in Australia; and how well Australia meets its obligations under this convention.

23. i name and nationality
    ii discrimination
    iii care and control

    iv discipline
    v education
    vi religion
    vii medical treatment
  viii contracts
    ix succession
    x autonomy

24. the *Adoption Act 2000* (NSW)

25. People over twenty-one, either single or as a married or *de facto* couple, can adopt a child.

26. The birth mother, the biological father and the child (if he or she is over twelve years old) must consent to an adoption.

27. Parents of a newborn child cannot consent to the child's adoption until thirty days after the birth and, generally, they must receive counselling before consenting.

28. The advance notice request system means an adoptive parent and adopted child or a birth parent can request that they be given advance notice before personal information is released, in order to make suitable arrangements. The advance notice cannot be longer than three months. If an adopted adult or the biological parents of an adopted adult do not wish to be contacted, they can lodge a contact veto, which makes it illegal for the other party to contact them.

29. Over the last thirty years, it has become increasingly difficult to adopt a child because fewer and fewer children are available for adoption, due to the increased availability of effective contraception and abortion, and because of the reduced social stigma attached to unmarried mothers and ex-nuptial children meaning these children are being raised by their biological parent.

30. The Hague Convention on Protection of Children and Co-operation in respect of Intercountry Adoption 1993 governs overseas adoption.

31. The *Family Law Act 1975* (Cth) governs divorce in Australia.

32. For a divorce to be granted there must be an irretrievable breakdown of marriage. To prove this, a couple must live separately and apart for a period of twelve months.

33. The 'no-fault' concept is the idea that neither party is to blame for the marriage breakdown. Before this act was passed, the spouse who committed adultery or who left the marriage was seen to be the party at fault. When the *Family Law Act 1975* (Cth) was first passed, many people felt that one party should be blamed for the breakdown of the marriage and that decisions about property division and the care of children should take into account which party was to blame for the marriage failure.

34. When proving a couple are living 'separately and apart':
    i there must be the intention to end the relationship on the part of at least one of the parties to the marriage
    ii there can be separation under one roof, which means a couple may be living separately and apart while still occupying a house together, as long as one has formed the intention to separate
    iii there exists a 'kiss and make up' clause, which means that couples who are separated may try living together again for one period of up to three months. If this does not work out, there is no need for the twelve-month separation period to restart.

35. The care of children and child maintenance are the two areas of law regarding children which become issues when parents separate.

36. The legislation governing the care of children by their parents is the *Family Law Act 1975* (Cth), as amended by the *Family Law Reform Act 1995* (Cth) and the *Family Law Amendment (Shared Parental Responsibility) Act 2006* (Cth).

37. This legislation applies to all children and parents, no matter what the relationship between the parents is.

38. The terms are: 'live with'; 'spend time with'; 'communicate with'.

39. The current law emphasises the rights of children and the responsibilities of parents.

40. A parenting order may deal with: who the child is to live with; who a child spends time with; who the child communicates with and how such communications take place; the allocation of parental responsibility, such as equal shared parental responsibility; the way in which parents communicate with each other regarding major long-term decisions; and any other aspects of the child's care.

41. The Family Court makes decisions in the best interests of the child.

42. The two primary considerations for the Family Court are the benefit to the child of having a meaningful relationship with both parents, and the need to protect the child from harm. Additional considerations include: the views of the child; each parent's willingness and ability to facilitate and encourage a close and continuing relationship between the child and the other parent; whether the orders made are likely to lead to further dispute; the effect of changing the existing living conditions of the child; the attitude to parenting of those who are applying for orders and their capacity to care for the child; the practical difficulties and expense involved in 'spending time' with and 'communicating with' a parent; the capacity of each parent and others to provide for the child's needs; the maturity, gender, lifestyle and background of the child and the parents; the nature of the relationship of the child with each parent and other people; any family violence or family violence order that applies to the child, or his or her family; any other circumstance the court thinks relevant.

43. If there has been family violence the Family Court must consider the effect on the child of this violence and must make orders consistent with any other family violence orders made in other jurisdictions.

44. The Chisholm report and two other reports released in January 2010 found that children may have to spend significant time with a person whom they fear because:
    i some women were scared to raise issues of violence, for fear that the court would view them as the unwilling or 'unfriendly' parent, and grant them less time with the children as a result
    ii the provision regarding awarding costs against a parent who either maliciously raises untrue allegations of violence or makes untrue denials discouraged women from making reports about family violence.

45. Equal shared parental responsibility means that the parents must consult each other and agree on 'major long-term issues', such as the child's education, religious and cultural upbringing, and the child's name. The

presumption of equal shared parental responsibility does not apply if there has been, or there is a risk of family violence. The presumption can also be rebutted (that is, one parent can argue that equal shared parental responsibility is not in the best interests of the child).

46. Spending *substantial and significant time* with one parent means that the child should spend time with the parent that includes weekends, weekdays and holidays, which allows the parent to share daily routines and special occasions with the child. A court is only required to grant such time if an order for equal shared parental responsibility is made and if it is in the best interests of the child.

47. According to three reviews of the provisions released in January 2010 there has been no significant effect on the welfare of children, though the number of children spending equal or substantial and significant time with both parents has increased from 9% in 2003 to 16% in 2010. The number of cases regarding the care of children has declined by 22% since the introduction of the provisions. The reviews also found that children whose parents are in conflict have more problems than those whose parents cooperate, no matter what the living arrangements.

48. *Maintenance* refers to a payment made by one person to help contribute to the care and welfare of another person.

49. The Child Support Scheme was introduced in 1988 because the amount of maintenance ordered by the court was often much lower than the real cost of supporting a child; and over 70% of parents avoided paying child maintenance.

50. The amount of maintenance a liable parent must pay is determined by: the income of each parent; the age and number of children to be maintained; whether the liable parent has regular overnight care of the children, defined as at least one night a week; the age and true cost of raising the child; and the cost of providing regular overnight care.

51. If necessary, the Department of Human Services can garnishee wages, seize and sell property, sequester an estate, and intercept tax refunds.

52. The *Family Law Act 1975* (Cth) as amended by the *Family Law Amendment (De Facto Financial Matters and other Measures) Act 2008* (Cth) governs distribution of property after a couple separate.

53. The legislation governing distribution of property applies to divorcing married couples and to separating *de facto* couples, both heterosexual and homosexual.

54. *Property* is everything owned by both parties including houses, cars, household goods, bank accounts, shares, gifts and inheritances, compensation, lottery winnings and superannuation, regardless of whose name the property is in.

55. The court considers: what property the parties own and its value; the financial and non-financial contributions of each party to the property in the past; the present and future needs of each party; and whether the proposed division is just and equitable in all circumstances.

56. Superannuation is treated differently from other property because this money is locked away until a person retires, but is still a financial asset of the marriage. If one party

has a substantial superannuation fund, and the other does not, this is often because one party has had the opportunity to work and accrue superannuation, while the other has made non-financial contributions to the relationship.

57. Parties can make a consent order regarding the distribution of their property (which is legally binding), or they can make a binding financial agreement which is enforceable if: it is in writing; it is signed by both parties; independent legal advice has been received by both parties; and enforcing the agreement would not lead to serious injustice.

58. *Domestic violence* is actual or threatened violence or harassment within a domestic relationship.

59. Any two of the following: domestic violence is the most common form of assault in Australia; domestic violence related assaults accounted for 37% of all assaults reported to NSW police in 2007; NSW police respond to approximately 120 000 domestic violence incidents each year (NSW Ombudsman, 2006).

60. Apprehended violence orders (AVOs), criminal charges and other court orders are ways that the law responds to domestic violence.

61. The *Crimes (Domestic and Personal Violence) Act 2007* (NSW) provides for Apprehended Domestic Violence Orders (ADVOs), made to protect people against behaviour from someone with whom they are or have been in a domestic relationship, and Apprehended Personal Violence Orders (APVOs), made when the protected person and the defendant are not and have not been in a domestic relationship.

62. An AVO can be obtained by a victim if he or she can prove, on the balance of probabilities, that he or she has reasonable grounds to apprehend (fear), and does in fact fear, personal violence, intimidation or stalking by the defendant.

63. The standard of proof required for an AVO is 'on the balance of probabilities' whereas, for an assault charge, the requirement is for the higher, criminal standard: 'beyond reasonable doubt'.

64. An AVO can prevent a defendant from doing a large range of activities such as: assaulting or threatening the victim; possessing firearms; approaching the victim's home; and stalking or intimidating the victim.

65. When an AVO is breached, the defendant can be arrested immediately and can be found guilty of a criminal offence, with penalties of up to $5500 in fines and/or two years imprisonment.

66. *Domestic violence offences* are crimes that involve violence between people in a domestic relationship and are illegal under the *Crimes Act 1900* (NSW). Police are required to apply for an ADVO if an offence committed is recorded as a domestic violence offence.

67. *Stalking* includes following a person, spying on them and frequenting a place where that person works or lives. *Intimidation* includes other behaviours such as nuisance telephone calls or other unwelcome forms of communication, and harassing or threatening someone. These behaviours can be criminal offences when a defendant engages in such acts with the intention or

reasonable foresight of putting a victim in fear of his or her personal or family's safety.

68. The Family Court can issue a court order, such as an injunction, which has a similar effect to an AVO. The Family Court must also ensure that any parenting orders it makes are consistent with family violence orders.

69. i the women's refuge program
ii the Staying Home Leaving Violence program
iii the Women's Domestic Violence Court Assistance Scheme
iv the Start Safely rental subsidy
v victim's compensation
vi personal injury claims

70. You need to discuss the factors which enhance, and those which limit the effectiveness of the law in protecting victims of domestic violence. Then you need to decide how effective the protection is, given the two sets of factors.

71. State Courts hear matters of: adoption; wills, inheritance and succession; most aspects of domestic violence; surrogacy and birth technologies; and the care and protection of children.

72. The two courts which deal with divorce in Australia are: the Family Court of Australia, which was established under the *Family Law Act* in 1975 and commenced operation in the same year; and the Federal Magistrates Court, which was established under the *Federal Magistrates Act 1999* (Cth) and commenced operation in 2000.

73. The Family Court of Australia only hears the more complex divorce matters, such as parenting cases which involve multiple parties, allegations of abuse or child welfare agencies; and complex financial matters. Of the 10% of divorce matters which need a court resolution, only 25% are heard by the Family Court.

74. Over 90% of divorces are finalised without a court hearing.

75. i Family Relationship Centres were established to provide dispute resolution on a range of matters.
ii It has been made compulsory for parents, in most circumstances, to attempt dispute resolution about the care of children before applying for a court order
iii A less adversarial legal process, 'child-related proceedings', applies to matters involving children.

76. You need to name the problems (divorce, the care of children after the parents separate, child maintenance, distribution of property after separation, and domestic violence) and describe the legal processes involved in dealing with each problem.

77. i physical assistance, such as food, clothing and household goods (The Salvation Army)
ii relationship support services (Relationships Australia)
iii domestic violence support for victims (women's refuges)
iv legal assistance (Women's Legal Service NSW)

78. The primary purpose of a lobby group is to pressure government to reform the law. A secondary purpose is to give a voice to people with particular common concerns who feel that they cannot be heard by the government when they voice these concerns individually.

79. i The Domestic Violence Committee Coalition (DVCC) pressured the government to establish the NSW Domestic Violence Death Review Team in 2010.
ii NSW Gay and Lesbian Rights Lobby has pressured parliaments to pass laws to equalise the status of same-sex couples with that of heterosexual couples.
iii Parents groups, such as Dads in Distress and the Lone Fathers Association, were instrumental in having the reforms to family law introduced by the *Family Law Amendment (Shared Parental Responsibility) Act* 2006 (Cth).

80. The media can pressure governments to change laws by publishing the views of particular lobby groups, persistently criticising a government for their policies, and giving publicity to current events.

81. The media coverage of the killing of Darcey Freeman by her father who threw her off the West Gate bridge in Melbourne on 29 January 2009 assisted in the government's decision to commission a review of the *Family Law Amendment (Shared Parental Responsibility) Act 2006* (Cth). The publicity given by *The Sydney Morning Herald* to domestic-violence-related homicides in November 2008 immediately preceded the announcement of the establishment of the NSW Domestic Violence Homicide Advisory Panel, whose report led to the announcement, on 25 November 2009, that the NSW Domestic Violence Death Review Team would be established.

82. First, you need to state the roles of both non-government organisations and the media in relation to family law. Next you need to give examples of non-government organisations and the media performing these roles; and then comment on the impact of these examples in the area of family law.

83. You need to identify the parties involved in relationship breakdown and then, for each party, discuss the factors which enhance, and those which limit the effectiveness of the law in achieving justice. Then you need to decide how effective the law is in achieving justice, given the two sets of factors.

84. The parties who may be involved in relationship breakdown are: parties to a marriage; parties to a *de facto* relationship; parents; children; other people with an interest in the children; and victims and perpetrators of domestic violence.

85. Homosexuality was first decriminalised in South Australia in 1975.

86. In 1982 the *Anti-Discrimination Act 1977* (NSW) was amended to prohibit discrimination on the grounds of homosexuality. In 1984 homosexual sexual activity was decriminalised in NSW.

87. In the *Property (Relationship) Legislation Amendment Act 1999* (NSW), same-sex couples were included in the provisions regarding property division that had applied to *de facto* couples since 1984. Other laws affected were those regarding family provision, intestacy, accident compensation and decision-making during illness and after death. NSW was the first state to pass legislation which extended the protection of the law to same-sex couples so comprehensively.

88. • The *Miscellaneous Acts Amendment (Same Sex Relationships) Act 2008* (NSW) meant that female

same-sex parents, who conceive a child through artificial means, are treated in the same way as opposite-sex parents. It also amended fifty-seven other pieces of NSW legislation to ensure de facto couples, including same-sex couples, are treated equally with married couples.

- The *Family Law Amendment (De Facto Financial Matters and other Measures) Act 2008* (Cth) means that, when their relationships break down, same-sex couples are treated in the same way in financial matters as *de facto* and married couples.
  The *Same-Sex Relationships (Equal Treatment in Commonwealth Laws—General Law Reform) Act 2008* and the *Same-Sex Relationships (Equal Treatment in Commonwealth Laws—Superannuation) Act 2008* were passed by the federal government in December 2008 to remove over 100 discriminatory provisions about same-sex couples in various pieces of Commonwealth legislation.

89. In 2010, the *Relationships Register Act* (NSW) was passed, giving same-sex couples the ability to register their relationship with the NSW Registry of Births, Deaths and Marriages, providing proof of the existence of the relationship for the purposes of the law. In September 2010, the *Adoption Amendment (Same Sex Couples) Act* was passed in NSW parliament, meaning that same-sex couples could legally adopt a child.

90. The recognition of same-sex relationships refers to the legal recognition of these relationships, which has usually followed rather than led societal acceptance and recognition.

91. The lobbying activities of various groups such as the NSW Gay and Lesbian Rights Lobby are a non-legal response to the recognition of same-sex relationships.

92. You need to describe the legal recognition of same-sex relationships that has occurred in NSW and Australia since 1975, outline the reasons for this recognition and non-recognition, and come to a conclusion about the effectiveness of the recognition of same-sex relationships.

93. Parental responsibility is defined in the *Family Law Act 1975* (Cth) as 'all the duties, powers, responsibilities and authority which, by law, parents have in relation to children'.

94. In 1900, women had no custody or guardianship rights over their children. The automatic guardian of any children born to a marriage was the father. If he died, he could, in his will, appoint another person guardian of his children rather than the children's mother.

95. In 1916, with the *Testator's Family Maintenance and Guardianship of Infants Act 1916* (NSW), widows were given automatic custody of their children when the father died. The *Guardianship of Infants Act 1934* (NSW) gave women with husbands still alive equal rights to the custody of their children.

96. When a divorce occurred, the party found to be 'at fault', was generally not awarded custody of the children and was made to pay maintenance to the custodial parent. Access and maintenance were linked in the minds of many divorced parents with the idea that, if maintenance was not paid, the liable parent had no right to see the child and, similarly, if the parent did pay maintenance he or she then did have the right to have access to the child.

97. The inclusion of ex-nuptial children in the *Family Law Act* in 1988 meant that it was recognised that both parents

had responsibility for the maintenance of their children no matter what their marital status.

98. The introduction of the Child Support Scheme meant that the amount of child maintenance payable by a non-custodial parent better reflected the cost of raising the child, and that it became harder for non-custodial parents to avoid paying maintenance. The introduction of this scheme reflected the idea that both parents were responsible for the upkeep of a child.

99. Article 9 of the United Nations Convention on the Rights of the Child 1989 emphasises the rights of the child (rather than the parent) to maintain contact with each parent, if it is in the child's best interest. Parental responsibility towards the child is emphasised, rather than rights of parents to the child.

100. The terms 'custody', 'guardianship' and 'access' were replaced with 'residence', 'parental responsibility' and 'contact' to emphasise the fact that parents do not have rights to a child, but that both parents have parental responsibility for the child, whether they are married, unmarried, divorced or separated.

101. Concerns about the 1995 reforms, which indicated that the idea of parental responsibility did not altogether replace the notion of parental rights in the minds of some parents, and strong lobbying from fathers' groups led to the idea of 'equal shared parental responsibility' which was introduced in the *Family Law Amendment (Shared Responsibility) Act 2006* (Cth).

102. i The increasing equality of women: In 1900, women had no rights to the guardianship or custody of their children. As women won the right to vote, they lobbied for equal rights of guardianship and custody which led to the passing of the *Guardianship of Infants Act 1934* (NSW) giving married men and women equal rights to custody and guardianship of their children.

ii The increasing number of divorces, combined with greater acceptance of unmarried mothers which occurred from the 1960s onwards, has led to many more separated parents and many more children who know only one parent. These societal changes have led to reforms to the law, such as the inclusion of ex-nuptial children in the *Family Law Act* and the introduction of the Child Support Scheme.

iii Fathers' lobby groups were very influential in legal changes made in 2006, introducing the notion of 'equal shared parental responsibility'.

103. You need to describe how the concept of parental responsibility has changed from being focused on the rights of the parents in 1900 to being focused on the responsibilities of parents and the rights of the child in 2010. You then need to outline the relationship between the non-legal and legal responses to the changing nature of parental responsibility, discuss the factors which indicate the effectiveness, and the lack of effectiveness, of the legal and non-legal responses to promoting the idea of parental responsibility, and then come to a conclusion about the effectiveness of legal and non-legal responses to the changing nature of parental responsibility.

104. *Artificial insemination* is a process whereby semen is medically implanted into a woman's reproductive system so that she can bear a child. *In-vitro fertilisation* (IVF) is a process whereby ovum and sperm are united in a test tube where they form an embryo which is then implanted into the woman's uterus. Artificial insemination and IVF are, together, referred to as *artificial reproductive technologies* (ART).

105. Laws in the area of birth technologies are a matter for state governments in Australia, though there are some areas in which national laws operate, particularly in the area of research. The National Health and Medical Research Council (NHMRC) provides guidelines and supervises some aspects of this technology, and federal legislation covers some research activities. The *Status of Children Act 1996* (NSW) and the *Assisted Reproductive Technology Act 2007* (NSW) contain much of the law that operates in NSW about birth technologies.

106. On 1 January 2010, the *Assisted Reproductive Technology Act 2007* (NSW) established a mandatory gamete donor register in order to assist those born from IVF who may experience 'genetic bewilderment' and/or want information regarding medical conditions which could be linked to genetic material.

107. While all women, no matter what their marital status, are permitted access to IVF treatment in New South Wales under the *Assisted Reproductive Technology Act 2007* (NSW), Medicare funding is only available to couples or single women who are medically infertile. Single women, whether heterosexual or homosexual, may seek IVF because they have no male partner, not for medical reasons. These women are considered 'socially infertile' and so are not eligible for Medicare assistance. They are, therefore, disadvantaged in their access to ART compared to women in heterosexual relationships, because it costs them considerably more money.

108. *Surrogacy* is when a woman agrees to become pregnant and bear a child on behalf of another couple who are usually unable to have children of their own.

109. Commercial surrogacy is banned under the *Surrogacy Act 2010* (NSW), though there is nothing to prevent private surrogacy arrangements taking place for altruistic reasons.

110. Two cases are that of *Re 'Evelyn'* (1998) FamCA 55 (15 May 1998) and *Re Mark* (2003) 31 Fam LR 162. Both these cases show that no matter what the parentage, the court will make its decision on what is in 'the best interests of the child'.

111. Seven legal responses are:
    i birth mothers and social fathers are the legal parents of children conceived through ART, and lesbian non-birth mothers can be registered as co-mothers (NSW)
    ii the Family Law Court can and does make orders about the care of children in favour of people other than the biological and/or social parents and, like all such decisions, these decisions are based on 'the best interests of the child' (Cth)
    iii gender selection is banned (Cth)
    iv cloning for reproductive purposes is banned, but restricted and tightly controlled research is allowed (Cth)
    v there is a mandatory donor register (NSW)
    vi all women have equal access to ART, but do not have equal access to Medicare funding
    vii commercial surrogacy is banned (NSW).

    Three non-legal responses are:

    i some people travel overseas to access gender selection of children and, sometimes, surrogacy arrangements, because these are not available in Australia
    ii most IVF clinics do not provide services to women over fifty
    iii private surrogacy arrangements can be made, but are not legally enforceable.

112. You need to: explain the questions and issues raised by surrogacy and birth technologies; describe the legal and non-legal responses to surrogacy and birth technologies; discuss the factors which may enhance, and those which may limit, the effectiveness of legal and non-legal responses to issues involving surrogacy and birth technologies; and come to a conclusion about the effectiveness of legal and non-legal responses to issues involving surrogacy and birth technologies, given that such issues are morally and ethically sensitive.

113. *Child abuse* means: assault of a child, including sexual assault; ill-treatment of a child; and exposing a child to behaviour that psychologically harms him or her.

114. The number of children in out of home care in Australia rose by almost 115% from June 1998 to June 2008. In NSW the figure more than doubled in the same period. In 2008, 8.4 children in every 1000 children in NSW were in out of home care.

115. Keep Them Safe is a five-year action plan launched by the NSW government to improve child care and protection in NSW and to implement the recommendations of the Wood Inquiry.

116. Children may be deemed 'in need of care' if they have been removed from their home because of neglect or abuse, if they have run away from home, or if they have no home or no-one to take care of them.

117. Such children can be placed in the care of relatives, foster parents or an institution.

118. Family and Community Services can:
    i do nothing
    ii undertake further investigations
    iii visit the child and family immediately if it seems that the child may be at immediate risk of harm
    iv notify the police if investigations reveal there may be criminal activity so a Joint Investigation and Review Team can investigate the allegations
    v arrange for support services to be provided to the family
    vi make an arrangement with the family for the child to be placed in a temporary care arrangement
    vii develop a care plan with the family to meet the needs of the child
    viii develop a parental responsibility contract with the primary caregivers of the child
    ix remove the child or young person from the family
    x make a care application to the Children's Court.

119. A *temporary care arrangement* is an arrangement made with Community Services for a child to be placed in the care of someone besides his or her family for a period of up to three months. A *restoration plan* is a plan setting out the circumstances under which the child will be returned to his or her parents. A *care plan* sets out the steps that will be taken by the family to resolve Community Services' concerns about the child. A *parental*

responsibility contract is a contract entered into by the child's carers which contains provisions aimed at improving the carers' parenting skills and making them more responsible for the child's wellbeing.

120. They are to be conducted with as little formality as possible; conducted in an non-adversarial manner; the Court must be satisfied on the 'balance of probabilities'; the child in question, any person with parental responsibility, Community Services and the Minister for Community Services have a right to appear before the Court; the child must be represented by a legal representative.

121. i an assessment order
ii an order accepting undertakings from the parent about how he or she will care for the child
iii an order for supervision
iv an order for the provision of support services
v an order allocating parental responsibility

122. i apprehended violence orders
ii victims compensation
iii Family Court hearings and orders which take child abuse into consideration when making decisions about children
iv legal aid
v alternative dispute resolution

123. These include:
i Family Referral Services which connect vulnerable young people and their families with locally available services which can help them
ii Child Wellbeing Units which are part of government departments that come across vulnerable children and coordinate with other government authorities to ensure the child is not at risk of 'significant harm'
iii NGOs which provide help to families and young people
iv AbSec which coordinates assistance for Aboriginal and Torres Strait Islander children and families

124. You need to: explain the extent of the problem of the care and protection of children in NSW; explain the reasons for the Wood Inquiry, and its findings; describe the legal and non-legal responses to the care and protection of children; discuss the factors which may enhance, and those which may limit, the effectiveness of legal and non-legal responses to the care and protection of children; and come to a conclusion about the effectiveness of the legal and non-legal responses to the care and protection of children.

125. The law encourages mediation to resolve family conflict and, in many cases, makes mediation compulsory before a court decision will be imposed.

126. The law provides for the breakdown of marriage by allowing married couples whose relationship has irretrievably broken down to divorce.

127. Family Relationship Centres were established by the federal government in 2006 to assist families to resolve disputes and reach agreement over a large range of matters.

128. Some same-sex couples would like to comply with marriage laws, but are excluded from them.

129. Compliance is less widespread for:
i laws regarding parental responsibility orders
ii payment of child maintenance

iii some laws regarding children, such as private surrogacy arrangements and overseas adoption
iv laws regarding domestic violence.

130. Marriage has become less popular and the drop in the marriage rate has corresponded to a rise in the number of *de facto* couples. These changes reflect the increased acceptance of sexual relations outside of marriage and the lessening stigma attached to unmarried couples and ex-nuptial children.

131. Under the *Family Law Amendment (De Facto Financial Matters and other Measures) Act 2008* (Cth), *de facto* spouses are treated in the same way as married spouses when they separate, which reflects the fact that these relationships are no longer seen as morally reprehensible.

132. Divorce laws reflect changing community values as shown by the introduction of the 'no fault' concept in 1975 and, subsequently, through the increased recognition of the impact of family violence, which is now taken into account when making decisions about parental responsibility and property settlement.

133. As society has increasingly recognised the right of the child to know both parents and the responsibility of both parents to care for a child, the law has changed so that both parents, no matter what their marital status, now both have equal responsibility for their child. This idea applies to all children, so ex-nuptial children are no longer discriminated against as they once were.

134. i Sperm donors have no legal status; the social father is the legal father.
ii The birth mother is the legal mother.
iii The non-birth mother in a lesbian relationship can be named as the co-mother.
iv Gender selection for non-medical reasons is banned.
v Strictly controlled therapeutic human embryo cloning is permitted.
vi There is a mandatory gamete donor register in NSW.
vii All women have access to birth technology, but those who are 'socially infertile' rather than 'medically infertile' must pay considerably more for the technology because they do not receive Medicare payments for the treatment.
viii Commercial surrogacy is banned.

135. *Child maintenance*: These laws were radically changed by the introduction of the Child Support Scheme in 1988, and the scheme was substantially reformed in 1998 and 2008.

Domestic violence: The *Crimes (Domestic and Personal Violence) Act 2007* (NSW) strengthened AVOs and introduced other reforms.

Responsibility for children: Reforms to the *Family Law Act 1975* in 1988, 1995 and 2006 have made all children subject to these laws, introduced family violence as a factor in determining the best interests of the child, and emphasised parental responsibility.

Adoption: The *Adoption Act 2000* (NSW) reformed the previous law in several ways, including making open adoption a common practice and ensuring that adoption is a service, first and foremost, to the child concerned.

De facto relationships: The *Family Law Amendment (De Facto Financial Matters and other Measures) Act 2008* (Cth) means that *de facto* couples, whether heterosexual or homosexual, are now covered by the same laws as married couples in matters to do with property and children after separation.

Birth technology: There have been many recent reforms in this area, including allowing lesbian co-mothers (2008), banning gender selection for non-medical reasons (2005), allowing therapeutic human embryo cloning (2006), establishing a mandatory gamete donor register and laws allowing restricted access to information on the register (2007), and banning commercial surrogacy (2007).

136. Any three of the following: recognition of same-sex marriages; reform of the operation of equal shared parenting laws and the consideration of family violence; legislating for altruistic surrogacy so it can be controlled; and allowing Medicare for 'socially infertile' women.

137. i protection of the rights of the child
   ii adoption
   iii domestic violence
   iv the roles of courts and alternative dispute resolution mechanisms in resolving disputes arising from the separation of couples
   v effectiveness of the law in achieving justice for parties involved in relationship breakdown
   vi recognition of same-sex relationships
   vii the changing nature of parental responsibility
   viii surrogacy and birth technologies
   ix the care and protection of children.

 Sample HSC questions (page 272)

Extended-response questions

Note: **EM** means Examiner Maximiser

Question 1

What you are asked to do

This question asks you to:

- describe the extent to which alternative family arrangements are recognised by the law
- evaluate how well this recognition reflects community values.

  EM In order to achieve top marks for your answer to this question, in your answer you should:

- identify the alternative relationships: Aboriginal and Torres Strait Islander peoples' customary law marriages; single-parent families; blended families; same-sex relationships; polygamous marriages; *de facto* relationships; and other family arrangements
- describe how the law recognises each form of alternative relationship in comparison to its recognition of marriage
- describe community values towards each type of family arrangement and assess whether the law reflects these values.

Your answer could follow the plan below.

Plan

Paragraph 1:

- State the traditional idea of family.
- State the ABS definition of *family*.
- List types of alternative family arrangements in Australia. Explain that many of these are recognised by the law to some degree. Explain that this recognition reflects community

values to a large extent, as the community has become more accepting of family relationships which are different from the traditional idea of family. **[4.1.1, 4.1.3 and 4.4.3]**

Paragraph 2:

- Define *Aboriginal and Torres Strait Islander peoples' customary law marriages*.
- Describe the recognition by the law of Aboriginal and Torres Strait Islander peoples' customary law marriages. Discuss the extent to which this recognition reflects community values. **[4.1.3]**

Paragraph 3:

- Define *de facto relationships*.
- State the past recognition of *de facto* relationships by the law.
- State the recognition by the law of *de facto* relationships today.
- Comment on the extent to which this recognition reflects community values. **[4.1.3, 4.1.4, 4.2.2 and 4.4.3]**

Paragraph 4:

- State the past recognition by the law of same-sex relationships.
- State the recognition by the law of same-sex relationships today.
- Comment on the extent to which this recognition reflects community values. **[4.1.1, 4.1.3 and 4.3.1]**

Paragraph 5:

- Define *polygamous marriages*.
- State the recognition by the law of polygamous marriages.
- Comment on the extent to which this recognition reflects community values. **[4.1.2, 4.2.1, 4.2.3, 4.2.4 and 4.4.3]**

Paragraph 6:

- Define/describe *single parent families, blended families*, and other family arrangements.
- State the recognition by the law of single parent families, blended families, and other family arrangements.
- Comment on the extent to which this recognition reflects community values. **[4.1.1, 4.1.3, 4.1.4, 4.2.2 and 4.3.2]**

Conclusion:

- State that the law recognises most types of families in Australia.
- List the types of families it recognises.
- State that all children have the same protection under the law, no matter what the marital status of their parents.
- List areas in which some types of families are not recognised to the same extent as others.
- State that this recognition reflects community values to a large extent, because the community has become more accepting of family relationships which are different from the traditional idea of family.

Question 2

What you are asked to do

This question asks you to:

- describe legal and non-legal responses to domestic violence
- evaluate the effectiveness of each response.

EM In order to achieve top marks for your answer to this question, in your answer you should:

- describe legal responses to domestic violence
- describe non-legal responses to domestic violence
- state the advantages and disadvantages of each response
- come to a conclusion about how effective each response is.

Your answer could follow the plan below.

Plan

Paragraph 1:

- Define *domestic violence*.
- Describe the extent of domestic violence.
- List legal responses to domestic violence.
- List non-legal responses to domestic violence.
- Make a statement about the effectiveness of these responses given that domestic violence is the most common form of assault in Australia. **[4.2.4]**

Paragraph 2:

- Describe the legal response of apprehended violence orders, particularly ADVOs.
- Cite relevant legislation.
- State advantages and disadvantages of ADVOs.
- Make a statement about the effectiveness of ADVOs, given the advantages and disadvantages. **[4.2.4]**

Paragraph 3:

- Describe the legal response of criminal charges in regard to domestic violence.
- Cite relevant legislation.
- State advantages and disadvantages of criminal charges.
- Make a statement about the effectiveness of criminal charges in regard to domestic violence, given the advantages and disadvantages. **[4.2.4]**

Paragraph 4:

- Describe the legal response of family court orders.
- Cite relevant legislation.
- State advantages and disadvantages of family court orders.
- Make a statement about the effectiveness of family court orders, given the advantages and disadvantages. **[4.2.4]**

Paragraph 5:

- Describe the problem of spousal murder.
- Explain the defence of battered woman syndrome.
- Describe the recent legal reform resulting in the establishment of the Death Review Team. Comment on the possible effectiveness of this reform. **[4.2.4]**

Paragraph 6:

- List and describe the non-legal responses to domestic violence, including support and lobby groups.
- Comment on the effectiveness of these responses. **[4.2.4]**

Conclusion:

- List legal and non-legal responses to domestic violence.
- Make a comment about the most effective response to the problem.

- Come to a conclusion about the effectiveness of the responses, given that domestic violence is the most common form of assault in Australia. **[4.2.4]**

Chapter 5: Workplace

KCq *Key Concept questions* (pages 365–9)

1. Workplace law is law about the relationships between employees and employers.

2. An *employer* is a person or organisation who pays wages or a salary to others for performing certain work. *Employees* are the people who perform the work and are paid a wage or a salary to do so.

3. low minimum wages, long working hours, and unsafe and unhealthy working conditions

4. The philosophy of laissez faire allowed poor working conditions to exist because the government did nothing to prevent them from occurring. Laissez faire relies on the parties to an agreement having equal bargaining power but, in the area of employment during the Industrial Revolution, this was not the case—employers had far greater bargaining power than employees.

5. State intervention first took the form of preventing trade unionism, through a series of *Combination Acts* which made trade unions illegal.

6. Any four of the following: minimum wages; equal pay for equal work; a forty-hour week; occupational health and safety laws; the right to form trade unions.

7. *Globalisation* is the growing economic and social interdependence and interconnectedness of countries worldwide. *Restructuring* means rearranging the duties in the workplace, usually in an attempt to make the workplace more efficient. Globalisation has put Australian businesses under pressure to increase productivity which has led to restructuring in many industries.

8. The number of people working longer hours (over 50 hours a week) rose from just over 13% in 1979 to just over 18% in 1994, and declined to 16% in 2006. The proportion of people working part-time (under 35 hours a week) has risen, from 25% in 1979 to 36% in 2006. The number of casual workers has doubled since 1982 (from 13% to 27%). The number of contract workers has also risen significantly.

9. You need to: describe early forms of employment, such as the gang system and the master–servant relationship; describe the effect of the Industrial Revolution and the philosophy of laissez faire on workplaces and working conditions; describe the growth of trade unions and state intervention in workplace law because of the hardships caused by the philosophy of laissez faire; and describe the impact of technological change in the workplace and changing working patterns in contemporary Australia.

10. A *contract of service* is a legally binding agreement made between an employer and an employee. Under a *contract for services* a person is hired to do a particular task or perform a particular service for a certain sum of money. There is no employee–employer relationship.

11. the contract itself, including express and implied terms; legislation; awards; and agreements

12. a contract for services

13. the control test and the multi-factor test

14. Materials would be supplied by the worker; a quote would be given for the job; a beginning and completion date for the job would be given; the worker would have the right to hire others to assist him or her; and the worker would pay his or her own income tax.

15. People under a *contract of service* generally receive an award wage, annual leave, superannuation, workers compensation, sick pay and other leave.

16. There has been a growing trend for people who would normally be employees to be hired under a contract for services. The law has 'deemed' some of these people employees so that they can have access to workers compensation and the other entitlements of being an employee.

17. Under the *Fair Work Act 2009* (Cth), an employer can be fined up to $33 000 if he or she misrepresents an employment relationship as an independent contracting arrangement, dismisses or threatens to dismiss an employee so as to engage him or her as an independent contractor, or makes a knowingly false statement to persuade an employee to become an independent contractor.

18. An *express term* of a contract of employment is one that is actually spoken or written into the contract by the employee and employer, while an *implied term* is a promise that is binding on the parties to the contract put in the contract by the law. An implied term is binding even though the parties to the contract may have never discussed it.

19. The rights and duties of employees and employers are found in the common law, legislation, enterprise agreements, awards, and express terms of contract found in a contract of employment or an AWA or ITEA.

20. The rights of employees and duties of employers are that the employee has the right to: be paid reasonable wages; be provided with work in certain circumstances; be repaid by their employer for expenses incurred during their employment; and work in a safe environment.

21. The rights of employers and duties of employees are that the employer has the right to insist that the employee: uses due skill and care; obeys lawful instructions; acts in good faith; and does not commit misconduct.

22. Modern awards are industry or occupation-based minimum employment standards which apply in addition to the National Employment Standards. They apply in the federal jurisdiction.

23. Modern awards must not contain conditions less than the NES, and they must contain a flexibility term and a dispute settling procedure.

24. Most NSW awards no longer operate because all private sector employees in NSW now come under the national system. Awards for public sector workers and some others still do operate.

25. An *enterprise agreement* is an agreement made collectively by all employees in a particular workplace (or workplaces) with their employer, which overrides existing awards or agreements.

26. An agreement overrides an existing award.

27. single-enterprise agreements; multi-enterprise agreements; and greenfields agreements

28. The Fair Work Commission

29. The conditions which must be met by a federal award are: the agreement must have been made with the genuine agreement of those involved; it must pass the 'better off overall' test (BOOT); it must not include any unlawful terms or designated outworker terms; the group of employees covered by the agreement must have been fairly chosen; the agreement must specify a date as its nominal expiry date not more than four years after the date of approval; the agreement must provide a dispute settlement procedure; and must include a flexibility clause and a consultation clause.

30. BOOT is the 'better off overall' test. To pass this test each of the employees to be covered by an agreement must be better off overall than they would be under the relevant modern award.

31. AWAs were individual contracts that must be registered with the government. Individual contracts have not normally been part of industrial relations in Australia. For the first time, individual contracts (in the form of AWAs) prevailed over existing awards or agreements.

32. AWAs and ITEAs are being phased out and replaced by modern awards and enterprise agreements.

33. Many employees were worse off under AWAs than they were under their previous award or agreement. AWAs were also criticised by the International Labour Organization who said that the provision of AWAs put Australia in breach of ILO Conventions No. 87 and No. 98, relating to the right to organise and collective bargaining, because AWAs override collective agreements.

34. NSW enterprise bargaining agreements may apply to employees of local councils, the NSW public sector and some state owned corporations, as well as to some deemed employees, such as contract truck and courier drivers and taxi drivers

35. Both the employer and 65% of the workforce or the relevant union must agree to be covered by an enterprise agreement for it to be adopted, it must meet the 'no net detriment' test, and it must comply with anti-discrimination legislation.

36. The NSW Industrial Relations Commission (IRC)

37. Both federal and state governments have passed many pieces of legislation in the area of employment law, covering many aspects of the relationships between employees and employers, which override any contradictory provisions which may be in the contract of service. This legislation provides minimum conditions of employment and other rights and obligations of employers and employees.

38. The National Employment Standards

39. the *Fair Work Act 2009* (Cth)

40. The NES apply to every employee in the national workplace system.

41. The ten NES entitlements are: maximum weekly hours of work of thirty-eight hours per week; provision for requests for flexible working arrangements for parents and carers; parental leave and related entitlements; four weeks annual leave; ten days paid personal or carer's

leave, and compassionate leave; up to ten days unpaid community service leave; long service leave; a paid day off on public holidays; provision for notice of termination and redundancy pay; and a requirement for employers to provide a Fair Work Information Statement.

42. *General protections* are employee rights protected under the *Fair Work Act 2009* (Cth).

43. If general protections are breached, legal action can be commenced and penalties of up to $6600 for an individual or $33 000 for a corporation can be applied.

44. industrial awards; agreements; termination of employment; dispute settling mechanisms; Australian Workplace Agreements (AWAs) and Individual Transitional Employment Agreements (ITEAs); state and federal tribunals; safety in the workplace; workers compensation; discrimination; leave

45. First, you should explain that workplace regulations come from: express and implied terms of the contract of service; industrial awards; workplace agreements, including AWAs and ITEAs until such time as these cease operation; and statute law, with particular reference to the NES. Second, you should explain the relationship between these sources of workplace regulations.

46. In order to describe the rights and responsibilities of employers and employees, you should describe: the rights of employees in the workplace; the rights of employers in the workplace; the responsibilities of employees in the workplace; and the responsibilities of employers in the workplace. You should explain and give examples of rights or responsibilities for **each** of the above as they arise from: terms implied into the contract of service by the common law; express terms in the contract of service; rights and responsibilities imposed by legislation, and rights and responsibilities contained in awards and in agreements.

47. *Industrial relations* refers to the relationships between employers and employees.

48. In regard to industrial relations, the 'state and federal framework' is the legislation and organisations, at both state and federal levels, which regulate the relationships between employers and employees.

49. Under the corporations power used to enact Work Choices in 2006, the federal government was able make laws about industrial relations for corporations, whether they operated within or between states. This gave the federal government the power to legislate for up to 85% of all employees in Australia.

50. Not only does the *Fair Work Act* cover all corporations, but all state governments, except Western Australia, also handed over the bulk of their industrial relations powers to the federal government operative from 1 January 2010. So the federal government now has jurisdiction over an even greater number of workplaces.

51. Fair Work Australia (FWA) and the Office of the Fair Work Ombudsman, which operate under the *Fair Work Act 2009* (Cth)

52. The NSW Industrial Relations Commission (IRC) and the NSW Industrial Registry which operate under the *Industrial Relations Act 1996* (NSW)

53. In order to eaxamine the legal framework for workplace law, you should: describe the division of power between state and federal governments in the area of industrial relations, explaining how there has been a fundamental shift of power from state to federal government; cite the relevant state and federal legislation; and list the relevant state and federal organisations.

54. Negotiations between employers and employees can take place between an individual employer and employee or between an employer and a group of employees.

55. The bargaining process is initiated; the employer notifies employees that they have the right to be represented in the bargaining process; employers and employees obtain bargaining representatives if they wish; bargaining in good faith occurs; Fair Work Australia may be applied to for assistance if required; when agreement between bargaining representatives is reached, terms of the draft agreement are explained to employees; voting on the agreement takes place; the agreement is accepted by a majority of employees; the agreement is sent to Fair Work Australia for approval.

56. To *bargain in good faith* means that employees and employers who are negotiating an enterprise agreement must: attend and participate in meetings at reasonable times; disclose relevant information in a timely manner; respond to proposals made by the other side of the bargaining process in a timely manner; give genuine consideration to the proposals of other bargaining representatives, and give reasons for the responses to those proposals; refrain from capricious or unfair conduct that undermines freedom of association or collective bargaining; and recognise and bargain with other bargaining representatives for the agreement.

57. strikes, demarcation disputes, work-to-rule and secondary boycotts

58. stand-downs and lock-outs

59. For industrial action to be protected it must be taken after an existing agreement has reached its expiry date; the action must be in support of a new enterprise agreement; in the case of employees, Fair Work Australia must have granted an order for a protected action ballot to be held and the employees must have voted to take the action; the required notice must have been given to the other party; and the parties involved must be genuinely trying to reach agreement.

60. FWA can suspend protected industrial action: when the action is causing significant economic harm; when the action threatens to endanger the life, personal safety, health or welfare of the population or of part of it, or to cause significant damage to the economy or an important part of it; and to allow a cooling-off period when the action threatens to cause significant harm to a third party. In the case of *CFMEU v Woodside Burrup Pty Ltd* (2010) FWAFB 6021, Fair Work Australia did not suspend industrial action, saying that even though it was causing harm to third parties, for the harm to be significant enough to warrant a suspension order, the harm must be out of the ordinary, and that effective industrial action will usually cause harm to at least the employer, and perhaps to third parties.

61. Fair Work Australia can make an order preventing the industrial action. If the order is ignored, the parties responsible can be fined and anyone who has suffered a loss can sue for damages.

62. An *industrial dispute* is any dispute about any matter which pertains to the relationship between employers and employees.

63. workplace resolution, mediation, conciliation and arbitration

64. Both the *Fair Work Act 2009* (NSW) and the *Industrial Relations Act 1996* (NSW) make it compulsory for all awards and enterprise agreements to contain dispute settling procedures which must be adhered to before an outside party will intervene in the dispute. This encourages resolution of disputes in individual workplaces.

65. First, the employees with the dispute meet with their immediate supervisor. If the matter is not resolved, then the employees meet with more senior management. If the matter is still not resolved, the employer may refer it to more senior management or a more senior national officer within the employer organisation. Finally, if the matter is still unresolved, either party to the dispute may refer to the relevant industrial relations tribunal for conciliation and/or arbitration. Throughout this process, employers may be represented by their employer association. The employees may be represented by their union.

66. This case made it clear that clauses about dispute settling procedures need not include compulsory arbitration of disputes, unless both parties agree.

67. Mediation may become unofficially part of workplace dispute settling procedures with either a union representative or an employer organisation representative acting as a mediator.

68. Conciliation occurs when the employer and employees meet with an Industrial Relations Commissioner privately and try to reach agreement. If no agreement is reached, the Industrial Relations Commissioner may arbitrate.

69. When arbitration occurs, the Industrial Relations Commissioner makes a decision on the disputed matters which then governs the terms of employment.

70. Today, compulsory conferences and arbitration no longer exist at the federal level, though they do under NSW law.

71. The large downward trend in the number of industrial disputes in Australia since the 1980s may mean that fewer disputes occur and that more disputes are quickly and informally resolved at workplace level.

72. In order to evaluate the effectiveness of dispute resolution processes, you need to: describe the processes involved, i.e. workplace resolution and conciliation and arbitration; describe the reduction in the number of industrial disputes in Australia in recent years, and what these figures may mean; compare the advantages and disadvantages of various dispute settling processes; and decide whether the current dispute settling processes in Australian workplaces are effective or ineffective, given the alternative dispute settling mechanisms.

73. Three types of legal institutions are tribunals, courts and government organisations. Four non-legal agencies are trade unions, employer associations, other non-government organisations and the media.

74. Fair Work Australia and the NSW Industrial Relations Commission (IRC)

75. i determining the safety net of minimum wages and employment conditions

ii ensuring enterprise bargaining occurs according to the law and approving enterprise agreements

iii overseeing awards

iv ensuring any industrial action occurs according to the law

v assisting in dispute resolution

vi making determinations about unfair dismissals

76. The NSW Industrial Relations Commission: makes awards relating to pay and disputes; settles disputes; conciliates in the area of enterprise bargaining and approves agreements; and determines applications regarding unfair dismissal.

77. the Federal Magistrates Court, the Federal Court and the Industrial Court of New South Wales

78. The Fair Work Ombudsman listens to and investigates complaints or suspected contraventions of workplace laws, awards and agreements, and litigates to enforce workplace laws.

79. NSW Industrial Relations: works with the Commonwealth's Fair Work Ombudsman to ensure NSW private sector businesses comply with their responsibilities under the national workplace relations system; administers NSW laws regulating shop trading hours, public holidays and long service leave; and also has the role of prosecuting breaches of awards and agreements.

80. Trade unions assist individual members with unfair dismissal claims, occupational health and safety matters, individual disputes with employers, and dispute settling procedures.

81. Trade unions assist members collectively by: negotiating with employers for better wages and conditions in awards and agreements; organising industrial action to support the claims of members; appearing before Industrial Relations tribunals for conciliation or arbitration; and lobbying governments to change laws and policies to better protect workers.

82. The ACTU is an organisation of trade unions. It provides support for unions and negotiates on behalf of unions in national areas, such as in minimum wage reviews.

83. In 1953, 63% of the Australian labour force were members of trade unions. This had dropped to just 20% by August 2009.

84. i Unions are seen by some as less relevant than in the past.

ii Changes to wage fixing mean that individual unions have had less involvement.

iii The NES have been established to protect all workers' basic rights.

iv There has been a rise in enterprise agreements, which can be made without a union.

v The number of casual and part-time workers has increased and these are far less likely to belong to unions.

vi The rise of independent contracting, particularly in the building and meat industries, means that unions can no longer represent traditional groups.

vii The principle of freedom of association has replaced closed shop and union preference arrangements.

viii There are now restrictions on the right to strike.

85. *An industry association* is an organisation that represents the interests of the businesses that operate in a particular industry and are members of the association. Examples include the Minerals Council of Australia (MCA) and the Australian Meat Industry Council (AMIC).

86. Employer associations: advocate on behalf of their members for policies that promote the interests of their members; promote the industry to the community; lobby governments to make legislative changes which are in the interests of employers; represent the views of various industries and employer groups to governments and the community; represent member businesses in international forums, such as the International Labour Organization; and conduct relevant research and policy development

87. trade unions and employer associations

88. The media can put pressure on governments and political parties to change their policies and can influence the outcomes of elections. For example, in the 2007 federal election campaign, media played an important role in publicising the messages of the 'Your Rights at Work' campaign, which was influential in ousting the Howard coalition government.

89. To assess the role of the legal system in regulating the workplace, you need to: describe the role in regulating the workplace played by legal and government institutions and agencies, including tribunals, courts and government organisations; describe the role in workplace regulation of non-legal organisations, including trade unions, employer associations, other NGOs and the media; and comment on the importance of the legal and non-legal institutions involved in workplace regulation.

90. Remuneration in Australia is determined through national minimum wage determinations, awards and agreements.

91. i 'Needs of workers' principle: wages should be sufficient to meet the needs of workers (that is, how much a worker and his family need to support themselves).
    ii 'Capacity to pay' principle: wage levels should take into account the capacity of employers to pay the wages.
    iii 'Cost of living' principle: rises in the cost of living should be taken into account in the determination of wage levels.
    iv 'Productivity' principle: wage rises are to be given to workers who have been able to show that they have become more efficient in their work.

92. The Minimum Wage Panel must consider:
    i productivity, business competitiveness and viability, inflation and employment growth
    ii increased workforce participation
    iii relative living standards and the needs of the low paid
    iv the principle of equal remuneration for work of equal or comparable value
    v provision of a comprehensive range of fair minimum wages to junior employees, employees to whom training arrangements apply and employees with a disability.

93. The Annual Wage Review 2009–10: set a new minimum wage of $15.00 per hour or $569.90 per week; increased the pay under all modern awards and some enterprise agreements by $26 a week; and determined that casual employees not under an award or agreement should receive an extra 21% of their wage as casual loading.

94. The level of an individual's wage or salary is determined by: the national minimum wage; the relevant award; the relevant agreement; the employee's age; the employee's experience; the employee's level of education; the employee's level of responsibility; and the nature of the employment.

95. A *penalty rate* is a higher rate of pay for work done outside usual working hours, such as late at night or on weekends or public holidays. *Casual loading* is an amount paid on top of the normal wage rate to casual employees to compensate them for not getting certain entitlements that permanent employees receive. *Part-time loading* is an amount paid on top of the normal wage rate to part-time employees to compensate them for not getting certain entitlements that full-time employees receive. *Overtime* is time worked in excess of ordinary hours of work, often paid at a higher rate of pay. *Allowances* are extra payments to employees because of special circumstances attached to the job.

96. Under the *Superannuation Guarantee (Administration) Act 1992* (Cth), employers are obliged to pay a minimum level of superannuation for their employees, currently set at 9% of an employee's earnings. If employers fail to do this they must pay a tax called the Superannuation Guarantee Charge.

97. To outline how remuneration is determined, you need to: define remuneration; briefly describe the different types of remuneration; explain that remuneration is determined by awards, agreements and by national minimum wage decisions; outline how awards and agreements are determined and how remuneration is determined within these industrial instruments; outline how national minimum wage decisions are made, and explain to whom they apply; and list other decisions made by the Minimum Wage Panel.

98. In order to evaluate the effectiveness of legal and non-legal responses in protecting and recognising workplace rights, you need to: identify the way workplace rights are protected; explain whether each method is non-legal or legal; discuss those factors which enhance the effectiveness of each method of protection; discuss the factors which limit the effectiveness of each method of protection; and decide how effective each legal or non-legal responses is in protecting and recognising workplace rights given the two sets of factors.

99. Legal responses for protecting and recognising workplace rights are: common law contracts of service; contracts for services; awards; agreements; statutory conditions; negotiation processes (these can be legal or non-legal); tribunals; courts; and government agencies.

100. Non-legal responses for protecting and recognising workplace rights are: negotiation processes (these can be legal or non-legal); trade unions; employer associations; NGOS; and the media.

101. *Discrimination* is the treatment of one person differently from another in the same situation because of that person's membership of a particular group in society (such as Aboriginal people, women, migrants or people with physical disabilities).

102. NSW legislation: *Anti-Discrimination Act 1977* (NSW) and the *Industrial Relations Act 1996* (NSW). Federal legislation:

Racial Discrimination Act 1975 (Cth), *Sex Discrimination Act 1984* (Cth), *Australian Human Rights Commission Act 1986* (Cth), formerly called the *Human Rights and Equal Opportunity Commission Act 1986* (Cth), *Disability Discrimination Act 1992* (Cth), *Equal Opportunity for Women in the Workplace Act 1999* (Cth), *Age Discrimination Act 2004* (Cth), and the *Fair Work Act 2009* (Cth).

103. *Adverse action* means: dismissing an employee, damaging an employee's ability to do his or her job, changing an employee's job to his or her disadvantage, treating one employee differently from other employees, refusing to employ a potential employee, and not offering a potential employee all the terms and conditions normally in a job.

104. Adverse action is illegal under the *Fair Work Act 2009* (Cth) if it is taken because of discrimination on the grounds of race, gender, disability, age, family responsibility, marital status, sexuality, transgender status, trade union involvement, or religious or political opinion.

105. The person suffering workplace discrimination should approach his or her superior and attempt to resolve the matter in the workplace.

106. Organisations able to conciliate in cases of discrimination are the NSW Anti-Discrimination Board, the Australian Human Rights Commission, and the Federal Fair Work Ombudsman in certain circumstances.

107. The NSW Administrative Decisions Tribunal, the Federal Court and the Federal Magistrates Court are able to make a determination about a discrimination grievance.

108. The Wongtas case shows that the Fair Work Ombudsman will pursue litigation on behalf of people who have been discriminated against in the workplace. The publicity surrounding the case in the media, and the fact that the Fair Work Ombudsman launched a publicity campaign at the same time as the case was brought, means that the issue of pregnancy discrimination and the powers of the Fair Work Ombudsman are now widely known.

109. The Australian Human Rights Commission can conduct inquiries and make recommendations to the federal government about what action it should take in matters of discrimination and can make determinations to resolve discrimination matters in its jurisdiction. However, it does not have the power to make its determinations legally binding.

110. Employers who discriminate can be made to pay damages of up to $40 000 under NSW state law, and federal courts can impose penalties of up to $33 000 per breach for companies and up to $6600 per breach for individuals.

111. The most far-reaching affirmative action program, governed by the *Workplace Gender Equality Act 2012* (Cth), requires private sector employers, community organisations, non-government schools, trade unions and group training companies employing over 100 people, as well as higher-education authorities, to implement affirmative action programs over a period of time.

112. Legal responses to the issue of discrimination are: legislation which prohibits discrimination in the workplace; state and federal government organisations, tribunals and courts; litigation in the NSW Civil and Administrative Tribunal (NCAT) or the Federal Court, which can be brought by the NSW Anti-Discrimination Board or the Federal Fair Work Ombudsman; and the imposition of penalties.

Non-legal responses include: workplace settlement of discrimination claims; approaching government bodies for information and advice; and conciliation by government organisations, such as the NSW Anti-Discrimination Board or the federal Fair Work Ombudsman.

113. To identify and investigate workplace discrimination, you need to: explain discrimination, both direct and indirect; list the grounds under which discrimination is illegal in the workplace; list the legislation under which discrimination is illegal in the workplace; describe the action that can be taken by employees to deal with discrimination, including the roles of government organisations, tribunals and courts; list legal and non-legal responses; discuss the factors which help ensure, and those which limit, the effectiveness of legal and non-legal responses to the contemporary issue of workplace discrimination; and come to a conclusion about the effectiveness legal and non-legal responses to the contemporary issue of workplace discrimination.

114. *Safety* in the workplace means that employees can perform their work in a safe manner in a workplace that is not injurious to their health.

115. Under common law, employers must not expose employees to unreasonable hazards.

116. Employers have the common law duties to: employ competent staff and provide proper supervision; provide safe plant and equipment; provide safe means of access to work; and to ensure a safe system of conducting work.

117. The common law duty to work with due skill and care means that employees are obliged to follow safety directions and to work carefully and skilfully, avoiding dangerous practices.

118. The *Work Health and Safety Act 2011* (NSW)

119. Employers must ensure the health, safety and welfare of their employees by: providing and maintaining a safe workplace, facilities, plant and work systems; ensuring the safe use, handling, storage and transport of equipment or substances; and providing proper information, instruction, training and supervision. Employees are obliged to take reasonable care for health and safety at work, and must cooperate with initiatives designed to ensure safety at work.

120. Penalties include fines of up to $825 000, seizure of offending articles, and orders to shut down machines and places of work that infringe safety regulations.

121. Workplace safety is hampered by: lack of sufficient funding for adequate government surveillance; increased use of part-time workers, casual workers and independent contractors; lack of adequate enforcement procedures when safety standards are breached; lack of prosecutions; insufficient penalties imposed by the courts; 'management by stress' practices; and the weakening role of trade unions.

122. The aim of workers compensation is to provide for people who are injured or whose health is adversely affected because of work.

123. the *Workers Compensation Act 1987* (NSW) and the *Workplace Injury Management and Workers Compensation Act 1998* (NSW)

124. Workers compensation is payable for any injury or disease that arises out of the course of employment. The injury does not need to be caused by the employer's negligence or breach of statutory duty. It is payable to all employees, certain 'deemed' employees and to the families of workers who die because of a work injury.

125. A *significant injury* is one which prevents a worker undertaking some or all of his or her normal duties for more than seven days.

126. If an employee suffers a significant injury, the employer must contact the insurer within forty-eight hours. The injured worker must obtain a medical certificate and give it to his or her employer. The insurer is then obliged to approach the employer, the worker and the treating doctor within three days to initiate an injury management plan.

127. SafeWork NSW administers workers compensation in NSW, and the Workers Compensation Commission settles disputes in this area.

128. An injury management plan is a plan made to ensure the swift and safe return to work of an injured worker and is made in consultation with the employer, the worker's nominated treating doctor and the injured worker when there has been a significant injury. The employer must provide suitable employment, where practicable, for workers who are able to return to work. The doctor treating the injured worker provides information on the worker's fitness for work and recommends suitable duties for the injured worker. The worker must make all reasonable efforts to return to work and to cooperate with the injury management plan.

129. A uniform national system of workplace safety laws is likely to be introduced in 2012, after all states, except Western Australia, agreed to work towards this in December 2009.

130. **Legal responses to the issue of safety in the workplace are:** common law duties of employers and employees; workplace safety legislation, most importantly the *Work Health and Safety Act 2011* (NSW) and its regulations; provision of inspectors and imposition of penalties for breaches of law; workers compensation, specifically, the SafeWork NSW scheme; provision of dispute settling procedures through the Workers Compensation Commission; and injury management plans. **Non-legal responses include:** workplace occupational health and safety committees; and union assistance and right of entry into workplaces when there are suspected breaches of safety legislation. Injury management plans can also be seen as a non-legal response because, even though they must be formulated under legislation, the details are determined by the parties involved, not the legal system.

131. In order to identify the issue of workplace safety and evaluate the effectiveness of responses to it, you need to: explain the meaning of safety in the workplace; describe common and statute laws which place obligations on employers and employees to ensure workplaces are safe; describe Australia's workplace safety record in recent years compared to that of other countries; explain workers compensation laws; describe the action that can be taken by employees who are injured during the course of employment, including injury management plans and dispute settling by the Workers Compensation Commission; describe the move towards national workplace safety laws; list legal and non-legal responses to the issue of workplace safety; discuss the factors which help ensure, and those which limit, the effectiveness of legal and non-legal responses to the contemporary issue of safety in the workplace; and come to a conclusion about the effectiveness of legal and non-legal responses to the contemporary issue of safety in the workplace.

132. *Retirement* occurs when a person finishes working and does not return to work for the rest of his or her life.

133. The federal government has increased the preservation age for superannuation funds and has increased the age at which people can be eligible for the Age Pension.

134. Australia's population is ageing and the number of retirees is a continually increasing proportion of the Australian population. As a result of this, the government needs to provide adequate incomes and health care for an increasing number of people. Forcing people to retire at a later age minimises this.

135. *Resignation* is the voluntary termination of the contract of employment by an employee.

136. *Notice* is the informing of one party to a contract of employment (the employer or employee) to the other party, of the intention to terminate the employment.

137. *Dismissal* occurs when an employer tells a worker that he or she is no longer required to work for the employer.

138. An employer may summarily dismiss an employee if the employee has been extremely incompetent, has committed serious misconduct or has performed a series of cumulative acts and the employer has made it clear each time that such acts are unacceptable.

139. It is lawful to dismiss an employee: if there is a genuine redundancy; if the dismissal is not 'harsh, unjust or unreasonable'; and if the dismissal is not unlawful.

140. The circumstances that will be examined are: whether a genuine reason was given for the dismissal; whether a warning was given; whether the employee was given a chance to explain or defend his or her actions; or whether the dismissal came about because of a genuine redundancy.

141. Federal law is relevant because of the corporations power in the Constitution and because NSW, along with other states, handed over its industrial relations power to the federal government. Since 1 January 2010, the vast majority of employees are part of the national employment system and are, therefore, protected by federal unfair dismissal laws.

142. It was estimated that 99% of all private sector employers became exempt from unfair dismissal laws under Work Choices, whereas the *Fair Work Act* 2009 (Cth) means that most employees now have access to unfair dismissal laws.

143. A dismissal is rendered illegal if it was due to: unlawful discrimination; temporary absence from work because of illness or injury; absence from work because of maternity or parental leave; temporary absence from work because of the carrying out of a voluntary emergency management activity; raising a complaint against an employer; union

membership or non-membership; or acting as an employee representative.

144. Any person employed in the national workplace system is entitled to make a claim about unlawful termination of employment, but some employees are not protected by unfair dismissal laws (including those who have not completed a minimum employment period of at least six months [or twelve months if the employer is a employs fewer than fifteen employees], those not covered by a relevant award or agreement or those earning more than $113 800 a year).

145. The Fair Work Commission or the Fair Work Ombudsman

146. An employer who unlawfully dismisses an employee can be fined, issued with a caution, required to enter into an enforceable undertaking or required to pay compensation to the employee.

147. A retrenched worker is entitled to at least four weeks pay if he or she has worked for the employer for more than one and less than two years, and is entitled to up to sixteen weeks pay if he or she has worked for the employer for between nine and ten years.

148. A retrenched worker may be entitled to unpaid wages, pay for unused annual leave, pay in lieu of notice, redundancy pay and unused long service leave.

149. The following are not entitled to redundancy pay: an employee with less than twelve months of continuous service; an employee employed for a specified period of time, a specific task or for a specific season; a casual employee; an employee who works for a business employing fewer than fifteen employees.

150. For a redundancy to be legal:
   i an employer must dismiss an employee because he or she no longer needs the person's job to be done by anyone due to changes in the operational requirements of the business
   ii an employer must follow the consultation requirements in the relevant award or agreement.

151. The *Fair Work Act 2009* makes the distinction between genuine and non-genuine redundancies to prevent employers stating that terminations are not redundancies in order to avoid paying severance pays, or for other reasons that disadvantage the employees, as occurred in the Cowra Abattoir case.

152. GEERS stands for the General Employment Entitlements and Redundancy Scheme. It can pay eligible people up to three months unpaid wages, all unpaid annual leave, redundancy pay, up to five weeks unpaid payment in lieu of notice, and all unpaid long service leave.

153. **Legal responses to termination of employment include:** legislation which prohibits forcing someone to retire because of his or her age; measures which encourage people to retire at a later age; summary dismissal provisions; NES provisions for notice requirements for employees who are being dismissed; major reforms introduced by the *Fair Work Act* in 2009 which provide most workers with access to unfair dismissal laws; protection from unlawful termination of employment for all workers under the national workplace system; the legislative definition of *redundancy* and the distinction between genuine and non-genuine redundancies; NES minimums for workers who are made redundant; and GEERS. **Non-legal responses include:** provision of conciliation by the Fair Work Commission; and information and advice from government agencies.

154. To identify and investigate termination of employment, you need to: explain the four types of termination of employment and that terminations can be initiated by employees or employers; describe the legislative measures which govern resignation; describe the legislation which protects workers from unfair dismissal and unlawful termination of employment; describe the protections given by legislation to workers who are made redundant; list legal and non-legal responses to the issue of termination of employment; discuss the factors which help ensure, and those which limit, the effectiveness of legal and non-legal responses to the contemporary workplace issue of termination of employment; and come to a conclusion about the effectiveness legal and non-legal responses to the contemporary workplace issue of termination of employment.

155. *Leave* means permission for an employee to be absent from work for a legitimate reason.

156. Legislation, awards or agreements all grant leave to employees.

157. The National Employment Standards (NES) contained in the *Fair Work Act 2009* (Cth)

158. The NES provide for annual leave, personal/carer's leave, compassionate leave, community service leave, long service leave and parental leave.

159. For an employee to *cash out* leave means for him or her to agree to receive money rather than take some of the leave he or she is owed.

160. Annual leave and personal/carer's leave can be cashed out, though the latter can only be cashed out if an award or agreement allows it, not under the NES.

161. Personal leave can be taken: because the employee is sick or injured; because the employer needs to provide care or support to a member of his or her immediate household or family because of illness, injury or unexpected emergency; or because of a death in the immediate household or family.

162. Full-time employees are entitled to ten days paid personal leave per year. Part-time workers receive a *pro rata* entitlement to personal leave based on the number of hours they work. A casual employee is also entitled to two days unpaid carer's leave on any one occasion.

163. Community service leave can be taken for jury duty and for voluntary emergency management activities, such as being a volunteer with the NSW Rural Fire Service and the NSW State Emergency Service.

164. In January 2011, the NES provided that entitlements to long service leave remained as they were in awards and agreements in force on 31 December 2009, or in state legislation.

165. If an employee would not have had an entitlement under an award or agreement if they had been employed in the same circumstances on 31 December 2009, in NSW their entitlement to long service leave generally comes from the *Long Service Leave Act 1955* (NSW).

166. The NES gives unpaid parental leave entitlements to all employees if they have completed twelve months of service with their employer.

167. The paid parental leave scheme was introduced on 1 January 2011 under the *Paid Parental Leave Act 2010* (Cth).

168. i the 'work' test, which means a person must have worked for at least ten of the thirteen months prior to the birth or adoption of their child, and must have worked for at least 330 hours in that ten-month period (just over one day a week)

   ii the 'income test', which means a person must have a taxable income of less than $150 000 in the financial year prior to the date of birth or adoption

   iii residency requirements, which means a claimant must be an Australian citizen or permanent resident, or be the holder of one of a number of temporary visas detailed by the Family Assistance Office

169. The NES entitlement is unaffected by the paid parental leave scheme.

170. Casuals workers are not entitled to any paid leave, unless eligible under the paid parental leave scheme. They are entitled to two days unpaid carer's leave and two days unpaid compassionate leave per occasion, as well as unpaid community service leave. In addition, casual employees who have been employed for at least twelve months by an employer on a regular and systematic basis and with an expectation of ongoing employment are entitled to unpaid parental leave.

171. Casual employees are compensated for their lack of leave entitlements through the payment of an hourly casual loading.

172. Legal responses are: the NES provides minimum standards for various types of leave, applicable to most Australian employees; awards and agreements apply if they are more advantageous to an employee than the minimum leave entitlements provided by the NES; provision of the ability to 'cash out' some leave entitlements under the NES and some awards and agreements; long service leave is provided under awards, agreements and state legislation, and there are plans for a national long service leave standard to be developed and to apply under the NES; and the paid parental leave scheme was introduced for parents who give birth to or adopt a child after 1 January 2011. A non-legal response to the issue of leave is that employees and employers are able to negotiate many aspects of leave arrangements to suit both parties, as long as they stay in the parameters set by the law.

173. To identify and investigate the issue of leave and evaluate the effectiveness of responses to this issue, you need to: describe the leave entitlements under the NES and to whom they apply; describe leave entitlements and provisions which arise under other legal instruments; describe the provisions of the *Paid Parental Leave Act* (Cth) 2010; describe any non-legal responses to the issue of leave; discuss the factors which help ensure, and those which limit, the effectiveness of legal and non-legal responses to the contemporary workplace issue of leave; and come to a conclusion about the effectiveness of legal and non-legal responses to the contemporary workplace issue of leave.

174. Any six of the following: allowing contracts of employment to be negotiated between employers and employees, though these cannot interfere with conditions in statutes, awards or agreements; allowing informal negotiations to take place between employers and employees about numerous matters, such as overtime or leave; providing for enterprise agreements which allow employers and employees to negotiate for pay and conditions that suit their particular workplace or business rather than be bound by an award; requiring employers, employees and their representatives to bargain in good faith when enterprise agreements are being negotiated; allowing for industrial action to take place to give force to negotiations between employers and employees; clearly delineating the role and the allowable actions of trade unions and employer associations so they can assist in workplace negotiations; providing for injury management plans for workers who have sustained a significant injury at work to be developed through cooperation between the employer, the injured worker and the worker's doctor; providing for the Fair Work Commission to arrange conciliation when there has been an unfair dismissal claim; and providing that both the Fair Work Commission and the Fair Work Ombudsman will try to bring employers and employees to a resolution about an unfair termination of employment claim before any determinations take place or any orders are made about the matter.

175. Any six of the following: dispute settling mechanisms must be contained in awards and agreements; the *Fair Work Act 2009* (Cth) prescribes a bargaining process for the negotiation of enterprise agreements, which minimises disputes and provides for dispute settling mechanisms if disputes do occur while negotiations are taking place; mediation can become part of unofficial workplace dispute settling mechanisms, with a trade union or employer association acting as the mediator; mandatory dispute settling procedures are in all awards and agreements to encourage the settlement of disputes in the workplace; conciliation and arbitration are accessible through tribunals, such as the Fair Work Commission and the NSW Industrial Relations Commission; federal and state courts can make decisions about disputes relating to a range of industrial matters; the Fair Work Ombudsman can investigate complaints and seek resolutions with employees for suspected breaches of workplace law as well as litigate on behalf of complainants; clear roles and the allowable actions for trade unions and employer associations in the settlement of industrial disputes have been defined; the NSW Anti-Discrimination Board, the Fair Work Ombudsman (Cth) and the Australian Human Rights Commission can provide conciliation in disputes about discrimination; provision of quick, inexpensive methods of dispute resolution can be achieved through the NSW Civil and Administrative Tribunal (NCAT), and through litigation by the Fair Work Ombudsman in the Federal Court on behalf of complainants if conciliation in discrimination matters is not effective; the NSW Workers Compensation Commission is a tribunal which provides independent, quick and inexpensive resolutions to disputes about workers compensation in NSW; and the Fair Work Commission makes determinations about unfair dismissal and unfair termination of employment claims and can impose penalties and order compensation.

176. **i** The Fair Work Commission: makes determinations in industrial disputes, unfair dismissal and unfair termination of employment claims. It also offers conciliation in these matters

ii the NSW Industrial Relations Commission: makes determinations in industrial disputes, unfair dismissal and unfair termination of employment claims. It also offers conciliation in these matters

iii the Fair Work Ombudsman: can investigate complaints and seek resolutions with employees for suspected breaches of workplace law as well as litigate on behalf of complainants in discrimination matters and termination of employment matters

iv the NSW Anti-Discrimination Board: conciliates in discrimination matters

v the Australian Human Rights Commission: conciliates in discrimination matters

vi the NSW Civil and Administrative Tribunal (NCAT): conducts hearings and makes orders in discrimination matters

vii the NSW Workers Compensation Commission: conducts hearings to resolve workers compensation disputes

177. There is sometimes a lack of compliance with workplace safety laws because of: lack of knowledge of the law; a desire to save money; carelessness; disagreement with the law and/or the values and ethics behind it; and media pressure.

178. Factors which may have contributed to the increase in workplace deaths include: lack of commitment to and non-compliance with safety laws by both employers and employees; insufficient inspectors; insufficient penalties; 'management by stress'; and the weakening power of the unions.

179. Employers with less than 100 employees did not need to comply with unfair dismissal laws under the Work Choices amendments in the federal sphere.

180. Any three of the following: lack of knowledge by both employers and/or employees as to what the five minimum standards were; employees may have been forced to accept conditions less than the legislative requirements; lack of scrutiny by trade unions; failure by the Workplace Authority to scrutinise the agreements promptly and ensure compliance; failure of the legislation to ensure compliance before an AWA took effect.

181. AWAs are no longer possible; most employees are covered by an award or agreement, and all workers in the national workplace system are covered by the NES, including being provided with a Fair Work Information Statement.

182. Unions can ensure that individual employers comply with the law. For example, in 2006, the CFMEU embarrassed JAL Landscape and Construction Pty Ltd, a Sydney construction company, into paying wages owed to two teenage employees.

183. For much of Australia's history, the ethical view that workers have rights which need to be protected has been a fundamental part of Australia's workplace legal framework.

184. One ideology, reflected in the *Workplace Relations Act 1996* (Cth), sees the freedom of individual employers and employees to make their own workplace arrangements as paramount, because it leads to more flexible and more profitable workplaces. So, AWAs overrode awards and agreements. This ideology seeks to lessen the role of unions and government organisations, such as tribunals in workplace arrangements. The conflicting ideology holds that government intervention in workplace arrangements is vital to protect the rights of workers, especially those who are most vulnerable. This ideology is reflected in the *Fair Work Act 2009* (Cth).

185. Any seven of the following reforms: the introduction of a national workplace system that is applicable to most employees in Australia; sham contracting arrangements being made illegal and penalties being applied to employers who attempt to make such arrangements; modern awards being made central to the conditions of employment in most industries; the establishment of the NES and general protections so that all workers in the national workplace system are protected by minimum conditions; the provision for the negotiation of enterprise agreements which must comply with a bargaining process prescribed in the act and must pass the 'better off overall' test (BOOT); allowing for industrial action to take place, as well as limiting the circumstances under which it can take place; dispute settling procedures being made mandatory in all awards and agreements, to encourage the settlement of disputes in the workplace; the establishment of government bodies, i.e. the Fair Work Commission and the Fair Work Ombudsman, to provide advice, assistance, conciliation and arbitration of disputes; the investment of the Fair Work Ombudsman with the power to litigate on behalf of complainants; the establishment of annual national wage reviews by the Minimum Wage Panel of the Fair Work Commission, which is required to hear submissions from all interested parties; changes to the ways in which discrimination issues can be dealt with in the federal arena, so that employees have greater access to remedies; making unfair dismissal laws apply to most workers; a distinction being made between genuine and non-genuine redundancies, to prevent employers attempting to disadvantage workers; and the provision of protections to redundant workers under the NES.

186. The case of *Scholem v NSW Department of Health* (NSW District Court, 27 May 1992) was the first passive smoking case in the world and led to many workplaces around Australia declaring themselves smoke-free so as to avoid similar claims from their workforces.

187. **i** changing social values, which led to the reform of the *Fair Work Act 2009* (Cth)

ii changing composition of society, which is reflected in the *Paid Parental Leave Act 2010* (Cth)

iii failure of existing law, which is addressed in the *Fair Work Act 2009* (Cth)

iv new technology, which is reflected in laws protecting workers who have been made redundant

188. Any four of the following reforms: the introduction of the NES under the *Fair Work Act 2009* (Cth) to protect the rights of workers; changes to the ways in which discrimination issues can be dealt with in the federal arena, so that employees have greater access to remedies; changes to workers compensation in NSW to make it more efficient and less costly; the introduction of national

workplace safety laws from January 2012; the introduction of the GEERS; the reform of unfair dismissal laws so that they have wider application; and the introduction of the paid parental leave scheme.

189. **i** dispute resolution mechanisms
ii the role of trade unions
iii protection and recognition of workplace rights
iv discrimination in the workplace
v workplace safety
vi termination of employment
vii leave

190. **i** contracts of service
ii contracts for services
iii awards
iv agreements
v statutory conditions
vi negotiation processes
vii the role of tribunals
viii the role of the courts
ix the role of government organisations
x the role of trade unions and employer associations
xi the role of other NGOs
xii the role of the media

 Sample HSC questions (page 369)

Extended-response questions

Note: **EM** means Examiner Maximiser

Question 1

What you are asked to do

This question asks you to:

- describe the law relating to termination of employment
- evaluate the effectiveness of the law in achieving justice in the workplace for each type of termination of employment.

EM In order to achieve top marks for your answer to this question, in your answer you should:

- list the FOUR ways employment may be terminated
- state that the law governs each type of termination, particularly those initiated by employers (that is, dismissal and redundancy)
- state that, for the law regarding termination of employment to 'achieve justice in the workplace', it should be fair to both employers and employees
- explain that there is both state and federal law about termination of employment, but that the discussion in this answer will focus on federal law.

Your answer could follow the plan below.

Plan

Paragraph 1 (Introduction):

- List the four ways employment may be terminated.
- State that the law governs each type of termination, particularly those initiated by employers (that is, dismissal and redundancy).

- State that, for the law regarding termination of employment to achieve justice in the workplace; it should be fair to both employers and employees.
- Explain that there is both state and federal law about termination of employment, but that the discussion will focus on federal law. **[5.2.1 and 5.3.3]**

Paragraph 2:

- Define *resignation*.
- Describe the law regarding resignation. **[5.3.3]**

Paragraph 3:

- Explain the factors which may *enhance* the effectiveness of the law regarding resignation in achieving justice in the workplace for both employers and employees.
- Explain the factors which may *limit* the effectiveness of the law regarding resignation in achieving justice in the workplace for both employers and employees.
- Come to a conclusion about how effective the law regarding resignation is in achieving justice in the workplace for employers and employees. **[5.3.3]**

Paragraph 4:

- Define *retirement*.
- Describe the law regarding retirement. **[5.3.3 and 5.3.1]**

Paragraph 5:

- Explain the factors which may *enhance* the effectiveness of the law regarding retirement in achieving justice in the workplace for both employers and employees.
- Explain the factors which may *limit* the effectiveness of the law regarding retirement in achieving justice in the workplace for both employers and employees.
- Come to a conclusion about how effective the law regarding retirement is in achieving justice in the workplace for employers and employees. **[5.3.3]**

Paragraph 6:

- Define *dismissal* and the kinds of dismissal that can take place: *summary dismissal*; *constructive dismissal*; *dismissal with notice*.
- State that there are two kinds of wrongful dismissal (that is, unfair dismissal and unfair termination of employment).
- Describe the law regarding dismissal, with particular reference to laws regarding:
  - unfair dismissal
  - unlawful termination of employment. **[5.3.3]**

Paragraph 7:

- Explain the factors which may *enhance* the effectiveness of the law regarding dismissal in achieving justice in the workplace for both employers and employees.
- Explain the factors which may *limit* the effectiveness of the law regarding dismissal in achieving justice in the workplace for both employers and employees.
- Come to a conclusion about how effective the law regarding dismissal is in achieving justice in the workplace for employers and employees. **[5.3.3]**

Paragraph 8:

- Define *redundancy*.
- Describe the law regarding redundancy. **[5.3.3]**

Paragraph 9:

- Explain the factors which may *enhance* the effectiveness of the law regarding redundancy in achieving justice in the workplace for both employers and employees.
- Explain the factors which may *limit* the effectiveness of the law regarding redundancy in achieving justice in the workplace for both employers and employees.
- Come to a conclusion about how effective the law regarding redundancy is in achieving justice in the workplace for employers and employees. **[5.3.3]**

Conclusion:

- Briefly summarise how well the current laws about termination of employment achieve justice for employers and employees.
- Summarise any limitations to the effectiveness of the law in achieving justice for both.
- Describe possible areas of reform. **[5.3.3 and 5.3.1]**

Question 2

What you are asked to do

This question asks you to:

- describe various approaches of the law to regulating the workplace
- explain how well each approach has reflected prevailing values and ethical standards.

EM In order to achieve top marks for your answer to this question, in your answer you should:

- describe various approaches the law has had to regulating the workplace and/or various changes that have occurred in the workplace and how the law has responded to these changes
- come to a conclusion about how each of the responses you described reflects society's values and ethical standards.

Your answer could follow the plan below.

Plan

Paragraph 1 (Introduction):

- List the various approaches the law has had to regulating the workplace and/or various changes that have occurred in the workplace.
- State that the law's response to change in the workplace and the law itself often reflect the prevailing values and ethical standards of the time.
- State that laws can also change because they fail to adequately reflect the values and ethical standards of the community, as occurred with the replacement of Work Choices with the *Fair Work Act 2009* (Cth). **[5.1.1, 5.1.3 and 5.4.3]**

Paragraph 2:

- Explain the philosophy of laissez faire.
- Explain how the philosophy of laissez faire reflected the ideas of the time.

- Explain how laissez faire was gradually replaced with state intervention.
- Explain how state intervention better reflected prevailing values and ethical standards. **[5.1.1]**

Paragraph 3:

- Explain that technological change in the workplace and globalisation have led to the need for greater flexibility in the workplace.
- Explain the impact of these changes on the workplace, such as changes in employment patterns and consequent legislative changes. **[5.1.1, 5.1.3 and 5.4.3]**

Paragraph 4:

- Explain that the rise in casual and contract workers reflect the attitude of many business owners that they need to make these kinds of workplace arrangements in order to be competitive in a global market.
- Explain that the conflicting view to the one above is that such workers are insufficiently protected by the law.
- Explain how the law has tried to balance these two sets of values and ethical standards by giving some protections to casual and contract workers.
- Describe the laws which have given these protections. **[5.1.1, 5.1.2, 5.2.5, 5.3.3, 5.3.4 and 5.4.3]**

Paragraph 5:

- Explain changes made to the law since 1996 to make workplaces more flexible, i.e. enterprise agreements, AWAs and Work Choices.
- Explain how these laws have been made in response to the globalisation of industry and to the attitude that workplaces need to be more flexible to be competitive.
- Explain that these laws reflect one set of values and ethical standards in the community.
- Explain that these laws were replaced by the Fair Work reforms which reflect a conflicting set of values and ethical standards and see the protection of workers' rights as of paramount importance, while also seeking to provide flexible workplaces. **[5.1.3, 5.2.4, 5.3.3 and 5.4.3]**

Paragraph 6:

- Explain that the reforms brought in by the *Fair Work Act* reflect the current prevailing values and ethical standards better than Work Choices did.
- List some of the reforms introduced by the *Fair Work Act*. **[5.1.3, 5.1.4, 5.2.1, 5.2.2, 5.2.4, 5.3.1, 5.3.3, 5.4.3 and 5.4.4]**

Conclusion:

- List the various approaches the law has had to regulating the workplace, and various changes that have occurred in the workplace and how the law has responded to them.
- Comment on the extent to which these laws reflect changing values and ethical standards. **[5.1.1, 5.4.3 and 5.4.4]**

Chapter 6: World order

 Key Concept questions (pages 418–20)

1. *World order* refers to the creation of global relationships and maintenance of world peace. It governs the relationships between nation-states and other global participants, including transnational corporations, regional federations, intergovernmental organisations and non-government organisations.

2. You need to explain that, without world order:
   i there would be international anarchy
   ii global destruction could eventuate
   iii global issues would not be adequately addressed
   iv economic development and globalisation would not occur.

3. You need to define world order, explain the consequences of a lack of world order, and explain that world order is an evolving concept.

4. *Expansionism* is the situation in which one nation-state pushes to increase its size or territories and/or increase its influence in the world community.

5. i The creation of borders split many modern nation-states with boundaries that cut across ethnic and cultural lines.
   ii Colonies were often left with poor infrastructure and with political and economic systems imposed on them by the colonial power.

6. Any three of the following: loss of land; destruction of culture; loss of life due to weapons and disease; poverty; lower life expectancy.

7. A *unipolar* world means a world in which there is one dominant power. A world in which there are two or more dominant powers is called a *multipolar* world

8. *Transnationals* are corporations that engage in foreign investment and own, or control, activities in more than one nation-state. Transnationals wield more economic power than the traditional nation-state and are extremely wealthy.

9. Nation-states are becoming increasingly interdependent because of:
   i a recognition of the need to work together to improve themselves and the conditions of their people
   ii a recognition of the need to cooperate to fight against common threats such as war, disease, human trafficking, the drug trade, terrorism, global warming, pollution and famine
   iii mutual benefit.

10. Any three of the following: transnationals; intergovernmental organisations; non-governmental organisations; the media; individuals.

11. The chief aim of the League of Nations is to maintain international peace and security.

12. The Pact of Paris (1928) was the first international agreement to renounce war.

13. You need to: explain that world order is constantly evolving and it must continue to do so as new challenges to resolving conflict and maintaining peace arise; outline major world events and international instruments that are essential to explain the evolution of world order to the present day; explain that the evolution of world order is also due to constantly emerging ethics, morality and values held by nation-states and their citizens; and describe the current challenges to maintaining world order.

14. *Intra-state conflict* is between opposing sides in the same nation-state. *Inter-state conflict* is between two or more different nation-states.

15. Any five of the following: guerrilla warfare; conventional warfare; border conflict; nuclear warfare; chemical and biological warfare; civil war; democide; communal killing; terrorism.

16. The Cold War began after World War II and ran from 1947 to 1991. Cold War is the name for the uneasy peace maintained between the two world superpowers, the communist USSR and the capitalist US.

17. *Terrorism* is the deliberate use of violence by an individual or group against the enemy in order to provoke fear. The 'enemy' in terrorism is difficult to define: it can be nation-states, rulers or their governments, an ethnic or religious group, or even international concepts such as communism or democracy.

18. i More 'traditional' types of conflict, such as conventional warfare, civil war and border conflict, are governed by a large body of international law, developed over a long period of time.
    ii Nuclear warfare is closely governed and controlled by the United Nations and international organisations, and there are several conventions and treaties applying to it.
    iii Genocide, democide and communal killing can also be classified as a traditional form of warfare and are clearly governed by international law.
    iv Chemical warfare and biological warfare are governed by a large body of international law which must be constantly reviewed as new forms of this type of warfare are developed.
    v Terrorism is proving to be the most challenging type of conflict in the current world order because the very definition of *terrorism* makes it a challenge, because traditional methods of governing the disputes between separate nation-states do not apply.

19. You need to explain the different types of conflict as described in Section 6.1.4 (pages 389–91), and discuss the implications about the attempts of nations to control these different types of conflict, as listed in the answer to Question 18 above.

20. i the behaviour of unethical transnationals and corrupt corporations
    ii corrupt regimes and undemocratic and repressive governments
    iii the legacy of imperialism and the repression of Indigenous populations
    iv inequitable free trade laws and the sanctioning of unjust trade practices

21. In 2005, over three billion people attended simultaneous 'Live Aid' concerts throughout the world, in an attempt to convince the G8 leaders to cancel African foreign debt—debt which is debilitating to the affected nations

and their peoples. This movement led to the G8 leaders promising some reduction of African debt.

22. The collapse of the Greek economy in 2010, and the subsequent bail-out by the remainder of the EU-currency countries (led by Germany), is one example of an IGO assisting smaller member states in the event of a crisis.

23. Wealthy UN member states have agreed to give 0.7% of GDP to foreign aid (but the UN has not been able to ensure that this occurs because it is a suggested target only).

24. Some transnationals move their manufacturing operations to countries in which the population can be easily exploited and the country itself gains no benefits from the huge profits made by the company. Coca-Cola's use of sugar obtained from plantations which use child labour in El Salvador is one example.

25. The corruption of transnationals in wealthy nations does not lead to wide scale internal conflict as it does in developing nations. This is because developed nations have the necessary infrastructure, resources and social systems to ensure that the corrupt actions of a few do not impact upon the nation-state as a whole.

26. i the United Nations
    ii international instruments (declarations and treaties)
    iii international courts and tribunals
    iv intergovernmental organisations (IGOs)
    v non-government organisations (NGOs)
    vi national governments, such as the Australian federal government
    vii the media
    viii political negotiation and persuasion
    ix force

27. *State sovereignty* means that each nation-state has the absolute right to control its own affairs within its borders and is not obligated to listen to any outside authority.

28. One of the following:
    i when pollution or disease crosses over into neighbouring states
    ii when a nation-state allows a human rights abuse or internal conflict to occur
    iii when a nation-state develops nuclear weapons

29. *Reciprocity* means nations comply with international agreements because they want other nations to do the same. *Legal responsibility* means that nations want to be seen as law-abiding by other nations.

30. You need to explain that state sovereignty has the potential to impede the resolution of world order issues, but the ideas of reciprocity and legal responsibility assist in resolving world order issues because both these ideas encourage sovereign states to resolve issues in their dealings with other nations. In addition, the right of the international community to intervene in the domestic affairs of a nation is recognised in some circumstances.

31. Any two of the following:
    i maintain international peace and security
    ii develop friendly relations between nation-states and strengthen universal peace
    iii achieve international cooperation in solving international problems of a social, economic, cultural or humanitarian nature
    iv promote respect for human rights

32. i All member states have full, and equal, sovereignty.
    ii All members will settle disputes through peaceful means.
    iii All members will refrain from force, or the threat of force, against the territorial boundaries or political independence of any state.
    iv Members will not intervene in the domestic matters of any state, subject to enforcement measures.

33. the General Assembly, the Security Council, the International Court of Justice (ICJ), the Economic and Social Council (ECOSOC), the Secretariat, and the Trusteeship Council (which is no longer in existence)

34. The Perm-5 are the permanent members of the UN Security Council. They are the UK, USA, France, China, and Russia. Each of these nations has veto powers over any Security Council decision.

35. A *treaty* is a written legal agreement between nation-states. Treaties are also called statutes, protocols, covenants or conventions. Treaties are binding on the nation-states that ratify them. A *declaration* is a formal statement outlining a set of values considered to be universally applicable, usually made by the UN General Assembly. Declarations are not binding on any nation-state.

36. *Ratification of a treaty* means that a nation-state agrees to ensure that domestic laws will be implemented to incorporate the requirements of the treaty.

37. *International customary law* is international law drawn from the common practices of governments which, over a period of time, become accepted as legally binding. Unlike a *treaty*, customary law applies to all nation-states, whether they have ratified a treaty or not.

38. The ICJ can hear disputes between nation-states and give advisory opinions.

39. The ICC will only hear cases if they are not being investigated or prosecuted by a national judicial system, unless the national system is not genuine.

40. Cases can be referred to ICC jurisdiction in three ways: by a signatory nation-state, by the UN Security Council or by the ICC prosecutor.

41. The International Criminal Tribunal for the former Yugoslavia, established in 1993 and the International Criminal Tribunal for Rwanda, set up in 1994. Both these tribunals hear cases of war crimes, genocide and crimes against humanity committed in those countries.

42. Any two of the following: the European Union Court of Justice; the European Court of Human Rights; the Appellate Body of the World Trade Organization (WTO); the International Tribunal for the Law of the Sea; The International Court of Arbitration; the International Centre for Settlement of Investment Disputes (ICSID)

43. Article 52 of the UN Charter allows regional organisations to handle matters pertaining to international peace as long as the aims of the organisation are consistent with the principles of the UN.

44. Examples of regional federations are: the European Union (EU); the North Atlantic Treaty Organization (NATO); the African Union (AU); the Commonwealth; the Association of Southeast Asian Nations (ASEAN); and the Arab League.

45. NGOs act as powerful political lobby groups, provide humanitarian aid and work closely with the UN and other specialised international agencies.

46. international humanitarian law and the Geneva Conventions

47. Section 51(29) of the Australian Constitution gives the power over external affairs to the federal government. This means the Australian federal government has exclusive powers over international affairs—meaning only the federal government can enter into international agreements.

48. Australia's state governments cannot enter into international agreements but can lobby the federal government to sign treaties on Australia's behalf, as they did when they urged the federal government to ratify the Kyoto Protocol 1997. States can also enact legislation to mirror international agreements.

49. i entering into international agreements for Australia
    ii passing legislation to put international agreements into effect
    iii contributing to foreign aid
    iv sending peacekeeping and other forces to areas of conflict
    v extradition of criminals
    vi maintaining membership of the UN and relevant IGOs, such as ASEAN
    vii taking part in diplomatic persuasion

50. You need to describe the seven roles the federal government plays in contributing to the maintenance of world order, giving an example of each one, and you need to explain the limited role of Australian state and territory governments.

51. One positive influence of media attention is that it can mobilise public action. For example, public action can call on governments and international organisations to settle conflicts, give aid, or uphold human rights.

    Any two of the following are negative influences of media attention:
    i the modern media tends to treat news as entertainment and, in the case of conflict, to show the drama and the violent images, with little or no exploration of the reasons behind the issues
    ii news items grow old very quickly and, once the initial drama is shown, the story is then ignored, even if the situation continues
    iii constant media coverage of tragedy can lead to 'compassion fatigue'.

52. Political negotiation is not always effective because mutual goodwill and willingness to find a solution must be present on both sides.

53. Any three of the following:
    i NGOs use persuasion by 'naming and shaming' offending states in reports
    ii the UN 'names and shames' offending nations in their reports and deliberations on human rights issues
    iii the threat of international sanctions, including economic and trade sanctions
    iv expressions of global disapproval, often through media coverage

v positive persuasion employed so that states must improve their behaviour if they wish to join world or regional intergovernmental organisations

54. Nations may use force legally only when acting in self-defence.

55. The concept of *collective self-defence* means, if a nation-state is threatened, its allies can legally come to its assistance. *Pre-emptive self-defence* describes the legal use of force by a nation-state that can prove it is about to be subject to invasion or force.

56. The general rule is that multilateral intervention is authorised by international law if the threat to peace is significant, as defined by the UN Security Council. An example is the use of force in Kosovo by NATO in 1999.

57. Five legal measures are: the United Nations; international instruments; international courts and tribunals; IGOs; and the Australian federal government.

    Four non-legal measures are: NGOs; the media; political negotiation; and persuasion.

58. Force can sometimes be legally used but is also sometimes used illegally.

59. You need to: list legal and non-legal measures of resolving conflict and working towards world order; explain those factors which enhance and those which limit the effectiveness of each measure in resolving conflict and working towards world order (using examples where appropriate); and come to a conclusion about the overall effectiveness of each measure.

60. i A nation-state has the first responsibility to protect its population from mass atrocities.
    ii If the nation-state cannot protect its population from the mass atrocities alone, then the international community has a responsibility to assist that nation-state by building its capacity to manage the situation.
    iii If the nation-state is manifestly failing to protect its population from mass atrocities and peaceful measures are not working, then the international community has the responsibility to intervene with force if necessary.

61. Humanitarian intervention is permissible:
    i when the UN Security Council decides that the actions of a nation pose a threat to international peace and security
    ii when a nation intervenes to protect its own citizens caught in a conflict (UN Charter, Article 41)
    iii when a nation is to be inspected for outlawed weapons.

62. Chapter VII (Article 42) of the UN Charter establishes the UN peace-enforcement powers and states that the UN Security Council can 'take such action by air, sea or land forces as may be necessary to maintain or restore international peace and security'.

63. In order to do this you need to: describe the RtoP principle and explain that it has no legal basis; explain the legal response of humanitarian intervention under the UN Charter; discuss the factors which may enhance, and those which may limit, the effectiveness of legal and non-legal responses for the issue of the principle of RtoP; and come to a conclusion about the effectiveness of the legal and non-legal responses to the contemporary world order issue of the principle of RtoP.

64. Any of the following:
    i the war on terror
    ii ongoing conflict in Afghanistan and Iraq
    iii illegal use of force
    iv the threat of nuclear warfare
    v the conflict between Israel and Palestine
    vi the behaviour of North Korea
    vii the incidence of mass atrocities

65. The legal basis of the mission in Afghanistan was through the exemption of self-defence under Article 51 of the UN Charter. The US argued it was attacked by Al-Queda, and the Taliban were harbouring them. This was accepted by the Security Council and the mission was declared legal.

    The legal basis for the mission in Iraq is more complex, and there is still dispute about whether the mission is legal (that is, backed by the Security Council). In the case of Iraq, the US and the Security Council cosponsored Resolution 1441 that gave the Iraqi government a final opportunity to comply with Resolution 687. It stated that Iraq would face 'serious consequences' for non-compliance. The US then used Resolution 1441 as the means to enter Iraq, stating that it was a 'measure of last resort' under Article 42 of the UN Charter. Article 42 says that when all other measures are deemed inadequate, the Council 'may take such action by air, sea, or land forces as may be necessary to maintain or restore international peace and security'.

66. India and Pakistan have had a dispute over who owns the territory of Kashmir since the 1950s and both acquired nuclear weapons in the 1990s. Iran also has a nuclear program in place and is not complying with UN requirements to show the peaceful nature of its nuclear program.

67. Any of the following: North Korea claims to be developing nuclear weapons; North Korea withdrew from the NPTT in 2003; North Korea refuses any arms inspections or international overseeing of its regime; North Korea torpedoed a South Korean warship in 2010; and North Korea has isolated itself from the rest of the world.

68. The international community has tried to address incidences of mass atrocities with *ad hoc* war crimes tribunals, the RtoP principles, and the ICC.

69. You need to: identify and describe the regional and global situations that threaten peace and security which are discussed in Section 6.3.2 (pages 408–12); explain the legal and non-legal responses to these situations; discuss the factors which may enhance, and those which may limit, the effectiveness of legal and non-legal responses for each of the situations described; and come to a conclusion about the effectiveness of the legal and non-legal responses to the contemporary world order issue of regional and global situations that threaten peace and security.

70. The United Nations is limited by:
    i the nature of modern conflicts (such as terrorism, internal conflict and border disputes) which directly challenge how the United Nations and intergovernmental organisations can work to resolve conflict
    ii humanitarian law and the Geneva Conventions appearing outdated when faced with modern conflict
    iii it being too easy for nation-states to ignore United Nations conventions without consequences.

71. Chapter VII (Article 47) of the UN Charter established a Military Staff Committee, which was to coordinate a UN 'force' that would enforce the decisions of the UN.

72. i Peacekeepers are sent into areas of conflict to assist in enforcing peace so that diplomatic measures can be used to negotiate an end to conflict.
    ii Agreement of the Perm-5 members of the Security Council is not required.
    iii Missions operate out of the UN Secretary General's department.
    iv The UN has requested troops from nations for each mission. Nation-states do not have to send troops, and they have the right to withdraw their troops at any time.
    v The UN raises funds for missions from contributions from nation-states, who are often slow to pay.

73. There have been sixty-four peacekeeping missions since 1948. There were thirteen missions in the first forty years of the UN, and fifty missions in the last twenty years. In the middle of 2010 there were sixteen peacekeeping missions in operation.

74. You need to: identify and describe the cooperative global measures of peace enforcement and peacekeeping; discuss the factors which may enhance, and those which may limit, the success of peace enforcement and peacekeeping as methods of global cooperation in achieving world order; and come to a conclusion about the effectiveness of the peace enforcement and peacekeeping measures in the success of global cooperation in achieving world order.

75. *International humanitarian law* applies to military personnel and civilians who are caught up in a conflict. It is different to human rights law, which applies to all people at all times.

76. The Geneva Conventions protect military personnel and combatants in a conflict, civilians in war, wounded combatants, military medical staff and prisoners of war.

77. You need to: identify and describe the rules regarding the conduct of hostilities; explain that the US, which promotes itself as an upholder of human rights, side-stepped the rules regarding the conduct of hostilities in its treatment of so-called 'unlawful combatants' in Guantanamo Bay; explain that pressure from the international community and NGOs encouraged the US to change its treatment of prisoners in Guantanamo Bay; and come to a conclusion about the effectiveness of the rules regarding the conduct of hostilities given the Guantanamo Bay example.

78. Nation-states are becoming increasingly interdependent because of: a recognition of the need to work together to improve themselves and the conditions of their people; a recognition of the need to cooperate to fight against common threats such as war, disease, human trafficking, the drug trade, terrorism, global warming, pollution and famine; and mutual benefit.

79. The concept of state sovereignty is being eroded by the increasing power of transnationals, and intergovernmental and international organisations. The wealth of transnationals means that they can impact on a state's decisions regarding environmental, industrial relations, resource and economic issues. The power of international organisations, such as the World Bank, means they can impact on the decisions of a state—particularly smaller and less powerful states.

80. Most nations that sign treaties do so for mutual benefit, so are unlikely to break a treaty.

81. Economic and political sanctions can put pressure on a nation to start complying with the law. For example, during the 1970s and 1980s, as a protest against apartheid and in an endeavour to make the South African government change its policy, OPEC countries, followed by the EU, then Commonwealth nations and the US, all gradually imposed sanctions, both political and economic, on South Africa. Many say that the sanctions eventually made economic conditions so intolerable that South Africa was forced to end apartheid.

82. Treaties and conventions are based on agreements between nation-states, so there is normally a large commitment from the signatories to treaties to comply with them. In an increasingly interdependent world order, it is generally in the best interest of nation-states to create and comply with international law.

83. Domestic laws have separate enforcement procedures. The police enforce law, and there are clear judicial processes and punishments when individuals do not comply. There are clear-cut, and unavoidable, consequences for breaking the law. When a nation does not comply with international treaties or judgements, then that nation can choose to withdraw from the treaty, ignore the decision and to even withdraw from international relations all together. There may be little consequence and, often, no enforcement of the law (unlike what occurs with a domestic police force).

84. political negotiation, persuasion (including political and economic sanctions), and force

85. The development of international copyright law and, more recently, protocols handling pornography and racial vilification on the internet are examples of new laws focusing on emerging moral standards.

86. International principles of *jus cogens* are the principles that have developed due to changes in what the global community will, and will not, accept. When a principle becomes *jus cogens*, it means that all treaties that conflict with it are no longer valid. For example, there were, in the nineteenth century, various treaties which allowed for slave trading between nations. As the moral and ethical views on slavery changed across the world, the prohibition against slavery became *jus cogens*, so that any treaty today that allowed for slavery would be invalid.

87. The International Law Commission affects reform by reviewing and reporting on legal issues. It writes reports on legal issues and remedies, and makes recommendations for treaties and conventions to the General Assembly.

88. Parliaments of nation-states bring about reform by enacting international treaties and conventions into domestic legislation, by reporting to international committees on their compliance with international law, and by grouping together on common issues to lobby the international community.

89. Non-legal agencies of reform are non-governmental organisations, the media and individuals. Individuals can influence reform by supporting grassroots movements and NGOs, or they may be academics or visionary leaders.

90. Over 30 000 children die each day due to extreme poverty, showing that this challenge has not been adequately addressed by the international community. The possibility of a global pandemic is more real today than ever with new strains of disease developing, and with international trade and travel leading to the quick global dispersal of these diseases.

91. State sovereignty and the consensual nature of international law limit legal responses to world order issues, because nation-states do not have to follow international law if they choose not to.

92. Restructuring the Security Council to give nations more equal representation is sometimes suggested, so that it better reflects the range of attitudes to world order issues. Reforms concerning how nation-states fund both foreign aid and the UN itself are also required, because there is a serious lack of funding currently.

93. The ICJ can hear disputes between nation-states only when each nation-state agrees to have the case heard, and then agrees to abide by the ICJ's decision.

94. The best mechanism for enforcement of the international law for individuals is still through their own nation's domestic tribunals and enforcement measures.

95. The 'Lockerbie case' is an example of individuals being successfully prosecuted and punished by a domestic court for offences against world order. The Dragan Vasiljkovic case is a case of an Australian citizen being successfully extradited to face an indictment for war crimes, by the International Criminal Tribunal for the former Yugoslavia.

96. Economic and other sanctions can help persuade a nation-state to change its laws when these laws go against international law. For example, sanctions imposed multilaterally against South Africa in the 1970s and 1980s helped to persuade the South African government to dismantle the system of apartheid.

97. Genocide, such as in Rwanda in 1994, can still occur. The fact that the global community did not intervene until after the worst of the genocide occurred in this case demonstrates that reform is needed in the use of the current Security Council powers to intervene in the affairs of a sovereign state when serious human rights violations are occurring.

98. Nuclear war remains a threat as long as nations are still acquiring and developing nuclear weapons, and as long as nations who already have nuclear weapons fail to disarm.

99. The threats to world order posed by terrorism are not being adequately addressed because there have been more terrorist attacks since the attacks of 11 September 2001 and these are ongoing. In addition, the UN was powerless to stop the US invading Iraq in 2003. Also, in response to terrorism, some states have enacted legislation that may infringe on the rights of individuals.

100. Some communities within a nation-state have more rights to review than others, particularly if their states are members of intergovernmental organisations, such as the EU.

101. New weaponry, including nuclear and biological weaponry, means that it is now far easier to implement mass destruction than it has ever been. In addition, the rate of change in technology means that the law is constantly playing 'catch-up'. New problems continue to emerge, such as gambling over the internet, and child pornography and violent pornography being distributed on the internet.

102. Nation-states are not equal in the current world order because: the Security Council has five permanent states (the Perm-5), all of whom have veto power; smaller, newer nation-states cannot lobby as effectively as stronger, more powerful states and are more likely to be influenced by larger states on international issues; and powerful international organisations, such as the World Bank, are predominately managed and staffed by citizens of powerful nation-states.

103. Australia has always played an important role in global affairs. For example, many Australian suggestions were implemented in the newly formed United Nations.

In terms of peacekeeping missions, Australia has also taken its responsibilities seriously since 1947, particularly in the case of peacekeeping in our region. It contributed 1.93% of the total UN peacekeeping budget as of February 2010, placing it twelfth among the world's contributors. However, Australia, like many developed nations, is giving much less than the 0.7% of gross domestic product (GDP) agreed upon. In 2010, the Australian government gave approximately 0.3% of GDP to foreign aid—one of the lowest levels of giving from rich developed nations.

104. Any two of the following:
  i The United Nations system has managed to avoid another major world conflict for over sixty years.
  ii Nuclear weapons have the potential to destroy the entire world, so all nation-states have a vested interest in avoiding conflict and maintaining world order
  iii *Ad hoc* war tribunals and the ICC have had effect in bringing to justice individuals and groups who have perpetrated war crimes.
  iv Intergovernmental organisations, such as the EU, are proving effective in maintaining order, security and prosperity for their member nations.
  v The media is effective in contributing to world order in that local issues are now global and its reporting instigates public awareness and action.
  vi NGOs are also having an increasing impact on creating and maintaining world order through humanitarian programs and the lobbying of governments.

105. Any two of the following:
  i A nation-state can refuse to be a member of the UN and to ignore international customary law and treaty law if it chooses to do so.
  ii The UN system of treaties and the ICJ have not been effective in stopping issues such as terrorism, and conflicts in Africa and Iraq
  iii The effectiveness of the ICC has not really been tested and the fact that some nation-states, including the US, do not recognise the jurisdiction of the ICC means its effectiveness is already limited.
  iv There is criticism that the UN is not allowing the use of force for humanitarian reasons when required.

HSC *Sample HSC questions* (pages 420–1)

Extended-response questions

Note: **EM** means Examiner Maximiser

Question 1

What you are asked to do

This question asks you to:

- choose and describe **two** legal responses to world order
- choose and describe **one** non-legal response to world order
- for the legal and non-legal responses you listed, evaluate the effectiveness of each in resolving conflict and working towards world order.

EM In order to achieve top marks for your answer to this question, in your answer you should:

- name the TWO legal and ONE non-legal response you intend to examine in the essay
- describe each of your chosen responses
- briefly sum up the effectiveness of each of your chosen responses in resolving conflict and working towards world order.

If focusing on the **legal** responses of international instruments, and courts and tribunals; and the **non-legal** response of the media, your answer could use the following plan.

Plan

Paragraph 1 (Introduction):

- Name the TWO legal and ONE non legal response to be examined in the essay. (In this example international instruments, and courts and tribunals are the legal responses and the media is the non-legal response.)
- Briefly sum up the effectiveness of the responses you named in resolving conflict and working towards world order.

Paragraph 2: Briefly describe the legal response of international instruments, with examples. **[6.1.3, 6.2.3, 6.2.7 and 6.3.2]**

Paragraph 3: Evaluate the effectiveness of international instruments in resolving conflict and working towards world order, by:

- looking at the factors which *limit* this response
- looking at factors which *enhance* this response
- coming to a conclusion about the effectiveness of this response. **[6.1.2, 6.3.2 and 6.4.4]**

Paragraph 4: Briefly describe the legal response of courts and tribunals, with examples. **[6.2.4]**

Paragraph 5: Evaluate the effectiveness of courts and tribunals in resolving conflict and working towards world order, by:

- looking at the factors which *limit* this response
- looking at factors which *enhance* this response
- coming to a conclusion about the effectiveness of this response. **[6.2.4 and 6.2.5]**

Paragraph 6: Briefly describe the non-legal response of the media, with examples. **[6.2.8 and 6.4.5]**

Paragraph 7: Evaluate the effectiveness of the media in resolving conflict and working towards world order, by:

- looking at the factors which *limit* this response
- looking at factors which *enhance* this response
- coming to a conclusion about the effectiveness of this response. **[6.4.5]**

Conclusion:

- List the responses you have discussed in the essay.
- State whether they are, on the whole, effective or ineffective.
- State which responses seem to be the most effective and which seem to be the least effective.

Question 2

What you are asked to do

This question asks you to:

- describe issues of compliance and non-compliance
- for each issue you described, explain how that issue affects the maintenance of world order.

EM In order to achieve top marks for your answer to this question, in your answer you should:

- explain what is meant by *compliance* and *non-compliance*
- list factors which affect compliance and non-compliance in relation to world order
- briefly state how issues of compliance and non compliance affect the maintenance of world order.

Your answer could follow the plan below.

Plan

Paragraph 1 (Introduction):

- Explain what is meant by compliance and non-compliance.
- List factors which affect compliance and non-compliance in relation to world order.
- Briefly state how issues of compliance and non compliance affect the maintenance of world order.

Paragraph 2:

- Explain that international law is based on consensus.
- Explain that because of its consensual nature, if countries do reach consensus, they are usually compliant, because they have agreed to the law in the first place. Give an example of treaty law.
- State that this consensus assists in the maintenance of world order in most cases. **[6.2.3, 6.2.4, 6.4.1 and 6.4.2]**

Paragraph 3:

- Explain the notions of reciprocity and legal responsibility and how they encourage compliance. Use international customary law as an example.
- State how these ideas mean that most nations are compliant with international law most of the time. **[6.2.1 and 6.2.2]**

Paragraph 4:

- Explain the idea of state sovereignty and how this can lead to non-compliance with international law. Give an example.
- State that the notion of state sovereignty can affect the compliance of nations and, therefore, the maintenance of world order. **[6.2.1 and 6.3.2]**

Paragraph 5:

- Explain that there are several ways to encourage nation states to comply with the law, including: political negotiations; persuasion which includes the use of sanctions; and the use of force.

- Describe, with an example, the use of political negotiations to encourage compliance.
- Comment on the effectiveness of political negotiations in assisting compliance with international law and, therefore, the maintenance of world order. **[6.2.9]**

Paragraph 6:

- Describe, with an example, the use of persuasion, including the use of sanctions, to encourage compliance.
- Comment on the effectiveness of sanctions in assisting compliance with international law and, therefore, the maintenance of world order. **[6.2.9 and 6.4.1]**

Paragraph 7:

- Describe, with an example, how the use of force encourages compliance.
- Comment on the effectiveness of the use of force in assisting compliance with international law and, therefore, the maintenance of world order. **[6.2.9 and 6.3.2]**

Conclusion:

- State that issues of compliance and non-compliance are very important to the maintenance of world order.
- State that the consensual nature of international law and the ideas of reciprocity and legal responsibility encourage compliance, as do political negotiations, persuasion (which includes the use of sanctions), and the use of force.
- State that the idea of state sovereignty limits compliance and non-compliance; even one state can cause major disruptions to world order.

Sample HSC Examination 1
(pages 423–6)

Note: **EM** means Examiner Maximiser

SECTION I

1. **C** is the correct answer. It describes the action which broke the law. **A**, **B** and **D** describe possible forms of *mens rea* for the crime. **[1.1.2]**

2. **C** is the correct answer. Murder is an indictable offence that is always heard by a judge and jury. It as an offence against the person, not an economic offence. **[1.1.5 and 1.1.6]**

3. **C** is the correct answer. **A** is an example of civil disobedience. **B** is an example of compliance with the law. **D** is an example of social crime prevention. **[1.1.8 and 1.1.9]**

4. **D** is the correct answer. People are not compelled to answer police questions when arrested or charged, but do have to produce their driver's licence upon request. **[1.2.1]**

5. **B** is the correct answer. The crime of assault is a summary offence and would usually be heard in the Local Court. So an appeal about the severity of the sentence would be heard in the District Court. **[1.3.1 and 1.4.5]**

6. **A** is the correct answer. **B** (remand) is what occurs if the court does not grant bail. **C** (charge) refers to the crime for which the alleged offender is to be answerable. **D**

(summons) refers to one way an alleged offender can be brought before the court.

7. **A** is the correct answer. This is an example of charge negotiation, also known as plea-bargaining. **[1.3.4]**

8. **A** is the correct answer. counterterrorism laws allow for detention without charge and so limit human rights in Australia. Freedom of movement (**B**) is not really restricted in Australia. **C** and **D** grant, rather than limit, rights. **[2.2.5 and 2.2.6]**

9. **B** is the correct answer. **B** protects Indigenous Australians from discrimination. **A** protects very few rights in Australia. **C** applies to all children, so is not specific to the rights of Indigenous Australians. **D** limits the rights of Indigenous Australians. **[2.2.5 and 2.2.6]**

10. **B** is the correct answer. **[1.3.1]**

11. **B** is the correct answer. This right is recognised in the ICCPR. **A**, **C** and **D** are economic, social and cultural rights. **[2.1.1]**

12. **A** is the correct answer. The defence of necessity is a complete defence where the defendant claims that the criminal act or omission was necessary to avert serious danger. **C** describes the defence of self-defence and **D** describes the defence of duress. **[1.3.8]**

13. **A** is the correct answer. A citizen must have a greater cause than just 'reasonable suspicion' in order to arrest someone. Police are not restricted in the ways described in **B** and **C**. Police generally do not need a warrant as stated in **D**. **[1.2.4]**

14. **A** is the correct answer. **[1.3.6]**

15. **D** is the correct answer. **A**, **B** and **C** are aggravating factors and would tend to persuade the magistrate to pass a more severe sentence. **[1.4.3]**

16. **B** is the correct answer. Generally people accused of a serious criminal offence do not have to pass a merit or jurisdiction test. Merit tests only apply to some criminal matters, such as appeals, and the jurisdiction test is largely irrelevant to criminal matters except for motor vehicle offences. **[1.3.5]**

17. **D** is the correct answer. **A**, **B**, and **C** all describe other characteristics of human rights, that is that they are universal (**A**), indivisible (**B**), and inherent (**C**). **[2.1.1]**

18. **C** is the correct answer. A criminal infringement notice does not incapacitate the offender and there is no evidence that it rehabilitates, so **A** and **D** are incorrect. Such notices are often ignored (**B**) but this is not an advantage. **[1.4.6]**

19. **C** is the correct answer. **A** refers to the division of powers. **B** and **D** are not accurate descriptions of governmental power allocation. **[2.2.5]**

20. **B** is the correct answer. It is a treaty between two nations only and, so, is a bilateral treaty. **[1.6.2]**

SECTION II

Part A

Question 21

EM In order to achieve top marks for your answer to this question, in your answer you should:

- choose THREE major international human rights documents. (There are several that you could choose from, discussed in Section 2.1.3 [pages 106–7].)
- name each document, with its date, and describe how it protects human rights.

One major international human rights document is the Universal Declaration of Human Rights 1948, which lists the human rights to which every person is entitled. Each of its thirty articles sets out a particular human right or set of rights. Another document is the International Covenant on Civil and Political Rights 1966 (ICCPR) which was drawn up in order to give legal force to the part of the Universal Declaration which protects civil and political rights. There is also the International Covenant on Economic, Social and Cultural Rights 1966 (ICESCR), which gives legal force to the second part of the Universal Declaration. It protects economic, social and cultural rights. These three documents are known as the International Bill of Rights.

Question 22

EM In order to access the top band of marks in your answer to this question, you should choose a human right. Choose one whose protection in Australia you know about. See Sections 2.1.1 (pages 95–7) and 2.2.5 (pages 114–19).

One of the few human rights that is protected by the Australian Constitution is freedom of religion, which is enshrined in Section 116 of the Constitution.

Question 23

EM In order to access the top band of marks in your answer to this question, you need to choose a contemporary human rights issue which you have studied and make sure you can answer both parts of the question (a and b). Your answer needs to include:

- the nature and extent of the issue
- one legal response to the issue, and its effectiveness
- one non-legal response to the issue, and its effectiveness.

The contemporary human rights issue which is used for the sample answer below is the treatment of refugees, which is discussed in Sections 2.3.1 to 2.3.3 (pages 123–8).

a The 1951 United Nations Convention relating to the Status of Refugees (the 1951 Refugee Convention) defines a refugee as someone who 'owing to a well-founded fear of being persecuted for reasons of race, religion, nationality, membership of a particular social group or political opinion, is outside the country of his nationality, and is unable to or, owing to such fear, is unwilling to avail himself of the protection of that country'. Refugees are a major human rights issue because of the large number of refugees worldwide. In 2009, the United Nations High Commissioner for Refugees (the UNHCR) reported that there were 15.2 million people in the world who fell under this formal definition of refugee and another 27 million who were uprooted from their homes in their own country because of internal conflict. Refugees need the protection of another nation-state to survive, because they cannot live in or return to their own country because of the likelihood they will be persecuted.

b There are several legal and non-legal responses to the issue of refugees, both international and domestic. One international legal response to the issue is the United Nations Convention relating to the Status of Refugees (the 1951 Refugee

Convention). This document defines a refugee, outlines refugee rights and establishes the refugee obligations of states. The rights of a refugee as outlined in the Convention include the right to freedom of religion and movement, the right to work, education, and accessibility to travel documents. A key provision of the Convention is that refugees should not be returned to a country where they fear persecution.

One international non-legal response is the work of NGOs in the care and protection of refugees. Amnesty International and Human Rights Watch are the two main NGOs working in this area. Their role is to: monitor refugee camps; monitor human rights compliance by states creating or hosting refugees; report on refugee situations to the UN; government and the media; and campaign for reform.

The effectiveness of both the 1951 Refugee Convention and the work of NGOs is limited by the sheer number of refugees, the increasing unwillingness of developed nations to accept large numbers of refugees because of terrorism fears and the global financial crisis, and unresolved long-term internal conflict within nations. The majority of the world's refugees have been living as refugees for five years or more. 80% of all asylum seekers live in cities in the developing world, usually in substandard refugee camps. Despite the best efforts of NGOs and aid agencies, and of the UNHCR, refugee camps are often overcrowded, unhygienic and lawless. A lack of funding for these bodies, as well as domestic political inaction, means refugees continue to live in these conditions for many years.

Part B

Question 24

EM In order to access the top band of marks in your answer to this question, you should explain the extent to which there is a proper balance between the rights of victims, the rights of offenders and the rights of society. In order to do this, you need to describe the rights of each group. Then decide if any of the groups have their rights protected at the expense of other groups.

Your answer could follow the plan below.

Plan

Paragraph 1: Describe the rights of the victims. [1.4.4, 1.4.7, 1.5.5 and 1.7.5]

Paragraph 2: Describe the rights of offenders, including those accused of a crime. [1.2.1, 1.2.5, 1.2.6 and 1.3.5]

Paragraph 3: Explain whether the protection of the rights of victims infringes upon the rights of offenders. [1.2.2, 1.3.8, 1.4.4 and 1.7.5]

Paragraph 4: Describe the rights of society and how those rights are protected. [1.2.1, 1.2.5, 1.2.6, 1.7.4 and 1.7.5]

Paragraph 5: Explain whether the protection of the rights of society infringes upon the rights of victims and offenders [1.2.1, 1.2.6, 1.7.4 and 1.7.5]

Paragraph 6: Come to a conclusion about whether there is a proper balance between the rights of the various groups. [1.7.5]

SECTION III

Question 25

a **EM** In order to access the top band of marks in your answer to this question, you should:

- identify ONE contemporary issue involving consumer protection. This should be an issue listed in Part III, Option1 of the syllabus, i.e. credit, product certification, marketing innovations, or technology. (The example plan below is based on the issue of marketing innovations.)

- describe the issue you identified

- describe legal and non-legal responses to the issue you identified

- evaluate each of the legal and non-legal responses by describing the advantages and disadvantages of each and deciding how well each response assists the consumer.

Your answer could follow the plan below.

Plan

Paragraph 1: As an introduction, describe the contemporary issue involving consumers to be discussed. (In this case, it is marketing innovations, which involves direct commerce and product placement.) State the legal and non-legal responses to the issue and their overall effect (in this case, there are several responses, legal and non-legal, and consumers are generally well protected). [3.3.3]

Paragraph 2: State the definition of direct commerce, and telemarketing. Describe the advantages to consumers of direct marketing, as well as the increase in telemarketing and the invasion of people's privacy this type of marketing represents. [3.3.3]

Paragraph 3: List three legal responses (which could include: general laws about advertising and consumer transactions; direct commerce laws; and the Do Not Call Register). [3.1.8 and 3.3.3]

Paragraph 4: Discuss factors which enhance, and those which lessen, the effectiveness of the legal responses. Discuss the overall effectiveness of the legal responses to direct marketing. Also list non-legal responses and discuss their effectiveness. [3.1.8 and 3.3.3]

Paragraph 5: Describe product placement and provide examples. Discuss the attitude to product placement in other jurisdictions. [3.3.3]

Paragraph 6: Discuss two legal responses to product placement:

- the ban on tobacco products.

- the disclosure standard and the John Laws case.

Discuss factors which enhance, and those which lessen, the effectiveness of the legal responses to product placement. Discuss the overall effectiveness of the legal responses to product placement. [3.3.3]

Paragraph 7: Discuss non-legal responses to product placement and their effectiveness.

Conclusion: Restate that the contemporary issue being explored is marketing innovations, particularly direct commerce and product placement. Summarise the effectiveness of the legal and non-legal responses. [3.3.3]

b **EM** In order to access the top band of marks in your answer to this question, you should:

- state that there is a wide range of legal and non-legal responses aimed at achieving justice for consumers

- list three or four examples of such responses

- describe legal and non-legal responses to the regulation of marketing and advertising

- evaluate each of the legal and non-legal responses by describing the advantages and disadvantages of each and deciding how well each response achieves justice for consumers.

Your answer could follow the plan below.

Plan

Paragraph 1: As an introduction, state that there exists a wide range of legal and non-legal responses aimed at achieving justice for consumers. Provide three or four examples of such responses and identify several responses, legal and non-legal, to the regulation of advertising, marketing and product certification. State that consumers are generally well protected as a result of these responses, although there have been some recent calls for tougher laws about exaggerated product certification claims. **[3.1.8, 3.2.1, 3.2.6, 3.3.2 and 3.4.5]**

Paragraph 2: Describe the general legal standards about advertising, providing an example of the laws in operation. Comment on the effectiveness of such laws. **[3.1.8]**

Paragraph 3: Describe the specific legal standards about advertising, providing an example of the laws in operation (telemarketing and the Do Not Call Register). Comment on the effectiveness of such laws. **[3.1.8 and 3.3.3]**

Paragraph 4: Describe the non-legal responses to advertising, providing examples of these responses in operation. Comment on the effectiveness of these responses. **[3.1.8]**

Paragraph 5: Describe the specific laws about product certification, providing examples of these laws in operation. Comment on the effectiveness of such laws. **[3.1.8 and 3.3.2]**

Paragraph 6: Describe non-legal responses to product certification, and comment on the effectiveness of these responses. **[3.3.2]**

Conclusion: Restate that there is a wide range of legal and non-legal responses aimed at achieving justice for consumers. List the legal and non-legal responses to advertising, marketing and product certification. Provide a general summary of the effectiveness of the legal and non-legal responses. **[3.1.8, 3.3.2 and 3.4.5]**

Question 26

Note: There are no sample answers provided for this Option.

Question 27

a **EM** In order to access the top band of marks in your answer to this question, you should:

- identify ONE contemporary issue involving family law. This should be an issue listed in Part III, Option 3 of the syllabus, i.e. recognition of same-sex relationships, the changing nature of parental responsibility, surrogacy and birth technologies, or the care and protection of children. (The example plan below is based on the issue of the care and protection of children.)

- describe the issue you identified

- describe legal and non-legal responses to the issue you identified

- evaluate each of these responses by describing the advantages and disadvantages of each and deciding how well each response assists in the care and protection of children.

Your answer could follow the plan below.

Plan

Paragraph 1: As an introduction, state that the contemporary issue to be discussed is the care and protection of children and that there are several legal and non-legal responses to this issue. State that the overall effect of the legal and non-legal responses is that the care and protection of children in

Australia, and in NSW particularly, is an issue of ongoing concern, though there have been major reforms in the legal responses to this issue in recent years. **[4.3.4]**

Paragraph 2: Describe the nature and extent of the issue of the care and protection of children, including a reference to the Special Commission of Inquiry into Child Protection Services in NSW 2008. **[4.3.4]**

Paragraph 3: State that the legal response to the issue of the care and protection of children are:

- Keep Them Safe

- amended legislation. **[4.3.4]**

Paragraph 4: Describe the role of the community services. **[4.3.4]**

Paragraph 5: Describe the role of the courts. State other legal responses to the care and protection of children. **[4.3.4]**

Paragraph 6: Describe non-legal responses to the issue of the care and protection of children. **[4.3.4]**

Conclusion: Restate that the contemporary issue being explored is the issue of the care and protection of children. List the legal and non-legal responses to this issue. Provide a general summary of the effectiveness of the legal and non-legal responses. **[4.3.4]**

b **EM** In order to access the top band of marks in your answer to this question, you should:

- list the parties involved in relationship breakdowns

- state that there is a number of legal and non-legal responses aimed at achieving justice for parties involved in relationship breakdowns

- describe legal and non-legal responses to protecting and recognising the rights of people involved in family law disputes

- evaluate each of the legal and non-legal responses by describing the advantages and disadvantages of each and deciding how well each response achieves justice for the parties involved.

Your answer could follow the plan below.

Plan

Paragraph 1: As an introduction, list the parties involved in relationship breakdowns and the responses, legal and non-legal, aimed at achieving justice for them. State that relationship breakdowns often involve much anger and distress and, while legal and non-legal responses attempt to minimise this, some of these emotions are inevitable. Also state that, overall, the effect of responses aimed at achieving justice for parties involved in relationship breakdown is that those parties are generally well provided for, though there is some concern that children may be exposed to violent parents. **[4.1.3 and 4.2.1–4.2.6]**

Paragraph 2: Describe how a divorce can be obtained—legal and non-legal responses. Also describe how the breakdown of non-married adult relationships occurs. Discuss the extent to which the legal and non-legal responses achieve justice for the parties involved. **[4.1.3, 4.2.1, 4.2.2, 4.2.3, 4.2.5 and 4.2.8]**

Paragraph 3: Describe the non-legal and legal responses to property division when relationships break down. Discuss the extent to which these responses achieve justice for the parties involved. **[4.1.3, 4.2.3 and 4.2.8]**

Paragraph 4: Describe the legal and non-legal responses to the care of children when relationships break down. Discuss the extent to which these responses achieve justice for the parties involved: parents, children and other parties with an interest in the child. [4.2.2, 4.2.4 and 4.2.8]

Paragraph 5: Describe the legal and non-legal responses to child maintenance when relationships break down. Discuss the extent to which these responses achieve justice for the parties involved. [4.2.2]

Conclusion: Restate that there is a range of legal and non-legal responses aimed at achieving justice for parties involved in relationship breakdown. List the legal and non-legal responses to relationship breakdown. Provide a general summary of the effectiveness of the legal and non-legal responses. [4.1.3 and 4.2.1–4.2.6]

Question 28

Note: there are no sample answers provided for this Option.

Question 29

Note: there are no sample answers provided for this Option.

Question 30

a **EM** In order to access the top band of marks in your answer to this question, you should:

- identify ONE contemporary issue involving workplace law. This should be an issue listed in Part III, Option 6 of the syllabus, i.e. discrimination, safety, termination of employment, or leave. (The example plan below is based on the issue of discrimination in the workplace.)
- describe the issue you identified
- describe the legal and non-legal responses to the issue you described
- evaluate each of the legal and non-legal responses by describing the advantages and disadvantages of each and deciding how well each response combats the problem of workplace discrimination.

Your answer could follow the plan below.

Plan

Paragraph 1: As an introduction, state that the contemporary issue to be discussed is discrimination in the workplace. Define *discrimination*. State that there are several responses, legal and non-legal, to this issue at both state and federal level. Explain that the overall effect of the legal and non-legal responses is that employees have effective legal avenues they can pursue if they have been discriminated against in the workplace—however, discrimination is very hard to prove. Explain that equal opportunity laws seem to have improved the position of women in the workforce to some degree, though the average remuneration of women is still significantly lower than that of men. [5.3.1]

Paragraph 2: Describe direct and indirect discrimination. State the grounds for which discrimination is illegal in the workplace. [5.3.1]

Paragraph 3: Describe the legislation about discrimination—a legal response. Discuss adverse action. [5.1.3 and 5.3.1]

Paragraph 4: State the NSW avenues for taking action against discrimination. List the four steps that can be taken by someone who feels he or she has been discriminated against:

- workplace
- advice and assistance
- conciliation
- ADT (with a case example). [5.3.1]

Paragraph 5: State the federal avenues for taking action against discrimination. List the four steps that can be taken by someone who feels he or she has been discriminated against:

- workplace
- advice and assistance
- conciliation
- court action (with a case example). [5.3.1]

Paragraph 6: Discuss the factors which enhance, and those which lessen, the effectiveness of legal and non-legal responses to workplace discrimination. Discuss the overall effectiveness of the legal and non-legal responses to discrimination in the workplace. [5.3.3]

Paragraph 7: State the responses to lack of equal opportunity in the workplace, and the factors which enhance and lessen the effectiveness of these responses. Discuss the overall effectiveness of equal opportunity responses. [5.3.3]

Conclusion: Restate that the contemporary issue being explored is discrimination, including the equal opportunity laws. List the legal and non-legal responses to the issue of workplace discrimination. Provide a general summary of the effectiveness of the legal and non-legal responses. [5.3.3]

b **EM** In order to access the top band of marks in your answer to this question, you should:

- state there is a wide range of legal and non-legal responses aimed at achieving justice for employers and employees
- describe legal and non-legal responses aimed at protecting and recognising workplace rights
- evaluate each of the legal and non-legal responses by describing the advantages and disadvantages of each and deciding how well each response achieves justice for employers and employees.

Your answer could follow the plan below.

Plan

Paragraph 1: As an introduction, state that there is a wide range of legal and non-legal responses aimed at achieving justice for employers and employees. List the legal and non-legal responses aimed at protecting and recognising workplace rights. Also state that, overall, the effect of the legal and non-legal responses is that workplace rights are generally well protected, particularly since the commencement of the national workplace system under the *Fair Work Act 2009* (Cth). [5.2.6 and 5.4.5]

Paragraph 2: Describe the role of statutory conditions in establishing conditions of employment—note these are legal responses. Discuss the extent to which these responses achieve justice for:

- employers
- employees, particularly in relation to protecting and recognising workplace rights. [5.1.3, 5.1.4, 5.2.1, 5.2.5 and 5.3.3]

Paragraph 3:

Describe the role of contracts, awards and agreements in establishing conditions of employment—note these are legal responses. Discuss the extent to which these responses achieve justice for:

- employers
- employees, particularly in relation to protecting and recognising workplace rights. [5.1.3, 5.2.5 and 5.2.6]

Paragraph 4: Describe the role of courts, tribunals and government organisations in establishing conditions of employment—note these are legal responses. Discuss the extent to which these responses achieve justice for:

- employers
- employees, particularly in relation to protecting and recognising workplace rights. **[5.2.4 and 5.2.6]**

Paragraph 5: Describe the role of trade unions and employer associations in establishing conditions of employment—note these are non-legal responses. Discuss the extent to which these responses achieve justice for:

- employers
- employees, particularly in relation to protecting and recognising workplace rights. **[5.2.4 and 5.2.6]**

Paragraph 6: Describe the role of other NGOs and the media in establishing conditions of employment—note these are non-legal responses. Discuss the extent to which these responses achieve justice for:

- employers
- employees, particularly in relation to protecting and recognising workplace rights. **[5.2.4 and 5.2.6]**

Conclusion: Restate that there is a wide range of legal and non-legal responses aimed at achieving justice for employers and employees. List the legal and non-legal responses aimed at protecting and recognising workplace rights. Provide a general summary of the effectiveness of the legal and non-legal responses. **[5.1.3, 5.2.4 and 5.2.6]**

Question 31

a **EM** In order to access the top band of marks in your answer to this question, you should:

- identify ONE contemporary issue involving world order. This should be an issue listed in Part III, Option 7 of the syllabus, i.e. the principle of 'Responsibility to Protect', regional and global situations that threaten peace and security, the success of global cooperation in achieving world order, or rules regarding the conduct of hostilities. (The example plan below is based on the issue of the rules regarding the conduct of hostilities.)
- describe the issue you identified
- describe the legal and non-legal responses to the issue you identified
- evaluate each of the legal and non-legal responses by describing their advantages and disadvantages and deciding how effective they are.

Your answer could follow the plan below.

Plan

Paragraph 1: As an introduction, state that the contemporary issue to be discussed is the rules regarding the conduct of hostilities. Describe the rules regarding the conduct of hostilities under Geneva Conventions of 1949 and the 1977 Additional Protocols. Describe the application of the rules regarding the conduct of hostilities in Guantanamo Bay. Also state that, overall, the effectiveness of the rules regarding the conduct of hostilities is that they are effective if nations choose to or can be persuaded to follow them, so they are dependent on the ideas of state sovereignty, legal responsibility and reciprocity. **[6.2.1 and 6.3.4]**

Paragraph 2: State what is meant by the *rules regarding the conduct of hostilities*. Describe the rules regarding the conduct

of hostilities and the legal instruments which apply to them. **[6.2.6 and 6.3.4]**

Paragraph 3: Describe the situation at Guantanamo Bay and how the rules regarding the conduct of hostilities are applied there. **[6.3.4]**

Paragraph 4: State the effectiveness of the rules regarding the conduct of hostilities, given the Guantanamo Bay situation. Discuss the ideas of state sovereignty, reciprocity and legal responsibility and the effectiveness of international law. Discuss the importance of non-legal responses in persuading nations to comply with international law, including the rules regarding the conduct of hostilities. **[6.2.1. 6.3.4 and 6.4.2]**

Conclusion: Restate that the contemporary issue being explored is the rules regarding the conduct of hostilities. Briefly state the legal and non-legal responses to this issue. Provide a general summary of the effectiveness of the legal and non-legal responses. **[6.2.1 and 6.3.4]**

b **EM** In order to access the top band of marks in your answer to this question, you should:

- state that there is a wide range of legal and non-legal responses aimed at working towards world order
- describe the legal and non-legal responses aimed at working towards world order
- explain how state sovereignty both assists and impedes the legal and non-legal responses to the resolution of world order issues
- evaluate each of the legal and non-legal responses by describing the advantages and disadvantages of each and deciding how well each response assists in working towards world order.

Your answer could follow the plan below.

Plan

Paragraph 1: As an introduction, state that there is a wide range of legal and non-legal responses aimed at working towards world order. List legal and non-legal responses aimed at working towards world order. Explain that the effectiveness of any legal or non-legal response to world order issues is impeded by state sovereignty and the consensual nature of international law, though state sovereignty can also assist in the resolution of world issues because of the ideas of reciprocity and legal responsibility. **[6.2.1, 6.2.10 and 6.4.5]**

Paragraph 2: Describe the role of the United Nations and international instruments in working towards world order—note these are legal responses. Describe the role of state sovereignty in assisting and impeding the effectiveness of these legal responses. **[6.2.1, 6.2.2, 6.2.3, 6.2.10 and 6.4.5]**

Paragraph 3: Describe the role of IGOs in working towards world order—note these are legal responses. Describe the role of state sovereignty in assisting and impeding the effectiveness of these legal responses. **[6.2.1, 6.2.10 and 6.4.5]**

Paragraph 4: Describe the role of international courts and tribunals in working towards world order—note these are legal responses. Describe the role of state sovereignty in assisting and impeding the effectiveness of these legal responses. **[6.2.1, 6.2.4, 6.2.10 and 6.4.5]**

Paragraph 5: Describe the role of NGOs and the media in working towards world order—note these are non-legal responses. Describe the role of state sovereignty in assisting and impeding the effectiveness of these non-legal responses. **[6.2.6, 6.2.8 and 6.4.5]**

Paragraph 6: Describe the role of political negotiation and persuasion in working towards world order—note these are non-legal responses. Describe the role of state sovereignty in assisting and impeding the effectiveness of these non-legal responses. **[6.2.9]**

Paragraph 7: Describe the use of force in working towards world order—note this could be a legal or a non-legal response. Describe the role of state sovereignty in assisting and impeding the effectiveness of this response. **[6.2.9 and 6.2.10]**

Conclusion: Restate that there is a wide range of legal and non-legal responses aimed at working towards world order. List the legal and non-legal responses aimed at working towards world order. Provide a general summary of the effectiveness of the legal and non-legal responses considering that state sovereignty both impedes and assist in the resolution of world issues. **[6.2.1, 6.2.10 and 6.4.5]**

Sample HSC Examination 2
(pages 427–30)

Note: **EM** means Examiner Maximiser

SECTION I

1. **B** is the correct answer. **A** and **D** are incorrect because it is criminal matters that are prosecuted and involve the state, not civil matters. **C** is incorrect because common law and statute law play a part in both civil and criminal matters. **[1.1.1 and 1.3.2]**

2. **C** is the correct answer. A strict liability offence is one where only *actus reus* need be proved. Both *actus reus* and *mens rea* need to be proved for answers **A**, **B**, and **D**. **[1.1.3]**

3. **D** is the correct answer. Treason is an example of an offence against the sovereign. **[1.1.5]**

4. **C** is the correct answer. Legal aid is only available for those who pass a means test, which is too low for everyone who needs legal aid to receive it (making **A** incorrect). There is no absolute right to legal representation in Australia, so **B** is incorrect. Legal aid is available for most criminal matters, not just serious ones, so **D** is incorrect. **[1.3.5]**

5. **D** is the correct answer. Public defenders only defend people who are eligible for legal aid and who have been accused of a criminal offence. **[1.3.3]**

6. **D** is the correct answer. **[1.3.6]**

7. **A** is the correct answer. Under anti-terrorist legislation police can detain a person for forty-eight hours without charge. Extensions to this time may be granted if police investigations are ongoing, but for other crimes the police do not have this power. **[1.5.1]**

8. **A** is the correct answer. Freedom of religion is protected by Section 116 of the Australian Constitution. **[2.2.5]**

9. **A** is the correct answer. Opinions can only be given by experts. **B** and **C** are permitted and **D** occurs during cross-examination. **[1.3.6]**

10. **C** is the correct answer. The right to peace is a collective right. Arguably it is also a moral and social right (**B** and

D), but **C** is the best answer of the alternatives given. **[2.1.1 and 2.1.2]**

11. **A** is the correct answer. **B**, **C** and **D** are not features of the adversarial system. **[1.3.2]**

12. **C** is the correct answer. Deportation (**A**) refers to the removal of a person from a country and the return of that person to his or her country of origin because of a crime committed in the country from which the person is being removed. In the case of extradition (**C**), the criminal is sent to the country in which he or she committed a crime, to face the consequences of their actions. A physical sanction (**B**) is placed by one country upon another, and a transnational agreement (**D**) is an agreement between countries. **[1.4.8 and 1.6.2]**

13. **B** is the correct answer. **A** refers to the ability of a nation to govern itself without interference from other nations. **C** refers to the allocation of power between the judiciary, the executive and the legislature. **D** refers to a system in which there is only one national government and no state governments, so a division of power is not necessary. **[2.2.5 and 2.2.1]**

14. **A** is the correct answer. A coronial inquiry may issue an indictment against a person involved in an unnatural death or an unexplained fire, but does not decide guilt or innocence (**B**). **C** occurs at a committal hearing, and **D** occurs at a bail hearing. **[1.3.1 and 1.2.5]**

15. **A** is the correct answer. Provocation is a partial defence to murder. **[1.3.8]**

16. **A** is the correct answer. The ICCPR protects civil and political rights, of which **A** is an example. **B** and **D** are economic, social and cultural rights. **C** is a collective right. **[2.1.1]**

17. **D** is the correct answer. Warrants are not generally used for **A**, **B** or **C**. **[1.2.3 and 1.2.4]**

18. **B** is the correct answer. Official warnings are only available for young offenders. **[1.4.6 and 1.5.4]**

19. **B** is the correct answer. **[1.6.1]**

20. **B** is the correct answer. This is the only body of those mentioned that can order compensation. The organisations in **A**, **C** and **D** can only make recommendations, they cannot make binding orders. **[2.2.2, 2.2.3 and 2.2.5]**

Section II

Part A

Question 21

EM In order to access the top band of marks in your answer to this question, you should:

- choose one domestic or international non-government organisation that is involved with the protection of human rights
- describe ONE way in which the organisation you chose protects human rights.

A non-government organisation (NGO) is one that works towards a certain cause and operates separately to any government. There are many NGOs which work both nationally and internationally in the field of human rights. One well-known international organisation is Amnesty International. In recent times, Amnesty International has assisted in the recognition of human rights in several ways. (Any of the following ways Amnesty international has assisted in the recognition of human rights will be sufficient to answer this question.)

- Amnesty International provides independent information to the United Nations about human rights violations (as it has done with violations in Darfur and Burma).

- Amnesty International publicises human rights abuses across the world in order to put pressure on governments to stop such violations.

- Amnesty International organises letter writing campaigns to urge for release of particular political prisoners in various nations.

- Amnesty International raises funds to assist those who are suffering from human rights abuses.

- Amnesty International monitors refugee camps and monitors human rights compliance by states creating or hosting refugees. **[2.2.2, 2.2.3, 2.2.5, 2.2.6 and 2.3.2]**

Question 22

Human rights are fundamental rights. They are things to which every human being is entitled for just being a human being. Generally, it is recognised that human rights are:

- universal (that is, to be enjoyed by all individuals regardless of their nationality, gender, race or status)

- indivisible (that is, all human rights are equally important)

- inherent (that is, they are the birthright of all humans and are to be enjoyed by all people simply by reason of their humanity)

- inalienable (that is, people cannot agree to give them up or have them taken away).

The indivisibility and universality of human rights is recognised in the Charter of the United Nations 1945 and in the Universal Declaration of Human Rights 1948.

There are three types of human rights: civil and political rights (such as the right to vote and freedom of movement); economic, social and cultural rights (such as the rights to education and to social security); and collective rights (such as environmental and peace rights and the right to self-determination).

The view expressed by the Chinese government in the quotation is referring to economic, social and cultural rights (such as an adequate standard of living and social security) and stating that these are more important than other human rights (such as civil and political rights). This goes against the notion that human rights are indivisible. **[2.1.1 and 2.4.3]**

Question 23

EM In order to access the top band of marks in your answer to this question, you should:

- explain the idea of self-determination

- describe ONE way in which the right of self-determination is protected in Australia

- describe ONE way in which the right of self-determination is protected internationally.

Self-determination means the right of peoples to govern themselves and to choose their own form of government. The right to self-determination can mean several things:

- the right of colonised peoples to establish their independence, which happened in many African and Asian countries in the 1960s

- the right of people within a nation to freely choose their own form of government and to elect their own government

- the principle of sovereign equality of all United Nations member states, irrespective of their size or power, which means that all member nations have an equal footing in the United Nations and all have one vote in the General Assembly

- the right claimed by Indigenous peoples to control their traditional lands and economy.

Internationally, the right to self-determination is protected by its prominence in the Charter of the United Nations 1945, where it is referred to in Articles 1(2) and 55, and by its inclusion in Article 1 of both the ICCPR and ICESCR. It is regarded as a fundamental principle of international relations.

In Australia, the right to self-determination is protected by the right to vote, which is enshrined in Section 40 of the Australian Constitution. The right to vote assures the second of the ideas about self-determination listed above. **[2.1.3]**

Part B

Question 24

Note: This question refers to stimulus which involves two people, Naomi and Lloyd, being convicted of burglary in two separate incidents.

EM In order to access the top band of marks in your answer to this question, you should:

- explain what happens in a sentencing hearing and briefly outline the factors which a court takes into account when deciding on a suitable sentence. You should compare the circumstances of Naomi and Lloyd.

- choose one penalty that could be given to Naomi, such as a good behaviour bond

- choose a diversionary program for Lloyd, such as referral to the Drug Court

- compare the effectiveness of each penalty you choose, by describing the advantages and disadvantages of each and deciding whether one is better than the other.

Your answer could follow the plan below.

Plan

Paragraph 1: Describe the process in a sentencing hearing. **[1.4.3]**

Paragraph 2: State that the court, under the *Crimes (Sentencing Procedure) Act 1999* (NSW) and other legislation, must take into account five factors when sentencing an offender: the maximum penalty; other legislative and judicial guidelines; the purposes of punishment; aggravating circumstances; and mitigating factors. **[1.4.3]**

Paragraph 3: Discuss each of the five factors you stated in paragraph 2, making references to the cases of Lloyd and Naomi. **[1.4.1, 1.4.2 and 1.4.3]**

Paragraph 4: State that Naomi could be given a good behaviour bond and explain what this entails. **[1.4.6]**

Paragraph 5: Discuss the advantages and disadvantages of imposing a bond in Naomi's case, and decide how effective it would be (taking into account the purposes of punishment, and Naomi's circumstances). **[1.4.6]**

Paragraph 6: State that Lloyd could be dealt with by the Drug Court and explain what this entails. **[1.3.1]**

Paragraph 7: Discuss the advantages and disadvantages of a Drug Court program in Lloyd's case, and decide how effective it would be (taking into account the purposes of punishment, and Lloyd's circumstances). **[1.3.1]**

Paragraph 8: Compare the two punishments and state how effective they would be for their respective scenarios. **[1.3.1 and 1.4.6]**

SECTION III

Question 25

a **EM** In order to access the top band of marks in your answer to this question, you should:

- describe what law reform is
- describe factors which have led to law reform in the area of consumer law, and describe the reforms themselves
- evaluate how well these law reforms have recognised rights of consumers in the modern consumer society
- describe areas of consumer law in which the law has failed to adequately protect the rights of consumers, and describe the reasons for this.

Your answer could follow the plan below.

Plan

Paragraph 1: As an introduction, define *law reform*. Explain how law is reformed. State the reasons why law is reformed: pressures to reform the law and factors which lead to law reform. State the importance of law reform in recognising the rights of consumers in a modern consumer society. **[3.4.4]**

Paragraph 2: Describe the pressures for law reform (examples: Law Reform Commissions, ACCC and 'green' certification). Comment about the role of such agencies in pressuring for law reform and their importance in protecting the rights of the consumer in a modern consumer society. **[3.2.5 and 3.4.4]**

Paragraph 3: Describe how the factors of changing social values and new concepts of justice lead to law reform (examples: 'green' certification, credit, mandatory standards and product liability). Comment about the responsiveness of the law to such issues, and the effectiveness of the legal response in protecting the rights of the consumer in a modern consumer society. **[3.1.5, 3.1.7, 3.3.1, 3.3.2 and 3.4.4]**

Paragraph 4: Describe how failure of existing law is a factor which leads to law reform (examples: mandatory standards, product liability, and product certification). Comment about the responsiveness of the law to this issue, and the effectiveness of the legal response in protecting the rights of the consumer in a modern consumer society. **[3.3.2]**

Paragraph 5: Describe how technology and marketing innovations are factors which lead to law reform (examples: internet shopping, telemarketing and product placement). Comment about the responsiveness of the law to such issues, and the effectiveness of the legal response in protecting the rights of the consumer in a modern consumer society. **[3.3.3, 3.3.4 and 3.4.4]**

Paragraph 6: Describe how international law is a factor which leads to law reform (example: standardisation). Comment about the responsiveness of the law to this issue, and the

effectiveness of the legal response in protecting the rights of the consumer in a modern consumer society. **[3.4.4]**

Conclusion: Restate why and how law is reformed. List some recent law reforms and their effectiveness in recognising rights of consumers in a modern consumer society. Discuss areas which present challenges for lawmakers, and the importance of the role of law reform in recognising the rights of consumers in a modern consumer society.

b **EM** In order to access the top band of marks in your answer to this question, you should:

- explain the ways in which the law encourages cooperation in regard to preventing consumer complaints
- explain the ways in which the law encourages cooperation in regard to settling consumer complaints
- state the extent to which the law encourages cooperation in regard to both preventing and settling consumer complaints.

Your answer could follow the plan below.

Plan

Paragraph 1: As an introduction, state the extent to which the law encourages cooperation in regard to both preventing and settling consumer complaints. List the ways in which the law encourages cooperation in regard to preventing and settling consumer complaints. **[3.2.1, 3.2.2, 3.2.3, 3.2.4, 3.2.5 and 3.4.1]**

Paragraph 2: Discuss the regulatory framework and monitoring of compliance by government agencies (example: merchantable quality and mandatory standards). State the extent to which the law encourages cooperation in regard to preventing consumer complaints, and the effectiveness of this in protecting consumers. **[3.1.5 and 3.1.7]**

Paragraph 3: Discuss the regulation of marketing and advertising (examples: the case of Prouds, and the case of Radio 2UE). State the extent to which the law encourages cooperation in regard to compliance with advertising and marketing laws, and the effectiveness of this in protecting consumers. **[3.1.8 and 3.3.3]**

Paragraph 4: Discuss self-help and consumer awareness. Discuss mediation and assistance from government authorities. State the extent to which the law encourages cooperation in regard to settling consumer disputes, and the effectiveness of this in protecting consumers. **[3.2.1, 3.2.2 and 3.2.3]**

Paragraph 5: Discuss industry organisations. State the extent to which the law encourages cooperation in regard to settling consumer disputes, and the effectiveness of this in protecting consumers. **[3.2.4 and 3.2.5]**

Conclusion: State that the law encourages cooperation to a very large extent. List ways the law does this: mandatory and statutory standards; penalties for non-compliance; product liability; marketing and advertising and compliance undertakings; sources of advice and assistance; and insistence on mediation. Restate that the law encourages cooperation to a large extent in both preventing and settling disputes.

Question 26

Note: There are no sample answers provided for this Option.

Question 27

a **EM** In order to access the top band of marks in your answer to this question, you should:

- describe what law reform is
- describe factors which have led to law reform in the area of family law, and describe the reforms themselves
- evaluate how effective these law reforms have been in achieving just outcomes for family members and society, and in meeting the challenges of modern family relationships
- describe the areas of family law in which the law has failed to meet the challenges of modern family relationships, and state the reasons for this.

Your answer could follow the plan below.

Plan

Paragraph 1: As an introduction, define *law reform*. Explain how law is reformed. State the reasons why law is reformed: pressures to reform the law and factors which lead to law reform. State the importance of law reform in achieving just outcomes for family members and society. **[4.2.3, 4.3.4 and 4.4.4]**

Paragraph 2: Describe the pressures for law reform (examples: government inquiries, the media and lobby groups). Comment about the role of such agencies in pressuring for law reform and the importance of them in achieving just outcomes for family members and society. **[4.1.2, 4.1.5, 4.2.7, 4.3.1, 4.3.4 and 4.4.4]**

Paragraph 3: Describe how the factors of changing social values and the changing composition of society lead to law reform (examples: *de facto* relationships and same-sex couples). Comment about the responsiveness of the law to issues brought about by changing social values, and the effectiveness of legal responses in achieving just outcomes for family members and society, and in meeting the challenges of modern family relationships. **[4.1.3, 4.2.3, 4.3.1 and 4.4.4]**

Paragraph 4: Describe how failure of existing law is a factor which leads to law reform (examples: care and protection of children, and domestic violence). Comment about the responsiveness of the law to issues brought about by the failure of existing law, and the effectiveness of legal responses in achieving just outcomes for family members and society, and in meeting the challenges of modern family relationships. **[4.2.4, 4.3.4 and 4.4.4]**

Paragraph 5: Describe how new technology is a factor which leads to law reform (example: birth technologies). Comment about the responsiveness of the law to issues brought about by new technology, and the effectiveness of legal responses in achieving just outcomes for family members and society, and in meeting the challenges of modern family relationships. **[4.3.3]**

Paragraph 6: Describe how international law is a factor which leads to law reform (example: rights of the child). Comment about the responsiveness of the law to issues brought about by international law, and the effectiveness of legal responses in achieving just outcomes for family members and society, and in meeting the challenges of modern family relationships. **[4.1.4 and 4.2.2]**

Conclusion: Restate why and how law is reformed. List some recent law reforms and their effectiveness in achieving just outcomes for family members and society, and in meeting the challenges of modern family relationships. State the areas which still present challenges for lawmakers. **[4.3.4 and 4.4.4]**

b **EM** In order to access the top band of marks in your answer to this question, you should:

- state that the law has an extensive role in encouraging cooperation as a way of resolving family conflict, through supplying mediation services and making these mandatory in many circumstances before a determination will be made on the matter by a court.
- explain the ways the law encourages cooperation in regard to resolving family conflict in a range of family matters.
- comment on the extent to which the law encourages cooperation in regard to resolving family conflict. Explain the unsuitability of mediation in situations where family violence is involved.

Your answer could follow the plan below.

Plan

Paragraph 1: As an introduction, state the extent to which the law encourages cooperation in regard to resolving family conflict. Explain why the law is reluctant to step into family conflicts in many circumstances. List the range of family conflict matters in which the law encourages resolution through cooperation: dissolution of adult relationships (including matters to do with property distribution and the care of children); adoption; succession; and the care and protection of children. Mention the unsuitability of mediation for situations in which family violence is involved. **[4.4.1]**

Paragraph 2: State the extent to which the law encourages cooperation in regard to family conflict in the area of dissolution of adult relationships. **[4.1.3, 4.2.1, 4.2.3, 4.2.5 and 4.3.1]**

Paragraph 3: State the extent to which the law encourages cooperation in regard to family conflict in matters to do with property allocation when a relationship dissolves. **[4.2.3, 4.2.5 and 4.4.1]**

Paragraph 4: State the advantages and disadvantages of dispute resolution under the *Family Law Act*. State the extent to which the law encourages cooperation in regard to family conflict in matters to do with the care of children when a relationship dissolves. **[4.2.2, 4.2.5 and 4.4.1]**

Paragraph 5: State the extent to which the law encourages cooperation in regard to family conflict in matters to do with adoption and succession. **[4.1.4 and 4.1.5]**

Paragraph 6: State the extent to which the law encourages cooperation in regard to family conflict in matters to do with the care and protection of children. **[4.3.4 and 4.4.1]**

Conclusion: State that the law encourages cooperation to a very large extent in family matters. List the areas in which the law does this: dissolution of adult relationships (including matters to do with property distribution and the care of children); adoption; succession; and the care and protection of children. Restate that the law encourages cooperation to a large extent in the resolution of family conflict, except where family violence may be involved. **[4.2.5]**

Question 28

Note: There are no sample answers provided for this Option.

Question 29

Note: There are no sample answers provided for this Option.

Question 30

a **EM** In order to access the top band of marks in your answer to this question, you should:

- describe what law reform is

- describe some reforms that have taken place in the workplace in recent years. For each one:
  - explain the factors which have led to law reform
  - describe the role of the reform in recognising rights and enforcing responsibilities in the workplace
  - evaluate how well the reform has met the challenges of the modern workplace.
- describe areas in which the law has failed to meet the challenges of the modern workplace, and describe the reasons for this.

Your answer could follow the plan below.

Plan

Paragraph 1: As an introduction, define *law reform*. Explain how law is reformed. State the reasons why laws are reformed, state the factors which lead to law reform, and list some recent law reforms:

- the *Fair Work Act* 2009 (Cth) and minimum standards
- laws about unfair dismissals
- the paid parental leave scheme
- laws about safety.

State the importance of law reform in recognising rights and enforcing responsibilities in the workplace, and in meeting the challenges of the modern workplace. **[5.4.4]**

Paragraph 2: Describe the *Fair Work Act* 2009 (Cth) and minimum standards. Discuss the factors which led to the reform represented by this act. Discuss the role of the reform in recognising rights and enforcing responsibilities in the workplace. Evaluate how well the reform has met the challenges of the modern workplace. **[5.1.3, 5.1.4, 5.2.1, 5.2.2 and 5.4.3]**

Paragraph 3:

Describe the reforms of laws about unfair dismissals. Discuss the factors which led to these reforms. Discuss the role of the reforms in recognising rights and enforcing responsibilities in the workplace. Evaluate how well the reforms have met the challenges of the modern workplace. **[5.3.3]**

Paragraph 4: Describe the paid parental leave scheme. Discuss the factors which led to this reform. Discuss the role of the reform in recognising rights and enforcing responsibilities in the workplace. Evaluate how well the reform has met the challenges of the modern workplace. **[5.3.4]**

Paragraph 5: Describe reforms of laws about workplace safety. Discuss the factors which led to the reforms. Discuss the role of the reform in recognising rights and enforcing responsibilities in the workplace. Evaluate how well the reforms have met the challenges of the modern workplace. **[5.3.2 and 5.4.2]**

Conclusion: Restate why and how law is reformed. List some recent law reforms and their effectiveness in recognising rights and enforcing responsibilities in the workplace, and in meeting the challenges of the modern workplace. State the areas which still present challenges for lawmakers. **[5.4.4]**

b **EM** In order to access the top band of marks in your answer to this question, you should:

- state that the law has an extensive role in encouraging cooperation in regard to preventing and settling workplace disputes.
- explain the ways the law encourages cooperation to both prevent and settle workplace disputes in several areas, including the

negotiation of working conditions, occupational health and safety, unfair dismissals and discrimination.

- explain that, in most of these areas, the legal system will not make a determination on a matter under dispute until the parties have tried to settle the dispute themselves, and that the law encourages parties to negotiate their own workplace agreements so that disputation will not occur in the first place.

Your answer could follow the plan below.

Plan

Paragraph 1: As an introduction, state the extent to which the law encourages cooperation in regard to preventing and settling workplace disputes. List the range of matters in which the law encourages cooperation in regard to preventing and settling workplace disputes: dispute settling mechanisms in awards and agreements; the provision of enterprise agreements; occupational health and safety; unfair dismissals; and discrimination. Explain that the law encourages parties to negotiate their own workplace agreements to prevent disputation from occurring. Explain that in most of the above areas, the legal system will not make a determination on a matter under dispute until the parties have tried to settle the dispute themselves. **[5.4.1]**

Paragraph 2: State how the law encourages cooperation by making dispute settling mechanisms mandatory in awards and agreements. State the extent to which the law encourages cooperation in regard to preventing and settling workplace disputes through these provisions. **[5.2.3]**

Paragraph 3: State how the law encourages cooperation by providing for the negotiation of enterprise agreements and procedures which must be followed while negotiations take place. State the extent to which the law encourages cooperation in regard to preventing and settling workplace disputes through these provisions. **[5.1.3 and 5.2.2]**

Paragraph 4: State how the law encourages cooperation in the area of occupational health and safety. State the extent to which the law encourages cooperation in regard to preventing and settling workplace disputes through these provisions. **[5.3.2]**

Paragraph 5: State how the law encourages cooperation in matters to do with unfair dismissals. State the extent to which the law encourages cooperation in regard to preventing and settling workplace disputes through these provisions. **[5.3.3]**

Paragraph 6: State how the law encourages cooperation in matters to do with discrimination. State the extent to which the law encourages cooperation in regard to preventing and settling workplace disputes through these provisions. **[5.3.1]**

Conclusion:

State that the law encourages cooperation to a large extent in workplace matters. List the areas in which the law does this: dispute settling mechanisms in awards and agreements; the provision of enterprise agreements; occupational health and safety; unfair dismissals; and discrimination. Restate that the law encourages cooperation to a large extent in regard to preventing and settling workplace disputes, and in providing dispute settling mechanisms when these provisions fail to result in agreement. **[5.3.2]**

Question 31

a **EM** In order to access the top band of marks in your answer to this question, you should:

- describe what law reform is

- describe the factors which have led to the reform of laws for promoting and maintaining world order:
  - changing values and ethics
  - changing composition of the world community
  - failure of existing laws
  - new technology
- list the reforms the listed factors resulted in
- evaluate how well these law reforms have met the challenges of maintaining world order in contemporary society
- describe the areas of international law in which the law has failed to adequately meet the challenges of maintaining world order in contemporary society.

Your answer could follow the plan below.

Plan

Paragraph 1: As an introduction, define *law reform*. Explain how law is reformed. State the reasons why laws are reformed: pressures to reform the law and factors which lead to law reform. State the importance of law reform in meeting the challenges of maintaining world order in contemporary society. **[6.4.4]**

Paragraph 2: Discuss the agencies of law reform, providing examples. Comment on the role of such agencies in pressuring for law reform and the importance of them in assisting to meet the challenges of maintaining world order in contemporary society. **[6.2.4, 6.2.6, 6.2.8 and 6.4.4]**

Paragraph 3: Discuss changing values and ethics as a factor which leads to law reform (examples in regard to: preventing world conflict; preventing slavery; upholding human rights; and preventing poverty). Comment about the responsiveness of the law to such issues, and the effectiveness of legal responses in meeting the challenges of maintaining world order in contemporary society. **[6.3.1, 6.4.3, 6.4.4 and 2.1.2]**

Paragraph 4: Discuss the changing composition of the world community as a factor which leads to law reform (examples in regard to: world opinion; Indigenous peoples; and transnational corporations). Comment on the responsiveness of the law to such issues, and the effectiveness of legal responses in meeting the challenges of maintaining world order in contemporary society. **[6.1.3, 6.3.4 and 6.4.3]**

Paragraph 5: Discuss the failure of existing law as a factor which leads to law reform (examples in regard to: reform of the UN; funding; and conflicts around the world). Comment on the responsiveness of the law to such issues, and the effectiveness of legal responses in meeting the challenges of maintaining world order in contemporary society. **[6.3.2 and 6.4.5]**

Paragraph 6: Discuss new technology as a factor which leads to law reform (examples in regard to: communications technology; and environmental issues). Comment on the responsiveness of the law to such issues, and the effectiveness of legal responses in meeting the challenges of maintaining world order in contemporary society. **[6.4.3]**

Conclusion: Restate why and how law is reformed. List some agencies and factors which help bring about law reform in order to meet the challenges of maintaining world order in contemporary society. State the areas which still present challenges. State the importance of law reform in meeting the challenges of maintaining world order in contemporary society. **[6.4.4]**

b **EM** In order to access the top band of marks in your answer to this question, you should:
- explain that international cooperation is the basis of the maintenance of world order
- explain how state sovereignty impedes cooperation and, therefore, the maintenance of world order
- explain the ways states are encouraged to comply with international law and cooperate in order to maintain world order
- state the extent to which state sovereignty has an impact on international cooperation in regard to maintaining world order.

Your answer could follow the plan below.

Plan

Paragraph 1: As an introduction, state that international law is consensual and is based on treaties and conventions. Define *state sovereignty* and explain how it is contrary to the idea of consensus between nations. Explain that, despite state sovereignty, most international law is followed, because it is in the self interests of each nation-state to cooperate. List the ways the international community encourages nations to cooperate, even when they wish to exercise their sovereignty in a manner contrary to the international laws that maintain world order. **[6.2.1, 6.2.9 and 6.4.1]**

Paragraph 2: Discuss international cooperation as the basis for world order. Discuss the interdependence of nation-states. State the importance of international cooperation in maintaining world order. **[6.2.3 and 6.4.1]**

Paragraph 3: Discuss the impact of state sovereignty (examples: Nicaragua; and nuclear weapons). Discuss the enacting of domestic legislation to comply with international law. State the impact of state sovereignty on international cooperation in regard to maintaining world order. **[6.1.4, 6.2.4, 6.3.2 and 6.4.1]**

Paragraph 4: Discuss political negotiations and persuasion—the use of sanctions. State the effectiveness of political negotiation and persuasion in overcoming state sovereignty to enable states to cooperate in maintaining world order. **[6.2.9 and 6.4.1]**

Paragraph 5: Discuss the use of peacekeeping forces. State the effectiveness of peacekeeping forces in overcoming state sovereignty to enable states to cooperate in maintaining world order. **[6.3.3]**

Conclusion: State that international law is consensual and is based on treaties and conventions. Explain that most states comply with laws to maintain world order because it is in their interests to do so. Explain how state sovereignty means that nations do not have to comply with international law. List the ways the international community encourages nations to cooperate: political negotiation and persuasion; the use of sanctions; and peacekeeping forces. Summarise the impact that state sovereignty has on international cooperation in regard to maintaining world order, noting that compliance is widespread most of the time. **[6.4.1]**

Index